LEXICON OF TRUST & FOUNDATION PRACTICE

Practical definitions and explanations on the law and practice of trusts and private foundations and associated subjects

By JOHN GRAHAM GOLDSWORTH

Mulberry House Press

Published in 2016 by
Mulberry House Press Limited
(Registered in England and Wales) Company No. 7802089

Registered Office:
The Old Bakery, 49 Post Street, Godmanchester, Huntingdon, Cambridgeshire
PE29 2AQ

Editorial Office:
The Barn, Waterloo House, High Street, Newport, Essex, CB11 3PG
www.mulberryhousepress.com

Typeset and design by:
theassociates, 87 bd de la Concorde, F-13009 Marseille

General Editor
John Graham Goldsworth

Associate Editor
Jennifer Mallyon-Crook

Production & Marketing Editor
Daniel East

ISBN: 978-0-9570843-1-5

Table of Contents

Preface

The modern international trust practitioner requires knowledge of many aspects of private law at his fingertips. Clients require their advisers to have a ready source of definition and explanation of the many branches of law and an appreciation of the international position of a structure that they may wish to recommend.

The trust practitioner or adviser must have an awareness which covers all the elements of asset planning to be able to inspire confidence in new and existing clients.

The ability to advise clients in a holistic manner only comes by continued exposure to the industry. Laws differ from jurisdiction to jurisdiction but the broad comprehensive approach in this Dictionary provides the conceptual principles essential to advise on the advantages of international trusts and other asset planning vehicles. Terms appearing in older testamentary and trust documents require a source of clear and concise explanation which can add depth to understanding modern terminology.

LEXICON OF TRUST AND FOUNDATION PRACTICE is a source of straightforward explanations of terms relevant to trusts and associated interests. The definitions are accompanied with a brief and straightforward explanation of advantage to the practitioner, administrator and student.

LEXICON OF TRUST AND FOUNDATION PRACTICE is the product of over 30 years' experience of practical trust and foundation formation and administration and reflects situations raised by international students on academic, professional and training courses. The idiosyncratic origin of this experience has created a unique reference tool that bridges the gap between a glossary and a practitioner's textbook – an essential work for trust and foundation management and an important adjunct to existing reference material.

LEXICON OF TRUST AND FOUNDATION PRACTICE is intended not only for trust and foundation practitioners and their legal advisers but also for bankers, insurers, litigators and others who need definitions and explanations of some of the seemingly obscure terms used in their businesses.

LEXICON OF TRUST AND FOUNDATION PRACTICE is particularly useful not only for people/students studying for qualifications but also for those who have recently qualified.

JOHN GRAHAM GOLDSWORTH

Guide to Usage

A word or term in SMALL CAPS indicates a related entry that can be consulted. This facility for cross referencing is a selective one and refers to the more specialised terms. This method is intended to direct attention to other entries which are particularly relevant to the word or terms being considered in the paragraph in which the SMALL CAPS appear. Although more commonplace words or terms, such as testator, will, trust deed, beneficiary and trustee etc., are not indicated in the same way, they are, naturally, presented in alphabetical order. More general cross references may be given at the end of an entry.

Italics are used to indicate: (i) words in a foreign language that have not been assimilated into the English language; (ii) certain Latin words or phrases that are italicised in the Oxford Dictionary of English (3rd edn) or, if they are not so listed in that dictionary, are in Roman type; (iii) a direction (e.g., see, see also); and (iv) title of a legislative Act or a book or publication. Decisions of a court or tribunal (case names or jurisprudence) are in bold italics.

Note: When reference is made to 'civil partnerships' this type of association may have been superseded, as in the UK, by 'civil marriages' between couples of the same sex. The term 'civil partnership' has not been amended to accord with such developments so as to avoid any confusion between these so-called 'civil marriages' and a civil marriage as understood in some jurisdictions as the formality which precedes or accompanies a religious ceremony.

Attention is drawn to the appended chapters of explanation on acronyms which appear in the text and a comprehensive glossary of Islamic terms.

"Knowledge is of two kinds. We know a subject ourselves, or we know where we can find information upon it."

SAMUEL JOHNSON

James Boswell, *The Life of Samuel Johnson Including a Journal of a Tour to the Hebrides, Vol.2*

Entries A - Z

A

Ab initio: 'From the beginning'; applied to circumstances which affect the validity of a legal relationship from the beginning. For example, where a settlor does not have legal capacity at the time of executing a trust deed the purported trust is void ab initio, i.e. VOID from the beginning: it never existed; the settlor was incapable of performing the act. The term 'void ab initio' may also describe circumstances where the authority of a person is affected by an act which occurs after the relationship commences, such as where a person has authority by law to enter the land of another and once upon the land commits a MISFEASANCE which constitutes a trespass; the person then becomes a 'trespasser ab initio', i.e. he is always considered to have been unlawfully present on the land from the beginning despite blameless conduct until the time the trespass was committed. This is only where authority is granted by law; where the person gains his authority from the landowner and not from the law and the abuse takes place after entering the land, then the person is liable only for the consequences of the offence and is not considered to be a trespasser ab initio.

Ab intestato: 'From an intestate person'; applied to SUCCESSION to property of a person who dies without disposing of the property by a valid will.

Abandonment: The giving up of an INTEREST or claim; particularly where the owner attempts to discard property finally and completely and is indifferent as to what becomes of it. Property can be relinquished but the law has never expressly recognised that property can exist but belong to no one. Where there is an attempt to abandon property, the English legal solution is to find that the property either is then held upon a RESULTING TRUST or that the property is treated as BONA VACANTIA and cedes to the state. In ***Vandervell v. IRC*** [1974] Ch 269, a beneficiary under a trust instructed his trustees to transfer a parcel of shares away from the trust with the intention of divesting himself of the entire EQUITABLE INTEREST in the shares. This did not succeed; the equitable interest that was unallocated passed back to the beneficiary on a resulting trust. This view was modified by Lord Browne-Wilkinson in ***Westdeutsche Landesbank Girozentrale v. Islington London Borough*** [1996] AC 669, who rejected the suggestion that the resulting trust would not arise upon any implication of the intention of the parties but operated automatically. The true position, he said, was that if the settlor abandons any BENEFICIAL INTEREST in the trust the interest is then vested in the Crown as bona vacantia. *See* INTEREST (2).

Abatement: The reduction of a legacy where the assets in the estate of the deceased are insufficient for the payment of expenses, debts and liabilities. Unless otherwise provided in the will, the general legacies will be used to pay the expenses, debts and liabilities before the specific legacies, i.e. general legacies abate before specific legacies. *See also* ADEMPTION *and* GENERAL LEGACY.

Abode: A habitation, dwelling or place of residence. This is not a precise legal term. It generally indicates where a person may have a place of business or where he lives. 'Abode' is distinct from the concepts of domicile or residence; although it denotes the place of a person's residence or business, temporary or permanent, without the legal precision attached to the other terms. The abode of a person is a question of fact rather than of law but is generally taken to mean where a person has a house or other residence in which he lives with his family and sleeps at night. *See also* RESIDENT *and* DOMICILE.

Absolute: Complete and unconditional; used legally to convey that an act or event is complete and not subject to any LIMITATION or prior INTEREST. For example, an absolute fee simple is a fee simple that is unlimited and in English law is the LEGAL ESTATE in land which cannot be enlarged. An interest in land is nonetheless absolute, although there may be a right of re-entry or similar rights. This does not affect the fundamental nature of the absolute fee simple. Similarly, an absolute interest means a full and complete ownership of that interest and, being a vested right in property, may only be determined by failure of successors in title. In connection with trust property, neither the trustees nor the beneficiaries have an absolute title until trust assets are awarded by the trustees to a beneficiary with no REMAINDER or other subsequent rights attached to those assets; the beneficiary then becomes the absolute owner of the trust assets and may do with them as he wishes. Similarly, a foundation is not the absolute owner because the assets are held subject to the express wishes of the founder. A foundation, acting through its foundation council, is unable to exercise the unrestrained rights of an absolute owner. When property is transferred, it is sometimes difficult to decide whether the transfer is meant to be absolute or to impose a trust. The word 'absolutely', when contained in a document transferring property, may be used in different senses and sometimes with contradictions in the same document, such as where an absolute gift is expressed to be made and then this seemingly all-powerful position is qualified by a provision purporting to give gifts over if certain circumstances arise, such as if the donee should die intestate and childless. This is a matter of construction because some absolute gifts may be accompanied by PRECATORY WORDS; for example, where the donor makes an unconditional gift but at the same time hopes that the donee will use the gift in a certain way. In that case, the donee takes absolutely and the precatory words are treated as repugnant to the idea of an absolute gift and are therefore legally void. On the other hand, there may be a gift expressed to be an absolute gift but which is accompanied by a valid limitation, such as the gift being made valid only upon the happening of some contingency. A variation on this is where a gift is made to a person absolutely but where the absolute nature of the gift is cut down by trusts that are imposed upon it. In this case, the absolute gift only takes effect if the trust lapses or is invalid for any other reason. Most difficulties arise due to problems of construction, such as in wills where there are precatory words, i.e. words expressing a hope, wish, desire, expectation or confidence that a legatee will use his inheritance in a particular way. Similarly, precatory words used in connection with the setting up of a gift, expressing a hope or expectation, may or may not constitute a valid trust but produce problems relating to the construction of the gift. Precatory words should therefore be avoided and there should be no doubt whether a gift is a gift absolute or a gift in trust. *See* INTEREST (2) AND (3), ABSOLUTE GIFT *and* PRECATORY WORDS.

Absolute assignment: *See* ASSIGNMENT.

Absolute discretion: A term sometimes applied to the powers of trustees or to a foundation council and others which indicates that the decisions which those holders of powers may make are subject to their sole discretion and cannot be challenged as to their content. Trustees and others who are given powers to dispose of property in their absolute discretion may need to show the steps they have taken and the investigations made in the assessments of the various interested parties in order to show that they have exercised their discretion knowledgeably, although the reason for the exercise in the direction which they have made is not disclosable.

Minutes of meetings of trustees and others need to take this into account.

Absolute gift: An unlimited and unfettered gift. Such a gift is unlimited by any other interest existing in the subject matter of the gift and where there is no condition or trust imposed on the freedom of the donee to deal with the subject matter as he wishes. An absolute gift is not diminished if the making of the gift is followed by an attempt by the donor to impose future gifts on the same property; for example, if the donee dies intestate or becomes incapable of managing his assets, the donor may wish the property to go elsewhere. Precatory words do not cut down an absolute gift. Any such attempt is void under the so-called 'doctrine of repugnancy'. *See* PRECATORY WORDS, ABSOLUTE, ABSOLUTE INTEREST *and* REPUGNANCY.

Absolute interest: An ESTATE that is transferred unfettered by any condition or trust. The donor cannot impose conditions or trust in respect of that property, real or personal, or provide, for example, if the donee does not spend it or give it away, that it should then pass to someone else. Nevertheless, there are several instances where absolute gifts are made that are then followed by gifts over if certain circumstances arise or certain events occur, such as where there has been an absolute gift on which trusts are engrafted or imposed, which have been judged that only if these trusts fail will the absolute gift then take effect. *See* ABSOLUTE GIFT *and* REPUGNANCY.

Absolute owner: A person with legal and beneficial rights in property; used to describe the power of trustees to sell, lease and manage TRUST PROPERTY to indicate the nature of their ability to deal in trust assets.

Absolute privilege: An exceptional advantage given to persons because of their status or office, allowing them to do certain things with protection against the consequences. The term is applied to a wide variety of circumstances, such as a legal professional privilege which protects confidential communications between a party and its lawyers, or between their lawyers. The extent that absolute privilege extends to communications between other professionals and their clients is unclear and probably does not exist between trustees and beneficiaries to the same extent as between lawyer and client. *See* CONFIDENTIAL INFORMATION AND TRUSTEES. Absolute privilege covers court proceedings and tribunals, and reports of such proceedings, as well as debates in Parliament. The absolute nature extends to the fact that it is immaterial whether the statement made was made with malice or otherwise. This goes back to the *Bill of Rights* of 1689, which stated that: 'The freedom of speech in debates or proceedings in Parliament ought not to be impeached or questioned in any court or place out of Parliament.' This has been extended to cover papers published by either House under the *Parliamentary Papers Act* 1840. Absolute privilege contrasts with 'QUALIFIED PRIVILEGE', which is less extensive. For example, qualified privilege is a defence to a defamation suit where the statement, although false, was made within limits of circumstances allowed by the law, such as statements made under the protection of fair comment or in the public interest. The term 'absolute privilege' is therefore fairly restrictive and it is a mistake to apply this term as an alternative to something which is purely confidential or private. *See also* PRIVILEGE.

Absolute right: A term that is now set out in the *European Convention on Human Rights* 1953 and cannot be lawfully interfered with no matter how important the public interest might be in doing so. Absolute rights include freedom of thought, conscience and religion and prohibitions on torture and inhuman treatment or punishment. This term must be distinguished from terms that also incorporate the word 'absolute', such as ABSOLUTE GIFT or ABSOLUTE INTEREST.

Absolute term of years: A LEGAL ESTATE in land that comprises one of the two legal estates which are permitted in land (the other being a FEE SIMPLE ABSOLUTE IN POSSESSION). In modern terminology, a holder may be described as a LESSEE or TENANT, the prime characteristic of which is that the term obeys the common law rules requiring certainty of term, which means a lease for a fixed period must have a certain beginning and a certain maximum duration. A lease is still an absolute term of years, whether in possession or in reversion, and may be subject to another legal estate or liable to determination prematurely by notice, re-entry, operation of law or by REDEMPTION or any other event, other than the ending of a life or the determination of a LIFE INTEREST, or one which does not take effect in possession within 21 years after the creation. Tenancies that run from month to month or from year to year are recognised and the tenancy extends and renews itself if neither party takes steps to bring it to the end after one of the periods. The term 'tenancy' is, in addition, used indiscriminately and often applied to arrangements when no legal estate is involved, such as when it is applied merely to a licence to occupy a property.

Absolute theory of sovereign immunity: A theory that a foreign state could not be sued before a municipal tribunal in any circumstances so as to uphold mutual respect between monarchs. This theory was eroded on the increase in the 20th century of industrial enterprises financed and controlled by states. *See* IMMUNITY.

Absolute title: Under the UK *Land Registration Act* 2002, Section 11, applied to a FREEHOLD estate in registered land which is absolute except for any interest on the Register at the time of registration or an unregistered interest which is an OVERRIDING INTEREST and other interests provided in the Act.

Absolute trust: A trust where the beneficiary has an absolute entitlement to the trust fund. Where there is more than one beneficiary, each beneficiary's interest in the trust is fixed and cannot be changed. A term used by some insurance companies to promote the use of trusts where a beneficiary has an ABSOLUTE RIGHT to the property, but which leaves many questions unanswered and is not a term to be used by trust professionals.

Absolute trust for minor: Unlike a BARE TRUST created for a person of full age and capacity, an absolute trust created by a settlor for a minor beneficiary may have extensive administrative powers consistent with statutory powers; for example, powers of maintenance and advancement under Sections 31 and 32 of the *Trustee Act* 1925. Such a trust cannot be considered as a mere repository and may be varied by the *Variation of Trusts Act* 1958.

Absolutely: With no limitation, restriction or qualification: totally; not determinable. Sometimes used in wills to describe bequests that are unconditional, immediate and not subject to any preceding or succeeding interest. When used to govern the holding of an income, it means the VESTED interest in the income is indefeasible, *Trustee Act* 1925, Section 33(2).

Absolutely entitled: Ownership that is free from any power or condition which may defeat that ownership. 'Entitled to the property ... absolutely' (*Trustee Act* 1925, Section 31(2)(i)(b)), when applied to PERSONALTY, denotes 'an interest which was not merely a vested interest in the entire capital and income of the property but was so vested free from any power or condition in future which might defeat it.' 'Absolutely entitled as against the trustee' means any person able to direct the trustee how to deal with the property and to give the trustee a good receipt for anything with which he has parted, *Finance Act* 1965, Sections 22 and 25, and *Finance Act* 1969, Schedule 19.

Absorption: A non-legal term used when two companies or operations become united by one of them merging with the other. *See* AMALGAMATION.

Abstention doctrine: A US term applied where the US Supreme Court declines to consider an appeal from a state court on a matter of state law or declines to exercise its federal constitutional jurisdiction.

Abstract of title: A written summary of the title deeds and other documents that the seller of land will put forward to show that he has a right to dispose of the land or an interest in it and which covers the LEGAL ESTATE and EQUITABLE INTERESTS. The abstract is presented to the purchaser who compares it with the original title deeds when they are produced or handed over on completion. In respect of registered land, the abstract consists of official copies of the entries in the register and other documents necessary to prove the owner's title, such as a marriage certificate where this is relevant.

Abuse of a position of trust: A term outside the law of trust where the word 'trust' is applied in its ordinary meaning when referred to in the *Children's Act* 1989 and the *Sexual Offences Act* 2003 in connection with an abuse of the position of trust with the person concerned.

Abuse of confidence: A breach in the duty owed by a FIDUCIARY to his principal where the fiduciary does not observe his duty of confidentiality and which can give rise to an action by the principal in equity. This term is also particularly relevant to commercial financial transactions and is sometimes attributed to an implied contractual obligation as opposed to a general fiduciary duty when it is required by law or in discharge of a public duty, especially in banking relationships. *See* FIDUCIARY *and* PROTECTION, EQUITABLE.

Abuse of direction: A US term applied where a person does not get a fair trial and which may justify a court of appeal reversing a trial court judgment. The term is applied only where a trial judge has made a serious error, such as making improper comments which might influence a jury, showing bias or excluding the testimony of an important witness, but does not apply to less than perfect judgments, which cannot be considered as having denied a fair trial.

Abuse of process: Usually means wrong, bad or improper use of the process of the court that is countered by the court having power to strike out or stay an action by the court itself. Abuse of process has been defined as 'using the court's process for a purpose or in a way which is significantly different from the ordinary and proper use of the court's process' (***Attorney General v. Barker*** [2000] 1 F.L.R. 759). The categories of abuse are numerous; for example, where a litigant raises issues that should have been determined in an earlier action and where a person is declared to be a VEXATIOUS LITIGANT. The categories of abuse are many and not closed. The term is also applied to abuse of civil process that may itself be actionable as the tort of malicious institution, such as where there is a malicious presentation of a bankruptcy petition or the malicious arrest of a ship. There is an analogous power of the court in connection with criminal matters, particularly where the criminal courts have the power and duty in upholding the law to protect their own purpose and functions. The court has the power to stay a criminal proceeding on the grounds of abuse where the court concludes that the accused cannot receive a fair trial or where it would be unfair for the accused to be tried.

Acceleration clause: A clause incorporated into financial contracts that impose an obligation to pay the amount owing before the contractual date due to some element of default. It is a question of law whether such payment in full constitutes a penalty and which is therefore unenforceable. For example, an agreement that a loan payable by instalments becomes payable in full on default is not a penalty but simply a provision in the loan contract requiring the outstanding instalments to be paid immediately. Also, where an ANNUITY is paid to a person during that person's lifetime and to others for three months after the annuitant's death and where, during his lifetime, he disclaims his interest in receiving the annuities, this acts to accelerate the payment to the others notwithstanding that the original recipient is still alive. An acceleration clause is often found in connection with promissory notes in the US for instalment payments for the purchase of real property and requires the entire amount of the notes to be paid immediately if the purchaser sells the property. This is known as a 'due on sale' clause, which is prohibited in some US states where a new owner of the property simply assumes the outstanding debt.

Acceptance of trust property: This is the taking of property into a TRUST, by which a trustee becomes the legal owner of the property. Before accepting property a potential trustee ought to consider whether there is a conflict between his personal self-interest and his FIDUCIARY duty. There may be a liability attached to the property that is unforeseen to a casual observer (such as liability for damages in respect of toxic waste below the surface of the land). The trustee must also be aware of whether there is a potential liability under any anti-money laundering legislation. *See* ANTI-MONEY LAUNDERING LAW. The duty of a trustee following acquisition of property is to acquaint himself with the nature of the property and the documents and to ensure that proper minutes are made in respect of the property. On accepting property, a trustee must ensure that the formalities relating to the acquisition of property have been followed and, where the property is held by CUSTODIANS, the trustee should ensure that the custodian agreement is adequate to a change of trustee.

Acceptance of trusteeship: The process through which a prospective trustee considers whether there could be a conflict between his personal interests and his FIDUCIARY duties as a trustee. Also relevant, which a prospective trustee should consider, is the onerous nature of the responsibilities; these include the validity of the proposed trust, the requirements to produce a transfer of assets and the anti-money laundering rules. *See* ANTI-MONEY LAUNDERING LAW. The taking on of a new trust, or becoming the trustee of an established trust, calls for care to be exercised by the new trustee to determine the extent of the potential liability. Relevant to taking on a trust are the questions of REMUNERATION OF TRUSTEES and an EXCULPATORY CLAUSE and the possible means of ultimately relinquishing the trust. Particular care needs to be taken when considering becoming a trustee, either as a sole trustee or as a co-trustee, especially where the co-trustee is in a different jurisdiction. Caution must also be exercised when considering the relationship between the trustee and the PROTECTOR and the protector's powers of supervision.

Access to Justice Report 1996: *See* PRE-ACTION PROTOCOL.

Accessory liability: *See* KNOWING RECEIPT AND DISHONEST ASSISTANCE.

Accord and satisfaction: Generally, a contractual concept where a person who has a right of action against another agrees that the person against whom action may be brought should do or give something which would be accepted in satisfaction of the obligation. The accord is the agreement and the satisfaction is the consideration for that agreement. Both aspects must be present in order to bar the right of action under the original claim. A typical example is where there is an agreement by a debtor with a number of creditors whereby each of the creditors agree with one another to take a sum less than the debt (***Slater v. Jones*** (1873) L.R. 8 Ex. 186). That is sufficient to bar an action by the creditors against the debtor for the full amount and illustrates that the essence of the doctrine is a contractual modification of the original bargain.

Account: An equitable remedy which, under the *Constitutional Reform Act* 2005, was assigned to the Chancery Division of the High Court. When an order for account is made, it requires the party to whom it is addressed to render to the other party a proper account of profits and other financial features of their relationship. A judge may, as an interim remedy, grant an order directing a party to prepare and file accounts. No action for account can be brought on any matter which arose more than six years before the commencement of the action (*Limitation Act* 1980, Section 23).

Accretion: *See* ACCRETION AND ACCRUAL.

Accretion and accrual: Terms indicating an increase in value to personal or real property usually by gradual or imperceptible accumulation or by an APPORTIONMENT according to established legal practice. The terms are used interchangeably to indicate such accumulations without a precise reference to a legal principle. For example, with real property, when the sea recedes, the land revealed accrues to the adjoining land onshore. Similarly, accrual occurs where a fund, share, estate, security or other property is increased by additions that take place *IPSO JURE* or *IPSO FACTO*. The additions are said to accrue either to the original property or to the person entitled to it. This can take place either by an act of nature (e.g. when applied to young animals) or where property is increased or added to by an act of the party or by a tenant, and where a fund is increased by additions that arise from the rule *accessorium sequitur principale* (an accessory thing goes with the thing to which it is accessory), such as the addition to a charitable fund from an increase in rents and from crops and fixtures that become part of the land to which they have been fixed. This is usually referred to as an 'accretion'. With companies that distribute profits in capital form, it is not clear, on the winding up, whether the payments to shareholders may include the capital and accumulated profits. The solution lies in the nature of the payment and the language used. Similar problems arise where there is a transfer of securities. These examples are usually referred to as matters of accretion and, where there is an increase in value of the assets in a trust or legacy following an apportionment to the interested parties, this is usually referred to as an accrual. Accretion as applied to trust assets occurs when the trust assets increase in value; for example, where there is a bonus issue made in respect of shares held by a trust for persons in SUCCESSION. The question arises of whether the benefit of that increase goes to the tenant for life, i.e. the person immediately entitled to the income of the trust (*see* LIFE TENANT), or should be added to capital that will be for the benefit of the REMAINDERMEN. Where there is such an accretion, the increased value must be apportioned; this is considered either from the point of view of apportionment as to time or apportionment as to subject matter. Examples of apportionment as to time occur where the settlor or testator is still alive and where accretions, and, in particular, dividends, are regarded as part of the settlor's property and are treated as capital even though they are not distributed until after the settlor's death, when there is a will trust, or when the trust becomes active when it is an inter vivos trust. Otherwise, the tenant for life takes all dividends and bonuses as income. A tenant for life takes the proceeds of accretions occurring after the settlor's death even if it was in relation to events before the settlor's death. On the death of the life tenant, his executors are not entitled to any income of the trust that was not declared payable during the life tenant's life. The *Apportionment Act* 1870 usually provides the answer to these problems. Apportionment as to subject matter into either income or capital usually arises when securities are transferred by trustees cum dividend, i.e. the purchaser obtains the right to the securities and the dividend associated with those securities. In that case, trustees would be expected to postpone the sale until the investments are quoted ex dividend and then there is no question that the price received needs to be apportioned between capital and income. Concerning other payments made in respect of TRUST PROPERTY there is no one rule for determining the rights of beneficiaries. The court will endeavour to give beneficiaries' rights corresponding to those they enjoyed in the property concerned or may order apportionment between income and capital in the absence of any statutory provision relating to the payment, such as provisions for compensation. Also, if dividends or accretions were declared during the settlor's lifetime, they are regarded as part of the settlor's property and hence treated as capital. There are exceptions in the case of SETTLED LAND.

Accrual: *See* ACCRETION AND ACCRUAL.

Accumulations: The aggregation, or putting by, of dividends, rents and other incomes that are then converted into principal by investing them and again investing the income arriving from the new principal, and so on. The legal consequences of accumulating income features in trust law, but in recent years the provisions relating to the accumulation of income over an extensive period have been relaxed. *See* PERPETUITIES AND ACCUMULATIONS *and* ACCUMULATION OF INCOME.

Accumulation and maintenance trusts: Trusts of a type that in the past qualified for favourable treatment for inheritance tax purposes but which were discontinued under the *Finance Act* 2006. *See* ACCUMULATION TRUSTS *and also* AGE 18-25 TRUST.

Accumulation of income: Under the *Perpetuities and Accumulations Act* 1964, in respect of trusts created before 6 April 2010, no person may settle or dispose of any property so that the income shall be accumulated for a period longer than any one of six periods stated in the Act. For trusts created after 6 April 2010 these restrictions were abolished and trustees will be able to accumulate income throughout the lifetime of the trust if this is required by the SETTLOR. The previous periods stated in the 1964 Act are: (1) the life of the GRANTOR or settlor, (2) 21 years from the death of the grantor or settlor, (3) the minority of any person living or expected at the death of the grantor, settlor or TESTATOR, (4) the minority of any person who would, if of full age, be entitled to the income, (5) 21 years from making the disposition, and (6) the duration of the minority of any person in being at that date. There are exceptions to these rules. A beneficiary under a trust that provides for accumulation may put an end to the accumulation that is exclusively for his benefit and demand the property under the rule in ***Saunders v. Vautier*** (1841) 4 Beav 115. This is a provision under the *Perpetuities and Accumulations Act* 1964, Section 14, but does not apply to instruments taking effect before the commencement of that Act. *See* PERPETUITIES AND ACCUMULATIONS.

Accumulation trusts: Trusts where the trustees accumulate income within a trust by adding it to the capital. This is a feature of trusts and continues until the beneficiary becomes legally entitled to the trust assets. These trusts should not be confused with maintenance trusts (*see* MAINTENANCE (1)).

Acquiescence: A tacit agreement to an infringement of rights, either express or implied from conduct, by which the right to equitable relief is generally lost. A trust beneficiary who is SUI JURIS with full knowledge of the facts may not claim a remedy from trustees for BREACH OF TRUST where the beneficiary fails to make adequate complaint or to take appropriate action within a reasonable period. Under these circumstances, the beneficiary is considered to have acquiesced in the breach unless the delay can be reasonably explained. The important thing to avoid losing a right by acquiescence is for the beneficiary or other person to make suitable protest. This should be made even though it is inappropriate to start an action in respect of the matter, for the time being. For example, a REVERSIONER is not automatically assumed to have acquiesced when he knows of a breach of trust and protests but takes no steps until he becomes entitled in possession. The acquiescence of a past breach does not constitute a licence for further breaches by the trustee to be committed by the trustee with impunity. Acquiescence is associated with ESTOPPEL, and in particular with LACHES, as where a potential claim is frustrated by 'laches, acquiescence and delay'. It is also associated with the limitation of a time where an action may be brought; time only begins to run from the date when the party first becomes aware of a right that has been infringed. Acquiescence can lead to an action which is otherwise justifiable being barred due to a deliberate abstention of asserting the rights under the limitation laws. *See* ESTOPPEL *and* LIMITATION OF ACTIONS.

Acquis communautaire: Also known as the 'community acquis', or the 'EU acquis': this is the whole body of European Community law comprising the treaty, regulations, directives, decisions and judicial opinions.

Act of God: More than a mere misfortune and something that is overwhelming, such as a storm or earthquake or other natural causes which could not have happened by the intervention of man and which could not have been prevented or avoided by any reasonable amount of foresight. *See* FORCE MAJEURE.

Acting trustee: A person who has taken upon himself to perform some of the duties of a trustee and, by doing so, incurs the liability of a trustee in respect of the act performed. This does not include a person who has refused to act, such as a trustee who selects the matters over which he will be concerned and matters over which he will not. *See also* CONTINUING TRUSTEE.

Action: Any civil proceedings commenced by writ or in any other manner prescribed in rules of court; the term was used before the CIVIL PROCEDURE RULES (CPR) were introduced to indicate proceedings in what were then called the UK's Superior Courts (now known as Senior Courts). Since the CPR applied, the words 'action' 'cause' and 'matter' as terms of art are not used. This results in a lack of consistency in the legislation governing the jurisdictions of the High Court and the Court of Appeal and other courts, and the useful differences in the meanings of these terms. Under the CPR, there is now a universally applicable term, 'claim', which is used in all courts.

Active trust: An EXPRESS TRUST that requires the trustee to do positive acts, such as administering and distributing the trust property in contrast to merely holding the TRUST PROPERTY and handing it eventually to the person entitled to it as with a BARE TRUST.

Actual: In many cases the word does not add or mean anything and could quite well be omitted. However, the word may have a constructive legal meaning and, when applied, will intensify the word which it describes and indicate that the situation occurred as a matter of fact and not merely as a matter of law.

Actual entry: An entry on land that requires a person to bodily place himself on the land in contrast to an entry in law where physical presence on land is deemed to have been made where actual entry was prevented by violence or fear of violence.

Actual notice: Knowledge possessed by an owner of land that another person has rights which take precedence over his own. For example, where a purchaser of UNREGISTERED LAND knows of an interest that need not be registered but which nevertheless persists (i.e. overreaches) a sale. In this case, the owner cannot plead that he did not know of that right if the other party can show that the owner actually did know of the existence of that OVERREACHING right. (With registered land the doctrine of notice plays no part as it has been replaced by the rules of registration.)

Actual possession: Physical possession of land or goods and the receipt of rents or profits as opposed to CONSTRUCTIVE POSSESSION or technical possession.

Ad hoc: 'For this purpose only'.

Ad litem: 'For the purpose of the legal action only': A term applied to a person or event that exists for the purpose of a legal action. It is particularly used in connection with guardianship where a GUARDIAN ad litem is a person appointed by a court to represent another person who is unable to act on his own behalf. This applies particularly in connection with judicial proceedings involving children.

Ad valorem: 'Based on value'.

Ademption: The complete or partial extinction of a specific legacy where the property (other than real property) ceases to be part of the testator's property in his lifetime. For example, by the testator giving away an item included in his will, during his lifetime. The legatee is not then entitled to any payment out of the general assets. Ademption also occurs if the asset has been changed into something different even if it is still in the testator's possession at his death unless the change is only in name and form, e.g. shares changed on a company reconstruction. It is immaterial whether the change comes about by external influences or by the testator's hand. A general legacy given to a child by a parent or a person in *LOCO PARENTIS* is subject to ademption if a PORTION is given to the child after the will has been executed. A general legacy to a stranger is not liable to ademption under similar circumstances unless it is clear that the testator did not mean to discharge such moral obligations more than once. Ademption is statutorily excluded from the proceeds of REDEMPTION of government stock (*National Debt (Conversion) Act* 1888) and from the stock of various nationalisation schemes. Ademption only takes place with specific legacies if the thing bequeathed has ceased to belong to the testator. Demonstrative legacies allow the best of both worlds. A DEMONSTRATIVE LEGACY is not liable for ademption by reason that the fund from which the payment is declared is not enough and that source has been deleted from the daily source book.

Adjective law: Also called 'procedural law'. The law relating to practice and procedure which is distinguished from SUBSTANTIVE LAW; the law that decides the relationship between parties. The distinction is not hard and fast and the question may arise as to whether a particular matter is one of substantive law or of procedural law or adjective law. No general answer can be made to these questions and any situation requires an analysis of the legal background in its factual context. Adjective law or procedural law is concerned with the machinery by which legal rights and duties are recognised, as opposed to substantive law which comprises the body of laws that give or define legal rights and duties or confers legal status. In international matters the adjective law is in the exclusive jurisdiction of each state, i.e. an action in the courts is governed exclusively by the adjective law of the jurisdiction in which the court is situated. A matter that is a part of the substantive law in one jurisdiction may be regarded as adjective law in another. This particularly occurs in connection with the award of COSTS of a proceeding where it is likely to be regarded by the courts as part of the substantive law. *See also* PROCEDURAL RULES.

Adjudicate: The settlement of a dispute by a judge or arbitrator in a court or tribunal.

Adjustment: The ability of trustees when overpaying a beneficiary to retain the amount of any overpayment out of other interests of the beneficiary such as future income; for example, when payments to the beneficiary should have been reduced to take into account the payment of tax. Adjustment does not apply where the trustee is also a beneficiary where no adjustment is allowed for overpayment by a trustee of himself as this would be a means of avoiding a BREACH OF TRUST claim.

Administration: The winding up of the estate of a deceased person, paying the debts and distributing the assets to those entitled or to trustees on their behalf. This was a task originally performed by the ecclesiastical courts with the Court of Chancery having a supplementary jurisdiction. Administration, such as the winding up and distribution duties of PERSONAL REPRESENTATIVES, contrasts with the duties of trustees who normally are required to hold the trust property and administer it in accordance with the trust deed. During the administration of a will, personal representatives have the control of the whole property of the testator. Beneficiaries have no interest in any assets until distributed by the personal representatives. Beneficiaries merely have the right to compel the due administration; these rights are subject to the limitation period; for example, a personal estate of a deceased person must be completed within 12 years. This is unlike the position with trusts where the right to recover trust property is barred after six years. Personal representatives conducting administration may act individually, unlike trustees which act jointly. The distinction becomes blurred; an individual may at the same time be both a trustee and a personal representative, particularly where a testator sets up a WILL TRUST and appoints the same person to be both executor and trustee; individual assets must be assessed separately.

Administration action: An application made by the personal representatives of the estate of a deceased person or by a beneficiary or creditor of the estate requesting that the court should issue an order to take over the administration of the estate. If made, such an order renders the powers of the personal representatives who deal with the estate to be inoperable without the sanction of the court.

Administration of estates: The regime introduced by the *Administration of Estates Act* 1925 by which the assets of a deceased person devolve on the deceased's PERSONAL REPRESENTATIVE and with it the responsibility for the disposal of the deceased's estate according to his will or according to the rules of intestacy. *See also* EXECUTOR *and* ADMINISTRATOR (1).

Administration order: An order made by the court for the administration of a trust where there are difficulties which cannot be resolved in some other way. This type of order is provided for in English law (under Part 64, Civil Procedure Rules (CPR), in the Practice Directions). Orders for the removal of trustees and for the appointment of new ones are frequent examples of such orders. Administration orders will not be given if the court considers that issues between the parties could be resolved in some other way. Frivolous applications are discouraged by making an applicant pay all the costs when, for example, a trustee merely wishes to be released or a beneficiary has no basis for making a complaint about the competence of the trustee. An applicant making a frivolous action will not get his costs despite making the application in GOOD FAITH where he had no good cause to expect success.

Administrative and managerial powers: *See* POWER.

Administrator (1): A person appointed as a personal representative of a deceased person when the deceased died intestate (the appointment of authority is contained in the Letter of Administration), or when the testator left a will but failed to appoint an executor, or where the persons appointed as executors refuse to act. The authority then, by what is known as a Letter of Administration with Will Attached, makes a suitable appointment. Where necessary, limited administrations may be granted, such as for the collection of assets of foreigners, where an infant is entitled to administration, where a person appointed is abroad or where the will is subject to litigation. There are other situations where limited administrators may be appointed. All these ancillary administrators are subordinate to the principal or original administrators. *See* EXECUTOR.

Administrator (2): A person who is appointed under the *Insolvency Act* 1986 to manage the affairs and properties of an insolvent company or partnership and who is qualified under the Act to be an insolvency practitioner.

Administrator de son tort: *See* EXECUTOR DE SON TORT.

Admitted Purpose Trust: A trust set up in several offshore jurisdictions whose legislation provides for the establishment of a PURPOSE TRUST that may also have individuals as beneficiaries, such as Bermuda, the British Virgin Islands and the Turks and Caicos Islands. The same objective is reached in other legislation by more complex provisions.

ADR, contracts for: *See* ALTERNATIVE DISPUTE RESOLUTION.

Advancement: The power of a trustee to apply part of the capital or income of a trust fund for the benefit of a beneficiary who is still a minor or whose interest is still contingent. Sometimes a trustee may extend an advancement to a beneficiary who is neither a minor nor whose interest is contingent. The word 'advancement' seems to be an abbreviation of 'advancement in the world' which implies the setting up of a beneficiary in a trade or profession. The word advancement has also been criticized as being a word appropriate to an early period of a beneficiary's life. This meaning is now regarded as too restrictive. Advancement is now considered to describe a power to make some permanent provision for a child or other beneficiary, such as an advance on the purchase of a house. *The Inheritance and Trustees' Powers Act* 2014 removed the limit on advancements for trusts which previously could not exceed one half of the beneficiary's interest in the trust property. This removal of the limit applied to advancement under trusts created or arising after the Act came into force. Also, under this Act, trustees could advance assets and not merely cash. This amendment applies to all trusts whenever established. The sum advanced or the value of assets advanced is brought into account when the beneficiary becomes entitled to a share of the capital (i.e. the sum advanced is brought into HOTCHPOTCH). Where there is a person entitled in priority to the beneficiary who might receive an advancement, then the consent of that person must be obtained before an advancement is made. An advancement results in the fund advanced being taken right out of the trust estate and is therefore distinct from the exercise of the POWER OF APPOINTMENT and thus may affect other beneficiaries. An exercise of the power of advancement by trustees may be accompanied by a postponement of the vesting of the beneficiaries' remaining interests in the trust fund. The provision of a power of advancement may appear in wills or settlements under an express power or, as far as trusts are concerned, may be left to the statutory powers contained in Section 32 of the *Trustee Act* 1925 as amended in 2014. Similar provisions appear in the trust laws of other jurisdictions. Laws on private foundations generally contain no similar specific provisions. Provided the person requiring advancement is a named beneficiary, or within the class of beneficiaries of a foundation, the award of a sum for advancement is then up to the ability of the foundation council to exercise their discretion and subject to whatever conditions they may decide.

Adverse claim: A claim to property made without a reasonable expectation of succeeding. A trustee must not set up or aid the interest of a third party who makes a claim against trust property that prejudices the interests of the beneficiaries. Trustees may not contest the rights of their beneficiaries to the trust assets. Where a trustee is faced with an adverse claim by a third party that damages the interests of a beneficiary, or where there is an adverse claim that would make the trustee personally liable, the trustee should continue as far as possible to fulfil the trustees' obligations towards the beneficiaries but apply to the court for directions of whether he should resist the claim.

Adverse party: Parties who are opposed to the other parties in a legal action. Sometimes parties may be adverse to each other on some issues but in agreement on others, such as where two beneficiaries under a will are in agreement in maintaining the validity of the will but in opposition when it comes to its interpretation.

Adverse possession: Occupation of REAL PROPERTY which is alleged by the true owner to be inconsistent with his rights but where there is nothing to show that possession is inconsistent with the true owner's title. To constitute adverse possession the person occupying the property must do so as of right with the intention of excluding all persons from it, including the rightful owner. *See NEC PER VIM, NEC CLAM, NEC PRECARIO.* Adverse possession may arise from the beginning of the occupation, such as occurs when a mere trespasser takes possession of another's property and retains it against him, or it may develop on the expiry of a lawful possession where, for example, a TENANT remains in possession after the end of his tenancy. Possession is not considered adverse if it can be referred to a lawful title, such as a permissive or FIDUCIARY title, or through an agreement or judgment of law, when all who claim under him are presumed to hold possession according to that right. A person holding under adverse possession is protected in his possession against all who cannot show a better title. If adverse possession continues for a prescribed period of time, it may extinguish the title of the true owner (*Limitation Act* 1980, Section 17); this will apply although the true owner is unaware of the adverse possessor being in occupation. The ordinary time limit under the Act for an action to recover land is 12 years, or 30 years in the case of Crown land or land owned by a spiritual corporation sole. Under the 1980 Act, adverse possession does not extinguish the title of any person where the period of LIMITATION has not had its effect. Registration of land under the *Land Registration Act* 2002 is now regarded as a protection against adverse possession. Under Schedule 6 of that Act an adverse possessor of land may be registered as a proprietor of a registered estate after 10 years and, failing action by the registered proprietor, the person in adverse possession may, after a further period of two years, reapply to be registered and, if still in adverse possession, the second application will be successful.

Adverse witness: A witness who discloses a hostile attitude to the party who calls for his testimony and may be cross-examined by the party calling him, particularly in connection with inconsistent statements. A witness is established as an adverse witness on consent of the judge, who then allows the party calling the witness to cross-examine.

Advertisement: A means by which trustees and personal representatives may protect themselves from failure to distribute assets to persons entitled to them and who they did not know existed. This has become more important due to the inclusion of illegitimate and other issue on the same footing as legitimate issue. Section 27 of the *Trustee Act* 1925 makes provision for advertisement in the *London Gazette* and in a newspaper circulating in the area in which land is situated and, where the trust is a personality only, then the advertisement should give equivalent NOTICE. A trustee only attains protection if the advertisement complies with the requirements of Section 27 of the Act.

Advisory board: A structure present in the law of private foundations in some jurisdictions, such as Austria. This is useful where the founder and members of the family are excluded by law from being members of the management board or foundation council when they are beneficiaries. Therefore, in addition to the management board or foundation council, it is prudent to establish an advisory board, which allows the beneficiaries some influence on the daily management of the foundation.

Advowson: The right to appoint a minister of the church to occupy a parish or other ecclesiastical post (if the gift is in the hands of a diocesan bishop, it is called a 'collation'). In modern terminology, this is 'a right of patronage': the owner of which is called the 'patron'. The ecclesiastical laws on patronage and associated rights have been revised in recent years and are now governed by the *Patronage (Benefices) Measure* 1986. An advowson can no longer be sold or transferred for a valuable CONSIDERATION.

Affiant: A person who signs an AFFIDAVIT and swears to its truth. The essential item is the giving of a promise or plighting of troth, as in affiance, which is the agreement between a man and a woman on marriage, i.e. in modern parlance described as 'engaged to be married'.

Affidavit: A signed statement by a person (the deponent) usually for use in judicial proceedings by which a person describes circumstances in a manner equivalent to an oath (in civil proceedings the use of an affidavit is governed by Civil Procedure Rules (under CPR 32.15-17 and the form governed by Paras. 2-16, Pt. 32), Practice Direction. However, for many purposes in civil proceedings, affidavits are now replaced by the less formal 'Statements of Truth'. Affidavits are used in criminal proceedings where the *Commissioner for Oaths Act* 1889 regulates the appointment and powers for Commissioners for Oaths who also take affidavits.

After acquired property: *See* SEPARATE ESTATE.

Age 18-25 trust: A trust created under the will of a deceased parent or step-parent or under the Criminal Injuries Compensation Scheme where the property is held for the benefit of persons aged under 25 so that the beneficiary becomes absolutely entitled to the whole property on or before their 25th birthday. Introduced in March 2006, where it was provided that the existing Accumulation and Maintenance Trusts created before 22 March 2006 only become Age 18-25 Trusts if the terms are rewritten to allow the beneficiary to be absolutely entitled on or before his or her 25th birthday. Failure to rewrite those trusts before 6 April 2008 resulted in the existing Accumulation and Maintenance Trusts becoming Relevant Property Trusts and thereby incurs the 10-year anniversary charge. *See* TRUSTS FOR BEREAVED MINORS.

Age discrimination: A person who has not reached the age of maturity does not have the CAPACITY to set up a trust, where the trust assets comprise a legal estate in land, since a minor is incapable of holding such an asset and therefore cannot settle a legal estate in land. This restriction does not apply to the ability of a minor to set up other settlements where capacity is treated in the same way as capacity to enter into contracts. Although settlements of personal property may be possible, a minor may plead *non est factum* if too young to understand the nature of the arrangements he purported to make. Also, any INTER VIVOS trust made by a minor, although it would bind the property if made by an adult, is treated as VOIDABLE but not VOID; a minor may repudiate it shortly after attaining his MAJORITY; if he does not so repudiate the settlement it will be binding except where, by the law of the child's DOMICILE or the proper law of the settlement, such ratification is not allowed. A child cannot make a settlement by will unless the child is a privileged testator, such as a soldier or airman in actual military service or a mariner or seaman at sea. Also, by Section 20 of the *Law of Property Act* 1925, the appointment of a child to be a trustee in relation to a settlement or trust is void. It is advisable to avoid making a child a member of the foundation council or appointing a child as a protector of a private foundation for similar reasons.

Agent: A person, individual or corporate, who acts on behalf of another, the principal. Although an agent may have a FIDUCIARY relationship with the principal, agency is recognised at common law. The relationship is contractual and does not depend upon ownership or passing of ownership of property. A trustee is not an agent. A foundation council may be an agent for the foundation. On the other hand, a person appointed as an agent may be a trustee, such as where the relationship is such that a RESULTING TRUST exists and in circumstances where an agent holds money on a CONSTRUCTIVE TRUST for a principal (see *QUISTCLOSE* TRUST). The appointment of agents, including NOMINEES or CUSTODIANS, is a fiduciary operation requiring the appropriate DUTY OF CARE. Trustees basically have no right to shift their duty to other persons, i.e. they are unable to appoint agents unless authorised by statute or the trust instrument. *The Trustee Act* 2000 made new provisions and trustees acting collectively may delegate most of their administrative duties to an agent unless the trust instrument provides otherwise. Trustees are unable to delegate their essential discretionary responsibilities, however.

***Agip (Africa) v. Jackson* [1991] Ch 476, 566:** A decision that demonstrates the benefit of EQUITABLE TRACING over common law tracing in that a claimant may be able to trace through mixtures of property and the bankruptcies of companies that are intended to obscure the involvement of stolen funds. The judgment also decided that either a principal or an agent can sue on the equitable tracing claim.

Agreement: A consensus of two or more minds expressing a COMMON INTENTION with a view to altering their rights and duties. A contract is an agreement that is legally enforceable. Also, in INTERNATIONAL LAW, an agreement between two governments indicates that their consensus is of a less formal nature than a treaty. *See* CONTRACT.

Agreement for a lease: A contract to enter into a lease which, if the period of the lease is not more than three years, may be made orally or by any kind of written agreement so long as it does not create a future lease; a contract for a longer lease must be in writing incorporating all the terms of the agreement and signed by the parties. A contract which does not meet these requirements is void irrespective of performance unless the arrangement can be construed as a constructive trust or resulting trust (*Law of Property (Miscellaneous Provisions) Act* 1989).

***Agricultural Holdings Act* 1986:** Where land is held on a tenancy where the actual or contemplated use of the land, the date of the contract, or subsequently, or subject to any other circumstances, is for the whole of the land to be let for agricultural purposes, then it is governed by the *Agricultural Holdings Act* 1986 and the whole of the land, whether or not agricultural, is held as within the terms of a tenancy governed by the Act. Under earlier Acts, which were intended to encourage domestic food production, tenants of agricultural holdings were given certain securities such as compensation for damage by game, against distress and length of notice to quit. This is reflected in the *Agricultural Holdings Act* 1986 but the *Agricultural Tenancies Act* 1995 introduces the concept of the farm business tenancy, which aims to encourage new lettings of farmland and diversity in the use of land by removing such security of tenure.

Airmen: *See* EXECUTION OF WILLS.

Aleatory: An uncertain occurrence and, applied to contracts, the effect of which, with respect to advantages or losses, depends on an uncertain event. Applied in civil law, aleatory describes what English law regards as a 'wagering contract' but, in common law usage, it has a wider meaning, such as in connection with circumstances that are beyond the control of either party; for example, most insurance contracts are aleatory because the insured may collect a large amount of compensation or even nothing in return for the premiums paid depending upon the interpretation of the contract.

Alienation: The transfer of property to another. The power of alienation is the power of an owner or tenant of property to dispose of his interest. With personal property the power appears to have always existed subject to particular rules as to the mode of the alienation. In contrast, the power to alienate real property was only acquired over a period of centuries due to the original concept that all the estates were at first only life estates held under the Crown. This continued until the Statute of *Quia Emptores* 1285, after which every freeman could then sell all his land. Now, under modern law, the term is frequently used to describe the effect of any condition imposed on the transfer of property to impose a restraint on any further transfer. This is known as 'a RESTRAINT ON ALIENATION' and is VOID where the purported transfer is of an ABSOLUTE INTEREST. This applies to any attempts of restraint of alienation with real or personal property. With trusts, if a person makes a settlement on himself so that his interest in the settlement determines upon bankruptcy, this is seen as a restraint on alienation under the *Trustee Act* 1925, Section 33.

***Alieni juris*:** The opposite of SUI JURIS and applied to a person who is subject to the authority of another, such as, in modern law, a child subject to the authority of a parent or subject to some legal constraint. A term originally used in Roman law to indicate that a person was under the power of a father, a husband or a master.

Aliens: An alien is defined in the *British Nationality Act* 1981, Section 50, as 'A person who is neither a Commonwealth citizen nor a British protected person nor citizen of the Republic of Ireland.' Aliens are under no disability with regards to BENEFICIAL INTERESTS other than property in British ships and aircraft. There is no prohibition against the appointment of foreign residents as trustees (*see* FOREIGN RESIDENT TRUSTEE).

Alimentary trust: *See* PROTECTIVE TRUST.

Aliquot share: A beneficiary, who is of full age and capacity, is entitled to request the transfer of a definite fractional share (an aliquot share) of each and every asset of the fund in which he has an absolute vested beneficial interest provided there is no difficulty in the division of the assets generally.

Allegation: A statement of fact or the presentation of reasons used in any court or legal proceedings including AFFIDAVITS, witness statements or statements of truth. An appellant in a civil case cannot recover damages in respect of any situation not mentioned in his or her allegation.

***Allhusen v. Whittell* (1867) L.R. 4 Eq 295:** A decision that comprised one of the four rules of APPORTIONMENT, which have been made optional for new trusts by the *Trusts (Capital and Income) Act* 2013 and which are still relevant in respect of older trusts. *See* APPORTIONMENT.

Allotment: The issue of previously unissued shares in a limited company in exchange for a contribution in cash or kind towards the capital of that company. Allotments usually are made on the public flotation of a company or on the privatisation of a state-owned industry. Before the shares are issued the company sends a letter of allotment to each potential shareholder stating how many shares have been allotted to that applicant. An increase in the total issued SHARE CAPITAL of a UK company is registered with the Registrar of Companies.

Alter ego: An indication that a settlor has retained so much influence over the affairs of a trust or foundation that the trust or foundation is truly a NOMINEE of the settlor. This results in the arrangement being ignored in any assessment of a settlor's or founder's assets, such as in court proceedings to determine taxable income and in matrimonial proceedings to determine the size of the settlor's or founder's personal assets which influences the amount allocated to each party. The concept is different from a SHAM as here the trustees' or foundation councils' discretion is overcome by the degree of dominance that the settlor can exercise in an otherwise valid trust or foundation. The court may feel justified in piercing the veil of a trust or foundation when the arrangement represents personal assets. This can happen despite the submission that the property is held in trust or by the foundation and is no longer within the settlor or founder's PATRIMONY. The court considers that by the exercise of the dominance of the settlor or founder the assets could be returned to him and used in the calculation of his personal wealth. The property is the alter ego of the settlor or founder. Although the alter ego concept is different from that of a sham, both are based upon evidence that could be used in either situation.

Alter ego trust: A Canadian concept where an INTER VIVOS trust is created by a person of an age of 65 or over where the property may be transferred into the trust free of Canadian capital gains tax in respect of the disposal by the settlor provided that no person except the settlor may obtain the use of the income or capital of the trust. The trust may provide a LIFE INTEREST in favour of the settlor's spouse to arise after his death with the REMAINDER in favour of the children. These trusts save liability to capital gains tax that would otherwise be charged if the same dispositions had been made by a simple inter vivos trust.

Alternative dispute resolution (ADR): A method of resolving civil disputes otherwise than through the normal trial process, which is now required in the UK under *Civil Procedure Rules* 1998 to encourage parties to use methods, such as MEDIATION and conciliation, to reduce delays and costs of resolving disputes. A party who fails to engage in ADR will be penalised in the award of costs of the litigation even though that person may eventually succeed. The equitable remedy of SPECIFIC PERFORMANCE does not apply to an agreement to appoint an arbitrator or engage in some form of ADR; the court has the power to stay an action where the subject matter should have been put to ARBITRATION, mediation or some other form of ADR. *See also* EQUITABLE REMEDIES.

Alternative Investment Market (AIM): *See* QUOTED COMPANY.

Alternative finance arrangements: A term used in UK legislation to indicate lending arrangements that comply with Islamic law which overcome the *Qur'anic's* (Koran) prohibition on *riba* (interest). *See* ISLAMIC LAW.

Amalgamation: A term applied to the merging of two companies, either by one of them going into voluntary liquidation and authorising the LIQUIDATOR to transfer the shares to members of the other company, or where two or more public companies transfer their undertakings (the businesses) to an existing or new public company, or by the purchase by one company of another company's shares by way of a takeover. Equivalent provisions control the amalgamation of industrial provident societies, building societies and friendly societies. It can also apply to trusts and foundations which can merge in a similar way, although there is no established practice for the amalgamation of two trusts or two foundations. Provisions for amalgamation should be included in a trust's documentation or in a foundation's charter.

Ambulatory: A legislative term applied if an enactment or instrument is to embrace future amendments. For example, a will is said to be ambulatory if it takes effect from the death of the testator and not from when it was made. This results in the inclusion in the terms of a will of unascertained property being bequeathed according to the will for the benefit of a class of beneficiaries as described in the will as they exist at that time of the death of the testator. An ambulatory will remains revocable until death. A constructive trust may be referred to as 'ambulatory' where the parties' intentions change over time. A document may be fixed in its terms but the interpretation may change before execution by a change in the circumstances; the document is then said to be 'ambulatory'.

Amendment, powers of: Generally, the power to correct some error or omission or the curing of some defect in judicial proceedings. In connection with trusts, the beneficial and administration terms and provisions may be amended if the trust instrument contains powers of various kinds such as POWER OF APPOINTMENT and powers of ADVANCEMENT. Otherwise, a specific power to amend may be included and which takes the form of power to add to, vary, modify or alter the terms of stated provisions. Such powers are intended to provide flexibility. The powers are not construed in a narrow or unreal way, although express restrictions must be complied with and cannot be amended, removed, etc. by the exercise of the power itself. Any power to amend is subject to any implied restriction, particularly in connection with pension schemes that must be operated in GOOD FAITH and not to damage the relationship between employer and employees. Similar protection can be anticipated to preserve the relationships between trustees and beneficiaries and to preserve the declared object of foundations.

American law: The law of the territory of the US comprising federal law, which is applicable throughout the entirety of the US, and state law. State laws can differ between states, some even belonging to different legal systems, e.g. French law in Louisiana. American law is historically built on English law, which was specifically adopted in the state of New York on 19 April 1775 when the common law and statutes then in force in England on that day were taken as the law of New York. A similar adoption took place in the other original states and those subsequently to the Union except the state of Louisiana. State laws, however, have been much modified by legislation and judicial decisions. American decisions cannot be quoted as binding in England but occasionally sited as illustration, especially of commercial law.

American Law Institute: An organisation established in 1923 in the US to define, summarise and restate the existing US common law. It achieves this by issuing 'restatements', none of which are intended to be enforced but are merely descriptive of the law in the various states. The most recent revision (the third) of the restatement (third of trust laws) has yet to be completed. *See* THE NATIONAL CONFERENCE ON COMMISSIONERS FOR UNIFORM STATE LAWS.

AML: *See* ANTI-MONEY LAUNDERING LAW.

Ancient documents: Documents that are 20 years old or more and which are produced from proper custody are presumed to have been duly executed. Thus, a conveyance or trust deed at least 20 years old and that has been duly signed and where necessary witnessed and which is produced from proper custody, say, from the care of a solicitor or from a bank, is then presumed to have been duly executed.

Ancillary relief: Incidental and supplementary relief in awards of the court that is additional to the principal award. For example, the term is applied where a plaintiff recovers damages for nuisance and at the same time an INJUNCTION to restrain the defendant from continuing the nuisance. The injunction is then by way of ancillary relief. In trust law, the term is mostly met with in connection with ancillary relief in matrimonial proceedings. Orders for financial provisions, property adjustments, pension sharing and other APPORTIONMENT of one party's financial assets are called ancillary relief, i.e. they are ancillary to the main action of divorce or separation. Trusts have featured substantially in actions for ancillary relief where a husband places a large proportion of his assets into a trust and claims that these assets are not available in calculating financial support for the former wife. These often involve a determination by the court of whether the trust set up by the husband has been properly formed and conducted or whether it is a sham, which means that the so-called trust assets revert to the husband and consequently are available as part of the calculation for ancillary relief. Ancillary relief orders can be made on or after granting the decree of divorce.

***Andrews v. Partington* (1791) 3 Bro CC 401:** A rule of construction applicable to settlements INTER VIVOS and will trusts that mitigates the harshness of the common law RULE AGAINST PERPETUITIES. The rule applies to realty and personalty and provides that a class of beneficiaries will close when the first member of that class becomes entitled in possession to his share of capital.

Annual return: A report that registered companies must make by law each year and which, in the UK, is sent to COMPANIES HOUSE. This return includes information about the type of company and its business activities, its registered office, directors, company members and certain company debts. The return is open to public inspection. Failure to file the return is a criminal offence and may lead to a penalty or, ultimately, to the company being removed from the Register and fined. If Companies House accepts an indication that the company is no longer wanted, then, in the absence of an annual return, the company will ultimately be struck off the Register.

Annuity: A periodic payment, usually annually, of a certain sum of money granted to another. An annuity can be payable under a personal obligation of the grantor or charged upon his personal estate, freehold or leasehold land. If the payment is made from both the real and personal estate it is a matter of construction as to its nature; an annuity under a will is prima facie regarded as the payment of personal property, but this does not exclude the possibility that the annuity could be constructed as a charge only on land. An annuity that is paid out under a trust instrument is primarily made out of income but may be apportionable between capital and income where a sum is payable under COVENANT by a testator by instalments. *See* ***PERKINS SETTLEMENTS TRUSTS, RE*** **[1912] WN 99** *and* ***ALLHUSEN V. WHITTELL*** **(1867) LR 4 Eq 295.**

Anstalt: A trust-type vehicle established in Liechtenstein, sometimes called an establishment, governed by the first section of Title Five of the *Persons and Companies Act* 1926, Articles 534-551. An *anstalt* is a legal entity that may be formed and operated by an individual person, firm, community, or an association of communes, or by another legal entity. The structure depends upon written articles and requires entry in the Public Register. Establishments are extremely flexible and have judicial personality and may be used for commercial, non-commercial or mixed purposes. *Anstalts* are unitary bodies, i.e. they are not divided into shares or other forms of participation, though the articles may allow for shareholders. Under a memorandum issued by the US Internal Revenue Service in 2009, *anstalts* are properly classified as business entities for US tax purposes (while *stiftungs* are more likely to be classified as trusts). *See also* BUSINESS TRUSTS, *STIFTUNG and* TREUUNTERNEHMEN.

Ante-nuptial agreements: Sometimes referred to as PRE-NUPTIAL AGREEMENTS or pre-nuptial contracts and comprise an agreement made between the husband and wife before marriage. The agreement provides for a future division of property between husband and wife on the breakdown of the marriage. Where, after making an ante-nuptial agreement, a person later makes a will distributing his property otherwise than in accordance with the agreement, then the court enforces the agreement and any provisions of the will which contradict the terms of the ante-nuptial agreement are VOID. In these cases, the promises made in the contract exist independently of the will. The validity of an ante-nuptial agreement depends on whether the parties have made full and frank disclosure of their respective financial affairs, whether they had independent legal advice and whether there was any UNDUE INFLUENCE of one party upon the other. Also taken into account is the question of one party to the agreement being mistaken as to the significance of the agreement and then there is the question of the needs of any children. A court must have regard to the terms of an ante-nuptial agreement when making an order for ancillary relief in the event of divorce. *See* ANCILLARY RELIEF *and* POST-NUPTIAL AGREEMENTS.

Ante-nuptial settlement: As an alternative to an ante-nuptial agreement, parties may enter into a TRUST whereby one party places assets in a trust for the benefit of both parties to the marriage. Such a settlement can be varied on divorce under the *Matrimonial Causes Act* 1973, Section 24,1(c). *See* POST-NUPTIAL SETTLEMENT.

Anti-avoidance provisions: Statutory provisions designed to stop arrangements that would reduce a taxpayer's tax liability. These are particularly aimed at lessening the impact of otherwise legal transactions that have a beneficial tax effect. Anti-avoidance provisions relating to trusts are mostly concerned with deeming the income or capital gains made by a trust to be those of the settlor if tax is not incurred and charged on the beneficiaries. *See* TAX AVOIDANCE.

Anti-Bartlett clauses: Clauses inserted into trust deeds absolving trustees from liability for loss to the trust by not interfering in the management or conduct of the business of a company in which the trust owns shares. Where the trust owns a majority of the shares the trustee shareholder is required to have a more detailed view of a company than is available to a normal shareholder; a seat on the board should be procured. This was the effect of the decision in ***Bartlett v. Barclays Bank Trust Co. Ltd*** and led to the insertion into trust deeds of EXEMPTION CLAUSES absolving trustees from any failure to obtain a more detailed view. Such clauses have no effect if the trustees have ACTUAL NOTICE of any irregularities. When the trustees do not have any actual notice, the clause will make it permissible for the trustees to leave the conduct of the business wholly to the directors and to rely upon the exemption clause if they are found wanting. Adequate drafting of the exemption clause is necessary to overcome the effect of ***Bartlett v. Barclays Bank Trust Co. Ltd.*** Effectiveness of the clause also depends on the willingness of the court to acknowledge the effectiveness of exemption clauses as in ***Armitage v. Nurse*** [1997] 2 All ER 705. *See* *BARTLETT V. BARCLAYS BANK TRUST CO. LTD* [1980] Ch 515 at 533-534.

Anticipation: Performing an act before the appointed time. It was particularly relevant in respect of settlements of property on a woman where, either in the settlement or the will, a 'Restraint on Anticipation Clause' was included to protect her from the influence of her husband by preventing him from depriving her of the benefit of future income. A term in the will or settlement was able to restrain the woman from alienating, by way of anticipation, the property to which she would one day be freely entitled, i.e. the woman could not act freely to alienate the property given to her by will or settlement before the will or settlement allowed and therefore the property was kept out of the hands of the husband's powers regardless of his persuasive influence over his wife. This restraint prevented a woman from anticipating an income so that she was unable to alienate it from the settlement and transfer it to her husband. A similar clause also appeared in wills. Various statutes modified this restraint and the *Law Reform (Married Woman and Tortfeasors) Act* 1935 abolished the doctrine of restraint upon anticipation in respect of future instruments and wills and future appointments under old instruments. The restraints on anticipation were abolished altogether by the *Married Woman (Restraint upon Anticipation) Act* 1949.

Anticipatory breach of contract: Where a party to a contract, before performing any part of the contract, renounces the contract or disables himself from performance, he is said to have committed anticipatory breach. The other party has two choices; first, he may affirm the contract and wait until the date set for performance and then sue for BREACH OF CONTRACT. Second, when the anticipatory breach occurs, he can immediately terminate the contract and immediately claim damages. In the latter alternative, he can respond at once and does not have to wait until the date of performance before being able to claim a breach; by accepting the anticipatory breach the relationship can be terminated immediately and the innocent party can claim damages.

Anti-money laundering law: A law that has the intention of preventing drug trafficking and organised crime through detecting and preventing the use of money obtained by these offences. Most jurisdictions, including the EU, have accepted the recommendations of the FINANCIAL ACTION TASK FORCE (FATF) and have adopted its recommendations into their own laws, which, in addition to anti-money laundering provisions, now contain anti-corruption measures.

Anti-suit injunction: An order directed to an overseas party not to pursue proceedings overseas on pain of contempt of court.

Anton Piller order: The original name given to orders granted by the High Court, which are now known as search orders. *See* SEARCH ORDER.

Appeal: The modern meaning is a challenge to a decision of a lower court or tribunal that is brought before a higher court as may be permitted as a right under a statute with the objective of revising or reconsidering the lower court's decision. The right of appeal is a right made under a statute and is not in itself a right under the common law. An appeal questions whether the order of the court from which the appeal is brought is a correct decision on the materials which the court had before it. The right of appeal is concerned with a matter of SUBSTANTIVE LAW and not of procedure. Appeals have been substantially affected by Article 2 of the Protocol 7 to the European Convention on Human Rights, which allows everyone, subject only to limited exceptions, to have a conviction and/or sentence reviewed by a higher tribunal. In the UK, an appeal may be available as a matter of right or only after permission is given by a higher court and may be limited to questions of law. An appeal court may restrict itself to examining the records of the proceedings in the lower court but if the appeal court thinks it necessary it may hear additional evidence. The result of an appeal may be to confirm or vary the decision of the lower court, substitute a new decision or to order a new trial.

Applicable law: The law that applies to a particular transaction or arrangement. This is often dictated according to international conventions. For example, the *Rome Convention* 1980 provides what shall be the applicable law in international contracts. *The Hague Convention on the Recognition and Enforcement of Trusts* lays down rules for the determination of the law that governs a TRUST to which the Convention relates under circumstances where the Convention applies. The law that applies to a particular situation is referred to as the PROPER LAW of the contract, trust, etc. The general trend is to permit the law chosen by the parties to be the proper law. This choice is made by a clause in the documents of the international transaction, e.g., the contract, the trust deed or the foundation charter. A CHOICE OF LAW will be recognised by most courts and where the proper law is different from the law of the jurisdiction in which an action is brought; the terms of the proper law have to be proved to the court as a question of fact and expert witnesses present their interpretation of what the law means and the judge then decides according to the law as presented to him as evidence. As well as a law of the transaction, many international documents contain a JURISDICTION CLAUSE by which the parties choose the jurisdiction in which a dispute will be heard. This is a different matter but one which, in practical terms, is closely associated with the choice of law clause for the proper law for practical reasons. *See also* PROPER LAW *and* GOVERNING LAW.

Appointment of trustees (1) General: Trustees may be appointed either under express powers in the trust instrument or by the statutory powers provided for under Section 36 of the *Trustee Act* 1925. Statutory powers apply where no contrary intention is expressed in the trust instrument and statutory powers take effect subject to the terms of that instrument, (*Trustee Act* 1925, Section 69(2)). In general, a corporation may be a trustee of personalty or land. A corporation may in general be a trustee for any purpose, e.g., trustee of a friendly society and may be co-trustee with an individual or another corporation. The *Trustee Act* 1925 encouraged the appointment of certain corporations as trustees; these corporations were referred to as a TRUST CORPORATION and included the Public Trustee, the Treasury Solicitor and the Official Solicitor and some charitable corporations or corporations appointed by the court. Corporations which are entitled to act as CUSTODIAN TRUSTEE are provided for under the *Public Trustee Act* 1906. A JUDICIAL TRUSTEE differs from an ordinary trustee in being an officer of the court who may obtain the direction of the court without a formal application. Individuals cannot be appointed as trustees if they are minors and, in any case, legal estate in land cannot be held by a minor. A conveyance of a legal estate to a minor on trust will only operate as a declaration of trust and will not pass any legal estate to him. If a conveyance is made to two or more persons, one of whom is a trustee, then the person or persons of full age take the legal estate. One case, ***Re Vinogradoff*** [1935] W.N. 68, provided that nothing prevented a minor from holding property on IMPLIED, RESULTING or CONSTRUCTIVE TRUST.

Appointment of trustees (2) New trustees: After a trust is set up, the settlor has no power to appoint trustees unless he has reserved such a power. In the absence of such a power by the settlor, there are four ways by which a new trustee can be appointed: (a) an express power may be conferred upon a person in special circumstances (this is now unusual due to the comprehensive power given by statute); (b) under some statutory power, such as the *UK Trustee Act* 1925, where a person is nominated in the trust instrument, or a surviving or continuing trustee, or the personal representatives of the last surviving trustee, or by the court. The circumstances where a new trustee may be appointed is where the last surviving trustee dies, remains out of the UK for more than 12 months, wishes to be discharged, refuses or is unfit to act, is incapable of acting or is an infant (where the trust is implied, resulting or constructive) or is removed under a power in the trust instrument; (c) under the *Trusts of Land and Appointment of Trustees Act* 1996, which entitles beneficiaries to appoint new trustees and to require existing trustees to retire under certain circumstances; or (d) by the court, which has a wide power of appointing new trustees in substitution for, or in addition to, existing trustees. Under the maxim 'Equity does not want for a trustee', the court has power to appoint new trustees in a wide range of circumstances, in particular where it is found that it is 'inexpedient, difficult or impractical to do so without the assistance of the court', and further powers were given under the *Judicial Trustees Act* 1896 generally where the ADMINISTRATION OF THE ESTATE by the ordinary trustees has broken down.

***Apportionment Act* 1870:** Unless the Act is specifically excluded in the trust instrument, then: 'All rents, annuities, dividends, and other periodical payments in the nature of income ... shall, like interest on money lent, be considered as accruing from day to day, and shall be apportioned in respect of time accordingly.'

Apportionment: The obligation of trustees to divide trust income between income and capital beneficiaries. Apportionment is based upon the principle that trustees must not favour one beneficiary or a class of beneficiaries over another and a fair balance must be made between beneficiaries who are entitled to capital and those who are entitled to income. The rules of apportionment by which certain returns and outgoings had to be shared in a particular way were contained in statute and case law and required complex calculations that exposed many trusts of small sums to excessive technicalities. In the UK, the traditional rules on apportionment were reformed by the *Trusts (Capital and Income) Act* 2013. The traditional apportionment regime was contained in four rules, which, under the Act, have been simplified for trusts created or arising on or after 1 October 2013:

1. Section 2 of the *Apportionment Act* 1870 entitled income beneficiaries to a proportion of income that was deemed to have accrued during their period of entitlement. There is no longer any requirement to apportion an income receipt where the entitlement of income has changed over the period in which it accrued. This is relevant to trusts where trustees have a power to maintain a class of beneficiary out of income to which they are not yet absolutely entitled; the income, as it arises, is available for the maintenance of those beneficiaries entitled to be maintained from it.
2. The first part of the rule in ***Howe v. Lord Dartmouth*** (1802) 7 Ves. 137/146 that required trustees to sell particular investments and reinvest the proceeds ('a duty to convert') applied to wasting or hazardous investments which were residuary personalty and which would have had a potential to prejudice the capital beneficiary. Now, trustees can exercise discretion in their context of 'general duty of care' where an immediate sale would be unwise; trustees have a power to sell rather than a duty. The second part of the rule is that where a trust for interest in succession holds unauthorised investments in hazardous or wasting property under a trust for sale, the income beneficiary will be entitled to the actual income as it arises.
3. The rule in ***Re Earl of Chesterfield's Trusts*** (1883) 24 Ch D 643 was that where a trust for interest in succession holds property that does not produce any income until it falls in possession (such as a REVERSIONARY INTEREST) such property now will be treated as capital when it comes into the possession of the trustees.
4. The rule in ***Allhusen v. Whittell*** (1867) L.R. 4 Eq 295 that apportioned between capital and income beneficiaries certain classes of payments which included debts, liabilities, legacies etc., out of residuary estate is disapplied. Such payments and other charges payable from the residuary estate will be paid only out of capital unless a contrary provision is provided in the trust instrument or in any power by which the trust was established.

The Act also provides that where a trust receives a tax-exempt distribution from corporate activities, such as in the course of a demerger, the receipt is to be treated as capital; income beneficiaries can be compensated under certain circumstances. Charities are also affected by the Act. Trustees of a charity that has a permanent endowment may invest on a total return basis by adopting a special scheme of the CHARITY COMMISSION.

Appropriation: The power of trustees to transfer an asset to a beneficiary who agrees to take the asset in full or partial satisfaction of his entitlement to receive a sum of money. Where the beneficiaries are infants, appropriation is valid if done fairly and at a proper valuation even though infant beneficiaries are incapable of giving consent. Appropriated assets are valued at the date of appropriation. If the value of the appropriated assets exceeds the value of the beneficiary's entitlement, appropriation can still be made with the beneficiary paying money to make up the difference. There are also extensive statutory powers of appropriation in connection with estates (Section 41, *Administration of Estates Act* 1925) and it is common practice for trust instruments to confer these statutory powers expressly on trustees.

Arbitration: Method of the settling of a dispute by the use of one or more independent third parties, i.e. the arbitrators, who are appointed according to a specific clause in an agreement. Although arbitrators apply the law, a more relaxed procedure is adopted than exists in courts. Arbitration in connection with trusts and wills does not feature largely.

Arm's length: The relationship between parties to an agreement made freely and independently of each other and without the existence of a special relationship or control. This term is frequently used in connection with financial and tax matters to indicate that no undue preference was given to one party or the other or that the impartiality of the parties was not affected by any outside influence.

***Armitage v. Nurse* [1997] 2 All ER 705:** A case concerning a trust of agricultural land created by a grandfather for his granddaughter. The farm was managed by a company run by the daughter's mother and grandmother. The daughter brought an action against the trustees for failure to monitor the company properly and for exercising a misplaced favouritism in favour of her mother's interests. The House of Lords held that a properly drafted EXEMPTION CLAUSE could exempt the trustees from liability for negligence or incompetence. The principle of this case has been followed widely and has focussed attention on the construction of exemption clauses.

Artificial legal person: The process by which a law confers independent legal status on a group or organisation establishing them as legal persons in a similar way to individuals. This may be by charter, Act of Parliament or registration under the law, such as under company law in the formation of a commercial company. In civil law countries, LEGAL PERSONALITY has given rise to much academic debate, but is considered more easily obtained than in common law countries. Private foundations, like foundations generally, are legal persons (unlike trustees) whose legal personality comes about by registration.

ARTs: *See* AUTOMATIC RESULTING TRUSTS.

As trustees: Words that may be used by trustees to indicate their status and to attempt to avoid personal liability. The general rule is that a trustee who enters into a contract will be personally liable under it like other contacting parties and this may incur an unlimited liability. Accordingly, a trustee may limit his liability to a specific amount or to the extent of the trust assets available if it is a contract that allows a limitation of liability. Entering into a contract 'as trustee' is an attempt to so limit the liability incurred to those trust assets which are available. However, personal liability is not limited by a party who describes himself simply as a trustee. More is required and this is subject to interpretation. Cases show that contracting 'as trustee but not otherwise' or 'as trustee only' have been held to limit a trustee's personal liability to the amount of the trust assets providing the contract admits limited liability. The words used are crucial. For example, if a trustee contracts to pay personally but then denies any personal liability, that proviso will be void on the grounds of REPUGNANCY so that the trustee's liability as a signatory is not limited at all. Where trustees took over a mortgage property and covenanted, for example in ***Watling v. Lewis*** [1911] 1 Ch. 414, to pay off the mortgage loan but did so: 'As ... trustees but not so as to create any personal liability on the part of them or either of them ...', it was construed by the court to make the trustees personally liable. Underlying that decision is the view that a signatory of a contract is liable and if a trustee signs and clearly indicates that he is doing so as a trustee then his personal liability is limited to what may be available under the trust to meet the liability; whereas in ***Watling v. Lewis*** the trustees attempted to avoid any liability whatsoever. In some jurisdictions, such as Jersey and Guernsey, if a trustee informs a third party he is entering into a contract as a trustee, then the liability is limited to what is available in the trust and personal liability is only incurred if he fails to inform the other party to the contract. A similar liability does not arise in the case of a foundation or a company as any member of the foundation council, or a director, enters into a contract merely as the agent for the incorporated body.

Assent: The confirmation by an executor that a legacy is due to a legatee before the legatee has a right to possession; the assent to a specific legacy can give rise to an ACTION to recover the legacy; in other cases, proceedings are taken out for the ADMINISTRATION OF ESTATES. Also, assent is used to indicate the means by which a personal representative transfers the title to property, both real and personal, to a person entitled to it following the death of the previous owner.

Asset protection trusts: Trusts set up in a jurisdiction that does not recognise the validity of judgments in the settlor's domestic jurisdiction to enforce a debt. The settlor, fearing future liability, transfers his assets to a trust in a sympathetic jurisdiction knowing that they would be safe against claims by future CREDITORS. These trusts were inspired to overcome well-established principles based upon the *Law of Property Act* 1925, Section 172, that were largely based upon the *Statute of Elizabeth* 1571 and upon Section 42 of the *Bankruptcy Act* 1914. These statutes provided that the transfer of assets 'with intent to defraud' rendered any transfer VOIDABLE. These provisions were construed widely and used to protect future or subsequent unascertained creditors; it was not necessary that a settlor was actually indebted when he created the settlement. Offshore centres followed the English legislation, particularly the *Statute of Elizabeth*, which was reproduced in the Australian states, Belize, British Virgin Islands, Gibraltar, Guernsey, Hong Kong and New Zealand. This resulted in several offshore centres countering these restrictions by principally limiting the period for which a transfer can be attacked by introducing legislation designed to protect the debtor. The Bahamas has introduced a provision whereby the creditor seeking to set aside a transfer must prove there was a wilful intention to defeat an obligation within a period of two years from the date of the transfer. In the Cook Islands, a disposition can only be set aside if the creditor brings, within two years, a specific action in respect of his debt and that the avoidance of the debt was the settlor's principal intent. Generally, an asset protection trust is a trust that is designed and intended to protect assets from claims by creditors and others; the settlor organises his affairs in advance to safeguard against claims which might arise from some future event and which results in a claim for damages in his home jurisdiction. These trusts developed from the explosion in litigation affecting professional practitioners, which, with the dramatic increase in professional indemnity insurance particularly for medical and legal professionals, resulted in some other means being required to protect assets. Some jurisdictions, for example England and Wales and the US, have specific provisions to prevent the transfer or disposal of assets so as to defraud or defeat the claims of creditors. These statutory revisions, particularly the *Insolvency Act* 1986 in the UK, have been applied by the courts in favour of creditors and represent a serious threat to the effectiveness of asset protection trusts. It would be difficult to justify any fraud on a creditor but some jurisdictions have legislation that is more favourable to the creditor by requiring claims by creditors to be brought within a shorter period of time than is permitted in the debtor's home country.

Assets: All property of any person or undertaking especially when in connection with the satisfaction of bequests and the property owned by trustees or by a foundation. Assets are usually divided into fixed (or capital) assets which have been held with the intention that they should be used over a long period without change, and current assets that comprise liquid, or quick, assets for use immediately to meet obligations or which can be converted into such a state almost immediately. Fixed assets comprise tangible assets, plant and buildings, fixed intangible assets, goodwill and deferred assets (long-term loans).

Assignment: A transfer, particularly of a CHOSE IN ACTION, that may be assigned by one person to another, from the assignor to the assignee. Both legal rights, such as a right under a contract, and EQUITABLE rights, such as a right under a trust, may be assigned. These are sometimes confusingly referred to as 'legal or equitable assignments'. Assignments may be by either an equitable assignment (whatever the nature of the right assigned) where no formality is required and is sufficient that the assignor demonstrates a clear intention that the right is to be transferred. For example, the mere deposit of title deeds to property can secure a debt on that property and this is an 'EQUITABLE MORTGAGE'. 'Legal assignments' are valid according to the *Law of Property Act* 1925. A statutory assignment is sometimes referred to as a legal assignment but since it may be for the purpose of assigning both an equitable chose in action, such as an interest under a trust, as well as a legal chose in action, such as the right to shares in a company, this is confusing; the term 'statutory assignment' is preferred. So there may be a statutory or equitable assignment of a right which itself is either a legal chose in action or an equitable chose in action. In an equitable assignment (whether the right assigned is an equitable or legal right) the assignor must be made a party to any proceedings by the assignee to enforce the right and if the assignor refuses then he should be made a co-defendant in the action. In contrast, where the assignment is a statutory assignment, the assignee can enforce the right in his own name without joining the assignor to the proceedings (again, whether it is a legal chose or equitable chose in action which has been assigned). For a statutory assignment to be valid it must be ABSOLUTE, i.e. it must be the assignment of the whole of the action and must be in writing and written NOTICE of it must be given to the person against whom the right is enforceable. If less than the whole interest in the chose in action is transferred, such as part of a debt, or any condition is attached to the transfer, such as requiring the consent of a third party, then the assignment is not absolute and therefore not a statutory assignment; at best it would be a subcontract. The fact that an assignment is not permanent does not prevent the assignment being absolute. There are statutory restrictions against some assignments, such as a prohibition against the assignment of salaries from a public office or rights to the performance of personal services or under contracts of employment. Some forms of property, such as intellectual property rights, must be assigned or transferred by a document in writing signed by the assignor. The term 'assignment' is also applied to the transfer of the whole or remainder of a term of a lease. A tenant may assign his lease unless there is a covenant in the lease against assignment. Assignments may be made of an interest under a trust especially where the beneficiary assigns his EQUITABLE INTEREST to another as a form of security; for example, where a LIFE TENANT raises money secured by his interest under the trust. This assignment of this equitable interest may be either by an equitable or a statutory assignment. Trustees may also be involved in assignments where they assign their legal title to the trust assets to other trustees.

Assurance: *See* INSURANCE.

Attestation: Is the signature of witnesses to the making of a WILL or DEED for the purpose of proving the document's authenticity. Under the *Wills Act* 1837, as amended, a testator must sign or acknowledge his signature in the presence of two witnesses who must both be present at the same time and who attest and acknowledge that the testator's signature has been made in their presence, and each must sign in the testator's presence. Each witness should be able to say that to his own knowledge the testator, without pressure from anyone, had signed the document and that he (the witness) had seen this signature. The testator's signature should precede the attestation and the signature and attestation should be attached to each other, appearing, for example, on the same page of the documents. The witnesses do not have to read the will but they must be present and remain in the same room until the formalities are complete. They must be present before signing begins. Beneficiaries cannot be witnesses to a will; the usual signatures must be used and the parties must insert their address and occupation. In some countries, e.g. the US, there is a movement to reduce or abolish the attestation of wills.

Attorney: A person who is appointed by another to act in his place with authority. Attorneys at law were formerly admitted to practise in the Superior Courts of Common Law after having studied the law with barristers in the legal inns until both attorneys and solicitors were expelled from the Inns of Court in 1574. The term 'attorney' was abolished in the UK by the *Supreme Court Act* 1873 and the title Solicitor of the Supreme Court Judicature was substituted. The term 'attorney', however, is still used in many countries.

Attorney General: The principal Law Officer of a government. In the UK, under the *Charities Act* 1993, the Attorney General protects CHARITIES and provides advice and assistance to the court in the administration of CHARITABLE TRUSTS.

Audit: The power of trustees under Section 24(4) of the *Trustee Act* 1925 to have the trust property examined or audited by an independent accountant not more than once in every three years; costs being payable out of the capital or income, or partly one or partly in the other, as the trustees think fit, unless there are any special dealings or other reasons requiring a more frequent exercise of the right. Where the trustees are the PUBLIC TRUSTEE then under the *Public Trustee Act* 1906 an application can be made by any trustee or beneficiary for an investigation and audit but not more than once a year.

Augmentation of capital: Where trustees are allocated shares in a company of which they are already a shareholder, which are paid for by the company, allocating unissued SHARE CAPITAL out of a reserve fund, the shares so allocated to the trustees are held by them as capital and as an ACCRETION to the shares already held of the company.

Austin, John: Professor of jurisprudence at University College, London, 1826-1833, and a barrister who developed the theory of legal positivism. This theory maintains that the law is a command issued by the SOVEREIGN which is backed by sanctions if not obeyed. The sovereign is the person or institution in each country which is habitually obeyed, such as Parliament in the UK, the Supreme Court in the US and, where appropriate, dictators or ruling monarchs. This view of legal positivism is the opposite of NATURAL LAW, which is the law dictated by nature embodied in mutual consent. The positivist theory was challenged on the grounds that in some countries there is no sovereign power as understood by Austin but which, nevertheless, maintain a system of law. Austin also attempted to separate moral rules from POSITIVE LAW. Austin was influenced by Jeremy Bentham (*see* BENTHAM, JEREMY).

Authorised capital: *See* CAPITAL OF A COMPANY.

Authorised investments: A description which formerly indicated the permitted investments by trustees in the UK that were specifically provided for under the *Trustee Investment Act* 1961. However, since the *Trustee Act* 2000, a far more permissive approach to investment has been adopted and the earlier mandatory rules for the administration and investment of trust funds have been omitted; even the terms of the latest Act may be excluded by express provision or by inference. Where the *Trustee Act* does apply, then the trustee may make 'any kind of investment that he could make if he were absolutely entitled to the assets of the trust'. This is referred to in the Act as a GENERAL POWER OF INVESTMENT.

Automatic resulting trusts (ARTs): A term used to describe automatic trusts that arise by operation of the law and independently of the settlor's intention. This doctrine, however, has been doubted in ***Westdeutsche Landesbank Girozentrale v. Islington London Borough Council*** [1996] AC 669 [1996] 2 All ER 961, where Megarry J suggested that where a BENEFICIAL INTEREST in TRUST PROPERTY is abandoned then it becomes BONA VACANTIA.

Autonomy of spouses: Expresses the independence financially and socially of spouses. It is significant in that married couples can possess their own independent assets.

B

Babanaft Proviso: A provision inserted into a worldwide FREEZING INJUNCTION (sometimes known as a freezing order) to make it clear that third parties who are situated outside the jurisdiction in which the freezing injunction is issued are not liable, under English law, for knowingly assisting a person to breach a freezing order and are not thereby guilty of contempt of court for interfering with the administration of justice. This provision is to protect branches of trust companies and banks with head offices within the jurisdiction of the English courts from attempts by those branches to evade the freezing injunction in foreign countries. However, where the freezing injunction made in England is declared as enforceable in a foreign country, a Babanaft Proviso does not apply to a knowing breach of that injunction in the foreign country. Moreover, a branch of an English bank or trust company situated in a foreign country needs to observe the terms (to determine if there is a Babanaft Proviso) of a freezing injunction made in England, otherwise any contravention by the branch may have repercussions on the head office in England. This proviso only applies to branches and not subsidiaries. The order was named after ***Babanaft International Co. v. Bassane*** [1990] Ch. 13, the case in which it was first proposed.

Backwards tracing: A form of tracing validated for the first time in a decision of the Judicial Committee of the Privy Council (JCPC) on an appeal from the Royal Court of Jersey (***Federal Republic of Brazil et al v. Durant International Corporation et al*** [2015] UKPC 35). The appeal allowed for the first time the victims of a breach of fiduciary duty and fraud to trace and recover sums lost. The action was against two BVI companies that held funds in a Jersey bank. The funds were derived from the deposit by two Brazilians of $10 million that they received as secret bribes which, before being deposited in Jersey, had been mixed with other funds through a bank in New York. The Royal Court of Jersey held that the depositors were liable, as constructive trustees, for the whole amount of the deposit. Previously, backwards tracing had not been allowed because tracing depends upon identifying new assets acquired in substitution for the original assets, which would have been the subject of a claim had they still been in the possession of the debtor. Allowing backwards tracing was a matter for the discretion of the court and it was allowed in this case because of the need to counter increasingly sophisticated and elaborate methods of money laundering involving credits and debits between intermediaries. The JCPC decided that it should not allow any camouflage to obscure the true purpose of transactions. *See* CONSTRUCTIVE TRUSTEE.

Bacon, Lord: Lord Chancellor from 1618 to 1621. Lord Bacon combined a legal career with politics, philosophy and literature. He promoted vast schemes of legal and political reform, including the union with Scotland, colonisation of America and the abolition of feudalism, and realised that the influence to carry out these schemes was only achieved by engaging in the intrigue which surrounded King James I. Although not entirely successful in these efforts, he laid the foundations of modern scientific thought in a work which King James I likened to 'the peace of God' because it passed all understanding. Lord Bacon's success was that he consolidated and completed the work of previous Lord Chancellors. A statue of Lord Bacon is prominent in the gardens of Gray's Inn.

Bad debt: An irrecoverable debt.

Baden rules: Rules for determining various classes of knowledge. *See* KNOWLEDGE.

Badges of fraud: Characteristics that when present in a transaction can be used as circumstantial evidence of fraud by one of the parties. These are matters of evidence and are not conclusive that fraud was the intention. These characteristics are variously presented but may be summarised as:

- One of the parties becomes insolvent because of the transfer.
- The lack or inadequacy of consideration for the transaction.
- The existence of a family or insider relationship among parties.
- The retention of possession, benefits or use of property in question.
- The existence of the threat of litigation.
- The difficult financial situation of the debtor at the time of the transfer or after the transfer.
- The existence or a cumulative effect of a series of transactions after the onset of the debtor's financial difficulties.
- The general chronology of events.
- The secrecy of the transaction in question.
- Deviation from the usual method or course of business.

Bad title: The failure of a person to establish a title to a chattel or piece of land is said to result in a bad title and consequently the person cannot be considered as the owner of the chattel or land.

Bahamas Executive Entity: A new private wealth structure established by the *Executive Entities Act* 2011 in the Bahamas which came into force on 1 February 2012 and is known as a BEE. The Act defines the BEE as 'The legal person established by charter to perform only executive functions and registered in accordance with the Act'. The name of a BEE must end with the words 'Executive Entity' or 'EE'. A BEE is used as a vehicle to carry out executive functions in private wealth structures provided these comply with the relevant regulatory law. The executive functions are limited to trusts or other arrangements domiciled in or regulated by the law of the Bahamas or another designated legislation. The BEE is set up by the submission of a charter, which contains details similar to those required in a foundation charter, to the Registrar who, provided the founder of the BEE has appointed an executive agent, will register the BEE. A BEE is run by an Executive Entity Council with a registered office in the Bahamas and may exist for a definite or indefinite period. A BEE is a separate legal entity and can sue and be sued in its registered name. Executive entity services must be rendered by a bank or trust company or registered service provider. A BEE has no shareholders or other ownership interests. This makes a BEE different from a normal nominee company in that there are no shareholders or other persons entitled to the profits of the operation. It also separates these nominee functions from any nominee and, as a stand-alone operation, insulates the BEE operations from a trust company or bank. A BEE can undertake to act as a process agent in structured finance, the holder of shares, the role of an officer of a company, a trusted protector or enforcer of a trust, a foundation council, a shareholder of a family company, the owner of a single premium life insurance policy, or as a settlor of a trust or founder of a foundation. Due to its nature as merely providing executive functions, there is no application of a beneficiary principle to this new structure and no concern that it has a self-serving principle and is free from the 'directly outward-related' criteria of foundation purposes. *See* DIRECTLY OUTWARD-RELATED FOUNDATION PURPOSES.

Bail: A general term to include, in criminal cases, some security given to the court that the accused (the BAILEE), if released from custody, will surrender at a certain place or time and, in civil cases, the security paid to the court to ensure that the defendant will obey the requirement of the court in connection with the civil proceedings. In admiralty cases, bail may be required to delay the arrest of a ship. Where bail is granted, the issue will be settled in due course by judicial proceedings but bail will not be granted if the court or other authority suspects that the person will default. If bail is granted and the person defaults, the bail is forfeited. This possibility requires a high degree of trust by the person providing the bail as to the reliability of the accused. The willingness of a person providing the bail to risk losing the security deposited acts as a reference for the accused person's promise to reappear. Bail is usually awarded by judges and may also be granted for minor offences by the police. The use of the term 'bail' in this context has nothing to do with the civil relationship of BAILOR and bailee considered under BAILMENT.

Bailee: A person who takes goods from another (the bailor) under contract of bailment. *See* BAILMENT.

Bailment: The delivery by one person (the bailor) of goods to another (the bailee) for a certain purpose. The types of bailment are numerous and cover the following situations where the liability of the bailor differs:

- A bare naked bailment of goods, a deposit, and the bailee is only answerable for gross negligence.
- Goods or chattels lent to a friend gratis, a *commodatum* where the liability of the bailor is that he must use the strictest care and diligence.
- Goods are left for hire with the bailee to be used by him, *locatio et conductio* where the bailee must use ordinary care.
- Goods delivered to the bailor as a pawn to be a security for money borrowed where the bailee must use ordinary care.
- Goods or chattels delivered to the bailor to be carried or subject to something to be done for a reward, *locatio operis faciendi*, where ordinary care is also needed unless the bailee is a common carrier.
- Where the bailee is to do something in respect of the goods without charge (*mandatum*) where the bailee is only answerable for gross negligence.

In the UK the *Tort (Interference with Goods) Act* 1977, Section 12, allows a bailee to sell goods that he has accepted for repair or other treatment when the bailor fails to pay and to accept redelivery according to the contract. The contract of bailment is concerned with the deposit of goods and chattels and does not expose either party to the rigours of a fiduciary relationship and therefore differs from trustee and banking situations. Where an investor or trustee requires a bank or other, as custodian, to carry out administrative duties in connection with securities and lodges those securities with the bank or trustee, then the duty of care owed by the custodian is high and approaches a level required of trustees' fiduciary duty.

Bailor: A person who commits goods to another person (the bailee) for a specific purpose. *See* BAILMENT.

Balance Sheet: A statement showing the assets and liabilities of a trading company, compiled according to the standards applied where the company has its registered office. An equivalent document is prepared for trusts and foundations. This should show the capital position of each beneficiary and a schedule of investments. A balance sheet shows the state of the organisation at the date of the balance sheet. Balance sheets are usually accompanied by other statements; a profit and loss account in respect of a trading company or a statement of expenditure and income for non-trading companies. Tax computations are based upon these accounts.

Bank: A financial institution, the chief characteristic of which is that customers deposit funds that are to be repaid on demand. The bank uses the money by lending it out and charging interest, or for other purposes such as discounting bills and cashing cheques for its customers. Unless contractual terms between a bank and its customers provides otherwise, a bank is entitled to charge interest on funds lent, but is not required to pay interest on funds deposited with it. The relationship between banks and their customers is that of debtor and creditor, not of trustee and beneficiary or principal and agent, so that any money lying untouched with a bank for six years, without any drawing by the customer or allowance of interest by the bank, becomes the property of the bank, although this right is rarely enforced.

Bank Administration Order: A form of administration applied to a bank in the UK that is, or is likely to be, in financial difficulties and which allows the court to appoint an administrator on application by the Bank of England. When part of a bank's business has been sold to a commercial purchaser or transferred to a bridge bank under the *Bank Act* 2009, called a *Special Resolution Regime*, then the administrator is obliged to fulfil the transfer, by sale or otherwise, and then to deal with the bank in the interests of the creditors in a similar way as an advisory company administrator.

Bank rate: Previously used to indicate the minimum rate of discount charged by the Bank of England for discounting bills. 'Bank rate' is now known as the Minimum Lending Rate.

Bankruptcy of a settlor: Bankruptcy is applied to an individual who has been adjudged bankrupt where an order vests the debtor's estate first in the official receiver and subsequently in the TRUSTEE IN BANKRUPTCY. Bankruptcy is the name given to a variety of judicial proceedings having for their main object the seizure and distribution of an insolvent person's property to his creditors (*see* CREDITOR). The bankruptcy of a settlor is a particular example of bankruptcy, notably in respect of the provisions which frustrate a person's distribution of property intended to overcome the consequences of his expected bankruptcy. Before the *Insolvency Act* 1986, a voluntary settlement of any property might be avoided if a settlor subsequently became bankrupt even if the settlement was not intended to defraud creditors. For this purpose, the definition of 'settlement' was broad enough to cover foundations. This provision was replaced by the *Insolvency Act* 1986, which is more concerned with transactions at an undervalue that take place after 28 December 1986. Section 339(1) of the *Insolvency Act* 1986 provides that where an individual is adjudged bankrupt, and has at a relevant time entered into a transaction with any person at an undervalue, the trustee of the bankrupt's estate may apply to the court for an order under this section. (***Note***, the trustee concerned here is the trustee in bankruptcy appointed under the *Insolvency Act* 1986 to administer the bankrupt's estate and not the trustee of any trust which the bankrupt may have attempted to set up.) For this provision to apply, the settlor must have been declared bankrupt. Bankruptcy denotes proceedings taken to make a person bankrupt and to administer his property for the benefit of his creditors. When a person becomes insolvent the property which he still owns rightly belongs to his creditors and should be distributed rateably amongst them towards satisfying their claims. This is administered by a trustee in bankruptcy from the date the order on which the bankruptcy commences. Under the *Insolvency Act* 1986, Section 284 prevents dispositions of property in the period between the presentation of the petition against a bankrupt and the bankruptcy order. Originally, bankruptcy was a branch of the criminal law but is now entirely covered by the *Insolvency Act* 1986. For these rules to apply in respect of a settlement, it is necessary that the transfer to the trustees of the settlement must be at an undervalue and made at a relevant time. A relevant time indicates one of two periods; first, if an individual enters into a transaction at an undervalue within five years preceding the presentation of the petition on which he was adjudged bankrupt, and second, if the transaction was only entered into between two and five years before the petition was presented, the time of the transaction is relevant only if the individual was then insolvent or became so in consequence of the transaction. There is, in addition, a presumption of insolvency where a transaction is entered into by an individual with an associate. 'Associate' is widely defined and covers spouses and relatives, and this would almost always include a family settlement. Insolvency, which is the criteria, exists if a person is unable to pay his debts as they fall due or the value of his assets is less than the amount of his liabilities taking into account the contingent and prospective liabilities (*Insolvency Act* 1983, Section 341). These provisions are of general application: the Insolvency Act is concerned with transactions and not the characteristics of the transferor whether settlor, founder or other. *See* VOLUNTARY CONVEYANCE.

Bare trust: A trust in which property is vested in one person on trust for another where no active duties or powers of management are imposed on the trustee; for example, where property is transferred to 'T' on trust for 'S' absolutely. T's duty is to obey any instructions that may be given on how the property should be disposed of. A bare trust is sometimes called a SIMPLE TRUST. Many nominee situations comprise a bare trust (a nominee situation can also arise by contract). A bare trust can exist where a beneficiary under a trust sells his entire equitable interest to another, in which case the trustee would then hold the property in trust for this other person and the original beneficiary, having given up his rights under the trust, drops out. A CUSTODIAN TRUSTEE is not a bare trustee as he has some active duties to perform and is therefore excluded from being within the concept of a bare trust. Bare trusts were omitted from the two statutory schemes relating to TRUSTS OF LAND, i.e. under the *Settled Land Act* 1925 and under the *Trust of Land and Appointment of Trustees Act* 1996.

Bare trustee: A trustee who has no duty to perform and who, on request, would be compelled or would be compellable to convey the assets to those persons legally entitled to hold them; sometimes referred to as a 'dry trustee'.

Barring of entailed interests: *See* ENTAILED INTEREST.

***Bartlett v. Barclays Bank Trust Co. Ltd* [1980] Ch 515 at 533-534:** This case confirmed the position outlined in an earlier case of Luckings Will Trusts, Re [1967] 3 All ER 726, [1968] 1 WLR 866, where Cross J expressed that trustees holding a controlling interest in a company ought to ensure, as far as they can, that they have such information on the company's affairs as directors would have, and also confirmed that a trustee should be in a position to make an informed decision when any action by the company is appropriate to protect its assets. The alternatives suggested in this decision were that more details should be supplied to trustee shareholders who would have had a controlling interest and, although every case will depend on its own facts, the trustees should receive an adequate flow of information in time to enable the trustees to make use of their controlling shareholdings for the protection of the trust assets, i.e. the shareholding in the company. *See also* ANTI-BARTLETT CLAUSES.

Base Erosion and Profit Shifting (BEPS): A project launched in July 2013 by the OECD at the request of the G20 Finance Ministers to overcome the failure of national tax laws which allow global corporations to avoid taxation in their home countries by pushing activities abroad to low- or no-tax jurisdictions. The OECD Committee on Fiscal Affairs (CFA) recognises the importance of developing new sets of standards to prevent double taxation and the need for closer international cooperation and greater transparency and greater data and reporting requirements. These remedies will be achieved through an action plan divided into three phases to be finalised by December 2015 by the creation of a multilateral instrument to amend bilateral tax treaties. To achieve this, the CFA operates through its subsidiary bodies, Working Parties 1, 2, 6 and 11, and the Forum on Harmful Tax Practices (FHTP) and the Task Force on Digital Economy (TFDE). In March 2015, the EU revealed plans to put forward a Commission Directive for the automatic exchange by multinationals of information. The terms of any such Directive would impose a compulsory obligation on the Member States, unlike a recommendation of the OECD, which is legally unenforceable.

Base Fee: An estate in FEE SIMPLE which, under the *Fines and Recoveries Act* 1833, arose where an issue IN TAIL was barred by a vesting declaration of the life tenant of a settlement of land with the consequences that the property is then held on a simple trust, but where a person claiming an estate as a REMAINDERMAN is not barred. Therefore, a base fee is an estate arising out of a fee tail which has been barred by a person whose power only extends to the ability to bar his own issue. A base fee under these circumstances extends only so long as such heirs or their issue survive and which thereafter becomes extinct. Base fees were converted by the *Law of Property Act* 1925, Section 1(3), from legal estates into EQUITABLE INTERESTS. The term, in a wider sense, is used to indicate an estate in land which has some condition attached to it.

Basel Committee on Bank Supervision: A committee established in 1974 by governors of central banks of the G10 countries. The committee is situated in Basel as part of the Bank for International Settlement and formulates supervising standards and guidelines for bank supervision. The committee also makes statements on bank practice that carry great weight with bank supervisors and its recommendations are recognised as a form of soft law. The requirements of Basel III supersede the previous standards comprising Basel II following the 2008 financial crisis.

Bearer: A person in possession of a bill or promissory note made payable 'to the bearer', i.e. for the benefit of any person who presents it and to whom the payment must be made by a banker unless its negotiability has been compromised.

Bearer shares: Shares in a limited company made out to 'the bearer', which means that whoever may present the share certificate is the person who is regarded as the legitimate owner of the shares stated on the certificate. Bearer shares may be transferred by simple delivery. Bearer shares were intended to simplify the payment of dividends in foreign countries by the presentation of a detachable coupon on the share certificate to an authorised agent. These shares were frequently used in connection with the financing by London banks of Argentine railways where shares were paid to non-UK shareholders by presenting the dividend coupon to an authorised agent. Such shares are now rarely issued as the beneficial owners of the shares are not disclosed and this non-disclosure runs contrary to the present insistence on transparency and the disclosure of the beneficial owners of the financial instruments.

Beddoe orders: An order by the court addressed to trustees which gives them leave to sue or defend an action against their trust and ensures that, however litigation results, the trustee is protected against any action by the beneficiaries and entitled to be reimbursed costs out of the trust's estate. This avoids trustees risking an inability to recover costs of litigation on the grounds that the expenses were not reasonably incurred and therefore not a true expense recoverable by the trustees. Trustees are advised to make a Beddoe application whenever litigation appears to be prima facie proper and in the interests of the trust with the expectation that the court will grant the trustees leave to sue or defend. So long as trustees make full disclosure of the strengths and weakness of their case, and they then act as authorised by the court, their entitlement to an indemnity and a lien over the assets is secure. If trustees do not apply for an order they will still be entitled to be reimbursed their costs if the action was properly brought or defended; however, if the action is unsuccessful the beneficiaries may resist the trustees' application for costs. Where there is hostile litigation, trustees should remain neutral and submit to the court's ruling.

Beneficial interest: Also known as EQUITABLE INTERESTS, indicates the interest of a beneficiary in trust assets. This interest, which may take the form of income or a right to occupy the property, is distinct from the legal interest or title in the property. In a trust, the beneficiaries collectively own the beneficial interest in the trust assets even if individual beneficiaries' interests cannot be identified. The separation of beneficial interests from legal ownership is a characteristic of trust and unknown in countries whose property rights are not based upon English law. This distinction is unknown in connection with foundation assets.

Beneficially entitled: Entitled to the beneficial interest in property.

Beneficial owner: An individual who enjoys the benefit of owning property or security despite the legal ownership being elsewhere. A beneficial owner may be able to control the legal owner's right to sell the property, although the existence of a beneficial owner may not be revealed by searches of the land's title or by enquiries such as when a trustee, the legal owner of trust property, attempts to sell for legitimate reasons or otherwise. In such cases, the existence of the beneficial owner and his interest may not be revealed. In some circumstances, the acquirers of land may take free of beneficial interests through the doctrine of OVERREACHING: *see LAW OF PROPERTY ACT* 1925, Section 2(1)(ii). The *Trusts of Land and Trustee Act* 1996 regulates the various forms of beneficial ownership.

Beneficial receipt: The unlawful receipt of misapplied trust property for the recipient's own benefit. The person actually receiving the trust property will not be liable if he receives it as the agent for a principal to whom he owes an immediate duty to account for the property. The principal is liable to the claimant in respect of the receipt of the property but his agent can still be liable for the tort of DISHONEST ASSISTANCE.

Beneficiaries' power to extinguish a trust: A beneficiary solely and absolutely entitled under a trust, or all those who may possibly benefit under a trust, whether it is a fixed trust, discretionary trust or under powers of appointment, and whose benefits may be concurrent or successive, may unanimously decide, if none are under a DISABILITY, to collectively extinguish the trust without reference to the wishes of the settlor or the trustee. Also, if the beneficiaries are of full age and capacity they may take joint action to rid themselves of unwanted trustees without the need to terminate the trust. This was originally used to counteract a trustee who insisted on accumulating the income of a trust thus depriving a beneficiary of any income. This principle was developed in ***Saunders v. Vautier*** (1841) 4 Beav 115, so that beneficiaries who are sui juris and together absolutely entitled to the trust property may exercise their proprietary rights and defeat the intentions of the testator or settlor. This doctrine adds substance to the principle that the trust assets are beneficially owned by the beneficiaries and that the legal interest of the trustees should not be a barrier to the enjoyment of these assets where the object to preserve and enhance trust assets for beneficiaries under the age of MAJORITY is no longer valid. The doctrine of ***Saunders v. Vautier*** is not universal in all trust jurisdictions; in particular, it is not included in many of the states' trust laws in the US.

Beneficiaries' rights to assign interest: A beneficiary of a trust of full age and capacity cannot be prohibited from assigning his or her interest. Any beneficiary who is absolutely vested with a beneficial interest in a share of the trust fund is entitled to an ALIQUOT SHARE of each asset. This allows beneficiaries who qualify to be able to mortgage or sell their interest.

Beneficiaries' rights to foundation information: Beneficiaries under civil and common law foundations are considered by most jurisdictions to be entitled to information concerning the affairs of the foundation. Unlike beneficiaries under trusts, no broad principle has yet become universally applied, although in most jurisdictions beneficiaries are entitled to information relating to important features of their foundation's financial position. The authority for any disclosure to a beneficiary about a foundation's affairs is found either in the law of the jurisdiction where the foundation is set up or by the constitutional documents of the particular foundation. As far as the law is concerned, the provisions are numerous and range from providing that the foundation council should provide information specified in the law with, in some cases, a restriction on the type of information that may be given out and distinctions between the information that may be given to different classes of beneficiaries. The powers of protectors or enforcers are also relevant in the event of the failure of any stipulated procedure; recourse to the courts can be used as a default situation in many jurisdictions.

Beneficiaries' rights to trust information: *See* DISCLOSURE BY TRUSTEES TO BENEFICIARIES.

Beneficiary (1): A person for whose benefit the trustee holds trust property. A beneficiary may be an individual or legal person and there may be more than one beneficiary. A settlor may be a beneficiary. Under a trust, a beneficiary has the BENEFICIAL INTEREST in the trust property and may hold that interest on behalf of others, i.e. where an interest under a trust is held on a further trust for some other person. The beneficiaries may enforce the terms of the trust through a PERSONAL ACTION against the trustees and, because the beneficiary also has an EQUITABLE PROPRIETARY INTEREST in the trust property, the beneficiary may TRACE the property into the hands of an apparent owner and claim the property for the trust fund or for himself. A person who is incapable of owning a legal estate in land directly because of incapacity or disability may be a beneficiary of a trust that includes land in the trust assets. Beneficiaries were formerly known as *cestuis que trust*.

Beneficiary (2): A person who receives or is entitled to receive a benefit under a will.

Beneficiary (3): A person, organisation or other entity that is entitled and identified as the party who will receive the net proceeds under an insurance policy.

Beneficiary liability: *See* PERSONAL LIABILITY.

Beneficiary principle: A requirement that there must be a beneficiary, corporate or individual, in whose favour the trust property is held in order for there to be a valid trust unless the trust falls within a very small category that has been given judicial approval, such as property held on trust for the maintenance of tombs and the maintenance of animals. The great exception to this principle exists for trusts that are created for a charitable purpose. In admitting charities as trusts, it is emphasised that charities, although trusts for purposes, are beneficial overall, although not for specific persons. This means that a CHARITABLE TRUST does not have CERTAINTY OF OBJECTS. The beneficiary principle is not an essential item with foundations. Foundations can exist to achieve a purpose that is not charitable, although currently it is recognised that a foundation's purpose must be externally related and not merely for the preservation of foundation assets. In many jurisdictions foundations may have both beneficiaries and purposes as the objective of the foundation. *See* DIRECTLY OUTWARD-RELATED FOUNDATION PURPOSES.

Beneficium abstinandi: In civil law the power of an heir to abstain from accepting an inheritance.

Benevolent purposes: A trust set up with vague objects of benevolence as its purpose and with similar well-meaning descriptions, such as philanthropic purposes, but which is not recognised as a charity, is void. Where assets could be used for charitable or non-charitable purposes without allocating the trust assets between the two classes, the trust could also be regarded as void for uncertainty. In jurisdictions that do not maintain this distinction, such a trust is valid and, where purpose trusts are permitted, the word 'benevolent' has its ordinary meaning, which is comparable to philanthropic or charitable. *See* CHARITIES *and* CHARITABLE TRUST *and see* UNCERTAINTY.

Benjamin Order: An order made by the court under the precedent established in ***Re Benjamin*** [1902] 1 Ch 723 for the distribution of assets on death when it is uncertain whether or not a beneficiary is still alive. The order authorises the personal representatives of the deceased to distribute the property on the assumption of the beneficiary's death and the personal representatives are thereby protected from being sued if the beneficiary is alive and claims to be entitled to the assets distributed. Such a beneficiary may trace the trust property (*see* TRACING). A Benjamin Order 'Does not vary or destroy beneficial interests. It merely enables trust property to be distributed in accordance with the practical probabilities.' (***Green's Trusts, Re*** [1985] 3 All ER 148).

Bentham, Jeremy (1748-1832): Philosopher, jurist and the founder of modern utilitarianism and regarded as the spiritual founder of University College, London; the leading theorist in the Anglo-American philosophy of law whose theories were developed by his student, John Austin (*see* AUSTIN, JOHN). Bentham developed the idea of the welfare state and the separation of church and state. He was strongly in favour of individual legal rights and an opponent of natural law and natural rights referring to them as 'nonsense upon stilts' and he thereby fuelled the positivist theory of law later developed by his student, Austin. Bentham was unsuccessful in his call for the codification of all the common law, despite some moderate success which followed in the US a generation later. An early advocate of animal rights, the freedom of expression, equal rights for women and the right of divorce, Bentham laid the seeds for many legal reforms over the next 200 years.

Bequeathed: Primarily applies only to property passing under a will and generally applied to personal property passing in this way; not itself a technical term.

Bequest: A gift by a will of personal property unlike a gift of real property, which is a devise, although the terms are now used interchangeably. Specific bequest is where a testator bequeaths all his property of a specific class or kind, but it is now commonly used as indicating a legacy of a particular item. An executory bequest is the bequest of an interest in personalty which is contingent or deferred.

Best evidence rule: The requirement that original pieces of evidence should be presented to the courts: this rule applies particularly in respect of documentary evidence. Original documents are considered to be superior to copies and this has led to the rule that if the original is available a copy will not be permitted as evidence.

Best rent: The maximum rent, below a commercial rent, that can be negotiated for the rental of property. The use of the term 'best rent' carries an implication that there are factors which prevent a commercial rent being obtainable.

Best title: A term indicating that a vendor of property falls short of being able to grant a complete title to the property but what he can provide may be adequate if the purchaser agrees by contract to accept.

Better equity: The claimant in a Court of Equity who is held by the court to be entitled to priority over the other claimants, either by way of priority in time or for some other reason.

Bias: Anyone acting in a judicial capacity who decides matters contrary to what the evidence properly requires on impartial consideration. May be applied to the acts of a trustee who is in a particular relationship with one beneficiary and where the other beneficiaries suspect favouritism. No judge can adjudicate in matters in which he has a pecuniary interest and the same applies to trustees or to a foundation council. Generally, bias indicates a failure to perform in accordance with the standard of even-handed justice.

Bien: The equivalent in a French will to the deceased's estate; may be used in the plural.

Bifurcate: To split into two parts; when applied to a court action a judge may decide that one issue may be heard to conclusion without trying all aspects of the case. For example, in trust litigation a judge may decide that he will hear legal arguments on the validity of a trust and leave questions as to the relative claims of beneficiaries until after the validity has been settled. If the trust is found to be invalid, then time is saved by not pursuing the relative interests of the beneficiaries any further.

Bilateral contract: A contract between two persons where each undertakes obligations towards the other, such as a contract for sale where one party is obliged to deliver the thing sold and the other party to pay the price. Bilateral contracts are distinct from unilateral contracts where one party promises to pay if the other party refrains from doing something.

***Bill of Rights* 1688:** A declaration by the Houses of Lords and Commons and afterwards enacted as a Statute (1 Will. & Mary, sess. 2, c. 2.), which asserted the freedom of speech in Parliament, the Protestant Succession to the UK Throne and the objection to various powers and financial corrupt practices. This is still frequently considered in cases before the courts and expressly preserved (*Parliamentary Standards Act* 2009, Section 1), and is used to support the principle that the proceedings in Parliament should not be interfered with by any court.

Bills of Sale: A deed assigning personal property either absolutely or as security for other transactions. The *Bills of Sale Acts* 1878 to 1882 provides a public registration system. Of uncommon use except where the title of personal property is conveyed to another but the property is retained by the original owner; for example, the transfer of the ownership of a family portrait as security for a loan whilst leaving the portrait in the possession of the family. A further use is where property is seized by an official under a court order and sold by a Bill of Sale to secure a repayment of a sum owed. In the case of registered ships, a Bill of Sale is the only method of transferring ownership.

Blackacre: A term used to describe a hypothetical piece of land for the purpose of illustrating various interests existing on that land such as rights of way and easements (*see* EASEMENT), particularly for teaching purposes where a technical topic is made more understandable by the employment of fictitious names to a property involved in the problem, such as where a person has an interest in 'Blackacre' or similar names such as 'Whiteacre'.

Blind trust: A trust where the settlor transfers property, usually money or existing investments, to trustees to be held on trust for his own and his family's benefit on the basis that he will not know at any time the identity of investments made by the trustees in their complete discretion. This prevents the settlor being vulnerable to accusations of conflict of interest between his private and professional life. A blind trust is often used on the appointment of a person to a position of authority where impartiality needs to be exercised; for example, in the government, to avoid a possible allegation of misconducting his power to award government contracts. This places a high burden of responsibility on the trustees. Also called a FROZEN TRUST.

Body corporate: A body of persons that is dealt with as a single unit by law and, depending on the context, does not necessarily indicate a separate legal person; for example, in the UK *Trade Descriptions Act* 1968, the term 'body corporate' includes a partnership. The term is often used, despite having this rather broader meaning, to describe a company. The term might also be applied to PRIVATE FOUNDATIONS.

Bona fide: A phrase used to indicate that a person has acted in good faith and honestly, without fraud or participation in any wrongdoing. The phrase expresses the mental approach to a situation and is used to describe a person's overall conduct rather than the physical nature of a particular act. The absence of bona fide conduct does not denote a fraud of the type which makes a contract or other transaction voidable between the parties, but indicates that there is some form of collusion or knowledge that taints the conduct of one party by generally taking advantage of the other party's weakness or ignorance and which may disentitle the party who lacks the good faith to set up a claim against a person who would otherwise be liable. For example, a bona fide purchaser of land for value without notice of the existence of EQUITABLE INTERESTS in the land will take the land free of those equitable interests. To do so, the purchaser must be bona fide, i.e. a genuine purchaser, with the intention of transferring ownership of the unencumbered property; this is in addition to not having notice of the existence of equitable rights and, in addition, a bona fide purchaser may mean a purchaser for real value and not pretended value. *See* GOOD FAITH, MALA FIDES *and* EQUITY'S DARLING.

Bona fide purchaser – equity's darling: A bona fide purchaser of a legal estate in property for value without notice of an existing equitable interest takes the property free of those equitable interests. This is a key principle of equity law; such a purchaser was referred to as the darling of the Court of Chancery by F. W. Maitland (Collected Papers, Vol. 3, page 350). This privilege has long been recognised in decisions and textbooks; for example:

> 'The "polar star of equity" thus became: legal rights are good against all the world; equitable rights are good against all persons except a bona fide purchaser of the legal estate for value without notice (i.e., "equity's darling") and those claiming under such a purchaser.' [*Stanhope v. Earl Verney* (1761) 2 Eden 81, 85.] *See* EQUITABLE INTERESTS *and* EQUITY'S DARLING.

Bona vacantia: Property, real or personal, in which there is no person taking an absolute interest, particularly on INTESTACY. This results in the estate of an intestate passing to the Crown (or the Duchies of Lancaster or Cornwall depending on where the property is situated) under the *Administration of Estates Act* 1925, Section 46(1)(vi). The term is also used to indicate an asset without an owner, such as abandoned CHATTELS or wild animals (subject to certain prerogative rights of the Crown), goods without an owner, or property held on trust which has failed where there is no beneficiary to benefit under a RESULTING TRUST, or property formerly owned by a company that has been dissolved. The term is also used in a general sense to indicate property without an owner.

Bond: A bond is an obligation by deed and frequently used to record an obligation to repay money and the interest charged on the money, i.e. as in government and corporate bonds.

Bonus issue: The issue of shares without charge to existing company members by a company to increase its share capital in proportion to each shareholder's holding and which is paid for out of undistributed profits of the company.

Breach of contract: The failure of one party to a contract to perform according to the agreed obligation and for which the injured party can usually claim DAMAGES. Where one party perceives that the other party to a contract will be unable to perform as required, then that party can claim ANTICIPATORY BREACH OF CONTRACT and himself rescind the obligation to mitigate exposure or continue with the obligation until an actual breach occurs.

Breach of trust: An omission by a trustee or an improper act of a trustee or other person in a fiduciary position which is contrary to the duties imposed upon him by the terms of the trust or by the fiduciary standards required by law. Although the breach may not be deliberate or dishonest, the trustee then becomes personally responsible for compensating the beneficiaries or the trust for any loss caused. Property acquired by trustees in breach of trust is held on CONSTRUCTIVE TRUST for the rightful owners. The most frequent breach of trust is the failure of a trustee to follow the direction given in the trust instrument. The term is also applied to a trustee's action performed at the instigation of a beneficiary where the trustee has a justifiable claim to be indemnified under the UK *Trustee Act* 1925, Section 62, for the loss caused to the trust by the beneficiary. A beneficiary breaches a trust if there is an act or omission which itself is a breach, such as the pledging of trust assets for an unwarranted purpose, and not merely where there is some act or omission that only constitutes a breach of trust by reason of want of care on the part of the trustee. A breach of trust may be innocent or fraudulent. The courts have operated a traditionally severe strict liability rule in connection with any breach of trust by a trustee. A trustee has a duty to act precisely within the terms of his obligations; excusing a breach of trust as merely a 'technical breach of trust' will not suffice nor will the argument that he did not intend to depart from his duty. This strict level of liability was established as an attempt to provide greater certainty for the beneficiaries. The courts have been disturbed as they have watched the era of strict liability be mitigated by an EXEMPTION CLAUSE in trust deeds. Where a trustee was a party to, or privy to, a fraudulent breach of trust, then the trustee incurs personal liability. Other examples of breach of trust include taking SECRET PROFITS, non-compliance with the terms of the trust, acting in a negligent manner and failing to distribute the funds according to the terms of the trust or failing to invest the trust funds in accordance with the *Trustee Act* 2000.

Bribe: A gift made to a person holding a position of trust with the object of securing an advantage by betrayal by that person of the trust. A term that is usually applied in regard to attempts to persuade a public officer to carry out his duties in a particular way. Acceptance of a bribe by a judicial or ministerial person, or to conspire with another to accept a bribe, is an offence at common law. The *Public Bodies Corrupt Practices Act* 1889 covers bribery of members of local government bodies. Bribery was made the subject of a statutory offence under the *Bribery Act* 2010 which made provision about offences relating to bribery and for connected purposes. *See* CORRUPTION.

British Overseas Territories: Formerly called British Dependent Territories until the *British Overseas Territories Act* 2002; these comprise: Anguilla, Bermuda, British Antarctic Territory, British Indian Ocean Territory, British Virgin Islands, Cayman Islands, Falkland Islands, Gibraltar, Montserrat, Pitcairn islands, St. Helena and Dependencies, South Georgia and the South Sandwich Islands, the Sovereign Base Areas of Akrotiri and Dhekelia in Cyprus, and the Turks and Caicos Islands. These territories have a substantial independence, conduct their own affairs and pass their own laws; several of these have passed their own trust Acts and foundation Acts.

Brother - Sister: The term is used in ordinary parlance to mean a person standing 'in the same relationship to one or both of his parents in which he himself stands'. Therefore, a gift to a brother or sister includes those brothers and sisters of the half blood. Construction of the term may be detected by the context in which it is used, i.e. as required by a settlor or founder, but there are limits. A gift to a brother or sister by the testator who knows that he himself was illegitimate, nevertheless, is a valid provision of his will to his putative brother and sister.

Brussels Convention on Jurisdiction and the Enforcement of Judgments in Civil and Commercial Matters 1968: An international convention which became part of a complex attempt to harmonise jurisdiction and enforcement in the EU, and which has been superseded (except in relation to questions arising with Denmark) by EU Council Regulation (EC 44/2001), which took effect in all Member States on 1 March 2002. As far as trusts are concerned, the regulation determines whether a trust is domiciled in a particular country and generally the regulation Article 5(6) operates to confer jurisdiction on the courts of a particular Member State if the trust is domiciled in that state.

Brussels Regulation (Recast): Introduced in Regulation (EU) 1215/2012 of the European Parliament and the Council of 12th December 2012 some improvements to EC COUNCIL REGULATION 44/2001. These amendments expand (Article 25) the ability of parties, regardless of their domicile, to agree that the courts of a Member State have jurisdiction to settle any dispute. Previously, such an agreement required one or more of the parties to be domiciled in a Member State. There is also an enhanced arbitration rule and new rules relating to the *LIS ALIBI PENDENS* provisions of the original regulation. (*See* ITALIAN TORPEDO). These amendments have been criticised as not being entirely fool proof.

Bubble Act: An Act passed in 1721 after the collapse of the South Sea Company with the intention of discouraging similar investment schemes. The South Sea Bubble was a speculative venture of the South Sea Company, a British trading company, which exploited the monopoly in trade with Spain's colonies in South America and the West Indies. The intention was to fund the British Government's debt incurred during the War of Spanish Succession 1701 – 1713 and the British Government believed that the exclusive trading rights offered by the South Sea Company would convince private investors to assume the Government's war debts. Shareholders assumed a total of £10 million government debt in exchange for South Sea Company shares. Eventually a proposal was made by the South Sea Company to purchase over half of the British national debt, which approached £25 million. The trading activities were quite modest but rumours of gold and silver in South America caused a speculative frenzy. In 1720, the stock prices increased from £128 in January to £550 in May; many purchased through option schemes. The same principle was then applied to other companies of great variety. These highly competitive companies were nicknamed 'bubbles' and stock prices in the South Sea Company leapt to £1,000 by August 1720, followed by an avalanche of selling, resulting in the bankruptcy of speculators who purchased on credit. Sir Isaac Newton lost £20,000, equivalent in modern terms to over £2 million. He remarked: 'I can calculate the movement of the stars, but not the madness of men.' The Act, passed in 1721, was intended to discourage similar schemes that would be designed as baits to extract money from the thoughtless.

Burden of proof, or the onus of proof: The obligation that a party who wishes to prove a particular fact must satisfy the court as to its truth. A party who fails to discharge this burden in respect of any material issue raised will normally lose the case. The standard of proof indicates the level of evidence required to discharge the burden of proof. In criminal proceedings, the onus of proof is to produce evidence to convince the court or jury that the plaintiff's case is proof 'beyond reasonable doubt' that the accused has been shown to have committed the offence. This incorporates the presumption of innocence. In civil proceedings the onus of proof is on 'the balance of probabilities'. The position is summarised in the old legal maxim that the onus of proof lies on the party asserting a proposition not on the one who denies it. This means that the burden of proof in criminal proceedings is on the prosecution and, in civil cases, on the claimants who seek redress for alleged wrongs. The burden of proof is sometimes reversed, i.e. the accused (and not the claimant) must satisfy the court that on the balance of probabilities his account of the situation is correct, particularly in relation to affirmative defences; e.g. where a defence is made to a claim that a certain state of affairs existed, it is then up to that person to prove the existence of that state of affairs. Thus, the burden of proof is then shifted to the defence case. In trust cases, a beneficiary alleging a breach of trust by the trustee has the burden of proving his allegation in the normal way on the balance of probabilities; in view of the nature of the trustee's duty, and a trustee's powers and discretions, this can be a heavy evidential burden on a beneficiary. The courts exercise a sympathetic approach towards a trustee in view of the difficult duties assumed by them and are clearly conscious of the need that the accuser, if a beneficiary, should show more than mere displeasure or disappointment when trustees carry out their proper independent assessment of the merits of each discretionary beneficiary.

Business trusts: A term of particular significance in the US and Canada, which applies to trusts established primarily for commercial purposes, where the likely consequence is that such trusts will be regarded as companies for tax purposes. There is some thought that purpose trusts may also be regarded as companies, but this depends upon the particular tax laws of the state in which the trust is situated. In many cases, these trusts are the product of statute or statutory regulation resulting in only limited similarity with personal trusts. The attraction for business use is the separation of the legal title from the management of the business assets and from the enjoyment of them. Business trusts have enjoyed a remarkable increase in popularity, particularly in connection with financial affairs, where the fundamental principles of trust law and practice are sometimes difficult to identify. A business trust can be used as a holding device in a variety of situations, including a trust to provide for the liquidity for partners to be able to buy out the interest of any one of them on death. The trustee holds the contributions made by the partners generally and, in the event of the death of one of them, the accumulated funds are passed to the deceased's estate as consideration for the purchase by the surviving partners of his share of the partnership. As an alternative to contributing funds to a trust, the funding is done through life assurance policies on each partner, the premiums for which are paid by the partnership. Shares or stocks in a company may also be placed in a trust and made available for purchase by employees over an extended period. Shares may also be placed in a trust for allocation to directors on their appointment or discharge at the discretion of the trustee. In some jurisdictions, a business trust is sometimes used as a substitute for an incorporated body because it is a much more informal and flexible device, particularly in conjunction with real estate transactions that may have, as in Canada, the additional advantage to the beneficiaries of flow-through depreciation allowances. This type of trust is also used for mutual funds and real estate investment trusts and oil and gas tax royalty trusts. *See* PENSION TRUSTS, PROFIT SHARING TRUSTS, COLLECTIVE INVESTMENT SCHEMES *and* COMMERCIAL TRUSTS.

C

Cancellation: A doctrine of equity not greatly used whereby a court may order a document to be delivered up and cancelled. This only occurs where a document appears to be valid but is VOID or VOIDABLE and its existence may be dangerous by being likely to facilitate some fraudulent claim. The REMEDY is subject to the same principles as applied to RESCISSION with the additional requirement that there must be some reason to destroy the document itself. Nowadays, a declaration that a document is void or has been voided is thought to be an adequate remedy.

Canon law (or ecclesiastical law): A term which is used imprecisely, but principally indicates the body of law applying to the church. The early law of the church developed in a local and AD HOC manner and remained unconsolidated despite various attempts at codification. Those attempts made during the Reformation produced little but, under the *Submission of Clergy Act* 1533, all Canons, constitutions, ordinances and synods which did not conflict with the common law and the King's prerogative were preserved and enforced. Different collections of Canons were subsequently assembled. An entirely new Code of Canons was enacted in 1964 and 1969 and these are, from time to time, amended by the General Synod. The term 'Canon Law' is now best reserved for the Canons of the Church of England and generally treated as a species of ecclesiastical law. In England, Canon law influenced the legal decisions given by the Lord Chancellor in the early days of the Chancery Courts because at that time the Lord Chancellor was a cleric. Eventually the common law took over. Canon Law retained its influence in continental Europe on the formation of civil law and played a part in the preference for foundations over the idea of trusts. This followed the application of Canon Law to those religious bodies that in the Middle Ages were considered to be separate legal persons; this concept was upheld by the Roman Catholic Church, which considered religious bodies to be of divine foundation.

Capacity: Capacity indicates the legal competence of a person to enter into a transaction. In this sense of the use of the word 'capacity' is the criterion that dictates whether the law will recognise a person as being capable of carrying out actions or transactions; for example, a person who lacks contractual capacity is unable to enter into a valid contract. Generally, a person who is a minor or who is mentally incompetent can be expected to lack capacity and the legal competence to enter into a trust, foundation or contract. Apart from this use of the term in relation to a person's total capacity and incapacity, the term is used in other situations. For example, a person may be said not to have the capacity to enter into a contract or other arrangement when the proposed transaction itself is contrary to the law. In that case, capacity is treated as part of the essential validity of a proposal and not something which is particularly attributed to the person concerned. One objection to this is that it may be possible for the parties to choose a law to govern a particular transaction that would give capacity to a person who did not otherwise have it under a different law that might, apart from the choice of law, govern the transaction. DOMICILE is now rejected as a test of capacity; capacity may now depend either upon the law of a person's domicile and residence or under the governing law of the contract objectively ascertained, i.e. the law with which the contract is most closely connected and not that necessarily chosen by the parties, although the law of the closest connection may not be discernable at the time when capacity is being debated. In contrast to the position of capacity under contracts and trusts, the position is simpler for assessing capacity to set up a private foundation as the capacity of the founder depends entirely on the place where the foundation is incorporated and follows the rules relating to capacity to set up companies and, as with companies, is distinct from the capacity to be a shareholder or a director. Capacity and trust law can overlap. Any person who would, if of full age and of sound mind, be capable of owning property may be a beneficiary. This means, in practice, anyone may be a beneficiary unless there are statutory provisions rendering in any particular circumstance the relationship of trustee and beneficiary as unlawful. A settlor or trustee may be a beneficiary, or one of the beneficiaries, under the trust which he sets up. But a sole trustee cannot hold property on trust for himself as the sole beneficiary. Under this situation, there can be no equitable interest created and therefore no trust; such a person is the absolute legal beneficial owner. But are these matters of capacity or of trust law? The *LEX SITUS* governs this distinction. The capacity of an intended person to act as a trustee is governed by the law applicable to the trust under the Hague Convention, Article 8(2)(a), but this is subject to the inevitable rule that an intended trustee must also have the capacity to receive property under the general law of the *lex situs*, which is not by-passed by the Hague Convention. The *lex situs* decides whether a person can act as trustee of a particular trust even though the *lex situs* applies a law of a different jurisdiction as the proper law of the trust. Any person who has power to hold or dispose of any legal or equitable estate or interest in assets may be a settlor or a trustee (i.e. have the capacity to so act); this includes individuals and corporate bodies. This depends upon their ability to hold the legal estate and therefore a minor who cannot hold a legal estate in land cannot settle property on trust (unless it is a privileged testator, such as soldier or airman on active military service). Other criteria are set out in the *Mental Capacity Act* 2005. Having capacity does not, *ipso facto*, authorise a person to act in a particular role; authorisation to do so which does not involve capacity may be required. For example, a corporation may require authorisation under the laws, such as the *Financial Services and Markets Act* 2000, to be a trustee. Similarly, the capacity of a beneficiary to receive a benefit is determined according to the Hague Convention by the *lex situs* at the time of the purported transfer of the property to the trustee and then whether a person with that general capacity is actually entitled under the trust to take a benefit depends upon the terms of the trust as governed by the applicable law. The role that capacity applies to the setting up of a trust can therefore be divided into two aspects. First, a settlor who wishes to transfer a property to a trustee intends to dispose of his property in the same way as he would if he simply gave it away or sold it to another person. He needs capacity to dispose of that property. The second aspect is whether the purported settlor has the capacity to create the trust structure with that property as a trust asset. This demonstrates the interplay between capacity, in respect of the ownership of property, and with trust law. A person, even though he has capacity to hold property, may be incapable of setting up a trust, i.e. the settlor may have the capacity to own and dispose of property but this is distinct from capacity to set up a trust under the trust's proper law. The capacity to act as a founder, member of the foundation council or similar body such as a protector/guardian, or to be a beneficiary, follows the rules relating to the equivalent positions in trusts as far as general capacity is concerned but, in the absence of guidance of an international Convention, the capacity to act in the individual roles will depend on the governing law of the foundation. Capacity is also relevant to international and legal entities that may act in a variety of roles. It is important to consider whether, in conjunction with any purported application, the party has that capacity. For example, governments engaged in a variety of operations may have a variety of capacities in respect of such operations. *See* HAGUE CONVENTION ON THE LAW APPLICABLE TO TRUSTS AND ON THEIR RECOGNITION, MENTAL CAPACITY *and* MENTAL DISORDER.

Capital and income: The distinction between capital and income is important for trustees and foundation councils where there are beneficiaries entitled to capital or to income. Also, trust or foundation expenses are required to be allocated between capital and income. A common metaphor to distinguish capital and income is to compare the ownership of a tree and the ownership of the fruits borne by that tree. Ownership of the tree, which is the source of the income, indicates the capital, whereas the fruit is the income which flows from the tree. This metaphor is detectible in many decisions but, in some cases, the comparison is too wide to be reliable in every case. The apportionment of additions to the trust and foundation assets between capital and income depends upon the character of the receipts. The distinction is a legal matter and any provision in the trust instrument which states that the trustees may make a binding distinction between income and capital is ineffective as being repugnant to the interests that may be conferred by the instrument and as an attempt to oust the jurisdiction of the court. A further complication is that trustees may be given discretion in the trust instrument to distribute income to beneficiaries entitled by the trust instrument to capital distributions and vice versa. Trustees may also be given the POWER to pay out as income expenses what would normally be regarded as capital expenses. This power has been regarded as an administrative power and not as a dispositive power. In connection with land, it is clear that the ordinary rents from land are income either under an existing lease or a new lease. In connection with TRUSTS OF LAND, the sale of timber which is cut to improve the growth of other trees constitutes capital; the tree being regarded as a capital asset. Receipts from the sale of underwood and thinnings made in the ordinary course of forestry management are interest. A variation of this is if land is bought and sold on a regular basis and in such a volume as to suggest that each parcel of land is regarded as an item of saleable stock, then profit on the sale may be regarded as income, a trading income. A contrary view to this is that assets which involve a large financial investment, either to buy or to sell, would be considered to be capital. The existence of a series of assets does not preclude them from being regarded as capital assets with a possible exception that if held by a trading trust, the parcels of land might be held as ordinary trading assets, the receipts of the sale of which would be income. Income includes rents and royalties received under a lease of an open mine, interest on mortgage debts even those receivable as a lump sum, and compensation under an indemnity for damages done to a park during the war. Capital receipts have included periodic receipts, such as receipts from another fund, compensation payable under various Acts and the proceeds of a compulsory acquisition of trust property. Dividends received from companies naturally belong to the beneficiary entitled to income allocations. A tenant for life is entitled to the fruit of the shares in the form of dividends which are duly declared during his lifetime even though the actual payment falls after his death. The payment of arrears of dividends on preference shares has been the subject of much litigation. A shareholder has no right to a dividend, whether cumulative or otherwise, until there are profits available. Complications arise when arrears of dividends are paid but one of the beneficiaries entitled has died during the period when payment of the dividends was not made. The question then is who is entitled to take the dividend as an income? Under these circumstances, if the arrears are paid during the lifetime of a life interest beneficiary, the payment goes to him, but if such a life tenant has died, the payment goes to the remainderman. Also, the *Trusts (Capital and Income) Act* 2013 has introduced new rules on APPORTIONMENT unless a contrary intention is expressed in any instrument creating the trust.

Capital assets: *See* ASSETS.

Capital Gains Tax: A tax on capital gains introduced in the UK in 1965 and consolidated by the *Taxation of Chargeable Gains Act* 1992 that affects individuals and other settlors when disposing of assets to trustees and on the disposal of trust assets when in the ownership of the trustees. The rules have been considerably changed since the tax was introduced to prevent tax avoidance, principally by techniques to transform income into capital gains and thereby enjoy what was a lower rate of tax on the latter. This tax planning opportunity has been substantially removed; changes in UK tax law have made capital gains and income taxable at the same rate.

Capital of a company: Means the money subscribed for the shares in that company where it is known as the 'ISSUED CAPITAL' as compared to the maximum amount that can be issued as share capital, which is known as the 'authorised capital'. The term is sometimes used to refer to the total of the capital assets of a company in the form of movable or IMMOVABLE PROPERTY without regard to the issued or AUTHORISED CAPITAL.

Capital Transfer Tax: A tax introduced in 1975 to replace estate duty from 13 March 1975 and which was itself replaced by the current regime of INHERITANCE TAX by the *Inheritance Tax Act* 1984.

Capricious trusts: Where trustees act without any apparent reason, the trust is said to be capricious and the decisions of trustees are open to review by the court. The term is also applied in other contexts to describe unjustifiable conduct. With trusts, this particularly applies where the trustees' behaviour cannot be construed on any reasonable view to benefit the objects or the beneficiaries of the trust or to fulfil the purpose for which the power had been created. Each situation is treated separately but, generally, capricious trusts are treated as void. The term 'capricious trust' applies first to trusts where the settlor gives capricious instructions to the trustees and, second, where the trustees ignore proper instructions and manage the property in a different manner (see Underhill & Hayton, *Law of Trusts and Trustees*, 17th edn, para. 8.185). The concept of 'capricious behaviour' has been described as where the trustees act in an 'arbitrary, absurd, wanton, oppressive, vexatious, mischievous or ruinous' manner (*see* Thomas & Hudson, *Law of Trusts*, Oxford University Press, para. 11.89). In practical terms, capricious conduct or actions have received little judicial comment. In one case, a trustee in bankruptcy decided not to sell a reversion of a CONTINGENT INTEREST that in counsel's opinion was an absurd exercise of the discretion of the trustee, but the court stated that it would not interfere unless the trustee 'is doing that which is so utterly unreasonable and absurd that no reasonable man would so act' (Lord Jessel MR in ***Ex parte Lloyd*** (1882) 47 LT 64). A practical way of defining capricious conduct is that it may constitute a failure to take into account relevant considerations or may give credence to irrelevant considerations. The word 'capricious' in this context differs from the ordinary meaning of the word, such as volatile, irregular or fickle, or sudden unaccountable changes of mood or behaviour. A trustee must give properly informed consideration to a problem and a failure to acknowledge plain facts or accept an unequivocal statement of the law may result in his conduct being properly described as capricious. A common factor in capricious actions seems to be a matter of a positive decision of a trustee rather than omissions. A trustee acts in a frivolous way when distinguishing between discretionary beneficiaries for reasons unauthorised in the trust deed, such as the colour of beneficiaries' hair or eyes or any other features. A trust set up by will with the intention of teasing and humiliating those who might otherwise have been beneficiaries but who did not find favour with the testator may be considered capricious conduct on the part of the testator. Such motive has no legal consequences provided the dispositions made in the will are legally acceptable. But this is different from the concept of capricious action of trustees as described above. Cases in which the principle of ***Hastings Bass*** has been applied have been considered as examples of behaviour which may broadly be described as capricious on the part of the trustees but are now regarded as a separate principle as they have received close judicial comment and are rarely labelled as capricious.

Carat: A weight used to describe the size of diamonds and other precious stones and also to indicate the purity of gold articles from 9 carat to 24 carat; the latter consisting of 916.6 parts of gold per thousand.

Case law: Principles of law derived from judicial decisions which are extracted from decisions of the higher courts and which are taken to be declarations of the law and applied in subsequent cases where the principle is shown by counsel's argument to be relevant. This is based on the declaratory principle of the common law where the judges are understood to know the law and, in giving judgment, are declaring what is the law. A PRECEDENT only arises in this way in so far as the conclusion reached in a previous case by a judge is relevant to his decision, i.e. the *rationale judicata*. Other comments that may be useful opinions on the law but which do not constitute a binding precedent are called *obitur dicta* (*see* OBITER DICTUM).

Causation: The relationship between an act committed and the actual harm or loss that is subject to a claim. For example, a fiduciary is bound to pursue activities on his principal's behalf, but where the fiduciary legitimately pursues a cause of action in his own interest and makes a profit, the object of the fiduciary duty needs to show that there is a connection between the profit and a breach of duty by the fiduciary, i.e. the act by the fiduciary or the breach of trust that led to a gain by the fiduciary contrary to his fiduciary responsibilities. In other words, the object of the fiduciary duty needs to show that the perverse action of the fiduciary is the actual cause of harm or loss that would otherwise have been avoided had the fiduciary acted in a proper manner.

Cause of action: A circumstance in which one party considers that he has a right of action for compensation or damages and where the cause of action is identified as a wrongful act by the person against whom the claim is made. A cause of action, i.e. the fact giving rise to a right to sue, may be a unilateral act such as destroying trust documents or it may consist of such a wrongful act and the consequent damages. This presupposes that the matter from which the cause of action is generated is a lawful situation or structure; thus, a trust deed that has not been executed by the settlor does not represent a valid trust and is not one from which any cause of action can be generated.

Certainties: A form of conduct or manner of expression that leaves no doubt as to its meaning and for which only one interpretation is reasonably possible. A term applied to one of the requirements of law so that the subjects of that law are in no doubt as to whether a form of conduct is legal or illegal or is applied to particular aspects of conduct, such as the terms by which parties commit themselves in contracts (*see* CERTAINTY OF CONTRACTUAL OBLIGATIONS). The concept of certainty has particular meaning in the law of trusts in that to constitute a valid trust there must be certainty on three principal elements, i.e. for the creation of a valid trust there must be three certainties usually contained in the words of a document or will that set up the trust. These words of the settlor must be imperative, i.e. that there is no ambiguity as to the intention of the settlor to set up a trust; *see* CERTAINTY OF WORDS. Then, the subject matter of the trust must be certain, *see* CERTAINTY OF SUBJECT MATTER; and the objects or persons intended to benefit by the trust must be certain, *see* CERTAINTY OF OBJECTS. With private foundations the emphasis on these three certainties is not so great, as the formation procedures are said to leave less opportunity for doubt due to the registration procedure of foundations. *See* PRIVATE FOUNDATIONS. Certainty in the drafting of a foundation's constitutional documents is nevertheless essential for the avoidance of disputes after formation; these disputes are likely to be based on an allegation that the certainty of the founder's intention, or of the subject matter or of the objects, was lacking despite the apparent adequacy of the words of the charter or regulations and that, on proper consideration, the lack of certainty could lead to a claim that the foundation was unenforceable. *See* CHARITABLE GIFTS.

Certainty of contractual obligations: A necessary element to be able to translate the legal agreement reached by an offer of one party being unequivocally accepted by another. Many contractual obligations may arise which may not pass a crucial test of this nature but which are adequate to allow the parties to the contract to fulfil their respective needs. A more stringent test of certainty is likely to be required if one party to a contract requires the court to issue an order of specific performance, i.e. an order that the respondent party should perform according to what was agreed. Although such a contract may have been sufficient, to be workable under the common understanding of both parties it may not be sufficient for a court to be able to determine exactly what the obligations of the parties are. This applies particularly to the party whose obligations characterise the nature of the contract, i.e. the seller of goods characterises a contract of sale; the obligations of the other party are merely to make payment and this obligation is not necessarily an essential characteristic of a contract of sale. In other words, the contractual obligation of the seller of goods must be sufficiently certain so that an order of specific performance can be workable. Consequently, the obligations of the parties must be expressed with such precision as to enable a court to consider whether an order should be issued to perform the obligation. Furthermore, specific performance will not normally be ordered with contracts to carry on an activity as opposed to contracts to achieve a particular result.

Certainty of objects: It must be possible to identify the beneficiaries or to determine how the actual identity of beneficiaries can be established. This must exist without doubt. This need for certainty extends beyond confirming the identity of beneficiaries and covers the extent and time that the trust or foundation assets, capital or income will be distributed. Naming the beneficiaries, or describing the class of persons who may be chosen by the trustees or a foundation council, is a method of securing this certainty of objects, such as naming the persons concerned or allowing the trustees at their discretion to select any person within a stated class; for example, anyone who played cricket for England in 2012. This latter method has its limitations in that, in view of the size of the trust or foundation, the criterion must be reasonable and be capable of being carried out. It is possible to add to a class of beneficiaries without making a trust uncertain, but a trust for 'my old friends' carries two uncertainties, identity and extent of the intended benefits, although it is possible that making a gift to 'dependents' may be valid where there is no difficulty in identifying them.

Certainty of subject matter: A property held on trust must be certain: 'the bulk of my personal assets' would not be certain but 25 out of 1000 shares of a named company, although not specifically identifying individual shares, would still be certain because each share is identical (assuming there is no doubt about the class of shares intended). A second meaning is that the beneficial interests to be taken by beneficiaries must also be certain; this applies both in respect of the identity of the property and how much each beneficiary is to have. In the absence of this certainty a trust fails and property in a will trust falls into residue or passes on intestacy. The maxim: 'equality is equity' may rescue a situation of apparent uncertainty by dividing the subject matter into equal shares or by relying on the trustees' discretionary power when such power is given to them, or where the beneficial interest is given to one beneficiary but the rights of others are uncertain, then the first beneficiary is entitled to the whole.

Certainty of words: Requires words to be used so as to show a sufficient intention to create a trust although a trust may be created without using the word 'trust'. The previous inclination of the Court of Chancery to construe a trust when precatory words were used, i.e. gifts with words of wish, hope, desire, confidence or similar, that the donee will dispose of the property in some particular way, are less likely to be recognised now than in the 19th century. Certainty of words is the leading factor in demonstrating the true intention of the settlor and where that intention is clear then there is less chance of the arrangement being regarded as a sham (*see* SHAMS (GENERALLY)). Also, in COMMERCIAL TRUSTS, the demand for clear words is sometimes less pronounced than in private express trusts.

Certificate: A term that describes a statement in writing by a person having a public or official status and with authority over and knowledge of the matter contained on the certificate. The term is used in connection with a variety of matters. When used in connection with land it formerly meant a certificate issued under the *Land Registrations Act* 1925 containing a description of a piece of land on the Land Registry, the name and address of the registered proprietor, the class of title, and other particulars. The certificate was PRIMA FACIA evidence of the matters contained within its terms. From 13 October 2003, however, land certificates have no longer been issued as they were incompatible with the electronic system of land transfer.

Certificate of incorporation: A certificate issued by an official of a jurisdiction, usually called a Registrar, stating that the body to which the certificate refers has been properly incorporated and is in existence as a legal person from the date stated on the certificate. These certificates are particularly prevalent in company and foundation law. Certificates of incorporation of companies state the date on which the company was incorporated. In some cases, where a foundation can be formed by the mere agreement between the parties prior to registration, the certificate is evidence that a foundation with the name contained on the certificate has been incorporated.

Certified copy: A copy of a document and signed as a true copy by the officer having the custody of the document, such as a company secretary certifying a copy of a resolution of directors, to be a true copy of a resolution passed by the directors at a board meeting.

Cestuis que trust / cestuis que use: Terms in Norman French that can be translated respectively as 'he for whom is the trust' and 'he to whose use'. Later on, particularly in the 19th century, the person to whose use lands or other hereditaments were held under a trust was referred to as a *cestui que use*. The modern equivalent is the cestuis que trust, or beneficiary. These Norman French terms are no longer in fashion but the position was summarised judicially in 1976:

> 'The full ownership in the trust property was split into two constituent elements which became vested in different persons: the "legal ownership" in the trustee, the "beneficial ownership" in the cestui que trust.' (Lord Diplock in ***Ayerst v. C & K Construction*** [1976] AC 167 at 177.)

Cestuis que vie: A person for whose life another person holds an interest in property. Generally, a person whose life is used to measure various things, such as the duration of a trust, a gift or an insurance contract, and also a person on whose life a policy of insurance is drawn. This expression is archaic and not of regular use.

Champerty: A form of 'maintenance' (*see* MAINTENANCE (2)) in existence until the criminal and tortuous nature of both champerty and maintenance was abolished by the *Criminal Justice Act* 1967 whereby a person, who has no legitimate concern in the outcome of litigation, agrees to support the action financially in consideration of a promise to receive a share of the proceeds of the action. Despite its abolition under the 1967 Act, equity will continue to refuse to give effect to assignments that involve or savour maintenance or champerty. The modern test requires an assessment of the facts of the particular case in order for the court to consider whether the agreement in question might constitute champerty and tempt a party for his personal gain 'to inflame the damages to suppress evidence, to suborn witnesses or otherwise undermine the ends of justice' (***R (Factortame Ltd) v. Transport Secretary (No. 8)*** [2002] EWCA Civ 932.)

Chancellor, Lord: An important figure in the development of the law of equity and trusts. The practice developed of referring petitions that were addressed to the King in Council for relief against unjust application of the law to the Lord Chancellor following the *Statute of Westminster* II, 1285. This custom was confirmed by an order of Edward III in 1349 when the Lord Chancellor acted at first in the name of the King in Council but from 1474 he was allowed to operate under his own authority and, for this purpose, developed a Court of Chancery that was independent of the King and his Council. The Lord Chancellor, at that period being a cleric, exercised wide but vague powers on the grounds of conscience guided by his understanding of universal and natural justice. This practice continued until the law of the Court of Chancery became secularised during the 16th century and his conscience then became the conscience of the Queen (Queen Elizabeth I being then on the throne). The Lord Chancellor was then designated the Keeper of the Queen's Conscience. During the remainder of the Tudor period, the Lord Chancellor's jurisdiction was extended and developed to cover the concept of the estate of married women, the RULE AGAINST PERPETUITIES and the rule of EQUITABLE WASTE. At this time the Lord Chancellors were drawn from the ranks of common lawyers and not, as previously, from ecclesiastics. This began the rise of the Lord Chancellor as an important legal and government official person, who was also the speaker of the House of Lords and thus combined judicial, executive and legislative roles. (*See* BACON, LORD (1618-1621), ELDON, LORD (1801-1827), ELLESMERE, LORD (1596-1617), HARDWICKE, LORD (1737-1756) *and* NOTTINGHAM, LORD (1673-1682)). The duties of the Lord Chancellor changed over the centuries; most of the previous duties having been taken over by other senior judges during the 20th century. The Lord Chancellor became a Minister in the Government of the day with responsibility for the procedure in the House of Lords and the progress through Parliament of legislative measures. The Lord Chancellor also nominated High Court judges, except the Lord Chief Justice, and had the power to remove county court judges. This combination of duties resulted in the Lord Chancellor becoming a senior Minister of the Government (a member of the Executive), the Head of the Judiciary (a member of the Judiciary) and a senior member of the House of Lords (a member of the Legislature). This combination shows the exception in English constitutional principles to the SEPARATION OF POWERS. The nature of the office has been completely transformed in the early 21st century. The Lord Chancellor's department was renamed the Department of Constitutional Affairs. The House of Lords (which had become the highest appeal court in the UK staffed by members of the House of Lords who occupied high judicial positions), was replaced by the Supreme Court of the United Kingdom. The election of a Lord Speaker to conduct affairs in the House of Lords legislature entirely transformed the office and established a better separation of powers than had previously existed. *See* SUPERIOR COURTS *and* SUPREME COURT OF THE UNITED KINGDOM.

***Chancery Amendment Act* 1858:** (Popularly known as the *Cairns'* Act) which for the first time allowed the Court of Chancery to award damages in addition to, or as an alternative for, a degree of specific performance or as an alternative to an injunction, e.g. in an action to restrain interference with ancient lights. The *Partition Act* 1868, also introduced by Mr Cairns, was also known as the Cairns' Act and the Lord Cairns' Act was a popular title of the *Land Transfer Act* 1875.

Chancery Division: A division of the High Court which replaced the Court of Chancery under the *Judicature Acts* 1873 and 1875 and which is principally concerned with matters relating to real property, trusts and the administration of estates, and also includes matters concerned with company law, patents and other intellectual property and confidentiality cases. The division is headed by the Vice Chancellor and acts alongside the Queen's Bench Division and the Family Divisions. Appeals from the Chancery Division, as with other divisions of the High Court, lay to the Court of Appeal and thence to the Supreme Court of the United Kingdom.

Changing the proper law: A clause in trust instruments, foundation charters and other legal documents, such as international contracts, which permits a change of the proper law (i.e. the law which governs the relationship). Associated with such a clause there is sometimes a FLIGHT CLAUSE which permits the trust or foundation to migrate from one jurisdiction to another with a consequent change of the proper law. Theoretically, merely changing the law applicable to the arrangement from one law to another does not change the jurisdiction in which that vehicle is situated but in practice such a change of the proper law usually accompanies a complete migration of the vehicle concerned. A change of the proper law without a change of the domicile of the vehicle concerned may mean that the newly adopted law has to be proved as a fact from the evidence of expert witnesses in the event of litigation in the law of the domicile of the vehicle, which considerably adds to the cost and complications.

Characterisation (or Classification): The process of allocating a particular matter to its most appropriate rules for the purpose of helping a court assess into which category that matter falls. For example, from the general law, the formal validity of a marriage (i.e. whether a marriage has been properly carried out) is usually allocated to the place of celebration, whereas whether one of the parties has the CAPACITY to marry is allocated to the law of the DOMICILE of each party; thus a person under age, according to the place of his domicile, does not have the capacity to marry anywhere and this is applied by a court to assess the requirement of parental consent prior to a marriage. In other words, is parental consent a matter of formal VALIDITY (governed by the place of celebration) or a matter of capacity (governed by the law of domicile of the party concerned)? Both these issues are important in relation to a trust's essential validity, i.e. is it a matter under dispute if the critical feature is concerned with the capacity of the parties or of the form of the arrangement? This dictates, in the absence of other considerations which might apply, such as choice of law provisions, which law, procedural or substantive, within a jurisdiction will govern the matter. The HAGUE TRUST CONVENTION merely describes some key properties but does not absolve a national court from deciding which provisions of the Hague Convention should be applied to any particular point. Characterisation by a court is therefore an essential element where the Hague Convention applies. Once having identified the applicable branch of law, characterisation has completed its purpose. Academic opinion favours a court adopting the applicable law to determine a structure's characterisation, which may not be the jurisdiction in which litigation is likely. With private foundations the registration of the foundation gives a clear indication of the applicable law and therefore there seems little reason for departing from the provisions of that law. The process of characterisation when a matter is subject to a choice of governing law, or a choice of forum, is beset with difficulties.

Charge: A charge, in the general sense, is a liability or an obligation which, when applied to property, refers to a security interest in that property when the property is held as security for the payment of a sum of money or the performance of an obligation. The property is then said to be 'charged with' the payment of the debt or the performance of the obligation.

***Chargeable Gains Act* 1992:** The UK Act that now governs the law on capital gains tax. This Act consolidated the provisions of the *Finance Act* 1965, which introduced a new tax on capital gains in the UK. The 1992 Act consolidated the legislation introduced for this tax and the Act itself has now been heavily amended. The provisions of the 1992 Act also apply for the taxation of capital gains of companies within the corporation tax provisions. The Act comes into play in various stages of a trust's life, such as on creation, where the settlor may dispose of property on which there is a deemed gain over the acquisition price. The Act may also apply on disposals by trustees, both actual and deemed and, with interest in possession trusts, where life interest determines other than on death. The Act will apply in a similar way to DISCRETIONARY TRUSTS. The application of the Act to trustees is complex, particularly in connection with the annual exemption to tax on individuals' gains up to a certain amount. *See* DISPOSAL.

Charges on property: An obligation established by one party on the security of the property owned by that party against default by him of any payment of a sum of money or for the performance of an obligation. A charge may be placed over REAL PROPERTY and PERSONAL PROPERTY; the term therefore covers mortgages, liens and other interests and also covers fixed and floating charges placed over a company's assets to secure a loan or other indebtedness. A charge can exist without the transfer of the asset charged (unlike a pledge when the asset is personal property). One aspect of the law on charges is that anyone claiming any interest in property previously owned by a now deceased person which, at the time of death, was subject to any charge, is primarily liable for the payment of the charge unless there was a contrary indication in the will, deed or other document and every part of such an interest according to its value is to bear a proportion of part of the charge. In other words, a charge over property goes with the property and whoever becomes the owner must bear the responsibility for repayment of the sum secured by the charge. A beneficiary who, prima facie, takes the property subject to the charge cannot call for the amount secured by the charge to be discharged out of the other assets of the deceased. The rule applies only as between beneficiaries and the right remains for the mortgagee or other persons entitled to the charge to obtain payment or satisfaction out of the other assets of the deceased. Also, there is no personal liability on the beneficiary in the event that the charge exceeds the value of the property. *See* MORTGAGE *and* LIEN.

Charging clause: Under the general law, a trustee is not entitled to charge for his services except where a clause in the trust authorises payment. The inclusion of a charging clause in the trust documentation formerly was the only source by which a trustee under English law could obtain reward for his services (and consequently the first clause a professional trustee searches for in the trust deed!). Since this was only possible with express trusts, no payment for trust duties would follow from becoming a trustee of a resulting or constructive trust without some supplementary documentation. This led to many offshore trust laws, including a provision whereby payment of the trustee is generally authorised. Now, under the UK law, the *Trustee Act* 2000, Section 29, establishes the ability for a reasonable remuneration to be claimed by a professional trustee, except for sole trustees or trustees of charitable trusts.

Charitable gifts: A gift given with a clear intention that the gift shall be applied for charitable purposes whether or not the objects of the charity are defined. The courts treat a charity as a legitimate donee and the mode of the gift does not affect its legitimacy. A distinction is drawn when considering the intention of a testator to distinguish between charitable intention, which must be clear, and the mode of executing it, which, though vague and indefinite, does not affect the validity of the gift. A charitable gift does not fail because the institution aimed at being the recipient cannot be identified. The intention of the testator is paramount. For example, a gift in a will that was void for uncertainty but which nevertheless demonstrated a general charitable intent was considered by an Australian court to take effect as a valid charitable gift that would be applied by the court CY-PRES (***Connery v. Williams Business College*** [2014] NSWSC 154; [2014] 17 ITELR, 251).

Charitable remainder irrevocable trust: A form of trust known in the US in which the donor (settlor) places funds or assets in an irrevocable trust and the trustee is required to devote the assets to charity only on the death of the donor; during the donor's lifetime the donor or specified beneficiaries will receive an income. This has been permitted by the IRS to allow a large donation in the year the trust is set up and where the tax savings are used to buy an insurance policy on the life of the donor and where the proceeds of such a policy will be paid to the donor's children. The overall effect is intended to allow the donor to make a gift to charity, receive a return on his money and still make a large gift to his children. The tax law outside the US impedes the adoption of this type of trust elsewhere.

Charitable trust: A trust whose purpose is charitable is enforceable under English law and is an exception to the English law rule that, generally, a purpose trust is unenforceable. This rule is omitted in most offshore centres trust laws where purpose trusts can be enforced and there is no distinction between those which are officially charitable and other purpose trusts which may have some philanthropic purpose as their object. Under English law, trusts that are philanthropic, or otherwise which have the appearance of being charitable, are non-enforceable unless that purpose qualifies officially for registration as a charity. Such registration enables the CHARITY COMMISSIONERS to act as the enforcer of that trust; otherwise English law sees no means of enforcing a general purpose trust. This absence of any means of enforcing a trust is said to be one of the main reasons why English law does not recognise non-charitable purpose trusts. Charitable trusts benefit from many advantages including exemption from taxation and the right to claim a refund of the tax paid by donors of the income of the charity when the donation was made by way of 'Gift Aid'. This allows the charity to reclaim the tax paid by the donor on his gift. To be charitable a trust must comply with the *Charities Act* 2006, which sets out in Section 2 a definition of charitable purpose. Prior to this Act, there was no statutory definition and reliance had to be held on the 'heads' of the charity identified in the decision of ***Commissioners for Special Purposes of Income Tax v. Pemsel*** [1891] AC 531 (***Pemsel's case***). The purposes contained in this decision are preserved in the definition in the Act. Under the Act, trusts are not the only vehicle that may qualify; companies and foundations may also qualify as charities. Whatever the legal structure, the status of being a charity comes about by approval being granted by the Charity Commissioners and recognised by the tax authorities. *See* TEMPORARY CHARITABLE TRUSTS *and* CHARITIES.

Charities: A type of non-profit organisation formed for a charitable purpose. In the UK this means an institution established for charitable purposes which is subject to the High Court and which operates in one of the 13 fields described in the *Charities Act* 2011. The categories of charitable activities listed in the Act are modern developments from the original spirit and intention of the *Statute of Elizabeth I* (43 Eliz., 1 c.4, 1601) as interpreted by the courts (***Pemsel's case***) and extended by subsequent legislation, *CHARITIES ACT* 2006 and most recently by the *Charities Act* 2011.* The vehicle must be for a public benefit within the various categories notwithstanding a limited number of persons are likely to avail themselves of that benefit even though it may be aimed at the relief of poverty. Also, the purpose must be exclusively charitable, i.e. every object or purpose of the vehicle has to be wholly charitable. These requirements under the Act require careful organisation, particularly where the charitable organisation wishes to carry out some ancillary operation to enhance its funds for charitable giving. This is usually achieved by the use of a subsidiary or associated separate organisation. In the UK the Charity Commissioner is the independent regulator of charities in England and Wales who ensures that each charity is worthy of public support by conforming to the law. Currently, the CHARITY COMMISSION is encouraging charities to provide their trustees with adequate knowledge and experience to meet their goals. Three priority areas have been identified by the Charity Commission for improvement: an increase by the trustees of their knowledge and experience of fund raising, charity law regulation and business development.

*The 13 fields are:

1. The prevention or relief of poverty.
2. The advancement of education.
3. The advancement of religion.
4. The advancement of health or the saving of lives.
5. The advancement of citizenship or community development.
6. The advancement of the arts, culture, heritage or science.
7. The advancement of amateur sport.
8. The advancement of human rights, conflict resolution or reconciliation or the promotion of religious or racial harmony or equality and diversity.
9. The advancement of environmental protection or improvement.
10. The relief of those in need, by reason of youth, age, ill-health, disability, financial hardship or other disadvantage.
11. The advancement of animal welfare.
12. The promotion of the efficiency of the armed forces of the Crown or of the police, fire and rescue services or ambulance services.
13. Other purposes currently recognized as charitable and any new charitable purposes which are similar to another charitable purpose.

See PUBLIC BENEFIT REQUIREMENTS.

***Charities Act* 2006:** Before this Act, charities comprised four principal divisions: the relief of poverty, the advancement of education, the advancement of religion, and other purposes beneficial to the community, all of which had to fall within the spirit of the 1601 Act. The *Charities Act* 2006 removed these four divisions and replaced them with 12 charitable purposes, which are all subject to providing an overriding public benefit. The *Charities Act* 2006 was consolidated by the *Charities Act* 2011, which revised what constitutes a charity. *See* CHARITIES.

Charity Commission: A body established in the UK by statute which oversees the proper management of charitable bodies in England and Wales. The Charity Commission also provides a special scheme that may be adopted by trustees of a charity with a permanent endowment to secure investment on a total return basis; this change was introduced by the *Trusts (Capital and Income) Act* 2013.

Charity Commissioners: Three persons appointed under the *Charities Act* 1993 who, together ,are referred to as the Charity Commission and who are responsible to the Home Secretary to promote the effective use of charitable resources by encouraging better administration, giving advice to charities and investigating and checking abuses. One of the principal tasks of the Charity Commissioners is to maintain a Register of Charities and to generally encourage the development of better methods of administration by giving charities information and advice and investigating and checking abuses. They do not have power to act in the administration of a charity; *see* TRUSTEES OF CHARITIES, OFFICIAL CUSTODIAN FOR CHARITIES *and* ATTORNEY GENERAL.

Charity Tribunal: A body established under the *Charities Act* 2006 to determine appeals against decisions of the CHARITY COMMISSION, to hear applications for review of decisions of the Charity Commission and to consider points of law on reference from the Attorney General relating to charities. The Charity Tribunal only has jurisdiction over decisions of the Charity Commission made on or after 18 March 2008.

Charter: A document that provides evidence of something to be done by a party, which, although it may involve other parties, is principally a unilateral act. Frequently applied to a document granting privileges by the Crown; for example, the setting up of a university or, internationally, for the constitution of some international body such as the Charter of the United Nations. In recent years the word has been used in connection with private foundations (following a civil law practice) whereby the founder sets up a private foundation according to the terms of a charter that he then submits for registration. The setting up of a foundation is a unilateral act by the founder; it may be said that the setting up of a trust by a trustee is equally a unilateral act but the word 'charter' is not normally applied to the fundamental document of an express trust, which is usually referred to as a 'trust instrument' or a 'trust deed'.

Chartered companies: Companies set up by Royal Charter to establish an activity as a separate legal person; originally, trading companies such as the Hudson Bay Company or the East India Trading Company, and also used to establish (as the Virginia Company) the founding colonies of North America. Royal charters are also used to set up colleges and universities and similar public-type institutions as separate legal persons for the purpose of holding and managing public interests, leaving private interests to be controlled under the law of trusts. Many other bodies, also called colleges, are incorporated as companies and not by Royal Charter. *See* CHARTER.

Chattels: A term which applies to any form of property that is not freehold and which is also colloquially used to describe what are more accurately 'chattels personal', a term which has the more precise definition set out below (*see also* LEASEHOLD *and* REAL PROPERTY).

1. 'Chattels personal' means movable property such as furniture, paintings, jewellery and animals according to a definition in the *Administration of Estate Act* 1925. Leasehold property is also personal property. Money and incorporeal personal property, such as patent and trademark rights and copyright, are not generally included in the term.
2. 'Chattels real' now abolished as a class of chattels mainly by the *Administration of Estates Act* 1925 were estates in, or arising out of, land and were distinguished from real estate by the uncertain duration of a freehold; a characteristic of freehold is its uncertain duration. This, before the Act of 1925, would have included leasehold property.

Child Trust Fund: An account for an 'eligible child' which satisfies the requirements of the *Child Trust Funds Act* 2004 into which the tax authorities in the UK (HMRC) make a payment to be held for the child. A further payment is made when the parents are in receipt of tax credits. Others may contribute to the fund.

Children Act 1989: There is no universal definition of 'child' in English law and therefore any act which concerns the affairs of children will contain its own definitions. The *Children Act* 1989 provides that a Financial Provision Order can be made in respect of a child up to the age of 18 and when there is a dependence beyond that age. Under the Act, the term 'child' describes the relationship between the deceased and the applicant in connection with the *Inheritance (Provision for Family and Dependants) Act* 1975. The term 'child' is traditionally construed to only mean legitimate children, but this was reversed by the *Family Law Reform Act* 1969, Section 15. The Act has had little direct bearing on trusts and foundations.

Chinese walls: An arrangement by which the affairs of clients are kept confidential from other members of a firm who may be dealing with or advising a competitor.

This may require personnel from one department to be excluded from entry into other departments and to be denied access to parts of the workplace where sensitive material is kept. Professional advisers who neglect to establish suitable Chinese walls could be liable for breach of those practices designed to maintain confidentiality and to be liable for any benefit obtained from transactions that breach this confidentiality; a constructive trust would result in favour of the clients of any benefit received. A firm may also be liable for tort or for assistance in breach of the firm's fiduciary duties. Liability for fraud or negligence may arise.

Choice of forum: Often called the 'choice of court clause', means a choice of the court that the parties to a written instrument have agreed shall be used to settle a dispute that might arise out of the relationship set up or evidenced by the written instrument. In many examples, the choice relates to a jurisdiction such as in the courts of England rather than to a specific court such as the High Court. This election of the forum is frequently accompanied by a CHOICE OF LAW: parties attempt to elect both the substantive law and the jurisdiction in which that law shall be applied. Practical difficulties restrict choices; the choice of law A for the law governing the relationship to be litigated in the courts of country B may not be practical on account of the expense and difficulties of presenting evidence and proving the law of A before a court in B. *The Hague Convention on the Law Applicable to Trusts and on their Recognition* makes no provision affecting the forum where trust disputes shall be settled. The Convention defines the law which governs a trust but not the jurisdiction in which that law is to apply in litigation. Recognition of trusts under the Convention takes place irrespective of the jurisdiction in which a judgment is obtained. The European rules on jurisdiction have been largely replaced by a Council Regulation, the *Brussels Regulation* (EC 44/2001). The Regulation provides that the domicile of the defendant is the jurisdiction where action should be brought except where there is a valid choice of forum, a voluntary submission to a particular jurisdiction or where the application of the FORUM NON-CONVENIENS doctrine dictates otherwise. This general rule is subject to much detail. As far as trusts are concerned a settlor, trustee or beneficiary of an express written trust may be sued in the Member State in which the trust is domiciled (DOMICILE is as defined in the Regulation). The traditional rules of private international law (i.e. the law concerned before the Council Regulation became effective) are still used to decide the domicile of a trust for the purpose of the Regulation. If more than one Member State has jurisdiction the Regulation solves the problem by awarding the case to the jurisdiction where the first court seized of the case is situated, i.e. the jurisdiction where the action is commenced first. The Regulation does not answer all questions relating to trust litigation; for example, the question of legal title to foreign immovable property is subject to the *lex situs* according to private international law and this rule is applied widely throughout the world and is not amenable to litigation in the domicile of the trust. The complications of the regulation have not been welcomed as being any improvement over the former rules. The above principles may apply to private foundations unless the law under which a foundation is set up makes particular provisions. *See* JURISDICTION CLAUSE, HAGUE CONVENTIONS *and* COUNCIL REGULATION EC 44/2001.

Choice of law: The process adopted by a court of determining the law that applies to a claim or part of a claim when there is some substantial connection with a foreign jurisdiction. This process only takes place after a domestic court has decided that it has JUSTIFICATION to hear a claim and then has to decide which law applies to the substance of the dispute. The courts of each jurisdiction have their own processes for choosing which law to apply. When, for example, an English court decides to apply a foreign law (i.e. a law other than English law) the court usually applies the domestic law of the foreign jurisdiction but may find, on investigating the matter, that the law which the foreign court would apply includes that foreign jurisdiction's CONFLICT OF LAWS rules. It may be that the foreign court might, under this procedure, decide that the matter should be settled by English law on account of, say, the place of residence of the beneficiary or trustee. The term 'RENVOI' is applied to this bounce-back of the applicable law. In making a decision on the choice of law issue, an English court always applies its own rules for assessing connecting factors. These factors include the type of asset under dispute, or the place of residence, or the nationality of litigants. There is occasionally an exception relating to whether a particular asset is movable or immovable property, which is decided according to the law of the place where the property is situated. The choice of law in the case of trusts is now substantially governed by the *Hague Convention on the Recognition and Enforcement of Trusts*. Under this Convention, it is provided in Article 6 that:

> 'A trust shall be governed by the law chosen by the settlor. The choice must be express or be implied in the terms of the instrument creating or the writing evidencing the trust, interpreted, if necessary, in the light of the circumstances of the case.'

And, in Article 7:

> 'Where no applicable law has been chosen, a trust shall be governed by the law with which it is most closely connected.'

These follow common law principles. Also relevant is Article 13, which provides that:

> 'No state shall be bound to recognise a trust the significant elements of which, except for the choice of the applicable law, the place of administration and habitual residence of the trustee, are more closely connected with states which do not have the institution of the trust or the category of trust involved.'

This latter provision was not adopted in the UK *Recognition of Trusts Act* 1987, which introduced the Convention into UK law. *See* HAGUE CONVENTION.

Chose: A French word for a 'thing', which features in English law to denote usually an incorporeal thing, the benefit of which requires legal recognition and not mere physical possession, as in, for example, the terms 'CHOSE IN ACTION', 'CHOSE IN EQUITY' and 'CHOSE IN POSSESSION'.

Chose in action: A personal right of property that may only be claimed or enforced by legal action and not by taking physical possession. The rights in a company as evidenced by ownership of shares are an example, as are rights under bills of exchange. A chose in action may be legal, such as a debt, a bill of exchange, a policy of insurance, a sweepstake ticket or a share in a company. Legal choses also include rights of proceedings in a court of law to pursue a sum of money; for example, on an insurance policy, or the repayment of a debt, for damages for the inflicting of a wrong or the non-performance of a contract. Alternatively, a chose in action may be equitable, such as a legacy, a legatee's right in an unadministered estate or a share in a trust fund, or an assignment by way of mortgage of an interest under a will of which notice was given to the testator. Such a chose, effective only in equity, may therefore be called a 'CHOSE IN EQUITY'. A chose in action, legal or equitable, may be an asset of a trust or of a private foundation even if it is not immediately recoverable by action. There is also a distinction between the transferable nature of a chose in action and the non-transferable nature of a remedy to enforce a chose in action. The remedy is not capable of assignment separately from the chose in action itself. For example, the right to rescind a mortgage cannot be assigned separately from the mortgaged property. Distinctions are also made between existing and future choses in action. Thus, an accrued right under an existing contract to a certain sum of money at a future date is an existing chose in action in contrast to a mere expectation of inheriting money, which is not. The latter, a mere expectation, contrasts with an expectation of receiving future uncertain sums of money under an existing contract. All choses in action depend entirely upon an express or implied contract; the only method of acquisition of a chose in action. A chose in action differs from a tangible item of property which is capable of being actually possessed and enjoyed, such as a painting or jewel; a chose in action is a right only to recover a debt enforceable by legal procedure where the right itself has no tangible property attached. Some assignments, such as salaries or pensions of public officers, or maintenance payable on a divorce, are not assignable as these items are not in the nature of property and the court has full power to alter or take them away. The term 'chose in action' is less used in modern judgments but nevertheless the characteristics summarised above are still legitimate legal concepts; it is judicial terminology that has changed.

Chose in equity: *See* CHOSE IN ACTION.

Chose in possession: Property in personal chattels may either be in possession, which is where a person has not only the right to enjoy but has the actual enjoyment of the thing concerned, i.e. owns the actual property, and has the right of actual possession.

Civil Code: A code of law enacted by Emperor Napoleon Bonaparte in France in 1804 that replaced the existing law with a new code which defined the principles of Roman law which had formed the background of the current legal system. The reception (that is, the official adoption) of Roman law in France in the Middle Ages was to overcome the difficulties and contradictions of a multiplicity of customary law. Bonaparte's codification brought the principles together and formed the basis of reform for most laws in Continental Europe in the 19th century. One of the motives for introducing this Code was to buttress the arguments and the authority of the new European rulers in their struggle to assert their SOVEREIGNTY over feudal nobility. The Emperor forbade any structure similar to trusts as he considered them as too feudal. Following the adoption in France of the Civil Code, or *Code Napoléon*, further Codes appeared in other parts of Europe: Austria in 1811, Germany in 1889 and Switzerland followed in 1889 and 1907. The Code also served as a model for the Codes of Louisiana and Quebec and most countries of Latin America. One effect of the Civil Code was that new foundations were no longer exclusively religious and trade-related and eventually became capable of being devoted to entirely private family interests as under the Liechtenstein Law of 1926. *See* CIVIL LAW.

Civil Law: A term used in various contexts. In particular, it is applied to a legal system based upon Roman law and describes the juridical systems in most Continental European countries that have been embodied in Codes: the *Code Napoléon* of France was an example of the drawing together of many remnants from Roman law into a modern system. Civil law is distinct from the English system of common law, which is based upon judicial PRECEDENT by which a judge decides a dispute on the basis that he is presumed to know the law, and the legal principles embodied in his decision serve as precedents for future application or refinement. A separate meaning is given to the term to characterise private law from other branches of law such as public law, military law and ecclesiastical law. A further meaning distinguishes domestic law of a jurisdiction from that country's international law; the law applicable within a jurisdiction's territories is now usually called municipal law in preference to civil law. *See* CIVIL CODE.

Civil legal aid: The provision of legal advice or representation that is provided free to persons who cannot afford to engage in civil litigation.

Civil list: Official expenses of the Queen's household paid by Parliament to pay for official functions in respect of the state and the Commonwealth. The civil list arrangement dates back to 1660 and developed in 1760 on the principle that the whole cost of civil government should be provided by Parliament, and an allowance is paid to persons on the civil list in exchange for surrender of the hereditary revenues of the Crown.

Civil marriage: A lawful marriage in England and Wales celebrated other than in a religious ceremony.

Civil partnership: A relationship between two people of the same sex that is registered under the *Civil Partnership Act* 2004 and which purported to be akin to a marriage; however, this aspect of a civil partnership has been superseded in England and Wales by the rights of same-sex couples to enter into a marriage.

Civil Procedure Rules: A code of procedure in England and Wales that, since April 1999, regulates civil proceedings. These rules revoked the previous procedural rules of the Supreme Court and embodied the reforms proposed by Lord Woolf's *Access to Justice (Final Report)* 1986 to govern the proceedings in civil cases of the Court of Appeal (Civil Division), the High Court and the county courts. The intention of this revision was to simplify the administration of justice. The most noticeable introduction was the requirement that the parties to a civil dispute should enter into some form of ALTERNATIVE DISPUTE RESOLUTION (ADR) before proceeding to court and this usually includes a form of mediation. The failure of a party in a dispute to engage in these alternative dispute resolutions may result in that party being penalised in the award of costs to subsequent court proceedings even though that party may succeed.

Civil standard of proof: 'A balance of probabilities' is accepted as the standard of proof required in civil actions in contrast with the criminal standard of 'beyond reasonable doubt'.

Claim form: *See* WRIT.

Class: A body of persons possessing a common attribute who are intended to be treated either as a group or in a similar manner to other members of the same class. Examples are rights attached to a particular class of shares and also to a class of beneficiaries such as the children of a settlor or founder. A 'CLASS ACTION' is an action brought by a group of people on behalf of themselves and others who have the same claim against the same defendant.

Class action: A legal action brought by one or more persons on behalf of themselves and the larger group of people who are similarly situated and is useful for people who cannot afford to bring an action entirely on their own behalf. Although such actions are difficult and expensive to file, the results are useful in establishing a liability of large organisations such as pension funds and insurance companies to accept responsibility for negligence or errors in their treatment of their clients.

Clayton's* case (1816) 1 Mer. 572:** The rule that payments are presumed prima facie to be appropriated to debts in the order in which they are incurred, i.e. a sum of money that is used to pay off debts is applied to the oldest of those debts. For example, with a bank account, in the absence of a different express rule, a fixed sum paid into an account is the first sum drawn out. This rule does not apply where a person in a fiduciary position pays money that he has held in his own bank account and which therefore becomes mixed with his own money. In that case, where the fiduciary draws money for his own use, he is deemed to have withdrawn his own money from the amount available in the account which, under the rule, leaves the trust money intact (Hallett's*** case (1880) 13 Ch.D 696); the rule was developed by the courts in situations where a trustee or similar fiduciary person mixed trust money with his own.

Clean hands: *See* EQUITABLE MAXIMS: "He who comes to equity must come with clean hands". A person may be refused equitable relief where he has acted improperly in relation to the matter for which relief is sought. An example is specific performance that may be refused where the contract is induced by misrepresentation.

Clog on the equity of redemption: A term inserted into a mortgage deed that intends to penalise a repayment or performance of a debt and is void. Redemption of a mortgage loan is always possible. To be a clog on redemption the term must be part of the agreement that sets up the loan. If the clause is part of a separate or collateral agreement then it is not void. The issue of debentures which are stated to be irredeemable is not treated as a clog on the equity of redemption as far as these instruments are concerned (Section 738, *Companies Act* 2006). An example of the application of this clause is where there is a contractual date for the repayment of a mortgage loan and the mortgage deed provides that the right shall not be executed by the mortgagor (borrower) for a substantial period after the loan was granted. This clog on the equity of redemption is void. The principle of equity is 'Once a mortgage always a mortgage'. This rule has no effect if irredeemable debentures are issued which delay the redemption of the sum borrowed. The agreement by the mortgagor and the mortgagee will only act as a clog if the term can be characterised as a term of the mortgage. If an agreement restraining redemption is only collateral to the mortgage agreement, it will not clog the redemption and then the rule is not so strictly applied as in the past.

Close company: A UK company under the control of its directors, or five or fewer individual participators, and for which purpose participators include those who have or are entitled to acquire a share or interest in the capital or income of the company and can include loan creditors. Close companies are subject to special tax provisions.

Closed-end funds or Closed-ended funds: A collective investment scheme in the form of a company whose shares are purchased and sold by investors on a stock exchange. These investment companies, as they are called, invest their capital in other companies and the prices of the shares of the investment company reflect the success of these underlying investments. Consequently, at any time, the value of the holding of the shares of an investment company may be greater (at a premium) or less (at a discount) to the value of the proportion of the total investment of the shares held by any one investor. The cause of these variations is subject to much theoretical debate but, broadly, it is based on the market's confidence and the investment manager's ability to produce a satisfactory income and capital appreciation. Other characteristics of closed-ended funds are that no new capital can be subscribed to the investment company after it begins operation; however, an investment company may engage in leverage and increase the amount it has available for investment. As a company, a closed-ended fund may provide for reserves that can be used to even out the amount of dividends paid to provide a more stable investment return.

Close investment holding company: Any close company that is not set up for the purpose of carrying on a trade on a commercial basis or which is to hold land that is rented to unconnected persons, i.e. a close company devoted to investments rather than active business. The term is mostly applied to family investment companies. Trusts and foundations, not being companies, are not involved. The significant aspect is that a close investment holding company is subject to corporation tax at the full rate of profits.

Codicil: A supplement to a WILL executed by the testator of the will to add, revoke or explain matters contained in the will itself and which is executed with the same formalities as a will in the UK under the *Wills Act* 1837. The codicil becomes part of the will to which it relates in the formalities following the death of the testator; the will and codicils comprise the total testament of the deceased.

Cohabitant: Each of two people who are not married to one another or in a civil partnership with each other and who live together as husband and wife or as civil partners.

Collateral (1): Means anything describing the relationship between people who share a common ancestor but who have descended through different lines of the family.

Collateral (2): In financial matters, collateral is security that is additional to the main security for a debt. For example, a lender may require as collateral the assignment of an insurance policy in addition to the principal security of a mortgage on the borrower's property.

Collateral advantage: Where there is a separate obligation in favour of a mortgagee running alongside the mortgage and which subsists only until the mortgage is redeemed. Such a covenant is upheld by a court order to enforce it. A collateral advantage running concurrently with the mortgage and which subsists only until the right to redemption is exercised is generally unobjectionable and enforceable by a court order. If that collateral advantage continues after the repayment of the loan then it is a 'CLOG ON THE EQUITY OF REDEMPTION' and after the loan is redeemed such clause is no longer enforceable. The term is also applied to an advantage that one contracting party obtains when he uses a stronger bargaining power than has been conferred upon him by the main contract. *See* COLLATERAL CONTRACT.

Collateral contract: A contract that exists in association with another contract known as the principal contract where promises made by one party in the collateral contract have induced the other party to enter the principal contract. For example, a party may agree to buy goods on the assurance given by the seller of the quality of the goods and this undertaking may be regarded as a separate or collateral contract and may be separately enforced. Associated with this are collateral guarantees, collateral securities and collateral warranties.

Collateralisation: Assets held by a third party, 'C', for the benefit of 'A', a party to a financial transaction with 'B', against the risk that B becomes unable to complete his part of the bargain. In that case, the secured party, A, becomes absolutely entitled to the assets held by the third party, C. C holds the assets on trust as a custodian. A variation on this is where both parties A and B transfer assets to the custodian, equal in value to their respective exposures to each other. This is known as a 'PLEDGE' and is used instead of a trust.

In its simplest form, collateralisation is where a custodian C, receives assets from the counterparty, B, to a contract, which are held under a bare trust for the benefit of A if B fails to fulfil his contractual obligations; C then holding the assets for the party who suffers the loss because of the default of the other. The assets held by C are held on trust. A problem with this arrangement concerns the subject matter of the assets held by C, particularly where these collateral assets are bonds that are not in bearer form, but which are issued under a global note held by the custodian. In that case, the investors only acquire an entry on a register to prove their entitlement but there is no certainty as to which bonds are held as security. This may cause the purported trust to fail for uncertainty of subject matter.

Collective investment schemes: An umbrella term frequently used in connection with regulation to embrace all schemes used for the investment purposes of funds from the public. *See* MUTUAL FUND, UNIT TRUST *and* INVESTMENT TRUST.

Comitology: The procedure whereby the European Commission consults special advisory committees of experts from various EU Member States to ensure that when implementing EU law the situation of each Member State is taken into account.

Comity: The courtesies extended from one state to another to ensure good relations but without accepting any legal obligation to behave in any particular manner. The doctrine is based upon the concept of sovereign equality among states and is expected to be reciprocal. Such practices may, over a period of time and with common use, develop into rules of customary international law (*see* JUDICIAL COMITY). Comity may also be described as the accepted rule of reciprocal mutual confidence existing between states. *See* INTERNATIONAL COMITY.

Commercial court: Constituted under the *Administration of Justice Act* 1970 as part of the Queen's Bench Division of the High Court that deals with commercial claims applying a simplified procedure and being capable of dealing with matters promptly using specialised judges.

Commercial law: May be public or private, national or international law, which is relevant to the conduct of business.

Commercial trusts: Trusts that carry on a business or make investments with the object of making money. Where the trust is a CHARITABLE TRUST, the trustees' obligations include the making of money either by receiving donations or by engaging in trading and investment activities for the benefit of the charitable purpose for which they were set up. Therefore, a charitable trust will operate very much along the lines of a company registered as a charity. In the case of private trusts, trustees must conduct business and remain aware that the beneficiaries take an equitable interest in the trust assets, i.e. the trustees must make no profit for themselves or any other person out of the business they conduct. Trusts conducting a business should not be used to achieve an abstract purpose as this is unlikely to be justified as a benefit to the beneficiaries and this would be a breach of the beneficiary principle and accordingly invalid (*see* PURPOSE TRUSTS). Trustees must balance their duties of trusteeship with the management of the trust's business activities. For example, the trustees may wish to invest the trust assets whereas the beneficiaries' prime interest may be to preserve their capital or take an income. The trust instruments may make this possible by granting wide investment powers to the trustees. The ring-fencing of the trust assets from the trustee's own assets must be clearly made known to any contracting party. Where trustees engage in commercial operations, an outside contracting party may not be willing to enter into the arrangements as the normal corporate disclosures and information will not be available. Creditors should therefore satisfy themselves as to the extent of the trustees' authority and the ways that are available to secure their rights under a transaction. Also, when trustees exercise a commercial decision outside of their authority and thereby incur a personal liability, they are denied any right to recover any costs payable from the trust funds. For these reasons it is unusual that a trust will enter business adventures directly but instead prefer to set up a wholly owned limited company and transact through that company in the normal corporate manner. *See* BUSINESS TRUSTS.

Commingling: The act of mixing the funds of one party with those of another, or the mixing of a party's funds with trust funds held for another. Commingling between spouses and business partners usually is without problem except that a spouse who allows his or her separate property to be commingled with the funds of the other spouse risks the whole being regarded as matrimonial property. Trustees, guardians or lawyers must be careful not to commingle clients' funds that they hold with their own funds to prevent a conflict of interest. The commingling of funds for an investment is still improper despite the possible benefit to each of the individual parties. If funds become temporarily or inadvertently commingled, prompt separation should take place with an accounting to the client or beneficiary. Generally, commingling is avoided by trustees and others setting up separate accounts for the trust funds.

Commissioner: A member, full-time or part-time, of a permanently constituted commission or board established by legislation for a particular purpose, such as the Charity Commissioners, the Church Commissioners and the Commissioners of Inland Revenue. The legislation establishing such commissions may apply the provisions of the *Commissioners Clauses Act* 1847, which contains standard clauses regulating such matters as the qualifications of commissioners. In particular, Section 60 of that Act provides that commissioners do not incur personal liability in connection with the proper exercise of their duties. This is a regular clause and now appears in legislation. The nature of commissioners' duties depends upon the Act under which they are appointed.

Commonhold: A new way of holding land introduced by the *Commonhold and Leasehold Reform Act* 2002 which is intended for developments in which individual properties, such as flats, houses and shops, are owned and occupied by separate persons but with common parts such as stairways and walkways, remaining in central ownership. This applies to land in England and Wales and is the equivalent to what other jurisdictions refer to as 'strata title' or 'condominium' devices.

Common intention: One of the elements under current law necessary to constitute a common intention CONSTRUCTIVE TRUST when real property is purchased (by A) as a home for more than one person (A and B). The common intention arises either expressly or implicitly, where, under the circumstances, one person (A) conducts himself, within a domestic consumer context, in a manner that would be inequitable to deny that the other person (B) should have a BENEFICIAL INTEREST in the property either at the time of acquisition or later. If the common intention does not reveal the extent of beneficial interest, then it is what is a fair share having regard to each person's financial and other circumstances. The second requirement for this type of trust to arise is that the other party (B) should have acted to his detriment in the belief that a beneficial interest was intended to be given. These two requirements distinguish common intention constructive trusts from PROPRIETARY

ESTOPPEL, where the former does not depend on the narrow or technical concept associated with ESTOPPEL but upon a broader basis of whether the repudiation of an ASSURANCE is or is not unconscionable in all the circumstances.

Common law: In the three centuries after the Norman Conquest (1066), the establishment of Royal Courts by the King began the process of centralising justice in England. At first, Royal Courts heard disputes between the Royal Revenues (the recipients of revenue on behalf of the King) and subjects but then developed to hear private disputes between individual subjects. The establishment of the Royal Courts and the attendance at them of itinerant judges from London resulted in the decline of local customary law. The certainty of Royal justice and the monopoly given to Royal Courts to hear disputes concerning land contributed to this centralisation. The law between state and subject, and subject and subject, was subsequently supplemented by the equity of the Court of Chancery which became part of the High Court of Justice under the *Judicature Acts* 1873-1875. The fundamental principle of this common law was STARE DECISIS whereby the decision of a judge (who is presumed to know the law) is followed in subsequent cases unless a new case can be distinguished on its facts. The common law's reputation was enhanced through the publication of judges' decisions in law reports where the decisions, together with the reasons, developed the system of judicial precedents and allowed general access to the law. This resulted in the common law being universally applicable to all men, although legislation took precedence due to the supremacy of Parliament and common law was regarded as the fundamental source of the law in England. The term 'common law' at one time was regarded as distinguishing the law from the Royal Courts and from the law of equity derived from the Court of Chancery. After the *Judicature Acts* 1873-1875, which removed barriers to the access to law between the components of the High Court, both sources are colloquially referred to as 'common law' – mainly owing to the use in these courts of judicial precedent. The term 'common law' also distinguishes the law derived from legislation and from various bodies of specialised law, such as canon law, ecclesiastical law and military law. The adoption of common law into the legal systems of many countries and territories outside England led to the development of the common law as one of the major legal systems of the world with only those based on Roman law being comparable. Two quotations by comparative lawyers suggest that common law is an English eccentricity and shows the characteristics of being a law derived from real adjudication of disputes with an antipathy towards centralised imposition of legal rules (as opposed to the centralised administration of the court system). For example, Pollock stated:

> 'Parliament generally changes the law for the worse, and ... the business of the judge is to keep the mischief of its interference within the narrowest possible bounds.' (Pollock, F., Essays on Jurisprudence and Ethics. 1882: Macmillan & Co.)

This has affected many attitudes, such as the opinion that legislation until the 19th century in England was tolerated only if it counteracted some specific social or economic mischief, about which distinguished comparative lawyers have stated:

> 'With their practical empiricism and a habit of going step-by-step, from case to case, the English would have regarded it as dangerous and unnatural to prescribe the outcome of comparable cases in advance by making general regulations to cover the whole area of life: "we will cross the bridge when we come to it".' (Zweigert, K. & Kötz, H. *An Introduction to Comparative Law: 1 The Framework*. Vol. 1, 2nd edn, North-Holland Publishing.)

Commorientes: A presumption of law relating to simultaneous deaths for the purpose of deciding who in law should have died first. At common law, there is no presumption of law as to survivorship amongst persons whose death was by the one and the same cause. Nor is there a presumption that all died at the same time. This question is one of fact, depending wholly on evidence which, if inconclusive, places the burden of proving SURVIVORSHIP on the party who puts forward the order of death. A statutory presumption was introduced in cases after 1 January 1926 where two or more persons died in circumstances which rendered it uncertain who was the survivor. Commorientes presumes, under Section 184 of the *Law of Property Act* 1925, that, in the absence of evidence to the contrary, the order of seniority dictates the order in which a group of people die and accordingly the younger is deemed to have survived the elder (the oldest died first and thereafter in descending age order). This rule means that any bequest made by the younger to the elder will lapse because the elder will have died before the bequest became effective. This statutory presumption may be rebutted by evidence leading to a defined and warranted conclusion that one died before the other. The presumption applies unless it is displaced by a contrary intention expressed in the will by the use of a survivorship clause. A different rule applies to husbands and wives on intestacy. Under the *Administration of Estates Act* 1925, Sections 46(2)(A), as amended by the *Law Reform (Succession) Act* 1995, Section 1(1), an intestate spouse's rights are contingent on the spouse surviving the intestate by 28 days. The commorientes rule does not apply for inheritance tax purposes where the *Inheritance Tax Act* 1984, Section 4(2), provides that where the order of death is uncertain, it is assumed that neither person survived the other. *See* INTESTACY.

Community Interest Company (CIC): A company limited by shares or by guarantee may, under Sections 26 and 36(5) of the *UK Companies (Audit, Investigations and Communities Enterprise) Act* 2004, register initially as a community interest company or may become one if the Regulator of Company Interest Companies considers that it meets the requirement that a reasonable person would consider its activities as being carried out for the benefit of the community other than political campaigning. A community interest company must provide, in its constitution, a limit to the distribution of its assets to members by capping dividend payments and restricting any other distributions. This structure could be appropriate for non-charitable altruistic purposes and could overcome the impossibility of forming a non-charitable purpose trust under English law and the difficulties of becoming registered as a charity.

Community legislation: Primary and secondary legislation and case law of the European Union that has a direct effect within Member States. Nowadays, 'European Community law' is applied strictly to legislation known as the 'first pillar' of EU law, which relates to economic and social rights and the setting up of the European Institutions. The term 'European Union law' denotes all three pillars, i.e. the first pillar; the second pillar, which concerns EU Common Foreign and Security Policy, and the third pillar, which comprises Police and Judicial Cooperation in Criminal Matters.

Community of property: The common ownership of property that exists between spouses according to the law of the place of domicile of a deceased owner, particularly in many civil law jurisdictions and some American states such as California.

Companies: Originally an association of persons created to undertake a common purpose. The term 'company' now generally refers to a company formed by registration under a company law enactment (in the UK in the *Companies Act* 2006). Companies are often referred to as 'corporations' in certain contexts, such as taxation where under double taxation treaties that follow the OECD Model, the term 'corporation' is defined widely enough to include registered companies and foundations. Registered companies are separate legal entities (as are most other structures within the general concept of 'corporation') and the participants, the shareholders, may have limited or unlimited liability. A company limited by shares is the most common form of company. A company is, for legal purposes, distinct from its shareholders. This contrasts with structures such as unincorporated partnerships and other associations and sole traders. This broad definition of 'company' is adequate to cover foundations but these are generally referred to as a separate type of structure. In addition to companies registered under the *Companies Act* 2006, there are other bodies created by registration in the UK under other legislation. These include building societies and friendly societies. The characteristics of these companies are found in the legislation under which they are set up; generally they may carry out any activity that is not of a personal nature whereas, in the past, their activity was limited by the terms of their objects clauses and anything outside these clauses was regarded as ULTRA VIRES and beyond the capability of the company. Therefore, a company can act as trustee of a trust or as a foundation council and may also be the settlor of a trust or the founder of a foundation or a beneficiary of either structure. In the UK under the *Companies Act* 2006, Section 3, a limited company can limit the liability of its members by shares or by guarantee. Without this limited liability, members are liable for the debts of the company to the full extent of their personal wealth. A company which is described in its Certificate of Incorporation as a 'public company' is indicated by the description of 'Plc' and must comply with the requirements for that type of company, in particular that of a minimum share capital requirement. A company that is not a public company is a private company, which is prohibited from offering any securities to the public; in order to do so, a private company must convert to a public company where the degree of regulation is more severe. A public company may become a quoted company, i.e. its shares may be quoted on a registered stock exchange. Not all public companies will be accepted by a stock exchange if they do not conform to the regulations of the stock exchange concerned.

***Companies Act* 2006:** The Act of Parliament in the United Kingdom that governs the registration and other formalities relating to limited companies in the UK and which has substantially taken over from the previous Act, the *Companies Act* 1985, which succeeded the *Companies Act* 1948. The latter forms the basis of company law in offshore jurisdictions which had previously been under British influence.

Companies, chartered: An incorporated body set up under the prerogative of the Crown that issues a charter to any number of persons desiring to be incorporated. These companies are legal persons but distinct from those set up by incorporation under the *Companies Act* 2006. Chartered companies remain dependent on a Royal Charter for their incorporation and featured as early forms of incorporation in the development of international trade. Charters are now rarely issued for trading enterprises but feature as the constitutional documents of public bodies, such as the BBC, nationalised industries and, in many cases, universities and colleges. Prerogative charters were given to the Africa Company, the East India Company and the Hudson's Bay Company, amongst others, of which the Hudson's

Bay Company alone survives. Chartered companies were issued for the purpose of founding the colonies in Virginia by the Virginia Company and in Massachusetts by the Massachusetts Company in 1609 and 1629 respectively.

Companies Court: The Companies Court is a specialist court within the Chancery Division of the High Court of Justice of England and Wales, which deals with certain matters relating to companies. These include those matters that are regulated by the *Companies Act* 2006, the *Financial Services and Markets Act* 2000 and the *Insolvency Act* 1986, where applicable to companies registered in England and Wales. Actions under the *Company Directors' Disqualification Act* 1986 must be commenced in the Companies Court.

Companies House: The name 'Companies House', strictly the building, which the Companies Registrar for England and Wales occupies but, in common parlance, it represents the name of the organisation that serves the Company Registrar and which is run as an executive agency of the government department with the responsibility for trade and industry. Therefore, 'Companies House' is said to represent the authority of the government over registered companies.

***Company Directors' Disqualification Act* 1986:** An Act that enables the courts, by a disqualification order, to disqualify a person from acting as a director or participating in the management of a company, either as an administrator, receiver or manager. Orders may also be issued by the court in respect of unfit conduct in insolvent companies and criminal offences connected with the *Companies Act* 2006. The Act can also apply to those who carry out the functions of company directors as well as those who have been formally appointed. A later Act, the *Insolvency Act* 2000, enables an administrator of a company to issue disqualification undertakings which are the administrative equivalent of a disqualification order. The disqualification undertaking or disqualification order is a potent tool against wrongdoing in the context of limited liability.

Company investigation: An investigation into the affairs of a company brought about by the Secretary of State (under Sections 431 and 432 of the *Companies Act* 1985), either of his own volition, at the request of company members, or when ordered by a court, by the appointment of one or more competent inspectors who are instructed to investigate the affairs of a company. The most celebrated company investigations are in connection with Robert Maxwell (***Re Pergamon Press Limited*** [1971] Ch. 388), and Mohamed Al-Fayed in connection with Harrods (***Fayed v. United Kingdom*** (1994) 18 EHRR 393). The evidence given in a company investigation cannot generally be used in later criminal proceedings (***Saunders v. United Kingdom*** [1998] 1 BCLC 362 and Section 447(a) of the *Companies Act* 1985).

Company Memorandum and Articles of Association: The two documents that are delivered to the Registrar of Companies which, on approval of the Registrar and registration, constitute the formation of a registered company. Under the UK *Companies Act* 2006 the Memorandum of Association states that the signatories wish to form a registered company and, in the case of a company that has a share capital, that each signatory will take at least one share (Section 8). The Articles of Association comprise the company's constitution together with any resolutions and agreements (Sections 17 and 29). The Articles of Association set out the detail of the internal management of the company, including the issue and transfer of shares, the payment of dividends, the appointment and retirement of directors and the conduct of meetings of the directors and of the shareholders (Section 33). The *Companies Act* 2006 provides that a default model set of articles can be provided by the Secretary of State, which may be accepted by subscribers. Subscribers may amend the terms of these default articles.

Company secretary: An officer of the company who deals with the administrative matters and who must satisfy qualification requirements under the UK *Companies Act* 2006, Section 273. An obligation to have a company secretary is now only essential for a public company. An analogous post is usually created by the founder of a foundation in the foundation charter who nominates a person to be foundation secretary for the carrying out of administrative matters.

Competent jurisdiction: A term indicating that a jurisdiction has power to hear a particular claim. In common law jurisdictions competence and jurisdiction are often used interchangeably.

Competing equitable interests: The general principle is that where there is a conflict between two equitable interests in property, other than registered land, the first in time prevails. This only applies where the equities are equal. This is illustrated where the interests of a trust beneficiary will not be postponed where the trustee has previously handed over, in breach of trust, the title deeds of trust property to a third party or has failed to register a transfer. Then, the equities are not equal and therefore the first in time does not prevail. The principle also applies where a beneficiary under a trust, or other holder of an equitable interest in property, successively assigns or mortgages his beneficial interest. Then, priority of the assignees of that interest depends upon the order in which notice of the individual assignments are received by the person responsible for the disbursement of the fund, i.e. in the case of a trust, the trustees. This rule applies unless an assignee has actual or constructive notice of a previous assignment when he advances money or acquires security.

Completion: The final stage in a transfer of real property which occurs upon the payment of the purchase money and, accordingly, any contract for the sale of land which stipulates that interest to be paid on the purchase money until completion means that outstanding purchase money can bear interest until such time as final settlement takes place in respect of the sale.

Compliance: Indicates the way in which a body should be conducted in conformity with legal and regulatory requirements and is achieved by the installation and support of an internal framework under the control of a compliance manager although responsibility remains with the board of directors. Compliance may embrace conformity with listing rules, health and safety, the environment, data protection and freedom of information. With financial organisations, compliance may take several forms which vary from compliance with international financial regimes applicable to that particular organisation, to anti-money laundering regulation and to conformity with tax rules, including conforming to the requirements of double taxation treaties and associated matters, such as exchange of information and conformity with transfer pricing rules. Compliance will become more arduous with measures arising out of the Base Erosion and Profit Shifting plans (BEPS) of the OECD and out of the automatic exchange of information between EU Members. *See* BASE EROSION AND PROFIT SHIFTING.

Compound settlement: A trust of land created by several instruments executed at different times; for example, land placed into trust by a will and by a subsequent instrument authorised by the will giving a special power of appointment to a trustee.

Compulsory purchase: The acquisition of land by a public body empowered by legislation that authorises the purchase. This is achieved by compulsory purchase orders which may be challenged by statutory review under the *Acquisition of Land Act* 1981 in the UK. Local authorities may be granted the power to acquire land if they think that acquisition will promote economic, social or environment well-being in their area.

Concealment: Non-disclosure by a party to a contract of a fact that is material to the other party and which concerns matters that affect the value of the contract but generally has no effect on the validity of the contract (the principle of CAVEAT EMPTOR illustrates this). An exception is in contracts of INSURANCE where concealment amounts to FRAUD, making the contract voidable at the option of the party deceived, i.e. the insurer. Concealment may also take place where one party makes a statement that is true only in part but does not disclose matters that would alter the whole effect of a statement, such as by telling a half truth or describing as a fact what is only a probability. The party from whom the facts are concealed is entitled to rescind the contract and, depending on the circumstances, bring an action for deceit. There is a tort of failure to disclose that arises where one party voluntary assumes a responsibility for disclosure. There are various statutory requirements to make disclosure, including some matters governed by the *Financial Services and Markets Act* 2000; these include providing information on the state of a company that applies for a stock exchange listing. Special limitation periods apply where there has been actual deliberate concealment: the limitation period does not start until the truth is discovered or when discovery might reasonably have been made.

Concessions, extra-statutory: Concessions issued by the UK Tax Authority (HMRC) that relieve a taxpayer from paying tax where the law may be ambiguous and these are generally regarded as having no legal basis as they may be withdrawn if they are used in any particular case for tax avoidance. Formerly unpopular with the courts, but now enjoying better approval when they are interpreted and consistent with Parliamentary intention and which are now also only permitted to make narrow concessions since 2005 (***R v. Commissioners of Inland Revenue Ex p. Wilkinson*** [2005] UKHL 30). Before the ***Wilkinson*** case it was thought that extra-statutory concessions could be used for more substantial matters, which, in that particular case, were the granting of a bereavement allowance to a widower. Tax concessions of this nature are likely to come within the European Commission's definition of tax rulings under attack for lack of transparency and which are recognised as the basis of the majority of tax avoidance techniques that exploit tax loopholes and mismatches. The Commission defines tax rulings broadly as: 'Any communication or other instrument or action of a similar effect, given by or on behalf of a Member State, regarding the interpretation or application of its tax laws.'

Concordat: Originally a treaty involving a public benefit between the Pope and any prince. Now used to describe a relatively formal agreement that, in appearance, is closely related to a treaty but differs in being non-binding. The Concordats of the Basel Committee on Banking Security are a well known example.

Condition: A term in a contract that expresses something which goes to the root of the contract or is of the essence of the contract, in contrast to a warranty, which is a term of lesser importance. If a condition of a contract is breached, this entitles the injured party to treat the contract as discharged as the transaction becomes materially changed, whereas a breach of warranty is remedied only by action for damages to compensate the injured party for not getting as good a bargain as he was entitled to under the contract. Conditions can be classified in a variety of ways, the most significant of which is as express and implied conditions and conditions precedent and conditions subsequent.

Conditional acceptance: Is where payment by the acceptor is dependent upon the fulfilment of a condition by the other party as stated in the contract. At that stage it is normal for documents sent by one party to another to be endorsed 'subject to contract'. This indicates that matters referred to have not yet reached the contractual significance of an offer being accepted to form a legally binding obligation.

Conditional fee: Is an equitable interest in property characterised chiefly by being of a limited length of time. The continuance of the interest in the land may be limited by the occurrence of an event. The event which terminates the fee can be anything that does not violate the RULE AGAINST PERPETUITIES; however, the event is frequently simple expiry of time. A conditional fee is frequently called a 'base fee'. This suggests that it is impure, defective or circumscribed; this is not true although a conditional fee is inferior to a 'fee simple'.

Conditional interests: An interest in a contract or trust that may be forfeited on the occurrence of a specified event or time according to the wishes of the person who created it.

Condominium trusts: A trust of real property consisting of a combination of separately owned/occupied premises that receives, on behalf of the owner, the rents and other income paid in respect of the occupancy of the separate premises. The trustees, sometimes called a condominium council, apply the receipts towards the cost of the insurance of the building and/or contents. Any receipts from the insurer are held by the trustees for division in a manner determined by the trustees for distribution to the residents in proportion to the loss suffered.

Confidential information and trustees: Obligations of confidentiality exist over a wide range of relationships especially with those concerned with trusts. This is illustrated by the situation where a family solicitor, who was not a trustee but who held a fiduciary capacity as an adviser to a family trust, made a personal profit through the use of information obtained when acting for the trust. The solicitor was held to be a CONSTRUCTIVE TRUSTEE of the profits acquired through obtaining shares that were unavailable to the trust. Despite informing the trustees of his acquisition the solicitor had misused confidential information (***Boardman v. Phipps*** [1967] 2 AC 46). This led to the principle that the misuse of confidential information by a fiduciary might cause the fiduciary to be a constructive trustee of any profit derived from using the information.

Conflict of interest by trustees: Where a trustee gains a profit from a conflict between his personal and fiduciary capacities. The profit will be held on a CONSTRUCTIVE TRUST for the beneficiaries. In other words, a fiduciary must not place himself in a position where his personal interests may conflict with his duty: the fiduciary is deemed to have acted according to his duty so that any profit generated for himself is treated as earned on behalf of the beneficiaries and so held on a constructive trust for them.

> '[The fiduciary] must not place himself in a position where his interest may conflict with his duty. If he has done so, equity insists on treating him as having acted in accordance with his duty; he will not be allowed to say that he preferred his own interests to those of his principal. He must not obtain a profit for himself out of his fiduciary position.

If he has done so, equity insists on treating him as having obtained it for his principal; he will not be allowed to say that he obtained it for himself. He must not accept a bribe. If he has done so, equity insists on treating it as a legitimate payment intended for the benefit of the principal; he will not be allowed to say that it was a bribe.' (P. Millett, *Bribes, and secret commissions* [1993] R.L.R. 7.) *See* SELF-DEALING PRINCIPLE.

Conflict of laws: The body of law existing in each jurisdiction that determines which law applies where there are cross-border disputes. Each jurisdiction has its own law but some principles are applied almost universally, such as that the parties to a contract are free to nominate the law which governs their relationship. With trusts, the law that governs the trust, the PROPER LAW, can be determined by the settlor by placing a CHOICE OF LAW clause in the trust instrument. In the absence of such a clause, then the general conflict of law provisions of a jurisdiction will provide. A wide range of jurisdictions will come up with the answer that the law which governs the trust in the absence of a choice will be the law with which the trust is most closely connected. This practice was adopted as the policy in the HAGUE CONVENTION ON THE LAW APPLICABLE TO TRUSTS AND ON THEIR RECOGNITION 1986, a conflict of laws Convention. Guidelines on this are given in the Convention to indicate how the 'closest connection' is determined. Offshore trust laws frequently provide that a choice of law provision can be made in the trust deed. With foundations, these conflict of laws provisions are of less importance since a foundation, through its place of incorporation, will usually be subject to the law of that place. Although a choice of law provision may not be impossible, it may be somewhat impracticable since any choice which differs from the place of incorporation will require the charter being interpreted by a different law from that according to which the charter was prepared.

Conservator: A protector, preserver or maintainer, a role which may take the form of a standing arbitrator for the purpose of adjusting differences that could arise between two parties. In some jurisdictions, such as the US, a conservator is a person appointed by a judge to protect and manage the financial affairs and matters of daily life of persons who are incapable due to physical or mental limitations or old age. This follows a petition to a local court by a relative or friend. If the court establishes the need, an open hearing is made before an appointment and the conservator is required after appointment to make regular accountings for approval by the court.

Consideration: A requirement in English law for the creation of a legally enforceable contract that is not made by deed. Consideration constitutes an act, forbearance or promise by one party to a contract that constitutes the price of the forbearance or promise of the other. In other words, it is some right, interest, profit or benefit accruing to one party or some forbearance, detriment, loss or responsibility given, suffered or undertaken by the other. Also, the consideration must be of value and must be sufficient, although it need not be adequate and must move from the promisor, although this requirement was abolished by the passing of the *Contracts (Rights of Third Parties) Act* 1999. The consideration may be executory (i.e. as yet to be given) or executed (i.e. given at the time the contract is made). However, past consideration, an act or forbearance that took place in the past before the promises were exchanged, is not adequate consideration; in other words, something done yesterday will not support a promise made today. All contracts under English law require consideration to pass except those that are made by deed for which no consideration is necessary; the formalities of entering a deed are deemed to be sufficient to show the reality of the intention of the parties. Consideration is not required in civil law to form a legally binding agreement, although the intention of the parties under civil law requires more agreements to be in writing than under common law. In both systems of law, the intention of the parties is the predominant issue. In English law, the giving of consideration is the concept which marks that intention. *See* VALUABLE CONSIDERATION.

Constituted: A trust is constituted at the time when all has been done by the settlor and the trustees to make the trust workable. This is usually achieved by the transfer of assets, according to the requirements of the trust deed, to the trustees and the acceptance of these assets by the trustees as trust property. Under Section 32 of the *Trustee Act* 1925, a trust created by will is constituted or created at the time the will comes into operation (i.e. on the death of the testator) and not when the power of appointment is exercised under that will.

Constitution of trusts: The means by which trusts are set up. One method is where an express trust is made voluntarily during the lifetime of a person who, by a declaration, declares himself to be a trustee of assets already in his name; this person, the settlor, therefore changes his assets from being beneficially owned by himself to being held by him as a trustee according to the terms of the trust that he declares. The declaration includes directions to the beneficiaries of how the trustee will hold the assets for them. The second method of constitution of trusts is a trust set up inter vivos, i.e. as an express trust whereby the settlor, by trust instrument, sets up the trust with separate trustees and agrees to transfer property to them. Third, a trust may be set up by will where the testator makes the necessary declarations in his will that the assets specified are to be held by the executors of the will who will transfer the assets to trustees who will then continue to hold the assets according to the terms of the trust embodied in the will. Such a trust can only be valid if there is a valid will. Fourth, the exercise of powers of disposition over property under existing trustees' power of advancement, which can create a new trust from the assets held by an existing trust subject to proper transfer of the assets from the old to the new settlement. *See* FORMAL REQUIREMENTS.

Construction lien trusts: A statutory provision of security by which the contract price payable to a development contractor is held on trust where the first priority over the assets held is for unpaid subcontracting supplies of goods or services. This type of trust is known particularly in Canada and gives subcontractors the advantage that they can be assured of payment. The owner of the land may himself be a trustee of the purchase monies. The owner may be informed that the work has been satisfactorily completed and the obligation to make the payment becomes due and the trust is discharged on making the payment. The trust holds money in favour of all who supplied goods and services and not just the head contractor.

Constructive fraud: Grounds for the rescission in equity of a contract where one party took advantage of the weakness of another, or where a breach of fiduciary duty or fraud was procured by the exercise of undue influence, is regarded as constructive fraud and actionable for compensation in equity.

Constructive notice: The knowledge that the law presumes a person to have because that person would have had the knowledge if he had carried out the investigation that he ought reasonably to have done in the circumstances. Constructive notice applies particularly in contracts for sale or purchase of land where the purchaser, with reasonable prudence, should have found a defect in the title to the property about to be acquired and where the failure to have had actual notice of the defect did not remove the disadvantage that followed the lack of notice. *See* ACTUAL NOTICE *and* IMPUTED NOTICE.

Constructive possession: A legal concept applied when a person does not have actual possession of an asset but has power to control it. For example, having the key to a safe deposit box gives the holder of that key constructive possession of the contents.

Constructive trust: A trust imposed by operation of the law without the express or presumed intention of the owner of the property to create a trust or retain any beneficial interest for himself. A constructive trust may arise contrary to the actual intention of the owner. For example, where a person in a fiduciary position makes an unauthorised profit for himself he is considered to hold that profit on constructive trust for the beneficiaries. Where a person commits such wrongful conduct, the constructive trust that arises is on the grounds that it would be unconscionable for the owner of the property to assert a beneficial ownership. This allows the proceeds of the defendants' wrong to be used to assess an award in an action for RESTITUTION. The term 'constructive trust' is also used in connection with strangers to a trust who have an ancillary liability, particularly those involved in the knowing receipt of trust property or of dishonest assistance. This so-called constructive trust is imposed solely as a basis for granting equitable relief. Trustees of a proper constructive trust are accountable to their beneficiaries particularly in respect of trust property. Persons who are under a purely ancillary liability whose acts are averse to both true trustees and the beneficiaries are liable to account in equity but as wrongdoers and not as true trustees. This matter was discussed in the decision of ***Williams v. Central Bank of Nigeria*** [2014] UKSC 10. *See* KNOWING RECEIPT AND DISHONEST ASSISTANCE.

Constructive trustee: A person who holds property on a constructive trust and who may be unaware that he is holding the property on a trust for another. The nature of a constructive trustee's duty may vary from case to case depending upon the circumstances. A constructive trusteeship arises where a fiduciary receives an unauthorised profit, or where a stranger renders dishonest assistance, or where property is received by another in breach of trust. Once this relationship has been established, the constructive trustee has a duty to the trust. The terminology used can be misleading and has been criticised (***Paragon Finance v. D B Thakerar & Co*** [1999] 1 All ER 400 (CA)). The matter was substantially clarified in a recent case: *See* CONSTRUCTIVE TRUST.

Consuetude: *See* CUSTOM.

Contiguous properties: Properties which adjoin each other.

Contingent: A description of an interest or right where its existence depends upon an uncertain event, which is called a contingency. *See* VESTED.

Contingent beneficiary: A person or entity named as a beneficiary but who will only receive the gift if a certain event occurs or certain circumstances happen. *See* CONTINGENT INTEREST.

Contingent interest: A contingent interest that comes into existence upon the occurrence of a specified event, e.g. rights under a trust if the purported beneficiary marries. A contingent interest only comes into being in the future and, if it involves property under UK law, gives rise to a trust of land under the *Trusts of Land and Appointment of Trustees Act* 1996.

This means that contingent interests are equitable interests only and must be distinguished from conditional or determinable interests.

Contingent remainders: A remainder in a will or settlement that depends upon an event or condition to occur before the interest becomes a remainder in possession. Where the event or condition never happens, or where it does not happen until after the termination of a preceding estate in the property over which the contingent remainder is created, it means that the remainder can never come into possession.

Continuing trustee: An imprecise term generally applied to a person, other than a retiring trustee, who is a replacement for a trustee who has retired or otherwise forsaken trusteeship.

Contract: An agreement to do or abstain from doing some act that is intended to be legally enforceable and which comprises an offer, and an acceptance of that offer, between parties who have the capacity to contract and who have the intention to enter into a legally binding relationship to pursue a legal purpose. In English law, a contract that is not made by deed requires consideration to pass to the other party in exchange for that other party's act or promise. Consideration may be the price of goods, an exchange of property or the promise to suffer some detriment at the other party's request. Also, it is essential to give an agreement legal enforceability to provide a sufficiency of terms so as to enable a court to decide what is expected of each party. Certainty forms a part of this. An agreement that is so vague or uncertain that a court cannot determine what the terms of the contract are would result in there not being a contract at all. Contracts can be made orally or in writing or by deed and may have some legal effect, although less than a complete contract, and then are known as a QUASI-CONTRACT. Separate rules apply to different types of contract, such as contacts for an interest in land and contracts of insurance, etc. Express trusts, foundations and wills are not contracts as all three are unilateral declarations and therefore do not have the consent of a body that will benefit by the terms. This relates to the substance of the trust, etc. A trustee may be appointed by a settlor under a contract but this is to serve as a trustee and is not a contract between the settlor and the beneficiaries. In some jurisdictions, the trust deed or the foundation charter are referred to as the trust or foundation contracts. This is incorrect when applying a strict definition of a contract but excusable as implying the formal document associated with these arrangements.

Contract, freedom of: A principle which allowed parties in law to enter into any contract they like and was strongly held as a fundamental right in the 19th and early 20th centuries. The principle, however, was strained by many exemption clauses imposed by parties who were in a strong bargaining position that enabled them to exclude claims against themselves for negligence, etc., (such as with the powerful railway companies). Modern legislation which includes matters affecting contracts of employment and contracts with consumers has further restricted this so-called freedom.

Contract, inducement of breach of: A tort that is committed where one party, 'A', persuades another, 'B', to breach his contract with a third party, 'C'. Although it is necessary to show that the loss has been incurred by the appellant, it is often assumed to flow from the breach of contract. An essential element is that the person causing the breach of contract must intend to interfere with a claimant's contractual rights. Deliberate indifference or inadvertence to the possibility of breaching the contract, as with recklessness in the sense of not caring, is sufficient to ground liability whether or not there is breach. This has exposed trade unions and their officials to extensive potential liabilities for inducing their members to breach their contracts by an unofficial strike.

Contracts (compared with trusts and foundations): Contracts differ from trusts because contracts are developed by the common law and give rights merely IN PERSONAM unlike trusts where the courts of equity confer rights IN REM. A trust can be set up by a unilateral declaration that assets already owned shall henceforth be held on trust for stated beneficiaries. With express trusts the settlor makes a similar statement, usually in writing, but with no participation by the beneficiaries or trustees. Contracts are legally enforceable agreements formed by an offer of one party being accepted by the other. Some transactions, especially commercial transactions, involve both trusts and contracts such as UNIT TRUSTS. *See QUISTCLOSE* TRUST. Private foundations (like foundations generally) are formed by a unilateral declaration and give no rights to the beneficiaries which are analogous to the right of one party to a contract against the other.

Contracts and wills: Unlike a will, which is always revocable, a testator may bind himself by contract so that his personal representatives when he dies, testate or intestate, must distribute his assets to give effect to such agreement. This is at the expense of beneficiaries under the will or intestacy. For an agreement to be valid in this respect there must be more than a mere statement of intention or representation and it must also show, with certainty, the subject matter of the gift. In addition, apart from contract, it may be possible to base a claim on the principles of PROPRIETARY ESTOPPEL, which may arise following the deceased's assurances that in return for benefits given, the plaintiff will benefit from the deceased's will and the court may allow the plaintiff's claim even though the deceased did not include anything in his will to that effect.

Contracts for the sale of land: Contracts for the sale or other disposition of an interest in land must be made in writing and incorporate all the terms which the parties have expressly agreed. The basic provision is that all terms have to be expressed in one document which both parties must sign and when the parties exchange contracts the terms must be expressed in each contract. This is subject to the power of the court to order RECTIFICATION of a written document so as to make it conform to the express terms of what had been agreed. Also, there is a provision that the terms may be in more than one document provided they are cross referenced (*Law of Property (Miscellaneous Provisions) Act* 1989, Section 2(2)). These provisions relating to writing in a sale of land are different from the previous well-known provision of Section 40 of the *Law of Property Act* 1925 which merely provided that the existence of a contract for the disposition of land, or any interest in land, had to be evidenced in writing. Such 'note or memorandum' (as it was called under the 1925 Act) therefore meant that the contract itself could be oral, the terms of which would have to be proved. Without this 'note or memorandum' a contract for the sale of land was unenforceable. Under the more detailed provisions of the 1989 Act, a contract that fails to comply with its requirements is not merely unenforceable - it is non-existent. So, in the absence of writing, there is no contract and any writing which does exist must conform to the detailed provisions of the 1989 Act (Section 2). A further change under the 1989 Act is that the doctrine of PART PERFORMANCE, in connection with the transfer of an interest in land, is no longer available. Under the previous law, part performance could validate or make enforceable a contract that did not conform to the then existing rules by one party performing an unequivocal act which clearly indicated that he was committing the act under a contract for the sale of the land. The impact of the law on the sale of land by resulting, implied or constructive trusts is preserved (Section 2(5) of the 1989 Act). These major changes in the law have given rise to a considerable amount of litigation due to the fact that the writing now constitutes the contract itself instead of merely evidence of the existence of a contract. Under the previous law steps in the negotiation were not regarded as a note or memorandum where the words 'subject to contract' were clearly endorsed on each document. This meant that any letter etc., that had been written and made subject to contract could not be regarded as a note or memorandum of the existence of a contract. Now the 'SUBJECT TO CONTRACT' formula prevents the document on which the words are endorsed from constituting or forming part of the contract itself. *See* FORMAL REQUIREMENTS.

Contributory negligence: A defence to a claim for compensation where the claimant, by his own negligence, directly and materially contributed to a loss unless the defendant had the last opportunity of avoiding the event or was, nevertheless, the real and effective cause of the loss. Contributory negligence was formerly a complete defence to an action for damages but since the *Law Reform (Contributory Negligence) Act* 1945, the loss is to be apportioned according to the judge's assessment of each party's share of the responsibility. This Act does not apply to claims in contract.

Contract under seal: A contract under seal, sometimes called 'a speciality contract', is a contract made in writing that binds the party or parties executing it to commit a future act or forbearance contained within the terms. Such a contract is sometimes called 'a DEED' and, although it necessarily involves an agreement between the party, or parties, its legal effect is solely derived from the formality of sealing and delivering and not from the mere fact of agreement. A consequence of this is that although a contract under seal resembles a simple contract, the legal force coming from the formality of sealing and delivery requires no consideration to be given to the agreement to give validity to such a contract.

Contra proferentem: Literally meaning 'against the party putting forward'. For example, a document is interpreted where there is any ambiguity against the party who drafted it, or against the person whose document it is. The basis for this rule is that a person who has drafted a document will be deemed to have looked after his own interests. Therefore, any ambiguity is interpreted in favour of the other person.

Conversion: A doctrine that is best explained by the part that it played before the *Trusts of Land and Appointment of Trustees Act* 1996 and its application to trusts for sale. Trustees of trusts for sale were obliged to carry out an immediate sale of the trust assets and hold the proceeds of the sale on trust for the beneficiaries in the proportions provided in the trust. This power of sale could be postponed and, by obtaining an order of the court (under Section 30 of the *Law of Property Act* 1925), could be postponed indefinitely if there was some collateral purpose that could be established. Such collateral purpose was recognised where a family home was placed in the hands of trustees by will and was subject to an immediate binding trust for sale but with a collateral purpose that the property was to be used as a home for the family. In a trust for sale, the interests of the beneficiaries were immediately deemed to be interests in the proceeds of the sale before an actual sale took place, i.e. the interests were converted from interests in real property to interests in money; interests in personalty. The purpose of a trust for sale was that the equitable interests that had existed in the land were shifted to interests in the proceeds of the sale, which meant that a purchaser acquired the land free from those interests. The converse applied. Where trustees were obliged to invest in land the money to be used for the purchase was considered to be land. Conversion is an example of the equitable doctrine of looking at: 'that as done which ought to have been done'. Conversion did not apply to strict settlements (the land stayed as land and was not converted). This aspect of the law of conversion was abolished by the *Trusts of Land and Appointment of Trustees Act* 1996. The automatic conversion under a trust for sale of land to personalty and vice versa became irrelevant after the Act because persons who are beneficially entitled to land, subject to a trust for sale, now look to the Act for their rights of occupation and not to the rules on conversion; now there is no dependence on a court to determine a collateral purpose if the intention is to occupy the land. Conversion continues to play a part in the administration of a deceased person's estate by the personal representatives and in contracts for the sale of land which are specifically enforceable. *See* TRUST FOR SALE. Under the 1996 Act beneficiaries who are of full age and entitled in an INTEREST IN POSSESSION can require the trustees to do as the beneficiaries may wish concerning the land so long as no provision of the trust is breached. The trustees must consult with the beneficiaries as far as it is practical. If the beneficiaries cannot agree as to which action is required the wishes of beneficiaries whose interests represent a majority of the value in the property will be followed. Interests of each beneficiary is in proportion to each beneficiary's relative value in the trust as assessed on an actuarial value taking into account each beneficiary's position under the trust. The court which has an obligation to consider the performance of trustees is required to consider the beneficiaries' wishes but not necessarily to concur with them. The abolition of conversion in respect of trust for sale removes the argument that a beneficiary of land is interested in the proceeds of sale and not in the land. This no longer prevents the beneficiary having a right in the land itself. The 1996 Act provides the circumstances under which a beneficiary may occupy the land (Section 12(1)) and the supervisory powers of the court (Section 14(1)). Conversion was important in the past in succession law where realty would pass to the heir at law and personalty to the next of kin. The doctrine of conversion worked so that the PERSONALTY (money) with which the land was to be acquired was itself regarded as being an interest in land and consequently the personalty passed to the heir at law as though it were land. For example, Lord Lechmere settled £30,000 to be spent on land and which remained unspent on his death and because the money was to be spent on land the doctrine of conversion applied and resulted in the money passing as realty to Lord Lechmere's heir at law and not to those entitled to the personalty. *Lechmere v. Earl of Carlisle*, 3 P Wms (1733) 2011.

Conveyance: The method by which property is transferred from one person to another and, where the formalities require a written instrument, the term also applies to the document itself. In its narrow sense, 'conveyance' simply signifies the instrument which is used in connection with an ordinary purchase of freehold land. The word 'convey' means to affect such a purpose. The conveyance of real property was, in the 19th century, governed by its own Acts but these were repealed and replaced and extended by the *Law of Property Act* 1925 in the UK except for the *Conveyancing Act* 1881, which had simplified the form of conveyancing and incorporated the effect of legal decisions valid at that time.

Cooperation treaties: Treaties entered into, usually by international financial centres with major countries, for the exchange of information relating to tax affairs of residents in their country. This is a generic term and covers several types of arrangement such as straight-forward tax exchange agreements between states that conform to the *OECD Model Tax Convention on Income and Capital*, and individual bilateral treaties of similar purpose. The term also covers agreements between two countries to ensure cooperation on regulatory and criminal matters.

Coparcener: A person who holds something in common with another, an accomplice, such as where land descended on intestacy to several persons. This legal right was abolished by the *Law of Property Act* 1925 where the entirety of a legal estate, which would have been shared by coparceners, vested in trustees for sale although coparceners retain their equitable rights to the proceeds of sale and in the land as equitable interests. No further creation of equitable interest in coparcenary has been allowed since the *Administration of Estates Act* 1925. The word appears very occasionally in WILL TRUSTS set up before 1925.

Corporation as trustee: Certain trust corporations, including the Public Trustee, the Treasury Solicitor, the Official Solicitor and certain charitable corporations and others appointed by the court as custodian trustees under the *Public Trustee Act* 1906, are eligible to be appointed as a trustee provided the trust is constituted under the law of the UK or any part of any Member State of the European Community. To be a trustee, a corporation must be empowered by its constitution to undertake trust business and must be either a company incorporated by special Act or Royal Charter to act as a trustee or a registered company with an issued capital of at least £250,000 of which £100,000 has been paid in cash. The term 'trust corporation' applies to a number of other corporations of a public or charitable nature, such as those in connection with health authorities. These official trust corporations must be distinguished from trust companies. Trust companies are companies set up under the relevant company law in the country in which they operate for the purpose of operating commercially as trustees and are frequently subsidiaries of major banks. A corporation may be a trustee, both of pure personalty and of land. *See* TRUST CORPORATION *and* PRIVATE TRUST COMPANY.

Corporation tax: A tax payable on income, profits and capital gains tax by companies and other bodies designated under the *Finance Act* 1965. Tax is payable for each financial year (a company's financial year depends upon the company's accounting reference date as defined in the *Companies Act* 2006). Profits are assessed in the same way as for non-incorporated businesses with some special provisions. The sources of law are the *Income and Corporation Taxes Act* 1988 and the *Corporation Tax Act* 2009 as amended by subsequent finance Acts.

Corporeal hereditaments: Items of TANGIBLE PROPERTY which comprise real property.

Corporeal property: Property that has a physical form and includes both real and personal property.

Corpus and income: The corpus of a trust means the capital assets held on trust as distinct from the income which those assets produce. The corpus and income of a trust each bear outgoings incurred by the trust. The corpus bears the capital charges which are incurred for the benefit of the whole trust's estate but any interest payable on such expenditure is born by the income. The income bears current expenses in respect of repairs paid to save freeholds but the courts may allow trustees to use either fund as the court deems necessary. The corpus will bear costs incidental to the administration and protection of trust property including legal fees that are incurred for the benefit of the whole estate unless they relate exclusively to a tenant for life.

Corpus Juris Civilis: Compilations of Roman law principally made by Justinian between AD 529–534, whose collections, known as the Institutes, Pandects and the Code, were influential upon the development of civil law.

Corruption: Any agent unlawfully accepting, obtaining or attempting to obtain from any person, any gift or consideration as inducement or reward for doing or forbearing to do, or for having done any act or for showing or forbearing to show favour or disfavour in relation to a principal's affairs, is guilty of corruption. Under the *Prevention of Corruption Act* 1906, in the UK this is an indictable misdemeanour, penalties for which were increased in 1916 and in 1967 by the *Criminal Justice Act* 1967, Schedule 3. The offence can also be committed by any person who knowingly gives to any agent, or any agent who knowingly uses with intent to deceive his principal, any false, erroneous or defective account or other document. Many offshore centres have also enacted anti-corruption legislation as an accompaniment to their ANTI-MONEY LAUNDERING LAW. *See also* BRIBE.

Costs: The amount that a lawyer is entitled to recover from his client, or person employing him, as remuneration for his professional services, which covers legal advice, attendances, drafting and copying documents, conducting legal proceedings and instructing counsel. In addition to these costs, which are known as solicitor and own client costs, a lawyer's bill may also include the costs of expert witnesses and court fees, which are known as INTER PARTES costs. If disputed, an assessment can be carried out by a court officer known as a 'costs officer'. In assessing the costs, the principle is that costs follow the event, i.e. the loser pays the winner's costs as well as his own. This principle is at the discretion of the court except that the party who makes numerous distinct claims in an action may be ordered to pay the other side's costs when he fails to prove eligibility for the claim. The court may order a percentage of one party's costs to be paid by the other party to reflect the degree of success achieved. If one party has acted unlawfully then that party may be required to pay the others' costs are incurred in establishing the unlawful conduct and, generally, the party who acted unlawfully should pay the respondent's costs of having to respond to the unlawful conduct. The intention is that each party should carefully consider the strength of any claim which they wish to make in a public court; the likelihood of paying costs of both parties, if their claim fails, is always a danger and, in any case, the court can award damages against either party if the court thinks fit. Since the implementation of the *WOOLF REPORT*, and the encouragement of mediation, a party may be penalised and not awarded costs even if successful in a subsequent action if he does not materially take part in a process of mediation to attempt to resolve the differences before embarking upon court proceedings.

Cotenancy: A situation where more than one person has an interest in real property at the same time. This may include a TENANCY IN COMMON or JOINT TENANCY.

Counterclaim: An action in civil proceedings brought by a defendant in response to a claim and which is dealt with in the same proceedings. A counterclaim asserts an independent cause of action but is not a specific defence to the claimant's case. *See* SET-OFF.

Court of Chancery: The court developed by the Chancellor that formerly ran alongside the Royal Courts of Law. The court dealt with complaints that had previously been addressed to the King, about the harshness of a literal interpretation of the law. These matters were eventually addressed to the Chancellor and heard in the Chancellor's court, which issued remedies to mitigate the harshness of the common law. Since the common law was Royal justice, the Chancellor could not directly go against that law but provided collateral measures to mitigate unfairness; for example, the Court of Chancery could not cancel a contract but could issue its own remedy that might penalise any party that tried to enforce it (a measure which eventually became known as an INJUNCTION). The two courts existed side-by-side, and it was frequently the practice that matters had to be referred to one court and then the other. No court had adequate power to grant complete relief. This incurred delay and great expense. Charles Dickens' *Bleak House* showed the gross injustices of this system in the 19th century, although at that time courts of law often applied the rule of equity where the equitable remedy was apparent. Attempts at reform were piecemeal; the *Common Law Procedure Act* 1854 gave the common law courts limited power of granting injunctions and *Lord Cairns' Act (Chancery Amendment Act* 1858) allowed the Court of Chancery to award damages. A major reform occurred in the *Judicature Acts* 1873 and 1875, which amalgamated the superior courts into what was then called the Supreme Court of Judicature of England and Wales. The Chancery Court was absorbed in this system but its specialist knowledge was retained in the CHANCERY DIVISION of the High Court. Under the modern court reorganisation the Chancery Division remains part of the High Court which itself comprises one of the Senior Courts. The term 'Supreme Court' is now part of the title 'Supreme Court of the United Kingdom' which took over the role of the ultimate appellate court previously performed as part of the House of Lords' judicial function.

Court of First Instance: Generally means the court in which any proceedings are initiated, as distinct from an action in the Court of Appeal or any other appeal court. In trust matters, the Court of first instance in the UK may be either the County Court or the Chancery Division of the High Court.

Court of First Instance, of the European Communities: An independent court of the EU created in 1989 to hear disputes at first instance and which is competent for all direct actions brought by natural and legal persons and Member States except those assigned a judicial panel and those reserved for the EUROPEAN COURT OF JUSTICE. This court may also deliver preliminary rules, as prescribed by statute. Appeals from this court may be heard by the European Court of Justice on points of law. This Court of First Instance has 27 judges and usually sits in chambers of three or five judges.

Court of last resort: A court from which no further appeal lies. In the UK it is the Supreme Court and in the EU, the European Court of Justice. It is sometimes necessary under a treaty or other agreement for an issue to be pursued to the ultimate court in the country in which the dispute arose, before the treaty remedies can be implemented.

Court of Protection: A court established under the *Mental Capacity Act* 2005 with considerable powers to make wills and settlements on behalf of persons lacking mental capacity. The Court of Protection makes decisions and appoints deputies to act on behalf of people who are unable to make decisions about their personal health, finance or welfare. The court has power to direct the execution of a will, making provisions for the disposing of property or the exercising of a power, or in other matters that a person with capacity could make by will. The court also has power to direct the settlement of property of any person suffering from an incapacity and may do so for the benefit of that person or for others. The making of wills and settlements on behalf of such people must be made pursuant to an order of the court and, in all cases, must be made in the best interests of the persons on whose behalf they are made in accordance with the general principles of the *Mental Capacity Act* 2005, Section 1.

Courts of Equity: Comprised in England of the Court of Chancery and the Court of Exchequer Chamber, until abolished by the *Judicature Acts* 1873 and 1875. These courts were concerned mostly with fiscal matters but which also had a limited equity jurisdiction. These courts were supplemented by two ancient courts: the Chancery Courts of Lancaster and Durham which were also abolished. The equity work is now undertaken in the Senior Courts particularly in the Chancery Division of the High Court. In some jurisdictions, separate courts of equity still continue to specialise in equitable justice.

Covenant: A promise expressed in a deed and used to refer to a contract made by deed. The term is of significance in conveyance of land or other contractual-based relationships whereby one party wishes to insist on an action, or restraint by another party. The term 'covenant' also includes a statement concerning the truth of certain facts; this type of covenant is frequently used in the transfer of business assets where the seller covenants that a certain state of affairs exists upon which the purchaser relies. A covenant may be made by DEED POLL and, following the revision of the law, a deed can now be signed, although originally it had to be sealed and signed, but the characteristic of such a deed containing a covenant is that it needs to be witnessed. The CONTRA PROFERENTEM rule applies particularly to a covenant, which means that a covenant is construed against the person making it, in favour of the other party. Covenants are personal obligations. Any obligation under a covenant must be performed within a reasonable time. Covenants, the benefit of which runs with the land, may be assigned; then the covenants come within the category of a CHOSE IN ACTION (the *Law of Property Act* 1925, Section 136). Restrictive covenants affecting land, made after 1925, must be registered as a land charge; otherwise they will not bind a subsequent purchaser even if he has notice of them.

Covenants to settle after-acquired property: Promises made by a person that at some time in the future he will settle property on trust which, at the time of making the promise, he does not own or in which he has no proprietary interest. The matter is often referred to as a purported trust over after-acquired property. Such a promise must be made by a covenant to be enforceable. The distinction between a simple promise and a covenant goes to the question of the unenforceability of a promise if made without consideration. The identities and positions occupied by the parties are critical. Does the promise have to be made to a potential beneficiary who has vested rights in the property (by being named in the covenant, for example) or does the *Contracts (Rights of Third Parties) Act* 1999 cover persons who are objects merely of a power of appointment, such as discretionary beneficiaries? Also, the nature of a covenant, being a contract, establishes only personal and not proprietary rights where there is no reason to think that the persons who may be named in the covenant as beneficiaries of the trust will have any proprietary rights in the after-acquired property and therefore no order for specific performance will be possible against the settlor to enforce the inclusion of the after-acquired property in the trust. However, if the property consists of identified property other than money an order of specific performance may be possible. The *Contracts (Rights of Third Parties) Act* 1999 is not clear on these points. There is also the question of whether the trustees can enforce the covenant (the trustees are most likely to be parties to the covenant; who else would the settlor deal with?). The established position is that trustees are barred from doing so; otherwise, beneficiaries would be able to do, through trustees, what could not be done directly; in any case the trustees would only recover nominal damages, as the trustees incurred no loss. Even if substantial damages were awarded, they would not go to the trustees but would be held on a resulting trust for the settlor, as would the property itself, pending transfer to the trustees. These matters have been subject to a great deal of discussion and a considerable number of academic articles which leads to the conclusion that until many of these questions are settled on appeal, a trustee will be prevented by the court from enforcing covenants to settle after acquired property (*see* chapter on 'Constitution of an Express Private Trust' in Thomas & Hudson, *The Law of Trusts*).

***Cradock v. Piper*, rule in (1850) 1 Mac. & G. 664 (41 E.R. 1422):** The old rule that a trustee held office voluntarily and was required to perform his duties gratuitously. The rule applied equally to a professional trustee, such as a solicitor, as to a layman. In the former case, the rule was strictly applied so that a solicitor trustee could not employ one of his partners if he himself might derive a direct or indirect benefit from such employment. A limited exception was allowed for a solicitor to charge his profit costs when he acted as a solicitor in an action or other legal proceedings on behalf of himself and his co-trustee jointly. This strict principle has long since been modified and a professional trustee now has a right to remuneration under the *Trustee Act* 2000, Part V. This position, that it is now more appropriate to consider that a trustee has a right to remuneration, represents the international position as it affects trustees' remuneration generally.

Creditor: A person to whom a debt is payable. Creditors claiming a share in the assets of bankrupts, companies in liquidation or persons dying insolvent, may be either secured creditors, i.e. persons holding a mortgage or charge or other security granted by the debtor over their property, or may be unsecured creditors who hold no security but within that class may be preferential creditors, e.g. the tax authorities. A beneficiary under a trust or foundation is not a creditor of that trust or foundation since the expectation of either is not based upon the repayment of debt.

Creditor subrogation: Generally creditors of trusts (i.e. persons who have had dealings with trustees) have no recourse against the trust assets but must sue the trustees personally in respect of any amounts due to them. The trustees are then entitled to an indemnity out of the trust fund for debts properly incurred. Creditor subrogation is where trust creditors step into the trustees' shoes with direct access to the trust assets. This may be used as a short cut, for example, where there is a considerable trust fund and where the trustee is unable or unwilling to meet a liability before exercising his indemnity against the trust assets. This concept is different from any beneficiaries' right IN REM to direct access to the trust property in the event of a breach of trust. *See* TRUSTEE INDEMNITY.

Cumulative preference shares: Shares in a limited company which have the right to be preferred over ordinary shares in respect of dividends of a company and in respect of capital on a winding up, and which also have the added attraction of being cumulative, i.e. shares of which, if the dividend is not issued in whole or in part in any years, the right to receive the balance remains until the whole is paid. *See* PREFERENCE SHARES *and* ORDINARY SHARES.

Custodian: A person who has the care and custody of the property of another. Where that property is trust property, the custodian is then known as a CUSTODIAN TRUSTEE. The role also arises in international asset management where shares and securities are purchased by a trust, or other investor, in a different jurisdiction and then a custodian is appointed in that other jurisdiction to care for the share certificates and to manage the investment such as taking up rights issues and obtaining dividends. A custodian has advantages in knowing the local law and knowledge of the necessary language and procedures. These custodians are frequently large international banks who operate an international custodian service. The question of whether a custodian generally is a trustee depends upon the circumstances of the appointment.

Custodian Trustee: Custodian trustees were particularly provided for under the *Trustee Act* 1925 and other Acts, and include the Public Trustee, the Treasury Solicitor, the Official Solicitor and certain charitable corporations and corporations appointed by the court who are entitled to act as custodian trustee under the rules made under the *Public Trustee Act* 1906. The corporations that may be entitled under the Act comprise any corporation constituted under the law of the UK or under the law of any Member State of the European Community which has a place of business in the UK, provided it is empowered by its constitution to undertake trust business and has an initial share capital of at least £250,000, of which at least £100,000 has been paid in cash. These provisions for a custodian trustee do not prevent any other company acting as an ordinary trustee.

Customary international law: A source of international law that depends upon the practices or customs of states recognised by the International Court of Justice. To be admitted as law a custom must be reasonably consistent and comprise a practice that is generally followed. There is no length of time that a practice needs to be followed before it is admitted as law but a custom based upon a practice of a short length of time requires strong evidence that the state regarded it as legally binding. In many cases, customary international law has been supplanted by the use of treaties: the prime example of this is the current law on human rights.

Cy-pres: The doctrine by which a court will apply the property of a charitable trust to some other charitable purpose as nearly as possible resembling the original purpose, if a charitable trust is either initially impossible or impracticable or subsequently becomes so. In addition to the need for an existing charity to become impracticable or unenforceable, the doctrine will only be applied if the donor of the funds to the charity has shown a paramount intention that the funds are to be employed for charitable purposes.

D

Damages: Money payable by one person to another to compensate for a loss caused by an infringement of a legal right. Damages may be either liquidated or unliquidated. In the former, a specific sum is claimed by the appellant, as in a BREACH OF CONTRACT, and in the latter, the compensation is left to the court to decide, as in the case of physical injury caused by negligence. A contract which provides, in the event of one party's breach, that a fixed sum is payable is a valid provision, provided that the amount agreed truly represents the amount of possible loss. Otherwise, the provision in the contract for the payment of a sum that is not geared to the likely loss will be unenforceable as a penalty. Damages may also be classified according to their purpose. Substantial damages are damages that compensate for the loss actually sustained by the claimant; nominal damages are a small sum that is awarded despite the plaintiff being correct in law but where the plaintiff does not show he has sustained any real damage. Contemptuous damages are awarded when the claimant has proved his case but the action never ought to have been brought, in the opinion of the court. Restitutionary damages (more properly described as 'payment made as restitution') are intended to reverse an unjust enrichment rather than to compensate for a loss to the claimant. Exemplary, punitive or vindictive damages are damages not only to compensate the claimant but also to punish the defendant, particularly in actions for malicious injuries, fraud, oppression and continuing nuisance. Damages may also be awarded in some equitable cases; for example to replace an award of specific performance or an injunction for breach of confidence. Where there is breach of a fiduciary duty or breach of trust, then equitable compensation is available; 'compensation' is the word used in preference to 'damages' in Chancery matters; *see* EQUITABLE COMPENSATION. Where the conduct and the circumstances or the character of the parties is particularly deficient, then aggravated damages may be awarded which are greater than would otherwise have been granted.

Data protection: The protection given under the *Data Protection Act* 1998, as amended, to personal information which is automatically processed or held as a part of a non-automatic filing system or which is recorded by a public authority. The control of personal data relating to a living individual where the data assists in identifying the person to whom the data refers, must be handled according to eight principles in the Act, which generally restrict the use and the length of time in which data may be preserved. The eight principles are that the data must be:

- processed fairly and lawfully;
- obtained for a specific lawful purpose and not subsequently processed for separate and inconsistent process;
- adequate, relevant and not excessive to the purpose for which it was collected;
- accurate and, where necessary, kept up to date;
- kept for no longer a period than is necessary;
- processed in accordance with the rights of data subjects;
- protected against unauthorised or unlawful processing and protected against loss, destruction or damage;
- kept within the EU and not elsewhere unless the law adequately protects the rights and freedoms of data subjects.

These principles are frequently required to be exercised with the consent of the data subject. Additional considerations apply where the information is sensitive personal data that is given a wide interpretation.

Data subjects have a right to find out what information is stored and to prevent it from being processed in a way likely to cause damage or distress. Data controllers are subject to the power of a Commissioner to provide information about the use of data. Many operations are partly exempt from compliance, particularly concerned with national security, the prevention and detection of crime and the collection of taxes. In addition to the UK Act there is also European Community legislation.

Dearle v. Hall*, Rule in (1828) 3 Russ 1:** A rule which governs the priority of competing interests following dealings with EQUITABLE INTERESTS in PERSONALTY. Before 1925 the rule only applied to legal interests but it was extended to dealing with equitable interests in land, capital money and securities representing capital money by Section 137 of the *Law of Property Act* 1925. Under this provision the priority of equitable dealings depends upon the order in which written notice is given by the assignee to the trustee. This applies to equitable interests in real or personal property. For example, the owner of an equitable interest assigns it to A, who fails to give notice of the assignment to the trustee or the debtor. A then assigns the interest over to B for a valuable consideration, who then gives his own notice of assignment to the trustees. B had no notice, neither did the trustees, of the earlier assignment to A. Under the rule, B has priority over A since B was the first to give notice of the acquisition of the title to the trustees. This rule now applies to assignments of equitable interests in realty as well as in personalty. The rule is subject to strict rules of compliance; for example notice must be given to trustees personally; notice to their lawyers will be of no effect. Notice should be given to all the trustees; the notice must be in writing and should state what the assignee is claiming. Amongst the other features of the application of the rule is that it does not have effect in determining the priorities of equitable rights to shares in companies. Section 126 of the *Companies Act* 2006 provides that no notice of any trust, express, implied or constructive, shall be entered on the share register in the case of companies registered in England; the rule in ***Dearle v. Hall which would otherwise govern the priorities of equitable rights is therefore inapplicable. This requires the assignee of any equitable interest in such shares to protect himself by serving a 'stop notice' on the company, the effect of which is to prevent any legal transfer of the shares without notice to him, thus giving an opportunity to obtain an order restraining the transfer. *See* PRIORITIES.

Death duties: A general term indicating duties and taxes payable on the passing of property at death. Revised over the years, these taxes and duties were given different names; in the UK the term 'INHERITANCE TAX' is now used since the *Inheritance Tax Act* 1984.

Death of a trustee: Where there is more than one trustee, the consequence of the death of one of them is that the responsibilities and the share of the legal ownership of the trust assets passes to the other trustees by the survivorship principle that follows from the status of trustees as JOINT TENANTS of the trust property. On the death of a sole or of a last surviving trustee, the trust property devolves upon the deceased's personal representatives who become the legal owners of the property and the trustees of the trust. This follows from the law expressed in Section 18 of the *Trustee Act* 1925 that when power is given to, or imposed on, two or more trustees jointly, the same may be exercised or performed by the survivors or survivor of them for the time being. This provision extends to the trustees of implied and constructive trusts. Where a trustee has a beneficial interest in the trust property the rule also applies, which means that any such beneficial interest passes to the deceased's trustees personal representatives. The *Trustee Act* 1925 specifically provides that the personal representatives of a sole trustee will be capable of exercising or performing any power or trust that was given to, or capable of being exercised by, the sole or last surviving or continuing trustee. The role of personal representative of a deceased sole trustee ceases when a new trustee is appointed.

Debenture: A debenture is an instrument issued, usually by a company or public body, to acknowledge a debt and to provide security for the money outstanding. A debenture contains, expressly or impliedly, a promise to pay the amount mentioned in it and secures the promise to repay usually by a charge over the whole or a part of the property of the borrower. The definition of 'debenture' in the *Companies Act* 2006, Section 738, includes debenture stock, bonds and other securities of a company.

Debenture stock: Debenture stock is a stock or fund representing money borrowed by the company or other body and which is charged on the whole or part of its property. It has been defined by Lord Lindley as 'borrowed capital consolidated into one mass for the sake of convenience'. The debt is secured through a debenture trust deed where the stockholders, the lenders, have an action usually against the trustees and not the company. Debenture stock differs from ordinary debentures in that the title of each holder of debenture stock appears in a register and this registration is necessary to prove ownership of the debt. This registration facilitates the transfer of the stock. Each holder of the stock receives a certificate representing the amount of his stock, which is handed over on transfer and the name of the transferee is inserted in the register in place of the name of the transferor. The trustees of debenture stock obtain security from the company through a debenture trust deed that vests a legal mortgage of the real and leasehold property of the company in the hands of the trustee to be held on trust for the stockholders, and the trustees may also take a charge over other assets of the company as further security.

Debt: A debt is a sum of money due from one person to another. There are various kinds of debt depending on their origin. Debts may be created under the provisions of various statutes, such as a penalty imposed by law or a debt of record, i.e. a debt that is proved by the official records of a court. Debts may also be incurred under contracts. Debts may be secured by the creditor taking possession of property of the debtor with a contractual right to sell the property on default. This gives the creditor a contractual right as a means of securing repayment. Where the security is real property, it is usually referred to as a mortgage that gives the creditor direct rights, on default, to sell the property. The varieties of security are many. The term 'debt' or 'debts' when used in a will has been interpreted in numerous cases and is usually restricted to outstanding financial obligations of the testator where the amount is known at death and does not include possible claims that have not yet been identified.

***Debtors Act* 1869:** An Act which abolished imprisonment for debt except in respect of debts due to the Crown, or to debts incurred by a defaulting trustee or solicitor, or by a judgment creditor who is able, but refuses, to pay. The Act is now only of historical interest, particularly to readers of Charles Dickens' *Little Dorrit*.

Deceit: A TORT which is committed when someone makes a false statement of fact knowingly, without belief in its truth, or recklessly, i.e., carelessly as to whether it is true or false, with the intention that it should be acted upon by someone else and that person does act on the false statement and thereby suffers damage (***Derry v. Peek*** (1889) 14AC 337 (HL)). *See* FRAUD.

Declaration of trust: The setting up of a trust where the legal owner of property declares that specified items of property which he holds would henceforth be held by him as trustee on trust for beneficiaries that he nominates. Although no specific words are necessary as long as the intention is certain, for evidential purposes usually the declaration of trust is made by some form of written instrument. This is advisable and necessary in any case where land is to be held on trust under the requirement that TRUSTS OF LAND must be made in writing according to the *Law of Property Act* 1925, Section 53(1)(b), which states that:

> 'A declaration of trust respecting any land or any interest therein must be manifested and proved by some writing signed by some person who is able to declare such trust or by his will.'

Declaratory judgment: A court judgment which merely states the court's opinion on a question of law or upon the rights of the parties concerned and where there is normally no request for, or no provision for, enforcement. The court states the position regarding the disputed right or existence of facts or interpretation of a legal principle or a document. An example is where the parties concerned with a trust request the court's interpretation of the rights of the beneficiaries. In the UK, declaratory judgments are controlled under CPR 40.20.

Declining trustee: A person who refuses to act after being nominated as a trustee or, without a positive refusal to act, behaves as if he has never accepted the trust. The payment of trust money into a court indicates that the payor is a refusing or declining trustee if no actions have been taken in respect of the money.

Decree: An order of the court now used mostly in matrimonial cases which was previously, before the *Judicature Acts* 1873 and 1875, applied to decisions of the Court of Chancery but since those Acts, the expression 'judgment' has been applied to all decisions coming from the High Court. Consequently, the term 'decree' is almost entirely used now in matrimonial affairs.

Deed: A formal written document that makes it clear on its face that it is intended to be a deed, i.e. a declaration of intent or obligation of the party. By a deed some interest, right or property passes, or a binding obligation is created; the terms of the deed may be an affirmation of some act whereby right or interest in property has passed. A deed is entered into by a formal process which previously required the deed to be signed, sealed and delivered to the other party in the presence of witnesses. Since the *Law of Property (Miscellaneous Provisions) Act* 1989, the sealing requirements have been abolished in many circumstances so a deed may now be said to be a written contract signed by the party entering into the obligations and whose signature is witnessed. This forms a written contract but, because it is a deed, it can be enforced free from the obligation to show consideration for the promise. Deeds are frequently used commercially to avoid any possible argument on the existence of CONSIDERATION.

Deed of covenant: A deed whereby one party covenants with another to do certain things. Frequently used where the act undertaken under the deed of covenant is incidental to obligations created in other instruments. Deeds of covenant are used principally in connection with the title deeds of property, and to secure the payment of money, or for the indemnity of a purchaser or mortgagee. The advantage of using a deed of covenant to secure rights supplemental to a principal contract is that the obligation to these rights can be created without consideration.

Deed of discharge: Where the trustees of a STRICT SETTLEMENT wish to declare themselves discharged from the trusts of the settlement, they enter into a deed of discharge.

Deed of family arrangement: *See* DEED OF VARIATION.

Deed of gift: A deed which declares that property described within the deed is transferred to another by way of gift, i.e. a unilateral obligation of the donor is created. By conferring a gift by deed, the gift is enforceable; no question of the absence of consideration can affect the situation as deeds are effective as contracts without consideration.

Deed of grant: Property is granted to another by a deed of grant but the use of the word 'grant' is not now necessary to transfer the property and other words of similar meaning, such as 'give' are just as effectual.

Deed of variation: This is a deed by which a beneficiary under a will, or on intestacy, indicates that the gift which he would otherwise have acquired should go to some other person, whether or not that person is a beneficiary of the estate. This must be done within two years of the death, and statutory requirements complied with in order that the redirection is not treated as a gift for inheritance or capital gains tax purposes, i.e. the new beneficiary takes directly from the estate of the deceased. Where an attempt is made to use a deed of variation to vary a trust which arises on the death of a person, that deed must be executed before the trust comes to an end.

Deed poll: A declaration to all the world of the grantor's act and intention, such as changing his name or giving a power of attorney. A deed poll is so called because the instrument is trimmed to be even or polled at the top as opposed to an indenture, which is a deed that shows, by an indented margin at the top or bottom, that it has been separated from a copy by the irregular cutting off.

Deemed: A word used to indicate a matter or state of affairs that is presumed or imagined to be the case. The word appears frequently in legislation, such as tax law, where a situation is deemed to come within a taxation provision; although, on strict interpretation, a different construction could be made of the legislation. The word 'deemed' is considered to be archaic; the process of 'deeming' being thought now to be unsatisfactory and frustrating. The tendency is to provide that something should be treated as, or taken to come within, a specified construction of an act.

Deemsters: Traditionally, the name given to judges in the Isle of Man.

De facto: In fact, or a term used to describe a reality rather than a legal position. *See* DE FACTO TRUSTEESHIP.

De facto trusteeship: A trusteeship that arises where the 'trustee', although not effectively appointed, believes, and therefore acts, as if he is. *See* TRUSTEES DE SON TORT.

Default provisions: Where, in any branch of the law, the parties neglect to make provisions for a particular issue, the relevant law or contract between the parties provides the outcome, i.e. a fall-back provision of a general nature to remedy a breach of another party's obligations. This is seen in private foundations where the governing laws of the jurisdiction are comprehensive but which give the parties the ability to make their own provisions and where failure to do so allows the statutory provisions to apply.

De jure: A matter of law and used to describe the legal status of a situation or event as opposed to the de facto (actual) situation.

Delaware Business Trust: An incorporated type of trust used since the 19th century as a holding vehicle to overcome inadequacies of corporate law. First called Massachusetts Trusts or Business Trusts, which primarily were intended to deal in real estate and which reappeared in Delaware and were renamed as Statutory Trusts from 2002. The Delaware Code, Section 3801, defines such a vehicle as an unincorporated association created by a governing instrument under which property is or will be held, managed, administered, controlled, invested, reinvested and operated by a trustee. The trust is created for business or professional activities with the object of making a profit for the benefit of the beneficial owner designated in the governing instrument. A characteristic of these trusts is the ruling out of the personal liability of the trustees. This has been repeated in Connecticut and approved for adoption elsewhere as a Statutory Trust Entity, which has been defined by the National Conference of Commissioners on Uniform State Laws as an authorised entity separate from its trustees and beneficial owners which may have any lawful purpose 'except for a prevailing donative purpose' and where the managers, the trustees, are not liable for the debts. *See* TREUUNTERNEHMEN.

Delay defeats equity: *See* MAXIMS OF EQUITY.

Delegation: Entrusting another with the power to act. The general principle is that it is not lawful for a person in whom POWER vests to delegate to another without the express authority of the donor of the power. As far as trustees are concerned, the office, being one of personal confidence, cannot be delegated in general. Any failure for example to supervise the directors when the trust possesses a block of shares in a company is not excusable on the grounds that the trustees had delegated their supervision to others. The general rule is expressed as *delegatus non potest delegari,* i.e. a delegated power cannot be delegated. This applies to trustees and holders of special powers of appointment, both of which are required to apply their own mind as to how their duties should be exercised. The principle is that trustees who take upon themselves the management of property for the benefit of others have no right to shift their duty on to other persons and if they employ an agent they retain responsibility towards their *cestuis que* trust. The application of this principle to trustees is now subject to wide exceptions. These exceptions include:

1. **The appointment of agents under the *Trustee Act* 2000, Section 11.** Trustees may authorise 'any person to exercise any or all of their delegable functions as agent'. These, in the case of non-charitable trusts, consist of any function except the way any assets of the trust should be distributed, power to decide payment out of capital or income, power to appoint a person to be a trustee or any situation where there is a power conferred by another enactment or the trust instrument to act as nominee or custodian where that other enactment or trust instrument confers authority. In the case of charitable trusts delegation can be of any function to carry out a decision of the trustees, any function relating to the investment of the assets or the raising of funds other than where this is an integral part of carrying out the trust's charitable purpose, and other functions prescribed by an order of the Secretary of State. A beneficiary may not be appointed. Agents may be appointed by the trustees subject to the terms of the trust instrument.
2. **Valuation of securities.** Trustees, under the *Trustee Act 2000*, have a duty to obtain and consider proper advice before making investment decisions and are subject to the standard investment criteria with a duty to review investments while taking into account rules concerning valuation and obtaining appropriate advice.
3. **Temporary delegation.** A trustee may delegate by power of attorney, for a period not exceeding 12 months, all the

powers vested in him as trustee either alone or jointly. This may take the form of a lasting POWER OF ATTORNEY. This delegation may be to a trust corporation.

4. **Delegation by trustees of land.** The *Trusts for Land and Appointment of Trustees Act* 1996, Section 9, entitles trustees of land to delegate their powers to any beneficiary of full age who is beneficially entitled to an interest in possession in land that is subject to the trust. Delegation under this provision is restricted to a delegation of the trustees' function only insofar as it relates to the land. This delegation is by power of attorney. Trustees must observe the STATUTORY DUTY OF CARE under the *Trustee Act* 2000 when deciding on delegation.
5. **Delegation by trustees with a beneficial interest in land.** A trustee with a beneficial interest in land, in the proceeds of land or income of land, may delegate his powers in connection with these interests by a power of attorney for an indefinite period, provided this power is not excluded by a trust instrument or the power of attorney itself.

Delivery: A final act that, in the past, concluded any operation conducted by deed. Now rarely performed, it involved the deed being delivered to the other party by handing over the document or saying such words as: 'I deliver this writing as my act and deed' or expressing the same in writing. These formalities are now obsolete and the mere transference of the deed is adequate.

Demand guarantee: An undertaking issued by a bank or other institution to compensate, on demand, a person who suffers a loss caused by a third party subject to the terms agreed by the bank or other institution as laid down in the undertaking. This is a form of guarantee where the person guaranteed instigates payment from the guarantor and operates independently of any other party. Unlike an ordinary guarantee, the guarantor undertakes a primary liability. The validity of the guarantee depends entirely on the terms of the undertaking. If the bank or other institution is called upon to make payment, then the recourse to any other party is entirely a separate matter. The International Chamber of Commerce has issued an optional set of rules for incorporation into demand guarantees. A demand guarantee, establishing a primary liability, is close in effect to an indemnity but avoids the contractual complications of identifying the precise factors over which the security is given. *See* GUARANTEE *and* INDEMNITY.

***De minimis non curat lex*:** 'The law does not concern itself with trifles'. Courts of justice do not take trifling and immaterial matters into account. This is one of the few Latin maxims that has survived incorporation into statutes and has been applied, for example, to a case where anti-terrorism measures relating to explosives did not require a licence to buy a box of matches.

Demise: An old-fashioned word which means 'to grant' and is sometimes used in a trust for land where the settlor demises an estate for a term of years to a trustee, which merely means that he grants the land to the trustee according to the description contained in the deed. When the word is used in connection with the grant of a lease, it implies an undertaking on the part of the lessor that the lessee, i.e. the tenant, will have quiet enjoyment of the property during the term of the lease. The term is also used in shipping charter parties.

Demonstrative legacy: *See* ADEMPTION *and* LEGACIES.

***Denley's Trust Deed, Re* [1969] 1 Ch 373 at 387:** Under the English Law of Trusts a purpose trust, to be valid, must be for charitable purposes; a trust that does not have ascertainable beneficiaries is void. In

Re Denley, a more liberal approach was adopted. In that case the trustees of a trust for sale to whom the land was conveyed were directed to maintain land as a sports ground 'primarily for the benefit of the employees of that company and, secondly, for the benefit of such other person or persons (if any) as the trustees may allow to the use the same'. The gift was held to be valid on the grounds that the trust, although expressed as a purpose, was directly or indirectly for the benefit of an individual or individuals and was considered to be outside the rule that made purpose trusts unenforceable in England because of a lack of a beneficiary. The decision was subsequently approved in ***Re Lipinski*** [1976] Ch.2 235, but the decision has not always been followed. *See* PURPOSE TRUSTS.

Dépeçage: The term applied where aspects of a trust are severable, particularly matters of administration, and which may be governed by a different law to that which governs the other matters. This is recognised by *THE HAGUE CONVENTION ON THE LAW APPLICABLE TO TRUSTS AND ON THEIR RECOGNITION* 1986 and depends upon a court recognising the intention of the settlor to so separate the governing law into different jurisdictions. The term also is used generally to describe a provision in a deed or contract where different laws are applied to different issues contained within the document. A usual example is where the law of England is applied to the formal requirements of a contract but the law of another country is applied to its interpretation. *The Hague Convention on the law Applicable to Trusts and on their Recognition* 1986 provides that a trust may be set up according to the law of a particular jurisdiction but that the trust instrument may be interpreted according to the law of somewhere else.

Deposit: A sum of money paid as security that the recipient will perform a contract according to its terms. Where the recipient fails to perform, the money must be returned. This may be considered as an application of the law of restitution; the recipient having received an UNJUST ENRICHMENT by accepting the deposit and then not performing his part of the bargain. RESTITUTION, by requiring the return of the deposit, reverses the unjust enrichment. On the other hand, a deposit paid as a GUARANTEE that the contract shall be performed is different from a part-payment, which is recoverable subject to a counter claim for damages if the contract is not performed. Deposits in the case of sales of land are regarded not only as part-payment of the purchase money but also as security that the contract shall be completed by the purchaser. Here, the court regards money so deposited to have been given for safekeeping pending litigation: in the case of a sale of land, the deposit is regarded not only as part performance of the purchase money but also as security that the contract will be completed. The same term is used in a different context. The normal meaning of 'deposit' in banking is where money is placed with a bank in return for the payment of interest. Also, the depositing with a mortgagee of security for the repayment of money borrowed for the purchase of land constitutes an EQUITABLE MORTGAGE and therefore does not require registration or complex documentation: the equitable interest gained by the person with whom the documents are deposited is not overreached by a conveyance to a purchaser, i.e. the deposit-taker's interests are preserved.

Deposit protection: A form of statutory protection provided by the state in the UK up to a declared amount for deposits of funds with authorised banks. Following the financial collapse of the UK banks in 2008, the system remains in force. From 1st January 2016 the protection for each qualifying account was reduced from £85,000 to £75,000.

Depository: The person with whom a deposit is made and the term is also applied to the place where it is kept. The depository (the person) has an obligation to keep whatever is deposited with reasonable care and, upon request, the property or thing deposited should be returned to the depositor in accordance with the terms of the agreement by which the deposit was made.

Depreciatory conditions of sale: Sales of trust property under circumstances which cause the trust assets to unjustly depreciate. Such a sale cannot be impeached unless beneficiaries prove the consideration for the sale was inadequate, and no sale can be impeached after the execution of a transfer against the purchaser unless the beneficiaries can prove the purchaser was acting in collusion with the trustee at the time of the contract.

Derivative trusts: A derivative trust is a trust of a benefit to be derived from an existing trust; for example, where a beneficiary, before he becomes possessed of an interest in possession, sets up a trust of his expectation. That is, where A sets up a trust for the benefit of B and after B's death to C. Then C sets up a trust of his expectation of succeeding to an interest in possession set up originally by A. Such derivative trusts are therefore only valid to the extent that the parent trust is valid and subject to general rules of validity, such as perpetuities. Generally a derivative trust may be described as a secondary deed of trust that can be used to enlarge, confirm, alter, restrain, restore or transfer the interest granted in the parent trust instrument. *See* SUB-TRUSTS *and* PERPETUITIES AND ACCUMULATIONS.

Derivatives: An investment that takes the form of an artificial concept based upon the perceived changing value of some real tangible investment but not on its current actual value. Derivatives are usually involved in some form of 'swap' product, normally arranged by using the standard ISDA (International Swap Dealers Association) form of contract. *See* SWAPS.

Determinable interests: An interest potentially of perpetual duration but which may automatically come to an end if a specified event takes place or there is a specified change of circumstances. For example, a grant of property by X to A on the terms that A's interest will be determined on A's marriage and will revert back to the grantor, X. As it is uncertain when the event in question will take place, the determinable fee conferred on A is not absolute and therefore cannot exist as a legal estate and will be an equitable interest which can only exist behind a trust of land, i.e. X's grant of property in this way is a setting up of a trust for land for A. If the grantor, X, dies before A's marriage without leaving a spouse or heirs, the interest granted to A passes on A's marriage to the grantor's beneficiaries under his will or under intestacy as an absolute interest. Difficulties frequently arise in distinguishing between a determinable interest (when) and a conditional interest (if). A particular form of determinable interest is an interest for life, which is made terminable upon the happening of a future contingency. The grantee (A in the above example) is given the power of a tenant for life under the trust. If the grantee dies without the contingency arising which determines his interest, the interest reverts to the grantor or those taking his real estate under his will. *See* CONTINGENT INTEREST.

Determinable life interests: *See* DETERMINABLE INTERESTS.

***Devastavit*:** A Latin term used to indicate a person who has wasted assets for which he is responsible. This term is applied to describe the personal liability of an executor or administrator for the diminution of a deceased person's estate in failing properly to gain control of the assets or for misapplying them. The action in *devastavit* ('he who has wasted') is against the personal representative personally and the remedy is payable from his own assets. The action is open to any creditor, legatee or residuary beneficiary, who is affected by that waste. *See* PERSONAL REPRESENTATIVES.

Devise: The succession of property by will. Strictly, the term is only applied to real property but in wills it may be construed to transmit personal property as well and may be used in addition to, or as an alternative to, 'bequeath' (the proper term to indicate a disposition by will of personal property). An original consequence of this was a testator 'who gave, bequeathed and disposed of' all of his 'estate, effects and property' did not have any effect upon the succession to his real property due to the absence of the word 'devise' in his instructions. However, this distinction is now antique and 'bequeathed' and 'devised' are used more indiscriminately without the consequences of the former distinction.

Devolution: The passing of an interest in property from one person to another not by voluntary transfer but by the operation of law. This can occur on death, or bankruptcy, or insolvency where a person's estate becomes invested in a personal representative or an official receiver or trustee.

Dictum: *See* OBITER DICTUM.

Direct taxes: Taxes which are assessed on and payable by individuals, such as income tax, inheritance tax and capital gains tax. In respect of corporations, the direct form of taxation is corporation tax. These taxes are distinct from indirect taxes which are taxes paid by individuals and corporations not to the tax authorities but to some other person who ultimately accounts for that tax to the authorities. Examples of these are value added tax, insurance premium tax and duties on alcohol, fuel and tobacco.

Directive: A form of legislation in the European Union. Under the *Treaty on the Functioning of the European Union*, formerly the *European Communities Treaty*, Article 249 provides that:

> 'A Directive shall be binding, as to the result to be achieved, upon each Member State to which it is addressed, but shall leave to the national authorities the choice of form and methods.'

EU Directives lay down certain end results that must be achieved in every Member State. National authorities have to adapt their laws to meet these goals, but are free to decide how to do so. Directives may concern one or more Member State, or all of them. Each Directive specifies the date by which the national laws must be adapted – giving national authorities the room for manoeuvre within the deadlines necessary to take account of differing national situations. Directives are used to bring different national laws into line with each other and are particularly common in matters affecting the operation of the single market (e.g. product safety standards). This means that Directives are required to be transposed into domestic law in whatever way the jurisdiction concerned finds suitable. This contrasts with Regulations, which, by Section 288, shall have general application; a Regulation:

> '[S]hall be binding in its entirety and directly applicable in all Member States.'

In the case of Regulations it is therefore not necessary to transpose a Regulation to make it effective in domestic law.

Directly outward-related foundation purposes: A limitation on the setting up of a purpose foundation, which has been highlighted by the *Liechtenstein Foundation Law* 2008. Under this law (Article 107(4)(a)) a public benefit or charitable purpose must be based on an intention to promote a common good of a charitable, religious, humanitarian, scientific, cultural, moral, social, athletic or ecological nature. This applies even if the intention is only to benefit a special class of persons. This indicates that a purpose foundation in Liechtenstein law has an element of conferring benefits even though those benefits are to unnamed and unascertained persons. This is the background to para. 1 of the *Foundation Law* 2008 which allows a founder to endow a foundation for purposes which are known as 'outward related specifically identified purposes', as an alternative to, or in addition to, the benefit of individuals. This means that all Liechtenstein foundations, whether for beneficiaries or purposes, must have a directly outward-related and specifically identified purpose. A foundation with beneficiaries fulfils this test. This requirement may be stated in another way which is that is a foundation cannot have what is really an 'investment clause' presented as a purpose; this would confuse a statement of the form in which the assets are held (investment clause) with their application (purpose). The identification of the purpose is at the heart of a foundation. A foundation may pursue any purpose (a purpose that is not illegal and not contrary to public policy) and may combine more than one purpose to be pursued simultaneously or successively. The crucial criterion is that a Liechtenstein foundation's purpose must be stipulated by the founder and not left to the foundation's organs or third parties to define. A foundation itself (acting through the foundation council) cannot determine the purpose. A foundation cannot adopt the attitude that the foundation itself has a decision-making process. This contrasts with the position of a company; a company through its directors can decide the purpose and activities of their company (ignoring the remnants of the ULTRA VIRES doctrine). This applies even though under certain circumstances a foundation council has the ability to amend the foundation documents if an existing purpose becomes unachievable, impermissible or unreasonable, or if the purpose acquires a completely different significance or effect from the intent of the founder. This leads to the conclusion that the purpose of private foundations in Liechtenstein cannot be separated from the benefits conferred; the test of conferring a benefit gives the foundation reality. In other words, there must be an outward- related purpose in the sense that the purpose must have an end in itself which is permissible by law and acceptable in Liechtenstein by the Land and Public Registration Office. This appears to be an additional test on purposes despite the law stating that the foundation may be set up for any lawful purpose; to be a purpose there must be this outward-related benefit. Otherwise the foundation is void AB INITIO. An example of such a void foundation is one with the purpose of merely holding shares in a company without any outward- related purpose. Therefore, the draftsman of the foundation charter must incorporate an outward-related purpose by directing that the dividends are to be held for the benefit of some cause outside the foundation.

Director: A person appointed according to the provisions of the company's Articles of Association and who may have either an executive or a non-executive position within the company (*see* COMPANY MEMORANDUM AND ARTICLES OF ASSOCIATION). In company law a director is a person elected by the shareholders or otherwise appointed to superintend the management of the company's business. All the directors of a company, the Board of Directors, have general management powers and these powers, or some of them, may be delegated to one of their number, the managing director. Directors are agents of the company and it is to the company that they owe a fiduciary duty; they owe a duty of care to both company members and employees, although company directors do not owe any duty directly to individual shareholders. Remuneration of directors is subject to the members' supervision in a general meeting. Directors, however, may also have executive posts with their remuneration for those duties settled by other means. Case law is also relevant; for example in defining the extent of individual liabilities of directors. It is also possible that a person is regarded in law to be a director where they carry out the functions of a director without having been formally appointed; such a person is known then as a DE FACTO director. Where a person is able to influence directors, and the directors are accustomed to act in such a way, that person is then known as a 'SHADOW DIRECTOR'. This position in companies is similar to the position of constructive trustees in trust law or to TRUSTEES DE SON TORT. Directors of companies can be compared and contrasted with members of a foundation council whose role and duties towards a foundation may be similar to that of directors but with the exception that a foundation council is not appointed by the members, as in a foundation there are no members or shareholders, and their relationship with the foundation is subject to the terms of the foundation's charter or regulations.

Directors' duties: To safeguard the interests of the company. Duties in all cases, whether executive, non-executive or as shadow directors, are owed to the company and not to individual shareholders. The nature of these duties may be provided by legislation, common law or equitable principles. In the UK the *Companies Act* 2006, Sections 171 to 177, sets out seven general duties. These are:

- The duty to act within the powers of the company's constitution and to exercise the powers for the purposes for which they are conferred (Section 171).
- The duty to act in good faith to promote the success of the company for the benefit of its members as whole (Section 172).
- The duty to exercise independent judgement (Section 173).
- The duty to exercise reasonable care, skill and diligence (Section 174).
- The duty to avoid conflicts of interest (Section 175).
- The duty not to accept benefits from third parties (Section 176).
- The duty to declare an interest in any proposed transaction or arrangement with the company (Section 177).

Disability: The absence of legal capacity to be able to engage in acts or to enjoy certain benefits. Disability may be 'general', i.e. the person is prevented by disability from doing all acts of a given kind (such as disability due to being under age or lacking mental capabilities), or 'special' where the incapacity is concerned with the inability to engage in a specific act (such as to bring a legal action after the expiry of the limitation period). The word is of general application and has no particular or special meaning when applied to trusts or foundations.

Discharge of trustees: A trustee is said to be discharged when he ceases to be bound by the trust; the trust then ceases to exist. For example, where trust property is conveyed entirely to the beneficiaries. It is particularly important to decide at which point the trustee is discharged. For example, a trustee is not discharged from all his obligations simply by ceasing to hold trust property, i.e. a person may cease to be a trustee but may still not be discharged from his obligations. In that case, he will be discharged when a final account of his trusteeship is taken and approved. A departing trustee should take the precaution of obtaining a release by the beneficiaries when he ceases to be a trustee.

Disclaimer of trusteeship: Where a person appointed as a trustee declines to act in that office. The disclaimer to act must be made before the person appointed has done anything showing his acceptance of the obligations; a person may disclaim trusteeship although he had previously accepted the office but had not been active. The disclaimer may be by a deed, word or by conduct or from the fact that a long time has elapsed since the appointment and the trustee has done nothing. Any informal disclaimer must be unequivocal. A disclaimer cannot be made after a person has accepted and performed any act as a trustee and, under a will, if the same person is appointed both executor and trustee, he will be deemed to have accepted the trust once he proves the will, that is, submits it to probate. A trustee cannot renounce probate and be discharged from the trusteeship; such a renouncement, however, may be some evidence towards showing a disclaimer. A disclaimer of part of a trust is not possible. A disclaimer by a sole trustee means that the property reverts to the settlor or his representative.

Disclosure: A term with several meanings in law, including disclosure of circumstances in contract law (*see* NON-DISCLOSURE *and* UBERRIMAE FIDEI). In company law, directors and promoters are required to disclose relevant information to the public which is valuable to investors and promotes good governance even if the information conflicts with the interest of those disclosing it. The term is also used in procedural law where parties to civil litigation are required to disclose documents in their possession, custody or power, which relate to matters with regard to the action; this was formerly called 'discovery and inspection of documents'. In criminal proceedings, disclosure of evidence is required relevant to an investigation; disclosure must be made to both the prosecution and the defence. Disclosure also has some statutory meanings, for example, in employment law when an employer is required to disclose to employees and their trade union representatives information relevant to collective bargaining and proposed redundancies. The term is also used in connection with the exchange of information under double taxation treaties and exchange of information treaties for the purpose of enhancing transparency to achieve a better identification of beneficial owners in international tax arrangements.

Disclosure by trustees to beneficiaries: A traditional right of a beneficiary to information about the trust in which he has an equitable interest. Because of the beneficial enjoyment in the trust assets, beneficiaries traditionally have had the right to call upon trustees for accurate information as to the state of their trusts. This general rule was supplemented by the right of a beneficiary, at all reasonable times, to inspect, at his own expense, the documents relating to the trust and to be furnished with copies of the documents. This did not apply, however, to all the documents held by trustees; there was a particular exception in connection with information which was concerned with the details of the reasons for trustees' decisions especially where the decision affected discretionary beneficiaries. The Privy Council in ***Schmidt v. Rosewood Trust Ltd*** [2003] UKPC 26, modified these rules and adopted the general principle that beneficiaries have rights to seek disclosure of trust instruments under a basic principle of trust law. This is in place of the right being attributed to a beneficiary's equitable interest in the trust assets. This revised principle comes under the court's inherent jurisdiction to supervise and, where appropriate, intervene in the administration of a trust. The principle that the right of disclosure was itself a proprietary right based on the beneficiaries' equitable interests in trusts' assets was not considered an appropriate basis on which to justify a right to disclosure as such an inherent right might be harmful to beneficiaries' interests. The court can apply its discretion to avoid harmful consequences. In exercising its discretion, the court may rely on some of the older cases especially as to the limits of disclosure to safeguard the interests of beneficiaries generally and to limit the use which may be made of documents or information disclosed.

Discretion: A term which means that a person may exercise a legal obligation with flexibility and perform it in a manner suitable for each individual case as the person thinks fit. This allows courts and persons with administrative duties, and those in a fiduciary capacity, to have latitude to make decisions suitable for individual circumstances. Where discretion is allowed, it may not be unlimited and may be restricted by legal terms appropriate to the discretion in question. Where a public body exercises discretion beyond the terms permitted by law, it will be overturned by the court if done in bad faith, or for an improper purpose, or if irrelevant considerations are taken into account, or relevant considerations disregarded and, similarly, if a decision is manifestly irrational or unreasonable. A Court of Appeal will interfere with a discretionary decision of a court below if it were to decide differently and also if the lower court has exceeded the scope of the discretion given to it. Generally with trusts, where a trustee has discretion in the management or application of the trust property, the court will not interfere with the trustee's discretion unless bad faith, fraud or negligence, or a grave misdirection of themselves by trustees, occurs. *See* DISCRETIONARY TRUSTS.

Discretionary trusts: Express trusts where the trustees are given a defined discretion as to the manner of distribution and the identity of the persons entitled to receive capital and income from the trust. The discretion may be specific or the settlor may give the trustees a power of appointment between a number of specified potential beneficiaries allowing the trustee to decide who should be entitled to receive some or all of the trust property: the performance by the trustees of the discretion is obligatory even allowing the trustees some room for manoeuvre as to how that obligation is exercised. This compulsory trust power of trustees must be distinguished from a straightforward power which allows the holder of the power not to exercise it; all a court can do in this circumstance is to compel the holder to show that he has considered conscientiously whether or not the power should be exercised (*see* POWERS). Typically, trustees are given discretion, i.e. the flexibility to pay trust capital and income to such of the beneficiaries, of a class laid down by the settlor, as they think fit. In addition to its obvious use, trustees are given discretionary powers simply to prevent any particular beneficiary being regarded as having an interest in possession which would result in that beneficiary being excessively taxed. Discretionary trusts are also used where the assets of the trust are at risk of being taken in the execution or otherwise attributed to a beneficiary's personal assets. The intention then is that by leaving the appointment of a beneficiary to the discretion of the trustees, no attachment to the assets can take place before the discretion is exercised as until then the beneficiary has no right in the assets. A trust may often be accompanied by a LETTER OF WISHES issued after the trust is set up in which the settlor describes his wishes so as to guide the trustees as to how they may wish to exercise their discretion: such a letter is not legally binding. With private foundations, the foundation council may be given a similar discretion.

Disentailing deed: A deed used in connection with SETTLED LAND for the purpose of converting an entailed interest into a fee simple: the process being referred to as a 'disentailment'. This form of barring an ENTAIL came into use after the *Fines and Recovery Act* 1833, before which an entail had to be barred by one or other artificial transaction involving a fictitious debt. The process of using a disentailing deed is referred to as a 'disentailment' and is an assurance expressed by deed by which the TENANT IN TAIL barred the entail so as to convert the settled property into his own fee simple, or a BASE FEE, and therefore be able to convey the land as an estate in fee simple absolute. This would defeat the rights of all persons claiming under or after the tenant in tail. Abuse of this power was restrained by the appointment of a protector under the instrument creating the entail whereby no disentailing deed could be executed by the tenant in life without his permission. In 1925 all entailed estates in land were converted into equitable interests after which the entailed interest could be converted into a fee simple by a conveyance which incorporated a bar on the entail. Since the abolition of the ability to create new strict settlements of land, this will no longer be of such importance. *See* FEE SIMPLE ABSOLUTE IN POSSESSION.

Dishonest assistance: *See* KNOWING RECEIPT AND DISHONEST ASSISTANCE.

Disposal: A term frequently used in judicial and statutory statements, the meaning of which depends upon the context but, generally involves the relinquishing of title or ownership to an asset which may, as a disposal, give rise to a liability to a tax on the capital gain. With trusts, where trustees using their discretionary power appoint trust assets to be held entirely on new trusts, this resettlement is not considered to be the creation of a new and separate trust so as to give rise to a disposal which otherwise would incur a capital gains tax liability. *See* RESETTLEMENT.

***Disposicions mortis causa*:** Disposals of property made on death, principally by will and frequently used in connection with trusts made by will to indicate that the trust was an arrangement which was dependent upon the death of the settlor/testator.

Disqualification: A term applied to the situation where a person loses the right to fulfil an office by financial or criminal misdemeanours. In the UK, under the *Company Directors' Disqualification Act* 1986, a court can disqualify a person from being a director of a company, building society, or of an incorporated friendly society. These orders are commonly made on the grounds of conduct indicating unfitness to be concerned in company management after the director or incorporated body has been involved in a company insolvency or certain criminal activities, breaches of competition law, or in wrongful or fraudulent trading. Similar provisions for disqualification can be included in foundation legislation which disqualifies a person from being a member of a foundation council. Without any formal order from the court or any other body, this disqualification occurs merely by the fact that the person has, by commission or omission, failed to conform to the legislation. The word 'disqualification' is not used in connection with trustees but similar restrictions apply to the ability of a person to act as a trustee where a trustee acts in conflict with the trust laws.

Disqualification order: An order made by the courts under the *Company Directors' Disqualification Act* 1986 which disqualifies a person from acting as a director of a company or participating in the management of a company. *See* DISQUALIFICATION.

Disqualification undertakings: *See* COMPANY DIRECTORS' DISQUALIFICATION ACT 1986.

Dissolution: The putting of an end to a legal relationship, such as a partnership, by operation of the law, such as on the death or bankruptcy of one of the partners, by agreement between the partners, or by the life of the partnership expiring according to the partnership deed, or by order of the court. The dissolution of companies is now covered by the *Companies Act* 2006 where dissolution takes place when the affairs of a company have been wound up and other formalities completed. The term 'dissolution' is also used in the Family Division when the court exercises its power to terminate a marriage.

Dividend: Applicable to various subjects but its ordinary meaning is a share of profits paid to shareholders, usually from a limited company limited by shares.

Divorce: A decree dissolving a marriage on the petition of either husband or wife under the provisions of the *Matrimonial Causes Act* 1973 and under the supervision of the Family Division of the High Court. The financial consequences of a divorce may have an impact upon trusts, particularly in respect of ancillary relief granted to one of the parties by the Family Division in order to justly divide the assets of the husband and wife between them. This has an impact on trusts with which the Family Division has a right to interfere. *See* MATRIMONIAL CAUSES ACT 1973.

Doctrine of incorporation of international law: Where applied, this doctrine makes rules of an international law automatically part of a jurisdiction's municipal law, in contrast to the doctrine of transformation, which only makes international law part of the municipal law if accepted as such by statute or judicial decision. In English law, the position is not clear as far as customary international law is concerned but, with treaties, the sovereign has the power to make and ratify treaties so as to bind England under international law; however, these have no effect on municipal law until approved by Parliament.

Dog-leg claim: A term given to an action by a beneficiary against the directors of a trust company in an attempt to recover compensation from the directors themselves for breach of their fiduciary duty. Such claims were brought where the trust company (the trustees), had no assets from which beneficiaries could claim compensation. The dog-leg claim was based on the idea that an action against the directors personally for a breach of their fiduciary duty in rendering the trust company without assets would produce some assets that would belong to the trust company and which would be available for compensating the beneficiary. This idea had some support from the courts until the judgment in ***Gregson v. HAE Trustees*** [2008] EWHC 1006 (Ch) decided that such claims fail for the principal reason that director's fiduciary duties are owed to the company and not to the beneficiary.

Domicile: The country which a person treats as his permanent home and with which he has the closest legal connection. Under English private international law, the concept of domicile may be a country from which the person has been absent or, in certain circumstances, has never been present. A domicile of origin is acquired at birth, which is normally the domicile of the father if the father is alive. Consequently, a person can acquire a domicile of origin in a jurisdiction in which he has never lived. That domicile of origin is retained until a separate domicile of choice is acquired by which the person makes another country his home, with the intention that it should be his permanent base. To obtain a domicile of choice requires evidence both of the intention and of the fact of a change by adoption of a way of life in the domicile of choice and the severance of connections with the previous domicile which leads to the conclusion that a new home has been acquired. The matter is important because it is the law of the person's domicile which regulates his civil status and which is used to determine jurisdiction and the recognition and enforcement of judgments in civil and commercial matters under EC COUNCIL REGULATION No. 44/2001 and is the connecting factor allowing a court to assume jurisdiction over that person. Domicile must be contrasted with HABITUAL RESIDENCE. *See* DOMICILE OF DEFENDANT *and* EC COUNCIL REGULATION 44/2001.

Domicile of defendant: The connection between a person with a jurisdiction which implies an element of permanence sufficient to make that person subject to that jurisdiction. But the test of domicile is subject to different criteria in each jurisdiction. Generally, a person's domicile is considered to be where the person regards, on a long-term basis, as his home. There are variations. Thus, in English law, the domicile of a person is the place the person regards as his home but, in the absence of certainty, that person's domicile of origin may be used instead and that can be a place where the person has never been even for a short time as the domicile of origin depends upon the person's father's or, in some cases, the mother's domicile. At the other extreme, in the US, domicile is the term used to denote more or less the same idea as 'residence'. Domicile of a person when potentially a defendant in a civil or commercial action is important particularly in connection with EC COUNCIL REGULATION 44/2001 and the Lugano and Brussels Conventions where all three regimes provide that a defendant 'domiciled' in a Member or Contracting state should be sued in the courts of that domicile, irrespective of nationality or other personal attributes. For this purpose 'domicile' is given the meaning which it has under the domestic law of the state whose courts are seised of the matter, although in the UK the ordinary concept of individual domicile is subject to special provisions contained in the *Civil Jurisdiction and Judgments Act* 1982 which states that an individual is domiciled in the UK if he is resident there and the nature and circumstances of his residence indicate that he has a substantial connection with the UK. There is a rebuttable presumption for this purpose that an individual who is resident in the UK, and has been there for three months or more, has the necessary substantial connection. A corporation is domiciled where it has its 'seat'. This term varies in the legislation and is sometimes referred to as 'statutory seat' or 'central administration' or 'principal place of business'. Despite this slightly varied meaning, a company which is incorporated in the UK with a registered office there, will nevertheless always be treated as domiciled in the UK *See* LUGANO CONVENTION ON JURISDICTION AND THE ENFORCEMENT OF JUDGMENTS IN CIVIL AND COMMERCIAL MATTERS 1988 *and* BRUSSELS CONVENTION ON JURISDICTION AND THE ENFORCEMENT OF JUDGMENTS IN CIVIL AND COMMERCIAL MATTERS 1968.

Domicile of trusts: A trust is domiciled where the trust has the closest and most real connection with a system of law. This is important in connection with any action to be brought against a trust under EC COUNCIL REGULATION No. 44/2001 on jurisdiction, and in the Brussels and Lugano Conventions. Under the Regulation and the Conventions, a claimant must seek out and sue the defendant in courts of the defendant's domicile. This raises theoretical problems with actions concerning trusts and trustees. As a matter of English law a trust cannot be sued because a trust is not a legal person but this is ignored under the Regulation, which in Article 5(6) permits certain actions to be brought in the courts of a Member State in which the trust is domiciled. Under the Regulation, domicile of a trust has to be determined in the jurisdiction of the court in which an action is commenced where the court determines the domicile by applying its own private international law (Article 60(3)). The Regulation gives no indication how domicile is to be determined but authorities suggest that the *HAGUE CONVENTION ON THE LAW APPLICABLE TO TRUSTS AND ON THEIR RECOGNITION* 1986, enacted in the UK by the *RECOGNITION OF TRUSTS ACT*

1987, will influence the determination of domicile by applying the traditional test of the closest and most real connection to the system of law. The matter is complicated by the application of Article 5(6) of the Regulation that provides an alternative to trusts in two circumstances. First, where the defendant is domiciled in a country which is within EC Council Regulation EC 44/2001 or the Brussels or Lugano Conventions, proceedings may be commenced in that country without the permission of the court provided that no proceedings are pending elsewhere in the Regulation or Conventions' territories. Second, in other cases (the defendant is domiciled outside Regulation or Convention territories) the permission of the court is required under UK CIVIL PROCEDURE RULES, Part VI, Rule 6.20, which provides detailed criteria to decide if the party or trust has substantial connection with the UK. *See* LUGANO CONVENTION ON JURISDICTION AND THE ENFORCEMENT OF JUDGMENTS IN CIVIL AND COMMERCIAL MATTERS 1988 *and* BRUSSELS CONVENTION ON JURISDICTION AND THE ENFORCEMENT OF JUDGMENTS IN CIVIL AND COMMERCIAL MATTERS 1968.

Donatio inter vivos: A gift between living persons. With this type of gift all that is necessary is that the donor shows an intention to give and does whatever is necessary to complete the gift, such as handing over the object given. There may also be constructive delivery which takes place where the subject of the gift cannot be handed over in a simple way. For example, constructive delivery of goods in a warehouse takes place with the handing over of the warehouse key or, in the case of land, of some written instrument.

Donatio mortis causa: A gift of property at the point of death of the donor, upon the express or implied condition that the gift is not to be absolute and complete until the donor dies. To be effective, the gift must be made in contemplation of, though not necessarily the expectation of immediate death although it is usual that death is expected to occur within the near future. Such a gift is revocable during the donor's life and ineffective if he does not die. These conditions will normally be implied from the fact that the gift was given when the donor was ill; in other words, it is a gift made in the present to take effect in the future. A gift *donatio mortis causa* has been described as being a gift which is neither entirely INTER VIVOS nor testamentary. The gift must be completed by the delivery of the subject matter, or something representing it. The donor must intend to part with the ownership and not the mere physical possession of the gift. Thus, a gift of chattels may be made by the delivery of the keys of a cupboard containing the keys of a safe in which the chattel lies; other means of making a symbolic delivery where the thing is not capable of immediate actual delivery may be enough. Cases show a variety of circumstances; for example, a gift of land was held to be within the rule of symbolic delivery by the delivery of title deeds. A gift of shares could not be the subject of a *donatio mortis causa* since property does not pass by delivery. Also, the gift of a cheque can only be made effective by obtaining payment of it in the donor's lifetime; it is revoked on his death, but delivery of a bank deposit book or savings certificates has been held to be a valid gift. A valid *donatio mortis causa* cannot be revoked by will and differs from a legacy in taking effect without probate or the executor's assent. *A donatio mortis causa* is subject to inheritance tax. Therefore, a deathbed declaration that an asset should be held on trust could be valid provided the delivery of the asset was capable of transfer by delivery and actual delivery was made. This also requires that the trustee makes a declaration that he would henceforth hold the asset on trust for identified beneficiaries. Additions to the assets of a foundation can similarly be made by deathbed delivery to a member of the foundation council.

Double taxation: The assessment to income tax or inheritance tax in two countries on the same amount of income or capital gains. Relief against double taxation may be granted by an agreement entered by the governments of each country, usually in the form of a Double Taxation Convention. These Conventions are bilateral and frequently based upon the Model Tax Convention on Income and Capital devised and published by the OECD (latest version, July 2014). Other Model treaties, as these Conventions are frequently called, are provided by the UN, which particularly favours the developing countries, and by the US. Although the prime purpose of double taxation treaties is to avoid double taxation, these treaties regulate the collection of taxes between two countries and, in particular, provide for the exchange of information between each country to allow the tax authorities to obtain information about possible tax evasion. Trusts are not subject to any specific provisions in a Convention; the taxation of trusts is left to the general provisions relating to individuals or to companies where the trustees are an incorporate body. Private foundations, being incorporated bodies, are taxed accordingly and subject to treaty relief under the Articles concerned with companies and other legal bodies. In practice, each Convention must be examined; the terms of the Model cannot be relied upon to represent the relationships between real states. Also important is to make sure that the treaty covers the income or gains in question.

Double taxation relief: Rules that are designed to reduce or avoid multiple tax charges where the same item of income is liable to be taxed in more than one jurisdiction. It is particularly important where taxation in different jurisdictions is based upon different principles, such as in the US where taxation is based upon citizenship and in the UK where taxation is based upon residence. Different methods are used to prevent double taxation; principally, relief under a treaty between two countries (*see* DOUBLE TAXATION TREATIES). Where an item of income or capital gains is not subject to treaty relief, there may be relief against double taxation by a straightforward credit in one country against the tax paid in another country. This latter method of unilateral relief depends upon the internal laws of the countries concerned.

Dower: A gift made in consideration of a marriage intended to furnish a newly married person with assets. Dower was made into an equitable interest by the *Law of Property Act* 1925 but is now an obsolete concept as the characteristics of dower have been gradually reduced over the years. The legal process of a writ or dower by which a wife could bring an action against her husband if he had deprived his wife of her right to her dower is also obsolete.

Due diligence: An investigation to ascertain that a business or an activity has been performed according to the appropriate standard of care. Used particularly to describe a process whereby an investor or purchaser in a company will examine the records of the business or company in order to be assured of its value and to determine whether there are any hidden problems. The term is also used in connection with investigations carried out by financial professionals to ensure that they do not become involved in money laundering or other financial irregularities.

Dummy trust: A term given by the Court of Appeal to a BARE TRUST of shares where the trustee is instructed by the beneficiaries over the administration of the shares even in the absence of terms in the trust to this effect.

Duties of trustees: The following are amongst the most significant:

- To obey the directions of the trust deed unless any deviation has been sanctioned by the court.
- To act impartially and even-handedly between the beneficiaries where any discretion awarded the trustees must not be operated unfairly or with discrimination.
- To sell improper property, i.e. to convert any trust asset that is a wasting asset into a permanent form of property.
- To balance the interest of the tenant for life (who naturally would like to see the trust assets develop for the purpose of income) and of the remainderman, whose instincts would naturally be to see capital growth, even if this meant a reduction in the current income.
- To make payments out of the capital of the trust or the income of the trust respectively, as appropriate.
- To exercise the reasonable care and skill required now under English law in the *Trust Act* 2000.
- To invest trust funds and, where necessary, to engage in appropriate financial advice.
- To distribute trust property only to beneficiaries or to the object of a power of appointment or the persons authorised under the trust instrument or general law.
- To receive property as custodian or portfolio manager for the beneficiaries or purpose of the trust.
- To refrain from delegating their duties or powers unless authorised under the trust instrument or the law.
- To act jointly where there is more than one.
- Not to set up *JUS TERTII*, i.e. allow claims to be established that are adverse to the trust or beneficiaries.
- To act gratuitously unless otherwise authorised, hence the importance attached to charging clauses by which trustees can receive adequate remuneration; although under the *Trustee Act* 2000 in the UK, trustees are not prevented from charging reasonable fees; professional trustees charge reasonable fees for professional services which they render for the trust.
- Not to profit from the trust and not to cause loss from a conflict between the trustees' fiduciary duty and self interest.
- To conduct the trust in a professional manner and to keep records and minutes of the meetings of trustees and to be ready with the accounts.

Duty of care: The general equitable duty of care is the care that an ordinary prudent business man would take in managing his own affairs except, in selecting investments, he has to consider that he is acting for the benefit of others for whom he is morally obliged to provide, thus ruling out speculative investments that an ordinary PRUDENT MAN OF BUSINESS might make for himself. For trusts which came into force from 1 February 2001, a STATUTORY DUTY OF CARE is imposed which is 'to exercise such care and skill as is reasonable in the circumstances'. The specific circumstances will be the fact that the trustees' investment function is for the benefit of others and whether the adviser on investments is acting gratuitously or being paid. This codification of the general equitable duty applies to trustee powers under the *Trustee Act* 2000 and to several powers in the *Trustee Act* 1925; for example, Section 15 permits a trustee, if authorised, to do certain things with the trust funds and to manage the repayment of debts to the trust and the trustee would not be responsible for any loss by any act provided it was done in good faith. Now, after the *Trustee Act* 2000, all that is required is that a trustee has discharged the duty of care set out in that Act. Similarly, under Section 22 of the *Trustee Act* 1925, the duty of care in the *Trustee Act* 2000 applies to actions by trustees in connection with reversionary interests and valuations and to the standard of care required in relation to the acquisition of land. However, this general standard does not apply to many of the functions of a pension scheme where trustees are already covered by the *Pensions Act* 1995. With constructive trustees, the standard duty of care only applies from the time the conscience of a CONSTRUCTIVE TRUSTEE is effective. *See* REVERSIONARY INTEREST.

E

***Earl of Chesterfield's Trusts, Re* (1883) 24 Ch D 643:** A decision that comprised one of the four rules of 'apportionment' which have been made optional for new trusts by the *Trusts (Capital and Income) Act* 2013 and which are still relevant in respect of older trusts. *See* APPORTIONMENT.

Earned income: Income arising from an individual's employment or pension or other allowances, deferred pay, money paid for compensation for loss of office, or which is given in respect of present or past services. Included as earned income for tax purposes are benefits to which an individual is entitled by virtue of his employment. These benefits include any income derived from a property, motor cars, rewards in kind or advantages received (such as accommodation, children's school fees and free car parking) and any income which is derived by an individual from carrying on, or the exercise of, any trade, profession or vocation.

Easement: A right or privilege which constitutes an intangible right over the land of another so as to require the owner of adjoining land to refrain from doing something or to permit the neighbouring owner to do something on the other's property. For example, the occupier of land, 'A', can compel the occupier of an adjoining piece of land, 'B', to refrain from erecting a building that would interfere with A's rights in respect of water supplies, or A has a right to enter B's land for a particular purpose such as to cross the land (as with a right of way). In these examples, A's land is the dominant tenement and land B's land is the servient tenement. The existence of these tenements in different occupation or ownership is an essential element of an easement; different persons must occupy each and the easement must accommodate the dominant tenement. An easement exists only for a particular purpose and cannot exist unless the right is capable of forming the subject matter of a grant. This means that the right must be capable of definition and not be vague and uncertain and must exist within the general nature of rights capable of existing as an easement. An easement is different from a right of property or ownership and from a PROFIT À PRENDRE, which is a right to the produce or profit of land; easements are only concerned with the user of land, such as a natural right to support or the right to drain water from higher to lower ground. Also, an easement must be distinguished from a public right, such as the right to use a public highway or statutory rights, such as a 'right to roam' which exist under the general law. The law does not recognise any easement of prospect or privacy. The principal rights of easements are in respect of water, and of air, of light, of rights of way and rights of support and in respect of party walls and fences. An easement in or over land can exist as an interest equivalent to an estate in fee simple absolute in possession or a term of years and can be conveyed or created at law. Other easements are equitable. A legal easement can only exist if it is created by deed and if the servient land is registered and any registration requirements are met under the *Land Registration Act* 2002. A legal easement may also be created by statute or by implication where the easement is of necessity or which gives effect to the common intention of the parties. The protection of easements depends if the servient tenement is registered under the *Land Charges Act* 1972. An easement can come to an end if both tenements come under common possession and then be revived if the unity of possession ceases. An easement can be created by a grant between the owners of the dominant and servient properties. In the absence of a grant, an existing easement could be justified as having been in effect since time immemorial but, to make proof easier, the legal fiction is employed of presuming a lost modern grant. Also, an easement comes to an end when there is severe and radical change in the use of the dominant tenancy, such as a change from agricultural to residential use when, for example, any easement to accommodate the flow of surface water will end. Where there is an express grant, the terms of that grant dictate the nature and the limits of the easement.

EC Council Regulation 44/2001: *See* EUROPEAN REGULATION ON JURISPRUDENCE.

Egmont Group, The: An informal group of offshore bankers whose endeavours to enhance mutual cooperation in the sharing of information is aimed principally at countering money laundering.

***Ejusdem generis*:** Something of the same kind that, as a rule of construction, is applied to the general words in a document which follow a specific description. The general words are meant to extend the scope of what is named or referred to specifically. This intention to amplify the meaning of a description can only be interpreted to mean an extension of the particular specific type of item described in a general sense. Thus, in an expression of 'goods, facilities and services', the word 'facilities' is limited to matters associated to goods and services and does not include a facility of a completely different nature. The assumption is that general words are inserted to guard against any accidental omission from the objects mentioned rather than to extend the provision to cover completely different items.

Eldon, Lord: Lord Chancellor from 1801 to 1806, and 1807 to 1827. As Lord Chancellor, Lord Eldon drew fine distinctions and discussed subtleties and niceties and would not decide a case until he had exhausted all its possibilities and examined it from every angle. The business of Chancery became slow and was steadily reduced to the position of unending litigation which Dickens had described in *Bleak House*. Nevertheless, his work completed the process where equity hardened into law and this enabled the *Judicature Acts* 1873 and 1875 to amalgamate law and equity and to authorise the administration of both legal and equity systems by the same court, within 50 years of his death.

Election: The exercise by a person, left to his own free will, of choosing to take or do one thing out of the possible alternatives available to him. This applies to both rights and liabilities and is also the obligation to choose irrevocably between two inconsistent claims or courses of action. To constitute election the choice must be unequivocal and made with full knowledge of the circumstances. The doctrine in equity means that a person who accepts a benefit under a written instrument must accept the whole of it and renounce every right that is inconsistent. For example, when 'A', by will or deed, confers a gift on 'B' and in the same instrument confers a gift on 'C' of property which currently belongs to B (say, a family asset previously given by A to B). B then must choose (i.e. B is put to an election). B may either accept the gift and make over the stated property to C or B may elect against the instrument by declining the gift entirely or accepting A's gift to him and paying compensation to C. By doing this, A effectively rearranges the ownership of the family assets. The principle is expressed in other jurisdictions that a person should not be allowed to appropriate and reprobate. The doctrine is known in Scottish law as that of Approbate and Reprobate. The equitable principle is to secure a just distribution in accordance with the general scheme of the instrument. The general rule is that a person cannot accept and reject the same instrument; a person cannot accept a gift under an instrument but renounce every other provision in that instrument which is inconsistent with that gift.

Ellesmere, Lord: Lord Chancellor from 1603 to 1617, who was noted for delivering very lengthy opinions but nevertheless when Lord Chancellor, through the issue of numerous orders on the procedure and organisation of the court, consolidated the Court of Chancery as a formal body. This was secured after a great struggle between him and the Lord Chief Justice Coke, who had prohibited suitors from going into the Equity Court, to which Ellesmere responded by prohibiting them from pursuing common law judgments. The deadlock was resolved by a decision in favour of the Chancery, thereby establishing it as an independent court and, despite dissention, there was no further serious threat to the court's independence.

Employee benefit trusts: Trusts set up by employers to confer present or future benefits on employees in addition to or apart from their general remuneration. This is achieved by the employer setting up an employee benefit trust, the trustees of which hold the payment until the trustees can distribute those benefits to the employee at a time when the employee has an advantageous tax position. As may be expected, these trusts provide a complex area of taxation in the UK to the extent that such trusts tend to be set up in a low-tax jurisdiction where the beneficiary is not resident for tax purposes and when he can be expected to become entitled under the trust before returning to his domestic high-tax jurisdiction.

Employee share ownership trusts: Trusts into which a company places shares that the trustees hold for particular employees as an encouragement and reward for hard work. The trustees comprise members that are drawn from the employees and from the company management and may include outside persons.

Encumber: The process of making land subject to a charge or liability, such as subjecting the land to a mortgage. A mortgage existing over property is an encumbrance (sometimes spelt 'incumbrance') over that property. In addition to referring to security interests, such as mortgages, charges, liens and trusts to secure money, any kind of interest in property that restricts the owner's right to deal with it as he wishes is said to encumber the land or lease.

Endow: Originally the gift to a woman in connection with the right to DOWER but now used in the sense of providing funds for a charity and sometimes for other institutions, such as a foundation, or even trustees, with property, with the intention of providing a permanent income. With charities, a permanent endowment is a gift to the charity with a restriction on the ability of the charity to apply the capital for its general charitable purposes; only the income may be so disbursed.

Endowment: A term traditionally used to describe property becoming permanently owned by a charity or a fixed income for the support of the charity. The term is frequently now used to express the donation of assets to a private foundation.

Enduring power of attorney: A term used in North America and elsewhere to describe a power of attorney, the English equivalent of which is the LASTING POWER OF ATTORNEY.

Enforcement: The term 'enforcement' appears in the full title of the *Hague Convention on Trusts* indicating that the Convention is concerned with how trusts can be made effective in the jurisdictions of the parties to the Convention. *See* HAGUE CONVENTION ON THE RECOGNITION AND ENFORCEMENT OF TRUSTS.

Enforcement of judgments: A process by which judgments and other orders of a court may be enforced. Under English law, this may be by obtaining a writ of FIERI FACIAS or a warrant of execution, or a third party debt order, a charging order, an attachment of earnings order, or for the appointment of a receiver. In Europe this is governed by the EC COUNCIL REGULATION 44/2001 and by the Brussels or Lugano Conventions.

Entail: An entail is where land is given to a person for his life and thereafter to the heirs of his body. That interest is then known as a 'FEE TAIL' and the land is said to be entailed. This is a particular form of trust relating to land where the trustees are not given a right to sell, even if the right to sell might be postponed. The *Trusts of Land and Appointment of Trustees Act* 1996, Schedule 1, Para. 5, made it impossible to create new entailed interests in England and Wales and any effort to do so would result in a trust of the FEE SIMPLE ABSOLUTE IN POSSESSION in favour of the grantee. Also, an attempt to declare oneself a TENANT IN TAIL is ineffective. New provisions are provided for trusts for land of a less complex nature. Existing entailed arrangements will continue. The entail of freehold land was a device intended to allow family estates to be kept within the family and not to be dissipated by an extravagant heir. Throughout the 18th and 19th centuries, the entail was a standard method to keep land in the family. By complex court proceedings, an entail could be ended; these proceedings were simplified by the *Fines and Recoveries Act* 1833, which provided a simpler procedure for barring an entail by the execution of a DISENTAILING DEED by which the tenant in tail barred his issue from becoming tenants in tail in due course and also barred the interests of the REVERSIONER, i.e. the person entitled to the property at the end of the entailed interest, with the consent of the protector of the settlement. The use of entailed interests continued throughout the 19th and 20th centuries until the *Law of Property Act* 1925 barred legal entails and provided that they could only exist as equitable interests. Entailed interests were continued in this way under the *Settled Land Act* 1925. *See* TRUSTS OF LAND.

Entailed interest: An entail or an entailed interest exists when land is limited to a person and the heirs of his body with or without prior estates. An entailed interest is also known as a FEE TAIL. An entailed interest descends on the death of the first owner to his children, then to his grandchildren and then to more remote descendents but not to ascendants or collateral heirs. Where there is no one left to qualify to become tenants of the entailed interest, the land passes to the reversioner or remainderman. An entailed interest could be created in different forms, it could be entailed male general (father to son to grandson) or entailed female general, or limited to a tail special (i.e. to a particular person or group of persons other than would be indicated by 'general') with a special limitation, or tail male special, or tail female special. *See* ENTAIL.

Equality is equity: A maxim of equity applied where there is no reason for any other basis for division of property and that those entitled to property shall share in its equity.

Equitable: Fair, an adjective derived from the noun 'equity' and used particularly when applied as a liberal construction of a law or legal rule. This is in contrast to the interpretation of the common law which is more restrictive and precise. The rules of equity are used to enforce what is equitable as opposed to the rules of the common law. An equitable right, estate or interest is one which was originally recognised and enforced only in the Courts of Equity, such as the rights of a beneficiary under a trust, or of a mortgagor after the day fixed for repayment of the mortgage loan had passed. The Court of Chancery was primarily an equity court but now equitable principles are applied throughout the UK courts without the need for separate proceedings in a separate court. Some wrongs were originally only remedied in Courts of Equity such as equitable fraud and equitable waste; these can now be remedied in any court.

Equitable apportionment: The agreement by two or more persons to divide a payment, such as a rent, between themselves, without the consent of the person making the payment. Also applied where two or more persons are liable to pay a sum of money and they agree on the proportion which each should pay without the agreement of the person entitled to receive it. Equitable apportionment also means apportionment according to the rules of equity and between tenant for life and remainderman under the rules in ***Howe v. Dartmouth*** (1802) 7 Ves. 146 (*Howe v. Earl of Dartmouth* (1802) 7 Ves. 137, and ***Allhusen v. Whittell*** (1867) L.R. 4 Eq 295, as opposed to apportionments made under the *Apportionment Act* 1870. *See* APPORTIONMENT.

Equitable assignment of debt: Where a debtor is given to understand that the debt has been made over by a creditor to some third person and where a legal assignment under the *Law of Property Act* 1925, Section 136, is not necessary. *See* TRANSFER OF EQUITABLE INTERESTS *and* EQUITABLE INTERESTS.

Equitable charge: A charge created over property simply by designating the property with the discharge of some debt or other obligation. No special form of words is necessary. Unlike a legal charge, all that is required is a clear intention. For example, where the owner of a property designates that property as a source of repayment of a debt this counts as an equitable charge. An informal mortgage made by deposit of title deeds is also an equitable charge over the property to which the deeds refer. Where there is an equitable charge and the creditor does not feel that the equitable charge is sufficient security for outstanding monies, the creditor may seek an order for the sale of the property from the court or for the appointment of a receiver. This gives the creditor no right to apply for foreclosure so as to make the property his own or a right to take possession. Evidence of an equitable charge usually requires some form of letter whereby the debtor reassures the creditor that a particular source of income will be used to pay off the debt.

Equitable compensation: Money awards made by Courts of Equity to compensate for actual loss or as a pecuniary substitute for actual performance as a consequence of a breach of equitable duty. The breach may involve infidelity or disloyalty. This may be because the duty itself requires fidelity or loyalty or because there was wilful disregard of the duty itself: in such cases, equity regards this as tantamount to fraud. The claimant will still need to show the breach was causative of his loss and that the claimant should have mitigated the loss. The debtor is not allowed in a claim for equitable compensation to rely on other limits that would, under a legal action, be permitted to reduce the debtor's liability. A breach of the duty of care which does not involve any infidelity or loyalty can be compensated for in a way similar to damages with the claimant's entitlement being affected by considerations of CAUSATION, remoteness of loss (*see* REMOTENESS OF DAMAGE), CONTRIBUTORY NEGLIGENCE and the claimant's failure to mitigate his loss. The test for remoteness will depend upon whether the equitable duty of care was imposed by the terms of the fiduciary relationship or assumed at a later date. Other monetary relief also may be awarded in equity after an action for account which may be brought for assessment of the loss. An action for account may be brought in equity to assess the damages for breach of legal duty. Monetary relief may be granted in substitution for, or in addition to, non-monetary equitable relief where appropriate.

Equitable easement: An easement which is created informally, i.e. without execution of a deed, or one which is not held in fee simple or for a term of years. Although equitable easements are registerable as a land charge in the UK, they are overridden by a registered legal easement. *See* EASEMENT.

Equitable estates and interests: Rights of property that exist where the legal ownership of property is vested in one person and the beneficial interests in another. Or, where there is an equitable owner who also holds the legal interest in property in a different capacity. These rights arise principally when (a) a person has the right to have property or an estate or interest vested in himself, such as by way of a contract or conveyance or assignment, that does not by law actually transfer or vest the legal estate or ownership in the transferee; (b) by mortgage or charge; and (c) whenever a trust arises, whether express, constructive, implied, or by other operation of the law. Originally where a person was entitled to the beneficial interests in property, it was merely a personal right to enforce the legal owner to carry out his obligation or trust. These rights gradually became regarded as rights of property as a result of legislation, starting with the *Statute of Uses* 1535. These rights persisted alongside the personal rights so that where there is only one beneficial owner, who is entitled to the sole right of any income from trust property, that person is not regarded as the property's legal owner. Simplification of the law on real property in 1925 resulted in the number of equitable estates in land being increased, with a consequent decrease in the number of legal estates. Over the late 19th century and early 20th century, equitable and legal estates in interest became more unified and to some extent harmonised the law between legal and beneficial owners under the rule that equity followed the law. In particular, the rules of descent were the same and the words of limitation were practically construed in the same manner and, finally, by the *Trusts of Land and Appointment of Trustees Act* 1996 the one matter which remains distinct, the settlement of land under the *Settled Land Act* 1925 which required particular treatment, was repealed. Under the doctrine of 'equity followed the law' legal incidents fell upon the legal owner who, in many cases, had a right of indemnity against the beneficial owner and the equitable right of the beneficial owner of land or any interest in land became treated as a charge upon, or attached to, the property itself, binding not only the legal owner but all persons deriving title under him except in the case of EQUITY'S DARLING, i.e. purchasers for value of the legal estate without notice. This remains the law. Another consequence of this harmonisation is that some equitable estates and interests may require protection as land charges or by entry on the Register of Title to the land to which they relate.

Equitable estoppel: The doctrines of proprietary and promissory estoppel are described as equitable estoppel because the doctrines were principally developed by the Courts of Equity to supplement the narrower rules of common law when they were applied to the unconscionable or inequitable conduct of a party. Some cases of equitable estoppel were derived from the maxim 'he who seeks equity must do equity'. This maxim can be regarded as the common feature of both promissory and proprietary estoppel, about which there are a number of distinct doctrines. *See* ESTOPPEL, PROMISSORY ESTOPPEL *and* PROPRIETARY ESTOPPEL.

Equitable execution: The appointment of an equitable receiver (a person not to be confused with the administrative receiver or *Law of Property Act* 1925) who is appointed by a judgment creditor whose interests in property cannot be taken in execution under the law. An appointment may be made as a protective measure before judgement or even the issue of proceedings, such as where an application is to be made for a FREEZING INJUNCTION (*see* MAREVA INJUNCTION).

Equitable interests: Interests in land which are enforced by a Court of Equity in situations where it would be against the conscience to permit the legal owner of the property to keep the benefit of the property for himself. A trustee has the legal estate in the property but is compelled to hold the property for the benefit of the beneficiaries. Equitable interests were originally solely a personal interest against the trustee but they have become recognised more as rights in rem or property rights. This affects a large range of estates, interests and charges in or over land since the number of equitable interests was dramatically increased by the *Law of Property Act* 1925, Section 1(1),(2) and which now take effect as equitable interests (Section 1(3)). The terminology is used in describing a trust where the trustees have the legal estate but the beneficiaries have a beneficial or equitable interest, or that the ownership of the trust property is shared between trustees and beneficiaries who may be said to have the beneficial ownership. Equitable interests must be distinguished from 'mere equities' which are procedural rights ancillary to some right of property such as an equitable right to have a conveyance rectified. There is also a great distinction between equitable interests and a floating equity, which is a term to describe an interest of a beneficiary under a will or intestacy where the beneficiary hopes to receive the property of the deceased if it is available after the payment of debts and other liabilities; the equity floats in that it is not yet crystallised into a real equitable interest. Also, there is a less precise meaning of equity which is sometimes attached to the right to obtain an injunction or other equitable remedy where the right is sometimes referred to as equity. *See* FORMAL REQUIREMENTS – LAND, FORMAL REQUIREMENTS – PERSONAL PROPERTY, TRANSFER OF EQUITABLE INTERESTS *and* TRUST.

Equitable lien: A lien which exists independently of possession (unlike a common law lien), such as a vendor's lien for the purchase money of property and the purchaser's lien for the deposit. An equitable lien is similar to a charge over property except that it arises by operation of equity rather than from the conduct of the parties. An equitable lien cannot be set up against a purchaser of the legal estate for value without notice of the lien. In other jurisdictions the term is applied to a lien on property imposed by a court to achieve fairness generally and particularly where someone has, in his possession, property that is held for another person.

Equitable maxims: *See* MAXIMS OF EQUITY.

Equitable mortgage or equitable charge: A term with several meanings. Principally, the term is applied to a mortgage where the mortgagee does not obtain a legal interest in land because the mortgagor only has an EQUITABLE INTEREST and so can only grant an equitable mortgage. For example, a mortgage granted by a beneficiary under a trust of land held in the trust can only be equitable because the beneficiary only owns an equitable interest in that property. The term also applies in the way in which the mortgage is created. If a mortgage is not made by deed, as is required in the case of creating a legal mortgage, the mortgage may be an equitable mortgage. Although it need not be made by deed, nevertheless, an equitable mortgage must be made in writing and may require protection by registration as a land charge to give notice to the world at large as to its existence – to establish its priority over later mortgages in the same land. The term also has the further meaning that: if a charge by way of legal mortgage of registered land is not entered into the Register, it takes effect in equity only.

Equitable orders: A series of remedies created in equity to mitigate the harshness of the common law and seen most frequently in relationships arising in trusts. The orders are available only when common law remedies are unsuitable or inadequate. All orders depend upon the exercise by the court of its discretion. Although these orders are now awarded according to recognised principles, they retain flexibility to meet new situations. The equitable orders comprise rescission of contracts, rectification of documents, specific performance and injunctions.

Equitable presumption: An assumption made in equity that in certain circumstances, where there is a given set of facts, there is an assumption that other facts follow. For example, where a father makes a voluntary transfer to his child there is an equitable presumption of advancement that he intended to make a gift. The presumption can be overcome by evidence to the contrary, such as documentation that what might be presumed to be a gift was, in truth, a loan.

Equitable proprietary interest: An interest in property, originating in Courts of Chancery, that it would be against the conscience of the legal owner of the property to keep or use the property for himself. For example, a trustee who holds the legal estate in the trust property is compelled to hold it for the benefit of a beneficiary whose interests are merely equitable. However, equitable interests, which are really rights IN PERSONAM against the trustee, have come to resemble proprietary rights or rights IN REM. Equitable proprietary interests arise whenever a person obtains a right to have property, or an interest in property, vested in him and whenever there is property held on trust, whether the trust is express, constructive, implied or by operation of the law. Although equitable interests are interests conferring a proprietary right, it remains the duty of the legal owner to carry out the obligations associated with ownership. The rights of beneficial owners gradually became recognised as more than mere personal rights enforceable only against the legal owner or trustee and they became closer to legal estates and interests. For example, in a trust, a beneficiary has a right to any income from the trust property, although not regarded as the property's legal owner who remains, in law, the trustee. Following the maxim 'equity follows the law', whether there is a legal or beneficial interest, the rules applied to ownership in property are the same. The rules are at the centre of the consequences of any sale of property although the equitable interest may be subject to words of limitation, such as those that previously arose under the *Settled Land Act* 1925. A beneficial owner of land has rights against the legal owner. These rights became treated as charges upon the land or as rights attached to the property itself and were enforceable against not only the legal owner but against all persons deriving title under him except for a purchaser for value of the legal estate without notice (EQUITY'S DARLING). This remains the law so that the legal owner still may be able to convey the land free from equitable interests. Under the *Land Charges Act* 1972, some equitable estates and interests require protection as land charges or can be protected by an entry under the title of the land to which they relate. These equitable interests will bind anyone who later acquires an interest or estate in the land. This is also applied to many interests in land that were formerly legal interests and which became personal interests. This includes the transformation of the interest of co-owners of land where the land was vested in trustees and also where trusts were either expressly declared or under some default statutory scheme. Also, due to the legal entailed interests being abolished in respect of future estates, any attempt to set up an entailed interest becomes a trust of land under the *Trusts of Land and Appointment of Trustees Act* 1996. From that point, except for established entailed interests, beneficial interest in land became equitable interests. Also, many easements other than those easements which were the equivalent of a fee simple absolute in possession became equitable interests. In respect of personal property, equity also followed the law although the legal incidents that fell upon the legal owner gave that legal owner a right of indemnity against the beneficial owner. These considerations do not apply to foundations where the beneficiaries are not possessed of any equitable interest in the foundation property. Neither do they have any interests in the foundation property until such time as the foundation council exercises its discretion in their favour and takes steps towards conveying or transferring the property. The exact nature of the beneficiaries' rights has not been properly explored by the courts; their rights may be described as 'rights under the foundation', that is, a new right of property derived from the unique character of foundations or it may be that the beneficiaries acquire ordinary equitable rights to receive the property concerned as the foundation council is then holding property on behalf of another, i.e. on behalf of the beneficiaries. *See* EASEMENT.

Equitable receiver: A person appointed to enforce an equitable judgment especially where interest in property cannot be taken under the law by a judgment creditor. The appointment of an equitable receiver is made as a protective measure and may be made before judgment or even before issuing proceedings, particularly in respect of a freezing order to prevent assets being taken out of a jurisdiction before the matter is heard in court.

Equitable relief: A relief awarded by a court in civil claims; for example, where a court directs a defendant to sell a piece of real property in accordance with the defendant's contractual obligations. Such a relief is an order for SPECIFIC PERFORMANCE and is one of two forms of equitable relief, the other being an INJUNCTION, primarily to prevent the defendant continuing with an action which causes the other party damage or inconvenience. The common feature of equitable relief is that it is awarded where money damages would be inadequate.

Equitable remedies: Remedies devised by equity to redress wrongs outside the limited scope of legal remedies. The main characteristic of equitable remedies is that they act IN PERSONAM: the defendant being exposed to an order to do what appears to the judge to be just and equitable. If the defendant thereafter failed to do what is ordered, he would be guilty of contempt of court. Equitable remedies are discretionary and allow the court to take into account the conduct of the parties, particularly those of the claimant under the maxim of 'he who comes to equity must come with clean hands'. The principal equitable remedies are SPECIFIC PERFORMANCE, RESCISSION, CANCELLATION, RECTIFICATION, ACCOUNT, INJUNCTION and the appointment of a receiver. These remedies can be granted by the High Court and in some cases by a lower court. There are other equitable remedies such as 'discovery' which require the disclosure and inspection of documents, such as '*QUIA TIMET* ACTIONS' to protect the claimant against injury that was merely threatened and 'bills of peace' to establish the right to secure protection from the prospect of incessant or multifarious litigation. Also, the remedy '*NE EXEAT REGNO*' aimed at preventing a person liable to some equitable claim for a liquidated sum leaving the country without giving security: this remedy is now only available if the debt was legal and often used in connection with a FREEZING INJUNCTION (formerly a MAREVA INJUNCTION) and with SEARCH ORDERS (formerly known as ANTON PILLER ORDERS) or to compel the attendance of a director of a company in liquidation for examination before the Companies Court.

Equitable right to redeem: The mortgagor's right to pay off a mortgage (loan) secured on his property at the legal date for redemption and this continues even though that date has passed. This is distinct from the equity of redemption which arises as soon as the mortgage is made. *See* EQUITY OF REDEMPTION.

Equitable title: *See* EQUITABLE INTERESTS *and* MAXIMS OF EQUITY.

Equitable tracing: The means by which a claimant can trace property when that property has been mixed with other property and where a part of that mixture represents or comprises money to which the claimant previously held an equitable proprietary right. Equitable tracing differs from common law tracing; tracing is only possible at common law so long as the asset is identifiable and so long as it has not been mixed with other property. A pre-existing equitable interest is essential in being able to use equitable tracing: the claimant must have a distinct equitable title to be able to trace property. This requirement has been criticised because it confuses the process of identifying the claimant's original assets with a presumption that the claimant has a proprietary interest in whatever is being traced. It must be possible to identify that the claimant had an equitable interest in the property or some other property in which he had an equitable interest, in the mixture against which the tracing claim is brought. This interest need not be a beneficial interest and it may be, for example, an equitable charge over the original assets or held subject to a fiduciary relationship before the claimant was separated from the original assets. This is particularly relevant where the claim is for money which at common law could not be traced if the money was paid into a bank account already holding other money; whereas, in equity, identification can follow the rule in *Clayton's* case (*see* CLAYTON'S CASE) which broadly presumes that the money first withdrawn from an account is drawn against the contribution of the party whose money was first deposited. The concept of 'BACKWARDS TRACING' has been allowed for the first time. The JUDICIAL COMMITTEE OF THE PRIVY COUNCIL, in a judgment, recognised that in particular cases of fraud or breach of fiduciary duty the victims may trace the proceeds of the fraud or breach even where there is no direct connection between the funds lost by them and other assets in the hands of the party causing the loss. In cautiously allowing backwards tracing, the Judicial Committee of the Privy Council said that it was a matter of judicial policy that the court may disregard the previous principle of tracing: that debits and credits in the various accounts of the parties should directly correspond to each other. The policy was that the court should not allow increasingly sophisticated methods of money laundering to camouflage interconnected transactions which obscured their true nature (***Federal Republic of Brazil et al v. Durant International Corporation et al*** [2015] UKPC 35). *See* *AGIP (AFRICA) v. JACKSON* [1991] Ch 476, 566; ***DIPLOCK, RE*** [1948] Ch 465 *and* TRACING.

Equitable waste: Where a tenant for life holds land with the privilege of non-impeachment for waste, equity will restrain any unconscionable abuse of the privilege of non-impeachment where the tenant for life commits wilful, destructive, malicious or extravagant waste, such as pulling down houses or cutting down timber too young; that is, waste which the Courts of Equity can prevent even though the type of waste was not impeachable at law. The remedies for equitable waste have been described as an unconscientious abuse of the privileges of non-impeachability for waste at common law. The remedy for equitable waste is an action for damages or an injunction.

Equity: That part of remedial justice which was formerly administered exclusively by a Court of Equity, later known as the COURT OF CHANCERY. This was in contrast to the law administered in a court of law, where the law is referred to as the COMMON LAW. For a long time equity was an indifferent collection of standards of right or wrong which derived haphazardly whenever the CHANCELLOR, acting on behalf of the King ('the fountain of all justice'), considered that an appeal to mitigate an injustice brought by an excessive literal application of the common law deserved a remedy. As its origins suggest, being derived from '*aequus*' (meaning equal) equity, in its primary sense, means fairness or rules of conduct that in the opinion of society generally, and the courts in particular, ought to be followed. The Chancellor was originally an ecclesiastic and 'keeper of the King's conscience' and did not feel bound by the rules of law but nevertheless could not contradict the King's laws. The Chancellor gave relief from the harshness of the law as he thought fit without actually contradicting the law. In doing so the Chancellor aimed to remedy the defects of the common law by granting relief that the strict law did not recognise and was therefore able to give more ample redress than the ordinary narrow course of law had power to do. The maxim of equity 'where the equities are equal, the common law must prevail' showed the respect which the King's Justice earned. Nevertheless, the power of the Chancellor developed and eventually became a senior position occupied by lawyers, with the title of Lord Chancellor. The haphazard nature of a Court of Chancery's decision became systemised and formalised by a famous Lord Chancellor (LORD NOTTINGHAM, 1673-1682) into a parallel legal system. The Courts of Chancery in administering equity and the Courts of Common Law ran concurrent but exclusive jurisdictions. This caused considerable delay in resolving a dispute, often requiring parallel proceedings. The *Judicature Acts* of 1873 and 1875 merged equity and law so that any court of law could, where necessary, deliver a judgment containing a principle of equity. The Court of Chancery was discontinued and reformed as a Chancery Division of the High Court showing the amalgamation of the two systems. Equity's most significant contribution to the law was the development of trusts. The trustees, having the legal ownership of property, might attempt to behave in a manner inconsistent with their instructions from the settlor. The Court of Chancery, with its ecclesiastical background and as a court of conscience, was able to prevent trustees from behaving contrary to their conscience and contrary to their mandate from the settlor, and was thereby able to restrain trustees from breaching their obligations. A Chancery Court under equity would produce a remedy for the benefit of the beneficiaries who had suffered a loss caused by excesses or failures of trustees. The definition of a trust in English law incorporates the concept that the trust is an equitable obligation. In other jurisdictions, where equity is not a separately administered system or derived from such dual jurisdictions that have followed the English law, equitable principles are applied automatically as equity has been an intimate part of common law for centuries.

Equity does not want for a trustee: A principle that a trust will not fail because of a lack of a trustee. If a settlor or testator fails to appoint trustees, or if the appointed trustees refuse or are unable to act or cease to exist and no replacements are appointed, then the court has wide powers to appoint a new trustee or new trustees. The wishes of the settlor and of the beneficiaries and the likelihood of any conflict of interest between the proposed trustee, the settlor and the beneficiaries, are considered by the court. The *Judicial Trustees Act* 1896 gives further power to the courts enabling the appointment of a trustee and may do so by appointing any fit and proper person nominated in an application which may be made by the trustees, settlor or beneficiary. Such a trustee is a judicial trustee and is an officer of the court and subject to its control and supervision. This Act is of less significance in modern law since the *Trustee Act* 1925, Section 36, which conferred wide powers to appoint and replace new trustees and of the *Trusts of Land and Appointment of Trustees Act* 1996 which entitles beneficiaries to appoint new trustees or to require existing trustees to retire in certain circumstances.

Equity of redemption: The right of a mortgagee to recover the unencumbered title to his mortgaged property at any time on the payment of the principal, interests and costs. This right exists although the contractual date for redemption may have passed. Anything which appears in a mortgage deed to prevent redemption of the loan by payment or performance of the debt obligation is known as a clog or fetter on the equity of redemption, i.e. it prevents the mortgagee from repaying the loan and receiving the title to the property unencumbered by the mortgagor's rights. Any such clog is void and therefore does not prevent a mortgagee at any time repaying the amount due. The equity of redemption is described as 'an equitable interest in the land consisting of the sum total of the mortgagor's rights in the property'; i.e. it amounts to ownership of the property subject to the mortgage of which the equity of redemption is one of the elements of that ownership. Separate agreements that a mortgage will not be redeemed within a certain time or under certain conditions may be outside the 'clog on redemption' principle. *See* CLOG ON THE EQUITY OF REDEMPTION.

Equity, maxims of: A series of axioms that are still cited in judgments but less frequently than they used to be. These axioms incorporate some of the principles of equity that have been distilled from judgments of the courts. There are an indeterminate number of them but the current edition of *Snell's Equity* (2015) lists 12 of them as the most significant. *See* MAXIMS OF EQUITY.

Equity securities: The ordinary shares of a registered company and other securities that may be converted into such shares, such as allotment letters. The term also includes pre-emption rights that may be conferred on existing shareholders when the company issues ordinary shares. The term is used to distinguish ordinary shares from PREFERENCE SHARES.

Equity's darling: A BONA FIDE purchaser of property for value without notice of any equitable interest in that property and who takes the legal estate in that property free from any equitable rights. The reason behind this principle is that such a purchaser has been an innocent victim of a breach of trust whereby the seller of the property did not disclose the existence of the equitable interests, and where the application of the maxim 'where the equities are equal the law shall prevail' is relevant. Under that maxim the bona fide purchaser for value without notice becomes the owner of an unencumbered interest free of the equitable interests which previously existed on that property. The existence of this principle does not allow a trustee to avoid committing a breach of trust nor does it absolve a purchaser from making the normal enquiries particularly at the Land Registry. The concept of a purchaser being without notice of any equitable interest is important when it comes to regarding the extent that a purchaser is required to make adequate enquiries. A purchaser also has to be aware of the doctrine of 'constructive notice'. The term 'equity's darling' is reputed to be derived from the papers of legal historian F.W. Maitland (*Collected Papers* 1911, Volume iii, page

350) although Maitland there refers to the holder of the equitable interest as the Court of Chancery's 'darling'. The term must be used with caution and now has little legal significance. There is a historical conflict between the modern definition as given above and Maitland's view that the holder of the equitable interest is in the cherished position and the darling.

Escrow: A matter in writing which has been completed, signed, and, if necessary, sealed and delivered to a stranger who holds the document until certain conditions are performed and then delivers it to the other party to take effect as a deed. The term is also used where a written document is delivered in circumstances that show it is to take effect only when and if such a condition has been performed. If that condition is not performed the document has no effect. The document delivered in escrow can only be recalled if there has been an unreasonable delay in performing the condition. Performance within a reasonable time is implied to any escrow deed relating to the conveyance of real property. Securing the payment of a purchase price for property may be arranged by delivering the transfer documents with a condition that they are only effective if the purchase price is paid within a stated time.

Escrow trusts: Securities issued to a trustee who is required to transfer them upon the happening of a certain event. Promoters of a company may use an escrow trust by placing their shares on trust both as protection against each other and as a demonstration of the protection thereby given to the public until the offering of shares has been completed. This avoids the possibility that the promoters could sell their shares in the newly formed company and neglect to properly ensure the success of the issue. In other words, the trustee holds the shares as trust property in escrow until the issue to all parties has been completed.

Essence of the contract: The phrase means an essential term in a contract without which the arrangement between the parties would not have constituted an enforceable contract. The breach of any contractual term which is 'of the essence' entitles the innocent party to rescind the contract.

Essential capacity: A term which defines whether a person can enter into a transaction. This commonly depends on whether a person has the appropriate age or mental capacity to enter the transaction or, in the case of an incorporated body, whether a proposed transaction is permitted by that body and whether it is *INTRA VIRES* the body's powers. For example, an underage person does not have the essential capacity to enter into a contract for the sale or purchase of land and any attempt to do so would be void. In connection with trusts, the distinction between essential validity and essential capacity can be difficult. For example, a legal rule in a jurisdiction which states that no person below a certain age can settle property in trust may be regarded as an issue of essential validity. On the other hand, such a rule may be directed at a person attempting to enter into the trust who is below the age necessary to be able to perform the act concerned; in that case, it is a matter of essential capacity. This interpretation is reinforced if the same age requirement is applied to persons who are resident inside and outside the jurisdiction, i.e. the rules on capacity are applied to a trust set up within a jurisdiction regardless of the settlor's capacity wherever he was resident.

Essential validity: The core of a transaction that must be valid to make the transaction enforceable. Essential validity is the need for the essential core of a contract to be legally enforceable as opposed to some fringe matter which, if it is not valid, may be guillotined off from the core of the matter agreed in the contract, leaving the core as an enforceable obligation.

Estate: Signifies the position in which a person stands with regard to real property in which he has an interest, and the term is also applied to that interest itself. Because no person in English law can be the absolute owner of land, the term 'estate' indicates the varieties of mode of ownership which a person can possess; in other words, a person cannot own land absolutely but he may have an estate in it and the nature of that estate defines his relationship to that land. Under the *Law of Property Act* 1925, legal estates in land are limited to freehold and leasehold. All other types of estates are equitable. The term also implies property and is used when talking about real and personal estate, partnership estate or a trust estate and especially when referring to the questions of administration when a deceased person's total property is referred to as his estate. The word is often used in conjunction with others such as 'real or personal estates or effects', 'estate and effects', 'estate, effects and property whatsoever and wheresoever', 'estate and interest', 'estate or interest in possession', which may, due to judicial pronouncements, modify or amplify the impact of the unqualified term. Estate, as used in English law, is closest to the civil law concept of 'patrimony'. *See* PATRIMONY.

Estate duty: A tax in the UK introduced by the *Finance Act* 1894, which, with its frequent amendments, remained the basis of the law until it was replaced in 1975 by CAPITAL TRANSFER TAX and then by INHERITANCE TAX.

Estate tail: *See* ENTAILED INTEREST.

Estoppel: A principal which precludes a party in certain circumstances from denying the truth of a statement of fact or a state of affairs that he has asserted to another party who, after relying on that assertion, suffers a loss when that assertion proves to be untrue. Estoppel at common law takes numerous forms that have been developed from the three main types identified in the 17th century by Coke (*Coke upon Littleton*: Co. Litt. 352a; *Termes de la Ley*) depending on how the statements were made. These were (1) estoppel by record (a doctrine preventing a person from reopening issues which have been finally settled by the court); (2) by deed (for example, a representation made by deed which could not then be denied); and (3) *in pais* (conduct which was relied upon by another party). By the 19th century the common law had developed an estoppel based on a representation of fact that was intended to be acted upon by the person to whom it was made. The person making the representation was not then allowed to plead that the facts were different from his representation. For example, an informal waiver of contractual rights and obligations that a contractual obligation would not be strictly enforced could not be denied. Such informal assurances were usually in connection with time requirements in a contract. This applied to prevent the maker of the statement ignoring the detriment suffered by the other party so long as the assurance did not amount to a permanent variation of a contract which required consideration and to be recorded in writing. Estoppel at common law is often referred to as estoppel by representation and has traditionally been treated as a rule of evidence and not as a cause of action; that is, no action can be founded upon an estoppel by representation of fact (the American counterpart of this is known as 'equitable estoppel'). The courts of equity developed their own forms of estoppel and recognised the limitation of the doctrine applied by the common law courts. This was particularly noticeable in the recognition of estoppel based upon a representation as to a party's future conduct rather than the common law's restriction of requiring a representation of existing fact. Now what is known as equitable estoppel is not restricted to such extensions of the common law principles centred around a representation although still feature in many judgments. Equitable estoppel depends on an underlying unconscionable or inequitable conduct of a party. A form of estoppel has appeared where no representation or promise is made but the parties to a transaction act on an assumed state of fact or of law. This is sometimes referred to as estoppel by convention and depends on some form of reasoning that it would be unconscionable and unjust to allow a party to contradict an assumption on which the transaction was based. This depends on the particular facts of a situation and is regarded as a variant of equitable estoppel. Equitable estoppel principally takes two forms, PROMISSORY ESTOPPEL and PROPRIETARY ESTOPPEL, based upon the unconscionable or inequitable conduct of a party. Equity does not demand such a clear prejudicial conduct as does common law estoppel. In equity, for example, estoppel can prevent unjust enrichment where an owner of property retains unfairly a benefit or improvement he has made to the property but, nevertheless, induces another party to believe that such benefit or improvement has been transferred in a transaction. Also, equitable estoppel can prevent a party from withdrawing from a contract because the formalities had not been complied with. These two situations; that is, improvement of land and part-performance, developed a general doctrine of proprietary estoppel. At the same time the doctrine of promissory estoppel also arose in equity. The distinctions in modern law between promissory and proprietary estoppel are that proprietary estoppel is concerned with statements in connection with the title to land or interest in property for which a legal relationship is already in existence. In contrast, promissory estoppel is concerned principally with obligations. Equitable estoppel supplements the narrow rules of common law by introducing equitable remedies to relieve against what otherwise would be unconscionable or inequitable conduct by a party, such as a promise made in relation to a contract but which does not form part of that contract and which therefore is unenforceable at common law, but which was material in convincing the other party to the contract to enter into the legal obligation. The word 'estoppel' is also used to describe how estoppel may occur in other circumstances, such as estoppel by word, estoppel by deed or estoppel by silence, which are used in many jurisdictions but are merely variations in terminology. *See* EQUITABLE ESTOPPEL.

Estoppel by representation of fact: The common law doctrine of ESTOPPEL which originated in a party being bound by assertions that were recorded by deed and other means by which acts were recognised as having the same effect as delivery of the taking of possession of land. This common law doctrine of estoppel by representation of fact prevents one party from denying the truth of a statement of fact if he or she has induced another party to rely on it to their detriment. *See also* PROMISSORY ESTOPPEL *and* PROPRIETARY ESTOPPEL.

European Court of Justice: One of three judicial bodies of the EU with the Court of First Instance and the Civil Service Tribunal. The court ensures that European law is observed by the EU institutions and in the Member States. It has no jurisdiction to rule on the interpretation of international law provisions outside Community law. Its main activities are giving preliminary rulings at the request of national courts, proceedings against Member States for failure to comply with EU obligations, actions for annulment of Community acts, and for Community institutions failing to act. National judges have discretion to refer to the court but national courts of last resort, such as the Supreme Court in the UK, are compelled to refer if they consider a point needs determination to enable them to give their judgment. Interpretation by the European Court depends upon the spirit of the point in question and not upon national rules of construction. The European Court has been accused of activism, i.e. declaring principles not expressly included in the treaties, such as the supremacy of EU law and the direct effect of its decisions and the principle of state liability.

European Regulation on Jurisdiction: The European Council Regulation 44/2001 on Jurisdiction and the Recognition and Enforcement of Judgements in Civil and Commercial Matters has displaced the previous rules relating to jurisdiction which were contained in the Brussels Convention and the Lugano Convention, as far as jurisdiction and enforcement of judgments is concerned, between EU Member States. This applies to all the Member States except Denmark, which opted out. The Brussels Convention and the Lugano Convention still exist in particular instances and both the regulation and the conventions contain very similar rules but there are some subtle differences which raise complications. The Brussels Convention still applies between Denmark and the other EU Member States and the Lugano Convention applies between EU Member States and Switzerland, Norway and Iceland. *See* BRUSSELS CONVENTION ON JURISDICTION AND THE ENFORCEMENT OF JUDGMENTS IN CIVIL AND COMMERCIAL MATTERS 1968 *and* LUGANO CONVENTION ON JURISDICTION AND THE ENFORCEMENT OF JUDGMENTS IN CIVIL AND COMMERCIAL MATTERS 1988.

European trust law: An academic proposal sponsored by the Business and Law Research Centre which established the International Working Group on European Trust Law. The intention behind the proposal was to examine the uses to which the trust concept has been put and to appreciate that these roles might play a useful part in local internal law in countries which do not naturally incorporate trusts in their spectrum of vehicles available for investment. The publication of their researches by Kluwer Law International as volume 1 of *Law and Business Finance* in 1999 contained an introduction of principles of European trust law with a useful comparison of the principles in common and civil law countries and a compact summary of the principles of trust law that were subsequently commented upon by reporters from various European countries.

Even hand: The duty of trustees to act in such a way that each beneficiary receives his entitlement under the trust and is not unfairly favoured or penalised in a way which no other beneficiaries share; the trustees act impartially. This is often referred to as that they 'hold an even hand' or operate 'even-handedly'.

***Exacta diligentia*:** The utmost diligence applied to the way in which a trustee should discharge his duties.

Excess execution: A power contained in an instrument exercised in a manner which calls upon equity to relieve against unfair and unseen consequences by the use of equity's power to remedy an excessive application of the common law rules. In other words, where a normal and literary interpretation of an instrument may lead to unfair consequences and unforeseen events, such as where a deed is executed by mistake or when an appointment is made under a power by a donee who had forgotten a previous appointment to the same person, i.e. the holder of the power made the same appointment to the same person twice. Such an event could lead to the deed being rescinded or cancelled in equity. This doctrine might overlap with the doctrine of fraud on the power but excess execution is concerned with the effect of the appointment or use of the power, that is, excess execution is concerned with how the power is exercised. The doctrine of fraud on the power, on the other hand, is concerned with the intention or purpose of the holder.

Exchange control: A measure adopted during the Second World War which, in the UK, severely restricted the ability to exchange British currency for the currency of another country with a view to preventing capital investment abroad. Consent of the Bank of England, which administered the *Exchange Control Act* 1947, would only be given if an investment served the national interest. The restrictions were particularly intended to prevent speculative movements of short-term capital and especially controlled the payments to persons abroad other than those in the sterling area countries. Exchange control has largely been abolished worldwide under the influence of the IMF.

Exchequer bills: Bills issued by the Treasury to raise temporary loans in anticipation of government costs authorised by Parliament, such as expenses incurred in carrying out public works. Exchequer bills were negotiable instruments but are no longer issued having been replaced, to a large extent, by Treasury Bills and Exchequer Bonds.

Exclusion clause: *See* EXONERATION CLAUSE.

Exclusive jurisdiction: A provision in an agreement which declares that there is an exclusive right to bring an action in a named jurisdiction. This statement is presumed to embody the parties' agreed intention that all matters in a dispute will be tried in that named jurisdiction.

Exculpatory clause: A provision in a contract, or a deed, such as a trust deed, which releases one party from responsibility. The actual meaning of the word 'exculpation' suggests that the party relying on it has been guilty of some offence but has been pardoned by the appearance of the clause. *See* EXEMPTION CLAUSE *and* EXCLUSION CLAUSE.

Ex debito justitiae: The remedy to which an applicant is entitled as of right in contrast to one that may or may not be granted, which is called discretionary.

Execute: To complete or to be made effective. This applies particularly to written instruments, such as written agreements, deeds and wills. In common law, to execute a deed required the party to sign, seal and deliver it to the other party. The consequences of this formality were that a contract entered into this way, that is, by deed and also called a 'speciality' required no consideration.

Executed contract: A contract where nothing remains to be done by either party, the transaction is both agreed upon and completed at the moment consensus is arrived at, such as where an article is sold and delivered and payment made immediately. This contrasts with an executory contract where some future act has to be done, or to do an act on or before some future time.

Executed trust: A trust in which the interest of all the beneficiaries has been set out and clearly defined by the settlor. An executed trust is a trust that has been completely constituted, i.e. no further act is necessary to be done by the trustees to give effect to the terms of the trust, and where the property has already been conveyed to the trustees, making the trust properly set up and then said to be executed. *See* EXECUTORY TRUST.

Execution of deeds: Originally this meant the signing, sealing and delivery of deeds by the parties. After the signing of the document, in the presence of witnesses, a declaration was made that the documents consisted of the signatories' own acts and deeds before being handed over to the other party. Now, the sealing requirement has been abolished in certain circumstances, particularly in connection with the transfer of real property.

Execution of judgment: The final stage in a court action where the judgment or order is enforced against the losing party who is referred to as a 'judgment debtor'. The most usual form of enforcement is the requirement to pay a sum of money. This can be done by various means, by a writ of FIERI FACIAS, or warrant of execution, a third party debt order, a charging order, a stop order or notice, an attachment of earnings order, a writ of sequestration, an order of committal for imprisonment or the appointment of a receiver.

Execution of judgements against trustees: Liability of trustees is personal and where a court finds there has been a breach of trust by trustees each trustee can be the subject of a separate court order to provide compensation. The extent of a trustee's duty depends upon any special knowledge or experience he has, or holds himself out to have or is expected to have, and whether he acts in the course of a business or profession. Consequently, not all trustees may be required to make the same level of recompense. Because the awards against trustees are individual to each trustee, the question of the enforcement of an award may raise separate legal issues in respect of each; these may cover matters concerned with the enforcement of a judgment outside the jurisdiction and the effect of any exemption or exculpation clause in the trust deed.

Execution of wills: The signing and witnessing of a will by the TESTATOR and the witnesses. To be valid, a will must be in writing and signed by the testator or by some other person in the testator's presence and by his direction. The testator's signature now has to be acknowledged by two witnesses in the presence of the testator but not necessarily in the presence of each other under the *Administration of Justice Act* 1982, Section 17. Previously the testator's signature had to be at the foot or end of the document but these requirements are now relaxed and all that is necessary is that 'it appears that the testator intended by his signature to give effect to the will.' Obliterations, interlineations, or other alterations must be executed in the same manner as the will. These formalities do not apply to wills of soldiers on actual military service or to any mariner or seamen being at sea, members of the Royal Navy or marines if on actual military service; in such cases, an oral will can be admitted to probate. Internationally a will is treated as properly executed if the execution conforms to the internal law in force at the place of execution or where the testator was domiciled or where he was a resident or where he was a national. This follows a recommendation of the *Ninth Hague Conference on Private International Law* 1960. In the UK this is made effective by the *Wills Act* 1963 where there are detailed rules on related matters.

Executive entities: *See* BAHAMAS EXECUTIVE ENTITY.

Executor: The person or persons nominated by the TESTATOR who have the duty of carrying out the provisions of the testator's WILL. The executor also has the duty of burying the deceased, collecting the estate, paying the debts and distributing the property amongst the persons entitled. A testator may bring actions against persons who owe money to the testator or who are in possession of the testator's property, which becomes property then belonging to the estate: these things may usually be concluded only after the executor has proved the will and obtained probate. *See* PROBATE. The appointment of the executor or executors must take place in the body of the will and any direction made beneath the testator's signature is ineffective. Where the appointment is unambiguous the court will not admit evidence to show the testator's intention lay elsewhere but the court may, in certain circumstances, such as insolvency, or any other special circumstances, pass over the executor named in the will and grant letters of administration to another person when a court thinks it is necessary or expedient to do so. The number of executors, under English law, is limited to four and may include a corporation or person appointed by someone nominated in the will. *See* ADMINISTRATOR. Any person capable of making a will can be appointed as an executor, including minors, although no grant of probate will be made to a minor until he achieves his majority. An executor is allowed a year, from the date of the testator's death, to realise the testator's estate before being bound to distribute it, this is called the 'executor's year', which means that interest does not dwell on legacies until the end of that year unless the will contains some special directions. When an executor dies before the estate is completely administrated, the executor's executor continues to administer the estate of the original testator. Therefore, if a testator, by will, sets up a trust or foundation, the executor has a year in which to transfer the assets to the trustees or to the foundation council. The identity of either of these bodies depends upon instructions given by the executor in his will. Before the property is assigned by the executor to the trustees or to the foundation, the executor is liable for any action which would be a breach of trust or a breach of his obligations under the foundation. If an executor neglects to secure the property or distributes the estate incorrectly he will be personally liable for any loss (a *devastavit*). Real property comprised in a testator's estate vests automatically in the personal representatives, that is, in the case of a will, in the executor.

***Executor de son tort*:** A person who takes possession of, or intermeddles with, any of the deceased's assets as if he were a properly appointed executor or administrator without taking out any grant of probate or letters of administration. More properly called 'an ADMINISTRATOR DE SON TORT'.

Executor trust: This is a term which is used in the US in connection with trusts set up by executors, which in English terminology refers to a WILL TRUST.

Executory: *See* EXECUTE.

Executory consideration: Consideration that is not performed until after the contract.

Executory interest: An interest in property that arises or passes to a particular person on the occurrence of a specified event.

Executory limitation: A limitation of a future interest by deed or will; if by will, it is called an 'executory devise'; that is, a dispositive provision that becomes effective by divesting a prior interest. The *Family Reform Act* 1969 restricted executory limitations of land by providing that any executory limitation that takes place on default or failure of any issue of a specified class becomes void and incapable of taking effect as soon as any living issue of that class attains the age of 18.

Executory trust: A trust where the trustee or the settlor must perform some further act or duty before the trust is completely constituted, for example, where some other event must take place before the trustee obtains legal property in the trust assets. Sometimes executory trusts are thought of as being instructions for trusts rather than the instruments in themselves being incomplete. Executory trusts are found mostly in marriage settlements and wills. The distinction has been much reduced – both in the decline in the use of marriage settlements in recent times and the need for words of limitation in creating an estate in fee simple although the use of PRENUPTIAL AGREEMENTS may revive interest in the distinction. An example of an executory trust is a will trust which provides that a certain sum of money is to be laid out by the executors in the purchase of land to be settled on a tenant for life and his children. The terms 'executed' and 'executory' refer to the creation of a trust and not the carrying out of its terms. Tests were established in one case to determine whether a trust was executed or executory which involved asking whether the settlor had been his own conveyancer or draftsman (an executed trust) or whether it was left to the court to make out from the general words the settlor's precise intention (an executory trust). The distinction is that with executed trusts words are construed rather more strictly than with executory trusts. With executory trusts the intention predominates. With foundations, the question of whether a foundation is executory or executed does not arise as no foundation exists until it is incorporated and therefore foundations are executed arrangements. *See* EXECUTED TRUST *and* MARRIAGE SETTLEMENT *and* WILL TRUST.

Exemplary damages, punitive damages: A kind of punishment awarded with a view to discouraging any future wrongs of a defendant. These damages are not merely pecuniary compensation for a loss actually sustained or suffered by the plaintiff. These damages are especially awarded in the case of arbitrary or unconstitutional acts by government servants and where the defendant had intended to make a profit for himself which might exceed the compensation otherwise payable to the claimant. Punitive damages maybe expressly authorised by statute. Historically no English court has awarded exemplary damages against a defaulting trustee even though the *Pensions Act* 1995, Section 10, authorises the imposition of civil penalties for maladministration of occupational pension schemes, but no cases are reported. The award of punitive damages against trustees in other jurisdictions is not a significant occurrence.

Exemption clauses: *See* TRUSTEE EXEMPTION CLAUSES.

Exoneration clauses: *See* TRUSTEE EXEMPTION CLAUSES.

Ex parte: An application in a judicial proceeding made by a person who is not a party to those proceedings but who has an interest in the matter. But usually this means an application by one party to proceedings in the absence of the other, such as with an application for an ex parte injunction where the injunction can be granted without the other party having notice of the application.

Express trust: A trust which is set up according to the intention of the settlor. The setting up of an express trust may take the form of a settlor who already holds what will be the trust property declaring that henceforward he does not hold the property for his own benefit but for the beneficiaries of the trust which he has declared. This form is known as a 'DECLARATION OF TRUST'. The more usual form is that the trust is set up by a written instrument, a deed, which lays down the terms of the trust, the duties of the trustees and details of the beneficiaries, which is executed by the settlor and witnessed; then the settlor transfers the trust assets to the legal ownership of the trustees. This trust instrument is then evidence of the establishment and the terms of the trust and is important if the validity of the trust is disputed, especially when the certainties of intention, subject matter and purpose are considered. *See* CERTAINTIES. An express trust set up by declaration is equally valid although the evidence to support such a declaration must be found from a variety of sources, according to the circumstances in which the declaration was made. *See also* CONSTRUCTIVE TRUST *and* RESULTING TRUST.

Ex tempore: A judgment given by the judge at the conclusion of the hearing. The judgment is given orally where the judge feels he does not need an opportunity to review the evidence, the law, and to prepare his judgment for a later day. An *ex tempore* judgment, once the normal practice in lower courts, is now less frequent.

Extraterritoriality: The exercise, or attempted exercise, by a jurisdiction of its laws in a foreign country. This exercise is generally regarded as a breach of sovereignty of the country in which the laws are expected to be exercised. The effect of some treaties is to secure such extraterritorial influence but, being an agreement between the sovereign states, this is permissible. For example, treaties often give the subject of one country rights in another in respect of their 'complete personal protection, assurance of satisfactory judicial tribunals, and such enjoyment of property for himself and for those who claim under him' that their national law would give them if in their home jurisdiction. The term 'extraterritoriality', is now used frequently to direct attention to the effect of one state wishing to control individuals or a state of affairs in another in the absence of a treaty; this applies particularly in questions of taxation or financial regulation.

F

Fact: One of two elements that are involved in any action. First, there is the question of the existence of a right or liability, which is a question of law; the second is whether there are circumstances which allow that right or liability to be applied; this is a question of fact. Facts must be proved by the prosecution and those facts that are relevant to the case in question are known as 'facts in issue'. This proving of facts is part of the law of evidence. For example, with trusts, the contents of a trust deed are a question of fact and the consequences of those contents are matters of law. Also, the existence of a person as a beneficiary is a matter of fact, i.e. whether that person falls within the class of persons eligible and, then, whether that beneficiary qualifies under the trust, is a question of law. Similar divisions occur in matters relating to foundations.

Fail: An expression used in numerous legal situations and sometimes given a particular meaning. For example, a trust is sometimes said to 'fail' where there is either a defect in the documentation, such as an uncertainty in the drafting, or that the apparent trust created in a document is not supported by the facts. A lack of CERTAINTY OF INTENTION is an example of this failure. Trustees are also said to fail when they do not operate according to the law or the trust deed. But the position is not clear due to conflicting judicial decisions on this point. For example, the words 'failure or determination of the trust' in a will or settlement have been held not to cover the failure of the trust on the grounds of a breach of the RULE AGAINST PERPETUITIES (***Re Hubbard's Will Trusts, Marston v. Angier*** [1963] Ch. 275), but the opposite view was taken in ***Re Robinson's Will Trusts, Public Trustee v. Gotto*** [1963] 1 WLR 628. A further example is where the holder of a life interest disclaims his interest in the trust income; this has been held not to be a determination or failure of the life interest within the terms of the settlement, thus preserving the benefit to others (***Re Young's Settlement Trust, Royal Exchange Assurance v. Taylor-Young*** [1959] 1 W.L.R. 457).

Fair dealing principle: An umbrella term used in many circumstances but, in connection with trusts, may be applied to validate the acquisition by trustees, or by other fiduciaries, of the interests of their beneficiaries. It is necessary to apply this principle to demonstrate that such a transaction was not procured by, and was not a result of, any abuse of the trustees' position. The trustees will be required to demonstrate that no details were concealed from the beneficiaries and that the price paid by the trustees was fair and that the beneficiaries were not required to rely entirely on the trustees' advice. Ultimately, in applying this principle, the court will ask whether a fair-minded and honest person would have agreed that the transaction was fair. The term is also often used in other connections, particularly in a non-consensual use of items protected by copyright for certain purposes, principally research and private study. *See* SELF-DEALING RULE.

Fair market value: The amount for which property would sell on the open market if offered for sale. Similar in concept to an ARM'S LENGTH price. Usually used to distinguish the actual value of property from the replacement value. The term is often used in an insurance context.

Falsa demonstratio non nocet: Literally meaning 'false description does not vitiate'; this is illustrated by an example where a testator, by will, left all his freehold houses, specifying the addresses, to a beneficiary but in fact the testator held the properties on lease. Under this principle the leaseholds passed under the will; the false description of the properties by the testator did not vitiate the substance of his gift.

False: Generally meaning not correct or untrue, around which various maxims have been constructed and which are frequently used in their Latin form. One example is *falsa demonstratio non nocet* (false description does not vitiate). Similarly, *falsus in uno, falsus in omnibus* (false in one, false in all), a maxim which cannot be implicitly relied upon since a person may give utterly false evidence in one case but may be perfectly reliable in other matters. The word is used in a wide variety of other legal situations, such as false pretence, false representation, false statutory declaration and false trade description, etc.

False accounting: This is an offence in the UK under the *Theft Act* 1968, Section 17. It is a serious offence for the purpose of the *Serious Crime Act* 2007, Section 2, and may be based upon an intention by the wrongdoer of obtaining a temporary gain.

Family constitution: *See* FAMILY GOVERNANCE.

Family governance: The way in which a family makes decisions as a family that embraces many considerations, such as which persons are in the family and how decisions are enforced. The opinion has been expressed that good family governance is more valuable than a good trust document (*see* B.R. Hauser, *Trusts in Prime Jurisdictions* 3rd edn). Relevant to establishing good family governance is the existence of a family council, which is a chosen smaller group to act on behalf of the larger family unit and which is given authority to make certain decisions and to communicate these decisions to the larger family. Family governance has the prime purpose of the well-being of the larger family and this may be assisted in many cases by the creation of a family constitution. The principle in a family business, for example, is that all family members should be concerned with the long-term future of the business and all members of the family should agree on various aspects of this to ensure continuity. When it is clear how each of the challenges identified by the family council is to be dealt with, the conclusions should be recorded in a family protocol for signature and agreement by all members. Family governance is particularly relevant in family businesses which are subject to Islamic law but is of a general application. The executive responsibility for complying with family governance may be delegated to a family management board which is approved by the family generally or by the family council.

Family protocols: *See* FAMILY GOVERNANCE.

Family settlement: A settlement, usually by a father or grandfather, where the beneficiaries are the children and the grandchildren and where the intention is to provide for the settlor and the rest of his family. A family settlement is called a 'MARRIAGE SETTLEMENT' when made before marriage. There, the intended husband is given the fee simple of the property to be used as the matrimonial home with the following provisions: (1) that there is security for the payment to the wife of two annuities: one paid during her husband's life called 'pin money' and the other payable after his death called a 'JOINTURE'; (2) to provide for the payment of gross sums of money called 'portions' (*see* PORTION) to such of the younger children of the marriage when they attain majority and; (3) to provide that the property shall go to the eldest son on the husband's death. The trustee is obliged to secure the pin money, the jointure and the portions by charges on the property, then the land is limited to the husband for life and then to the eldest son with the remainder to the sons of the marriage successively in tail. If there are no sons, the land is limited to the daughters as tenants in common in tail and then, failing issue to the daughters, it is then limited to the settlor in fee, i.e. the property reverts to the estate of the original settlor. These basic provisions were frequently modified to secure a better tax position. Under the *Trustee Act* 2000 no new strict settlements can be made. An attempt is made to achieve some of the same stability between married couples by the use of pre and post-nuptial agreements. The term 'settlement' is now loosely applied to such agreements. On the granting of a decree of DIVORCE, NULLITY OF MARRIAGE or other matrimonial measures, the court may make an order varying the benefit of these arrangements to the parties of the marriage (*Matrimonial Causes Act* 1972, Section 174(1)(c)). Settlements may also be varied under the *Inheritance (Provision for Family and Dependents) Act* 1975, Section 2(1)(f)). Family settlements became important to mitigate the severity of an old rule under the *Wills Act* 1837 that a testator had complete discretion on how to dispose of his estate even if this involved cutting off his wife or children. The main protection for spouses and children was a marriage settlement where provision for their income was made in the original settlement. Under the modern law there are extensive provisions to allow the court to intervene in settlements, especially on death, where the court has extensive powers to order the payment of lump sums and instalments and to adjust the ownership of property and settlements in order to support dependants. Similar provisions apply under the *Civil Partnership Act* 2004.

FATCA (*Foreign Account Tax Compliance Act* (FATCA) 2014): A US law aimed to reduce US tax evasion by requiring foreign firms to provide the IRS with information about the offshore accounts of US persons, including US-owned foreign entities. The Act is implemented by non-US governments entering into an agreement with the US. These agreements are: (a) Model 1 Inter-governmental Agreement, by which financial institutions in the non-US country register with the IRS and report information on US accounts to their own tax authorities who then exchange this information with the IRS; and (b) Model 2 Agreement where the financial institutions have to enter into an agreement directly with the IRS. The Model 1 Agreement in many cases is preferable to the Model 2 Agreement since financial institutions using Model 1 will not be subject to a FATCA withholding tax and will not have to impose the tax on any payment to any other non-US financial institution or to any other non-US entity that fails to provide the financial institution with sufficient information to determine their statement (recalcitrant account holders). With Model 1 Agreements, financial institutions do not have to close accounts with recalcitrant account holders.

FATF: *See* FINANCIAL ACTION TASK FORCE.

FATF mutual evaluation reports: These are reports on each member state of the FATF to monitor the implementation by each of the FATF's recommendations. These reports are shared with the regional bodies of the FATF (FSRBs), the Offshore Group of Banking Supervisors (OGBS), the IMF and the World Bank and provide strong stimulus to encourage states to implement the recommendations.

Fee: A legal estate, other than leasehold, in land capable of being inherited but, since 1925, its only modern significance is in the phrase 'FEE SIMPLE ABSOLUTE IN POSSESSION'; all other estates are now equitable interests only. The term 'fee' indicates that the property can descend to a legatee of the owner.

Fee-conditional: *See* CONDITIONAL FEE.

Fee holders: The holder of a fee, such as the holder of a freehold or leasehold estate.

Fee simple absolute in possession: The term 'fee simple' indicates ownership that is not liable to end upon any person's death or by the passage of time or failure of particular heirs. 'Absolute' means the owners' rights are not conditional or liable to be terminated on the occurrence of any event and 'in possession' means the owners' rights are immediate, thus excluding future interests, but possession need not imply actual physical occupation.

Fee tail: A legal estate in land that was abolished under the *Law of Property Act* 1925 and which became an equitable interest known as an 'entailed interest' and not a legal estate. Under the *Trust Act* 2000, new entailed interests cannot be created and any attempt to do so results in the fee simple being transferred to the person nominated as tenant for life. *See* ENTAIL.

Feoffee: A person who is enfeoffed or put in possession.

Feoffer: One who makes a feoffment, i.e. transfers land, etc. An ancient term not now used.

Feoffment: An old term indicating a transfer of freehold land or of a tenement made by delivering actual possession of the land or tenement with a suitable oral statement. At one time it was the only means of conveying freehold land to the person in possession and originally required the overt or public delivery of the possession by the owner to the grantee or purchaser, which was made with a ceremony called 'livery of seisin', i.e. an act which evidenced the handing over of the freehold to the occupier, such as the delivering of keys or other means of exclusive access. However, for the sake of convenience, the terms of a conveyance, instead of being declared by a verbal ceremony, were put into writing to record the terms of the transaction. After the *Statute of Frauds* 1677, writing became necessary to evidence an agreement for a transaction in land and the actual transfer was made by a deed; a written conveyance. This became the normal method of transfer of real property and remains so.

***Fideicomiso*:** A term used in many Latin American countries for a trust-like structure which, although lacking many of the characteristics of the English type of trust, nevertheless complies with the description of trusts for the purpose of the Hague Convention and, if it does not, it is likely to be an ancillary structure under the Convention and to which the Convention then applies.

***Fideicommissa*:** A structure developed in Roman law some centuries after the *FIDUCIA* fell into disuse, which had some similarities to common law trusts. Under the doctrine of *fideicommissa*, it was common practice for a testator to direct, by will, that a beneficiary under that will should hand over property to some other person. Similar practice could be achieved by instructions contained in a separate document or by word of mouth. These gifts were not enforceable in the Republic of Rome but Emperor Augustus ordered them to be carried out under special circumstances where there was glaring dishonesty and where it would be perfidious not to enforce the gift. This arrangement became recognised and legally enforceable under the authority of a special officer, a *praetor fideicommissarius*, although the practice did not seem to become part of the general law and probably survived only under the personal authority of Augustus. According to Buckland, *fideicommissa* were developed out of the Roman inability or willingness to frame a theory for a number of miscellaneous groups and group activities (W.W. Buckland, *The Main*

Institutions of Roman Private Law, 1931). A parallel in English law exists today where many associations are recognised but are neither in law partnerships nor corporations. Although *fideicommissa* is said to be something like a trust, Buckland points out that in all probability the idea was not present in the minds of those whose thoughts eventually flowered into the idea of a trust. It would be excessive to attribute trusts as a descendent of *fideicommissa*. We are warned that where people try to make a modern work, such as a film, using antique texts, the natural result is what Buckland has happily called 'Wardour Street Roman Law', i.e. more cinematic fiction rather than historical truth. The early intimations of legal personality and the rudimentary ideas of *fideicommissa* of establishing separate interests served to inspire the further development of separate legal personalities and influenced civil law practices and, historically, are closely connected with foundations.

Fiducia

1) A trust-like structure present in the Canadian province of Ontario, which differs from the English type of trust in that the beneficiary (and not the trustee) is the legal owner of the property. The structure nevertheless generally conforms to what is required for recognition under the Hague Convention.
2) An arrangement known in the Roman Republic and early Roman Empire where funds were transferred to a trusted person who would be morally obliged to carry out the donor's wishes. This was a contractual matter but proved to be cumbersome in practice; it deprived the borrower of the ownership of the assets transferred without security that they could be recovered. The *fiducia* died out under the later Roman Empire and did not contribute to the development of either trusts or foundations. *Fiducia's* role was taken over by *fideicommissa*.

Fiduciary: A description of the duty of trust and confidence as required by equity: a term of ancient pedigree and somewhat shrouded in mystery. The concept has been called 'A concept in search of a principle' as in English law the concept of a fiduciary is sometimes vague; it is a legal concept of indistinct features and defining characteristics. Despite the uncertainty, the term is of prime importance in the law of trusts. In addition to describing the nature of the duty, it describes the persons who occupy positions of peculiar confidence towards others. The US Internal Revenue Code (Section 7701(a)(b)) states:

> 'The term "fiduciary" means a guardian, trustee, executor, administrator, receiver, conservator, or any person acting in a fiduciary capacity for another person.'

US Treasury Regulation (301.7701-6(b)) contains a similar description. A fiduciary relationship exists between agents and principals, partner and partner, company directors and their companies, trustees and beneficiaries and a foundation council member and the foundation. The categories are not closed; the courts are prepared to consider other relationships as fiduciary. The phrase 'FIDUCIARY DUTY' is used in a way which sometimes gives rise to a mistaken assumption that all fiduciaries have the same duties in all circumstances. This is not correct. A fiduciary (a person owing the fiduciary duty) may, in connection with the person to whom the duty is owed, also have other relationships. However, the core liability has several facets. A fiduciary must act in good faith; he must not make a profit out of his trust; he must not place himself in a position where his duty and his interests may conflict; he may not act for his own benefit or for the benefit of a third person without the informed consent of his principal. This list is not exhaustive but expresses the general nature of the duties of a fiduciary. A fiduciary is someone who has undertaken to act for or on behalf of another in a particular manner in circumstances which gives rise to a relationship of trust and confidence. Something stricter than the morals of the marketplace is required – which was described by US Judge Cardozo as:

> 'Not honesty alone, but the punctilio of an honor the most sensitive, is then the standard of behavior.'

The total scope of the duties is moulded according to the nature of the relationship and the facts of the case. One significant application of a general fiduciary conflict principle is the rule that trustees and executors are generally entitled to no allowance for their care and trouble. This rule is based on the conflict of duty and interest principle – an entitlement to remuneration would be in conflict with the duty to take care that no improper charges are made. This principle extends to other fiduciaries, such as a director of a company who is not entitled to remuneration for services rendered as a director unless there is a specific exception which is agreed by the shareholders. Similarly, a trustee is not entitled to remuneration but this general rule is subject to some important exceptions, principally where there is a charging clause in the trust instrument where Section 28(2) of the *Trustee Act* 2000 authorises a trust corporation or a trustee acting in a professional capacity to charge for professional services and for non-professional services as authorised under the Act, or by an order of the court or by consent of the beneficiaries or under statutory provisions apart from the *Trustee Act* 2000 applicable to certain kinds of trustees. The provisions of the 2000 Act have diminished the importance of orders of the court and the consent of the beneficiaries. Entitlement under other statutory measures applies in favour of the public trustee and custodian trustees. The provisions now relating to the remuneration of trustees under the Act are precise and heavily dependent upon interpretation of what falls within a professional capacity of a trustee (*see* FAIR DEALING *and* SELF-DEALING). The rule that a trustee or other fiduciary cannot, without authority, make a profit directly or indirectly from the beneficiary, or from any other person to whom he acts as a fiduciary, is strictly applied. (***Keech v. Sandford*** (1726) Sel. Cas. Ch 61; 2 Eq. Cas. King 61). Any profit made without proper authorisation cannot be retained. The rule is inflexible and applies regardless of the existence of skill or risk-taking on the part of the trustee and regardless also of whether the profit could not, or would not, have been obtained for the beneficiaries and whether or not the beneficiaries have been prejudiced by the transaction. No relief is given where the trustee has acted in perfect good faith and without any deception or concealment or where the trustee was acting in the best interests of the beneficiary. The rule has been questioned in circumstances where there is no possible conflict between duty and interest, such as where the trustee obtains for himself a profit by dealing with trust assets or affairs in a way which could not be done to provide a profit for the beneficiaries. *Lewin on Trusts*, (19th edn., page 725) considers the extent to which the rule against a fiduciary making a profit depends for its validity on a conflict arising so the profit rules may not apply where there is no possibility of conflict. This position is debatable under present rules. Where a trustee makes an unauthorised profit, that profit is held upon a constructive trust for the beneficiaries subject to a lien in respect of any costs incurred by him in making it. This proprietary remedy ensures that a trustee is not allowed to retain any advantage. A fiduciary can be made liable for damages for breach of trust if an unlawful profit is made as in ***Target Holdings Ltd v. Redferns*** [1995] UKHL 10.

Fiduciary duty: *See* FIDUCIARY.

Fiduciary relationship: A relationship founded on trust and confidence in equity between the parties. These include agents, partners, trustees and company directors. The categories are not closed. In a fiduciary relationship parties are not allowed to make secret profits (and this includes taking a bribe) or expose themselves to a conflict of duty and interest. Any property received contrary to this strict rule holds that property on constructive trust for the true owner. This traditional view was reconfirmed in ***FHR European Ventures LLP and others v. Cedar Capital Partners LLC*** [2014] UKSC 45 by the UK Supreme Court in 2014, where the difference between holding a property on trust and merely being liable for payment of equitable compensation was summarised by Lord Neuberger:

> 'If the bribe or commission is held on trust, the principal has a proprietary claim to it, whereas if the principal merely has a claim for equitable compensation, the claim is not proprietary. The distinction is significant for two main reasons. First, if the agent becomes insolvent, a proprietary claim would effectively give the principal priority over the agent's unsecured creditors, whereas the principal would rank pari passu, i.e., equally, with other unsecured creditors if he only has a claim for compensation. Secondly, if the principal has a proprietary claim to the bribe or commission, he can trace and follow it in equity, whereas (unless we develop the law of equitable tracing beyond its current boundaries) a principal with a right only to equitable compensation would have no such equitable right to trace or follow.'

Fiduziarische Treuhänd: A structure created under German law by the transferring of assets to the *Treuhänder* where, at the same time, the *Treuhänder* enters into a contract with the transferor and undertakes to manage the assets in a particular way for the benefit of the beneficiaries. The arrangement is purely contractual. Beneficiaries usually have a right to enforce the contract by way of a direct claim against the *Treuhänder*. This allows beneficiaries only ordinary contractual rights *IN PERSONAM*. The dual ownership, legal and equitable, on which trusts are based, is unknown in German law, although the *Treuhänder* is subject to a fiduciary obligation either explicitly according to a contractual term or as imposed by the court.

Fieri facias: Literally means: 'that you cause to be made'; abbreviated as fi.fa. and pronounced 'fy fay', which is a writ of execution to enforce a judgment debt by a judge commanding a court officer to take possession of goods and chattels of a debtor for the sum to be recovered by the judgment and to dispose of them for money.

Final judgment: A judgment is final where it at once affects the status of the parties so that it is conclusive. Where a further step is necessary to perfect a judgment it is not final but interlocutory. This can include findings by a judge of the Chancery Division on facts where the issues had not been agreed at the commencement of the trial. The decision there is the final judgment on the facts although the judgment on the issue brought to the court is as yet untried.

Financial Action Task Force (FATF): A body established by the G7 summit in 1987 to combat the increase in misuse of world financial systems by criminals laundering drug money. By 1990, the FATF had issued its 40 Recommendations, which were supplemented after the incident of 11 September 2001. By October 2001, the FATF had its mandate extended to deal with all issues relating to terrorist financing and added 8 Special Recommendations to the existing 40 and a 9th Special Recommendation was added in 2004. The 40 original Recommendations were amended twice, in 1996 and 2003, to become more effective. The influence of the FATF is considerable as it now covers the sheltering of the proceeds of crime and includes corruption. The Recommendations are implemented through the 36 members and other jurisdictions, who observe the FATF Recommendations through the activities of eight regional boards; a total of 180 jurisdictions are committed to carrying out the combating of money laundering. The FATF identifies countries with inadequate anti-money laundering regimes and works with them on improvement.

Financial Conduct Authority (FCA): A UK body structured as a guarantee company that operates independently of the government and which regulates the conduct of retail and wholesale financial firms. Created by the *Financial Services Act* 2012, in conjunction with the Bank of England Policy Committee and the Prudential Regulatory Authority, to replace the previous Financial Services Authority. The FCA has power to investigate organisations and individuals and may ban financial products for up to one year whilst considering an indefinite ban. The FCA also has power to require firms to modify or remove promotions which the FCA finds to be misleading. In addition, the FCA has taken over the regulation of the consumer credit industry and has substantial powers in connection with the conduct of banks, mutual societies and financial advisers.

Financial dispute resolution: Commonly known as 'FDR'. The procedure by way of a meeting in the course of an ANCILLARY RELIEF claim made between spouses, ex-spouses, civil partners or ex-civil partners. An FDR is held for the purpose of discussion and negotiation and the judge merely conducts the appointment to make any consent for order or further directions as agreed between the parties. The parties attending must use their best endeavours to reach agreement on the issue between them. The appointment may take many forms depending upon the judge conducting the meeting.

Financial Intelligence Unit: Centres established under the FATF regime to receive reports of money laundering. These are the Financial Intelligence Units (FIUs) which are the centres for the exchange of information between member countries and which in many cases also operate as investigating bodies.

Financial Services Authority (FSA): The term frequently applied to a state's international financial regulatory body. An alternative name is 'Financial Services Commission'. Variations on the term are used around the world. A prominent organisation given the title FSA in the UK was set up as a company limited by guarantee and funded entirely by fees charged to the financial services industry. It had independent quasi-judicial authority and regulated the financial services industry between 2001 and 2013. A division of the FSA, the Financial Capability Division, broke away from the organisation in 2010 and became known as the Money Advice Service. The FSA was abolished on 19 December 2012, with effect from 1 April 2013, by the *Financial Services Act* 2012. The FSA's responsibilities were split between two new agencies, the Prudential Regulation Authority and the Financial Conduct Authority which, with the Bank of England, share the responsibility for financial regulation in the UK.

***Financial Services and Markets Act* 2000:** An Act that came in to force for most purposes in the UK on 1 December 2001 and provided an all-encompassing regime of financial regulation which was made the responsibility of the UK's then single regulator, the Financial Services Authority, until the changes of 2012 (*see* FINANCIAL SERVICES AUTHORITY). The wide range of regulated activities under the Act is concerned generally with matters relating to the dealing, managing or advising on investments. The Act does not provide for the registration of trusts or trustee operation or matters relating to private foundations or the monitoring of any action in a way which would be incompatible with EU or other international obligations.

FinCEN: The Financial Crimes Enforcement Network in the US Treasury Department which issues regulations in connection with the declaration of financial accounts by taxpayers and covers any entity created, organised or formed under the laws of the United States.

Fines and recoveries: An old action brought against a tenant in tail as a mere procedural matter to enable a court to give a judgment on the nature of a claim for a fine or recovery of land so as to enable the court to give a decision which resulted in the property being no longer an entailed estate. This artificial procedure was abolished by the *Fines and Recoveries Act* 1833, which then enabled a TENANT IN TAIL to bar the entail by a deed. *See* DISENTAILING DEED.

Firewall: Safeguards against unexpected hazards.

First in first out rule: The payment of a debt from a current or running account opened without contrary intention by the parties where the debt is paid off from the earliest deposit made into the account. Where there are frequent deposits and withdrawals in a trust account, the operation of the rule requires careful calculation. For example, if A deposits £1,000 of trust money into a trust account, which is followed by a further deposit of £500 by the trustee of his own money into the same account, a payment of £1,000 to the beneficiaries consumes all the trust money in the account. The rule distinguishes withdrawals that represent trust business from those which are the trustee's own. A further example is where a trustee buys a painting using a withdrawal from the trust account and then withdraws money from the same account for his own personal use; the beneficiaries can be reassured that if the painting was purchased by money from the account which was original trust money then the painting is trust property. Deposits made by the trustee after the original trust money was deposited do not affect the application of this rule. In the example above the 'first in first out' rule was concerned with dealings by the trustee on behalf of the trust. Complications of this nature can arise where a trustee is a relation of the beneficiaries under circumstances where the trustee does not consider it necessary to establish a separate bank account for the trust business. This is in contrast to professional trustees who maintain strict discipline over using a trust account only for trust business.

Fit and proper: A term used in various connections requiring that the persons involved should be competent in their operation and well informed and equipped. The precise meaning is taken from the context in which the phrase appears.

FIU: *See* FINANCIAL INTELLIGENCE UNIT.

Fixed assets: Assets that are normally expected to be permanently available for the purpose of carrying on a business and a term which may be used in a debenture to define the property which is security for the loan made to a company and where the charge is then constituted as a fixed charge.

Fixed charge: A specific charge which, without further process, attaches to an ascertained and definite item of property, or property which is capable of being ascertained and defined, to secure a loan or other financial commitment of a debtor. This contrasts with a 'floating charge', which is ambulatory, shifting in its nature and which hovers over the entire property of the debtor until some event occurs or some act is done which causes the floating charge to settle on the subject of the charge, whatever it may be, from time to time. In other words, the floating charge is said to crystallise and the property affected is then subject to a fixed charge in favour of the debtor. A fixed charge grants property rights which are enforceable in the event of the debtor's insolvency and is a means of allowing the claimant, a creditor or an assignee of the creditor's rights, to be paid the amount of money secured by the charge and, on default of the debtor, to seize the property to satisfy the claim. The claimant can only extract from the property the amount which is owed to him. Where the book debts of a company are subject to a fixed charge, it is necessary that the book debts are put into a separate account which is then made subject to the fixed charge. If this is not done, the charge is then a floating charge; the charge is not over an ascertained and definite item of property. *See* FLOATING CHARGES.

Fixed trust: An express trust in which the identity and interests of the beneficiaries are laid down as opposed to a discretionary trust. A fixed trust is sometimes called an 'interest in possession trust': the beneficiaries know what their entitlement is or will be and, although they may not have immediate possession, they possess an equitable interest in the trust assets. *See* UNIT TRUSTS, DISCRETIONARY TRUSTS *and* INTEREST IN POSSESSION.

Fixtures: A term of no precise legal meaning but which is generally applied to articles of personal property that have been affixed to houses or lands and which, in its most extensive sense, means that anything annexed to the freehold becomes part of that freehold. Despite the variation in the meaning of the term in various contexts, the general rule is that if the owner or occupier of land fixes or annexes anything to the freehold it becomes part of that freehold and ownership of it passes with the freehold. The chattels fixed to freehold pass with freehold on the bankruptcy of the owner and, similarly, no fixture can be taken in distress for rent. Exceptions to the rule permit fixtures left on land by a testator or tenant for life to pass to the personal representatives with its other chattels. The rule is also relaxed between tenant and landlord. There, fixtures are divided into landlord's fixtures, those which belong to the landlord that go with the property and cannot be removed by the tenant, and tenant's fixtures. The latter may be removed by the tenant at any time during his tenancy. These tenants' fixtures are either trade fixtures, i.e. articles erected by the tenant solely for the purpose of trade or manufacturing, such as machinery, or ornamental fixtures put up for domestic use or ornamentation, such as bookcases and marble chimney pieces; if not fixed to the soil they are not fixtures at all and may be removed at will. The latter are sometimes referred to as 'fittings'. The term is subject to a variety of constructions of definitions in different contexts. Chattels fixed to property held in trust are subject to the general rule.

Flight clause: A clause in a trust deed or in a foundation's charter or regulations which enables a trust or foundation to forsake its present jurisdiction and move to another and thereby become subject to the laws of that new jurisdiction. The decision for a trust or foundation to emigrate from one country to another is usually made, as required by the constitutional documents, by the protector, as such a decision is outside the normal ambit of trustees' and foundation councils' competence. A flight clause can only be brought into effect in the event of some major crisis which is defined in the constitutional documents. These crises may be civil unrest, revolution or impending onerous tax rates, where a decision to change jurisdictions may be taken for the benefit of a trust or foundation and for the advantage of the beneficiaries on the grounds that setting up elsewhere would be advantageous. Before a trust or foundation can emigrate it is necessary that the law of the place of the existing jurisdiction in which the trust is resident, or the foundation is registered, includes in its law a provision that emigration is possible. It is also required that the jurisdiction of choice has a provision in its law that trusts and foundations may migrate into that jurisdiction. The law will lay down the procedures or formalities by which a foreign trust or foundation can transform itself into a structure under the new jurisdiction. In the event of a flight clause being implemented, a change of trustees may be desirable. Therefore, the procedures for a change in the legal ownership of the trust assets into that of the new trustees must be considered. If there is no change in the trustees, then perhaps some notification in respect of the trust's property should be lodged with companies, registries, banks etc., in connection with the change of address of the trust, even though the trustees remain the same. If one subsidiary of an international bank ceases to be trustee, and another subsidiary takes over the job, the formalities of transfer will be required. If an international trust management subsidiary of an international bank, which operates as trustee in several jurisdictions, is to continue as trustee, it need not carry out any of these changes.

Floating charges: A form of a charge that has an identified value and which takes effect over a fluctuating pool of property only crystallising at a point in time identified in the loan agreement. This is opposed to a fixed charge which requires that property at issue be held immobile for the purpose of establishing a property right in the chargee that is subject to the charger's performance of the relevant payment obligations. A floating charge permits a person or company charging the property to use it for the purpose of the business without tying that property down. The owner of the property can use the property as though he is the absolute owner and may dispose of it. Where a person takes out a floating charge and then purports to create a trust over the property which exceeds the value of the loan secured by the floating charge, there may be a problem as to whether the certainty of intention to create a trust existed and over the certainty of subject matter due to the difficulty in defining the exact property over which the trust would exist. *See* FIXED CHARGE.

Floating trust: A trust that is not unlike a 'Whatever is left' trust. The term was applied by Brightman J in ***Ottaway v. Norman*** [1972] Ch. 698, following an Australian case, ***Birmingham v. Renfrew*** (1937) 57 CLR 666, where a trust would remain in suspense during the life of the trustee and crystallise on the death of that trustee to whatever property was comprised within the trustee's estate. This is best explained by the facts of ***Ottaway v. Norman*** where Miss Hodges' employer, Mr. Ottaway, bequeathed his house to her on the terms that she would leave it by her own will to Mr. Ottaway's son. There was evidence that Miss Hodges also undertook to leave to Mr. Ottaway's son the furniture and other contents of the house including her own money. Miss Hodges died and in her will purported to leave all her property to a cousin. Brightman J considered that there was a constructive trust upon the house in the hands of Miss Hodges' executors. He also concluded that there was a secret trust over the furniture and fixtures which Miss Hodges had received under Mr. Ottaway's will. The undertaking during Miss Hodges' life that she would include her own property and money in her will in favour of Mr. Ottaway's son was considered by Brightman J to be held in a floating trust based upon the Australian case. He was not convinced that such an arrangement had been accepted by Miss Hodges but, had this been her intention, he accepted that this obligation could be enforced against her estate. The assets of the floating trust remained in suspense during her life to be crystallised on her death. The trust assets would be whatever personal assets and money she had at her death (thus precluding the making of even small pecuniary legacies of her own). A comparison can be made between assets that are comprised in a floating trust and the assets of a company that are subject to a floating charge. Similar reasoning was applied to mutual wills in ***Re Cleaver*** [1981] 1 WLR 939, without clearly considering whether property not received under a mutual will was bound by a floating trust. If the construction of the facts did not go so far as to indicate the existence of a floating trust and the MUTUAL WILLS were interpreted as enforceable contracts, there would have been no need to consider the floating trust idea as the survivor would have simply taken the property under the mutual will and thereafter could have set up a trust according to the terms of that mutual will. *See* 'WHATEVER IS LEFT' TRUST *and* SECRET TRUST.

Flow-through provisions: An indication that a provision in an agreement or stage in an arrangement, which usually has a financial implication, is ignored in so far as the monetary or tax obligations are calculated without regard to the effect of that provision or stage of the arrangement. The term is sometimes applicable to trust income when distributed to a beneficiary where some types of income retain the nature they had when received by the trustee; these include income derived from interest, capital gains or dividends and which when paid out to beneficiaries are allowed by flow-through provisions to be treated in the hands of the beneficiary as retaining the same form, i.e. the payments are treated as interest, capital gains or dividends. These items are included in the beneficiaries' tax returns in the same category in which they were received by the trustees. Beneficiaries are then entitled to the same tax reliefs as if they had been earned directly.

Flying freehold: A term without precise legal meaning used to describe freehold property built over land belonging to another, such as a room built by 'A', the freehold owner of neighbouring property that is built over a passageway belonging to 'B' who also owns the freehold of the land. These are unattractive to buyers and sellers because they sometimes produce problems concerning access and support and insurance and covenants to repair. The converse situation is where the occupier of a basement or cellar of one property extends under the property of an adjoining house which might be termed 'creeping freehold'.

Following: A rule by which the physical location of a tangible thing is identified for the purpose of a legal claim where the possession of the thing has passed to a different number of persons in sequence. The word 'following' is used to determine the thing's physical location; a purely physical exercise that must be distinguished from tracing, which is more concerned with identifying whatever has been received in substitution for the original thing. For example, if a car is stolen the victim can generally exercise his interest against any subsequent purchaser of the car; the victim is not looking at any substitute asset. *See* TRACING.

Forced heirship: A principle adopted in many civil law jurisdictions under which a person's estate on death may only devolve between specified relatives who each receive a predetermined proportion, and which cannot be overridden by will, and where the testator only has a percentage of his/her assets for free distribution. The avoidance of forced heirship is a frequent use of international trusts and foundations where the settlor or the founder places assets in one of these vehicles for the benefit of beneficiaries, or for a purpose, during his lifetime or by will to become effective on his death or at some subsequent time.

The intention is that the settlor or founder's personal estate will be permanently diminished during his lifetime by diverting capital to either a trust or foundation and thus reduce the value of the estate on which forced heirship payments will be levied. International trusts frequently contain a clause stating that no action shall be brought under a trust by anyone claiming forced heirship rights. Such a clause will be valid in the jurisdiction in which the trust is set up and in other jurisdictions if the trust of the deceased's assets is recognised according to the proper law of the trust.

Force majeure /*vis major* /Act of God: French, Latin and English equivalents applied to forces of nature of irresistible compulsion that may be included in a contract to excuse non-performance of the contract by a change of circumstances of such overwhelming coercion. The term is also used to excuse liability due to the effects of inevitable accidents that are not caused by nature but which nevertheless occur notwithstanding reasonable precautions having been taken. The preferable term is 'force majeure'; the term 'Act of God' might imply positive intervention of the Deity, which might be apparent in severe climatic events but not in other situations in which the term force majeure is applied, although the event has been brought about by the act of man. This phrase is of no direct application to trusts or foundations but relevant in connection with losses of trust and foundation assets and their insurances.

Foreclosure: The action brought by a MORTGAGEE (the lender) when a MORTGAGOR (the borrower) fails to pay off the mortgage debt within the proper time. The mortgagee can bring the action to deprive or debar the right of the mortgagor of his right of redemption, i.e. the mortgagor loses his rights to receive the property free of any encumbrance. The mortgagee is then entitled to seize the property and sell it. If the mortgagor obtains more on the sale of a property than he is due under the mortgage, he holds the balance on a RESULTING TRUST for the mortgagee. Hence the expression 'REDEEM UP, FORECLOSE DOWN' expressing fundamental rights attached to a mortgage, which summarises the right of the mortgagor to repay (redeem) the loan at any time and the rights of the mortgagee to foreclose in the event of default.

Foreign judgments: A judgment of a foreign court cannot be enforced in the UK without first being recognised by the UK legal system. This recognition takes several forms, the most significant of which in Europe is the recognition of judgments from a court within the EC recognised under Council Regulation EC No. 44/2001. Judgments from other courts, i.e. those outside the EU, depend on their enforcement upon the identity of the foreign court that gave the judgment. Upon this is determined the set of rules that are applied. A judgment from a Swiss court depends upon the Lugano Convention, which is a parallel to EC Regulation 44/2001 and applies between EC states and states of the European Free Trade Zone (EFTA) (OJ L1998 319/9). Common law rules govern judgments made in a US court. These common law rules in the UK depend upon the merits of the claim: the foreign judgment must be final and conclusive, for a fixed sum of money, and the judgment does not involve the enforcement of a foreign penalty or revenue or other public law measure and is not in conflict with provisions relating to the protection of trading interests of the enforcing state. A further source on which enforcement can be based is the *Foreign Judgment (Reciprocal Enforcement) Act* 1933, which provides that a foreign judgment may be registered when a judgment comes from a foreign state which gives reciprocal treatment to UK judgments. A judgment registered under this Act takes effect in the UK as if the judgment had been awarded by a UK court. This will apply to judgments from a wide range of foreign countries; for example, judgments from an Israeli court. Reciprocal treatment under the Act, which is required for registration, requires that the judgment closely mirrors the requirements for registration as provided by the common law. An earlier Act, the *Administration of Justice Act* 1920, applies to judgments of colonial and commonwealth superior courts. A judgment there depends upon it being just and convenient and that the judgment should be enforced in the UK and be interpreted in accordance with the common law rules without actually repeating them. Where none of these regimes apply, a foreign money judgment can be pursued as a claim for a debt under English common law. *See* LUGANO CONVENTION ON JURISDICTION AND THE ENFORCEMENT OF JUDGMENTS IN CIVIL AND COMMERCIAL MATTERS 1988 *and* EC COUNCIL REGULATION 44/200.

Foreign law: For the purposes of conflict of laws and private international law, foreign law in England means any law other than that of England and therefore includes the law of Northern Ireland, Scotland, the Channel Islands, the Isle of Man, the law of each American or Australian state or Canadian province and New Zealand, as well as the laws of other countries with different legal systems. English courts retain an overriding power to refuse the enforcement or recognition of foreign law that is against English public policy or that is a matter of foreign penal or revenue law, or that is based on discriminatory law. Foreign law, when raised in UK courts, is a question of fact that must be decided by the judge on expert evidence produced before him. Where the terms of foreign law have not been proved, it is presumed that the foreign law is the same as English law. In some countries the establishment of foreign law is a question of law and this imposes a duty on the judge, whereas in English law it is a question of fact to be proved by the party relying on it. Evidence of this question of fact must be provided by a practising lawyer or a judge from the country concerned.

Foreign resident trustee: Although not prohibited by law, the appointment of a trustee resident abroad may require justification before a UK court unless permitted by the trust instrument. The appointment of a foreign resident trustee of an English trust may be regarded as improper, or at least questioned, unless exceptional circumstances apply. Also, if such an appointment is made improperly, it may be set aside by a beneficiary who has not consented; the exceptional nature of circumstances is for the appointer to decide. A significant reason for appointing foreign resident trustees is where the beneficiaries are abroad. Formerly, approval was given for local administrative purposes but nowadays the pre-eminent concern is with tax. The matter usually comes before the courts in connection with the court's jurisdiction to approve variations of trusts, particularly where the variation request is that the trust should no longer be resident in the UK for which purpose foreign resident trustees are necessary (***Re Weston's Settlements*** [1968] 3 All ER 338).

Forfeiture clause: A clause which is designed to protect against the validity of an arrangement or contract being challenged and, in connection with trusts, a clause in the trust deed designed to protect a trust from any beneficiary's attempt to challenge its validity or any of the dispositions of the trust assets. Also called 'NO CONTEST CLAUSES', these have existed for centuries, particularly in wills. Where the clause is framed in the nature of a threat, it is not valid and where the original beneficial interest is to be forfeited there must be a specific clause that can effectively transfer the assets to specified beneficiaries or to the testator's estate where the clause is contained in a will. Also, in connection with forfeiture clauses in wills, any attempt to prevent a statutory claim is contrary to public policy. In *AN v. Barclays Private Bank and Trust (Cayman) Limited* [2006] 9 ITELR 630, a judgment on a forfeiture clause, in an INTER VIVOS trust, attempted to exclude as a beneficiary under the trust anyone who contested the validity of the trust or the provisions relating to the transfer of any property to the trustees. The court held that such a provision was void for uncertainty and repugnancy as it would have prevented beneficiaries having recourse to the court to properly enforce the trust. A superior court took a different view and examined the context of the whole settlement which was clearly intended to be a trust that was to be enforceable by the beneficiaries notwithstanding the possible exclusion of those who contested the validity of the trust; the trustees should have observed this principle, valid under Cayman Island law, which governed the trust, before bringing their action for forfeiture.

Forfeiture rule: A rule which is frequently referred to in connection with the imposition of constructive trusts that prevents a person who unlawfully kills another benefitting from the crime. For example, the basic rule was expressed by the UK Law Commission as:

> "In *Re DWS (deceased)* [[2001] Ch 568 (CA)] a person killed both his parent, neither of whom left a will. The killer was not allowed to inherit from them, under a rule of law known as the forfeiture rule. The Court of Appeal decided that not only the killer, but also his son, was excluded from inheriting. The inheritance went instead to the couple's other relatives."

Before the *Estates of Deceased Persons (Forfeiture Rule and Law of Succession) Act* 2011, a victim's will was construed on the basis that the gift of property to the killer was avoided by the arising of a CONSTRUCTIVE TRUST. If the deceased died intestate, then the rules of intestacy were similarly construed. The rule applied widely and included manslaughter, murder, incitement to murder, suicide pacts and where death followed because of the diminished responsibility of the offender, but judicial decisions tended to restrict the rule's application to murder or in situations where the killing was deliberate or intentional. From 1 February 2012 the Act provides that the victim's estate devolves as though the killer died immediately before the victim. This results in the killer's own children not being barred from inheriting despite the killer forfeiting the property which he might otherwise have received. Previously any gift to the killer was avoided by the constructive trust and would not have passed to the killer's own children. The rule is applied differently in Canada, Australia, New Zealand and in some courts of the US where a constructive trust is imposed on half of the victim's estate. The forfeiture rule may be wholly or partially relieved by the discretion of the court where a person is convicted of unlawfully killing except in the case of murder.

Formal requirements – land: The word 'formal' is sometimes used to imply additional significance or importance of the manner or form by which something is done. It may be used to attempt to diminish the significance or importance of the substantive matter, e.g. by describing requirements of a deed as being 'merely formal'. Sometimes formalities are necessary. Any declaration of trust concerning land, or any interest in land, must be made manifest and proved in writing and signed by the person who was able to declare such trust (Section 53(1)(b), *Law of Property Act* 1925) or made by will. This requirement of a written declaration only applies to express trusts since resulting and constructive trusts arise by operation of the law and may be enforced in the absence of writing. The transfer of an equitable interest or trust existing at the time of the disposal must be in writing (Section 53 (1)(c)) signed by the person disposing of the trust or interest or by his authorised agent. In this case the declaration must actually be made in writing, not merely evidenced in this way, although it may be in two documents of which only one is signed provided that reference is made to the other. That is, a disposition of an equitable interest or trust must be in writing and this applies for any equitable assignment falling within this provision, such as a direct assignment of an interest under a trust to an assignee or to an assignee's trustees or where trustees are directed to hold property on behalf of an assignee of an equitable interest or a trust. On the other hand, assignments that are not subject to these provisions or other similar statutory provisions may be made informally, even by way of mouth. A trust, when set up, is considered incompletely constituted until the trust assets are transferred to the trustees. The nature of this transfer depends upon the nature of the assets concerned and the transfer may require some formalities to be completed, such as a transfer of company shares into the legal ownership of the trustees. This does not affect the creation or operation of resulting, implied or constructive trusts, such as where a trust is declared orally for value, and although there is no memorandum required, as required under Section 53(1)(b), it is a contract that is capable of specific performance. Also, SECRET TRUSTS and a HALF-SECRET TRUST may come within the exclusion as do common intention constructive trusts. Writing may be required with procedural matters which are subject to the laws of the forum that governs matters of procedure. Therefore, in respect of foreign land, the procedure depends upon the law where the land is situated, where a trust of land may not need to be declared in writing but may require to be 'manifested and proved' in writing, i.e. there must be some written evidence of the existence of the trust. With foundations, the existence of a foundation depends upon the intention of the parties. This is normally recorded in the foundation charter and therefore the question of whether writing is necessary is irrelevant. In the past, various events have needed to be evidenced in writing to prevent mistakes occurring. This originated under the *Statute of Frauds* 1677 where some evidence in writing was required to prevent an allegation of fraud being maintained. *See* TRANSFER OF EQUITABLE INTERESTS *and* CONTRACTS FOR THE SALE OF LAND.

Formal requirements – personal property: Personalty, or personal property, consists of all property that is not realty and includes money, goods, chattels, cattle, stocks and shares, securities and debts, and also leaseholds. The term 'personalty' covers either personal property in possession or in action; the latter applies where the person is not in actual occupation of the thing, but only has a right which arises from a contract that enables possession of the personalty to be recoverable by action at law. The formal requirements to acquire personalty vary according to the personalty concerned; in particular, leaseholds (which are personal property despite being almost indistinguishable from realty) require a conveyancing procedure similar to that of realty and require a registration of the property at a Land Registry. The transfer of stocks and shares and securities may require the execution of a transfer form by the transferor and submission to the registered office of the company or other organisation concerned for registration with sometimes the issue of a new share certificate or an entry into an electronic record if it is a paperless transaction. Ships are another form of personalty that have a formal transfer registration and where a transfer of ownership requires registration at the Ships Registry in the jurisdiction in which the ship is registered. This requires a Bill of Sale; BILLS OF SALE are required to transfer personal property when a more formal procedure is required, i.e., where the object sold is of public importance, or where the goods are sold by order of the court, or where the object sold is left in the possession of the seller, such as where a painting is sold but left hanging on the wall of the transferor's property. Then, the Bill of Sale is registered under the *Bills of Sale Act* (1878) Amendment Act 1882. This registration acts as the evidence that the property has been transferred. Documentary evidence is traditionally used where there is a transfer of other personalty when the registration takes place in another manner, such as on a transfer of an aircraft. Where the personalty transferred is incorporeal, such as a chose in action, the transfer of possession, as evidence of the transfer, is more difficult. It may then be necessary for the transferor to execute a formal deed of assignment by which he transfers his interest in the incorporeal asset to the transferee and gives notice to all persons concerned. This applies particularly when a debt is assigned; the transferor issues a notice to the creditor of the transfer (among other reasons so that the creditor knows to whom he must pay the amount owed to clear his obligation). However, no formality is necessary for the majority of other transfers of personalty, although the purchaser may ask for a receipt as evidence that he has paid the purchase price.

Formal validity of a will: The proper execution of a will which conforms to the legal requirements of the law which governs the formalities for wills, and which is usually considered to be where the testator has a foreign domicile or owns assets.

Forum: The place or country in which a case is being heard.

Forum conveniens* and *forum non-conveniens*:** *Forum conveniens* means the convenient forum for a dispute to be heard. The doctrine was developed in Scotland during the 19th century by which a court may decline to accept jurisdiction over a case so as to allow the matter to be tried in an alternative and more appropriate forum, usually a foreign court. The doctrine was accepted in England in ***Spiliada Maritime Corp. v. Cansulex Ltd [1987] A.C.461, and may be applied completely at the court's discretion. The party, usually the defendant, must submit the identity of the alternative jurisdiction and then satisfy the court that the foreign court is available, competent and will provide justice. Factors which affect a court's decision include the location of the witnesses and of the documents, the language of the witnesses and the citizenship of the parties. Generally, the burden of proof rests upon the defendant to persuade the court to exercise its discretion, then the burden shifts to the claimant to show that there are special reasons why the action should not be moved and that the trial should take place in the claimant's chosen court. The doctrine has been curtailed by the European Court of Justice following the *Brussels Regulation* (44/2001). The doctrine of *forum non-conveniens* is the reverse of this; the appellant to the court claims that the court is not the most suitable one in which to hear the complaint, and similar procedures have to be complied with.

Forum shopping: The choosing of a country by a party, or the parties to an agreement or other transaction, so that any subsequent legal proceedings should be brought in the chosen forum on the basis that the chosen forum's laws are most favourable to the party or parties' situation. This may happen in choosing a forum in connection with business operations with a view to monitoring gains and profits. It applies particularly to the choice of the jurisdiction to which a financial transaction should be subject, on account of the application of an advantageous tax regime.

Foundation council: The governing body of a foundation, particularly of PRIVATE FOUNDATIONS, and authorised according to the terms laid down by the founder in the foundation CHARTER. The number of individuals comprising a foundation council is decided according to the governing law or the charter, on which also depends whether corporations or other foundations can be members. The foundation council operates with a FIDUCIARY DUTY to the foundation itself, unlike trustees who have a fiduciary duty to the beneficiaries.

Foundations, generally: A legal entity set up by a founder for public or philanthropic purposes which invests and uses assets provided by the founder or other persons for the furtherance of its purposes. Foundations (sometimes referred to as public foundations) are common structures in civil law countries, where there may be some advantage to the founder or to his family but where the benefit is ancillary to the main purpose of benefiting the foundation's public or philanthropic interests. For example, tax relief may be available on the amounts given to endow the foundation. The term is also used imprecisely and non-legally to describe an organisation that has a dignified status or purpose, such as a hospital, college or philanthropic organisation, whose legal form may be a trust or company. An example of this is the setting up under the National Health Service in the UK of hospital foundations which are entitled to manage their own finances and administration. A foundation in a civil law jurisdiction established solely for philanthropic or charitable purposes may be set up informally under the civil law's ability to recognise the formation of a legal entity without the need for registration and approval as is required under common law. A foundation of charitable or philanthropic purposes differs from a private foundation which has, as its objects, primarily the preservation of family assets and their distribution according to the wishes of the founder. *See* PRIVATE FOUNDATIONS (SOMETIMES CALLED PRIVATE INTEREST FOUNDATIONS).

Foundation, private: A foundation based upon civil law principles and which exists to administer its assets, principally provided by the founder, for the benefit of beneficiaries or for a purpose according to the instructions of the founder contained in the foundation charter; a legal entity without members. Private foundations have been introduced in common law countries by legislation, *see* FOUNDATION, PRIVATE, LEGISLATION, with the objective of adding private foundations to their range of asset planning vehicles as an alternative to trusts. A formal definition of a private foundation is:

> 'A private foundation is a self-governing separate revocable or irrevocable legal entity, managed by a foundation council or similar body in conjunction with the founder or protector, according to the foundation constitution and the law. A private foundation is set up by the declaration, registration or incorporation, by or on behalf of a founder to hold, administer and distribute the foundation's endowment for the benefit of beneficiaries, or for a purpose, where the ownership of the foundation assets rests with the foundation council, according to the charter and the law under which the foundation is set up.'

When a jurisdiction introduces foundations by legislation, there is frequently no distinction made in the legislation between private foundations and those set up for charitable or philanthropic purposes. The distinction is made within a foundation's individual constitution. In some cases, the inclusion of charitable or philanthropic foundations in the same law as private foundations has been made for the purpose of widening the attraction of a jurisdiction's laws, although the main reason for introducing foundations is to provide an investment vehicle as an alternative to trusts. The term 'private foundation', as used in the US and Canada, has a different meaning whereby donations can be made to a private foundation and the tax advantages permitted for those payments are granted because the donation is for charitable purposes and neither the founder, his family, nor any other individual, can obtain any interest under the arrangement. In both countries, these private foundations are subject to complex tax provisions.

Foundation, private, legislation: Legislation introducing private foundations in both common law and civil law jurisdictions for the purpose of attracting investment business into the jurisdiction. The legislation is frequently drafted widely enough to also allow the formation of public foundations, i.e. foundations for charitable purposes. Also, in addition to the special laws on private foundations listed below, many established civil law countries' laws on foundations may also confer favourable tax exemptions on the founders under certain circumstances. Jurisdictions in which special laws have been enacted introducing private foundations include:

Anguilla: The Anguilla Foundation Act 2008.

Antigua and Barbuda:International Foundations Act 2007.

Austria: Federal Act on Private Foundations 1993 (Amended 2001, 2005, 2008 and 2010).

Bahamas: The Foundations Act 2004 (Chapter 369D of the Statute Law of The Bahamas, 2000 edition).

Belize: International Foundations Act, Act No. 2 of 2010.

Cayman Islands: Companies Law (2013 Revision), as amended by the Foundations Law.

Cook Islands: Foundations Act 2012 (No. 11 of 3 July 2013).

Curaçao: The Corporate Code (Book 2 of the Curaçao Civil Code), Revised 1 January 2012.

Guernsey: The Foundations (Guernsey) Law, 2012.

Indonesia: Law No. 16, 2001 on Foundations (Yayasan), as amended by Law No. 28 of 2004.

Isle of Man: Foundations Act 2011.

Jersey: Foundations (Jersey) Law 2009, the Foundation's (Continuance) (Jersey) Regulations 2009, the Foundations (Mergers) (Jersey) Regulations 2009, and the Foundations (Winding Up) (Jersey) Regulations 2009.

Labuan: Labuan Foundations Act 2010 (Act 706), in conjunction with the Labuan Islamic Financial Services and Securities Act 2010 (Act 705).

Liberia: Chapter 60, Title 5, Association's Law as Amended 2002.

Liechtenstein: The Foundation Law, 1 April 2009, as Art. 552, §§1-41 Personen-und Gesellschaftsrecht, 'PGR'.

Malta: 2nd Schedule to the Civil Code, the Civil Code (2nd Schedule) (Fees) Regulations, the Civil Code (2nd Schedule) (Notifications and Forms) Regulations, and the Amalgamation of Organisations Regulations.

Mauritius: Foundations Act 2012.

Netherlands: The Dutch Civil Code, Book 2 (Legal Persons), Book 4 (Law of Inheritance) with an additional provision regarding foundations formed by will (Art. 4: 135).

Nevis: The Multiform Foundations Ordinance 2004, as amended.

Panama: Law 25 of 1995 and Executive Decree 417 of 1995 (on the public registry, formation and extension).

St Kitts: Foundations Act 2003 (No. 8 of 2003).

San Marino: Article 4(3) of the Law of 13 June 1990 (No. 68 Company Law).

Seychelles: Foundations Act 2009.

Founder: The person who sets up a private or public foundation. The term is used generally to cover the person or persons (including corporate persons) who contribute the original assets. Subject to the governing law, anyone who subsequently provides assets for the foundation is not regarded as the founder.

Fraud: A term covering all forms of DECEIT aimed at making illicit gains or inflicting illicit losses, and which is generally concerned with money interests. Common law fraud is an unfair advantage obtained by means of a false representation of fact made knowingly or without belief in its truth or recklessly not caring whether it is true. Fraud itself may constitute a tort of deceit and in litigation any collateral allegation of fraud may taint the evidence of a party. In equity, fraud is more generally a breach of rules of fair dealing which may not always imply the same sense of unlawfulness as fraud at common law. Fraud and the adjective 'fraudulent' are applied to a wide range of activities. *See* FRAUD ON A MINORITY, FRAUD ON A POWER *and* FRAUDULENT CONVEYANCE.

Fraud on a minority: The exercise of voting powers by a majority of members of a company where the votes do not benefit the company as a whole but are intended to produce an advantage for the majority at the cost of the minority shareholders.

Fraud on a power: The exercise of a special POWER OF APPOINTMENT by an unjustified person or with an unjustified intention or an improper use of the power for a collateral purpose. The exercise of a special power of appointment that is not BONA FIDE and not for the intended purpose but which is outside the purpose of the instrument creating the power, and which cannot be justified, is said to be a fraud on the power and equity holds it to be bad. The term 'fraud' is used to indicate an excessive exercise of a power and, as stated in ***Vatcher v. Paul*** [1915] A.C. 372:

> 'The term fraud in connection with frauds on a power does not necessarily denote any conduct on the part of the appointor amounting to fraud in the common law meaning of the term or any conduct which could be properly termed dishonest or immoral. It merely means that the power has been exercised for a purpose, or with an intention, beyond the scope of or not justified by the instrument creating the power.'

The doctrine of fraud on a power is concerned with the intention or purpose of the holder and contrasts with the doctrine of EXCESS EXECUTION.

Fraud on creditors: A transfer of assets by a debtor with the intention of avoiding payment to a creditor or creditors in respect of a debt or debts which exist at the time of the transfer. Any such transfer is known as a 'FRAUDULENT CONVEYANCE' and may take any of the following forms:

- a transfer when the debtor was insolvent or was rendered insolvent by the transfer;
- where the conveyance was made without a fair consideration where the transferor was left with unreasonably small capital;
- conveyances made without fair consideration when the transferor believes he will incur debts beyond his ability to pay as the debts mature; or
- conveyances made or obligations incurred with the actual intent to hinder, delay or defraud present or future creditors.

The common feature in fraudulent conveyance requires the intention of harming creditors. The intention is difficult to prove and the courts have laid down standards known as 'badges of fraud' (a list of 10 factors which, if any is present, might be regarded as evidence of fraud having been committed by one of the parties), which was first established in 1602 (***Twyne's case*** (1602) 3 Co Rep 80b). The consequence of a transaction found to be fraudulent is that it will not be enforced; thus a trust or foundation set up as a fraud on creditors will be illegal and invalid. The principle was first enacted by the *Statute of Elizabeth* 1571. The present law in the UK is under the *Insolvency Act* 1986, Section 423(5). The principle frequently appears in offshore legislation and in US and other common law jurisdictions. *See* BADGES OF FRAUD.

Fraudulent conveyance: The conveyance of property to another to avoid the property being used for the benefit of creditors. Such a transfer is termed fraudulent since the intention is to place property outside the reach of creditors to whom a debt is owed at the time of the conveyance. For example, the transfer of part of land without valuable consideration with the intent of defrauding a subsequent purchaser is a fraudulent conveyance. *See* BADGES OF FRAUD *and* FRAUD ON CREDITORS.

Freehold: A term that denotes the TENURE by which land may be held where the duration of the estate is uncertain. This common feature applies to freeholds of inheritance, i.e. FEE SIMPLE ABSOLUTE IN POSSESSION or to freeholds which were not of inheritance but for life; both being freehold estates, the duration of which is uncertain. However, since the *Law of Property Act* 1925, only the fee simple absolute in possession and a TERM OF YEARS ABSOLUTE can exist as separate legal estates. The consequence is that all other estates are equitable. A term of years, although a legal estate, is not freehold but known as 'leasehold'; by its nature, a leasehold estate is not of uncertain duration. The other freehold estates converted into equitable estates are limited in duration as life estates and therefore outside the concept of freehold.

Freezing injunction: Previously known as 'a MAREVA INJUNCTION' (from the case where it was first formulated in ***Mareva Compania Naviera SA v. International Bulk Carriers SA (The Mareva)*** [1980] 1 All ER 213), which was renamed in the UK Civil Procedure Rules 1998 (CPR 25.1(f)). A court order in the UK Civil Procedure Rules CPR 25.1(f), to restrain a person involved in an action, or likely to be imminently so involved, from removing assets from a jurisdiction or dealing with assets wherever located when such behaviour is likely to frustrate any claim by the other party for damages or compensation. A freezing injunction may be made ancillary to the consent by the court to allow an appellant to bring an action in a foreign jurisdiction. The injunction may be made by a High Court judge and any others authorised to make such injunctions, with limited powers only to do so in County Courts. Thus, where a beneficiary claims that the trustees of a trust have been in breach of the terms of the trust by making excessive distributions to one or more of the other beneficiaries, an application for a freezing order to restrain the trustees may be made to prevent any further distributions until the matter is settled. Similarly, a beneficiary of a foundation who is allowed by the applicable law to bring an action may follow a similar procedure.

Frozen trust: *See* BLIND TRUST.

Frustration: A situation which renders a contract for transaction impossible to perform by reasons arising outside the control of the parties after the contractual or other relationship was established which prevents any performance of the obligations. The original principle was that when a contract was rendered void any benefit or loss which had been incurred lay where it fell. This principle was changed under the *Law Reform Frustration of Contract Act* 1943. If a contract becomes frustrated any benefit conferred by one party to the other has to be paid for; the Act requires a reasonable sum to be paid.

Fully constituted: A requirement that the property to be held in trust has been transferred to the trustee (or a person who is properly committed to be a trustee) or, as an exception, that the transferor, probably the settlor, has done all in his power to effect the transfer which only requires a formality to complete, such as the issue by a company of a new share certificate, the settlor having done all that is necessary with the transfer forms etc. A rule which is closely associated with equity's principles for dealing with gifts and the equitable maxim that 'equity will not assist a volunteer' would apply unless the transfer of the assets into the legal ownership of the trustee had been completed.

Fungible property: A term applied to things which are of such a nature that they could be replaced by equal quantities and qualities of the same thing, such as a quantity of wheat, shares in a company or bank notes, but not to a particular horse or an antique china vase where any replacement, although similar, would not be identical.

***Furniss (Inspector of Taxes) v. Dawson*:** [1984] A.C. 474, [1984] 1 All ER 530. A trust case in the House of Lords (now the Supreme Court) which laid down the rule that where an unnecessary step is introduced into a chain of reactions in order to give a tax advantage, and where such steps have no real value, then that step may be ignored in determining a tax liability. For example, where a transfer of value is made by associated operations carried out at different times under the rule, it may be treated as made at the time of the last transfer. This may mean that an earlier transfer of value can be ignored in assessing the overall gain on a disposal if the earlier transfer was carried out in order to achieve a lower assessment.

Future interests: In equity there are two interests which confer the right of enjoyment in land in the future. The two interests are a REVERSION and a REMAINDER. Between them they represent how future interests can be created. A reversion comes about by a grantor not disposing of his whole interest. For example, where a settlor who owns land in fee simple disposes of the land to another but fails to do so absolutely and retains the fee simple. In other words, he confers a life interest that, on expiry, allows the complete absolute fee simple in possession to revert to the settlor or to his estate. A remainder is an interest which takes effect upon the termination of a prior estate, for example, an interest for life to 'B' and thereafter to 'C' for life, and thereafter to 'D' in fee simple. During the life of B, C has a remainder in interest, i.e. on the termination of B's interest the land passes to C then similarly, onwards to D who then is entitled to the fee simple in possession. With this arrangement there is no return to the settlor or grantor; the property ultimately ends up with a fee simple passed to D. The term 'future estates' carries the same meaning as 'FUTURE INTERESTS'.

Future property: An assignment of property by a person who does not actually possess the property concerned but which is treated in equity as an agreement to assign it when the person does actually acquire it. Agreements to transfer after acquired property are frequently found in a MARRIAGE SETTLEMENT (sometimes called an ante-nuptial trust) where one prospective spouse undertakes to assign to the marriage settlement specific property which will be acquired in the future for the benefit of the parties to the marriage. The terms of the assignment will dictate the consequences if that property is not acquired. Future estates in land are EQUITABLE INTERESTS which may be disposed of so that, on the termination of the prior estate, the property is then in the hands of anyone to whom the future estate was assigned.

G

Gazumping: The practice of withdrawing, usually at the last minute, by a vendor from a sale of land or property in order to take advantage of a higher offer from another purchaser. This may take place even after the seller has agreed to sell the land but by the use of the term 'subject to contract' prevents any legal contractual obligation arising. Therefore, the withdrawal may be without any recompense to the disappointed party unless there is a collateral contract between the parties that the vendor will not offer it to anyone else without the purchaser's agreement – a 'lock-out' agreement. Lock-out agreements have been recognised by the UK Parliament as one method of preventing gazumping.

Gazundering: A technique whereby a purchaser during contract negotiation for the purchase of property demands a reduction in price at the time the other party, the seller, is expecting the purchaser to sign the contract. The purchaser usually argues that there is some fault in the property, but the practice is purely to obtain a reduction in the purchase price where the seller is well advanced in his next purchase, which could cause the transaction to collapse.

General anti-avoidance rule: A provision in tax legislation which creates a general proposition to counter TAX AVOIDANCE. The avoidance is made illegal no matter what type of tax or method of taxation is concerned. This rule aims to counter vigorous tax planning on the basis that the manipulation of tax rules to avoid tax is offensive to the spirit of tax law. Such rules exist in Australia and Canada. In the UK the matter was debated over the last 20 years when commentators suggested that such legislation to counter tax avoidance in general would provide certainty for both sides of any transaction as to its tax consequences. A study group led to a consultation exercise on a 'general anti-abuse rule' and provisions were made to introduce such a rule in the *Finance Bill* 2013: the new rule came into force on 17 July 2013.

General equitable charge: A charge on property not secured by the deposit of documents relating to the legal estate of the property. Such a charge does not affect an interest arising under a trust or a settlement and is not a charge given as an indemnity against payment of rent on land, or other charges on land, or against the breach or non-observance of covenants or conditions. A general equitable charge is not included in any other class of land charge but is registerable independently as a Class C(iii) land charge under the *UK Land Charges Act* 1972.

General legacy: *See* LEGACIES.

General power of investment: The power of trustees of a trust governed by English law to make any kind of investment that could be made if the trustees were absolutely entitled to the trust assets. Trustees are restrained, however, by the terms of the trust instrument and are subject to financial regulations which affect various investments. Under the *Trustee Act* 2000 trustees are subject to a STATUTORY DUTY OF CARE in relation to their general power of investment or any other powers of investment conferred upon them by the trust deed. This duty of care is 'such skill and care as is reasonable in the circumstances'. Trustees are also required to have regard to the 'STANDARD INVESTMENT CRITERIA'.

Generation skipping: Gifts made through trusts by a grandparent to a grandchild, thus skipping the intermediate generation, made by US grantors to defer or avoid federal gift or estate taxes. The gift is usually made through a generation skipping trust. Such gifts are now subject to a generation skipping tax or, if made directly without using a trust, they are subject to tax as any other large gift. However, in the US, although generation skipping no longer avoids taxes, a grandparent can still give or leave gifts of under $10,000 a year to a grandchild without incurring gift tax.

Genuine transaction rule: A variation on the 'FAIR DEALING PRINCIPLE' and which has received no overall judicial comment but which may be applicable to trustees to prevent a breach of trust where a trustee may attempt to avoid the two-party rule by transferring an item that he owns personally to himself as a trustee. Such a transfer would not involve two separate parties. A trustee can only lawfully sell trust property to someone with whom he has no personal connection, i.e. he can only deal with persons at arm's length. Otherwise, the sale is ineffective although there may be a transfer of the legal title. Transactions, other than a sale, may also be bad for this reason, such as a grant of a lease of property to a trustee's nominee. The genuine transaction rule expresses the substance of a two-party rule to cover such a reverse situation, such as where a trustee is in conflict with the general principle by an attempt to sell an item of property which he personally possesses and owns himself, as trustee, and intends by the sale to make the item part of the trust assets. *See* SELF-DEALING RULE *and* TWO-PARTY RULE.

Gift: The transfer of property without the recipient giving a consideration to the donor. This gratuitous nature distinguishes a gift from a GRANT. A grant is made in return for some consideration or equivalent. The only proviso for making a gift valid is for the donor to have done everything in his power that is necessary in order to transfer the property, such as signing the necessary documents of transfer or handing over whatever is the gift. Unless this is done, the law will have no effect. The maxim 'equity will not assist in completing an imperfect gift' applies. However, the mere assertion that the intended donor is a trustee does not allow protection against all circumstances. The only exception to this is where the donee is a personal representative of the donor or already a trustee of the property in question, i.e. a gift by the beneficiary back to the trustee of a trust asset. The personal representative or the trustee then obtains the legal estate in the trust property as a result of the gift or the voluntary transfer and then holds the legal ownership of the property transferred but holds it on trust. There is an exception to the maxim quoted above, where the court will perfect an imperfect gift if the conditions for a *DONATIO MORTIS CAUSA* (gift in contemplation of death) are satisfied. Otherwise, there is no gift, such as in connection with payments by a husband into a joint bank account; these are not gifts from the husband to his wife; also, shares settled on trust for employees are not personal gifts.

Gift Aid: A relief on a UK tax liability in respect of donations to UK registered charities by individuals who pay income tax or capital gains tax. The advantage is that the charity receives the amount actually donated which is grossed up by the tax already paid by the donor on that amount so the charity then receives the actual amount plus the basic rate of tax already paid.

Gifts to non-charitable unincorporated associations: A gift intended to be for a club or other group of persons which is unincorporated may be a gift to each member or to a body of persons, the association or the club. Where there is a contract between the members, each member will be treated as a joint tenant of the gift.

Either method would enable the donor to impose conditions upon its use. The further alternative of making a gift to a trust may result in the gift transgressing the rule under English law that a gift to a trust for non-charitable purposes is unenforceable. Therefore, a gift in any form of trust structure to a football club, for example, would be unenforceable unless the rule in *Denley's Trust Deed, Re* [1969] 1 Ch 373 could be made applicable. In that case, a gift was made to a trust for the purpose of providing sporting facilities for former employees of the donor. The exclusion of purpose trusts from the scope of English trusts was overcome by the fact that there was an ascertainable and limited membership which allowed each potential recipient of the gift to be identified. On these grounds the trust was judged to be valid.

Giuliano-Lagarde Report: A report on the HAGUE CONVENTIONS explaining their purpose and background, published in OJ C282/1 at 15, 1980.

Global Forum: A worldwide group of government officials who operate several international consulting bodies, each of which is a Global Forum of their speciality. These bodies are set up by the OECD to carry forward an OECD policy. The Global Forum has semi-autonomy under an independent chairman and is usually financed by the participating governments with the intention of formulating guidelines or other items of soft law to achieve the policy of the OECD as inspired by the needs of the G20 countries. The current most significant group is the Global Forum on International Taxation, which, by examination of each cooperating state's legislation and by assessment of each country's practice by assessors drawn from the members of the Global Forum, reviews the extent that each jurisdiction is compliant with the standards of transparency and the exchange of information on international tax matters with other jurisdictions. There are also Global Fora set up by the OECD on transfer pricing and on competition, development, environment, agriculture, trade and VAT.

Good faith: The performance of an act done honestly and with no ulterior motive whether or not done negligently.

Goodwill: A term applied in several ways but principally to express the benefit of a business having been carried on for some time in a particular place or manner and represents a value based on the probability of old customers continuing, although there has been a change in the firm or place of business. The term 'goodwill' is also generally used to express the attractive force which brings in business and constitutes an intangible personal property attached to a business name or a trade name and which may be protected by the common law tort of 'passing off'. Further, the term extends to apply to personal characteristics of reputation and image.

Governing law: The law to which parties in a transaction or relationship refer in order to determine their duties, obligations and liabilities; also referred to as the applicable law or the proper law. Where a relationship or transaction takes place entirely in one jurisdiction there is no question about what constitutes the governing law: it is the law of that jurisdiction. Where the parties are in different jurisdictions or the nature of the relationship spans several, then in most situations it is generally acceptable in private law matters that the governing law is the law which is chosen by the parties in an express or implied agreement or, failing that, the law most closely associated with the matter. This rule applies to trusts and this provision is incorporated in the HAGUE TRUST CONVENTION. The governing law may be chosen by the parties. Under the English law of trusts, the governing law does not alter simply because there is a change of the place of investment or the place of residence of the trustees or the domicile of the beneficiaries. A trust instrument may give power to the trustees to change the governing law. When the trustees have this power, the trustees may, with the agreement of the beneficiaries, change the governing law and thus create a new settlement. The ability to resettle a trust in a different jurisdiction and thereby create a new trust is a valuable facility. A foundation may also have a clause in its charter stating the governing law. CHOICE OF LAW clauses are recognised in most jurisdictions; thus, if a trust is made subject to the law of Jersey and an action is brought in the Cayman Islands because, for some reason, the trust is in Cayman Island's jurisdiction, then the Cayman Islands judge will construe the trust and its implications by applying the law of Jersey to the best of his ability. It is usual that when a foreign law is applied the applicant or plaintiff must prove to the satisfaction of the court what the applicable foreign law is, as a matter of fact. A governing law clause is distinct from a jurisdictional clause which states that actions and disputes under the arrangement concerned shall be brought in a particular jurisdiction. It is therefore sensible and economical, when nominating a governing law, also to nominate the same jurisdiction as the forum for any action.

Grant: The creation or transfer of the ownership of property by written instrument. The term is used in this context in connection with an ESTATE or interest in land or the transfer of ownership of a chattel.

Grantor: An expression used mainly in connection with US trusts, with the same meaning as a settlor under English trusts. In the US a 'grantor trust' is a trust where the grantor is the beneficiary.

Ground rent: A rent payable on property which represents the value of the land excluding any buildings on it. A lessee of property may develop the land or sell a sublease for a period that is less than the unexpired period remaining of the lease. If there is a sale of the lease, it is sold subject to the ground rent. If it is sublet then the lessee remains responsible to the freeholder for payment of the ground rent and can recoup it by a term in the sublease. Where the property is redeveloped, the lessee can charge an increased ground rent, referred to as an improved ground rent. At the end of the term of lease of any buildings on the land, the buildings, together with the land, revert to the freeholder.

Grupo Torras: The name of a Spanish subsidiary of the Kuwait Investment Office which features in a number of cases in the UK and Jersey where attempts were made to recover funds stolen by the former chairman of the subsidiary who had been convicted in the English High Court of having conspired to defraud his company, ***Grupo Torras v. Al Sabah (No. 6) Sub nom-Esteem Settlement, Re: Abacus (CI) Limited v. Al Sabah*** [2002] WTLR 337, of approximately US$450 million which he had placed in trust in several jurisdictions.

Guarantee: *See* SURETY.

Guarantee company: A registered company where the liability of members is limited to the nominal amount that each member agrees to contribute to the assets of the company on liquidation, i.e. the amount agreed by each member as his guarantee is the limit of that member's liability. Liability does not require a provision of cash unless the company goes into liquidation or other instances arise which call for implementation of the guarantees. A guarantee company is used where a company is chosen as a vehicle for an activity but where capital is not raised by the issue of shares as capital may not be necessary, and where the members of the company are not intended to share in the company's profits or assets. A typical use of a guarantee company is in the form of a social club or learned society where the activities do not call for substantial assets. This has enabled guarantee companies to be adapted to be used as an alternative to foundations by dividing the shares of the guarantee company into two classes. The holders of the first class are those responsible for the administration of the company and the holders of the second class, the guarantee members, are there in the event that the company is in financial distress. The company can then manage a purpose; a function which a trust would in many jurisdictions be unable to carry out. The use of guarantee companies in this way has diminished since the wide adoption of private foundations but guarantee companies can still be used as alternatives to private foundations in Gibraltar and in the Isle of Man.

Guardian: An appointed person who takes care of someone else who, due to incapacity, is incapable of looking after their own affairs. This is usually due to either youth or mental incapacity. The word has become used in connection with private foundations as an alternative to 'PROTECTOR', where an individual or company is appointed as guardian with the duty of ensuring that the foundation council performs its duties properly. The guardian is not a member of the foundation council but, nevertheless, owes fiduciary duties to the foundation, as specified in the individual foundation documents or the law of the jurisdiction in which the foundation is incorporated. Guardians are also appointed to monitor trustees' performance in international trusts, especially where the trustees are geographically remote from the beneficiaries where a guardian who, by closer proximity to the trustees and family affiliations, is better informed of the circumstances and potential needs of beneficiaries than are the trustees. The guardian is therefore in a position to authenticate any request made by beneficiaries for assistance from the trust. A similar role can be performed by a guardian to a foundation. A guardian/protector is necessary in a private foundation in the absence of any power of the beneficiaries to protect their rights. *See* FOUNDATION, PRIVATE.

H

Habitual residence: A term introduced into English law from private international law conventions which distinguishes between the ordinary residence of a person and a temporary residence within a jurisdiction. The term is a connecting factor in private international law that is applied particularly when determining which country's courts have jurisdiction over a person. It is different from other terms in which the word 'resident' or 'residence' appears, such as 'resident' or 'ordinary resident', which is significant in determining the tax status of a person; these are different concepts from that of 'habitual residence'.

Hague Convention on the Law Applicable to Trusts and on their Recognition: This Convention, established on 10 January 1986 and frequently referred to as the 'Hague Convention on Trusts', aims to 'establish common provisions on the law applicable to trusts and to deal with the most important issues relating to the recognition of trusts.' The Convention is therefore a conflict of laws convention. States adopting the Convention are required for private international law purposes to recognise trusts falling within the Convention's scope. The Convention covers matters which may be the subject of dispute after a trust comes into existence, such as the role of the trustee, the administration of the trust and the relationship between the beneficiaries and trustees. The preliminary matters relating to the creation of the trust, the capacity of the settlor, the vesting of the trust property in the trustee, the powers of the trustee and the identity of the beneficiaries and questions concerning the general formal validity of the instrument are matters for the national law of the jurisdiction in which the trust is established. If a dispute arises calling for the forum and the proper law governing the trust to be determined, then the Convention's terms apply. On the resolution of the dispute, the Convention provides that the signatory states will enforce the resulting judgment. This applies whether or not a signatory to the Convention involved in the dispute includes a law of trusts in its national law. It requires that a judgment should be worded to give a remedy that is practical in a non-trust jurisdiction. The Convention is not confined to trusts that adopt the principles of English law. The Convention omits any reference to equity in the description of trusts to which the Convention applies. This description merely describes the characteristics of trusts for the purpose of the Convention. The Convention itself does not define trusts precisely. The Convention can therefore include various ancillary structures which, although not conforming strictly to the Convention's description of trusts, are nevertheless used for similar purposes. These are numerous and cover arrangements that would never be recognised as legitimate trusts under English law. The Convention, as well as breaking down difficulties of operating internationally, has raised the perception that the transfer of assets to another person in order to benefit a third party is not the monopoly of English law nor does it necessarily require an understanding of English legal practices. The Trust Convention was drafted in 1985, which came before the worldwide development of private foundations. The nature of some of the ancillary arrangements that have been recognised under the Convention differ from those of the English trust to such an extent that it can be questioned whether if foundations had been in wider use they might have been recognised as ancillary vehicles.

Although the matter was not considered in the drafting of the Convention, academic opinion has been given that foundations could not come within the Convention as foundations have legal personality. The Trust Convention was intended to give international standing and recognition to arrangements that did not depend on the formality of incorporation. Perhaps the draftsmen of the Hague Convention considered that the recognition given to a structure created by incorporation did not need amplifying within a treaty on the recognition of trusts. The Convention introduced some essential elements that distinguish a trust from other arrangements. Under the Convention, trusts must be created voluntarily and evidenced in writing unless an oral trust is subsequently reduced to writing. In the absence of a choice of law expressly stated in the trust document, the Convention provides that the governing law is the law with which the trust is most closely connected. This represents a principle familiar in common law countries. The Convention governs the validity, construction, effects and administration of a trust. The Convention has been adopted by disappointingly few jurisdictions. Nevertheless, it has been influential in internationalising the trust and, in particular, drawing attention to ancillary structures. The omission of any dependence upon equitable principles has also widened the meaning of a trust and although the English trust dependent upon equity may still be said to be unique, it is not alone.

Hague Conventions: Agreements signed by States at The Hague under the auspices of the Hague Conference on Private International Law. The most significant are the Hague Conventions of 1890 and 1899 to 1907 on the laws of war that deal with the conduct of hostilities (the Geneva Convention runs in parallel and deals with the protection of victims of the conflict). International Opium Conventions were also signed in The Hague in 1912. The term 'Hague Regulations', also known as 'The Hague Rules', is based upon an Annex to the Hague Convention No. IV of 1907 and deals with the law on customs of war on land. Many of the provisions have been modernised and adapted in the Geneva Protocol. The description 'Hague' is used in numerous Conventions, in particular the Hague Convention on Trusts, and the rules contained in the International Convention for the Unification of Certain Rules of Law relating to Bills of Lading are known as 'The Hague Rules'. These rules were amended by a protocol in 1968 and the amended rules are known as 'The Hague-Visby Rules'.

Hague Trust Convention: The full name of this Convention is 'The Convention on the Law Applicable to Trusts and on their Recognition' (*see* above).

Half-secret trust: A trust whose existence is declared in a will or other document but where the beneficiaries are undisclosed, although known to the secret trustee, i.e. the existence of a trust is known but the details are secret. *See* SECRET TRUSTS.

Hardwicke, Lord: Lord Chancellor from 1737 to 1757. With the advantage of 20 years' uninterrupted tenure, Lord Hardwicke was able to carry out a systematic policy of restating the basic principles of equity, harmonising the precedents with the philosophic notions of his age. Thereafter, it was possible to advise with some confidence on the probable result of an action in Chancery. The recording of proceedings enabled him to examine the principles to be drawn from precedents and where there was no guidance he would resort to Roman law and the modern systems based on that law. His reports were gathered and made available for practitioners and hundreds of his judgments became embodied into the very structure of equity.

Hastings-Bass*, Rule in:** The so-called rule in ***Hastings-Bass has played a considerable part in breach of trust actions against trustees since 1975, particularly since 1990. An explanation of the rule is best considered in seven parts.

1. The original ***Hastings-Bass*** decision (In ***Re Hastings-Bass, Deceased*** [1975] Ch. 25 CA) concerned a plan to save estate duty by terminating a life interest and passing settled property on to the next generation as a beneficiary in a new settlement. The creation of the life interest did not breach the rule against perpetuities but the remaining trusts did so and were void. The Court of Appeal considered whether the whole advancement was ineffective but upheld the life interest on the grounds that the exercise of the power could only be upset if the result was not for the benefit of the beneficiary intended. The crucial words in the Court of Appeal by Buckley LJ gave rise to the so-called rule in ***Hastings-Bass.*** Buckley LJ said that:

   '[W]here ... a trustee is given a discretion ... under which he acts in good faith, the court should not interfere with his action notwithstanding that it does not have the full effect which he intended unless (1) what he has achieved is unauthorised by the power conferred upon him, or (2) it is clear that he would not have acted as he did (a) had he not taken into account considerations which he should not have taken into account, or (b) had he not failed to take into account considerations which he ought to have taken into account.'

   This passage led to many conflicting decisions. In short, the passage means that the trustee took into account matters he should not have done or avoided others which were relevant. That case was not about mistake. The original decision is still valid in its narrow context.

2. The decision in ***Hastings-Bass*** was considered in ***Metoy Pension Trustees Limited v. Evans*** [1990] 1WLR 1587, which involved the replacement of a company pension scheme with a new one that was ineffective owing to an error about the trusteeship. The new scheme had to be wound up due to the financial position of Metoy. The trustees raised questions of whether the new deed was wholly invalid and whether a clause for the winding up in certain circumstances affected the validity of the scheme and consequently the priority of claims in a winding up and in the disposal of any surplus money. It was clear that the trustees had not fully considered the matter and this led to the dispute. Warner J reformulated what he understood was the rule in ***Hastings-Bass*** by deciding that:

   'Where a trustee acts under a discretion given to him by the terms of the trust, the court will interfere with his action if it is clear that he would not have acted as he did had he not failed to take into account considerations which he ought to have taken into account.'

   This reformulation became known as 'the rule in ***Hastings-Bass***'. The so-called rule which had been endorsed by the Court of Appeal led to many difficulties of application and interpretation due, according to Lord Walker of Guestingthorpe in the Supreme Court, to difficulties in principle and practice.

3. The above remarks made by Lord Walker in the Supreme Court judgment in ***Pitt v. Holt*** and ***Futter v. Futter*** both reported under the citation [2013] 312 AC, overruled the ***Metoy*** rule and followed the reasoning of the Court of Appeal in ***Pitt v. Holt*** and ***Futter v.***

Futter. In these cases the Court of Appeal felt bound to follow the precedent of the previous cases but provided arguments substantially relied upon by the Supreme Court in overruling the ***Metoy*** case. The Court of Appeal had analysed the techniques by which trust law controlled fiduciary powers. The issue in the Court of Appeal was concerned with the scope of the power rather than the nature of the decision-making process. In the wide number of circumstances where the rule had been applied the court had been concerned with the consequences to the trust when incorrect tax advice was relied upon by the trustees. The two cases (***Pitt v. Holt*** and ***Futter v. Futter***) that went to the Supreme Court concerned applications to the Lower Courts that trustees' action should be judged to be void and accordingly ignored on the grounds that the trustees had been in breach of trust in following incorrect advice and that a different path should have been followed which would have given the trustees the chance of avoiding the tax traps into which they had fallen. Following the ***Metoy*** case, judicial decisions had varied in their approach. The position remained unclear and produced conflicting academic and judicial opinions of whether particular situations rendered trustees' decision void or voidable. A distinction was drawn between alleged breaches of fiduciary duty following the taking of advice and those where the trustees took no advice but proceeded to make wrong decisions without the intervention of any outside or independent opinion. In the latter event, the only excuse which could be made by the trustees was that they had been mistaken in the soundness of their action, i.e. the remedies available for a mistake should be allowed. The applications became notorious. In ***Futter v. Futter*** it was revealed in the High Court that the trustees had confessed to have acted in an un-trustee-like fashion; they had failed to exercise a power vested in them and then wished openly to take advantage of their failure in performing their fiduciary duties in the expectation that their action would be declared void. Norris J said that this case was:

> 'Another application by trustees who wished to assert that they have acted in an un-trustee-like fashion and so have failed properly to execute a power vested in them.'

The trustees claimed that they had exercised their power (in fact there were two powers, advancement and enlargement) in the expectation that the gains which would have been made by the trust would have been offset by losses but they had failed to take into account a capital gains tax provision (Section 2(4) of the *Taxation of Chargeable Gains Act* 1992) that provided otherwise. This was despite the trustees having taken legal advice. Norris J felt obliged to apply the rule as he said the High Court was not the place to consider revising the rule although he added that 'the rule in ***Hastings-Bass***' may have been diverted from its true course. Longmore LJ in the Court of Appeal stated this view more strongly:

> 'Examples of the comparatively rare instance of the law taking a seriously wrong turn, of that wrong turn being not infrequently acted on over a 20-year period but this court being able to reverse that error have put the law back on its right course.'

The Supreme Court's remedies are considered in the next paragraph.

4. Neither of the circumstances considered by the Supreme Court in ***Pitt v. Holt*** and ***Futter v. Futter*** concerned express trusts. ***Pitt v. Holt*** was concerned with monies awarded as damages in respect of an accident and which were placed on a discretionary trust that

had been set up with no regard for inheritance tax consequences. A large liability arose that could have been avoided by taking advantage of privileges awarded by statute to meet these circumstances. The claimants sought a claim that the settlement should be set aside and therefore inheritance tax avoided due to a failure by the first claimant to take account of a material consideration that would have avoided the tax liability. The Court of Appeal had held that 'the rule in ***Hastings-Bass***' did not apply. The claimant's action in setting up the trust had been within the terms of a power that had previously been conferred by a court. This was followed by tax advice from a proper source. Despite the inaccuracy of that advice, the claimant had not been in breach of fiduciary duty. The belief that there were no adverse tax consequences was a mistake, not as to the legal effect of the settlement but as to its consequences, that the claimant was not entitled to avoid. Accordingly, the settlement was neither void nor voidable according to the Court of Appeal. The Supreme Court, however, allowed the appeal by applying its equitable jurisdiction to set aside a voluntary disposition on the grounds of a mistake which was so grave that it would be unconscionable to refuse relief. This was on a principle quite separate from the rule in ***Hastings-Bass***. The Supreme Court made an objective judgment on the grounds that there was a mistake either as to the legal character or nature of the transaction or as to some matter of fact which was basic to the transaction and that it would be unconscionable or unjust to leave the mistake uncorrected. The mistake was that the trust could have saved tax without any artificiality or abuse by taking into account a provision of the *Inheritance Tax Act* 1984. In ***Futter v. Futter*** the claimant settled assets on two discretionary trusts of which the claimants were trustees. The trustees exercised their power of enlargement on one trust by allowing the first claimant to be absolutely entitled to the fund, and then exercised their power of advancement under the second trust to appoint £12,000 to each of three children immediately. The purpose of the transactions was to avoid incurring a charge to capital gains tax but the legal advisers overlooked a statutory provision which undermined the basis on which the transactions were based. A large capital gains tax liability arose. The Court of Appeal held that the enlargement and advancements had been within the claimant's powers and they had not acted in breach of trust although they did receive wrong advice from appropriate solicitors. The trustees were mistaken as to those consequences; the enlargement and advancements were neither held to be void nor voidable. The Supreme Court added that the trustees had acted within their powers but had obtained and acted upon apparently competent professional advice and were not in breach of duty merely because the advice was wrong. In short, the Supreme Court appeals in these two cases decided that the court will only have jurisdiction to intervene following a trustee's flawed decision where the trustees acted within the limits of a power but were in breach of duty in taking that decision. This removes from the application of the rule any attempts by trustees to avoid the consequences of acting on bad advice and then claiming that such bad advice should be declared void or voidable on the grounds that taking the advice constituted a breach of their fiduciary duty.

5. The principle of the Supreme Court will doubtlessly be followed in subsequent cases although distinctions will

no doubt attempt to suggest that a different approach may be appropriate in the case of straightforward express trusts.

6. Following the Supreme Court's decision in ***Pitt v. Holt*** of 2013, the present characteristics of the so-called rule in ***Hastings-Bass*** have been summarised as follows:
   (a) Trustees exercising a discretionary power must take into account relevant matters and ignore irrelevant ones.
   (b) Fiscal consequences of any proposed exercise of a power are relevant matters.
   (c) Failure in (a) above may lead to a challenge on the exercise of the power.
   (d) A challenge will be on the failure to give adequate consideration to the exercise of the power which is distinct from the trustees making a mistake; ignorance or careless thinking may be enough for a challenge.
   (e) Such a challenge does not make the exercise void but voidable with relief being discretionary and subject to equitable defences.
   (f) Incorrect professional advice does not lead to a challenge unless the trustees were at fault by failing to take a given matter into account, such as adverse tax consequences. (Incorrect professional advice may be challenged on other grounds.)
7. The consequences of these Supreme Court decisions have been considered in other jurisdictions that follow the English practice. For example, in Jersey the *Trusts (Jersey) Law* 1984 has been modified by the *Trusts (Amendment No.6) (Jersey) Law* 2013, which, on the transfer or disposition of property into a trust or on the exercise of powers in relation to a trust or trust property, requires a mistake to be of so serious a character as to render it just for the court to make declarations. Otherwise, where a trustee has failed to take into account any relevant considerations in connection with the exercise of fiduciary power or in relation to trust property, there is no necessity to show that there was a breach of trust (this contrasts with the revised position in England and Wales after the two Supreme Court decisions). Revisions have taken place or are contemplated in the laws of other jurisdictions, including Guernsey and the Isle of Man.

Head lease: An original lease between a landlord who is a freeholder and the tenant. The tenant may, in turn, sublet or assign the lease so that a person other than the original head tenant may be in occupation of the property. A head lease may often cover an entire building occupied by many subtenants, each of whom can occupy their part of the building under a sublease from the head lessee. Subleases run for shorter periods than head leases.

Headnote: In a law report the headnote precedes the judgments. The headnote summarises the facts of the case and the matters in dispute and is a short summary of the court's findings, followed by a list of cases quoted by counsel or by the judges. A headnote is a useful summary of the principles involved in the case, but is compiled by the editor of the law report and does not form part of the judgment.

Hedge fund: A fund, often open-ended, in the form of a limited partnership or limited company with a diverse range of investments made available generally to professional investors aimed at achieving a positive result on their investments whether the markets rise or fall. Hedge funds have avoided regulations that cover other investments by not being made available to the general public. After the 2008 financial crisis, the regulations introduced in the US and the EU were intended to give governments greater insight into hedge funds and eliminate some regulatory gaps. In the US, regulation is through the *Dodd-Frank Wall Street Reform Act* 2010 and requires the registration of advisers with more than US$150m in assets, and of funds with more than 15 US clients and investors managing US$25m. In Europe, hedge funds are regulated primarily through advisers' managers and in the UK these managers are required to be authorised by the Financial Conduct Authority (FCA). The registration of hedge fund managers has been required since November 2010 in the EU. The Directive of Alternative Investment Fund Managers (AIFMD) requires managers to disclose information on a frequent basis; it also requires hedge fund managers to hold large amounts of capital and introduces potential limitation on leveraged investment. Hedge funds are sometimes called PROFESSIONAL FUNDS.

Heir: A person entitled, under common law and statutory rules, to inherit the freehold land of someone who has died intestate. This term was abolished by the *Administration of Estates Act* 1925. *See* ISSUE (OFFSPRING).

Hekdesh: An Israeli trust-type of structure set up by contract and, because it possesses many characteristics similar to Austrian, Panamanian and Liechtenstein foundations, the name 'Hekdesh' is also used to describe an Israeli foundation.

Hereditaments: Every kind of property that can be inherited, including property that a person may have had by descent from ancestors and also property that he has purchased which his heir could inherit. The term is now of limited use only to denote a unit for taxing purposes.

HNWI (high net worth individuals): An imprecise term generally meaning wealthy persons. The term is sometimes used to refer to individuals with disposable wealth of as little as US$500,000 which is free from any encumbrance and available for investment. Variations on this are used, such as VHNWI (very high net worth individuals), i.e. those with assets between US$5 million and US$50 million, and UHNWI (ultra-high net worth individuals), those considered to be individuals with assets above US$50 million. UVHNWI (ultra and very high net worth individuals) is used to refer to both VHNWI and UHNWIs.

Holder in due course: A banking term that refers to a person holding a cheque or promissory note or other bill of exchange that is complete and regular on the face of it. This means that the item has been received by the holder for value and received in good faith with no suspicion that it might not be good or subject to a claim by another, or that it is overdue, or that it has previously been dishonoured by, for example, a bank refusing to pay on it. A holder in due course is entitled to payment by the issuer.

Honesty and good faith: *See* quotation in IMPOSSIBILITY.

Hostile witness: *See* ADVERSE WITNESS.

Hotchpotch: A device in equity to secure fairness amongst a group of persons entitled to receive payment where one of them receives a payment in advance of the others. Under this doctrine, the person who receives an advance payment is required to bring the amount of that payment into account as part of his share when apportioning the balance of the total sum amongst his co-creditors, i.e. the amount which he has received in advance is deducted from his total entitlement to avoid him deriving an unfair advantage. This can apply where co-guarantors have to make good an amount owing under a contract and the debtor is unable to recompense the guarantors in full. However, if one of the guarantors received recompense of the amount which he had provided in advance of the others, then that early recipient would bring the amount he received into hotchpotch so that the co-guarantors then were recompensed equally. *See* SURETY.

***Howe v. Earl of Dartmouth*, Rule in, (1802) 7 Ves. 137**: A decision that comprised one of the four rules of 'apportionment' that have been made optional for new trusts by the *Trusts (Capital and Income) Act* 2013 and which are still relevant in respect of older trusts. *See* APPORTIONMENT.

Human rights: *The Human Rights Act* 1998 bringing into force the Convention for the Protection of Human Rights and Fundamental Freedoms appeared at first as though it would affect trustees of ordinary private trusts and council members of private foundations. This has been found to be incorrect. The Act applies only to the acts of public authorities which exclude interfering with trusts and private foundations. There may also be an exception for public trusts, such as charitable trusts, as the Public Trustee which oversees charitable trusts is not considered to be a public authority when it is acting in relation to the administration of private trusts (apart, possibly, from interlocutory procedures under the *RSC Order of the Civil Procedures Rules*, which are actions carried out in the absence of affected parties and could be within the scope of the Fair Trial Provisions of Article 6 of the Convention). Also, the *Human Rights Act* 1998 recognises the Convention may influence the future development of equity through Section 6 of the Act which forbids the courts as public authorities from acting in a way incompatible with Convention rights but this does not seem to have had any effect on the way trustees or foundation councils exercise their discretion. This is the opinion of the editors of *Lewin on Trusts* 19th edition. However, the editors of *Snell's Equity*, 33rd edition, consider that the *Human Rights Act* 1998 may offer a remedy for breach of Article 8 of the European Convention on Human Rights in respect of the infringement of a person's private and family life, home and correspondence, when private information is misused. This may also have an impact on the doctrine of breach of confidence but this has to be balanced by the rights of others under Article 10 which protects freedom of expression. This is, at the moment, not thoroughly explored and developments will depend upon how the courts define some of the concepts in the Act and the conflicting interests of the parties concerned. *See* UNLAWFUL AND FRAUDULENT ULTERIOR PURPOSES.

Hypothecation: The act of pledging a thing as security for a debt without parting with the possession. Basically a civil law concept, but usually seen in English law in connection with bottomry bonds in maritime law. A civil law term occasionally used in common law to describe the charging of property with the payment of a sum of money or the performance of an obligation but where the person in whose right it exists acquires neither the right of the possession of the property nor the right to sell it. The lender is left with only a right to realise the debt by judicial proceedings in the event of default. The term 'hypothecation' has a separate meaning when used to describe taxes that are collected for a specific purpose.

I

ICVC: (Investment Company with Variable Capital). *See* OEIC.

If they/he shall think fit: A phrase used in connection with the exercise of a power where the donee of the power may determine at his discretion whether the occasion has arisen for the exercise of the power. In the absence of MALA FIDES, that determination is then final.

Illegal: An illegal act is one that the law directly forbids or one which, by law, does not create any right except the right to a remedy for an injury caused by that action. A contract may be illegal if it involves the commission of a legal wrong or is contrary to public policy. Examples of illegal contract include agreements to commit a crime or to let property for illegal purposes. Similar principles apply to trusts. Illegal trusts are trusts whereby there is an illegal element in the transfer of the assets, in the way the trust is administered or in the intention of the settlor. The unlawful nature need not be criminal or morally reprehensible, as a trust may be considered illegal if it offends the RULE AGAINST PERPETUITIES or ACCUMULATIONS. More conventional examples of illegality are where a trust contains conditions that are directed at supporting or fulfilling an illegal purpose or a purpose which is contrary to public policy. Other factors which would make a trust or private foundation illegal are attempts to impose conditions *IN TERROREM*. Illegality will render a trust or a private foundation wholly void or, dependent upon the situation, the element that is illegal may be cut out and effect may be given to what remains of the trust or foundation if it is then legal and workable.

Illegal trust: *See* ILLEGAL.

Illegality rule: The rule of public policy that makes an unlawful trust or contract or other illegal conduct unlikely to receive the support of the court and is therefore unlikely to be enforced through legal proceedings.

Illicit: *See* UNLAWFUL *and* ILLEGAL.

Illusory trust: A term used particularly in US law for a trust in which the settlor retains so much control over the trust property that the trust has no real effect, and is generally an arrangement that gives the impression of being a trust but in fact does not fulfil the necessary certainties to be valid. *See* SHAM TRUSTS.

Immigrant trust: A trust set up by a potential immigrant who has placed his assets or those of his family in trust so that on immigration into another country, the immigrants arrive without the legal title to the property that they formerly held. Depending on the trust laws in the country to which they go, the income of the trust and the capital may then not be subject to tax for some years, with the probable general exception that any income received by the immigrants in their new home could be taxed (remittance basis of taxation). The purpose of an immigrant trust is therefore to denude the immigrants of their wealth, as far as the legal title is concerned, so that they arrive without income and without capital. This practice has been adopted by immigrant executives to a country who place their assets in trust before moving in order to honestly claim that they arrive without assets.

Immoral contracts, trusts and private foundations: Void and unenforceable arrangements due to being illegal or contrary to public policy. The same may apply where the contract, trust or private foundation is tainted because the whole arrangement is a means to an end that is illegal or immoral. In contract, it is not necessary that the actions or intentions of both parties need to be immoral. If one party's consideration is immoral, this is sufficient to vitiate a contract.

Immovable property: A term applied by the civil law to land and other real property and which in civil law is distinguished from moveable property, which term covers all other types of property. The term 'immovable property' is used informally in English law to cover both freehold and leasehold property and therefore involves both real property, such as freehold, and personal property, such as leasehold; the distinctions between real property and personal property being the categories into which property is placed in the common law. The term 'immovable property' may be used in a will, subject to English law, when it is interpreted as including, as well as what is real property, leases, rents, crops and the like but not debts, except for debts secured on land, which is an immovable, as such debts are considered to be interests in land. It appears that the terms 'moveable' and 'immovable' are not technical terms in English law (in the opinion of Cozens-Hardy M.R., in ***Re Anziani*** [1930] 1 Ch. 407), but the principle that courts of one country, in general, have no jurisdiction over immovables situated outside that country has been recognised in ***British South Africa Co. v. Compania de Mozambique*** [1893] AC 602.

Immunity: A general or particular exemption from the application of the law or the jurisdiction of a court. The widest immunity is that of the Crown under English law and it exists through immunity of ministers, government departments and Crown servants, although in recent years this has been reduced, e.g. the Crown is now liable in tort; proceedings may be taken under the *Crown Proceedings Act* 1947. The *State Immunity Act* 1978 gives immunity to foreign officials, servants and agents in respect of acts of a governmental nature but this does not extend to activities such as torture and other crimes under international law. In private law, immunity may be granted either by the terms of a contractual document or, for example, an EXEMPTION CLAUSE in a trust deed giving the trustee immunity from action. Immunity may also be granted to individuals by statute and in respect of activities conducted in the exercise of certain professions, although this has been abolished in respect of advocates in their pre-trial activities. This immunity generally comes under attack in other spheres, such as the immunity presently enjoyed by expert witnesses. Immunity in favour of a foreign government and administration arises out of respect for the territorial integrity and political independence of other states under international law. The modern rules on immunity have developed from the doctrine of SOVEREIGN IMMUNITY, which originally was centred on the political independence of the sovereign, and the allegiance that was owed to him by all prevented the sovereign being subject to legal process. From this exclusion the concept developed that a sovereign could not be sued in foreign courts. This developed into an abstract concept of immunity. Until the United Nations, in 2004, adopted the Convention on Jurisdictional Immunities of States and their Property, international law relating to sovereign immunity relied upon domestic case law. The idea of immunity from jurisdiction is a concept closely related to that of sovereign immunity and asserts that in particular circumstances a court is prevented from exercising the jurisdiction that it possesses. In the former, sovereign immunity, the principle of immunity goes to the jurisdiction of the court and becomes a principle of international law, whereas the latter constituted a prudential doctrine of domestic law. They both reflect the need to respect the sovereignty of other states. The distinction is not now so important since the absolute theory of sovereign immunity became modified, due to the growth in the commercial activities of states. The number of governmental agencies and public corporations, nationalised industries and other state organisations changed the attitude towards absolute sovereign immunity on the grounds that it would enable state enterprises to have an advantage over private corporations. This led to the doctrine of restrictive immunity that denies immunity where the state is engaged in commercial activity; the distinction is between acts *jure imperii* and acts *jure gestionis*. The restrictive approach first appeared in Austria in the 1950s. The UK was slower to adopt this approach than other countries but, by 1977, in ***Trendtex Corporation Ltd v. Central Bank of Nigeria*** [1977] 2 WLR 365, the Court of Appeal accepted the validity of the restrictive approach as representing international practice. The US *Foreign Sovereign Immunities Act* 1976, Section 1605 provides the grounds upon which a state may be subject to the jurisdiction and the UK *State Immunity Act* 1978 provides a general rule of immunity from the jurisdiction, with a range of exceptions. This has added another practice to analyse between acts that benefit from immunity and those which do not. This is helped by the inclusion in legislation of acts that lie outside a general rule of immunity. The UN Convention on Jurisdictional Immunities of States and their Property 2004 states that:

> 'A state enjoys immunity in respect of itself and its property, from the jurisdiction of the courts of another state subject to the provisions of the present Convention.'

In addition, the Convention provides that the term 'state' includes various organs of government, constituent units of a federal state or political subdivisions and agencies or instruments of the state or other entities to the extent that they are entitled to perform acts in the exercise of sovereign authority and, finally, representatives of the state acting in that capacity. The restrictive theory of immunity therefore now requires distinctions to be made between activities that are sovereign and those that are non-sovereign and the focus is therefore on the nature of the transaction rather than its purpose. In addition to sovereign immunity there is also the question of immunity under diplomatic law. Special customs developed on how ambassadors and other special representatives should be treated. The legal principle of state sovereignty is now applied to ambassadors, high commissioners and such other representatives of foreign states. The necessity for diplomatic privileges was given recognition by the Vienna Convention on Diplomatic Relations in 1961, Article 3.

Imperfect obligations: An obligation in the form of a moral duty which cannot be enforced by law, such as the expectation that a person should devote part of his estate to charity, or obligations that are said to arise out of a feeling of gratitude.

Imperfect trust: An executory trust that has not been adequately declared or constituted, i.e. something remains to be done to create the trust. This frequently occurs where the trust deed has been executed and the trustees appointed, but the trust assets have not been conveyed in law to the trustees. Until the settlor does all that he needs to do to transfer the assets, the trust is said to be imperfectly constituted and is not a trust and is unenforceable. *See* EXECUTORY TRUST *and* INCOMPLETELY CONSTITUTED TRUSTS.

Imperfect trust provisions: An expression formerly used in connection with trusts primarily for charitable purposes that could be used for providing other benefits.

These trusts were validated by the *Charitable Trust (Validation) Act* 1954. This concept is no longer of relevance under the modern charities law but the expression survives in connection with trusts that are intended to have a non-charitable purpose as their object. *See* CHARITIES *and* PURPOSE TRUSTS.

Implied consent: A consent which is taken to have been given after considering the surrounding circumstances although no direct express or explicit words of agreement have been given; this is provided that a reasonable person would believe that consent had been given. Implied consent is an illustration of how implications are relied upon in law when some elements of a situation cannot be provable directly but which are drawn logically from the available evidence. Something may be implied when it is necessary or inferred from the words produced in evidence.

Implied contract: A contract that is not expressly made by the parties but which is inferred by law from acts, circumstances or relationships or by the application of equity.

Implied covenants: The implied covenants in connection with the sale of land are those which are provided for in the *Law of Property (Miscellaneous Provisions) Act* 1994. Since 1994, the covenants implied are those of 'full title guarantee' or 'limited title guarantee'. The details of the contents of these covenants are specified in the 1994 Act. Previously, there were numerous implied warranties that had been attached to a CONVEYANCE of land by the *Conveyancing Act* 1881, including implied covenants that the seller conveyed the property as beneficial owner, settlor or trustee, amongst others. The covenants were implied in the conveyance because any implied term or covenant in the contract of sale that preceded the conveyance became of no effect after the conveyance; the obligations in the contract merged in the deed of conveyance and once the contract had been completed by the conveyance, no action lay for breach of any such contractual obligation. Hence the effect of the implied terms is preserved by being included in the conveyance.

Implied term: A term in a contract that, although not expressed, is implied in order to make commercial sense of the contract either by statute or by the courts. In the *Sale of Goods Act* 1893 there are implied terms in a contract for the sale of goods that the goods are reasonably fit for the purpose for which they are sold, that they are of merchantable quality and that they conform to the description given to them. The expression generally denotes the term inherent in the nature of the contract that the law will imply in every case, unless the parties agree to vary or exclude it.

Implied trust: Where a trust arises by operation of the law or without any express intention of the settlor. Implied trusts arise by the construction placed by equity upon the facts, conduct or the positions of parties. These trusts may be implied, first, because of the presumed intention of the parties, such as where property is purchased in the name of another there is an implied trust that the property will be held on trust for the benefit of the actual purchaser. Second, an implied trust may depend upon some intention that arises by operation of the law, e.g. the implied trust where a company director owes a fiduciary duty to his company. Implied trusts sometimes overlap with RESULTING TRUSTS or CONSTRUCTIVE TRUSTS. *See* PRESUMED INTENTION RESULTING TRUST (PIRT).

Impossibility: A general term applied to trusts or foundations if the purpose or objects of either cannot be achieved. This results in the arrangement being invalid and the assets that had been transferred to the trustees or foundation reverting, on a resulting trust, to the settlor or founder. Also, a gift that is made with impossible conditions attached to it results in the gift being invalid; the conditions may be imposed before or after the gift is made and the conditions are particularly relevant if they are the sole motive for making the gift. The concept of 'impossibility' is not capable of precise definition and depends upon a judge's interpretation of the facts of any particular situation.

Impracticable: Something that may not make commercial sense or which is inconvenient. In the case of a foundation or trust, if the impracticality amounts to impossibility, i.e. it can only be done at an excessive or unreasonable cost or effort, then the trust or the foundation is void; if it is merely inconvenient or difficult, that is another matter.

Improvement of land: A person in possession of land or in receipt of the rents or profits derived from the land may obtain approval under certain circumstances, particularly when concerned with agricultural land, to borrow or advance money for the purpose of improvements, and may obtain an order charging the amount of the loan and the interest on the inheritance of the land. This could apply to trustees or foundations that administer land, but this should not be necessary if the trust deed or foundation charter and regulations are properly drafted to accommodate incidents relating to the holding of land for beneficiaries' advantage in the future.

Improvident leasing or letting and purchasing: Similar principles apply as described under IMPROVIDENT SALE.

Improvident sale: Sales made by trustees or by a foundation council of real property without exercising reasonable diligence, e.g. in failing to invite competitive offers, or under circumstances where the land is subject to WASTE, thus exposing the trustees or foundation council to personal responsibility. The real value of the property must be understood by the trustees or foundation council and a reserve price placed on the property. Offers below the reserve price should not be accepted. An independent valuer should be employed and adequate notice in the sales details should emphasize the existence or potential of planning permission.

Imputation: The word 'impute' denotes something that is attributed elsewhere or connected or associated with another thing or person.

Imputed notice: Notice that is not as clear and unequivocal as actual notice, nor given according to the law, such as constructive notice. Imputed notice is considered to have been given following the true construction of the facts where, for example, the action of one party is construed as having made another party aware of a situation. The notice, actual or constructive, possessed by an agent is normally imputed to the principal, provided that the notice is obtained by the agent in the same transaction. Also, the notice must have come to the agent as such and only affects the principal if it is material to the transaction so that it constitutes a duty of the agent to communicate it to the principal. Thus, a lawyer conveying property to a trustee may, in the course of his work, obtain notice that there are rights attached to the property that is being conveyed. This notice is imputed to the principal. The question of whether an agent has actual or CONSTRUCTIVE NOTICE of the matter that can be imputed to the principal is an objective one; 'a nod is as good as a wink' type of awareness by an agent is in many cases unsatisfactory and indefinite, and should not be relied upon as imputed notice of the principal.

In absentia: In the absence of.

Inalienability, rule against: This is a rule that prevents setting up a trust so that the trust property is inalienable by being held for a specific purpose for an indefinite time. The same rule prevents income from being accumulated indefinitely. The rule does not apply to trusts established and approved for charitable purposes or to private foundations. *See* PERPETUITIES AND ACCUMULATIONS.

Incapacity: A term equivalent to disability and the opposite of 'capacity'. *See* CAPACITY.

Incentive trusts: Trusts where trustees are required to consider guidelines when making discretionary distributions so as to overcome the possibility of beneficiaries possessing too much easy wealth. The guidelines have been changed in recent trusts and now firm instructions are given to trustees on the approach they must follow. In the United States these have become known as 'incentive trusts', which provide that desirable behaviour, such as good academic grades, good jobs, etc., will be rewarded by distributions from the trust fund, and bad behaviour, particularly concerned with drugs, will be punished by withholding trust distributions.

The encouragement of careers, marriage and the purchase of a home have been accepted as incentives in traditional trusts, but there have been policy concerns when beneficiaries are required to meet certain less discernible standards before a distribution is made. This is illustrated by the 'Restatement (Third) of Trusts', which states:

> 'In cases of this type, society's interest in a property owner's freedom of disposition must be weighed against the risk of excessive influence on a personal decision significantly affecting the life of the beneficiary and perhaps others. The social concerns here involve not only the increased risk of an unsuitable decision being made or adhered to by the beneficiary but also the burdens and difficulties of judicial interpretation and enforcement of such interpretations.'

Incidental beneficiary: A person who, without being a beneficiary of a trust or a foundation, nevertheless enjoys, through a person who is a beneficiary, some enjoyment such as would be provided by a parent who is a beneficiary of a trust to his children. A term used in US practice but of no legal implications.

Income: *See* CAPITAL AND INCOME.

Income splitting trusts: Designed mostly for estate planning purposes where income, which would otherwise have come into the hands of one person or which would be held on trust for the benefit of one person, is paid to a variety of recipients with the intention of reducing liability to estate duty or inheritance tax.

Income tax: A tax applied on the income of persons and companies, although with the latter the term 'corporation tax' or similar is frequently used. Income tax also applies to the income of foundations and trusts that have sufficient connection with a jurisdiction to be liable for tax. The connection depends upon the residence of the taxable person. With trusts and foundations residence depends on where the structure is managed and controlled. This follows the principle applied to companies. As far as trusts are concerned, this is where the majority of the trustees are resident or where they meet to manage the trust. With a private foundation it may be that income tax, or similar, may be paid where the foundation is registered or, alternatively, where the foundation council manages the foundation, i.e. generally where the members of the foundation council are situated. With private foundations the powers retained by the founder and the powers given to a protector have to be taken into account to decide where the authority of the foundation is exercised.

Incompletely constituted trusts: Where a property intended to be held in trust has not been vested in the trustee, then the trust is said to be incompletely constituted and the arrangement then may not give rise to the trust that was intended. Where the intended trustee has no title to the property, there are only a few special circumstances where the intended beneficiary may obtain a court order to compel the settlor to complete the vesting of the property. For example, such an intended beneficiary may enforce the proper constitution of a trust where all that remains are formal steps to procure the transfer of the legal interest to the trustees. This depends upon the nature of the formal steps necessary. The GIFT may be considered to have been completely fulfilled if the donor, i.e. the settlor, has taken all the steps that lay exclusively in his power and completion depends upon action by others. For example, a transfer of shares by the settlor may be considered to be fulfilled if the settlor has signed the share transfer form and submitted it to the registered office of the company concerned. The issue of a new SHARE CERTIFICATE to the trustees depends upon the speed with which the company reacts. The rule was extended in equity and the gift was considered to be effective if it would be unconscionable for the donor to back out of his intention. In both circumstances, the donor is considered to hold the assets on trust for the beneficiary, i.e. the donor has done all that is necessary to declare a trust on behalf of the beneficiary but which is incomplete pending the transfer of assets to the trustees; in the meantime, the settlor is regarded as holding the assets on a separate trust for the beneficiaries. This principle is an exception to the EQUITABLE MAXIM that equity will not assist a volunteer.

Incorporate: To establish a legal entity. The method of incorporation varies from country to country. Incorporation usually involves the registration of documents by the promoters of the company in return for a Certificate of Registration. Another form of incorporation is by Royal Charter, which only occurs in connection with non-commercial and non-private organisations such as universities, colleges and cultural organisations operated by Government. The most frequent organisation that is incorporated is the limited liability company, which has the attraction that the participants, the shareholders, have no liability financially beyond the nominal price of their shares that is usually paid when the shares are acquired, thereby allowing the shareholders to incur no further liability. This makes limited liability companies attractive for commercial purposes and preferable to individuals acting as sole traders or with others in partnership where in both cases the liability is unlimited. Trusts are not incorporated and thereby incur no limitation of liability. Trustees can be liable to the full extent of their personal assets for any breach of trust. A foundation, although an incorporated separate legal entity, is liable to the full extent of the foundation's assets but no further liability is attached to either the founder or members of the foundation council. The growth of new structures, such as limited liability partnerships (LLPs), now allows limitation of liability without incorporation. *See* LIMITED LIABILITY PARTNERSHIPS.

Incorporeal hereditament: A right issuing out of a thing. It is not the thing itself, but something concerned with, annexed to or exercisable in association with and dependent upon a corporeal object. For example, in connection with land, houses or jewels, an incorporeal hereditament is an advantage collateral to the property itself; this includes a rent or income derived from a corporeal object. Also, incorporeal hereditament may consist of an annuity, patent rights or copyright and therefore comprise property that is intangible but which can be inherited. It is not necessary that the corporeal thing and the incorporeal hereditaments are owned by, or are in possession of, the same person.

Indemnity: An obligation to make good a loss that a person suffered in consequence of an act or by default of another. The act providing the indemnity is called 'indemnification'. A person who promises to indemnify, or actually does formally indemnify, to hold a person free from a designated loss, undertakes a primary liability. Consequently, unlike liability under a guarantee, an informal oral promise to indemnify will be adequate. This is contrasted with a guarantee where the guarantor undertakes a secondary liability where he is only bound if the other party does not perform the guaranteed obligation, in which case evidence in writing is required to prove the existence of such an obligation; whereas an indemnity is a primary liability where no evidence in writing is required. In practice, the terms 'indemnify' and 'guarantee' are used indiscriminately and the actual obligation undertaken needs to be examined to determine the correct nature. Indemnities are often used in association with insurance contracts. *See* GUARANTEE *and* SURETY.

Indicia: Signs used in respect of circumstances which show that something is probable, such as in connection with property where possession over a long period may be said to be the indicia of ownership.

Inferior courts: Under English law inferior courts are those that have jurisdiction to hear and determine civil cases other than the High Courts of Justice, the Court of Appeal and the Supreme Court. Inferior courts include a range of courts, such as County Courts, Lord Mayor's Court, industrial tribunals and local valuation courts. Inferior courts are limited to the types of actions they can hear and, where an inferior court has the jurisdiction of a matter that can also be heard by the High Court, the inferior court is limited to the amount of compensation or damages it may award and, in any case, has a lower scope for ordering imprisonment for contempt of court. Cases in the UK are limited to those which no request for compensation greater than £30,000 is claimed. A similar series of inferior courts is found in Northern Ireland, the US and Ireland, as well as other jurisdictions.

Informed consent: An agreement or consent to do something or allow something to happen after all relevant facts are known. Without a person being given full information about a course of action proposed, a subsequent action may be regarded as a criminal or civil offence, such as the absence of a full explanation prior to surgery might lead to a criminal offence of assault or to an action for negligence. Although the term is not usually applied in a trust or foundation context, there is nevertheless an analogous need to explain to a settlor the full consequences of entering into a trust. This is achieved by the normal practice of informing the settlor before a trust deed is executed of the true nature of the trust and removing any illusions by the settlor that a trust is an alternative to a bank account that he may use for his own purposes.

Infra: Below. Used in a book to refer the reader to a subsequent page or part of the book as opposed to supra (meaning above). *See* SUPRA.

In good faith: A phrase used to indicate honesty in connection with the manner in which a transaction is performed. It is best defined in the *Sale of Goods Act* 1893, Section 62(2), where a thing is done 'in good faith' 'when it is, in fact, done honestly, whether it be done negligently or not'. Similar conditions have been used in other Acts, such as the *Leasehold Reform Act* 1967. The concept of good faith appears to have originated from Section 90 of the *Bills of Exchange Act* 1882, which emphasises that 'in good faith' depends upon the subjective honesty of the party concerned. A person who is 'honestly blundering and careless' is distinct from one who has not acted honestly and with the intention to defraud.

Inheritance: The passing of property from one person to another on death either by WILL or INTESTACY. Once subject to considerable detail in interpretation, the word 'inheritance' is now used in a more straightforward sense and is often expressed in statute without definition.

Inheritance tax: A tax on the transfer of capital which operates primarily on transfers that occur on death. Anti-avoidance measures apply the tax retrospectively on certain lifetime gifts. When applied to INTER VIVOS transfers, the tax is generally charged at a reduced rate. Exemptions exist in respect of gifts between husbands and wives, and gifts to charities. Other classes of gifts are liable to inheritance tax if the transferor should die within seven years of making the gift. The rate of tax applied is reduced on a descending scale year by year for seven years. These gifts are known as 'POTENTIALLY EXEMPT TRANSFERS' or PETs.

In his own right: No precise and defined legal meaning, but an expression used to indicate that the holder of a company share, or money, or bill of exchange, holds without regard to any other interest in so far as the holder may deal with the property held. For example, the registered shareholder holds shares in such a way that the company that issued the shares can safely deal with him in respect of them, whatever his interest may be in those shares. However, a shareholder is not in that position after receiving notice from a trustee in bankruptcy that another person is claiming those shares. This means that a liquidator of a company does not hold 'in his own right' the shares of the company which he is liquidating. Therefore the phrase is not synonymous with 'beneficial owner' as the interest of the holder may not be a beneficial one, but it is clearly used to distinguish property that a trustee may hold in his own right (with a right to it not subject to that of anyone else and which he holds in a way that is good against all the world) and that which he holds as a trustee (on behalf of a beneficial owner) in the way that a liquidator does not hold shares of a company which he is liquidating in his own right. When applied to a bill of exchange, 'in his own right' means something more than one who does not acquire a bill in a representative character; it means that the holder has a right to the bill against all the world and is not subject to any other person's right. Therefore, a person holding something 'in his own right' means he has a right to hold it against all the world whatever his interest may be. The legal interest in a thing is a different matter from the right to hold. Similarly, money paid to a child's guardian or as maintenance under an order of the divorce court is not money to which the child was entitled 'in his own right'; the child's right was to be maintained and not to receive the money.

In-house Counsel: A lawyer employed by an institution, company, government or firm to provide advice to the employer on compliance with the law and matters relating to the employer's business. In this context, the word 'counsel' does not imply that the person described by this term is necessarily a barrister. Generally, in most jurisdictions, it is not appropriate for an in-house counsel to advise clients or customers of his employer on the grounds that, in addition to any professional barriers which may be based on the uncertainty of in-house counsel's standing within the legal profession, there is likely to be a conflict of interest. For example, an in-house counsel working for a trust company should not advise a potential settlor of a trust or founder of a private foundation as to the appropriateness of a standard form trust deed or charter used by his company, although there appears to be no harm in pointing out the characteristics of the terms of these deeds so long as the potential client is advised in writing to obtain his own professional advice as to the suitability of the proposed instrument.

Injunction: A court order directing a party to the proceedings to do, or refrain from doing, a specified act. An injunction is an EQUITABLE REMEDY and accordingly is granted in cases where a monetary compensation is inadequate. Injunctions are of various types. These are as follows:

- A perpetual or final injunction, which is granted after an infringement of an established justiciable right, or to forestall a future infringement. This is called perpetual because it is granted at the final determination of the party's right despite that it only be required to continue for a certain period, such as the length outstanding under a lease.
- An interlocutory, or interim injunction, which is granted before the trial of an action to keep matters relating to the party's business or other circumstances at a standstill until the issue has been determined.
- A prohibitory or restrictive injunction, which requires a person not to do a wrongful act. These are sometimes called preventative injunctions.
- A mandatory injunction, which is an order that requires a person to remedy some wrongful omission or to undo the consequences of a wrongful act.
- Common injunctions, which are to restrain a person from proceeding in the common law courts or from executing a judgment obtained there.
- A special injunction, which is granted to give effect to an equitable right or to provide an additional remedy.

In lieu: In the place of or instead of. The precise meaning depends upon the context of where these words appear.

In loco parentis: In the position of a parent. A person is in loco parentis towards a child when he is not a parent but is able to exercise some of the functions of a parent. A step-parent may acquire some parental responsibility and is then said to be in loco parentis in respect of those rights. Such a status could be acquired under certain circumstances by a trustee administering family assets to a child when there is no other person to do so. Normally this is avoided by a trustee, before a trusteeship is accepted, by ensuring that there is a person who might fulfil the role if a natural parent or relation is unable to look after the child. Where a person is in loco parentis there is a presumption of equity against double portions, such as where a parent or person in loco parentis incurs an obligation to provide a PORTION for a child and then that person subsequently makes a will making provisions for that child. Equity presumes that the child is not intended to benefit both from the portion and under the will.

In perpetuity: Forever, used to indicate the rights to retain an income or profit without any time limit, such as the rights to keep the profits from the land in perpetuity. *See* PERPETUITIES AND ACCUMULATIONS.

In personam – in person: A term used to distinguish a right or an obligation the enforcement of which is directed to a person. This is opposed to a right against property, an IN REM situation, where an action is brought directly against the property concerned. The consequences are that a remedy in personam is only applicable to the actual person concerned, whereas a remedy in rem asserts a right of property that can be enforced against the world at large. Actions in trust law are generally actions in personam against the trustees for breach of trust but where it is necessary to recover trust property an action in rem may sometimes be brought.

In re: A term used in proceedings in Chancery matters and bankruptcy to indicate the particular estate, person or matter to which the proceedings relate. The reports of such cases often do not have the names of the plaintiff (appellant) and defendant but relate to the property matter concerned preceded by the word 'Re'.

In rem: A term applied to civil actions where the action is brought against property, as opposed to actions against persons, actions IN PERSONAM. Actions in rem are generally concerned with the status of some particular subject matter such as land or ships and can be used to restore trust property when an action in personam against trustees is inadequate.

Insider dealing: Where a person deals in securities using unpublished, price-sensitive information to make a profit or avoid a loss. In the UK, under the *Criminal Justice Act* 1993, dealing by such persons, known as insiders, or others who have acquired information from insiders, may commit a criminal offence by dealing, by improperly disclosing such information or by encouraging others to deal.

Insolvency: The inability to pay debts as they become due. The term 'insolvent' is applied to a person who is or who is about to enter bankruptcy proceedings; it also applies to a person who enters an Individual Voluntary Arrangement to undertake to pay creditors agreed amounts at stated intervals until such time as the debts are repaid. The insolvency of a company generally leads to liquidation, administration or administrative receivership or, as an alternative, to a Company Voluntary Arrangement whereby the creditors agree not to bring liquidation procedures in exchange for an undertaking by the company to conduct its affairs in such a manner that the debts may eventually become repaid. This course of action is frequently adopted on the grounds that an immediate liquidation will produce nothing for the creditors but with a Company Voluntary Arrangement there is a chance that some business will continue and at least some of the debts can be repaid. The law in the UK governing insolvency is the *Insolvency Act* 1986.

Institutional trust: A trust that arises automatically when a person deals with the property of another knowing that his actions are unconscionable. Under English law, a person who is adversely affected by that unconscionable action can claim to be a beneficiary under a constructive or other trust which is imposed from the moment of that action. Because of the institutional nature of English trusts, the court's role consists only of recognising the existence of such a trust and that it arises at the time the defendant was aware of his unconscionable act. A simple example of such a trust is if A paid money to B under a mistake and a week later B was made aware of the mistaken nature of the payment. A CONSTRUCTIVE TRUST only arises at the time B knew of the mistake, i.e. at the time B gained some knowledge which would affect his conscience in relation to his dealings with the money. The English courts do not originate new proprietary rights but protect existing rights, employing, if necessary, such institutional trusts implied by law. As an alternative to acknowledging these constructive trusts, it is said that the doctrine of EQUITABLE TRACING will permit pre-existing property rights to be followed into property acquired by another and that equitable tracing could be a vindication of those pre-existing rights. This is in contrast to the American remedial constructive trusts that arise not at the date of the unconscionable action but at the date of the court's order at the end of a trial. With this remedial constructive trust the terms and extent of the trust are matters for the discretion of the court, i.e. the court is creating new rights as a remedy. With the institutional trust, the right arises at the moment of the unconscionable action. *See* REMEDIAL CONSTRUCTIVE TRUST.

Instrument: A general term applied to formal legal writing, such as a charter, deed or agreement and often used where the user wishes to refer to some written document without specifying its actual legal nature. The term is used in a variety of contexts and is subject to many legislative and judicial interpretations. The term can have an individual meaning, such as a power that is stated to be conferred by 'deed, instrument or will' and can be properly created by mere writing, which is neither a deed nor a will.

Insurable interest: A concept developed out of the INDEMNITY basis of insurance and adopted to distinguish insurance from undesirable wagering. Contracts of wager were considered unenforceable after the *Marine Insurance Act* 1745 and more so after the *Marine Insurance Act* 1906, which imposed an absolute requirement that a contract of insurance must be in connection with an insurable interest or the expectation of an insurable interest at the time of its formation. This means that the insured has an interest in the item for which insurance has been arranged other than the possibility of receiving monetary compensation for its damage or loss under the contract. This distinguishes insurance from wager where the only interest of a gambler on a horse race, for example, is that the horse may win and a profit may accrue to the gambler; this is the only interest which the gambler has in the horse. An owner of a horse, on the other hand, has many interests in the horse: its health, value and breeding potential, all of which are insurable interests.

Insurance: Despite a lack of any authoritative definition, insurance is a commitment by contract by which an insurer agrees to make a monetary provision to the insured upon the occurrence of some event or against some risk. The concept was analysed in ***Prudential Insurance Co. v. Commissioners of Inland Revenue*** [1904] 2KB 658 as: (1) securing a benefit when a stated event occurs in return for the payment of the premium by the insured; (2) an element of uncertainty as to whether the event will happen; and (3) the event must be PRIMA FACIE harmful to the interests of the insured, i.e. there must be an insurable interest. These characteristics require some modification with respect to certain types of insurance. The main types of insurance are: indemnity insurance, by which the insured is compensated when any event causes financial loss either with the payment of an agreed amount or on the assessment of the amount of the loss suffered; and life insurance (sometimes called 'assurance'), which is a term used to describe insurance in respect of events that are certain to take place, such as death, and sometimes used as an alternative to a trust whereby, after the payment of a single premium, the occurrence of the contingency, such as the insured person's death, results in the payment of a sum of money to a third party. A contract of insurance is one of UBERRIMAE FIDEI, which is one of utmost good faith: if a party fails in preliminary negotiations to disclose a fact that is material to the risk and the assessment of the premium then the insurance is voidable. *See* LIFE ASSURANCE.

Insurance policy: After a contract of insurance is arranged, a formal document is issued by the insurer setting out the terms of that insurance. Although in law policies are not required to be in writing, the general practice is that an insurance policy is a written document that is preceded in practice by a cover note, which represents a temporary contract of insurance.

Intangible property: Property that does not have a physical form but which nevertheless represents value and which may be vindicated through court action, such as shares in a company and INTELLECTUAL PROPERTY. Sometimes applied to characteristics that cannot be conventionally valued but which nevertheless add to the value of a thing or organisation, such as GOODWILL of a business.

Intellectual property: A collective term embracing certain INTANGIBLE PROPERTY rights and other related rights, and is generally taken to include patents, designs (registered and unregistered), trademarks, copyright, geographical indications (relating to the source of goods), trade secrets, plant breeding rights and rights associated with electronic information. These items are protected according to the individual laws of jurisdictions and international conventions. Trade secrets are not strictly property rights, although they are frequently characterised as such in books and articles.

Intention: In civil and private law, intention means that a person is responsible for the natural consequences of his act, whether or not the person concerned directed his mind to achieving the outcome of his act. Where there is a court or a jury, the decision must be made whether the defendant did intend or could foresee that the natural and probable consequences of his actions produced that result. The term is also used to describe the conscious or deliberate entry into financial arrangements; the intention is one of the requirements to constitute a valid trust (*see* CERTAINTIES). A similar stringent analysis is not usually carried out in the case of private foundations, as the evidence of incorporation is adequate to show that the foundation has been properly set up in the same way that the intention of a subscriber to a company is not usually of critical significance. Also, the intention of a testator, as expressed in his will, is what the court will enforce. The evidence of intention may be challenged and rules of construction are applied to enable the testator's intention to be ascertained when it is not otherwise clear.

Intention to create legal relations: This intention is one of the key elements of a contract. An agreement is only enforceable as a legal contract so long as this intention is present and therefore family and social arrangements are not binding as contracts as they do not intend to create legal relationships. In the commercial environment there is a reverse presumption that anyone entering into an agreement of a commercial nature will be taken to have the intention to create the legal relationship.

Inter alia: Amongst other things. The expression is often used to highlight one of several items with the intention of focussing on that particular item as one amongst many of similar status.

Interest (1): In financial terms, interest is a charge made for borrowing a sum of money. Although there is no statutory definition for tax purposes, it was defined in ***Bennett v. Ogston*** [1930] 15 TX 374 by Mr Justice Rowlatt as 'payment by time for the use of money', and further defined in *Halsbury's Laws of England* as 'the return or compensation for the use or retention by one person of a sum of money belonging to, or owed to, another'. An excessive payment cannot be interest (***Cairns v. MacDiarmid*** [1982] STC 226). The interest may be either simple interest or compound interest. Interest may also arise on unpaid damages for personal injuries. *See* CAPITAL AND INCOME.

Interest (2): In general legal terms, an interest exists in a thing when a person has rights, advantages, duties or liabilities, or has incurred a loss connected with the thing either present or future, ascertained or potential, so long as the connection is not too remote. The double meaning of the term 'interest' is seen in connection with land. The word 'interest' is used when the word 'estate' would be incorrect to denote rights in property that are not derived from ownership. The term was used to denote certain rights closely connected with the actual land itself, such as licences for profit and *PROFITS À PRENDRE*. *The Law of*

Property (Miscellaneous Provisions) Act 1989, Section 2(6)) defines in a circuitous manner what the law understands to be 'an interest in land'. This, the Act states, is 'any estate, interest or charge in or over land'. Therefore, interest is defined to distinguish an interest from other rights in land, such as a licence. Any piece of land may be subject to a variety of interests at the same time. For example, this will apply in the case of land if held by trustees which, concurrently, may be subject to a rent charge, a legal charge, a lease, a right of way and restrictive covenants, each held by separate individuals. Since the *Law of Property Act* 1925, Section 1, the only estates in land capable of subsisting or being created by law is an estate in FEE SIMPLE ABSOLUTE IN POSSESSION and the TERM OF YEARS ABSOLUTE, i.e. freehold or leasehold. Interests and charges that can be created at law are easements, rights or privileges in or over land for 'an interest equivalent to an estate in fee simple absolute in possession or for a term of years absolute.' Other interests in land take effect as EQUITABLE INTERESTS.

Interest (3): Frequently used in conjunction with the term 'EQUITY' or 'EQUITABLE'. For example, the 'EQUITABLE INTEREST' that a beneficiary has under a trust, thereby distinguishing the beneficiary's interest from that of the trustees, which is a legal interest. The term 'interest' may be used on conveyances to denote a beneficial right in the property or in a trust or in trust assets.

Interest (4): The term has also been used in connection with insurance to indicate the interest in the insured property using the term 'insurable interests'. *See* INSURABLE INTEREST.

Interest (5): The term has a variety of other meanings and, used in conjunction with other words, for example, personal interest refers to the interest a person may have in participating in public affairs or other pursuits.

Interest in possession: A present right or present enjoyment of property. Where an individual has an interest in possession over trust property, then any charge to inheritance tax is computed by bringing into that person's estate the full capital value of the property over which he has an interest in possession. Equally, a founder may be regarded as having an interest in possession of the foundation assets where he excessively duplicates the roles so that he may treat the foundation's assets as his own. A lease for life is treated as an interest in possession and trusts are often categorised as falling into three categories: bare trusts, discretionary trusts and interest in possession trusts where, in the latter, the beneficiaries have a present interest in the trust property for a fixed period or until death. A trust that is a sham because the settlor retains too great an interest in the trust property may result in the settlor being attributed to the whole value of the trust assets as an interest in possession. The term 'interest in possession', however, lacks precision and inheritance tax statutes do not define the term. *See* NON-INTEREST IN POSSESSION TRUSTS.

Interim orders: Orders issued by an English court in connection with matters being litigated in order to preserve the possibility of something arising that requires a court order to allow a proper conclusion of the case. The two most important are FREEZING ORDERS *and* SEARCH ORDERS.

Interlocutory: An application to the court or proceedings that is peripheral to the main hearing, such as an application for disclosure. Also used in connection with judgments; an interlocutory judgment refers to a judgment in default where the amount payable has to be decided later on by the court. The word has been largely replaced under the CPR by the word 'interim' in English law.

Intermeddle: A term that takes on several aspects. A person who is neither a trustee nor a person authorised by trustees who interferes in trust matters is said to intermeddle with the trust and, by doing so, makes himself a *TRUSTEE DE SON TORT* and becomes personally liable to account to the beneficiaries and, at the same time, establishes himself as a CONSTRUCTIVE TRUSTEE. This result is distinct from the personal liability owed by a trustee of a constructive trust. In the case of a *trustee de son tort*, or an intermeddler, it can apply even though that person did not receive any trust property. The intermeddler is better described as being merely unaccountable in equity and this clarifies his position and makes sure he is not taken to be a trustee at all. A person who is not a trustee but who lawfully receives trust property from the trustees as their agent, and who then deals with the property in a way which he knows is inconsistent with the trust is personally liable to compensate the beneficiaries. Similarly, a person who dishonestly assists in a BREACH OF TRUST or other FIDUCIARY DUTY will be personally liable to compensate the beneficiaries and to forfeit the profits made by his wrongdoing. A further form of intermeddling is where a person knowingly and dishonestly receives trust property for his own benefit; it also applies where a person receives trust property innocently and then subsequently acquires knowledge of the default but uses the property for his own benefit.

International comity: Rules of conduct that are observed by states on the grounds of courtesy, which sometimes is regarded as an item of international or customary law.

International European trust law: A study conducted by a group of scholars in 1996 the main object of which was to introduce Dutch lawyers to the common law concept of trust and trust-like arrangements. The study consisted of a hypothetical proposed European trust enactment with explanations, followed by national reports for various countries, to illustrate the diversity which the trust concept takes in various common law and civil law countries.

International financial regulation: Measures adopted with the intention of procuring harmonised control over financial functions to avoid exploitation of investors through inadequate financial regulation. These measures may either be formal international public law, in the form of treaties, or supranational law, such as the law from the EU. These measures are aimed at controlling the practices of particular activities of industries internationally; for example, banking. Laws enacted in a jurisdiction that controls activities within that jurisdiction may be based upon guidelines or codes of practice of international bodies which, in many cases, are respected as representing a form of best practice and, although not legally enforceable, they take on the appearance of being authoritative statements. The authority given to these measures has led to them being called 'SOFT LAW' which, on enactment, may become part of that state's domestic laws. The chief international bodies associated with financial regulation are the International Monetary Fund (IMF), the World Bank (WB) and the Financial Security Bureau (FSB), which, following the initiative of the G10 in 2012, now represent a more coordinated group of organisations that are authorised to secure international regulation in a more consistent and effective way than previously. In addition to these official bodies there are numerous others, such as the Basel Committee on Banking and the International Organization of Securities Commissions (IOSCO), which are recognised as authoritative bodies in the banking and securities fields although their recommendations on proposals can only be regarded as soft law but, necessarily, carry much authority. International financial regulation contrasts with the way in which world trade law is devised and administered by the World Trade Organization (WTO). As there is no world financial authority, each of the specialist bodies puts out its guidelines, codes or practices, or other announcements of standards, which have no legal authority but some of which are recognised as embodying international standards.

International law: A system of law regulating the relationship of sovereign states and their rights and duties with regard to one another and as 'PUBLIC INTERNATIONAL LAW' is distinguished from 'PRIVATE INTERNATIONAL LAW', also known as 'CONFLICT OF LAWS', which concerns the relationship between individuals when two or more legal systems are involved. International law governs legal aspects concerned with the formation and recognition of states, the acquisition of territory, war, the law of the sea and space, treaties, the treatment of aliens and human rights, the laws of which are derived particularly from conventions, treaties and international customs so far as there is evidence of a particular form of behaviour. The trend is that international law in some of its forms can now affect directly the behaviour of individuals. It might therefore be subject to proceedings if some aspects of international law are contravened, such as the law of human rights and of war crimes. Also, international law is influenced by the activities of international agencies and trade organisations who issue guidelines and other non-enforceable regimes that are often referred to as 'SOFT LAW' and which sometimes are recognised as being effective in regulating international affairs and, consequently, are considered to be an aspect of international law.

International trusts and foundations: A trust or foundation that contains elements involving more than one jurisdiction and where the place of administration is likely to be situated in a financial or offshore centre and used for asset planning purposes for individuals and their families. The management of these trusts and foundations may also involve the use of protectors or guardians to whom the trustees or foundation councils refer in matters about which more information is required so as properly to allocate the trust or foundation income and assets. The intention of offshore trusts and foundations developed around the need to separate the legal ownership of assets away from the settlor or founder and, by discretionary clauses, withhold the legal ownership from passing to the beneficiaries until such time as it was tax-advantageous to do so. This advantage was based on the liability to tax being restricted to the legal owners of capital and income, but this advantage has been diminished in recent years by many diverse and complex rules against tax evasion and tax avoidance, and has been severely affected by the requirement of transparency. *See* PROTECTOR *and* GUARDIAN.

***Inter partes*:** Court proceedings when both parties are present in court. This contrasts with EX PARTE proceedings, where the other parties are not present. Since the introduction of the Civil Procedure Rules these terms have been changed to 'on notice' or 'without notice' applications respectively.

Interpretation: The processes that are applied to determine the true meaning of a written document; also called 'construction'. The process is carried out in accordance with a number of rules and presumptions and, so far as they are relevant, these rules and presumptions apply to private documents such as deeds, wills and trust and foundation instruments, as well as to legislation. The principal rule that is applied is the literal rule by which words are given their ordinary meaning in the absence of any provision to the contrary. Also, the *Interpretation Act* 1978 provides a number of important principles that must be used in construing every Act and statutory instrument unless a term is expressly given a different meaning in the instrument concerned. In constructing statutory instruments, the reader is presumed to know the provisions of the Act, which lays down some accepted principles of interpretation.

In terrorem: Literally meaning 'by way of terrifying' and may be used in the case of a will or trust where a beneficiary is entitled to some benefit if he does or does not engage in a particular act, such as whether he does or does not marry a particular person, or does not contest a will or a trust instrument. In such cases, where there is no gift over, i.e. to another person, in the event of the named person failing to comply with the condition, then the condition is void and the term is said to be *in terrorem*, i.e. an attempt to frighten the beneficiary. Otherwise, the condition will be effective if there is a gift over. The expression is often used to describe penalty clauses in contracts.

In trust: The placing of assets in trust means the transfer of those assets to a trustee accompanied by instructions on how the trustee is to manage and distribute the assets in due course. The term is more accurate than the colloquial expression of 'setting up a trust' because the latter implies that a trust is a separate entity, whereas 'in trust' contains a greater implication that the assets are held by a person or persons subject to an obligation. This concept of an obligation indicates the essence of a trust. The phrase of 'in trust' or 'on trust' may frequently mean less than a formal trust structure or one with legal significance (such as a resulting trust) and merely means that something is entrusted to a person. Thus a keeper of goods in a warehouse may notify his customers that all goods are 'held in trust and covered by insurance' or that property is 'held in trust for an infant'. The term is frequently used in an insurance policy, such as where the insured is indemnified against loss or damage to goods 'belonging to or held in trust by' him. The literal meaning of the phrase is that some property is held on behalf of another and does not necessarily imply the existence of a legal, express or resulting trust and is not subject to all the detailed aspects of a formal trust.

Inter vivos: An event that takes place between living people. When a trust is created by a living settlor it is referred to as an inter vivos trust, as distinct from a trust set up on the settlor's death, which is referred to as a WILL TRUST.

Intestacy: When a person dies without having made a valid will, that person is then said to have died wholly intestate. Where there is a valid will that fails to dispose of all his property, then the term 'partially intestate' is applied. A person is also wholly intestate where the will only appoints an executor but does not dispose of any property, or when a will is invalid because it was not properly executed, or where the testator lacks testamentary capacity. A partial intestacy arises where a will deals with only part of a testator's estate; intestacy applies to the part that is not dealt with. Where there is intestacy, the rules of the jurisdiction in which the deceased was domiciled may reflect the importance given to familial relationships and may result in a surviving spouse being given, under the law of the deceased's domicile, a share in the deceased's estate under the prescribed rules on FORCED HEIRSHIP. The management of an intestate estate in the UK has been subject to numerous Acts of Parliament from 1884. The current law, the *Intestates' Estates Act* 1952, has been subject to many amendments particularly by the *Inheritance and Trustees' Powers Act* 2014 whereby a deceased's spouse or civil partner benefits from the deceased's assets absolutely when the deceased leaves no issue. This benefit is reduced by half when there is issue. Also, the definition of 'personal chattels' is amended to cover all tangible moveable property except for money, or security for money, or property which was solely or mainly used for business purposes or as an investment at the time of death.

Intra vires: Is an act carried out by a body, such as a company or public authority, which is within the limits of the powers conferred upon that body by statute. The rules on *intra vires* limiting the activities of registered companies have been diminished under the rules of the EU and there is now no distinction in the objects of a company in connection with *intra vires* and ULTRA VIRES objects clauses. Literally meaning 'within the powers' and continues to be applied to an act by a person or corporation that is within the scope of a person's or a company's powers or authority; the opposite of ultra vires.

Inventory: A schedule of chattels made by trustees to preserve evidence of the nature and value of the chattels in the event of loss by the neglect or fraud of others.

Investment company: A company that is either private or public where the object of the company is the holding of shares in one or more other companies as investments. Investment companies may be subject to a greater rate of taxation than trading companies and may also have to give special notice to the Company Registrar and may be subject to special provisions in relationship to dividends. Investment companies are an important way of investing in one vehicle that itself invests widely or specifically in other companies. An investment company is a closed-ended incorporated body (CLOSED-END FUND), i.e. investments are made by the purchase of that company's shares, which are limited in number. This differs substantially from unit trusts that are open-ended arrangements which can create more units the greater the investment demand. An investment company has only the authorised and issued share structure of a limited company to offer investors. Investment companies which are public companies and offer their shares to the public are sometimes referred to (erroneously) as 'investment trusts'. This is because mutual investment was originally conducted through trusts but now these types of investments are made through companies, although the misnomer persists. *See* UNIT TRUSTS, MUTUAL FUNDS *and* OEIC.

Investment of trust funds: Trustees have an obligation in relation to the investment of funds of EXPRESS TRUSTS. Following the *Trust Act* 2000, in English trust law the trustees' obligations are divided into three: first, those obligations imposed by statute; second, those entered into by virtue of express trust powers; and, third, the development of principles governing investment laid down in decided cases. The *Trust Act* 2000 sets out a statutory code relating to the investment of trust monies and the delegation of trustees' duties to agents, custodians and nominees. There is a general power of investment whereby trustees can act as though they were the absolute owners of the trust property. The duty of trustees to invest the trust funds, where appropriate, imposes a standard of care, and a further duty to consider the standard investment criteria provided by the statute, and the need to take proper advice on investment policies and decisions. Trust documents usually provide a code of powers and obligations imposed on trustees in respect of investments, and trustees will generally abide by that code in order to limit their own liability. The overall duty developed by case law requires a trustee to act prudently and safely, to act fairly between beneficiaries and to act in the beneficiaries' best interests. The duty of the trustees is not to take imprudent risk. There is a contradictory duty that the trustees should obtain an optimum return for the trust and this may be in opposition to fulfilling some other objective, either of an ethical or non-financial nature. Before making or changing investments, the *Trust Act* 2000 imposes an obligation on trustees to seek professional advice unless it appears unreasonable for the trustee to do so. 'Proper advice' is considered to be advice from someone whom the trustee reasonably believes to be suitably qualified. The investment of trust funds may be in stocks and securities and may be, under the *Trust Act* 2000, investments in freehold and leasehold land for any purpose. As well as seeking professional advice, trustees may appoint a nominee or bare trustee to act in relation to any of the assets in which they invest. Trustees also have powers to appoint a custodian and to take custody of any trust assets. The standard of care in connection with investments is the statutory duty of care imposed by the *Trust Act* 2000, which imposes a duty of 'such skill and care as is reasonable in the circumstances'. The Act provides, in Section 1, that the duty of care and skill is reasonable in the circumstances with regard to any special knowledge or experience, that the trustee has or holds himself out as having or, if he acts in the course of a business or profession, then any special knowledge which is reasonable to expect that person in the course of that business or profession to possess. Therefore, in appointing investment advisers, that standard of care will apply; circumstances can be indicated either by the trust deed or otherwise by the settlor and on the size of the investments to be made and other considerations such as repatriation of profits, dividends and taxation.

Investment trust: Originally a trust set up to make investments for subscribers to a trust, but the term is now misleading, as this type of operation is now conducted through an investment company, which is an ordinary registered company that invests the company's capital. *See* UNIT TRUST *and* INVESTMENT COMPANY.

Ipso facto: By the very act itself.

Ipso jure: By the act of the law.

Irrevocable: Incapable of being revoked. Trusts and foundations may be set up without containing any provision relating to revocation. If the settlor or the founder retains a power of revocation, this may be seen as preserving the power of the settlor or founder to repossess the assets of the trust or foundation and may be subject to an order of a court, especially a matrimonial court, to carry out the revocation in order to increase the wealth that is available for sharing with a former spouse. On the other hand, for the benefit of certainty, a settlor or founder is usually advised when setting up their respective organisations to state in the documents the period for which the trust or foundation is to survive. With trusts, this has to be done with the rules relating to perpetuity in mind. The settlor or founder may provide that the trust or foundation may be ended by themselves or by some other person authorised to do so, and this should be stated in the relevant constitutional documents. *See HASTINGS-BASS.*

Islamic law: *See* ISLAMIC LAW - GLOSSARY.

Issue (offspring): The issue of a person includes his children, grandchildren and all other lineal descendants. The term 'issue' under the *Family Reform Act* 1987 now includes, in all instruments, illegitimate descendants. Because the position of adopted, illegitimate and surrogate children may vary from jurisdiction to jurisdiction, it is advisable with international trusts or foundations not to refer generally to issue or children as beneficiaries but to specify more precisely the identity of the beneficiaries. *See* HEIR.

Issued capital: *See* CAPITAL OF A COMPANY.

Italian torpedo: A technique to delay an appeal in a commercial action under EC COUNCIL REGULATION 44/2001 that took advantage of the *LIS ALIBI PENDENS* (first in time) rule, which awarded exclusive jurisdiction to the courts first seized of a case. At the first sign of trouble, an action commenced in the courts of Italy (or Greece) would block the hearing of the dispute in any jurisdiction chosen by the parties to an agreement. This was regarded as abuse of the *lis pendens* rule and the BRUSSELS REGULATION (RECAST) has provided that the court designated in an exclusive jurisdiction clause can proceed without waiting for the court first seized to stay its proceedings on application by a party that such an action was in breach of the exclusive jurisdiction clause in an agreement.

J

Joinder: The joining of actions or parties that are concerned with the same (or a very similar) principle of law or facts, or where several separate actions can well be tried together and where the outcome will be applied to the individual parties.

Joinder of causes of action: Several court actions may be put together (joined) into one when the dispute is between the same parties, provided the court does not consider it more convenient to order separate trials. The rule is now simply stated in the Civil Procedure Rules that: 'A claimant may use a single claim form to start all claims which can be conveniently disposed of in the same proceedings.' Then the court, under its general case management powers if it does not agree, may direct proceedings to be dealt with separately. This reflects the equitable procedure of an application to strike out the joinder as an abuse of powers when an attempt is made to introduce too many issues in a single claim. The term 'joinder' is used in a similar context of joining together several matters, as in the phrases 'joinder of issue' and 'joinder of parties'.

Joint: Combined or shared amongst several. Applied to property (other than CHOSE IN ACTION) it means that property held jointly passes, on the death of one of the owners, to the survivors, providing that the deceased has not previously disposed of his interest. When all the parties have died except one, that person takes the whole by SURVIVORSHIP. This distinguishes joint ownership from OWNERSHIP IN COMMON (*see* TENANCY IN COMMON) and, in the case of land, from COPARCENARY. When bonds, covenants, contracts and other chose in action are jointly held so that the item is vested in two or more persons any action in respect of the bond, etc. must be a joint action. This contrasts with a bond where ownership is SEVERAL and where each of the parties therefore has a separate interest and may take action alone. Whether a bond, covenant or similar is joint or several depends more upon the subject matter than upon the words employed. Similarly, two or more persons may be jointly liable for the same debt or demand; each is liable for the whole claim yet they are all considered to form one person and must all be sued together; a voluntary release to one will discharge all the parties. If one party is compelled to pay the whole debt, he is entitled to receive contributions from the others to the extent of their shares. On death, liability passes to the survivors except where property is held by a partnership where, on the death of a partner, the estate of the deceased remains liable in equity for all partnership debts then existing. The term is also used in contrast to 'concurrent', which is often seen when power is vested in two persons, jointly, which requires the two of them to act in concert but to be individually responsible. In the case of trustees, trustees own jointly the legal estate in the trust property. The beneficiaries' equitable interest must also be held jointly unless the trust instrument defines the shares of the assets, which are then held severally by the trustees for those beneficiaries. Where property is held in trust by more than one trustee, the trustees hold it jointly and, because they hold it on a discretionary basis, the equitable interest of the beneficiaries must also be joint until such time as the trustees' discretion is exercised by an allocation to individual beneficiaries. This position is not yet supported by any judicial interpretation.

Joint account: An account that exists where two or more persons deposit money in a bank in their joint names or where two or more persons advance money and take security jointly. Each is, in equity, deemed to be separately entitled to his proportion of the money the rights to which pass, on his death, to his personal representatives and not to his surviving co-lender(s). Therefore, where money is advanced by trustees, it is usual to insert in the loan instrument or mortgage deed a declaration that the money belonged to the lenders on joint account in equity as well as law, and that the receipt by the survivor or survivors can give a full discharge for any money due on the security. If money has been advanced by trustees and none of the trustees is alive on repayment, the personal representative of the last surviving trustee can give a full discharge. Under the *Law of Property Act* 1925, Section 111, it is sufficient to say merely that the money is advanced by the lenders out of money belonging to them on joint account. With a joint bank account it may be possible for the surviving depositor to become beneficially entitled to the money in the joint account, but if not available the money will be used to satisfy any outstanding judgment against the deceased.

Joint and several liability: An obligation involving two or more persons where all are liable jointly and each is liable severally (i.e. individually). Where trust beneficiaries suffer damage as a result of a breach of trust caused by more than one trustee or where trustees have collectively breached a trust, or where one trustee commits the breach and others stand by with a knowledge of the breach or have failed to remedy a breach of which they are aware, then the whole of the amount of the damage can be recovered from any or all of the trustees; their liability is joint and several. Otherwise, trustees are liable for their own breaches of duty and are not vicariously liable for breaches by their co-trustees, but third parties participating in a breach of trust will be jointly and severally liable with the trustees and with one another for harm suffered by the beneficiaries. The third parties involved are *TRUSTEES DE SON TORT*; the term covers persons involved in KNOWING RECEIPT AND DISHONEST ASSISTANCE of misdirected trust funds. A trustee who is liable to pay compensation to a beneficiary for breach of trust may recover a contribution from any other trustee who is liable to pay. This contribution was always available under the general principles of equity and is now available under the *Civil Liability (Contribution) Act* 1978 provided the trustees concerned became trustees after 1978.

Joint spousal or common law partner trusts: A trust, best known in Canada, where the settlor transfers property to a trust and is not liable for capital gains tax on the disposal of the assets to trustees as long as the settlor, or the settlor with his spouse or common law partner, is entitled to receive all the income of the trust that arises before the death of the settlor and the settlor's spouse or common law partner. These trusts must be made INTER VIVOS by a settlor aged 65 or over who is resident in Canada and where the trust is also resident. These trusts are similar to an ALTER EGO TRUST.

Joint tenancy in law and equity: A form of co-ownership where all the joint tenants together own the entire interest in the property in undivided shares and individually own nothing. When one of the joint tenants dies the doctrine of SURVIVORSHIP allows the deceased person's rights to continue to be held by the surviving joint tenants; the deceased person's rights do not pass into his estate. A joint tenancy continues until there is only one surviving joint tenant, who then becomes the absolute owner. Joint tenancy of the legal title in land can only be held when a conveyance of the property is made to the co-owners; this requires that the land be conveyed to persons of full age in undivided shares; the conveyance shall operate as if the land had been expressed to be conveyed to the grantees or, where there are more than four, then to the first four named in the conveyance. No SEVERANCE of a joint tenancy of a legal estate is possible. On the other hand, a joint tenancy in equity is where the persons acquire equitable interest in property with unity of time, title, interest and possession, provided they had the intention to be joint tenants. An equitable joint tenancy may be severed, i.e. a separation of the shares of the joint tenants allowing the concurrent ownership to continue without the rights of survivorship. This results in the beneficial joint tenancy becoming a beneficial tenancy in common in undivided shares and the right of survivorship no longer applies. Severance in equity can apply where one joint tenant alienates his right in the property by sale or mortgage of his undivided share, or upon the bankruptcy of one of the tenants, but not where one joint tenant creates a will transferring his share in the property as part of his estate. Severance can also occur where one joint tenant serves a notice in writing of severance on the others or where one joint tenant acquires some greater interest in the property than the others. This greater interest can arise by the acquisition of another's reversion so that the joint tenant who acquires that reversion acquires a greater interest than the others. Severance may also occur by mutual agreement in the course of dealing by the parties where one of the joint tenants' interests merges with another. Severance also occurs in limited circumstances in connection with divorce. The common law always preferred joint tenancies because under the doctrine of survivorship the property would vest in one person, making the performance of feudal duties easier. This is different from TENANCY IN COMMON, where there is no right of survivorship and which was preferred by equity (with no interest in feudal obligations) leading equity to prefer tenancy in common. *See* TRUSTS OF LAND.

Jointure: Generally a provision made by a husband for the support of his wife after his death. The term is generally used in connection with trusts of land, having originated from provisions in deeds relating to settled land.

Joint will: A will attempting in one document to dispose of property belonging to two or more testators. The success of this type of will depends on the ease of enforcement by the survivor. Difficulties arise in determining the nature, scope and effect of the trust that arises which then holds the property of the deceased and of the survivor. This revolves around whether the trust is a constructive trust or an implied trust, which affects the powers of the survivor to deal with, or dispose of, both the joint property and his own. The position appears to be that the survivor may revoke his participation in the joint will in respect of property not included in the joint will. Property in the joint will, nevertheless, will remain affected by the trust imposed by the terms of the agreement. MUTUAL WILLS are now preferred.

Judgment: A determination or decision of a court by a judge on questions or issues determined in the court after the judge has heard evidence and arguments presented at the trial or earlier. The term 'judgment' is also used to refer to the reasons for that decision, which may be reported as a law report if the RATIO DECIDENDI is of value as a PRECEDENT. Judgments may be either *EX TEMPORE* given immediately after the conclusion of the final submissions or in a reserved judgment, i.e. in writing, a draft of which is provided to all concerned in advance and then the final text is formally handed down as a judgment. A judgment IN REM decides the status of a person or thing and a judgment IN PERSONAM binds only those who are parties to the claim, such as in the case of the arrest or sale of a ship on the one hand and ordinary actions in contract and tort on the other. A judgment given in one country may be recognised in another according to the conflict of the laws in the jurisdiction where the parties seek to enforce the judgment, or according to the EC COUNCIL REGULATION 44/2001. Judgments affecting the terms or validity of a trust are subject to special rules under the Hague Convention for the Recognition and Enforcement of Trusts which provides that a trust judgment in one Convention country can be enforced in another without formal proceedings.

***Judicature Acts* 1873 and 1875:** Acts of the UK Parliament to remedy the delays caused in actions in English courts by common law and equity being administered in separate courts. The result of the 1873 and 1875 Acts was the creation of the present-day High Court and Court of Appeal by the amalgamation of the pre-existing Superior and Appellate Courts. These Acts, which allowed COMMON LAW and EQUITABLE REMEDIES to be awarded in any court, started a series of amending Acts that were consolidated into the *Supreme Court of Judicature (Consolidation) Act* 1925 and eventually replaced by the *Senior Courts Act* 1981. The delays before the 1873 and 1875 Acts were notorious and resulted in a case being brought in the common law court until an opinion on an equitable principle was needed, which necessitated a separate action being brought in the Chancery Courts. Charles Dickens illustrated this well in his novel, *Bleak House*, where the proceeds of an estate were the subject of litigation for many years between many parties until the final solution was reached, by which time the assets of the estate were found to have been exhausted by legal costs.

Judicial comity: The principle where the courts of one state or jurisdiction will give effect to the laws and judicial decisions of another. The rule also applies between the different courts in the High Court of Judicature in the UK.

Judicial Committee of the Privy Council (JCPC): A tribunal created by the *Judicial Committee Act* 1833 as the Court for Final Appeal for all British possessions outside the UK, until the Statute of Westminster 1931 enabled independent dominions to establish their own Courts of Final Appeal. Most territories which became independent followed this practice of establishing their own Court of Final Appeal. The court, however, retained some jurisdiction over appeals from a few Commonwealth countries and the UK's Overseas Territories and Crown Dependencies. The committee performs other roles, such as hearing ecclesiastical cases and appeals on disciplinary matters from various professional bodies. The members of this committee are the judges of the SUPREME COURT OF THE UNITED KINGDOM and other privy councillors who are past or present holders of high judicial office in the UK, or senior judicial officers in certain Commonwealth countries. Technically their decisions are not judgments but they are advice to the Crown and, to become effective, must be incorporated in Orders in Council. The committee's decisions are not binding as precedents upon English courts but, because of the high ranking nature of their members, are given considerable respect and are a 'PERSUASIVE AUTHORITY'. In 2009 this committee moved into the Supreme Court building in Parliament Square, London.

Judicial discretion: The ability of a judge to decide matters in the course of a trial, such as the power of the judge in a trust case to decline to name the beneficiaries of the trust or of the foundation if in his judgment identifying such persons could cause them embarrassment or danger. The limits of judicial discretion are important and form part of the training for judges given by the Judicial Studies Board.

Judicial notice: A matter of which a court does not require any proof, as any such matter is deemed to be within the inherent knowledge of the court, such as the existence of a war or of the basic principles of a relationship or of the characteristics of a structure, such as a trust or company. In other matters it is incorrect to presume that the court is aware of every matter. 'Who are the Beatles?' illustrated that, despite that group's notoriety, their identity could not be assumed to be within the scope of judicial notice. The question by the judge was for the purpose of establishing the identity of a group of entertainers that was not within the then inherent knowledge of the court.

Judicial precedent: Also called 'authorities' which are judicial decisions to which a court must have regard when dealing with the same or similar legal issues. Precedents vary in their authoritative weight but represent a fundamental element of the COMMON LAW of England and Wales. Precedents arise in English law from decisions of the Senior Courts of England and Wales. Decisions from courts of other common law jurisdictions can be of persuasive value but any such decisions require adoption by an English court before they become part of the law of England. Other common law jurisdictions adopt the same principle. The authoritative weight depends upon the respective levels of the courts concerned with decisions of higher courts binding on lower courts. A decision of a lower court may be embodied in the decision of a higher court and forms part of that higher court's *RATIO DECIDENDI*; any other statement is OBITER DICTUM.

Judicial review: The supervision exercised by the UK High Court over UK public authorities in accordance with the doctrine of ULTRA VIRES. More significantly, however, in the European Union the European Court has a judicial review function provided under Article 230 of the EC Treaty. Under this Article, Community acts, which are legally binding on Member States, can be challenged by means of judicial review on the grounds of lack of competence, or infringement of an essential procedural requirement, or infringement of the treaty, or any law relating to its application or misuse of powers. Actions may be brought by an institution of the EU, a Member State or, in certain limited circumstances, an individual.

Judicial trustee: A trustee appointed by the court under the authority of the *Judicial Trustee Act* 1906. This trustee was an officer of the court and subject to the court's control who operated as a sole trustee or as a co-trustee. He was appointed on the application of a person creating or intending to create a trust, or of a trustee, or of a beneficiary. The judicial trustee acted under the direction of the court. The procedures were consolidated into the Judicial Trustee Rules 1983 (SI) 1983/370. Comparatively little use has been made of the Act and the role has been replaced in current practice by the *Public Trustee*. *See* EQUITY DOES NOT WANT FOR A TRUSTEE.

Junior barrister: Any barrister who is not a 'QUEEN'S (OR KING'S) COUNSEL'.

Jurisdiction: Has several meanings, first, the power of a court to hear and decide a case or to make a judicial order. This is based upon the nature of the case and the power of the court as laid down in legislation. Second, the term also means the territorial limits within which the authority of a court can be exercised; anywhere else is said to be outside the jurisdiction. Third, the territorial scope of the legislative competence of Parliament and, fourth, jurisdiction over a person means the ability to require a person to attend judicial proceedings, which, under English law, merely means being within the geographical jurisdiction of the English courts.

Jurisdiction and enforcement: Two concepts that go hand in hand and deal with the ability of a court of any country to hear a dispute (*see* JURISDICTION) and the enforcement of the decision. Jurisdiction and enforcement is generally a domestic matter but enforcement may be required outside the country in which the remedy was obtained. This then is a question for the conflict of laws. International enforcement is frequently controlled by Convention or by other means of accepting selected judicial decisions obtained elsewhere. These matters have achieved significant notoriety since the mistaken efforts of the EU to attempt to achieve harmony. In Europe the Regulation on Jurisdiction and Recognition and Enforcement of Judgments in Civil and Commercial Matters (EC COUNCIL REGULATION 44/2001) was presented by its creators as a uniform set of jurisdictional rules for EU Member States. However, the resulting situation is complex. This regulation, known as Brussels 1, entered into force on 1 January 2002 and superseded rules previously contained in successive versions of the BRUSSELS CONVENTION ON JURISDICTION AND THE ENFORCEMENT OF JUDGMENTS IN CIVIL AND COMMERCIAL MATTERS 1968 (known as 'the Brussels Convention'). Brussels 1 was made under Article 65 of the EC Treaty, which applies to judicial cooperation in civil matters having cross-border implications in so far as is necessary for the completion of the internal market. Brussels 1 applies to questions of jurisdiction between EU Member States in respect of proceedings instituted after 1 March 2002. Being 'instituted' refers to when the process was issued and not when it was served on the defendant, i.e. Brussels 1 applies at the earliest moment steps are taken to bring an action. Complications arise because of a series of exceptions to Brussels 1. For example, Brussels 1 does not apply to Denmark and its disputes with other Member States. This leaves the recognition and enforcement of Danish judgments in England to be settled by the earlier Brussels Convention. Then there is the Lugano Convention, which acts in parallel to the Brussels Convention. This Convention applies between EU Member States and certain EU non-Member States and continues to be applied in English courts to jurisdictional disputes between Member States and Iceland, Norway and Switzerland. *See* LUGANO CONVENTION ON JURISDICTION AND THE ENFORCEMENT OF JUDGMENTS IN CIVIL AND COMMERCIAL MATTERS 1988.

Jurisdiction at common law: The influence of common law on the principles of jurisdiction where common law practice challenges the validity of bringing an action in a court that might otherwise have legal authority. Based on a doctrine evolved from Scottish law, the common law recognises that there could be injustice if a case was heard in a court that otherwise had jurisdiction to hear the case when there was a more appropriate forum overseas. A defendant may use this doctrine as a means of escaping the jurisdiction of an English court if it can be successfully maintained that English proceedings would be vexatious or oppressive. This depends upon a two-stage test, following the decision in ***Spiliada Maritime Corp v. Cansulex Limited*** [1987] AC 460, where the defendant must prove there is an alternative forum that is more appropriate to resolution dispute. If this is successfully pleaded, the burden then passes to the claimant, who may then attempt to resist a stay of proceedings in an English court if he shows that it is unjust to require him to bring the action outside the UK. Evidence which may convince the court that the natural forum is overseas centres on the place of residence of the parties, the factual connection of the litigation to a particular court, the law applicable to the dispute and the availability of evidence, as well as the position of other parties (i.e. witnesses). *See FORUM CONVENIENS AND FORUM NON-CONVENIENS.*

Jurisdiction clause: A clause in an international agreement that designates the jurisdiction in which any dispute shall be heard; these are also called 'CHOICE OF FORUM' clauses. These clauses are essential in international contracts, trust deeds and shipping agreements, especially where transactions occur in more than one jurisdiction. Such clauses accompany choice of law clauses that dictate which substantive law shall apply to a dispute. There is no reason why parties living in 'A' and 'B' countries should not provide that the law of country 'C' shall apply to the substantive issues and that the jurisdiction clause designates that disputes shall be heard in the courts of country 'D'. Country D is therefore the law governing any procedural matters. To avoid expense and complications, the choice for both jurisdiction and governing law is frequently the same place, such as 'this contract shall be subject to the law of England and disputes held in the English courts'. A jurisdiction clause may be exclusive, which means that any attempt to pursue proceedings elsewhere would be a breach of the terms of the instrument in which the clause appears. The jurisdiction clause may be a non-exclusive clause that will preclude a party from arguing subsequently that the forum in which the action was brought was not appropriate on grounds foreseeable at the time of the agreement. If that happens, the parties will be taken to have been aware of the matters at the time of the agreement and a plea of '*forum non conveniens*' will ordinarily fail unless the factors relied upon were unforeseeable at the time. Choice of law and jurisdictional clauses are not always clearly drafted to identify the intention of the parties in respect of both of these issues. Where reference is made to 'exclusive jurisdiction' it does not always amount to a provision conferring jurisdiction on the courts of the designated country (*see* *FORUM CONVENIENS* AND *FORUM NON-CONVENIENS*, CHOICE OF LAW *and* HAGUE TRUST CONVENTION).

Jurisprudence: Strictly means the science or philosophy of law that, as an academic subject, attempts to ascertain and classify the principles on which legal rules are based and to show their relationship with one another; natural law, analytical jurisprudence and normative jurisprudence are topics considered, as well as the ultimate effect and the advantage or disadvantage that law brings to the community, but excludes questions of moral or political policy. The essential elements of the legal institutions of various countries, as revealed by comparative law studies, enable the underlying principles to be analysed. Also, the word is more widely used to mean 'law' generally and in civil law countries the word 'jurisprudence' is used to describe case law and decisions of the courts. Equity or trust jurisprudence, for example, then means nothing more than the law relating to trusts with no implication of any deeper analytical analysis. Similarly, when the term is used to describe the jurisprudence of a particular country, this simply means the laws and legal system of that country.

***Jus civile*:** The Latin term for 'CIVIL LAW'. When used properly it means the whole system of Roman laws which were used in the design of the civil law codes of Continental Europe, particularly the French civil law. It is sometimes used to describe municipal law in order to distinguish it from international law. *See* CIVIL CODE.

***Jus cogens*:** A source of public international law which refers to matters of such a fundamental nature that all states without exception are bound by those principles. To qualify as *jus cogens* a principle must be recognised as such by the international community as a whole. Examples consist of the laws prohibiting slavery, genocide, piracy and acts of aggression or illegal use of force. Some suggest that certain human rights provisions, such as prohibiting racial discrimination, also come under this category.

Jus gentium**:** Literally means 'law of the people', but is used also to indicate the law of nations and is really an out-of-date term in public international law that refers to rules of law which are common to all civilised nations.

Just and equitable: An indication of a standard to be applied to conduct that conforms both with the requirements of law (just) and the standards of equity (equitable). The expression 'just and equitable' was used in numerous statutes concerned with the power of the court to wind up a company but the expression has gone substantially out of use. Similarly, under the *Insolvency Act* 1986, Section 122(1)(g), a court may issue an order for the winding up of a company under circumstances where the court finds that it is 'just and equitable' to do so. Again, the phrase has gone out of use and in modern insolvency law it is now unusual since minority shareholders can now seek a wide range of other remedies, such as an order that the majority should buy the minorities' interests to avoid an 'unfair prejudice' against the minority. These alternative remedies are more specific; however, the essence of what is just and equitable is still maintained in trust law. For example, where there is a power in the nature of a trust which the holder of the power fails to execute, the court will execute it on his behalf under the maxim 'equality is equity' and will distribute the property in equal shares to those who are entitled. Equally significant under this doctrine is that a court will make a distinction between matters of substance and form.

Jus tertii**:** The right of a third party, sometimes called 'the third party defence,' to defend a claim and to redirect it elsewhere. For example, 'B', a person who is PRIMA FACIE liable to 'A', sets up as a defence that the money or property claimed by A does not belong to A but belongs to another person, a third party, 'C'. This is the defence of *jus tertii*. As a general rule, this defence does not work where B has obtained the goods by fraud or other wrongful act. The *jus tertii* defence is then not available since the defendant B committed an offence by seizing the goods in the first place. This means that an agent (a defendant) cannot refuse to account to his principal or dispute the principal's title by setting up the *jus tertii* unless the agent is able to do so with the authority of the third party that he claims is the legitimate owner. *Jus tertii* expresses really a simple situation: A claims goods from B; B's defence is that A has no rights to those goods because they belong to C – the *jus tertii* defence. This does not work if B obtained the goods from C illegally; under these circumstances the defence is not available.

Justice: The moral or social aim to uphold the rights of individuals, the protection of rights and the punishment of wrongs which is achieved through the enforcement and practice of law. The relationship between justice and law can be illustrated by representing the rights of individuals by one circle and the legal principles by another circle. The objective is that the greater the overlap between the two circles, the greater success law achieves in protecting rights. Justice has also been defined as the virtue by which we can give to every man what is his due or right as opposed to injury or wrong. Variously interpreted over the ages, justice is now regarded in two contexts, both derived from Aristotle's views. First, distributive justice monitors regulations between the state or community and the individual in the distribution of burdens and benefits, e.g. taxation. Second, there is commutative or rectificatory justice which regulates transactions voluntarily or involuntarily between individuals and provides reparation or restitution where appropriate. Under modern terminology, distributive justice is now often called 'social justice' and forms a matter of political policy.

The commutative or rectificatory justice equates, or should equate, to the rule of law, although this is not an absolute since strict application of the law between the parties may have had unjust results in some cases and was a prime reason for the rise of the system of EQUITY *and* RULE OF LAW.

Justiciable: The nature of matters to be examined in courts of justice. This includes disputes that are non-legal in nature, such as the regulation of universities and other matters that are appropriate for a court to examine and which would benefit from the skills of a judge. The term was not generally applied to legal matters as such, but the practice has developed of using it to indicate a matter that should be examined before the English courts, such as the justiciability of social and cultural rights.

K

***Keech v. Sandford*, Rule in, (1726) Sel. Cas. T. King 61 and 62:** Trustees cannot themselves profit out of trust assets or in dealing on behalf of a beneficiary; to do so would be a breach of their fiduciary duty. In this case, a trustee applied for a renewal of a lease for the benefit of an infant beneficiary. The landlord refused. The trustee, however, obtained a renewal of the lease for himself personally. The court decided that the trustee must hold the lease on trust for the infant because the trustee was in a fiduciary relationship with the beneficiary and therefore could not obtain any benefit for himself in any way that was connected with his role as a trustee. This rule binds other types of fiduciaries, such as partners where a partnership business is carried on in those same premises and where some of the partners take on the new lease to the exclusion of the others. The rule that fiduciaries should not make a profit out of their relationship is one of the key elements in defining a fiduciary obligation. *See* FIDUCIARY RELATIONSHIP.

Kin: Relationship by blood, including half blood, that is used where the closest relation to a person is referred to as the next of kin, which is relevant in connection with wills and intestacy.

Know-how: A category of information the significance of which is that possession of it calls for a duty of confidentiality on the person who obtains it. This can occur under a variety of circumstances but generally relates to a manufacturing process or a commercial advantage about which a person in a fiduciary position with an employer or client should maintain confidentiality. The information remains the property of the employer or client. When information becomes possessed by a person in a fiduciary position, a constructive trust arises in favour of the employer. 'Know-how' as a type of confidential information is difficult to define, as are the circumstances under which unlawful disclosure is actionable. Accordingly, a court, when deciding whether the recipient of the information ought to have understood that the information was passed in confidence, will take into account the standard practices in the industry or market and apply the test of whether a reasonable person would have considered that the information should have been held in confidence, particularly where the transfer of information was originally made for a limited purpose.

Knowing receipt and dishonest assistance: Actions concerned with a third party's involvement with the misapplication of trust funds. In the first category, knowing receipt, the defendant receives the money beneficially under circumstances where the state of knowledge at the time of receipt makes it unconscionable for him to retain the benefit. The test depends upon an assessment of the defendant's knowledge and the extent to which he would be expected to have investigated, knowing what he did know, the impropriety of receiving the money under the circumstances of the payment. A third party guilty of such knowing receipt is required to make restitution. It is necessary to prove that the claimant's equitable interest existed at the point when the third party received the money so that if the third party received the money as a bona fide purchaser for value, a claim for beneficial receipt could not arise. The rules of FOLLOWING OR TRACING are relevant to show that the defendant received the money that was properly attributable to the claimant. The defendant's liability is not strictly restitutional since he was not enriched by receiving the money in a beneficial capacity. Where a person handles money in a ministerial capacity a higher degree of fault is required and a breach of fiduciary duty is required that involves dishonesty. The need for dishonesty draws knowing receipt closer to dishonest assistance. Liability for knowing receipt occurs therefore where a person receives, or assists in procuring, a breach of trust in connection with assets held. This can be summarised as where a person knowingly receives, contrary to the terms of the trust, trust property or its traceable proceeds. The second category is dishonest assistance, where a person does not receive trust assets but assists in a breach of trust by acting dishonestly as an accessory to another person's breach. Both lead to personal claims for an order for an account to be presented to the beneficiaries as if the persons against whom the claim is made were in the position of trustees. Under the circumstances in which these claims arise the person guilty of 'knowing receipt' or 'dishonest assistance' is considered to have the obligations of a CONSTRUCTIVE TRUSTEE (although no trust exists). Both these offences have been subject to judicial interpretation and are part of a range of claims that may be brought by beneficiaries in the event of a breach of trust. The element of knowledge in 'knowing receipt' is distinguished from that in 'dishonest assistance' in that the latter requires some fraud to exist in the misapplication of the trust funds. In the case of ***Royal Brunei Airlines v. Tan*** [1995] 2 AC 378, a radical distinction was introduced between a test for dishonesty and a test for knowledge. As pointed out by G. Thomas and A. Hudson in *The Law of Trusts* (Oxford University Press, 2004, p. 993):

> 'The courts have not tended to apply the Baden categories of knowledge [a classification of knowledge derived from a case of this name, *see* BADEN RULES] slavishly as though they were a strict test.'

If evidence can be produced that there was actual knowledge, such as written records of meetings, the question does not need to be debated but, in relation to the test (in the BADEN RULES), the wilful and reckless failure to make enquiries was applied and held to be a crucial test of whether the defendant 'ought to have been suspicious' that trust property had been misapplied. The question may also arise of whether knowledge may be forgotten, i.e. once a person has knowledge, can it be forgotten and can the person therefore proceed without knowingly engaging in the action of which he is accused? A further complication arose after the Court of Appeal's decision in ***Twinsectra Limited v. Yardley*** [1999] Lloyd's Rep Bank 438; [2002] WLR 802, where it was laid down that the applicable test for both 'knowing receipt' and 'dishonest assistance' was that of dishonesty as set out in ***Royal Brunei Airlines v. Tan*** [1998] 2 AC 378. Although this point was not considered on appeal in the House of Lords, it suggests a movement away from knowledge as a receipt-based claim. Knowledge was not discussed in this case in the Court of Appeal, where the concentration was on honesty and dishonesty. This means that the present situation relating to knowledge is not clear. The movement away from the old test based upon knowledge where the judge needed to decide whether or not the defendant 'ought to have been suspicious' may result ultimately in the practical test comprising a combination of subjective and objective factors. Where knowing receipt or dishonest assistance occurs, liability for a fraudulent breach of trust arises against an accessory who is considered to be a constructive trustee of any advantage gained; this imposes a basis for granting EQUITABLE RELIEF and is distinguished from a true constructive trust because, in the latter, the trustee assumes duties with respect to the trust property. *See* CONSTRUCTIVE TRUST.

Knowledge: Something that is known. Knowledge must be something about which the person holding it is committed to being true rather than merely having a suspicion or considering that the matter is likely to be true. Knowledge in law is used in a variety of situations. For example, a binding contract can only be construed on the basis of knowledge had by each of the parties at the time the contract is alleged to have been set up. Absence of knowledge is also relevant in other situations; for example, property transactions allow 'a bona fide purchaser for value' (*see* BONA FIDE PURCHASER – EQUITY'S DARLING) to have rights over the property free of any encumbrances or liability when the purchaser is ignorant of a pre-existing situation. There are occasions where a purchaser will be 'put on notice' in respect of various aspects and will be deemed to have knowledge of those situations. Some statutory provisions are drafted in the way that only specific and actual knowledge will be sufficient to give rise to a liability. Knowledge is also an element in various factors indicating a legal relationship such as intention, recklessness and dishonesty, particularly in criminal matters where knowledge and its opposite, 'ignorance', constitute vital elements in establishing criminal responsibility. In trusts, knowledge is particularly relevant in the case of 'knowing receipt', which exists where a person receives trust property in the knowledge that the property has been passed in breach of trust or otherwise misapplied (*see* KNOWING RECEIPT AND DISHONEST ASSISTANCE); the property passed must be done knowingly, i.e. with knowledge that the property is subject to a trust. The key is whether the defendant receives trust property knowing that receiving it will constitute a breach of trust. This concept of knowledge is different from the imputed notice in conveyancing law or a situation where undue influence may be inferred. The elements of knowledge were considered in ***Baden v. Société Generale*** [1993] 1 WLR 509:

(a) first, actual knowledge;
(b) wilfully shutting one's eyes to the obvious;
(c) wilfully and recklessly failing to make inquiries which an honest person would have made;
(d) knowledge of circumstances which would indicate the facts to an honest and reasonable man;
(e) the knowledge of circumstances which would put an honest and reasonable man on enquiry.

The first three categories are taken to indicate forms of actual knowledge. The fourth and fifth categories are broader and are indicators of constructive notice. These five categories were reduced to a more manageable three in ***Re Montagu*** [1987] Ch 264, i.e. actual knowledge, wilfully shutting one's eyes to the obvious and wilfully and recklessly failing to make enquiries that an honest person would have made. This indicates that the knowledge here in any category includes either wilful or deliberate behaviour on the part of the defendant in circumstances where the defendant cannot be proved to have actually known of the facts that were alleged. These categories are not rigid and have been subject to various other interpretations, such as 'actual knowledge', 'Nelsonian knowledge' and 'naughty knowledge' (A. Underhill & D.J. Hayton, *The Law of Trusts*. 16th edn, 2002, p. 974). Possessing knowledge is a necessary constituent in establishing a person being a CONSTRUCTIVE TRUSTEE; therefore, the innocent receipt of property by a person subject to an equitable interest does not itself make the recipient a trustee, despite the severance of the legal and equitable titles, due to the fact that the recipient had no knowledge of that equitable interest.

L

Laches: Unreasonable delay in pursuing a legal remedy that results in a claimant forfeiting the benefit. Such a delay may be used by a defendant as an equitable defence. Laches must be distinguished from a defence under the *Limitation Act* 1980, which fixes a time limit for bringing an action at law to enforce a claim. With laches there is no prescribed period of limitation. For example, if a person discovers that he has suffered a breach of a fiduciary relationship but waits an unnecessary length of time before taking proceedings to remedy that breach, laches will disentitle him to relief. That person is nevertheless entitled to a reasonable time to make enquiries and obtain advice, etc. The essence of laches is that a claimant has neglected to pursue his rights with reasonable promptitude; the defendant must show the claim has been neglected and that it would be inequitable for the claimant to succeed. The maxim 'DELAY DEFEATS EQUITY' illustrates this.

Land: In its broadest sense land includes houses, buildings and other structures to which the law of REAL PROPERTY applies. Land includes any objects or equipment that are attached to or growing on the land. When land is transferred the structures that are fixed to the land also pass. This includes things which would otherwise be treated as personal property. The consequences of attaching objects to the land depend upon the intention of the parties but, as a rough test, the more damage it would take to remove the item the more likely it is that parties intended it to become part of the land. The decision in ***Holland v. Hodgson*** (1872) L.R. 7CP, 328 at 335, stated:

> '[A]n article which is affixed to the land, even slightly, is to be considered part of the land, unless the circumstances are such as to show that it was intended all along to continue [as] a chattel, the onus [of showing the nature of the object] is on those who contend that it was a chattel.'

Therefore, with regard to things that are only lightly attached, they become part of the land unless it can be shown that the intention was otherwise. For example, an open-air exhibition of large pieces of sculpture would imply an intention that the sculptures should be part of the land and it is the responsibility of the owners of the sculpture, or of the land, to show clearly that the intention of the parties was that the sculptures should not become part of the land by including a suitable clause in the exhibition contract and the other literature, programmes, etc. relating to the exhibition. Rights attached to the occupation of land project upwards into space only to such a height as is necessary for the ordinary use and enjoyment of the land and far enough to be able to protect the land from nuisance and trespass. Contrary to popular belief, no one owns the airspace. The transfer of land passes whatever is under the land, although minerals such as coal, oil and natural gas vest in the UK in the Crown by statute and cannot be exploited without licence. Naturally, these rights narrow the deeper under the land to which attention is directed in line with the curvature of the earth. The term 'land' also covers, in addition to buildings and other structures, any land covered with water and any ESTATE, INTEREST (2), EASEMENT, SERVITUDE or right in or over land following the definition of land in the *Interpretation Act* 1978, Schedule 1. This means that water is treated in law as a species of land so that in order to recover possession of a pool or rivulet of water, action must be brought for the land, e.g. 10 acres of land covered with water. In English law, the *Law of Property*

Act 1925, Section 205(1)(ix) includes in its definition:

> 'Land of any tenure, and mines and minerals, whether or not held apart from the surface, buildings or parts of buildings (whether the division is horizontal, vertical or made in any other way), and other CORPOREAL HEREDITAMENTS; also a MANOR, an ADVOWSON, and a rent and other INCORPOREAL HEREDITAMENTS, and an EASEMENT, RIGHT, PRIVILEGE, or benefit in, over, or derived from land; but not an undivided share in land.'

This means that land is divisible horizontally and vertically, allowing one person to own the surface of the land and another to own the minerals under it, or one person may have the fee simple in one storey of a house while the rest may belong to another. Although theoretically land is not the subject of ownership in English law, in practice rights in land can be of two types: the right of ownership and other rights which include EASEMENTS, PROFITS and RESTRICTIVE COVENANTS between FEE HOLDERS that normally restrict the use of the land over which these rights exist. The word 'land' has often been construed in court to include trusts where the trust asset is land and also money to be laid out in land. This will pass as land under a will under the general description of 'all the deceased's lands'. *See* CONVERSION.

Land certificate: A document that was formerly issued by the Land Registry to the proprietor of land as proof of his ownership. These have been discontinued and no further certificates have been issued since October 2003 as the Register is kept entirely in electronic form. The owner of land receives a Title Information Document containing a printed copy of the entry in the Register. *See also* CERTIFICATE.

Land charge: Until the *Land Charges Act* 1925, a purchaser of land could only discover matters affecting the land that were not revealed by the title deeds by making different searches and carrying out different enquiries. The *Land Charges Act* 1925, replaced by the *Land Charges Act* 1972, enables the Land Charges Department to maintain registers on: land charges; pending actions; writs and orders affecting land; deeds of arrangement affecting land; and annuities. An index of all entries is maintained which records the charges made in the registers. An entry in a register does not constitute evidence of the validity of the matter registered, but failure to register renders any registerable matter void against certain purchasers who buy the property for valuable consideration. Personal searches may be made of the Land Charges Registers. The detailed matters on land charges under the Act are governed by the Land Charges Rules 1974. In practice, the registration of a land charge is notice that the land is committed to some purpose in favour of a third party, i.e. the third party is protecting his interest in the land.

Landlord: Covers many judicial and statutory definitions and constructions that depend upon their context for precise meaning. Generally, it is a person who holds freehold land or a leasehold tenancy who rents out the property to another.

Landlord and tenant: The relationship of landlord and tenant arises whenever there is a tenancy, i.e. when the owner of an estate of land, sometimes known as the lessor or landlord, agrees expressly or by implication to allow another person, the lessee or tenant, to have exclusive possession and use of the land for a period less than the landlord's own estate (i.e. for a period less than the unexpired period of a landlord's lease where the landlord only holds a tenancy) in return, usually, for the payment of a rent or the rendering of a service. Whenever a tenancy is granted, the landlord's retained interest in the land is called a 'REVERSION'. The terms 'tenancy' and 'landlord and tenant' are generally used in connection with the lease of a house or land for the purpose of occupation. Leases, or tenancies, may be for any agreed period: for a year, or from year-to-year, at will, or for a great number of years such as 999 years. The granting of a tenancy implies that the landlord shall allow the tenant quiet possession and enjoyment of the premises during the term, free from any disturbance by the landlord or persons claiming against him or by superior title. The tenant undertakes in the lease or agreement to rent to abide by the terms of any covenant contained in the documentation. This enables the freeholder to constrain the tenant from unacceptable conduct, such as keeping pets or conducting a trade from the premises. Such covenants, when obtained from more than one tenant, enable the freeholder to preserve the appearance and dignity of a building or even a residential development. Hence, the tendency to offer property on 999-year leases. The general rule is that the landlord gives no implied warranty that the premises are fit for a purpose, with the particular exception that furnished premises should be fit for habitation. Also, where a house is let for a very low rent it is implied that the house must be fit for habitation at the start of the tenancy and that the landlord will maintain it in such a state. Where a house is let for less than seven years, the landlord is obliged to keep the structure and exterior of the house in repair and to keep the installations in it for the supply of water, gas, electricity, sanitation and heating in repair and in proper working order. These obligations are the personal obligations of a landlord and cannot be contracted out to other parties. The tenant, in return, is liable for the payment of the rent, which can be recovered in an action for debt in the event of default. The tenant is compelled to use the premises in a tenant-like manner and to return the premises at the end of the lease in the state in which he entered it subject to natural deterioration. The purposes for which the premises are let imply the standard that has to be fulfilled, otherwise the tenant is under no implied obligation to repair or reinstate the premises if destroyed or damaged, which means that the landlord is responsible for insuring the premises. The trend of legislation in recent years has been to offer more protection to the tenant in respect both of the state of the property and the security of tenure. A tenant generally agrees to allow the landlord, at reasonable times, to inspect and enter the agreed premises, but otherwise the tenant has an exclusive right of possession even against the landlord during the term of the lease. If there is non-payment of rent, there may be a forfeiture of the lease.

Land Register Online: In England this is an online service that enables members of the public to search the Register for the title-holder of land and for a plan of what any registered title comprises by reference to an address. The Register provides ownership details and, for most properties that have changed hands since April 2000, the property price information. Other online services include a Land Registry service for business users. *See* LAND REGISTRY.

Land registration: The system of registering at the Land Registry certain legal estates or interests in land. Under the *Land Registration Act* 1925, compulsory registration was introduced in specified areas by Order in Council. This Act was superseded by the *Land Registration Act* 2002, which, although it did not make it necessary for existing owners to register land on any transfer of land or any interest in land, such as sale, gift or mortgage, the new proprietor of that interest was required to register it to secure his rights in the property. The Register consists of three parts: the property register, which describes the land and any additional rights incidental to it, such as rights of way over adjoining land; the proprietorship register, which names the registered proprietors of the land and notes any restriction on their powers to dispose of it; and the charges register, which details interests adverse to the proprietor.

Land Registry: A non-ministerial government department headed by the Chief Land Registrar, who is appointed by the Lord Chancellor with the main statutory function of keeping registers relating to freehold and leasehold land throughout England and Wales. The Land Registry Department guarantees, on behalf of the Crown, titles to registered estates and interests in land. State-backed registration gives greater security of title and provides protection against claims of adverse possession since those who might claim should have registered their interest. *See* LAND REGISTER ONLINE.

Lands Tribunal: An independent judicial body set up in 1949 to resolve disputes concerning land. The main types of cases are concerned with rates or local taxes, disputed valuations of compulsorily purchased land, compensation claims for loss of value because of public works, and similar matters.

Lassence v. Tierney*, Rule in, (1849) 1 Mac & G 551:** A rule that applies to gifts of real property, the principle of which also applies to dispositions by will or by deed and to gifts by joint effect of a will and other instruments, as well as to the exercise of powers of appointment and to gifts through the interposition of trusts as well as direct gifts. In the law of trusts this is usually dealt with under dispositions on trusts that fail to exhaust the beneficial interest. The rule that was first known as the rule in ***Lassence v. Tierney is also known as the rule in ***Hancock v. Watson*** [1902] AC 14, where the principle was clearly annunciated as:

> 'It is settled law that if you find an absolute gift to a legatee ['W'] in the first instance, and trusts [to 'SD' and then for SD's children] are engrafted or imposed on that absolute interest which fail [trusts to SD failed for remoteness], either from lapse or invalidity or any other reason, then the absolute gift [to SD after the death of W] takes effect so far as the trusts have failed to the exclusion of the residuary legatee or next-of-kin as the case may be.'

In ***Hancock v. Watson*** a testator gave property to trustees in trust for his wife, 'W', for life and after her death to be divided into five portions. He gave two of these portions to another married woman, 'SD', on the basis that SD would hold those two portions in trust for her life and after her death for her children upon reaching 25 years of age. In default of any such issue, there was a gift over to the children of 'C'. It was held that the limitation after the life estate to SD was void for remoteness but the original gift remained. This meant that all which had been intended by the testator in respect of those two portions after the death of SD were to no effect but the original allotment to SD on the death of W remained, and on the death of SD the property in the two portions passed to her personal representatives and not to the testator's next of kin or to those nominated by the testator after the death of SD. The remoteness stopped the descent of the property with the consequence that SD took the property unencumbered by any trust. The question is one of intention. It is noticeable that, although the principle in the case prevented a resulting trust arising in favour of the settlor or testator, it did not prevent a resulting trust arising elsewhere. For this rule to apply there must be an attempt at a disposition on trust.

Lasting power of attorney: A power of attorney made in the UK under the *Mental Capacity Act* 2005, Sections 10 to 23. Unlike other powers of attorney, a lasting power of attorney is of indefinite duration and may continue to be effective after the donor loses MENTAL CAPACITY provided the power is in the prescribed form and registered with the COURT OF PROTECTION. *See also* ENDURING POWER OF ATTORNEY.

Law: A code of conduct with which persons are obliged to perform. The term is also applied to an individual principle of conduct within the broad meaning of law that is observed by an individual, or class of persons, and which may be limited to a section of the community, or imposed upon all persons who consent to its application or who are unable to resist its application and the sanctions imposed for non-compliance. Where a sanction or penalty is imposed for non-compliance of a law by the authority of the SOVEREIGN of the jurisdiction whose law was not complied with, the law becomes known as 'positive' law. The positive school of law, according to AUSTIN and BENTHAM, defines law as a command non-compliance with which will involve a sanction imposed by the sovereign. Positive law forms the basis of the study of the modern theory of law or JURISPRUDENCE. Alternative theories embrace the notion of law being based on customs or of NATURAL LAW. Also, the positive theory of law inevitably makes a distinction between international law and domestic law where the absence of an international sovereign to impose sanctions for non-compliance results in international law often being regarded as not being proper law. Domestic law is law applicable in a sovereign state where the sanction is imposed by that sovereign and is sometimes called 'territorial' or 'municipal' law and is derived from judicial precedence, legislation or custom. The nature of the enforcing power, the sovereign, varies from country to country and indicates where the ultimate power in that country rests and may vary from, as in the UK with Parliament, and in the US with the Supreme Court, to the personal powers of dictators. Judicial precedents give rise to law in common law countries where the principle invoked in an earlier decision is regarded as being declaratory of the law, and where the judge follows a previous declaration of law or distinguishes such a previous decision according to the individual facts of the case that he is considering. The judge then annunciates the principle which applies with his reasons and so his declaration becomes a new precedent that may be followed or distinguished in subsequent cases. The principle that judges annunciate is based upon the declaratory theory where judges are presumed to know the law. This is the basis of the COMMON LAW. Law that is derived from legislation is called 'statute law'. Custom, as a source of law, is now a fairly rare event due to most surviving customs having been considered and, where appropriate, embodied in the common law. Another classification of law is written and unwritten law, the former being principally statute law and the latter principally common law, i.e. law not embodied in written statutes. The distinction between public and private law is that public law is part of the law that involves the state (i.e. the sovereign or government) enforcing rights applicable to it through the legal system and to actions by individuals as to their rights against the state or such rights against other individuals. Public law includes constitutional law, which regulates the divisions of the sovereign power and the administration and the matters relating to state security, such as criminal law and the prevention of crimes and general matters such as public health, poor law and the relief of poverty. What is known as 'private law', sometimes called CIVIL LAW (the use of the term not to be confused with the civil law of Continental European countries), deals with the relationships between individuals in which the state does not directly have an interest; this includes matters such as contracts, trusts, wills and property. The tendency now is for public law to intrude into private law by laying down requirements with the aim of achieving political objectives.

Law Commission: A statutory independent body required by the *Law Commissions Act* 1965 to keep the law under review and to recommend reform. It is guided by the principle that the law should be as fair, modern, simple and cost-effective as possible. The Law Commission conducts research and consultations in order to make systemic recommendations for consideration by Parliament to assist in codifying the law and eliminating anomalies, repealing obsolete and unnecessary enactments and reducing the number of separate statutes. From time to time matters relating to trusts and related subjects are considered and the Law Commission's consultation papers provide a concise summary of the topics under review. The Law Commission's publications include:

- Capital and income in trusts: classification and appointment.
- Charities – social investment.
- Company directors: regulating conflicts of interest and formulating a statement of duties.
- Easements, covenants and *PROFITS Á PRENDRE*.
- Fiduciary duties of investment intermediaries.
- Illegal transactions: the effect of illegality on contracts and trusts.
- Insurance contract law: insurable interest.
- Intestacy and family provision claims on death.
- *Limited Partnership Act* 1907.
- Matrimonial property, needs and agreements.
- Trustee and exemption clauses.
- Trustees' powers and duties.
- Trusts (*Trustee Act* 1925, Sections 31 and 32).

The Law Commission's 12th Programme of Law Reform includes a proposal of the Trust Law Committee and the Chancery Bar Association to investigate arbitration as a means of settling disputes between trustees and beneficiaries. The issues refer to how settlors can require trustees and beneficiaries to use arbitration rather than litigation, and how an arbitration award made between persons of full capacity can be made binding in a trust context. The Law Commission admits that other projects should be given higher priority as they are likely to benefit more people and target more vulnerable groups. Also, between 2015 and 2018 there will be a review of the Law of Wills focussing on testamentary capacity, formalities, rectification and mutual wills and on reducing the likelihood of wills being challenged after death.

Law merchant: A system of law covering commercial and maritime matters, developed originally in southern Europe, which became internationally applied due to its use by merchants in their itinerant business with other countries. This gave rise to a system of law for international trade that was administered outside the main judicial system by borough courts administered by the local mayor or other local dignitaries. These courts were known as 'Pie Poudre' courts ('court of the dusty feet' or 'court of the peddlers') and were separate courts which decided summarily on matters of trade; they are now only of historical importance and one of the most remembered is the Tolzey Court in Bristol (which was demolished on 1 January 1972 by the *Courts Act* 1971). Merchants in the UK were subject to common law and did not play as important a part as merchants from Europe; English judges felt free to reject the rules of the Law merchant which they regarded as incompatible with common law or with equitable principles.

Law of nations: An old-fashioned term superseded by the term 'PUBLIC INTERNATIONAL LAW'; however, there is a difference. The term 'law of nations' is derived from the translation of the Latin phrase *JUS GENTIUM*, which means the rules of law that are common to all civilised nations, and it therefore differs from what is now understood by the narrower meaning given to 'public international law' as the law governing relations between states.

Law of Property Act 1925: An Act amended in 1926, 1929, 1932, 1964 and 1969 that consolidated and brought about fundamental changes in LAND LAW. The main purpose of this Act was to simplify the law and protect purchasers of land against interests attached to the land about which they had no notice, as well as protecting owners of equitable interests in land. This Act restricted legal estates in land to estates in FEE SIMPLE IN POSSESSION and a TERM OF YEARS ABSOLUTE (leasehold). All other estates and interests in land became EQUITABLE INTERESTS.

Law of the forum: The law of the place or the court in which a remedy is sought, i.e. the law applicable to the jurisdiction in which an action is commenced. This law governs the practice and procedure by which any dispute is settled and therefore distinguishes what is substantive law from what is procedural law. This may make a difference to the outcome of any action; for example, the question of damages or other remedies may be regarded as substantive law or procedural law, depending on the forum. Also, on a matter of enforcement, any decision takes on the characteristics of a decision of the country of the forum. This may be relevant in seeking enforcement under a Convention that may list the jurisdictions whose decisions are recognised for the purpose of the Convention.

Law reports: A published account of legal proceedings comprising the facts of the dispute, the argument by counsel on each side, the relevant law and previous decisions used to support the argument made by each side. Law reports are an essential element in the development of the common law as they contain a statement of how the established principles of law are relied upon and extended to meet the facts of the case. A new judgment extends the judicial precedents that will be applied in future cases. Where a decision is given by a majority, the dissenting opinions of the minority are recorded. Law reports are therefore the lifeblood of the common law. The earliest reports were the Yearbooks published annually between 1283 and 1535 by anonymous editors. They were superseded by reports written by lawyers that were identified by the name of the authors until 1865. Thereafter, reports were compiled and published as private enterprises with the reporters usually being accredited by the Chief Justice of each court. In 1865 the Incorporated Counsel of Law Reporting for England and Wales (ICLR) began to publish monthly reports called the 'Law Reports', which became known as the official Law Reports. A separate series for each branch of the Supreme Court of England and Wales (as it was then known, i.e. Queen's Bench, Chancery and Family Courts and the Court of Appeal) was published. These courts are now known as the SENIOR COURTS, which maintain their individual law reporting publications. Reports of decisions of the House of Lords (now the Supreme Court of the UK) and the Judicial Committee of the Privy Council are published separately from those of the Senior Courts. Currently the ICLR also publishes the Weekly Law Reports and specialised series on industrial and business cases. The rule now is that where a case has been reported in the official Law Reports any citation must come from that source; however, the ICLR has no monopoly in producing Law Reports and theoretically any report made by a member of the Bar, or since 1990 any solicitor having the right of audience, may publish a report that may be cited. Most of the private law reports are on specialised areas of the law, with the exception of the All England Law Reports, which are comprehensive. In all cases care is taken to ensure that the reports are prepared accurately, usually from a shorthand note of the court proceedings and the judge approves and modifies these reports before publication. The publishers prepare summaries of the issues consisting of the arguments of the crucial matters of law that are considered. These are called the 'HEADNOTES' and provide the invaluable indication of what the case is about. A well-prepared case report also contains a list of previous cases that have been referred to in a court and to other sources of the existing law used by counsel. International trust reports are frequently used in jurisdictions other than where the case was held; this is a principal means by which international trust law has adopted common principles. A jurisdiction that does not have a system of law reports that are freely available remains an unknown quantity and accordingly less attractive to potential investors.

Law Society: A regulatory professional body in London, which is the Registrar of Solicitors and which acts as the solicitors' professional body by enforcing professional standards. The Society is run by a council that has general power to act on behalf of the Society; it also oversees the various activities such as supporting legal reforms. The Society acts through local law societies established in various parts of England and Wales. A separate body, the Scottish Law Society, exists in Scotland.

Leading case: A case decided in the courts that is significant and where the legal reasoning establishes important principles of law that are referred to in subsequent cases and which may be followed or distinguished if counsel appearing in court can show that the principles in the quoted cases should not apply. In that case, another leading case is created by the judgment which refines and expands the precision of the common law. *See* LAW *and* LAW REPORTS.

Lease: A grant of property, also known as a 'tenancy', under which the owner of property, the landlord or lessor, grants to another, a tenant or lessee, exclusive possession of property for an agreed period in return for a rent. The person granting the lease is the 'lessor', who grants to the tenant, the 'lessee', a lease for a shorter estate or term than he himself has in the property. An essential element is that the lessee enjoys exclusive possession of the property. Without exclusive possession there is no lease but there may be a LICENCE. A lease is a part contractual relationship and partly an assignment of real property. A lease of real property for a term of years is a legal estate; other leases are equitable interests. In order to create a legal estate, a lease must be made by deed, except for leases taking effect in possession for a term not exceeding three years, and at the best rent that can be reasonably obtained. A lease for a shorter period may be made otherwise than by deed simply in writing or parole. If made in writing, it must contain all the terms expressly agreed and signed by both parties, otherwise no contract arises. Around this distinction there is much complex law. A lease must be for a specific purpose or period after which the possession of the property reverts to the owner of the freehold. A lease contains various covenants by which the landlord, i.e. the freeholder or leaseholder in the case of subleases, undertakes not to derogate from his grant. The landlord promises quiet enjoyment and that, in connection with residential accommodation, the premises are fit for habitation. In return, the tenant has an obligation, either express or implied, to pay the rent, to pay the ordinary rates and taxes, not to commit waste of the property and to use the property in a manner which is reasonable. A current practice is to use the terminology of the lease to describe an arrangement by which things other than land are hired out under a formal arrangement, such as a lease of machinery or equipment by which the owner of the equipment or a commercial bank enters into a lease with a commercial operator under conditions which mirror some of the terms of a lease of real property. Currently, ships are chartered and subject to special maritime laws, but aircraft can be leased where more concepts of real property are drawn upon. *See* LEASEHOLD.

Leasehold: Real property held under a LEASE for a term of years. Leasehold is a form of legal estate in land and, since the *Law of Property Act* 1925, has been, along with freehold, the only legal estates that survived. Leaseholds are personal property (as opposed to freeholds, which are real property) under English law. This is a historical distinction. An estate in freehold would go to a deceased's heir and a freehold estate in land dictated many other financial, social and political responsibilities. Leasehold, which was originally purely a contractual arrangement, became an estate in the land whilst preserving its contractual nature. Outside the common law system, no such distinction is made; the civil law equivalent of owned property and rented property are both described as 'immovables'. Sometimes in English law the distinction between personal property and real property is unwieldy; for example, in the *Administration of Estates Act* 1925, Section 55(xix), leaseholds are included in the term 'real estate' and by the *Wills Act* 1837, Section 26, a general devise of lands or land and tenements includes the testator's leasehold interests unless a contrary intention appears. The term 'leasehold' is sometimes liberally interpreted; for example, property held on a lease for life is leasehold. A contract to sell leasehold property will not be taken as covering property held on a sublease and will not be enforced if the seller only holds property on an underlease.

Legacies: Strictly, a legacy is a gift of a personalty by will, but the term is often used informally to denote a gift of realty by will. The person to whom the property is given is called the 'legatee', and the gift or property is called the 'BEQUEST' or, more strictly when it comes to land, a 'DEVISE'. Legacies are typically divided into three kinds: specific, demonstrative and general. This classification is not followed precisely by the courts. Each will must be constructed individually and looked at as a whole. Therefore, attempts to classify legacies can be imprecise as a result of small variations in the wording of the will changing the type of legacy. The clearest of those classifications are specific legacies, which are a bequest of a specific part of the testator's personal estate, such as 'all the money in my bank account at the time of my death' or a bequest of a particular object. A SPECIFIC LEGACY must be paid by the executor in preference to the general legacies and must not be used for the payment of debts until the general assets of the testator are exhausted. However, a specific legacy is subject to ADEMPTION. A DEMONSTRATIVE LEGACY is a gift of a certain sum directly to be paid out of a specific fund, i.e. it is paid out of a specific fund and is not a gift of the whole fund (that would be a specific legacy). A demonstrative legacy is not adeemed by disposals of the fund by the testator in his lifetime but has the advantage of being paid in priority to the general legacies if the total assets are sufficient. A GENERAL LEGACY is payable out of the general assets, such as where the testator bequeaths a certain sum of money or a certain amount of stock without referring to any particular stock, i.e. a legacy is a general legacy when it does not amount to bequest of a particular thing. Thus a gift of £1000 of a named stock, or a horse, without any reference to a particular holding of the stock or to a particular horse, is a general legacy. If valuable consideration was given to the testator in return for the specific legacy, then abatement does not occur in respect of that legacy as the payment to the legatee is regarded as repayment of a debt. The principal differences between these types of legacies relate to the effect of the concepts of ademption and abatement and which are important where a testator sets up a will trust by means of a legacy to executors. A demonstrative fund will be payable out of other assets, if available, and a demonstrative legacy will not abate because of a general deficiency of assets so long as the fund out of which it is payable is adequate. The general rules are that general legacies abate before specific legacies but general legacies are not within the principle of ademption. This is important in respect of the assets intended for a will trust. **Note:** A legacy is adeemed if the property is changed into something different even if the value of the changed item still exists on the testator's death. The principle of ademption applies, for example, to a specific legacy of the shares of the testator's company where that company no longer exists on the death of the testator either because of actions of the testator himself or because of external influences. However, there is no ademption if the subject matter is changed only in manner and form; a mere reconstruction of the testator's company by which the testator would receive shares in the new company in place of his shares in the old is not within the concept of ademption so that these new shares will satisfy a specific legacy expressed in terms of shares of the former company. The question is whether what he possesses on his death is substantially the same thing as that which is stated in his will. There is some statutory prevention of ademption in respect of government stock in the event of public amalgamations and nationalisation of companies. A demonstrative legacy has the advantage of immunity from ademption and, unlike a general legacy, it will not be affected by the alienation or non-existence of a specific fund primarily designed for the payment of a demonstrative legacy. Where a testator bequeaths more than one legacy to the same person, either in one instrument or several, the question arises of whether the second gift is meant to be cumulative to the first or a substitute for it. The answer lies in the actual wording of the testamentary instruments but the classical rule is that if different instruments give legacies of equal, greater or lesser sums to the same person without expressing the reason for the gift, there is a presumption that the testator intended to give more than one gift. The legatee will receive all the legacies. On the other hand, if the different instruments give the same motive and the same gift, the court presumes that the testator was merely repeating a former gift. Another difference is where a testator states that a legacy is to be paid or becomes payable at a certain stated age then the gift is considered to vest immediately so that if the legatee dies before that age then the legacy is payable to the legatee's executor or administrator. Such a legacy is regarded as being a debt from the moment the bequest is written but to be paid in the future; the time is annexed to the payment and not to the gift. This contrasts with a legacy bequeathed to a person at the age of 21; then, if the person named dies before that age, the legacy lapses. Where a testator provides that interest on a legacy should be paid to the legatee (or makes a provision for the legatee's maintenance until the time for payment that is equal to the amount of the interest) then the amount vests in the legatee unless the legacy is payable out of land. *See* WILL TRUSTS.

Legal age: In the UK from 1 January 1970 the age of majority was reduced from 21 to 18 years of age and a person who attains the age of 18 is now under no general legal disability even in relation to the exercise of a power of appointment. A person under the age of 18 cannot make a will or a testamentary trust unless he is a soldier on active military service or a mariner or seaman at sea. A settlement made by a minor INTER VIVOS is not void but voidable. If a minor, when he reaches the age of majority, elects to affirm the settlement or covenant, the election is binding upon him; if he does not do so, he must repudiate it within a reasonable time after attaining his majority. In the absence of a repudiation the settlement or covenant will become binding. This requires some qualification in connection with settlements and covenants to settle real estate in land, as a minor cannot hold a legal estate in land and consequently is unable to set up a trust.

Legal disability: *See* DISABILITY.

Legal estate: Ownership of land or an interest in land that is either a fee simple absolute in possession or a term of years absolute. These are the only forms of ownership that can exist as legal estates in land. All other forms are equitable only.

Legal incapacity: *See* INCAPACITY.

Legality of trusts: Trusts that are unlawful are ineffective, contrary to the general rule that the intention of the settlor is to be carried into effect. If trusts contravene the policy of the law they will not be enforced and are known as illegal trusts. There are several areas where trusts may be regarded as unlawful. These are:

- Trusts to carry out an illegal purpose.
- Trusts for an immoral purpose.
- Trusts contrary to some international standard.
- Trusts contrary to public policy; such as trusts imposing conditions in restraint of marriage; trusts discouraging entry into the Armed Forces; trusts which tend to separate parent and child; trusts where the property does not vest within the rules relating to PERPETUITIES AND ACCUMULATIONS; where there are restrictions on alienation; trusts that contradict the policy of insolvency laws; and trusts that prejudice creditors.

Legal mortgage: *See* MORTGAGE.

Legal personality: The characteristic of being a separate legal person and treated as having legal rights and obligations. Natural persons and corporations have legal personality. This means that private foundations have legal personality but trusts do not. This is shown in the way that most jurisdictions treat foundations as subject to taxation as a legal person, whereas trusts, being separate legal persons, may have uncertain tax characteristics. Tax, however, is not a reliable indicator of legal personality as some bodies, such as partnerships and, in some jurisdictions, trusts, are deemed to be individual taxable subjects as a matter of convenience.

Legal professional privilege: A rule of evidence that exempts communications between lawyers and their clients from compulsory disclosure of the nature of their communications in legal proceedings. This professional privilege has two components, the first being 'advice privilege' and the second being 'litigation privilege'. Both apply to communications between lawyer and client. Litigation privilege is broader and extends also to communications between the client's legal advisers and third parties if those communications are made in confidence for the purpose of pending or contemplated litigation. This privilege, which originally was restricted to communications between clients and their legal professional advisers, may be extended in some jurisdictions. In regard to trusts, it is doubtful whether this privilege extends to communications between beneficiaries and trustees, although it will doubtless be in existence between trustees and their lawyers, for example, if a situation arises where a trustee may be seeking advice, or where there is an actual case either pending or contemplated for breach of trust. The existence of this legal professional privilege is indirectly for the public interest in promoting access to justice and the efficient resolution of legal disputes. It does not exist for the benefit of lawyers. The client is at liberty to waive his privilege, which means that thereafter the lawyer has no basis for refusing or opposing disclosure.

Legal representatives: A term with numerous judicial or statutory definitions. It is generally applied to the persons who manage the affairs of a deceased, either as executors, being persons appointed under the will, or as personal representatives where the deceased dies intestate. The meaning is governed by the context and will generally mean next of kin.

Legatee: A person who receives a legacy that has been left to him. The correct meaning is the person who receives personal property, such as an object or money, in distinction to a devisee who takes real property, although the word has been used to cover both.

Legitimacy: *See* CHILDREN ACT 1989.

Legitimation: *See* CHILDREN ACT 1989.

Lessee: A person who rents property under a written lease from the owner. The lessee is the tenant and the lessor is the landlord.

Lessor: A person, individual or corporate, who lets another occupy or possess anything under a lease.

Letter of credit: An authority usually issued by a bank guaranteeing to provide a customer the ability to draw funds from the issuer automatically on the presentation of the specified documents. The authority is given by the purchaser of the goods, who undertakes to recompense the bank, who pays the seller on presentation of the specified documents. Letters of credit are particularly used in connection with the international transfer of goods or to effect drawdown of instalments in an international loan.

Letter of wishes: A letter issued by a settlor addressed to the trustees expressing how the settlor would like the trustees to exercise their DISCRETION. Such a letter should not be issued in a form that would allow it to be regarded as one of the trust documents so as to prevent the letter of wishes appearing to be the exercise by the settlor of excessive powers to control the trustees. Such retention of excessive power may invalidate the trust. To prevent this occurring, it is the practice to issue such a letter on a date after the establishment of a trust to which it relates and generally to frame the letters in terms which distance the expression of preferences of the settlor from the duties of the trustees. The letter of wishes should be framed in general terms and in such a way as to encourage the trustees' interest in family (or other circumstances) that they might find valuable in properly exercising their discretion. Letters of wishes have become more frequent with trusts established in offshore jurisdictions in order to enable trustees, remote from the settlor's family, to be advised on the circumstances that will enable them to exercise their discretion in an appropriate manner. The best use of letters of wishes is to advise the trustees on the nature, personality and prospects of different beneficiaries. It is advisable that a letter of wishes should not be regarded as part of the trust documentation that is open to disclosure; this may avoid embarrassment, as the beneficiaries will not then know whom the settlor favoured.

Letters of administration: A grant issued to a PERSONAL REPRESENTATIVE of a deceased who died intestate, or where the deceased failed to name an executor, or where the named executor could not or would not take out a grant of probate (a grant of probate is the normal authority given to an executor of a will to deal with a deceased's property). The person to whom letters of administration are granted is authorised to wind up the intestate's estate. On intestacy the next of kin are entitled to a grant of probate and, in the absence of a grant being made to the NEXT OF KIN, a grant will be made to a creditor or to the Treasury Solicitor. Where there is a will but no executor is named, the court will grant letters of administration with the will attached to the person having the greatest interest under the will, usually a residuary beneficiary or a creditor. *See* ADMINISTRATOR (1) *and* ADMINISTRATION.

Leverage: The borrowing of money to finance the purchase of real estate or other commercial assets and the use of such money to purchase these assets for financial advantages where the security for the loan is generally the asset purchased. Leverage is a term that indicates a degree of borrowing of a speculative nature. The point of leverage is to increase the amount of funds available to investment managers so as to increase their financial base.

Levy: To charge or impose the payment of a sum of money as in levying a penalty or a tax. There is no difference between a tax and a levy.

Lex: A Latin term for 'law' (which originally applied to a resolution of the Roman populous in the Comitia) and which is now used with other words to indicate some item of law. The following selections are applicable to trusts, foundations and property.

- ***Lex causae***: A term used in the conflict of laws to indicate the law that governs a particular question when there may be doubt as to which law applies in international transactions or trusts. In international trusts it is usual to state that the trust is governed by the law of a particular jurisdiction.
- ***Lex contractus***: The law of a contract. The law governing a contract that may be chosen by the parties.
- **Lex fori**: The place where an action is brought. The lex fori governs the remedies, the proceedings, the rules of evidence and other procedural matters. A judgment, when awarded, is regarded as a judgment of the place where the action was brought. If a judgment is to be enforced in a different country then that enforcement must be according to the laws on the enforcement of foreign judgments of that other country. Parties to a contract, trust or foundation may elect in the documentation that sets up the relationship that any proceedings shall be brought in a named jurisdiction. This constitutes a choice of the lex fori (as distinct from the *lex causae*). Any action brought outside the lex fori risks being dismissed. Such a different jurisdiction (a jurisdiction other than the lex fori) is considered as a *FORUM NON-CONVENIENS*.
- ***Lex informatica***: The law of the Internet; so far, only a proposal that there should be a separate law for those using the Internet. It is considered by some to be a development similar to that of the law merchant which arose spontaneously by parties involved in commerce.
- ***Lex loci***: The law of the place. This term is usually qualified as in *lex loci contractus* (the place where the contract was entered into), or *lex loci solutionis* (the law of the place of payment), or *lex loci actus* (the law of the place where some formal act, such as the transfer of property, has been performed), or *lex loci delecti* (the place where a wrong or tort is committed), or *lex loci celebrationis* (the place where the marriage is celebrated), or *lex domicilii* (the law of a person's domicile).
- ***Lex non curat de minimis***: The law takes no heed of trifles. A Latin maxim which is still current and is used to describe the dismissal of frivolous actions about trivialities. Also expressed as *de minimis non curat lex*.
- ***Lex situs***: The law of the place where property is situated and particularly

relevant in the case of immovables where the general rule is that immovables, including land, are governed by the *lex sitis*, i.e. the law of the country in which the property is situated. Sometimes called *Lex loci rei sitae*.

- *Lex specialis*: A doctrine of interpretation embodying the principle that a specialised rule or law will always take precedence over general law; frequently used in the civil law system, otherwise the equivalent of *lex specialis deroget generali* (a special statute overrules the general one).
- *Lex successionis*: The rule that governs the validity of a will and provides the rules of the administration of wills and of succession.

***Lex Koller*, Rule in:** A Swiss law that restricts the acquisition of property in Switzerland by foreigners. This law applies whenever an individual person abroad (as defined in the law) wishes to acquire residential property whether as a main residence, second residence or holiday residence. Such acquisition can only be made after authorisation but the law prohibits any fiduciary acquisition or any acquisition through a company of these categories of residential properties. Also, if consent is given it is given only to individuals abroad and not to legal entities. This law therefore conflicts with the provision in the HAGUE TRUST CONVENTION entered into by Switzerland that entitles a trustee who desires to register an asset 'to request its registration in his capacity as trustee or in such other way as existence of the trust is disclosed ...'. (In the UK this can be by a specific entry of a trust relationship involving land to be made in the Land Register.) However, the *Lex Koller* rule makes exceptions to the need for authorisation in the case of acquisition of REAL PROPERTY that is only used for commercial purposes (offices, hotels, restaurants, factories, etc.); this enables the transfer of such properties into trust. This is irrespective of whether the trustee personally, or a lessee or tenant, carries out the economic activity. Also, under the law acquisition does not require authorisation when the person acquiring a property is a relative or a spouse or is already a co-owner of the property. The law generally is complex.

Liability of a retired trustee: Liability persists for breaches of trust committed during a person's trusteeship but not after retirement unless it is proved that the trustee retired to enable the breach to be committed.

Liability of executors: An executor, being a trustee, is liable only for his own acts and not for those acts of co-executors, with exceptions. *See* LIABILITY OF TRUSTEES.

Liability of personal representatives: Liability is limited normally to the assets which come into the possession of a personal representative or to another on his behalf. This limitation does not apply to debts that the personal representative himself may owe to the estate; these will be treated as assets in his hand and should be made available on the repayment of the debt by the personal representative for distribution amongst the beneficiaries. Liability also exists for what he might have received but for his wilful default and for losses caused by neglect or a mistake of law. The personal representative is then considered to have committed a *DEVASTAVIT*. Generally a personal representative is in the same position as a trustee as far as general liability is concerned.

Liability of trustees: A liability arises if a trustee fails to do what his duty requires or if he does something that he is not entitled to do. Liability may arise from a broad spectrum of activities that range from the fraudulent conversion of trust funds to purely technical failures of duty which cause no harm, and even to the undertaking of unauthorised transactions even though they may result in substantial profits for the trust. Overall, any activity by a trustee that exceeds the trustee's equitable authority under the trust instrument or the general law leads to a liability to make good any losses which result. Generally a trustee is not liable for acts and defaults of others unless he himself is at fault by, for example, allowing a fellow trustee the opportunity to defraud the trust. Also, a trustee may incur liability for the default of a co-trustee particularly where one trustee is active in the administration of a trust and the other is passive. A trustee may be liable for a co-trustee's breach which he might reasonably have anticipated or where a trustee conceals a breach which he discovers and, generally, where a trustee neglects his duty to watch over his fellow trustees.

Liable: An expression to indicate that a person is 'under an obligation' or under a duty enforceable at law. It is also used to mean 'responsible at law'. However, the word 'liable' does not necessarily indicate that there is an existing liability; to say a person is liable in law may mean that the obligation has not yet crystallised into a responsibility or an obligation to perform.

Libel: A form of defamation in a permanent form, in contrast to slander, where the form of the defamation is temporary. Any false defamatory words, if published, can constitute a libel even if the publication is only made to one person provided the statement is made as a fact and not clearly as an opinion. There are three defences to actions for libel: justification (the statement was true); fair comment (a mere expression of an opinion); and privilege (such as the absolute privilege of statements made in Parliament). A libel is actionable PER SE, i.e. proof of special damage is not required.

Licence/License: Consent by one person to another to do some act without which the act would be unlawful or legally ineffective. The term is applied to licences granted by public authorities, of which there are a great number, especially licences to engage in activities that are restricted or regulated in the public interest and licences to control the number of people engaged in an activity such as a profession. There are also private licences that are granted by the owner or occupier of land permitting the licensee to enter land for specific purposes. Licences in the form of contracts confer consent to engage in activities which otherwise would be unlawful; for example, where there is a licence to use a patent or other form of intellectual property. Generally a licence is personal, not transferable and revocable at will by the licensor. These aspects may be modified where a consideration is given by the licensee to the licensor where the rights concerned in the licence are a matter of contract. The distinction between a licence and other consent to use property is that a licence passes no interest in the property itself.

Liechtenstein Trust Enterprise: *See* *TREUUNTERNEHMEN*.

Lien: A right only to retain possession of property belonging to another. A lien may be classified as legal or equitable and particular or general. A person possessing a lien may only sell the property to recover amounts owed to him with a court's permission. For example, a repairer who is unpaid and who still has the possession of the object that he has repaired may apply to the court for permission to sell the object in order to recover his costs. Common law liens are frequently annexed to contractual rights in some way but general equitable liens may be imposed by the courts. An equitable lien is a right accepted by equity to detain property giving rise to an equitable charge and when, as a consequence of this EQUITABLE CHARGE arising, the holder obtains a proprietary right in the asset concerned. The charge on property created differs from an equitable charge in that the lien arises from the relationship of the parties rather than from a deliberate act. An equitable lien exists independently of a continuation of possession but, as a creation of equity, will be ineffective against a purchaser for value of the legal estate without notice of it. A legal lien arising as a right to retain goods persists until payment is made of all claims existing against the owner. This only applies to goods and not to real estate.

Life: A presumption of the continuance of the existence of a thing or being unless it is shown that there is an inevitability that it must have terminated. Life is presumed to continue unless there is any presumption of fact recognised by law that that life has terminated. With human life there is no presumption that it must terminate after any length of time. Under the *Cestui que Vie Act* 1666 human life must be presumed to have ended after an absence of seven years.

Life annuity: An annual payment to be made during the period of any given life or lives. An arrangement, usually in the form of a policy with a life assurance company, that in return for a lump sum paid by the annuitant or another a periodical payment will be made for the life of the beneficiary where, on death, no further payment is made and there is no return of any part of the lump sum.

Life assurance: A purchase of a reversionary sum (i.e. a sum of money to be paid in the future according to the terms of the contract) in return for the present payment of money (the premium) or for an annuity in return for the premiums paid during the life of the person insuring. The term 'assurance' is generally used in respect of securing a sum payable on a person's life, and 'insurance' applies to other forms, although the term is frequently interchangeable, 'insurance' being more of a generic term.

Life estate: The right to occupy and use real property for the person's life.

Life insurance trusts: A trust that comes into operation on the death of a person who has insured his own life and has nominated the trust to receive the proceeds for distribution to the beneficiaries. This may be either by the insured taking out a commercial insurance policy with an insurer that establishes a standard form trust whereby the proceeds of the insurance are paid not to the estate of the deceased but are held by trustees (a subsidiary of the insurer) for the benefit of those nominated by the insured. This allows the proceeds of the insurance to be kept out of the insured person's estate (and therefore not subject to inheritance tax). The proceeds are then distributed by the trustees directly to the beneficiaries independently of the deceased's executors or personal representatives. Alternatively, the same effect is obtained where a life insurance policy is one of the investments held by a trust where the trust is also a vehicle for a number of INTER VIVOS property transfers. The purpose of these trusts is that on the death of the insured the proceeds are not payable to the deceased's estate and this thereby avoids an increase in the value of the deceased's estate, thus reducing the liability to estate or inheritance tax.

Life interest: An interest in property that persists only for the life of the person to whom it is granted or for the length of the life of some other person. The latter being called an estate '*pur autre vie*'. A life interest in land only exists as an equitable estate, which, until 1997, created a settlement governed by the *Settled Land Act* 1925. Since then it is known as a trust of land governed by the *Trusts of Land and Appointment of Trustees Act* 1996.

Life policy: A policy of insurance that will continue unless terminated for legitimate reasons during the life of a person. When a life policy forms part of the assets of a trust or a foundation, the trustees of the trust or the management of the foundation are required to maintain payments of the premiums unless there is a considered reason for not doing so which, when such a reason arises, should be recorded in the trust or foundation minutes and the consent to discontinue payments obtained, where appropriate, by any protector or guardian or under the reserved powers of a founder.

Life tenant: A person who is the beneficiary of property for the period of his life. *See* LIFE ESTATE.

Limitation: A method of limiting an estate or interest by defining in a conveyance or will the maximum period for which the interest or estate will continue. For example, a gift to A for life and after his death to B, known as 'words of limitation', show that A's interest in the gift persists only for his life; on A's death the property does not pass to A's estate but passes to B, who, since there is no further limitation, takes the estate absolutely. A limitation is different to a condition or other method by which an interest can be terminated before the time fixed for its longest duration, but the difference is sometimes only one of form as sometimes words of limitation are used to put an end to an interest that could continue. For example, if A transfers land to his widow for life on condition that she does not remarry, this may be regarded as a limitation or a means of defeating her interests. A true limitation does not cut down an interest; it defines when that interest ends without any involvement of the person who holds the interest. Similarly, there may be a limitation (so called) that is collateral to some other event, thus a gift to A until A qualifies as a surgeon and then to B. *See* REMAINDER.

Limitation of actions: The process by which the law provides a period in which actions must be brought. It has long been considered that it is in the public interest that persons with a claim should not be allowed to delay seeking redress for an unlimited period; stale claims are unfair to defendants and potential defendants should not be under pressure to preserve their records indefinitely. The practical element is that evidence of what happened long ago, and which may depend upon witnesses' memories, would be unreliable if there was undue delay. The *Limitation Act* 1980 consolidated the existing law that had evolved. Generally two principles have been applied. First, on the expiration of the limitation period, the right itself is extinguished, i.e. the cause of any action has disappeared. Second, the right may not be extinguished but after the limitation period the remedy is barred although the right continues to exist and can be enforced unless a limitation defence is pleaded. The first approach is generally adopted in respect of legal title of a chattel or piece of land; otherwise future holders of the land could never obtain an unencumbered title if previous neglected claims could be revived. Generally in private law it is the second approach which operates. For example, a simple debt on a contract can only be recovered for those who remain unpaid and unacknowledged for six years. One consequence of the debt remaining in existence, although unenforceable if the limitation period is pleaded, is that a creditor can exercise a right of lien by sale of goods of the debtor in his lawful possession to recover the debt, or part of it. However, since the debt itself is unenforceable, the amount of the debt, which has been recoverable through the exercise of the lien, cannot be brought into account to reduce, by set-off or counter-claim, any separate debt owed by the original creditor to the debtor; otherwise this would be an indirect enforcement of the original debt which is now unenforceable due to limitation. The limitation periods vary according to the nature of the action. For simple contract debts the ordinary limit is six years; for contracts made under seal, the limitation period is 12 years; for actions for negligence, the period is reduced to three years and, in defamation cases, to one year. Actions for the recovery of land must be brought within 12 years or 30 years if the land belongs to the Crown or to a church. Limitations run from the period when the right accrues, but the tendency is to delay the start of the limitation period until a certain other event occurs, for example, for persons who claim damages for a disability incurred, the limitation period does not begin to run until the disability ceases and then an action must be brought within six years. This applies to disabilities such as infancy or mental incapacity. This allows the full amount of loss to be determined. In contractual matters, if a creditor gives a written or signed acknowledgement of a debt, this has the effect of extending the period of limitation; the period starts from the date of the acknowledgement. Some situations are not subject to any limitation, for example, there is no limitation on actions brought by beneficiaries under a trust in respect of any fraud or fraudulent breach of trust by a trustee, or on actions to recover trust property in a trustee's possession, or where a trustee has converted a property for his own use. This exemption is contained in Section 21(a) of the *Limitation Act* 1980. But, where trustees have committed an innocent or negligent breach of trust, the six-year limitation period exists for actions against them or for proprietary claims for trust assets against innocent strangers, unless the strangers derive their title by fraudulent means, in which case there is no limitation period. The question arose of whether a stranger to a trust who dishonestly assists in the breach of trust, or knowingly receives trust property paid out in breach of trust and who is considered to hold the unlawful gains on a constructive trust, is a trustee within the meaning of the limitation. In ***Williams v. Central Bank of Nigeria*** [2014] UKSC 10, the Supreme Court in the UK held that such strangers to a trust and who are regarded as holding the unlawful gain on a constructive trust are not trustees within this exemption. The law contains many modifications to the general principles, particularly in connection with the power of the court in personal injury cases and where the defendant has been fraudulent. *See* LACHES.

Limited liability: The restriction of liability that accompanies a financial venture through the use of a legal structure where this advantage is an integral part of the legal nature of the structure used. The most significant example is the use of limited companies that are registered as limited by shares or by guarantee. A member of a company (a shareholder of a company limited by shares or a guarantor of a guarantee company) is liable only to the company for the nominal value of the shares which are held (whether or not the holder has paid more or less than that nominal value to a third party for the shares) or by the amount a participator in a guarantee company undertakes to pay in the event of the company becoming insolvent. A shareholder of a limited company usually has subscribed the maximum amount for which he is liable when he buys the shares as fully paid; where the shares are partly paid, the future liability is the difference between the amount paid and the full amount. In the case of a company limited by guarantee, the limit is the amount which the members have undertaken to contribute to the company's assets if the company is wound up. Other corporate bodies, under the legislation by which they are set up, offer similar protection such as industrial and provident societies, building societies and friendly societies. In the absence of fraud, the courts are reluctant to extend the liability of members of corporate bodies by lifting 'the VEIL OF INCORPORATION'. Limited liability also exists by members of LIMITED LIABILITY PARTNERSHIPS and by the limited member of a LIMITED PARTNERSHIP. In other fields, a limited liability may be achieved by a clause in a contract or in the case of ship-owner's liability under shipping law and the Convention Limitations Liability for Maritime Claims and the ***Hague-Visby*** Rules (rules for the international carriage of goods by sea). There is no limitation on liability for trustees who in the event of default of their duty may have unlimited liability. Foundations are liable to the full extent of the foundation's assets.

Limited liability partners: Members of a LIMITED LIABILITY PARTNERSHIP.

Limited liability partnerships (LLP): A partnership incorporated under the *Limited Liability Partnership Act* 2000 and which is further regulated by a range of statutory instruments that apply some of the Company Act regulations and other matters relevant to corporate bodies. An LLP is a corporate body. It has separate legal personality and unlimited capacity. Its members have a limited liability for the partnership's debts up to the amount they have contributed or agreed to contribute with the exception that there is no limitation on liability on any partner who commits a TORT in the course of the partnership's business. Unlike limited partnerships, with an LLP there is assumption that all the partners will take part in the management. The partners have an obligation to each other fully to account for profits, fully to share business information and not to compete with the LLPs business. An LLP is governed by an incorporation document that is registered with the members designated on incorporation and responsible for compliance with the regulations and for filing information. If there are no designated members, all members are responsible. LLPs are taxed as partnerships and all the profits are taxed as part of the income of the partners. An LLP cannot issue share capital to raise finance. An LLP is a hybrid of a limited company and a partnership but is unable to issue share capital or to raise finance. A limited liability partnership is governed in the UK by the *Limited Liability Partnership Act* 2000, supplemented by a range of statutory instruments and is used by professional organisations who are required to act as partnerships but ensures that each partner suffers only a limited liability. This structure came about due to the increase in the financial risks associated with work conducted by many accountants and solicitors where unlimited liability of the practitioners concerned would have been untenable. *See* LIMITED PARTNERSHIP.

Limited owner: A term of property law applied to tenants for life in tail and other persons not having a fee simple absolute (such as a tenant by courtesy). The holding of property as an entailed interest was a frequent form in which estates were held in the late 18th and 19th centuries. The law was codified by the *Settled Land Act* 1925. In the early 19th century, a tenant for life or other limited owner could only deal with his own estate unless there had been express power granted to him under the will or settlement. The limited owner's powers were extended in the mid-19th century to being able to sell the fee simple provided there was protection for the other beneficiaries. New entailed interests have not been possible since the *Trusts of Land and Appointment of Trustees Act* 1996. A limited owner's position is now an equitable interest under the *UK Inheritance Tax Act* 1984.

Limited partner: A term that originally described a limited partner under the *Limited Partnership Act* 2007 but which, since the introduction of limited liability partnerships, has been extended to cover members of both.

Limited partnership: A form of partnership, subject to the *Limited Partnership Act* 1907, similar to a general partnership except that there are one or more limited partners (LPs) in addition to one or more general partners (GPs), of which there need only be one. The GPs have management control and share the right to use partnership property and to share the profits in pre-defined portions with joint and several liability for the debts. The LPs have a limited liability whereby they are only liable for debts incurred by the firm to the extent of their registered investment. LPs have no management authority and they receive a return on their investment which is usually defined in the partnership agreement. This gives limited partners a similar veil to that of corporate shareholders which, however, is more difficult to pierce because limited partners do not have any formalities to maintain and, as long as the LPs and GPs do not mix their funds, they maintain their limited liability. In some jurisdictions the continuance of limited liability of limited partners depends upon their not participating in management. Limited partnerships are distinct from limited liability partners in which all the partners have limited liability. Limited partners are sometimes referred to as sleeping partners, i.e. those who provide the capital for the partnership activities but who take no part in the management. *See* LIMITED LIABILITY PARTNERSHIP.

Liquidated damages: The amount of damages agreed at the time a contract is entered into to be paid as compensation for breach of contract and intended to be recovered whether the damages suffered by the innocent party constitute more or less than the agreed amount. Where the estimate of the likely loss has been arrived at fairly and truly represents a genuine estimate then a liquidated damages clause will be enforced. Where a liquidated damages clause is included in a contract but does not fairly and truly represent a genuine estimate of likely loss to an injured party, this will not be enforced as it is likely to be a penalty. *See* PENALTY.

Liquidator: A person appointed on the winding up of a company to act for the creditors. Where there is a member's voluntary liquidation, that is, a company wound up on the resolution of the members, one or more liquidators are appointed by the company. Where a company is wound up by creditors, the creditors and the members each nominate a liquidator. The liquidator nominated by the creditors then has preference unless an application is made to the court within seven days. Where there is a compulsory winding up by the court, a provisional creditor is appointed by the court at the same time as the petition for winding up is presented (under the *Insolvency Act* 1986, Section 135) and, thereafter, when the winding up order is made, the official receiver is the liquidator until some other person is appointed. In all cases the duty of a liquidator is to get in and realise the assets of the company and distribute the proceeds to the company's creditors and, where possible, particularly on a member's voluntary winding up, to any person entitled to a surplus. The procedure of each liquidator is governed in the UK by the *Insolvency Act* 1986. This Act provides that a liquidator appointed by the creditor has the role of securing the amount owed to the creditor. In other cases, the duties of a liquidator are to get in and realise the assets of the company by selling the assets and then distributing the proceeds to the creditors and, if there is any surplus, to those so entitled.

***Lis alibi pendens*:** A legal action which is pending (also called simply *les pendens*). The plea of *lis alibi pendens* is frequently grounds to prevent a claimant bringing proceedings in another court against the same defendant for the same object and for the same cause of action. This doctrine, aimed at preventing duplication of litigation, was fundamental to the European Union's approach to jurisdiction under EU COUNCIL REGULATION No. 44/2001, the Brussels II Regulation No 2201/2003 (concerned with family law, divorce, child custody and child abduction) and the LUGANO CONVENTION ON JURISDICTION AND THE ENFORCEMENT OF JUDGMENTS IN CIVIL AND COMMERCIAL MATTERS 1988. (*See* BRUSSELS REGULATION (RECAST) *and* ITALIAN TORPEDO.)

Lis pendens: *See LIS ALIBI PENDENS.*

Litigation friend: A person who must be appointed to conduct proceedings on behalf of a child under 18 years of age or a protected party on the grounds of such a person's lack of legal capacity. A litigation friend may be appointed by the COURT OF PROTECTION or otherwise must be a person who is competent and fair in the conduct of proceedings and has no interest against the child or protected party and who can undertake to satisfy any order for costs.

Living trust: A trust set up and in effect during the lifetime of the grantor. Also called INTER VIVOS TRUST. Particularly a term used in North America to distinguish trusts made INTER VIVOS from trusts created by wills.

Living will: A misleading term, but one which is colloquially used to mean something that is an advance directive and associated with the wishes of a person as to future care. An advance directive is given by a patient before becoming incapable about his or her future treatment or care. An advance directive is not made subject to the *Wills Act* 1837 and does not need to be in writing and signed, nor need witnessing, and can be revoked orally, even if made under seal, and is not restricted to revocation, as is a will, by visible destruction or by a subsequent replacement in writing. Consequently, a living will has no application to the disposal of assets after death.

Loan: The lending of or giving to another person anything on the condition of return or repayment. This condition is implied unless it is clear that a gift is intended or that circumstances for which a presumption of ADVANCEMENT can be made. A borrower must take proper care of the thing borrowed, use it according to the lender's intention and restore it at the proper time and in a proper condition. Accordingly, the lender must allow the borrower to use and enjoy the thing lent during the time of the loan and according to the original intention, and is compelled to reimburse the borrower from any extraordinary expenses to which he has been put in connection with the preservation of the thing lent.

Loco parentis: In place of a parent. Normally used in connection with exercising some parental function where the assumption of parental responsibility is implied from the acts of a person, such as where he pays for the maintenance or education of a child or establishes him in life without actually being the parent. The characterisation of *loco parentis* can be acquired even though the father of the child is living although if the child resides with the father and is maintained by him there is an inference against another acquiring a *loco parentis* status.

Longus usus nec per vim: Long use without force. *See NEC PER VIM, NEC CLAM, NEC PRECARIO.*

Lord Chancellor: *See* CHANCELLOR, LORD.

Lost document: The normal rule is that the content of a document is proved by the production of the original. However, if it can be proved that a document has been destroyed, and cannot be found after a proper search, it may be proved by secondary evidence, such as by a copy or oral evidence of the contents.

Lugano Convention on Jurisdiction and the Enforcement of Judgments in Civil and Commercial Matters 1988: A Convention in almost identical terms to the

Brussels Convention but the Lugano Convention was applicable to deciding jurisdictional matters with Switzerland and Iceland. The Lugano Convention was similarly replaced by Council Regulation 44/2001. *See* BRUSSELS CONVENTION ON JURISDICTION AND THE ENFORCEMENT OF CIVIL AND COMMERCIAL MATTERS 1968.

M

Magna Carta: The Great Charter of 1215, subsequently regarded as the foundation of constitutional government in England. The content was mostly declaratory of ancient customs. The charter granted by King John set out some fundamental rights; such as, no man shall be imprisoned, etc. except by lawful judgment; and no man shall be denied or suffer any delay in justice or right. The Charter also restricted royal interference with military tenure of knights' service and other matters beneficial to the nobles. This became important to the system of land tenure. The King was restrained by the Charter from introducing further mesne estates, which prevented the chain of feudal land tenure growing longer than it was. Almost all the actual contents of the Charter have been replaced but the Magna Carta remains of great symbolic importance and represents the idea of limiting power by the monarch, which developed into political systems that deny absolute authority to a head of state or a sovereign controlling body.

Main purpose rule: The practice of a court of looking at the whole of a written instrument and determining its main purpose. This may lead to a rejection of words in an instrument or even all its provisions if they are inconsistent with what the judge can see as the main purpose of the instrument (derives from ***Glynn v. Margetson & Co*** [1893] A.C. 351 HL). This rule is applied in a variety of contractual contexts. In trusts it may be applied more restrictively where, if there are meaningless clauses, these may be rejected provided that there is sufficient certainty in what remains to form a valid trust. The rule may also apply to foundation documents. With trust and foundation documentation this rule is seen to be applied where a court looks at the documentation and perhaps decides that the trust or foundation may be the expression of the alter ego of the settlor or founder in that the main purpose of the structure is to preserve the settlor's or founder's authority over the assets.

Maintenance (1): The power of trustees over all settled property to apply the income or capital of the trust towards the maintenance and education of a beneficiary who is still a minor or whose interest is still contingent. This power may be expressed individually in a trust instrument if particular features are required, but maintenance is usually given under the statutory provision of the *Trustee Act* 1925, Section 31, as amended. Under the Act, trustees may, at their sole discretion, pay, or otherwise apply, to a beneficiary's parent or guardian trust income for the beneficiary's maintenance, education or benefit. This may apply to the whole, or such part of the income, as in all circumstances is reasonable, so long as there is no contrary intention expressed in the trust instrument. This provision was amended by the *Inheritance and Trustees' Powers Act* 2014 to give trustees an unfettered discretion when deciding whether and how much income to apply for maintenance under trusts created or arising after 1 October 2014. Contrary intentions include any express directions to accumulate income until a certain age. Since maintenance is normally paid out of income, where there is a trust without income there is nothing to support the power. Maintenance is paid at the trustees' discretion and may be made whether or not there is another fund available for the same purpose as long as the payments are reasonable and made with regard to the minor's age and requirements and to the general circumstances. Any income not paid in this way must be accumulated and invested. Also, apart from the provisions in the instrument and in the Act, a court has inherent power to allow a minor's property to be used for his maintenance; only income will be used for this purpose, although exceptions exist where the fund is very small and there is necessity. Foundation councils may be given a similar discretion if the law of the jurisdiction that governs the foundation so provides and then the founder may include such a provision in the foundation charter or regulations. The term 'maintenance' is also a colloquial term used for periodic payments made as part of a divorce, nullity or separation arrangements of a marriage or civil partnership.

Maintenance (2): The giving of assistance or encouragement to a party to a civil action by a person who has neither an interest in the action nor any motive recognised by law justifying that interference. The term 'maintenance' includes in this context CHAMPERTY where the assistance is given in consideration of a promise to share the proceeds or subject matter of the action if it succeeds. The origin of this prohibition of maintenance and champerty was that this conduct would act against public justice and keep alive strife and contention which would make law into an engine of oppression. But the modern courts have taken a broader view of what constitutes lawful support of a party. In recent times this has been extended to allow insurers, trade unions, trade associations and friendly societies to assist their clients to sue even if they have no financial interest in the outcome. The original strict prohibition has given way to a greater emphasis on facilitating access to justice. The offences in crime and tort involving maintenance were abolished in 1967 (*Criminal Law Act* 1967, Sections 13(1) and 14(1)), although maintenance contracts are still treated as contrary to public policy. Under the modern regime, conditional fee arrangements between solicitors and their clients and litigation funding arrangements have become lawful in certain circumstances, although the general illegality remains in respect of contingency fee agreements. The exception against maintenance does not apply where a person encourages, whether or not for a share of the proceeds, a beneficiary under a trust to bring an action against the trustees. The grounds for bringing an action against a private foundation council are generally vague.

Maitland, F.W. (1850–1906): An English barrister and historian who became the Downing Professor of Law at Cambridge University where he was held in high regard and his students published in 1909 their edited notes from his lectures. 'Equity' records Maitland's lectures on the law of trusts which are noted for their clear exposition of the then salient principles and the volume is still in print. Maitland edited many volumes of the Selden Society on English legal history. He is particularly well known for his work in conjunction with Sir Frederick Pollock for the classic 'History of English Law: Before the time of Edward I', which was first published in 1895 and continues to be the authoritative work on early English law. 'Maitland's Collected Papers', published posthumously in 1911 in three volumes, is still in print. In his paper on the 'Origin of Uses' Maitland shows the 'precarious life' the use had in English law until it found protection in the equitable jurisdiction of the Chancellors where, after many adventures, the use appears as 'equitable ownership'. In another paper, 'Outlines of English Legal History 560–1600', Maitland refers to the activities of the Inns of Court and the Inns of Chancery in developing a 'laborious system of legal education'; the conclusion being that under the fostering care of those societies English jurisprudence became an occult science and he describes the professors as 'the most unlearned kind of most learned men' but credits them as 'rigorous logicians afraid of no conclusion that was implicit in their premises' (*The Collected Papers of Frederick William Maitland*, Vol. 2, William S. Hein & Co. Inc.,. Buffalo, N.Y., first printed Cambridge University press 1911).

Majority (1): In English law the full age of a person, i.e. 18 years according to the *Family Reform Act* 1969. A person now attains the majority of 18 years at the first moment of his or her 18th birthday.

Majority (2): The greater number. Relevant in a deliberative body where questions are usually decided by a majority of those present at a meeting (provided there is a quorum at the meeting) and applied to the principle that the majority of members are entitled to control a company. Also, under the *Juries Act* 1974, Section 17, a majority verdict may be accepted under a trial by jury.

Mala fide: In bad faith, as opposed to BONA FIDE.

Mala fides: Bad feeling or intention.

Malfeasance: The commission of an unlawful act as contrasted with nonfeasance, which is the non-performance of something that ought to be undertaken. These terms are usually applied to the acts of public authorities where a distinction is made between something badly done and something that has not been done at all. *See* NONFEASANCE *and* MISFEASANCE.

Malpractice: The performance of an act, or of a statutory duty, with a lack of regard to whether the performance is indifferent to the likelihood of harm caused to other people if a reasonable standard of care is not taken.

Mandamus: An earlier name of a prerogative order to compel performance of a duty where an injured party has no other means of compelling the performance of something that he has a right to be performed. Now known as an Order of Mandamus in the UK under Part 54 of the Civil Procedure Rules 1998.

Mandate: A direction or a request. Thus, an agent is given a mandate by the principal, which is instructions on how to conduct business on behalf of the principal. Trustees have a mandate from the settlor of how to manage a trust and the foundation council has a mandate according to the foundation charter. The term is also used in connection with the bailment of goods without reward. A mandate requires the mandatory (the person to whom the mandate is addressed) to do the act with which he is charged, to apply care and diligence and to render an account of his doings to the mandator. The term is also applied by a bank to the instructions that a bank requires of a customer when the customer seeks to open an account. This is usually a printed form that details how the account will be operated and the terms and conditions under which the bank will accept the business. This procedure ensures the bank is only required to do what the bank is willing to do.

Mandatory: Compulsory; for example, mandatory duties, which are duties that are intended to be enforced, in contrast to those duties that are not compulsory. The distinction applies independently of whether a facility or requirement contained in a trust deed comprises either a trust or a power. A mandatory injunction is an injunction requiring the performance of some act, such as the removal of a building. A court has a greater reluctance to grant mandatory, as opposed to prohibitive, injunctions; with the former, the court requires a much higher degree of assurance that the application is justified. When the term is applied in conflict of laws situations, it indicates that the mandatory rules are to be applied before the conflict of laws rules, i.e. the local law takes precedence over an otherwise applicable foreign law.

Mareva injunction: *See* FREEZING ORDER.

Marketable security: An investment instrument that is capable, according to the use and practice of stock markets, of being sold and bought on that exchange. A company's debenture is ordinarily a marketable security, not being transferable by mere delivery and subject to a mortgage AD VALOREM stamp, but a debenture of a private trading company, which does not invite subscriptions for its shares, and where the debentures are subject to special conditions, is not a marketable security.

Marketable title: The title to real property which is free from any mortgage, trust, lien, claim or other objections which would render it less than a desirable property. A court will not enforce a contract to buy and sell real estate if there is not a marketable title unless the contract reveals that the impediment over the title has been declared and is acceptable to the purchaser.

Mark-to-market: Not a legal term but the means of establishing a present value of transactions that will mature only in the future and which is used for the purpose of determining the amount of collateral that a party is required to deposit to cover the value of a transaction as it proceeds towards maturity. This is an amount equal to the value of the obligation that is outstanding to the counterparty at any identified payment date. This value includes the amounts that stand to be paid on amounts owed in the future. The value of the amount of collateral required is then termed 'mark-to-market value' of all obligations at the valuation date, i.e. an estimation of the present value of what will be needed to enable the payment to be made in the future; in other words, the present value of a future obligation.

Marriage settlement: An arrangement whereby real or personal property is placed in the hands of trustees for the benefit of the husband and wife and their issue. The object is to retain the property in the family, particularly where the husband has the fee simple in the property and a settlement is made with the object of providing for the wife by securing the payment to her of two annuities. One of these annuities is paid during her husband's lifetime and is frequently called 'pin money' and the other payable after his death, called a JOINTURE. In addition, the settlement may provide for the payment of gross sums of money called 'PORTIONS' to such of the younger children of the marriage who have attained their majority. It is likely that the deed provides that the property charged with providing money for these portions should go on the death of the settlor to the wife and younger children before the remainder goes to, say, the eldest child. A marriage settlement often contains covenants to include in the settlement all property that exceeds an agreed value which may be acquired by each after the marriage. Such a covenant generally binds the covenantor to settle not only property in which he or she may have no interest at the time of the marriage but also interests that are only contingent. In some cases, this includes property which is vested at the time of the marriage such as REVERSIONS. Where there is a marriage settlement, on granting a decree of divorce or nullity or judicial separation, the court may make an order varying the benefit of the parties to the marriage and their children. This can be applied by the court to any ante-nuptial or post-nuptial settlement and may even extinguish or reduce the interests of either in the settlement under the *Matrimonial Causes Act* 1973, Section 24(1)(c). Settlements may also be varied under the *Inheritance (Provision for Family and Dependents) Act* 1975, Section 2(1)(f). Marriage settlements are sometimes referred to as anti-nuptial trusts. *See* SETTLEMENT *and* FUTURE PROPERTY.

Married woman's property: At common law a husband on marriage became absolutely entitled to all assets belonging to his wife in her own right and included those acquired after marriage and for all the rents and profits of her lands during the marriage except in respect of such property which was specifically made the separate estate of the wife. This rule was abolished in the *Married Woman's Property Acts* 1870 and 1882 and now has no part to play in the assets of a married couple. Subsequent legislation and court decisions have enlarged a wife's entitlement to assets that are deemed to have been acquired jointly by the husband and wife during marriage. As the rule no longer applies, and is of historical interest only, the term is still sometimes used in a non-legal context to describe the separate property of a wife.

Material breach: A serious or important breach in a pre-existing arrangement, such as a partnership or trust deed, usually applied where the breach is significant in the nature of the arrangement and which is serious enough to justify litigation.

Material validity: The validity of a contract or other arrangement that is effective notwithstanding minor inaccuracies where there is something in the nature of the substance of the contract which overcomes minor faults or omissions.

***Matrimonial Causes Act* 1973, Section 24(1)(c) and (d):** Powers of the Family Division of an English court which are broad and extensive for the purpose of varying trusts upon divorce, or to the granting of a decree of judicial separation which allows the court to make one or more orders varying the benefit of the trust to the parties to the marriage and to the children of the family, or either of them. Any anti-nuptial and post-nuptial settlement may also be the subject of a court order amending the interests of either of the parties under any such settlement according to the merits of the parties as assessed by the court.

Matrimonial property: '[T]hose things which are acquired by one or other, or both, of the parties with the intention that they should be continuing provision for them and their children during their joint lives and used for the benefit of the family as a whole ...' (***Wachtel v. Wachtel*** [1973] Fam. 72 at 90 (CA)). This quotation distinguishes between property built up during a marriage by the parties' common endeavours from property acquired independently of marriage (non-matrimonial property). The non-matrimonial property includes property that the parties bring with them into the marriage or acquire by inheritance or gift during the marriage. The distinction is important in connection with the dissolution of a marriage where the court has discretion under the *Matrimonial Causes Act* 1973 to supervise the division of the matrimonial property between the parties. The distinction between matrimonial and non-matrimonial property does not appear in the legislation. A claim by one party for a greater share of these assets than is acceptable to the other party is referred to as a claim for ANCILLARY RELIEF. A court, faced with such a claim, will be concerned when the property is held on trust if the other party, the settlor of a trust, can succeed in a call for discretionary distributions. The source of the assets and the participation of both parties in obtaining these assets will also be considered. Claims for ancillary relief frequently are the subject of high profile claims with sometimes large sums of money in dispute and are of particular interest where the husband sets up a trust in a different jurisdiction than that of the matrimonial home. A similar situation could arise with foundations where extra attention is likely to be given to the reserved powers of the founder. The trend is for the courts to intervene to restore into the pool of matrimonial property those assets which appear to a family court to have been unfairly put aside by one spouse into a trust or foundation, thereby decreasing the amount of matrimonial property available for division. This is sometimes done by one spouse with disregard to the basic law concepts.

Maxim: An axiomatic statement or general principle. Maxims in the past were more frequently quoted as embodying general principles of law. In modern law, maxims are not rated so highly as in the past and have been considered by judges to be misleading, expressing principles that are too wide and which do not cover all situations implied by the statement. They have been described as 'minims' rather than 'maxims' as they only encompass a small amount of information. Because the maxims do not cover exceptions or qualifications to the principle that they express, they are considered by some to be bad abstracts of the law. However, this is to misunderstand the use of maxims as an expression of broad principles which are useful as starting points but which may be modified by qualifications and exceptions. In the past, law dictionaries included large collections of these maxims; for example, 1,500 are found in *Bouvier's Law Dictionary*. Francis Bacon, 1561–1626, former Lord Chancellor of England, collected 800 maxims but only felt fit to publish 25. However, the maxims of equity are frequently referred to in textbooks on equity and should be taken as illustrating general principles, mostly of equitable procedure. One general maxim, however, retains great force and is relied upon regularly – *DE MINIMIS NON-CURAT LEX*.

Maxims of equity: Equity was never intended to be a complete system of law. Some of the general principles have been embodied in a series of general principles called the 'maxims of equity'. These maxims vary from authority to authority. In any case, the maxims are not a code of positive laws that will be applied literally but merely show the principles which can be discerned from many of the detailed rules that equity has established. These maxims were given more significance in previous years and are still useful expressions of important equitable principles. Sometimes there are overlaps between each of the 12 maxims listed here, which are considered in *Snell's Equity* (Sweet & Maxwell, 31st edn, 2015, Ch. 5, p. 93):

(1) **Equity will not suffer a wrong to be without a remedy.** This underlines the whole jurisdiction of equity that no moral wrong should be allowed to go without remedy provided that it is capable of being remedied by a court of justice. The Courts of Chancery were established to overcome the gap where the common law courts failed to remedy many wrongs, but equity cannot remedy every moral wrong. The maxims only apply to those which are capable of remedy by legal process. This maxim applies particularly to the enforcement of trusts where the abuse of confidence by a trustee is clearly a wrong. The maxim also covers the 'auxiliary jurisdiction', which originated in the Courts of Chancery to assist litigants in the enforcement of their legal rights, particularly where it was necessary for a party to obtain disclosure of facts which were only in the possession of the other party and where the common law courts had no power to order such disclosure.

(2) **Equity follows the law.** Equity never claimed to override the common law. Equity interferes only where some important circumstances are disregarded by common law rules, i.e. equity does not interfere with a man's legal rights. Equity remedies the excesses of the common law by restraining an individual from taking advantage of his legal rights in an unconscionable way despite his strict rights at common law. This would not deny the primacy of the common law but secures a relaxation of the excesses. This originated when the Lord Chancellor

was a cleric in Holy Orders and felt entitled to protect the conscience of persons who appeared in his court. This maxim can also be expressed as 'equity acts on the conscience' and it has also been stated that 'equity follows the law but not slavishly nor always'.

(3) **Where there is equal equity, the law shall prevail.** This maxim and the following one are concerned with the priority of rival parties to claim the same property in equity.

(4) **Where the equities are equal, the first in time shall prevail.**

(5) **He who seeks equity must do equity.** A person claiming equitable relief must be prepared to do what is right and fair to the defendant. This rule has many applications and covers the refusal of a court to order repayment of a loan to an unregistered money lender. Another example is that a mortgagor who wishes to exercise an equitable right to redeem his mortgage must give the mortgagee reasonable notice of his wish to do so.

(6) **He who comes to equity must come with clean hands.** Similar to the maxim above except that (5) applies to conduct in the future. This maxim applies to the claimant's conduct in the past. The combined effect of (5) and (6) is that a claimant must not only do, at the time of a claim, what is right and fair but must also show that he has behaved appropriately in the past.

(7) **Delay defeats equity.** Sometimes expressed as 'equity aids the vigilant and not the indolent'. Where a party has neglected his rights and put up with a breach of those rights for a considerable length of time then this is sufficient to prevent that party obtaining an equitable remedy (*see* LACHES). The maxim does not apply to cases where a situation is covered by the statutes of limitation expressly or perhaps by analogy (i.e. where a claim is not expressly covered by any statutory period but is closely analogous to one which is). Since the *Limitation Act* 1980, various equitable claims have been brought within the statutory period, such as claims by beneficiaries to recover trust property or in respect of any breach of trust.

(8) **Equality is equity.** This principle applies to the presumption of TENANCY IN COMMON and is behind the rules on the severance of JOINT TENANCIES. Persons entitled to property should have the certainty and fairness of equal distribution: 'Equity did delight in equality' (***Petit v. Smith*** (1695) 1 P Wms., 7, 9.). This principle of equity applies in the absence of any sufficient reason otherwise.

(9) **Equity looks to the intent rather than to the form.** This is the principle where equity makes the distinction between what is matter of substance and what is matter of form and if it finds that by insisting on the form the substance is defeated, then it would be inequitable to allow a person to insist on such form.

(10) **Equity looks on that as done which ought to be done.** This applies only in favour of persons entitled to enforce a contract specifically. It does not act in favour of a volunteer, i.e. a person who has not given consideration for the other parties' promise. For example, a person who enters into possession of land under a valid and enforceable agreement for a lease is regarded by the courts to be in the same position between himself and the lessor as if the lease had actually been granted to him. The maxim has also been applied to confer an equitable interest under a Property Adjustment Order – thus awarding the wife a priority to the property over the husband's trustee in his subsequent bankruptcy (***Mountney v. Treharne***

[2002] EWCA Civ. 1174).

(11) **Equity imputes an intention to fulfil an obligation.** Where a man does something that is capable of being regarded as the fulfilment of an obligation, the act will be so regarded. The maxim puts a favourable construction on a man's act, thus where a husband covenants with trustees of a marriage settlement to provide £50,000 for land to be settled on the trust of the settlement and separately purchases property for the same amount, it is presumed that the lands have been purchased by the husband in pursuance to his covenant and the lands are therefore subject to the trusts of the marriage settlement (***Sowden v. Sowden*** (1785) 1 Bro. C. C. 582).

(12) **Equity acts in personam.** Equity originally did not interfere with the defendant's property but merely made an order against the defendant personally and the court would, as a means of enforcement, issue an order of commitment if the defendant failed to comply. Sometimes an equitable court used the process of sequestration under which sequestrators were appointed to take possession of both the property in dispute, and further sufficient property if necessary, until the defendant did the act which he had been ordered to do. This maxim is of less application than formerly but liability still exists by trustees who, on breach of trust, are faced with actions against them personally, IN PERSONAM. The maxim may also apply in respect of property situated abroad over which an English court has no jurisdiction but can exercise its judgment against the person who owns the foreign property and who is within the English jurisdiction.

Strong dislike has been expressed from time to time about the maxims. For example:

'I need hardly repeat that I detest the attempt to fetter the law by maxims. They are almost incorrectly misleading: they are for the most part so large and general in their language that they always include something which actually is not intended to be included in them.' Lord Esher MR in ***Yarmouth v. France*** (1887) L.R.19 Q.B.D. 647 at 653.

Mediation: Settlement of a dispute by an independent third party. The process is usually initiated by the parties or may be ordered by a court. Mediation became more prominent after the profound change in civil procedure which followed the publication of the report by Lord Woolf, 'Access to Justice: Final Report', in July 1996, where the attention of litigants was focused on the desirability of resolving disputes without litigation. This was one of the purposes of establishing pre-action protocols to make both parties well informed of the procedures involved at the outset of litigation and was intended to ensure, as early as possible, that the parties to a dispute had the relevant information with which to define their claims and make realistic offers to settle. Protocols have been produced for guidance in various categories of action; the first were in respect of personal injury claims and the resolution of clinical disputes. Following the adoption of the CIVIL PROCEDURE RULES which were inspired by Lord Woolf's Report, mediation has been adopted in the UK courts under the Civil Procedure Rules (CPR, Rule R.1.4(1)). The courts are required to engage in the active management of cases. This process includes encouraging parties to use alternative dispute resolution procedures (ADR). The inducement to do so is that if the parties and their lawyers turn down the chance of ADR when suggested by the court, they may have to face uncomfortable cost consequences. With trusts, trustees need to know whether they have a duty to resist a claim against them before they can proceed to mediation. This is closely bound with the ability of the trustee to recover costs from the trust fund. Trustees have no duty to litigate at their own personal expense. With claims against the trust or trust property trustees are usually required to be neutral and this may merit a Beddoe-type application or an application for a pre-emptive costs order (***Alsop Wilkinson v. Neary*** [1995] 1 All ER 431) (*see* BEDDOE ORDERS). The Centre for Effective Dispute Resolution also defined mediation in 2004 as:

> 'A flexible process conducted confidentially in which a neutral person assists the parties in working towards a negotiated agreement of a dispute or difference, with the parties in ultimate control of the decision to settle and the terms of resolution'.

The European Parliament and the Council of the EU adopted Directive 2008/52/EC which provided, in Article 3, that mediation:

> 'Means a structured process, however named or referred to, whereby two or more parties to a dispute attempt by themselves on a voluntary basis to reach an agreement on the settlement of their dispute with the assistance of a mediator.'

Mens rea: An essential element in establishing criminal liability. The term refers to the mental state and therefore to the intent of a defendant in connection with the act which led to a criminal accusation. Different crimes require different mens rea, such as intention, recklessness or negligence. Some crimes, known as strict liability offences, do not require any mens rea from the defendant. These sorts of crimes are increasing, particularly in the areas of safety and environment where the general rule indicates that an offence is committed only where criminal conduct is accompanied by some element of fault.

Mental capacity: Mental capacity refers to the independent ability of a person to make a decision. A person does not have CAPACITY if he 'is unable to make a decision for himself in relation to a matter because of an impairment of or disturbance in the functioning of the mind or brain' (UK *Mental Capacity Act* 2005, Section 2). A person who lacks capacity cannot make a valid will or act as a trustee or, indeed, set up a will, a trust or a private foundation. *See* VALIDITY OF SETTLEMENTS. A trustee who becomes unable to act may be replaced subject to provisions in the trust instrument under the *Trustee Act* 1925, Section 36. Similar provisions exist in a number of laws on private foundations. *See* CAPACITY *and* MENTAL DISORDER.

Mental disorder: Under the *Mental Health Act* 1983, Section 1, mental disorder is defined as comprising any disorder or disability of the mind. This definition is wide and covers both mental impairment and PSYCHOPATHIC DISORDER as well as learning deficiencies; the latter are not within some of the provisions of the Act. That a person suffers from a mental disorder, or is detained pursuant to other powers in the Act, does not necessarily mean that he is incompetent and does not have the MENTAL CAPACITY to make a will. Each case is considered with reference to general definitions and with medical and psychiatric evidence. A valid will can be made by a person with a mental disorder if it is shown that the will was made during a lucid interval. The Act expressly provides that a person shall not be deemed to be suffering from any form of mental disorder by reason only of promiscuity or other immoral conduct, sexual deviancy or dependence on alcohol or drugs. The *Mental Health Act* 1959 conferred a wide general power on the court with respect to the property and the affairs of a mentally disordered person and, subject to this general provision, confers special powers to manage and deal with the patient's property in the patient's name and to make settlements or gifts of the patient's property. The Vice Chancellor has issued guidelines on how this jurisdiction should be exercised. The crucial consideration for the court is whether the patient can make a disposition of his property objectively (***Re D (J)*** [1982] Ch 237, 2 All ER 37). The terms of the *Mental Health Act* 1983 included four categories of mental disorder; this was mostly replaced by the *Mental Health Act* 2007, but one of the categories of mental disorder in that earlier Act was 'mental impairment'. This term is still used outside definitions concerned with mental health to describe generally a significant impairment of intelligence and social functioning and abnormally aggressive or seriously irresponsible conduct. *See* CAPACITY *and* MENTAL CAPACITY.

Mere powers: The ability to do something lawfully which otherwise would be unlawful. There are many variations centred upon whether a power may be public or private, legal or equitable. Within the context of a trust or similar transaction, a mere power can be regarded as the authority of a person to deal with or dispose of property of which he is not the beneficial owner; the exercise of which depends upon the power holder's discretion. Consequently, powers must be distinguished from trusts; trusts are imperative whereas powers are discretionary. This is complicated by the existence of a category of powers called 'trust powers' or a 'power in the nature of a trust' which gives the holder a power that he is obliged to perform in order to achieve the objects of a trust. This is in contrast to a mere or bare power which imposes no obligation to act on the holder.

Mesne: An encumbrance, or person, or process that is preliminary or subordinate to another, such as 'mesne process' which means a preliminary, but not a final, process.

Mesne profits: Profits derived from land that have been improperly withheld, such as rents and profits which a trespasser has, or might have received, during occupation of the premises and which the trespasser must pay over to the true owner as compensation for committing trespass; for example, a jury is not bound by the amount of rent but may give extra damages. A claim for arrears of rent and mesne profits may be joined with a claim for possession.

Migration: When applied to trusts and foundations means the ability of the trust or foundation to change its domicile and, by registration in a different jurisdiction, become a trust or foundation of that new jurisdiction. A provision in the law of both jurisdictions is required for a migration to take place. Migration requires re-registration of the existing trust or foundation in the new jurisdiction. Following migration, the trust or foundation becomes a body of the new jurisdiction without the cost and procedure of winding up the old vehicle and re-establishing elsewhere. This avoids liquidating and reacquiring the assets but does not remove the need for informing company registrars and land registries of the change and fulfilling the necessary procedures which these separate bodies may require. One further consequence of migration is that the double taxation conventions which were formerly applicable will be replaced by those treaties that have been entered into by the new host jurisdiction. The new domicile will require a reappraisal of the trust or foundation's position in connection with international enforcement and recognition laws. An emigration tax may be levied when a trust or foundation departs from a country.

***Milroy v. Lord* (1862) 4 De G. F. & J. 264:** A principle derived from a case of that name which states: 'There is no equity in this court to perfect an imperfect gift', i.e. where a person gives a cheque made out to another without endorsement or where there is an attempt to transfer a lease without going through the necessary assignment; equity does not supply an endorsement or deed or force the donor to complete the gift in any way. The principle in this case does not apply in connection with acts done by a donee or trustee to complete a change of ownership where the person has done everything which he can to effect the change (e.g. where a change of share ownership awaits only the issue of a new share certificate from the company secretary).

Misappropriation: A term applied to unlawful dealings with assets particularly through fraudulent dealings with property by a fiduciary where money or other property is put to a fraudulent use.

Misfeasance: The exercise of a duty by a trustee but where the duty is done badly although not necessarily in an unlawful manner. *See* NONFEASANCE *and* MALFEASANCE.

Mistake: The term 'mistake' is used to describe something incorrect or an error of judgment. The legal relevance of mistake depends upon the context in which it is used. Mistake features prominently in CONTRACT law and has a separate application in connection with trusts and other EQUITY matters. The broad interpretation of the doctrine in equity is that if someone is paid money under a mistake and the recipient knows of the mistake but nevertheless retains the money, then the money is held on a CONSTRUCTIVE TRUST. There is much CASE LAW on this principle which also impinges on the idea of UNJUST ENRICHMENT. Further applications connected with the law of equity are divided between circumstances which are not dependent on mistake occurring in connection with duties owed by non-fiduciaries and those which are so owed. With non-fiduciary duties a voluntary transaction, whether the mistake is of law or fact, may be set aside if the court is satisfied that it was made as a result of mistake as distinct from ignorance, inadvertence or misprediction. This may lead to RESCISSION or RECTIFICATION. Mistakes under circumstances dependent upon duties owed by fiduciaries are within the revisions in the case of ***Pitt v. Holt*** to the so-called principle of ***Hastings-Bass***, the substance of which concern the exercise of powers under trusts where the trustees acted under a mistake.

Mixed trust: Where the trust instrument provides different and distinct sets of trusts. For example, an authorised purpose trust of capital or income which, at the same time, includes a discretionary trust and a discretionary dispositive power over capital or income, i.e. a trust that has both a purpose and beneficiaries. The term 'mixed foundation' can also be applied to foundations combining purposes with beneficiaries.

Moiety: Meaning a half part but is frequently misapplied to indicate an equal part or share.

Monetary awards: Sometimes made under actions against trusts where no other action is possible and where money is made to compensate a person's interest under equity for a loss. Only used when no other equitable remedy, such as injunction or specific performance, is adequate.

Money due: Debts, or for monies otherwise arising under a contractual obligation.

Money had and received: Where a person receives property belonging to another, or money is paid by mistake on a wagering contract, or as an overpayment of a mortgage, the real owner is able to bring a personal claim against the recipient for debt. A claim is based upon the owner having legal title to the property and the common law in these cases imposes a strict liability upon a recipient subject to the defence of the recipient having altered his position in good faith. Frequently used in the case of money paid under a contract where the recipient was unable to perform his obligation formerly expressed as 'money paid in respect of a consideration which has wholly failed'. The term is less frequently used in modern law owing to the rise of the doctrine of RESTITUTION where there has been undue enrichment as where money is unjustly obtained and which merits the remedy of restitution. Money paid under a mistake of law is not recoverable and is not said to be money had or received.

Money into land: The common law distinguished between real and personal property but, through the doctrine of conversion, equity avoided some of the severities of this distinction. For example, if land is conveyed to trustees with instructions that the trustees should sell the land and pay the proceeds to a named person or, conversely, if trustees are instructed to invest money in land to be conveyed to another person, then, under equity, the land or the money, although still in its original form, takes the identity of the asset to which it was to be converted. Under the *Trusts of Land and Appointment of Trustees Act* 1996 this doctrine was abolished in the case of express trusts for sale although it is necessary to ascertain whether a beneficiary's interest is in land or in personal property. The doctrine still applies under a statutory trust or under an order of court or under a contract for the sale or purchase of real property under which real property is treated as part of a vendor's personalty from the moment when a specifically enforceable contract exists for the sale of the property; this also applies to cases of options to purchase property but not to mere pre-emption rights. *See* CONVERSION.

Money laundering: Defined in the UK in the *Proceeds of Crime Act* 2002 as the concealing, disguising, converting, transferring or removal of criminal property. Where a bank or other person knows or suspects that it is dealing with criminal property, it must make a disclosure to the Serious Organised Crime Agency. Similar rules exist in most countries based upon the recommendations of the Financial Action Task Force (FATF) against money laundering and in accordance with the 3rd Directive of the EU on Anti-Money Laundering. The laws generally introduce the crime of 'TIPPING OFF' where a bank or a person informs a suspect that he is being investigated for money laundering offences and who then is therefore likely to disappear or withdraw the money. In the UK it has been decided by a case (***Shah v. HSBC Private Bank*** (UK) Ltd [2009] All E.R. (D) 204 (Jan)) that it is appropriate for a bank simply to inform its customer that the transfer of funds requested will not take place for the reason that the bank is complying with its statutory duties. The European Commission announced in 2012 that following a revised set of international standards on 16 February 2012 by the FATF, the Commission was committed to rapidly updating the EU legislative framework. Prospective settlors of trusts are subject to increasing amounts of scrutiny. Under the trend to classify tax evasion as a criminal offence more rigorous 'know your customer' procedures are required. The current antipathy of regulatory bodies towards tax avoidance, or even straightforward tax planning structures, may subject the use of arrangements that are now legal to closer examination.

Mortgage: A conveyance of some interest in land or other property as security for the payment of a debt or the discharge of some obligation. A mortgage may be a legal mortgage where the property so committed is a LEGAL ESTATE (i.e. freehold or leasehold interest) or it may be an equitable mortgage where only an equitable interest is applied as security. Also, a mortgage will be an equitable mortgage where only an equitable interest can be used because the interest of the mortgagor is equitable or where an attempt to convey a legal estate is unsuccessful. When the debt or other obligation secured by a mortgage is satisfied then the mortgagor has the right to redeem and recover full ownership of the property (colloquially, the mortgage is 'paid off'). Although a mortgage was originally the creation of a borrower to secure a loan already in existence, a mortgage is now used extensively for the repayment of a loan made available by the mortgagee to enable the MORTGAGOR to acquire the property that is subject to the mortgage arrangements: the purchase and the mortgage taking place simultaneously. A mortgage consists of two legal devices in parallel: first, a personal contract by the MORTGAGOR to repay the debt with interest; second, a dispositional charge on the mortgagor's estate or interest as security for the repayment. Where the mortgaged property is land with a registered title, the mortgage is made through a charge by deed. A property not subject to the *Land Registration Act* 2002 leaves the relationship between the mortgagor and MORTGAGEE to depend upon the contract between them, including equity's right to allow the mortgagor to retain the right of REDEMPTION. An equitable mortgage is one where the mortgagor gets no legal estate; this occurs when either the mortgagor only has an equitable interest or because the mortgage is not created with the formalities required for a legal mortgage, for example, an equitable mortgage for a house can be created by a mere deposit of the title deeds and an agreement to repay a loan advanced against the value of the house. The main examples of equitable mortgages are mortgages by beneficiaries under trusts which require an equitable assignment by the beneficiary of his chose in action, i.e. the right under the trust to receive a benefit in the future. An attempt to create a legal mortgage that fails for a lack of formality will be treated as an agreement to create a mortgage and the principle that equity treats 'as done that which ought to have been done' results in such an agreement constituting an equitable mortgage. Also, an equitable mortgage by the deposit of title deeds creates a mortgage based on a contract to create a mortgage and which under Section 2, of the *Law of Property (Miscellaneous Provisions) Act* 1989 is required to be in writing and signed by both parties. An equitable mortgage of personalty may still be created by deposit of evidence of title, such as depositing a share certificate as security for a loan. *See* EQUITABLE MORTGAGE OR EQUITABLE CHARGE *and* EQUITABLE INTERESTS.

Mortgagee: The party to a mortgage transaction who provides the money, i.e. the lender. *See* MORTGAGE *and* MORTGAGOR.

Mortgagor: The person who conveys property in favour of another person as security for a payment, i.e. the borrower. *See* MORTGAGE *and* MORTGAGEE.

Moveables: Goods, furniture, jewellery and other personalty.

Multi-form foundations: A feature of foundations created in Nevis under the *Multiform Foundations Ordinance* 2004, which accepts that for an entity to become a foundation it does not necessarily have to be a specified corpus and, in recognising this legislation, allows existing entities, subject to the terms of the legislation, to be recognised by Nevis law as foundations. This enables trusts, limited companies, limited liability companies and other associations to be recognised as foundations. This means that the multiform foundation is a legal entity shell into which the subscribers can self-design the form of a foundation, subject to the provisions of the Act.

Muniment: A deed or writing recording claims and rights that depend on documentary evidence, such as title to real property. Such documents may be kept in a special room known as a 'muniment room', i.e. a house or room of strength in a public building purposely made for keeping deeds, charters and other writings.

Mutatis mutandis: A term usually used in connection with the correction of a draft written instrument, where one correction on a point in detail then requires necessary changes to accommodate that change in the rest of the document. The alteration is then said to apply mutatis mutandis.

Mutual fund: A form of investment where an individual's contribution is used in conjunction with others so as to enable a greater spread of opportunity and less concentrated risk than each individual sum used independently could achieve. These mutual funds are subject to mandatory regulatory control before they may invite contributions from the public. A mutual fund may either be a unit trust or an investment company. A unit trust is a trust subject to special regulatory rules to accommodate the various parties involved in a public participation, such as managers and custodians. These are 'open-ended investments' in which each subscriber takes a proportion of all the investments made by the manager of that unit trust. The other traditional forms of mutual funds are investment companies (sometimes referred to as 'investment trusts', an old name which applied when they were actual trusts). Nowadays, investment companies are ordinary limited companies in which the public can purchase shares through the stock exchanges. Investment companies can borrow money to gear up their investment activities and, as companies, can make reserves that can be used to iron out fluctuations in the dividends paid to the shareholders in the lean years. *See* UNIT TRUSTS, INVESTMENT TRUSTS, OEIC *and* REIT *and* OPEN-END FUNDS.

Mutual promise: A promise made in exchange for another promise in consideration of a promise to create a simple contract between two or more persons. The essential requirement in a contract in English law is for each party to provide consideration to the other. With mutual promises, the consideration shown by each party is a promise to the other. *See* CONSIDERATION.

Mutual wills: A legally binding agreement between two parties to make and not revoke mutual wills. When the first testator dies, having performed his part of the agreement, the second testator is barred from revoking his will; this makes the second testator's estate the subject of a constructive trust. For example, two testators can make mutual wills containing reciprocal provisions and agree they will not revoke their wills and then, on the death of the first of them, the survivor holds his property on trust for whomever it was agreed should benefit from both. The deceased's property remains held on trust by his executors who become his trustees pending the availability of the assets of the second testator on the second testator's death. This has the effect of barring the survivor from revoking his will on the death of the first testator. This distinguishes a mutual will from a joint will where either testator can revoke his part of the will at any time whether before or after the death of the other. Mutual wills have been regarded as analogous to secret trusts. Mutual wills are usually made by two separate wills. Theoretically, it is possible to make a mutual will by two persons making a joint will. This is unlike a usual joint will where either testator can revoke his part at any time whether before or after the death of the other. The making of separate wills in identical form does not give rise to any presumption that the wills were executed as mutual wills.

Mutuality: The requirement that the parties to an agreement must have, as far as the essentials of the agreement are concerned, reciprocal obligations so that each understands how his obligation matches that of the other party so that the object may be achieved. This is known as 'mutuality of obligation'. 'Mutuality of assent' is where both parties give a simple affirmation of the terms of the contract. 'Mutuality of remedy' is where each party can enforce the contract against the other, i.e. the purchaser can enforce the vendor to play his part in a contract of sale and vice versa.

N

Naked trust: *See* BARE TRUST.

Name: An appellation that distinguishes an individual person, thing or place from others, although not of universal application as others may have adopted or have been given an identical designation. An individual's original name appears on his birth certificate but, when of full age, a person is free to add to it or change it to any name he pleases, subject to certain necessary procedural requirements. The names of companies and limited liability partnerships are subject to detailed rules. In connection with the acquisition of securities by a trustee, the purchase 'in the name of' a trustee does not authorise a trustee to purchase bearer securities (because a bearer security does not incorporate the name of the purchaser). A trustee may nevertheless purchase such securities when the agreement to purchase is expressed to be 'in the name, or under the control of' the trustee or 'in the name and on behalf of' the trustee.

Name and arms clause: A clause in a settlement, common in the 18th century, which provided that a beneficiary under a settlement would forfeit his entitlement unless he used a specified surname and, if appropriate, a coat of arms at all times. Such clauses were inserted by the settlor to preserve the family name and identity and frequently imposed a condition by which a son-in-law would be entitled to continue a family's fortune.

National Conference of Commissioners for Uniform State Laws: A body created in the United States in 1892 consisting of more than 300 lawyers, judges and law professors appointed by the states to draft proposals for uniform and model laws. In 2000, the conference proposed a Proposed Uniform Trust Law intended to be the first national trust law. *See* UNIFORM TRUST CODE.

National Land Information Service (NLIS): In the UK a joint initiative between central and local governments to provide an online service to deliver information relating to land or property in England and Wales. The information is that which is stored by various organisations such as the Land Registry, local authorities, etc. This service may be used by applying through one of the registered channel providers, such as a solicitor or licensed conveyancer, who passes the enquiry to the NLIS hub. The NLIS hub seeks information from each of the data providers concurrently and reports back to the registered channel provider, which consolidates the results for delivery to the original enquirer.

National law: The law of a sovereign state applied to domestic issues within the jurisdiction of that state unless the parties to any dispute legitimately choose the issue to be tried by the law of a different state or where the issue is subject to some international law or convention. National law is the most likely law to be applied to a trust or foundation unless the basic documentation of either type of body shows an express choice for the application of another country's laws; a reference to the law of another country is a reference to that country's whole law, including its conflict of laws principles. *See* CONFLICT OF LAWS.

Natural justice: The requirement of procedural fairness and the collection of rules and principles to be followed by any decision-maker. This generally requires that people involved in a dispute are told of their right to be heard and to have their dispute settled free from any personal interest (i.e. bias) in the outcome, and that the decision-makers act on the basis of logically provable evidence. The rules are unofficial, variable and flexible, and the term is used mostly to imply an instinctive fairness in the relationships between persons.

Natural law: Rules derived from traditional moral principles, from God or from the writings of Roman jurist consults, as opposed to law derived from man and man-made organisations. The concept has passed through many different stages, both religious and secular, and became more adaptable and practical when it was treated as the law that existed between all states and which had been accepted by them, and then called the 'law of nations', as distinct from the 'law of nature'. The principle is that laws are divided into arbitrary or natural laws; the latter are essentially good and just and binding in all places where they are observed. This is distinct from arbitrary law, which is indifferent to morality and the natural law that exists. The idea of natural law is the opposite of positive law that is created by mankind through a state sovereign. *See* POSITIVE LAW.

Natural persons: Human beings or individuals as distinguished from artificial or legal persons, such as corporations and foundations. An unborn person is not generally regarded in law as a person, but such a child is a 'person in being' for the purpose of the law against perpetuities and is, nevertheless, owed a duty of care so that if subsequently born alive, the child has a right of action in respect of disabilities from wrongful acts before its birth (*Congenital Disabilities (Civil Liability) Act* 1976).

Natural rights: A natural right is something that is inherent in nature and is not imprescriptible and not capable of withdrawal or becoming inoperative by lapse of time. Natural rights supplement direct rights and may, when concerned with ownership, impose duties on other persons. For example, every owner of land has PRIMA FACIE the right to pure and free light, heat, rainfall and wind in respect of his land. These rights exist as a matter of course in connection with ownership or occupation of land, and are only subject to the rights of adjoining owners, who must also have similar rights with which the natural rights of a person should not interfere. Natural rights contrast with rights that may be acquired, such as easements, franchises and *PROFITS À PRENDRE*. The term is also applied in connection with human rights. An example of the persistence of natural right principles is seen in land law under the concept of *NEC PER VIM, NEC CLAM, NEC PRECARIO* (meaning not by force, secrecy or consent) as a precondition of acquiring title by prescription of land, such as by adverse possession, which must be occupied for 12 years by the claimant as of right and not by force or done secretly or with the consent of the landowner.

Near thereto as circumstances will permit: An antique expression used to permit property to be acquired for a trust, although not specifically described in the trust instrument. This was mostly used in strict settlements to allow assets not within the contemplation of the settlor to be brought within the settlement.

Necessaries: An expression most frequently used in describing when an infant may incur liability for the acquisition of things that are necessary to maintain the particular infant in his station and degree; these things extend beyond those that are necessary for the support of life (food, shelter, etc.), which can be referred to as 'necessities'. In contrast, 'necessaries' include a wide variety of objects which, under the circumstances, an infant requires to fulfil his academic and social position. Although an infant is incapable of binding himself by contract, he is bound to pay a reasonable price for the necessaries that have been sold and delivered to him. These items must be suitable to his condition in life and his actual requirements at the time of sale or delivery. Similar rules apply to persons of unsound mind. This is mostly of use in connection with the sale of goods. Also, if a person fails to provide the necessaries to a child under the age of 16, this may amount to an offence of cruelty to the child. This aspect is particularly relevant to trustees who have underage beneficiaries within their care. What is a necessary is judged by the usage of society at the time but, over the years, the following have been held to be necessaries: engagement and wedding rings, a racing bicycle for a youth, a regimental uniform for an enlisted soldier and the hire of a car to fetch luggage from a station six miles away. On the other hand, fancy waistcoats for a Cambridge undergraduate were not considered by the court to be necessaries as the undergraduate already had been sufficiently supplied with clothing. Lessons in flying for a law student, a horse for an impecunious cavalry officer and a second-hand sports car were similarly judged not to be necessaries on the facts pertaining to these items.

Nec per vim, nec clam, nec precario: Not by violence, stealth or permission. These three elements must be absent to succeed when a claim is made for the acquisition of property or interest in property by prescription. For example, to gain acceptance of the interest claimed, such as the right of way over property of another, or for the acquisition of a title to land by adverse possession, the claim must be one of right over the land itself and not obtained by force, secrecy or consent. The legal maxim expressing this is *longus usus nec per vim, nec clam, nec precario. See* ADVERSE POSSESSION.

Ne exeat regno: A writ issued by the Chancery Division of the UK High Court restraining a person from leaving the UK without licence of the Crown or leave of the court. It is implied when a person, against whom another has an equitable claim for a sum of money, is about to leave the country to evade payment and where the absence of the defendant would be materially prejudicial to a plaintiff's case; usually only now applicable to claims against debtors under the *Debtors Act* 1869.

Negligence: The mental element that must be present, in many circumstances, to constitute an act as a TORT, or an independent tort that is a breach of a legal duty to take care and which results in damage to a person or property; the tort of negligence. The classic definition of the tort of negligence is that a person must take reasonable care to avoid acts or omissions which he can reasonably foresee would be likely to injure a person who is so closely and directly affected by his action that he ought reasonably to have them in contemplation (***Donoghue v. Stevenson*** [1932] A.C. 562, the famous case of the snail in the ginger beer bottle). This general statement has been refined over the years in various branches of the law. Particularly relevant is the decision in ***Hedley Byrne & Co. v. Heller & Partners*** [1964] A.C. 465 HL, which concerned the presence or absence of a legal liability for negligence of a person who makes a statement on financial matters which, when relied upon, results in a loss where the statement is made under circumstances that may encourage the hearer to rely on it. Investment advisers owe a duty of care to their clients; advice is often accompanied by a disclaimer that no liability will be incurred by the adviser for any loss in following the advice given. This has a twofold purpose; first, to protect the adviser's position in any case; and, second, to cover circumstances where the adviser was incorrect in his assessment of the market. To be wrong does not necessarily mean that there was negligence and a disclaimer, if properly drafted, could cover both situations. The circumstances under which a potentially liable statement is made are also relevant; casual remarks in a social context are unlikely to come within the principle as it may not be reasonable to assume that a duty of care exists between the parties in such circumstances. To be the basis of an action of damages or compensation, the negligence must be to the prejudice of a person towards whom a duty of care exists; for example, negligence of a trustee towards a beneficiary would be actionable, although probably referred to as a breach of trust. It is essential for an action for negligence that the loss is caused by a person who owes a duty of care to the person suffering the loss. This shows the difference between trusts and foundations. A foundation council owes no duty of care to a beneficiary of the foundation; a foundation council's duty lies towards the foundation itself; directors of companies owe no duty of care directly to the shareholders, and the directors' duty is towards the company. Individual professional practitioners owe a duty of care to their clients.

Negotiable instruments: An instrument, the holder of which has a contractual right to property and where the right to receive the advantage can be transferred to another person who acquires it in good faith and for value. Negotiable instruments are exceptions to the rule that choses in action are not assignable. These instruments are also an exception to the *NEMO DAT QUAD NON HABET* rule, i.e. the transferee gets a better title to property than the transferor had. Negotiable instruments are, primarily, instruments relating to commerce and finance and include cheques and promissory notes where the payee can negotiate title to the amount on the face of the cheque or promissory note to another by a suitable endorsement on the instrument itself, usually on the back. Where this occurs, the desirability of the instrument depends upon the creditworthiness of the most recent person to whom it is negotiated in place of the creditworthiness of the original payee or other intermediate persons to whom it is negotiated. The principle of negotiation of a bill of exchange, promissory note, cheque or other negotiable instrument for the payment of money is to transfer it for value by delivery and usually by endorsement by the transferee of his name on the instrument. Certain instruments may be negotiated by delivery, e.g. bearer bonds, etc. The category of negotiable instruments is not closed; negotiation can be established by usage and by the expectation of the parties using that instrument; the issue of whether travellers' cheques are negotiable instruments is sometimes raised. Opinions are varied. Instruments that are traditionally negotiable, such as cheques, may be made non-negotiable by being so endorsed. The *Bills of Exchange Act* 1882 in the UK contains the law on the negotiation of bills of exchange, promissory notes and cheques.

Nemo dat qui non habet: *Nemo dat quod non habet: Nemo plus iuris in alium transferre potest quam ipse habet*: meaning, generally, that no one is able to transfer to another more rights than he has himself, i.e. no one can give a better title than he holds. Frequently applied in the sale of goods, but may also apply to other property, including real property, except where the *Settled Land Act* 1925 or other enactments apply. A trustee holding legal title to trust assets is able to transfer the legal title to those assets, and the recipient, on the strength of this rule, should not obtain complete and good title to them, as the trustee could not transfer the beneficial rights which he did not possess. The knowledge of the purchaser is relevant here and it is a rule of equity that if the purchase is made without knowledge of the existence of beneficial interests then the purchaser obtains a complete and good title to those assets. *See* EQUITY'S DARLING.

Nephew and niece: The sons and daughters of brothers and sisters, but the term is used frequently by testators describing persons who are not strictly and properly so related. The terms 'nephew' and 'niece' have been used by popular language to include nephews and nieces by marriage, and the sons and daughters of a half-brother or half-sister, a great nephew and even an illegitimate nephew, have been accepted to allow distributions to such persons under wills. There is no such popular extension with the regard to the term 'cousin'. Despite the liberal interpretation given in respect of legacies, the better policy is for a testator to actually name those whom he wishes to benefit.

New trustee: A person newly appointed, and not an existing one, to whom power is given to act in the stead of another existing trustee as well as himself.

Next friend: A term formerly used to describe a person appointed under the Rules of the Supreme Court (RSC Order 80, Rule 2) who is permitted to bring an action on behalf of someone who is suffering from a disability, such as being underage or a mental patient. The term is still used unofficially; under the present Civil Procedure Rules (CPR 21) it has been replaced by a 'litigation friend'. As a general rule, a person under disability can only bring an action by a litigation friend. A child, on the other hand, may sue without a litigation friend where leave is given or where the lawyer acting for the child considers the child is capable.

Next of kin: A term which has no precise and general legal meaning but essentially means a person's nearest relative or someone nominated by a person to whom information should be given in case of an emergency. A common selection of a next of kin is a person's partner, children or parents. However, the *Mental Health Act* 1983 lists a person's next of kin as follows:

Husband or Wife
Son or Daughter
Father or Mother
Brother or Sister
Grandparent
Grandchild
Uncle or Aunt
Nephew or Niece

To avoid doubt in case of accident, a person may carry a 'next of kin card' which details the people who should be contacted in an emergency in order to avoid problems, especially as an unmarried partner may be selected who would otherwise risk being ignored. Such a card does not have to follow any specific form. Also, the identification of a person's closest relative is relevant in matters relating to intestacy and to the distribution of assets on death, where the deceased nominates in his will his closest relatives, sometimes referred to as his 'next of kin'.

Nisi prius: A Latin phrase meaning 'unless before' and previously applied to the practice of entering a trial before judge and jury at Westminster to indicate by the use of the phrase that there had been no previous trial on the matter concerned.

No-contest clauses: A clause in an instrument, such as a trust deed, that aims at discouraging one party from contesting the validity of the arrangement that has been set up or witnessed by the instrument. For example, a trust deed may provide that discretionary beneficiaries will be removed as potential beneficiaries if any of them contests the performance or conduct of the trustees. Trustees with this power may be in contempt of court if they are considered to be attempting to oust the court's jurisdiction for discouraging what might be legitimate litigation. Where the power of trustees to remove a beneficiary is non-discretionary these provisions, on the whole, are not invalidated but may nevertheless fail for other reasons, such as the IN TERROREM principle. This prohibition does not apply if there is a gift over on the termination of the interest to which the no-contest clause applies. To be valid, a no-contest clause needs to be drafted so that a court is able to determine with reasonable certainty the exact event that will trigger the no-contest clause and result in the termination of the interest of a beneficiary. A no-contest clause could also be regarded as unlawful if the effect would be that no beneficiary could enforce his interest without incurring the consequences of such a clause. *See* FORFEITURE CLAUSE.

Nominee: A person who holds legal title to property for the benefit of another without having any real duties to perform except upon instructions from the beneficiaries. This distinguishes a nominee relationship from that of trustee. A nominee is usually established by contract to secure confidentiality as to the ownership of the property concerned, or as an administrative matter to pass the management of assets on to another person. The relationship may also be fiduciary, as in the case of bare trusts, where the nominee is a trustee but has no other duties other than to hold the property on behalf of the settlor.

Nominee trust: *See* PASSIVE TRUST.

Non-charitable purpose trust: *See* PURPOSE TRUST.

Non-charitable unincorporated associations: A body of two or more persons bound together for common purposes in an organisation, not being for business purposes, and where each of the persons is bound by mutual duties and obligations. The organisation so created will have rules that identify the person in control, the terms on which its funds are held and details of who may join and who may nominate the persons that might leave. Such an organisation is not a legal person and is incapable of owning property in its own right; for example, a sports or social club where property is owned by a selection of members as trustees for the benefit of the other members. *See* GIFTS TO NON-CHARITABLE UNINCORPORATED ASSOCIATIONS.

Non-disclosure: *See* CONCEALMENT.

Non-discretionary trust: A trust where the trustee has no discretion or decision-making power over property existing in trust. The trustee is directed how to invest trust assets and has no decision-making power in the distribution. Not a term frequently applied except to indicate the nature of a trust where there is an absence of trustees' discretionary powers. *See* DISCRETIONARY TRUST.

Non-executive director: A director of a company or other corporate body who is not employed full time. Their part is to attend board meetings and to challenge constructively and help develop proposals on strategy, to scrutinise the performance of management and to assist in appointing and removing executive directors and fixing their remuneration. Non-executive directors are frequently employed on the basis of their previous useful experience and contacts.

Nonfeasance: The failure of a person to do some act which he ought to do. Usually applied in contractual situations where there is no breach of contract but simply a failure to perform a duty, especially towards the public, and where an individual sustains some damage due to the non-performance. Frequently the term is applied in connection with failure by highway authorities to repair roads where a member of the public suffers some damage. A trustee who neglects to fulfil a requirement under a trust causing a loss to the trust or to a beneficiary could be accused of nonfeasance. This is a failure to perform rather than causing a loss through a bad performance, which may be called 'MISFEASANCE'; it is sometimes impossible to distinguish between nonfeasance and misfeasance. A trustee may attempt to complete the legal ownership of the trust assets unsuccessfully and then neglect to pursue the matter, which results in the trust being void as not properly constituted. It then matters little whether the failure of the trustee is considered nonfeasance or misfeasance. Where trustees are given mere powers, they can only be brought to court for misfeasance, not for nonfeasance, as generally there is no duty to exercise MERE POWERS. There is a different point where a trustee fails to carry out a fixed trust obligation, i.e. where the trust deed lays down a positive duty for the trustees then the court will compel the trustee to perform that duty or will order what is to be done. *See* MISFEASANCE.

Non-governmental organisation (NGO): A wholly or mainly voluntary organisation that is national or international and is independent of any government control. An NGO is likely to be engaged in humanitarian and/or political objectives and may have charitable status that is not prejudiced by receiving some government funding.

Non-interest in possession trusts: A trust where there is no INTEREST IN POSSESSION, i.e. where there is no beneficiary who is currently entitled to a benefit. Such trusts can cover a wide range of situations where the trust is not used as an immediate means of providing for an adult beneficiary, i.e. where the trust instrument does not specifically allocate a discernible benefit to a beneficiary who is entitled to immediate payment, or to a life tenant or other person. For example, a trust fund was settled on a beneficiary for life but subject to an overriding power of appointment amongst a discretionary class, and then subject also to a power given to the trustees to accumulate the income for 21 years. The House of Lords reversed the lower court's decision that the life tenant had an interest in possession on the grounds that the true test of an interest in possession was whether the person had a 'present right to present enjoyment' ***Pearson v. IRC*** [1981] AC 753, i.e. an undefeatable right to the trust income independent of any exercise by trustees of a power. Here there was no such right; a beneficiary has an interest in possession only if he is entitled to receive the trust income as it arises.

Non-intervention, principle of: A court will not restrain or compel trustees to exercise a power when the trustees have been given an absolute discretion whether to exercise it or not, provided their conduct is informed, BONA FIDE and uninfluenced by improper motives.

Non-resident: *See* RESIDENT.

Notary: An internationally recognised legal officer concerned with documentation, particularly prevalent in civil law countries where they are responsible for conveyancing and other matters relating to documents. In English law the functions of a notary are limited to witnessing signatures on documents, except for the City of London notaries, appointed by the Archbishop of Canterbury, who have a wide range of duties as a branch of the legal profession. These notaries are concerned with acting impartially and in connection with documents; formerly they were independently employed by banks and others when it was necessary to select which investors should first be repaid loans, etc., and thereafter indirectly affect the composition of further tranches. This function is now done electronically. City of London notaries are also skilled in the translation of legal documents.

Notice (1): Knowledge or awareness of a fact that is given or made available to another person or which that other person is taken in law to know about. The giving of notice to a person is to bring it clearly to his attention but notice 'means something less than full knowledge'. What is considered sufficient notice varies from case to case. The term in this sense is widely used and notice may constitute actual notice (express notice), constructive notice or imputed notice.

(a) **Actual notice** or express notice is that which is given in plain words from one party in a transaction to another. In the UK, under the *Land Charges Act* 1972, registration in a Land Charges Registry constitutes actual notice to all persons connected with the land but only in so far as documents and matters that must be registered. This applies unless it is impossible to search the names of all persons who may have registered the charge; in this case, the actual knowledge of the matter that affects the land does not depend on registration. Notice and land charges generally are of considerable complexity.

(b) **Constructive notice** is notice where the knowledge of a fact of which a person ought reasonably to be aware and which would have come to his knowledge by making an enquiry of a nature that people under similar circumstances would reasonably make.

(c) **Imputed knowledge** is notice which an agent, solicitor, etc. is given and which the principal is considered to have received, although that presumption can be rebutted if the agent was a party to fraud or acted in a way which indicated that he would not deliver the notice to his principal.

Notice in respect of a trust is subject to special provisions; for example, a stamp on a transfer of mortgage does not by itself give notice of a trust (*Law of Property Act* 1925, Sections 112 and 113). A person dealing in good faith with a mortgagee does not have to enquire into trusts of the mortgage money. Also, a trustee or personal representative acting for one trust or estate is not affected by notice obtained through acting for another in the absence of fraud (*Trustee Act* 1925, Section 28). The law of equity plays a large part in the law on notice. The principle is embodied in the maxim that legal rights are 'good against all the world' but equitable rights are good against all persons except a BONA FIDE purchaser of a legal estate for value without notice (EQUITY'S DARLING) and those claiming under such a purchaser. This explains the rationale behind the doctrine of notice; a bona fide purchaser for value will only be bound by equitable rights if he has notice of them. This restriction only applies to purchasers; a person who takes land without giving value in exchange, such as a donee, executor or a beneficiary under a trust or foundation, takes the land subject to all its legal and equitable encumbrances. The general principle, however, has exceptions as purchasers for value continue to be affected by notice of trusts, unless the concept of overreaching operates, where a purchaser will acquire property free from the interest of the beneficiaries even though he has notice of those interests. *See* OVERREACHING.

Notice (2): A form of providing information usually under the law or some legal situation where certain facts must be given to other parties usually in writing, such as notice to terminate employment, notice to quit tenancies or notice to treat when a public body has powers of compulsory purchase of land.

Nottingham, Lord: Lord Chancellor from 1675 to 1682. Lord Nottingham brought to the post immense legal learning that served as the basis of a policy of conservative reform. His most celebrated contribution was the 'Statute of Frauds' in 1677. An important dictum of Lord Nottingham was that a Chancellor's conscience was politic and civil rather than internal and natural and that, therefore, equity was a matter of rule and not discretion:

> 'It is infinitely better for the public that a trust, security or agreement, which is wholly secret should miscarry, than that men should lose their estates by the mere fancy and imagination of a Chancellor.'

Nottingham pioneered the making of the doctrines of equity into fixed doctrines (based upon judicial precedents), a process which was not completed until the end of the 17th century. For his influence on the principles and character of equity he is frequently referred to as the 'Father of Modern Equity'.

Novation: A term derived from the civil law meaning that a new contract is substituted for an existing contract either between the same parties or between different parties, the consideration being the discharge of the old relationship by both parties to the original contract. In financial matters, a novation of a contract includes a release of an existing debt with the debt being taken up by the party to whom the contract is novated.

Novus actus interveniens: A new act that takes place and which prevents a person being liable for damage done. The chain of causation between a negligent act, e.g. by a person and the suffering of damage by another, is broken by some participation by a third party that was unforeseeable and which is then said to intervene and which affects the liability of the person committing the original negligent act. *See* REPARATION CLAIMS.

Nullity of marriage: A marriage that is void or which has been made so by the exercise of a voidable condition. A void marriage is one which is regarded by every court as never having taken place and can be so treated without the necessity of any decree annulling it. A voidable marriage is one which will be regarded by every court as valid until it is annulled by a court of a competent jurisdiction.

Nunc pro tunc: (Now for then). A court may direct a document concerned with a court action to be dated earlier than that on which it was actually performed, such as predating a judgment if the entry has been delayed by an act of the court or if the plaintiff died between the hearing and the date the judgment was delivered. This is referred to as entering a judgment *nunc pro tunc*.

O

Obiter dictum: An opinion expressed by a judge which is not essential for judging a case and which does not form part of the judgment. Obiter dictum is something explanatory or illustrative of the circumstances surrounding the case and consequently does not contribute to establishing the judgment as a JUDICIAL PRECEDENT because those particular matters were not in contention. Such opinions, however, are frequently useful to illustrate how a judge approaches a situation and may be indicative of useful arguments to be made by counsel in future cases.

Objects: The reason for setting up a trust and the destination of the trust's benefits. Where a trust exists to benefit individuals, those individuals are the objects which require clear definition and CERTAINTY. Where a trust is set up for charitable purposes or to benefit a purpose, philanthropic or otherwise, the object of the trust is the purpose. *See* CERTAINTY OF OBJECTS.

Objects clause: A clause in the constitutional documents of a company or other incorporated body that describes the activity of the organisation. The objects clause was originally essential to describe the permitted activities of a company so that any activities not covered by the objects clause were ULTRA VIRES. Now, under Section 31 of the *Companies Act* 2006, a company need no longer have an objects clause, but there may still be restrictions to be imposed upon business activities and these may be included in the Articles of Association. A foundation also has an objects clause to describe the purpose or the individuals who are to benefit from the foundation and such a clause confines the foundation council and others to act within the limits specified. In some jurisdictions there is a mixture of terminology and it is not always clear that the reference is to what here is called the 'objects clause' (a purpose or beneficiary or mixed foundation) or whether it is solely a foundation for a purpose. The meaning, however, is usually clear in considering the context in which these expressions are used.

Objects of a power: The person or persons in whose favour a power may be exercised by the holder of the power. For example, the trustees may have the power of advancement in favour of the named beneficiaries of a trust. These beneficiaries are the objects of the power of advancement.

Occupancy: In connection with a property it means the state of being in physical control of that property either by agreement or otherwise. The term does not imply any right to legal possession, ownership or enjoyment of that property. When applied to goods, it allows goods and chattels to be acquired through occupancy but is of limited application.

Occupation: Possession and the act of taking POSSESSION when applied to property. Occupation refers to factual possession and control of personal or real property and to the rights and obligations which flow from that possession and control. The doctrine is limited to occupation by the consent of the proprietor of the land or thing so that anyone, for example, who has no more than personal permission to be on the land, such as a guest in a hotel or employee in an office, does not have possession and control and is classed in law as a LICENSEE, i.e. a person who has the consent of the owner to be present on the land but has no rights in the property. Occupation of land is protected by law against everyone except someone who has a better right.

Occupational pension scheme trusts: Trusts set up by employers to establish occupational pensions. These are subject to general trust law. Also, the trustees have particular duties and powers that are contained in the trust documentation. These provisions are invariably complex to allow the appropriate administration of a pension scheme. The powers of the trustees of this type of trust are particularly important, especially the trustees' power of amendment that has been described by the Pensions Ombudsman as an important tool to ensure that a pension scheme fulfils its purpose. This power is a fiduciary power.

Occupier: A term generally used to indicate a person residing in or upon or having the right to reside in or upon land, house or place. The precise meaning is subject to the context of the occupation. For example, in the context of liability towards visitors, occupier means the person in control of the premises. The liability of such an occupier extends to all visitors including licensees or invitees where the duty owed is the 'common duty of care', i.e. the duty to take such care as is reasonable in all the circumstances and to see that the visitor will be reasonably safe in using the premises for the purpose for which he is invited or permitted to be there. Liability of an occupier is governed by the *Occupiers Liability Act* 1957. Under the Act, the occupier is the person with immediate control and supervision of the premises and who possesses the power of permitting and prohibiting the entry of others. However, a warning notice or contractual term might discharge the occupier's duties provided the notice is not invalidated under the *Unfair Contract Terms Act* 1977. Originally an occupier was not liable to trespassers or non-visitors but since the *Occupiers Liability Act* 1984 liability is imposed for dangers about which the occupier is aware and has reasonable grounds to believe that a trespasser is, or will be, close to danger and that the risk to such a trespasser is one which the occupier ought to have in mind as something that he should attempt to prevent.

Occupiers' liability: *See* OCCUPIER.

OECD: The Organisation for Economic Co-operation and Development (OECD) developed from the Organisation for European Economic Co-operation (OEEC) established in 1948 to run the US-financed Marshall Plan for the reconstruction of a continent ravaged by war. Individual governments, by recognising the interdependence of their economies, paved the way for a new era of cooperation that was to change the face of Europe. Encouraged by its success and the prospect of carrying its work forward on a global stage, Canada and the US joined existing OEEC members and established the Organisation for Economic Co-operation and Development (OECD) on 30 September 1961. Membership of the OECD now includes all the developed countries of the world. The OECD is the source of economic and social data concerning international business and is well known for its Model Tax Convention on Income and on Capital which first appeared in 1955 when 70 bilateral general Conventions had been signed that aimed at eliminating double taxation. The effect of the Model Convention now extends outside the OECD countries. The OECD also promotes anti-tax avoidance measures through various global forums. The work of the Global Forum on Transparency and the Exchange of Information is particularly relevant to practitioners concerned with trusts and foundations. The most recent global forum has been set up to establish the use of a multilateral Convention on the automatic exchange of information. Further global fora exist on transfer pricing. *See* OEEC *and* BASE EROSION AND PROFIT SHIFTING (BEPS).

OECD Model Tax Convention on Income and Capital: (Sometimes colloquially referred to as the OECD Model Tax Treaty). A Model Tax Convention devised by international consultation under the organisation of the OECD which is a means of settling on a uniform basis the most common problems that arise in the field of international double taxation. It originated in 1963 in a Draft Convention which was superseded by the 1997 Model Convention, which, after amendment, is now the effective measure. The Model Convention has facilitated bilateral negotiations between OECD member countries and is also used as a basic document between member and non-member countries. The Model Convention provides model provisions for international taxation of income and capital and lays down the respective rights of states to tax the different classes of income. In a number of cases, the Model provides an internationally acceptable regime for the exclusive rights to tax by one contracting state that has entered into a double tax Convention along the lines of the Model. The Convention contains some special provisions, such as the elimination of tax discrimination in various circumstances, the establishment of a Mutual Agreement Procedure between Convention parties to eliminate double taxation to resolve conflicts, the exchange of information between tax authorities and for the assistance by contracting states in the collection of each other's taxes. Further special provisions exist that provide for the taxation of members of diplomatic missions and consular posts as well as for the territorial extension of the Convention. Each Article of the Convention is accompanied by extensive Commentaries that assist in the interpretation and application of the individual Articles. These Commentaries have had some substantial influence on the interpretation of taxing provisions under the Conventions and under international practice.

OECD Model Treaty: *See* OECD Model Tax Convention on Income and Capital.

OEEC: Organisation for European Economic Co-operation. *See* OECD.

OEIC: An open-ended investment company which is a type of company or fund in the UK with the purpose of investing in other companies and which has the ability to adjust its size and investment criteria. OEICs' shares are listed on the London Stock Exchange where the price is based on the value of the underlying assets of the fund; buyers and sellers trade at the same price. These companies are sometimes referred to as investment companies with variable capital (ICVCs). OEICs are similar to European SICAVs (société d'investissement à capital variable - investment company with variable capital) and US mutual funds. In the UK OEICs have become the preferred legal forms of open-ended investment over the older unit trust. OEICs were first introduced after the Open-Ended Investment Companies (Investment Companies with Variable Capital) Regulations 1966 and more recently by the Open-Ended Investment Regulations 2001 under the *Financial Services and Markets Act* 2000, Section 262, which ensured a level playing field for unit trusts and ICVCs.

Offer: An essential part of an agreement or contract. An offer made by one party, on unconditional acceptance by the other, can lead to a legally enforceable agreement or contract. If the acceptance is not unconditional, this is in effect a counter-offer and does not constitute an acceptance of the original. An offer may be withdrawn at any time before it has been unconditionally accepted, and an offer lapses whenever the party to whom it is made refuses it.

Official Custodian for Charities: A public official to whom the property of a charity may be vested in order to avoid the necessity of transferring the property held on trust when there are changes in the identity and number of charitable trustees.

Offshore centre: A jurisdiction that has developed legislation and commercial facilities to attract non-resident investors and business organisations to set up headquarters, or subsidiaries, for the purpose of conducting international financial and business operations. Such jurisdictions invariably offer opportunities for tax planning which leads to their reputation for being centres for the encouragement of tax avoidance. The term 'offshore' is a misnomer as these activities are developed by countries that are neither islands nor countries entirely devoted to this type of business; Dublin, Liechtenstein, Luxembourg and Switzerland are frequently referred to as offshore centres although none of these countries can be considered as offering their facilities mainly to non-residents. Many main financial centres, such as London, New York and others that do offer such incentives are not regarded as offshore jurisdictions. These anomalies have come about in using the term 'offshore centres' as a modern alternative to 'tax havens'. *See* OFFSHORE FINANCIAL LAW.

Offshore corporation: A company or corporation set up in an offshore centre which offers favourable tax conditions for the purpose of servicing commercial activities of a parent or associated company. An activity which usually involves acting as a conduit for commercial transactions so that profits can be accumulated in the offshore corporation rather than being directly repatriated and exposed to a higher rate of tax. For many years offshore corporations have been an essential part of corporate tax planning but, under the influence of the G20, these activities are likely to be severely curtailed under the campaign concerned with BASE EROSION AND PROFIT SHIFTING (BEPS).

Offshore financial law: Described in the case of ***Re Asia Credicom Ltd.*** (Sup Ct, BVI No. 20 of 1999) as:

'[L]egislation, legal practices and law concerned with investment, financial arrangements and entities created by non-residents of a particular jurisdiction but structured within that jurisdiction. Such investments or arrangements are typically focussed on some business advantage, tax avoidance, protection from creditors and judgment debtors or privacy.'

Offshore foundation: A term which has not generally been applied but, by analogy to the term 'offshore trusts', an offshore foundation is a private foundation set up in a jurisdiction that offers facilities for founders who are from outside. An offshore centre may provide that any foundation registered under its law and set up by a founder from outside that jurisdiction shall be entitled to exemption from domestic tax provided that the foundation does not possess any assets in the jurisdiction.

Offshore fund: A collective investment scheme or similar investment structure constituted by a company which is resident in an offshore jurisdiction or in a jurisdiction with lower regulatory and tax restraints. In the UK a unit trust scheme with trustees resident outside the UK, or any other arrangement which takes place outside of the jurisdiction, is described in the *Income and Corporation Taxes Act* 1988, Section 756(a), and is likely to be subject to tax regulations made under the *Finance Act* 2008, Section 41.

Offshore trusts: Trusts set up according to legislation that has been developed in an offshore centre. Such trusts borrow heavily on the traditional English trust concept. Variations include increased powers of a settlor without prejudicing the validity of the trust, the degree of confidentiality granted to the offshore trusts and the ability of the trust to resist challenges made under foreign legislation in respect of claims of creditors, forced heirs and taxation authorities. Offshore trusts set up in a jurisdiction are often limited to international trusts, i.e. where the settlor and assets are from outside the jurisdiction, and not to purely domestic arrangements. *See* VISTA TRUSTS *and* STAR TRUSTS.

Offspring: A vague expression that should not be used; it has no precise meaning and is only a variation on 'issue' and 'dependants'. Offspring usually indicates children or more remote descendants but is too imprecise to be used in a trust or will document.

Omissions: Omissions by a trustee to do something that a prudent trustee ought to have done. This may result in an enquiry to determine what the trustee might have received if he had been less neglectful of his duties. The trustee's failure to carry out his duty, a breach of trust, may not involve conscious wrongdoing.

Open-end funds: A collective investment scheme that can issue or redeem shares (or units) at any time. A popular form of investment of this type is the unit trust, which is an investment operation where subscribers buy units and the manager of the scheme then purchases more shares and when a unitholder sells units the manager sells enough shares to provide repayment. Investors deal with the manager and not through a stock exchange. Consequently, a holding of units represents a proportion of the net asset value of the entire investment and neither discount nor premium exists. The structure of an open-end fund, or unit trust, is basically a trust that holds the individual shares which is administered by a manager with other administrative bodies employed for marketing or to act as custodians. An important characteristic of an open-end fund is that the sale of investments caused by redemption of units may upset the balance of the underlying investments held; the tendency is to liquidate the most marketable securities and this may make a fund unbalanced and left with the least popular and least marketable shares.

Operative words: In a formal instrument, such as a conveyance, lease, mortgage, trust deed or foundation charter, the operative words are words which state the intention of the party signatory(ies), or create the obligation, or transfer the property by a clear statement of purpose. These words appear in a deed after the recitals have described the general intention of the parties and constitute the operative part of a deed; they set out the obligations of the parties. On a matter of interpretation, the operative part takes precedence over the RECITALS.

Option: A contract whereby one party pays a specified sum of money to another for the right to call for the delivery of property within a stated period; alternatively, the right may be to deliver property to the other party, or both: the consideration being agreed at the time the option contract was set up. For example, A enters into a contract with B on 1 January in which A has a right to require B to deliver to A 1,000 shares in Google on 1 March at a price of $100 per share. If A exercises his option he can call upon B to present the stated number of shares for which he will pay $100 per share whatever their market value may be. This is a 'call option'. If, on the other hand, the arrangement is that A requires B to take delivery of the shares at a stated price (rather than selling the shares to A) this would be called a 'put option'. Options relating to securities play an important part in alternative investment schemes. Options can be entered into for any type of property, real or personal. If the option concerns land in the UK, then that option must be registered with the LAND REGISTRY as an estate contract; if it affects unregistered land then the purchaser of the option should place a notice in the Land Registry under the *Land Charges Act* 1972 as an estate contract. If a notice is not inserted in the Land Registry then the option will be void against the purchaser for money or money's worth and thereby unenforceable, although the grantee of the option (as A was the grantee of the option in the above example) would be entitled to damages against the grantor (B in the above example), who made it impossible that the grantee could perform the option by not inserting a notice and thereby making it known to any stranger. If the holder of an option changes his mind about exercising his right (in the above example if the price of the shares falls below the option price) he can walk away from the arrangement. The money paid for the option would not be returnable. The only prohibition in law concerning options is that under the *Companies Act* 1985 directors, shadow directors, their spouses and children, are prohibited from buying or selling options in the shares of companies which they control in the UK. An option can also be concerned with non-performance, i.e. the acceptance by one party to an existing contract for an extra sum of money entitles the other party to perform differently or decline his part under the original contract; that is, have a separate contract to permit variation or cancellation.

Oral assignment: An assignment by word of mouth of an equitable or other interest. These are legally valid, provided evidence is available of the statement. Despite being legally valid, these assignments are often reduced to writing for evidential purposes. Oral assignments reduced to writing must be distinguished from those made by deed and those which are required to be evidenced in writing for the purpose of legislation. In the UK the *Law of Property Act* 1925, Section 53(1)(c), requires assignments concerning trusts containing land to be made in writing. This supplements the requirement of Section 52 of the Act that any trust containing land must be set up by deed.

Oral declaration of trust: *See* DECLARATION OF TRUST.

Order of creation of interests: At law and in equity, estates in interest rank in the order in which they are created. There is a difference between the law and equity. At law the result is generally expressed in terms of the transferor's ability to transfer a good title under the doctrine of *nemo dat quod non habet* (no person can confer a better title than he himself has). This means that the transferor takes the interest subject to any prior interests in the property. In equity the time of the transfer takes on greater significance; the maxim is *qui prior est tempore potior est jure* (he who is earlier in time is stronger in law), which means that where there are two competing equitable interests the equity attached to the property earlier will be entitled to priority over the other. The maxim is also stated as 'where the equities are equal, the first in time prevail'.

Ordinance: A form of legislation equivalent to an Act or law, usually the name given to legislation in UK dependencies where the authority for those provisions is based on the Royal prerogative.

Ordinarily resident: The position describing a person's connection with his ordinary residence.

Ordinary resident: A concept that is distinct from residence or domicile. Ordinary residence has been referred to as a man's abode in a particular place or country which he has adopted voluntarily and for settled purposes as part of the regular order of his life for the time being, whether of short or long duration (***R v. Barnet LBC Ex p. Shah*** [1983] 2 A.C. 309). Accordingly, temporary absence does not cause ordinary residence to cease. A person is generally treated for tax purposes as ordinarily resident in the UK if he or she spends 183 days or more in the country in one year; also if a person spends, in four consecutive years, between 91 and 183 days per year in the UK. The term is used, in particular, to assess the status of a person for UK capital gains tax liabilities and may be applied to a person who may not at the time be actually resident in the UK, such as a person who is in a foreign jail or a person who is voluntarily outside the UK. The term is also used in connection with some UK matters relating to eligibility for tax credits for children, etc. *See* RESIDENT.

Originating summons: A procedure to commence a claim in the High Court which was replaced by a similar form under Part 8 of the CIVIL PROCEDURE RULES (CPR) entitled 'Alternative Procedure for Claims' and intended for cases where there is no substantial dispute of facts. This is most common in Chancery proceedings to obtain the court's decision on trust administration.

Ouster: Dispossession of a rightful owner of hereditaments, corporeal or incorporeal, and where the wrongdoer gets actual occupation of the property, leaving the lawful possessor to seek legal remedies to restore possession and for damages sustained. Ouster may be performed for legitimate reasons.

Ouster of jurisdiction: An attempt to prevent a court from having jurisdiction over a matter which it would otherwise have had. This ouster may be a consequence of the interpretation of a statute, or a restrictive clause in a written instrument between parties which provides how a dispute will be settled in a way that attempts to exclude any immediate or eventual recourse to the courts. Statutes and other documents, such as contracts, are interpreted with the presumption that they do not oust the jurisdiction of the courts in which matters relating to the documents would be heard. As a rule, ouster in a statute can only take place by an express provision; there is a presumption against construing legislation as authorising ouster. Clauses in contracts that go beyond a legitimate choice of law and jurisdiction will be void if they are construed as attempts to oust the jurisdiction of a court which would be the natural court for hearing any dispute. On the whole, ousters of jurisdiction are very controversial.

Overdue: A bill or promissory note is not overdue if it is paid before the day after the stated date of payment, i.e. payment is not overdue until after midnight on the stated day. A bill or promissory note stated to be 'payable on demand' is overdue if it is not paid within a reasonable time. A reasonable time, in this context, depends upon the nature of the underlying contract and any other circumstances, including the previous expectations of the parties.

Overreaching: A doctrine by which an interest in land does not affect a purchaser who takes the land free from that interest. The burden of that interest is detached from the land and falls upon the purchase money that has been paid. This means that a person who holds an interest over land may find the land has been sold and that person is therefore deprived of that interest, but he is not without remedy since the benefit of that interest has now passed to the money received by the vendor and against whom the value of that interest can be recovered. For example, the interest of a mortgagor is transferred from the property to the purchase money on the sale of the mortgaged property. The concept also applies to any conveyance of land by trustees who pass the land to a purchaser free from the equitable interests of the person entitled under the trust. The beneficiaries of the trust may lose interest in the land but their interest is then against the money received by the trustees. That is, provided that the purchaser takes the land free from any notice of the beneficiaries' interests: the well-known 'EQUITY'S DARLING' concept. This doctrine also applies to any conveyance by a tenant for life under an entailed interest whether or not a purchaser of the land knows of the interest of the tenant. Where there is a trust for land under the *Trusts of Land and Appointment of Trustees Act* 1996, a conveyance by two or more individuals approved or appointed by the court, or a trust corporation as trustee, will overreach other equitable interests in the land which have had priority to the actual trust, such as other equitable interests that were in existence when the trust of land was created. This means that such a purchaser will obtain a better title to the land than possessed by the trustees because he is free from the burden of those other equitable interests over the property. However, in this context, overreaching is now of minimal practical importance because most of the interests which would have been overreached have particular statutory protection by being registered under the *Land Charges Act* 1972.

Overreaching clause: A clause in a resettlement deed which preserves the effect of powers incorporated in the original settlement, i.e. the terms of the old settlement survive and will still apply to the new settlement. These clauses are now irrelevant since they ceased to be of significance after the *Settled Land Acts* 1882 to 1890 and especially after the abolition of new entailed interests after the *Trusts for Land and Trustees Act* 2000, but are of interest to illustrate that had a RESETTLEMENT been made without such a clause the powers annexed to the estate by the original settlement would be lost. *See* ENTAILED INTEREST.

Overriding interests: Interests in land where a person in actual occupation has either an equitable interest or a mere equity that is not protected in the Land Registry is an overriding interest unless he fails to disclose his interest in response to an enquiry by a prospective purchaser. Overriding interests are binding on persons who acquire an interest in the registered land whether on first registration or where there has been a registerable disposition of an already registered property. The term is not used in the *Land Registration Act* 2002, which, instead, refers to unregistered interests that override first registration or registered dispositions. The most important of these are leasehold estates, interest in persons in actual occupation, easements and *PROFITS À PRENDRE* that persist despite other registered interests. Overriding interests bind the whole world irrespective of notice. Overriding interests were a major obstacle in achieving an electronically-based conveyancing system. The *Land Registration Act* 2002 tries to minimise the existence of these overriding interests by providing mechanisms to ensure that they are registered whenever possible. The Registrar may now make a note of those interests if adequate information is provided to him with the consequence that the interest then loses its overriding status. Trustees and foundation councils should ensure that the necessary steps are taken over any such overriding interests.

Overriding trust: A trust that takes precedence over other trusts previously declared. The validity of such a trust depends upon the settlor's intention and whether measures have been taken to adequately annul previous dispositions of assets to trustees of previous trusts.

Overseas divorce: Divorce taking place outside the jurisdiction of the place where the marriage occurred. The validity of such a divorce will depend upon the law of the jurisdiction in which the divorce action is arranged. For an overseas divorce to be valid it is necessary that the original marriage should be recognised in the territory where the parties intend to bring proceedings. The question then arises of whether the court of that territory has jurisdiction as the place of the divorce. If the marriage is not recognised there is no marriage to dissolve. Then, the question of jurisdiction arises. The court must be able to involve both parties of the marriage or, if it can act on the application of one party, convincing evidence of the reasons for divorce must be provided. The recognition in the other countries of an overseas divorce will affect the validity of the divorce settlement in that the matrimonial property will be divided according to the law or the decision of the court where the divorce was obtained.

Own benefit: Where a trustee uses trust property for his own benefit, such as using trust funds in a commercial venture of his own, he will be liable for all the losses but the beneficiary will be entitled to any gains. This is consistent with the principle of trust law that beneficiaries are entitled to any benefit received by the trustee as a result of the fact that he holds trust property. This rule applies also to other fiduciaries, such as a solicitor who must account for the interest earned on money which he holds on behalf of his clients, despite the difficulty in allocating it between them.

Ownership: This is the ultimate right a person can have by law over a thing, corporeal or incorporeal. The ultimate right is ownership IN REM with the consequence that the owner can exclude all other persons. Ownership gives the right to possess and enjoy the thing and the rights to what it produces and other accessions and the right to encumber, alienate, or even destroy the property (unless restricted in various ways, mostly statutory, to preserve the property or to protect others). The owner may divest himself of some of his rights or limit them in favour of another person. This diminishes the absolute concept of ownership but, nevertheless, the owner retains an indefinite right that he is still the owner. In other words, any party who has a right to use the owner's property has a definite right, i.e. something that is defined and limited, for example, where there is a right of way over another person's land the owner of that land continues with the otherwise unrestricted indefinite right. Conversely, if the owner parts with the indefinite right and retains only a definite one, he ceases to be the owner of the property generally; his ownership is restricted to the definite rights that he retains, such as a right of way. In trusts, there is a nominal and beneficial ownership where both trustee and beneficiary are the owners, although the trustees cannot derive any benefit and may only exercise defined rights while the beneficiary has the real benefit of the thing held in trust. The trustees are regarded as the legal owner and may exercise what goes under the concept of legal ownership leaving the beneficiary to have the beneficial ownership. With foundations, there is no equitable right of beneficial ownership until such time as the beneficiaries are identified and approved of by the foundation council. Until such an apportionment, there is no question that the foundation itself owns the foundation property. The question then arises of who owns the foundation. Opinions are divided. Some maintain that the foundation owns itself, which is a strange concept. The basic position is that a person is the owner of a thing where that person has the ultimate power to transform or to end its existence. In many cases, this situation clearly makes the founder the owner, particularly in view of the type of powers which the founder may reserve to himself, although the absolute rights of that ownership may be considerably curtailed by the rights the founder has given to the foundation council and to others, principally the protector.

Ownership in common: *See* TENANCY IN COMMON.

P

P.L.C.: Public limited company (PLC) introduced in the UK by the *Companies Act* 1980. Only a PLC may offer its shares to the public. A PLC must comply with the requirements of the Act, such as maintaining a minimum SHARE CAPITAL. A PLC must use the suffix 'public limited company' or 'plc'. A company must be a PLC to obtain a listing on a stock exchange. Being a PLC does not automatically entitle a company to such a listing because the PLC must conform to the requirements of the stock exchange in addition to what is required under company law.

Pacta sunt servanda: Agreements to be kept and treaties to be observed; a fundamental aspect of international contract law and customary international law.

Paid-up capital: The amount actually paid by subscribers for shares in a company that have been allotted to them. If a shareholder makes a full payment of the purchase price then the amount received is referred to as fully paid-up capital and the shareholder has no further obligation to make any financial contribution to the company; otherwise partly paid-up capital leaves the shareholder liable to be called upon to pay the balance to the company when required.

Palm tree justice: A term used much in the past but nevertheless a useful concept that means a form of justice dispensed by a cadi sitting under a palm tree but without being concerned with the law or precedents. This still exists in some offshore jurisdictions where a judgment is based on a judge's personal views of the relationship of the parties and is not a judgment based on the law. However, the term is sometimes used to express indignation when a legal principle or the entire rule of law is ignored or where a statement of a legal principle is too wide. For example, the statement that 'fraud unravels all' falls into this category. This phrase indicates that where fraud is present, many other concepts in tort and contract no longer apply. This was commented upon in ***Total Network SL v. Her Majesty's Revenue and Customs*** [2008] UKHL 19, per Lord Neuberger:

> '[S]imply to invoke the doctrine ... would seem to me to involve palm tree justice. In other words, one would be relying on a general sense of morality or indignation, without regard to principle or the rule of law. Such a course would be inconsistent with principle, especially in the context of a taxing statute, and would effectively represent carte blanche for any tribunal to do what it likes.'

Parcels: Property that is the subject of a conveyance, mortgage or other assurance. An old-fashioned word which was used when land, or pieces of land, had been referred to in an accompanying document and are brought up collectively using the word 'parcels' in some further discussion.

Parent and child: A relationship that requires a parent to provide necessities (**Note:** necessities is a different word from NECESSARIES) for their child and, in respect of a child of compulsory school age, to receive suitable full-time education. Where the parents of a child are separated, the authorities may impose maintenance requirements on the non-custodial parent which then implies that there is a wide range of rights which that parent must exercise, including the provision of necessities, education and other matters affecting the welfare of the child. The relationship between a parent and child may be severed by an adoption order.

Parental responsibility: All the rights, duties, powers and responsibilities, etc. which a parent of a child has in relation to his/her child and the child's property. If the child's father and mother are married to one another each has this responsibility. If they are not married the responsibility is that of the mother. Then, the father may acquire responsibility, for example, on registration or re-registration of the birth or with an agreement with the mother, or by court order. A step-parent may, with the agreement of both parents, undertake parental responsibility that may be supported by an order of the court. This responsibility may be ended by an order of the court on the application of any person with parental responsibility or with the leave of the court by application of the child itself. Also, a person appointed as a guardian under the *Children Act* 1989, Section 5, will have parental responsibility for the child concerned. Such an order must be made by the court when it makes a residence order in favour of the father and, where the court makes a residence order in favour of a person who is not the parent, the court must also make an order that the person shall have parental responsibility. This order cannot be refused by the person to whom it is addressed.

Pari delecto: In equal wrong.

Parol evidence: Literally by word of mouth and legally something that is put into writing but not under seal. A parol contract is therefore a contract that is not under seal although it may be evidenced in some written form. Proof of a document brought before a court may be either oral, i.e. parol evidence, or by means of a copy. Parol evidence is not a substitute for a written document, but parol evidence can defeat written evidence on the grounds of fraud or mistake but cannot add to, vary or alter the express terms of a deed except to explain ambiguities and to explain matters within the particular knowledge of the witness. This latter use of parol evidence may occur where it is necessary to explain circumstances in connection with a trust or foundation that are known only to a trustee or protector.

Partnership: A relationship that exists between two persons carrying on business in common with a view to profit other than as a company. Colloquially referred to as a 'firm', the essential element is that two or more people come together with the intention of making a profit, as defined in the *Partnership Act* 1890. A partner may be an individual or an incorporated body. The characteristic that every partner participates in the management of the business (unless otherwise agreed between them) establishes a joint liability on each partner for debts incurred in their joint participation. This liability exposes the whole of a partner's property. If required, each partner may be called upon to make a proportionate contribution to the partnership's liabilities. Each partner may be an agent for the entire business within the ordinary scope of its business. Each partner has a personal and fiduciary relationship with the other partners. The role of partner is a personal one and a partner cannot put another in his place without the consent of the others. This makes the transfer of a partnership share complicated and requires a reconveyance of all the partnership's assets from the names of the old partners into the names of the new partners, even though only one partner may change. This applies unless the law where the partnership operates provides that a partnership may operate under the partnership name with the partnership property held by a smaller number of senior partners on trust for the partners as they may exist from time to time. An alternative is for the partners to use a management company to hold all the assets of the partnership regardless of the actual makeup of the partnership list. If a partnership becomes insolvent it can be wound up, placed into administration or made subject to a voluntary arrangement as an unregistered company under the *Companies Act* 2006 in conjunction with, and distinct from, bankruptcy or corporate insolvency proceedings in respect of the individual partners. Previously there was a limitation on the number of persons who could constitute a partnership but this limitation was removed from December 2002 under the Regulatory Reform (Removal of 20 Member Limit in Partnerships etc.) Order 2002. *See* LIMITED PARTNERSHIP *and* LIMITED LIABILITY PARTNERSHIPS.

Partnership, limited liability (LLP): *See* LIMITED LIABILITY PARTNERSHIPS.

Part performance: An equitable doctrine that was made redundant by the *Law of Property (Miscellaneous Provisions) Act* 1989. This Act required all contracts for the sale or other dispositions of an interest in land to be made only in writing and incorporating all the terms which the parties had expressly agreed. Before the Act, contracts for the sale of land or an interest in land required some evidence in writing signed by the party to be charged. Without such written evidence, as a general rule, the contract was not enforceable. An exception to this existed where one of the parties had partially performed his part of the contract, such as where the seller of a house allowed the prospective purchaser to obtain possession of the property before completing the purchase, and where it would be fraudulent if the party who had permitted such part performance pleaded lack of evidence as a defence when refusing to complete the transaction. Although there was no express abolition of the doctrine, it is plain that it no longer exists. An oral contract is now irrelevant as far as property or an interest in property is concerned; there is either a written contract as required or there is no contract. There is, therefore, no place for part performance. However, if a party orally agrees to grant or sell an interest in land, the party may refuse to perform the agreement in the absence of a complete written contract even if the other party has done something in part performance. To remedy this there may be some degree of protection in the doctrine of PROPRIETARY ESTOPPEL, which will allow the oral agreement, although void as a contract, as evidence to satisfy the prospective purchaser's equity. This remedy, however, depends upon a court's discretion, making reliance upon the doctrine of propriety estoppel more uncertain than part performance.

Passing off: A wrong committed when a person sells goods or carries on business in a way which will mislead the public into believing that the goods or business are those of another. This can be achieved by applying a business name, a mark, a design or a description with the prime intention of misleading the public. Passing off is a common law action in tort and is useful when there may be an absence of an offence under INTELLECTUAL PROPERTY rights, i.e., no offence has been committed under trademark, patent or trade description law; nevertheless, there has been an intention to mislead the public even to the extent of where a person uses his own name (not an offence in itself) but uses it in a way which suggests that the business is that of an established and reputable organisation of the same name.

Passive trust: A term used to describe a trust where the trustee has no active duty to perform. This is an antique term which is not currently used but has considerable historical importance. Before the *Statute of Uses* 1535, a passive trust would escape provisions of the common law that had grown up to execute the trust, i.e. the legal ownership of the trust property passed to the beneficiaries. This was enacted in the *Statute of Uses* 1535 and subsequently passive trusts were revived to guard against forfeiture of a legal estate for life and were resorted to by the use of settlements to preserve contingent remainders and in order to preserve DOWER. Under modern law, a trust where the trustee has no active duties to perform is usually referred to as a 'BARE TRUST' or 'NOMINEE TRUST', where the trustee is virtually a nominee for the beneficiary.

Past consideration: *See* CONSIDERATION.

Patent ambiguity: Where the terms of a written instrument raise doubt as to its actual meaning and which can only be explained by argument on the construction of the document itself and not by parol evidence. *See* PAROL.

Paterfamilias: A civil law term indicating the head of a family. To constitute this position the person has to be SUI JURIS and not suffering from any incapacity.

Patrimony: A hereditary estate or the right to property that is usually descended from ancestors or which is added to in such a way that it is a part of a person's property that descendants can expect to inherit. Generally a civil law term. There is no immediate English term equivalent to this, the nearest being 'ESTATE', which in English law is normally used to express a similar right to property, but is used mainly when the person concerned has died. In Scotland the term is used in connection with a patrimonial loss, indicating a loss of property rather than physical damage or bodily injury. In Scotland 'personal patrimony' has been defined as 'the aggregate of a person's rights and liabilities'. This definition appeared in the Scottish Law Commission's Discussion Paper No. 133 in October 2006 on the Nature and Constitution of Trusts. The essence of their conclusion is that where a person becomes a trustee he acquires a second patrimony: he then has his private patrimony, as before, and a trust patrimony. The trust patrimony consists of the trust fund that is owned by the trustee and any obligations he has incurred in the proper administration of the trust. Although owned by the same person, the private patrimony is a separate legal status from the trust patrimony. This is in agreement with the general concept that although a trustee is the legal owner of the trust assets, these are separate from assets owned by the trustee in a personal capacity.

Pauline Action: An action which can be traced back to Roman law and to French law preceding the Civil Code and which is currently applied in the Jersey Courts in connection with the recovery of property after fraud by a debtor. The principle of these actions can be summarised as:

> 'No debtor can assign or transfer property by deed defrauding his unsecured or personal creditors, although the transferee may ignore the fraud; if he does those defrauded creditors shall be entitled to claw back the disposition' (Panico, P. *International Trust Laws*, Oxford University Press, 2010, p. 500).

In the Jersey actions in ***Re Esteem Settlement and The No. 52 Trust*** [2002] JLR 53 a disposition of assets claimed by the Kuwait Investment Office was set aside by application of a Pauline Action. This action is distinct from the English principle based on the *Statute of Elizabeth* 1571 where transfers of assets may be set aside if made with the intent to defraud creditors.

Payment into court: A method of payment where there is no other way of obtaining a discharge from an obligation. Trustees may obtain a discharge by paying into court any trust money or securities which they have under their control. The receipt or certificate from the proper official is a sufficient discharge. There are two ways of doing this: (1) if the trustees are unanimous they may make payment into court after filing an affidavit or by submitting a witness statement; and (2) if only a majority wishes to fulfil a commitment in this way, they must obtain an order of the court. Payments into court are most common under Section 3 of the *Trustee Act* 1925, where a trustee or executor cannot trace a beneficiary and, by payment into court, the trustee obtains a good discharge of his obligation. The term is also used where payment into court is required in connection with the provision of security for costs or where an order is made subject to a condition as to the payment of a sum of money into the court under the court's general case management powers. This applies particularly in connection with a summary judgment as a prior condition for the court to give a defendant permission to defend. This demonstrates that a party is willing to meet his obligations and, in modern English law, this has been replaced under Civil Procedure Rules (CPR) Part 36. Generally, where money is paid into court then an order for payment out has to be made. Payment may be directed to a beneficiary of a trust when that beneficiary, previously untraceable, is ascertained, or the sum may be applied to satisfy any claim awarded by the court.

Peer review: An examination or evaluation, frequently of a person's performance at work. It is not a term with any clear legal meaning.

***Pemsel's case (Income Tax Special Purpose Commissioners v. Pemsel* [1891] A.C. 531 at 583):** Lord Macnaghten's speech in this case is frequently quoted as a summary of the characteristics of a charity following the repeal in 1888 of the *Statute of Elizabeth*.

> '"Charity" in its legal sense comprises four principal divisions: trusts for the relief of poverty; trusts for the advancement of education; trusts for the advancement of religion; and trusts for other purposes beneficial to the community, not falling under any of the preceding heads. The trusts last referred to are not the less charitable in the eye of the law, because incidentally they benefit the rich as well as the poor, as indeed, every charity that deserves the name must do either directly or indirectly.'

This classification echoed a similar classification issued earlier in ***Morice v. Bishop of Durham*** (1805) 10 Ves. 522, affirming (1804) 9 Ves. 399, which emphasised the relief of poverty, education, religion and benefits to the community as charitable objects, to which may be added recreational charities. The modern definition of charities in the UK is governed by the *Charities Act* 2011. *See* CHARITIES.

Penalty: A sum of money that is payable and which acts as an equivalent to a punishment for an injury or breach of contract and that does not truly represent compensation for the actual loss suffered by the person to whom it is payable. Penalties are a feature of the criminal law, such as by the Commissioners of Revenue and Customs for defective tax returns and other offences where the likelihood of incurring the penalty is intended to encourage compliance with the law or regulation concerned. The term is also applied to penalties agreed upon by the parties, such as in a bond, with a condition that the borrower agrees to pay a penalty if the conditions of the bond are not complied with, e.g. if the borrower makes late repayment of the bond amount. This penalty may be justified as a reasonable compensation to the lender. The general position in the law of contract is that if one of the parties agreed, in the event of a breach, that he shall pay a specific sum of money to the other as LIQUIDATED DAMAGES, then this sum will be irrecoverable if it is regarded by the courts as a penalty. This will occur whatever form of words are used if it appears that on a true construction of the instrument there was no genuine pre-estimate of the amount of loss likely to have been caused by the breach. In that case, the sum is treated as *IN TERROREM* and called a 'penalty' which is irrecoverable and where only damages actually sustained for the breach will be awarded.

Pension: Income paid to a person who has reached retirement age either from employment or under the state pension scheme. Pensions paid by employers are often arranged to come from a trust set up by the employer into which contributions from the employee and the employer are paid, and by that means the fund from which pensions are paid is kept separate from the assets of the employer and therefore safe in the event that the employer becomes insolvent. *See* PENSION TRUSTS.

Pension trusts: Trusts set up by employers to hold contributions made by the employer and employees for the purpose of providing a means of paying pensions to the employees. This is frequently conducted through insurance companies. The funding party, frequently the employer (or the employer's parent company), will be the settlor of a trust, and will sometimes be called the sponsor, who declares in the trust instrument the terms by which the funds will be held by the trustees. The trustees may be called the pension committee. This body ensures the proper investment of the funds or, where the investment is placed in the hands of investment managers, acts as custodian. Large schemes are often coordinated by a 'master trustee' for the benefit of the other trustees. In this type of trust it is not unusual that an employee who contributed to the scheme was in the past entitled to a refund of his own contributions if he left that employment. Under modern rules, this is no longer possible and the employee has either transferable rights into other companies' schemes if he moves employment, or the pension is held in suspension and becomes payable when pension age is reached. The advantage of holding pension funds in trust is that they are held separately by trustees. In the UK greater access has been permitted by legislation to allow contributors to be able to treat their eventual pension as a bank account and to withdraw money from it.

Per capita; *Per stirpes* (By heads or by family): Two schemes by which property is divided to descendants or relations when there are two or more persons entitled. Distribution per capita means that those entitled form one class and each member takes an equal share, i.e. a gift by will to be shared by the testator's descendants means that the descendants (as defined in the jurisdiction concerned) such as children, grandchildren, great grandchildren, each take an equal share. The *per stirpes* principle is where those entitled are representatives of their respective ancestors or relations, i.e. the system takes account of the descendants from the original beneficiaries. Thus, if 'X' bequeaths his assets to his three children, A, B and C, and if on X's death A is still alive, B has died leaving three children, and C has also died leaving two children, then on a *per stirpes* distribution the property will be divided into three parts and each part will be distributed to the children or their descendants, i.e. A takes one part, the three children of B share another part, and the two children of C share the remaining part. The intention of the testator dictates which principle is followed. The term is also used in connection with distribution on intestacy.

Per curiam: Sometimes abbreviated to be 'per cur' which literally means 'through want of care'; often applied to the decision of a judge who has given his judgment without taking into account matters which he should have considered.

Perfect trust: *See* EXECUTED TRUST.

Performance bond: A bond frequently obtained from a bank or insurance company which is required when a contractor wins a tender and is awarded a contract to ensure that the contractor fulfils his part of the contract on time and in a manner acceptable to the client. The proceeds to be paid if a performance bond is called upon are calculated to be adequate to obtain completion of the work by another contractor. Similar bonds under a variety of names are frequently used to ensure performance of various aspects of a complex contract, particularly in the construction industry. Performance bonds are frequently disputed.

Performance in equity: Performance in equity is regarded as notional rather than actual performance, i.e. if a person has not fully performed a covenant but has done some act which is regarded as having been a step towards the performance, then the property concerned will be attributed to the performance of the agreement. This follows the maxim that 'equity imputes an intention to fulfil an obligation' and this applies, for example, where there is a covenant to purchase and settle land, and a purchase of land has been made; this land will be treated as the land to be used to satisfy the covenant relying on the maxim, rather than any legal designation. *See* LECHMERE V. LADY LECHMERE (1735) Cas. T. Talb. 80.

Perpetuities and accumulations: Two legal rules known as the RULE AGAINST PERPETUITIES and the rule against excessive accumulations are distinct but related and, under the modern law, are principally applicable to trust interests. With both rules the intention is to prevent assets, originally land, being tied up for an excessive length of time – in perpetuity. The rule against excessive accumulations, unlike the rule against perpetuities, originated as a statutory rule and operates independently. The rule came about when a danger was perceived in the 18th century that the ability to accumulate income indefinitely could result in such a concentration of wealth in private hands that it might compromise the economic independence of the nation. The close association of the two rules is seen in the most recent amendments to both rules in the *Perpetuities and Accumulations Act* 2009. The two rules can be dealt with separately.

(1) The rule against perpetuities was derived by the courts to prevent land being tied up for an excessive length of time (i.e. 'in perpetuity'). The remedy was to make any attempt to do so void, i.e. ineffective from the beginning. The question was therefore what period should be regarded as a perpetuity and the interests to which the rule applied. The perpetuity period under the common law was defined in the terms of the lifetime of a living person and for a further 21 years from the end of the life of that person. The person selected need not have been connected with the property. The choice was frequently made of a young person (so giving the possibility of a long period under the rule) whose death could be traced. The common law rule was amended in the UK by the *Perpetuities and Accumulations Act* 1964. Under that Act a future interest was made to be no longer void from the start if there was only a mere possibility that the property might vest after the perpetuity period has expired. In other words, retention in perpetuity was only a possible event (as opposed to an actual event) and was no longer considered to be prejudicial to a future interest. This means that an interest that could possibly only vest outside the perpetuity period would no longer be avoided from the moment the provision was written and would only be considered to offend the remoteness rule if it did not eventually vest within the permitted period. This 'wait and see' rule allowed a disposition to be treated as valid until it was shown that the interest must vest, if at all, after the end of the perpetuity period. This 'wait and see' rule did not save a gift if a gift was designated to an unborn person and the gift would not have vested within 21 years. When the 'wait and see' rule provisions did not save the gift then the period was reduced, not to 21 years after the life of the person named, but to an age nearest to that consistent with the gift being valid. The *Perpetuities and Accumulations Act* 2009 removed the uncertainty caused by the 'wait and see' provisions of the 1964 Act. After 6 April 2010 all trusts, including will trusts but excluding charitable trusts, will have a perpetuity period of 125 years beginning on the date the trust was created. This period will apply even if the trust instrument specifies a longer period. Individuals may specify a shorter period and give the trustees power to bring the

trust to an end at any time during the new perpetuity period. For trusts created before 6 April 2010 a perpetuity defined by reference to lives in being can have that period replaced with a 100-year fixed period if the trustees can demonstrate uncertainty as to whether the relevant lives in being have ended. The rule against perpetuities does not apply to incorporated bodies including foundations although the latter exclusion is not certain in all jurisdictions. Other interests, such as easements, restrictive covenants, options and preemption rights are excluded from the rule. The rule against perpetuities has been abolished in some offshore jurisdictions or significantly altered (by extending the perpetuity period) in at least 21 states, according to a review in 2005. The Uniform Trust Code, the model trust law in the United States, provides no uniformity for the rule against perpetuities, preferring to leave that issue to each individual state.

(2) The rule against excessive accumulations before the 2009 Act permitted accumulations for the lifetime of the settlor or 21 years from the date of the creation of a trust, or 21 years from the death of the settlor, or for the minority of any person living at the death of the settlor. The amendments made by the 2009 Act abolished the provisions restricting accumulation for non-charitable trusts created on or after 6 April 2010. Trustees will now be able to accumulate income throughout the lifetime of the trust if this is required by the settlor. This does not prevent individuals imposing restrictions on accumulation of income in wills and trusts if they so wish. In many trust jurisdictions there is no rule restricting the period of accumulation.

See AMERICAN LAW INSTITUTE. *See also* ACCUMULATIONS *and* POWER OF APPOINTMENT.

Personal action: An action to enforce a remedy against a person that contrasts to a real action, the purpose of which was to recover a thing, the *res* itself. Thus an action in contract is a personal action while an action to recover land is a real action. In the law of trusts there can be both: a personal action against the trustees for breach of trust, which is the preferred remedy, then, if this fails, there may be a real action to recover the trust property from the trustees or from others through the doctrine of TRACING. This is a valuable right existing only in equity and valid against everyone who receives trust property other than a person who receives the property without notice that it is subject to a trust and without giving valuable consideration. *See* EQUITY'S DARLING.

Personal liability of strangers to a trust: Liability incurred by a person who is not a trustee but who lawfully receives trust property as a trustee's agent and who subsequently deals with that property knowing that it is inconsistent with the trust. The person liable will be required to compensate the beneficiaries for the loss caused by the dishonest dealing and required to give up any profits acquired. Receipt of the trust property is not a prerequisite to incurring this liability, known as 'dishonest assistance', and results in a secondary liability for assisting in the breach of a trust by a trustee or other fiduciary who is exposed to a primary liability. The question of dishonesty has been subject to much litigation, particularly ***Royal Brunei Airlines Snd Bhd v. Tan*** [1995] 2 AC 378 and ***Twinsectra Ltd v. Yardley*** [2002] UKHL 12, [2002] 2 AC 164 at 171 and 195. *See* KNOWING RECEIPT AND DISHONEST ASSISTANCE.

Personal property: Personal property is all property that is not real property. The term 'personal property' covers a wide variety of things that are classified as property which is in possession, sometimes called a 'CHOSE IN POSSESSION', such as a chattel or animals or machinery unattached to real property where the thing can actually be held in possession. Alternatively, an item of personal property may be a 'CHOSE IN ACTION' where the things can only be enforced by actions, like shares in a limited company and things protected as intellectual property; these require an action at law to implement the effects of ownership.

Personal representative: Executors and administrators, whether acting in regard to personal property or real property. *See* EXECUTOR *or* ADMINISTRATOR.

Personality of laws: A civil law term generally meaning all the laws concerning the condition, state and capacity of persons. This contrasts with reality of laws, which means all laws that concern property and things. This distinction was applied to emphasise the universality of certain laws which should be applied to a person wherever an action is brought on the grounds that this is a personal statute. The term is also applied in connection with the classification of statutes into real, personal and mixed statutes. The term is now hardly used, although it was formerly of greater importance when deciding the choice of law, practice and theory which applied to any circumstance.

Personalty: Personal property as distinguished from realty or real property; a term which is frequently used in English law.

Per stirpes: *See* PER CAPITA.

Persuasive authority: A decision or other pronouncement of law that although not binding is respected because of the quality of the judgment or the seniority of the court. *See* OBITER DICTUM.

***Piaecausae*:** A word that is used to describe early foundations that were administered directly or indirectly by the church and which existed in the Byzantine Empire. *See* FOUNDATIONS, GENERALLY.

Piercing the corporate veil: Looking behind a company as a legal individual, particularly to examine the opinions and motives of the shareholders, which, as a general rule, are irrelevant on incorporation. In other words, matters which have gone into the formation of the company and its administration are irrelevant when judging the conduct of the directors or the company as an individual legal person. Similar concepts exist in respect of foundations and trusts. Exceptions to this general rule exist where there is evidence that the corporation or other body was established to engage in fraudulent practices either by the body itself or persons dealing with it. Although no cases have become apparent as to whether the veil of incorporation of a private foundation can be pierced, it is likely that enquiries will take place on the motives for setting up a foundation if there is suspicion of fraud or where the terms of the constitutional documents of a foundation are suspected of not representing the true intention of the founder, i.e. when the foundation, although properly incorporated, is set up for fraudulent purposes or is a sham. The current movement to a greater exposure of beneficiaries of company shares, trusts or foundations, although not called 'piercing the corporate veil', have much in common with this doctrine in that there is a 'looking behind' the vehicle as it is incorporated (a foundation or a company), or set up as a trust.

PIRT: *See* PRESUMED INTENTION RESULTING TRUST.

Place of abode: The place of residence.

Place of performance: When used in connection with contractual obligations, commonly used as a connecting factor to determine the law governing the contract, such as where the contract has to be performed. *See* *LEX CAUSAE*.

Plaintiff: A person who brings an action, now under English law called a 'claimant' since the Civil Procedure Rules 1998 became effective.

Pledge: 'The contract of pledge is a bailment or delivery, of goods and chattels by one man to another to be held as security for the payment of a debt or the performance of some engagement, and upon the express or implied understanding that the thing deposited is to be restored to the owner, as soon as the debt is discharged or the engagement has been fulfilled.' (***Bristol & West of England Bank v. Midland Railway Co*** [1891] 2 QB 653). For example, in a pawnbroking transaction the pawnbroker (the pledgee who, in this example, is also a bailee) is required to retain the chattel and not dispose of it except in a manner provided in the terms of the contract between the pawnbroker and the pledgor. That is, the pledgor raises money by transferring possession of a chattel to the pawnbroker (the pledgee) who must retain it according to the terms of the contract, which allows the pledgor to recover possession of it by repaying the sum advanced with commission or interest to the pawnbroker. Also, a chattel may be pledged as security for the performance of an obligation where, upon failure to perform the obligation, the pledgee may sell the chattel. The pledgor may redeem the chattel on the performance of the obligation; i.e. by repaying the sum advanced. Unless otherwise provided in the contract, the obligation is for the pledgee to return, on redemption of the pledge, the property. A contract of pledge is distinguished from a contract of HYPOTHECATION because with hypothecation there is no transfer of possession. Also, a pledge differs from a contract of mortgage because with a pledge there is no transfer of the ownership during the continuance of the contract.

Pooled investment trusts: *See* UNIT TRUSTS.

Portfolio theory: The duty of a trustee traditionally has been described as taking such care as 'an ordinary prudent man would take if he were minded to make investment for the benefit of other people for whom he felt morally bound to provide'. In doing so, the application of a modern portfolio theory to trustees' investment duties has to be considered. The major insight of this theory is that risks specific to investment in any particular company may be eliminated by holding diverse portfolio shares in other companies. This means that the prudence of an investing trustee will not be judged on the risk associated with any one particular company and that under this doctrine a trustee will manage his risk by spreading his investments across the market. This does not eliminate risk of a collapse of the market as a whole but it diminishes the risk in investing if the trustee had invested only in a few companies; under the portfolio theory the risk should be further diminished by investing in other markets, such as property.

Portion: Property that is provided, or settled, in a trust in favour of children or their issue. With personal property direct trusts are normally used in favour of children immediately after the death of a parent or parents. Where land was settled in strict settlement, say, for a husband for life with the remainder entailed to the eldest son, it was usual to provide for the payment of a sum of money to the younger children who did not have the advantage of the entailed estate or, in the case of daughters, a sum payable from the estate on marriage. These payments were called 'portions'. In order to provide portions, the trustees could mortgage the estate. The power to provide portions preceded the settlement of the estate for life or in tail, and this method was preserved in the *Settled Land Act* 1925 as an equitable interest. The concept of providing portions from entailed property is now archaic since no further settlements under the *Settled Land Act* 1925 can be made after the *Trusts of Land and Appointment of Trustees Act* 1996. Since the abolition of any further settlements in land because of the *Trusts of Land and Appointment of Trustees Act* 1996, a specific provision is now advisable in respect of portions in any trusts of land. Portions are usually made in writing with a provision for HOTCHPOTCH and for the maintenance of children and for the advancement of capital before the period of vesting, subject to 'the rule against double portions'. *See* SATISFACTION *and* ADVANCEMENT.

Positive justice: Justice that is in accordance with the POSITIVE LAW of a jurisdiction and, at the same time, accords with the concept of fairness or reasonableness or any other principle of natural justice. The aim of society is to achieve a close overlap between the two so that any transgression against the positive law of a state is not regarded as unfair or as an injustice in the broader sense of the term.

Positive law: Law that is laid down and enforced by a sovereign (e.g. legislative bodies with unlimited powers) that may apply or authorise a sanction if the law is not obeyed; a fundamental characteristic of the positive school of law of BENTHAM and AUSTIN and more recently by KELSEN. Positive law is distinguished from natural law, which is a series of propositions as to what the law ought to be, or the law which is acceptable without the authority of a sovereign. Trust and foundation laws are positive laws with a source from legislation or from judicial precedents by judges whose authority comes from the sovereign power of the jurisdiction concerned. *See also* NATURAL LAW.

Possession: The exercise of physical control over a thing, either against all the world or against all the world except certain persons. Possession has three requisites: first, there must be actual or potential physical control; second, the intention to possess; and, third, the evidence of the intention must be visible or evidenced by some external sign. If a thing is put in the hands of a sleepy or drunken person, he has not got possession of it because of the lack of intention to possess. Also, there may be no signs of intention to possess or of being under anyone's control where land or any other thing has been abandoned or deserted: then, the possession is said to be vacant. The question of whether land is vacant is important in actions to recover possession. As with other things, possession of land is where a person has sufficient physical control or control together with the intention to exercise custody and control on his own behalf and for his own benefit. Under the *Law of Property Act* 1925, Section 205(xix), possession includes the receipt of rent and profits and the right to receive them, if any. Possession of land, whether obtained rightly or wrongly, entitles the possessor to bring an action of trespass against any person who enters the land without his consent. If that person has a better right to possession then no action for trespass can be maintained. Possession of land may be of several categories; these include: actual possession, where the person enters into land conveyed to him, or where possession may be apparent, which is presumed from the title by which that person holds the land, such as where land descends to the heir; or naked possession, which is where there is mere possession without any element of right to such possession. In other contexts the primary meaning of possession is physical control. Possession does not necessarily imply the right to use or enjoy the property. It is particularly relevant to trustees who may have the right to possess trust assets but who do not have the accompanying right to enjoy the benefit from them. Similarly, a foundation may possess and have title to the foundation assets but does not have the right to enjoy them. This demonstrates that possession and legal ownership are two separate concepts and, under trusts and foundations, the beneficial enjoyment is another concept.

Possessory title: An item for registering with the Land Registry if the Registrar considers that the person is in actual possession of the land (either freehold or leasehold) or is in receipt of rent and profits of the land by virtue of the estate and there is no other class of title which may be registered. This class is most likely to be registered if the applicant claims to have acquired the title by adverse possession or where the title deeds have been lost or destroyed. Registration with possessory freehold title or possessory leasehold title has the same effect as registration with absolute freehold or absolute leasehold titles, except it does not affect the enforcement of any estate, right or interest which is adverse to the proprietor's title at the time of registration. A person registered with possessory freehold title may be upgraded by the Registrar to absolute freehold title if the Registrar is satisfied as to the applicant's title to the estate; that is, the Registrar is satisfied that evidence shows that registration of an absolute title is justified, or where title to a freehold estate in land has been entered as possessory for at least 12 years.

Post-nuptial agreements: An agreement made between husband and wife after marriage as to the possible disposal of their assets if the marriage should be terminated. This is simply an agreement without the formalities of the transfer of assets to a trust. Post-nuptial agreements are deemed unnecessary on the grounds that they add little to the general law on joint ownership and have no legal validity. *See* PRE-NUPTIAL AGREEMENTS *and* ANTE-NUPTIAL AGREEMENTS.

Post-nuptial settlement: A settlement made after marriage. It is generally deemed to be voluntary unless made in fulfilment of written undertakings made before marriage and entered into by each party. On or after granting a decree of divorce, or a degree of nullity, or a judicial separation, a court may order any post-nuptial settlement to be varied for the benefit of the parties or for the children of the marriage, other than a variation in the form of a pension arrangement, under the *Matrimonial Causes Act* 1973, Section 24(1)(c). Under the Act the court may extinguish the interests of either of the parties. Similar powers exist in the case of civil partnerships. *See* MARRIAGE SETTLEMENT.

Potentially exempt transfer (PET): Where a transfer is made by one individual to another it is a potentially exempt transfer that is free from inheritance tax if seven years has elapsed from the date of the transfer without the transferor dying. If the transferor dies in that period then the potentially exempt transfer becomes a transfer on which inheritance tax is payable on a reducing scale.

Pour-over will: An American term by which a testator bequeaths assets to the trustees of a trust which he earlier set up during his lifetime. These will be assets that the grantor (the settlor) kept in reserve or which were subsequently acquired. On his death, through his will, he 'pours over' the balance of his assets into the trust. This presupposes that the trust set up during the testator's lifetime is valid. As a safeguard, a pour-over will often provide that if the first trust is wholly or partially invalid, then the distributions under the will are to be held in a will trust on the same terms as the earlier trust and the assets from the invalid trust will be transferred into that new trust.

Power: 'An individual personal capacity of a donee of the power to do something' (***Re Armstrong*** (1886) 17 QBD 521). Applied to trusts, this is an authority or mandate conferred upon a trustee to deal with, or dispose of, property which the trustee holds according to the terms of the power. A power gives the trustee capacity to deal with the property without compelling the trustee to do so. Thus, powers generally must be distinguished from what a trustee must do as a matter of fulfilling the trustee's duty under the terms of the trust, i.e. powers may not be mandatory, in contrast to trust duties, which are compulsory. Some powers are given the mandatory force of trusts in the trust instrument. These are sometimes called 'powers in the nature of a trust' and trustees may sometimes be given powers which they must exercise even though they may have discretion as to the manner in which they do so (*see* DISCRETIONARY TRUSTS). Powers are now classified according to the purpose for which they are created or conferred; administrative or managerial powers for the purpose of managing the trust property, or dispositive powers that authorise a trustee to appoint out of a class of persons who is to be a beneficiary, or the disposal of beneficial interests or other rights in property which the holder of the power does not himself own. Powers of appointment may be a general power exercisable in favour of whoever the trustee pleases, or a special power exercisable only in favour of certain specified persons. There may also be hybrid (or intermediate) powers, which are powers to appoint anyone in the world with the exception of such persons or groups of persons specified by the settlor. Powers of trustees generally are created in the trust instrument and these are supplemented by those powers conferred upon trustees under the *Trustee Act* 1925. The trust instrument may omit or modify the statutory default provisions. Statutory powers include powers of maintenance, advancement, powers relating to sale and other dealings with land under the *Trustee Act* 1925. The *Trusts of Land and Appointment of Trustees Act* 1996 gives trustees powers to give receipts, powers to compromise, to pay statute debts, to appropriate trust assets, to conduct business and to lend trust monies, and to borrow. Generally, any power must be exercised unanimously by all those who have been given the power. A majority has no power to bind the minority unless in a trust deed there is an express provision permitting them then to do so. Trustees must exercise their powers in the light of the circumstances existing at the time and cannot bind themselves or their successors as to how they will or will not exercise a power in the future. In the exercise of the power, the trustees' duty is to consider the estate as a whole and not the effect of the exercise of any powers between some beneficiaries and others. *See* MERE POWER.

Power of appointment: A power given by deed or will in which a person directs an interest in property to devolve on anyone including himself, known as a general power. If the power is in favour of a specified person, or members of a specified class, it is a special power. *See* POWER.

Power of attorney: A formal document by which one person (the principal or donor) transfers to another (the attorney or donee) the right to act on his behalf either generally or in specific circumstances. Where a power of attorney is given to execute a deed then that power of attorney must be created by deed which may form part of a deed containing other matters. For example, a deed of dissolution of partnership may contain a power of attorney for the retiring or continuing partner to wind up the business and collect the assets. A power of attorney may be a general power where the attorney is given power to do all acts of a certain class from time to time, such as carrying on business, collecting debts, etc. Alternatively, it may be a special or particular power which is confined to a specific act or acts, such as completing the conveyance of a house or other property in the future owner's absence. There is also a limited power which contains precise instructions as to the way in which it is to be executed. The deed appointing an attorney may be proved by means of a photographic copy certified by the principal or his solicitor. Where powers of attorney are given as security they are irrevocable. The attorney is not liable for acts done after revocation if he did not know about it and a person dealing with such an attorney is nevertheless protected. A general power may confer on the attorney the power to do anything which may be lawfully done by the principal except where the principal is a trustee, a personal representative, a tenant for life or statutory owner. A power of attorney becomes void when the principal ceases to have the MENTAL CAPACITY to realise that a power has been awarded. This prevents an attorney being appointed to attend to the principal's affairs at a time when most needed. This shortcoming can be remedied by the use of a LASTING POWER OF ATTORNEY. A lasting power of attorney confers on the attorney the power to make decisions about the principal's personal welfare generally, and to look after his affairs when he no longer has capacity. The *Mental Capacity Act* 2005, Section 9 provides detailed restrictions and other matters concerned with lasting powers of attorney and refers disputes arising to the Court of Protection. *See* POWERS OF ATTORNEY AND TRUSTEES.

Power of disposition by will: The power to create interests by will that are recognised by law and which are within the extent of a testator's interest in property. For example, a testator cannot create an EASEMENT that operates independently of property (sometimes referred to as 'in gross') or any disposition which offends the rule against perpetuities.

Power to insure trust property: A power that trustees have under statutory provisions of the *Trustee Act* 2000 and the *Trustee Act* 1925 to insure any trust property against risks of loss or damage that occurs whenever the trustees exercise the care and skill of the ordinary businessman.

Powers of attorney and trustees: Powers of attorney are sometimes given to trustees so that they may delegate their power; for example, where a trustee has a particular function in connection with land. By a POWER OF ATTORNEY, a trustee may appoint a beneficiary of full age to be entitled to an interest in possession of trust land (*Trustee Act* 2000, Section 9(a)) to act for him. This is subject to any contrary intention expressed in the trust instrument or restrictions included in the instrument creating the power of attorney. Where a trustee suffers from a MENTAL DISORDER, detailed provisions are given in the UK under *Trustee Act* 1925, Section 36, as amended, and the *Trusts of Land Act* 1996, Section 20. Members of a foundation council are generally required to have MENTAL CAPACITY in order to act but there is no established rule as to their powers to delegate their powers by power of attorney. The powers of a PROTECTOR, or some other officer, should be sufficient to replace any member of a foundation council who lacks capacity to act.

Pre-action protocol: A procedural step introduced following the *Access to Justice Report* 1996 to promote settlements of disputes in a way that is satisfactory to both parties after they have been given the information which will help in coming to a settlement. The intention is to build on and increase the benefit of an early settlement and avoid unnecessarily prolonged and expensive litigation. The important provisions in a pre-action protocol are a timetable for the provision of letters of claim and response, the provision of information and documents and the procedure for instructing experts. Specific protocols are provided by the courts of the UK in respect of claims for personal injury, clinical negligence, construction, defamation, professional negligence, judicial review, disease and illness claims, and matters concerned with housing. The parties are not compelled to abide by the terms of protocols but failure to do so may result in adverse orders for costs, interest on awards and interest on costs, even if parties so penalised are successful in the eventual litigation in court. Although formal pre-action protocols are not at present available in connection with all types of action, there is a need for parties to a dispute to engage in some alternative dispute resolution and adopt procedural steps similar to those of the pre-action protocols before resorting to court action, in order to avoid being penalised for costs.

Precatory trust: A phrase used to describe a trust that a court finds to be in existence although no trust intention was expressed by the parties; it is a trust construed to be in existence by the court although there had been no clear expression showing an intention to create a trust. A trust is construed by the court from words of recommendation (of prayer or suggestion, or the like). The phrase 'precatory trust' was applied to these circumstances but was referred to as an abominable phrase in ***Re Sanson*** 12 T.L.R. 142 per Chitty J, and was condemned as: 'nothing more than a misleading nickname' (***Re Williams*** [1897] 2 Ch. 12, 18-19, page 27). In the same case, the judge stated that once a trust is established by will it is equal to a trust formed by other means and has the same effects and incidents of a trust whether declared in clearly imperative terms or deduced upon a consideration of the whole will. The Court of Appeal in the leading case, ***Re Adams and Kensington Vestry*** (1884) 27 Ch.D. 294, held that the wife of a deceased took the beneficial interest in the property of her deceased husband, who had given all his land and personal estates for the absolute use of his wife, her heirs, executors, administrators and assigns: 'In full confidence that she will do what is right as to the disposal thereof between my children ...'. In that case, the words attached to the ABSOLUTE GIFT that she would do what is right between several parties, did not show a clear intention to create a trust. There have been a few cases where precatory words have been held to constitute a trust although the majority have denied the existence of a trust when precatory words were used. Since the ***Re Adams*** decision, the doctrine of CERTAINTY OF WORDS expressing intention has gained a more dominant position as an essential element of a valid trust. This makes the use of precatory words in the drafting of trust deeds and wills a dangerous uncertainty.

Precedent: *See* CASE LAW.

Preference shares: A class of shares in a company that take preference over other shares (usually called ordinary shares or, in North America, 'common shares') in the payment of dividends or in the repayment of capital. The Articles of the company define the rights attached to preference shares, which frequently include entitlement to a dividend of a fixed amount before any dividend payment is made to ordinary shareholders. Preference shares may also be 'participating' in that the holders may be entitled, in addition to their fixed dividend, to participate in the financial prosperity of the company with an extra dividend. Payment of dividends to preference shareholders is contingent upon the profits of each year or half year being sufficient, otherwise the holders of preference shares have to forego their dividends but, if preference shares are set up as being cumulative, any unpaid dividends accumulate and are a debt that is payable in priority to any future payment of dividend on the ordinary shares. Also, the Articles might provide that preference shares may be 'redeemable' or 'convertible' by the company into ordinary shares. In the case of liquidation, preference shares take priority over ordinary shares in the distribution of capital.

Pre-incorporation contract: A contract entered into by a person purportedly on behalf of a company at a time when the company had not been incorporated. The consequences vary from jurisdiction to jurisdiction. In some countries a pre-incorporation contract may be confirmed by the company after formation and become enforceable against the company. In other countries, the person who purportedly acts for the company is made personally liable on any pre-incorporation contract and consequently is able to enforce the contract as a personal contract (*Companies Act* 2006, Section 50, 51).

Pre-nuptial agreement: An agreement entered into by couples before marriage with the intention of limiting the claim that one spouse can make against the other on divorce. In the UK these agreements are not binding but are taken into account by the court in determining how to split the assets and income on a divorce or judicial separation. Previously, these agreements were considered to be against public policy as they would discourage the permanency of marriage but they have now become influential, particularly where the agreement has been properly drawn up after appropriate disclosure and signed after legal advice (*see* ***Crossley v. Crossley*** [2007] EWCA Civ 1491). *See also* POST-NUPTIAL AGREEMENTS *and* ANTE-NUPTIAL AGREEMENTS.

Pre-owned asset: A new regime introduced into the UK by the *Finance Act* 2004, Schedule15, which provides that a person who disposes of any asset after 17 March 1986 but who continues to enjoy a benefit from it is charged to income tax based on the rental value of the asset for the tax year. This income tax charge is applied to three classes of asset: land, chattels and intangible property.

Presumed Intention Resulting Trust (PIRT): An inaccurate term to describe a trust that is claimed to arise as a RESULTING TRUST but which gives effect to a presumed intention of the settlor. The terminology has not been universally accepted for obvious reasons. A resulting trust is a trust that arises in law when there appears to be no other justifiable course of action. This is frequently where an express trust cannot be performed and a resulting trust in favour of the settlor results. Such a trust is founded purely by trust law. It has no relationship to the intention of the settlor. If the settlor's intention is known or can be determined and recognised by the court, then there is no need to involve the concept of a resulting trust. The contradiction is to attribute a resulting trust, a creation of the law, as being under the influence of the settlor's intention. Alternatively, where a trust is set up according to a settlor's intention, it is inappropriate to consider the trust as a resulting trust; intention is one thing and the nature of a resulting trust is another.

Presumption of death: A person who is missing can be presumed dead under the UK's *Presumption of Death Act* 2013 if a 'Declaration of presumed death' is issued by the court. Such declarations can be made under three circumstances that follow an application made to the court by an interested person. First, a declaration can be issued where the court is satisfied that a missing person has died or has not been known to be alive for a period of at least seven years. Then the declaration states the date and time at which the missing person is presumed to have died. Second, where the court is satisfied that the missing person has died but is uncertain when death occurred during a period when the person was missing, then the declaration states that the missing person is presumed to have died at the end of that period. Third, where the court is satisfied that the missing person has not been known to have been alive for a period of seven years but is not satisfied that the missing person has died, the finding is that the missing person is presumed to have died at the end of the period of seven years beginning with the day after the day on which he or she was last known to have been alive.

Presumption of sanity: The law presumes that the state of things should continue to exist unless the contrary is proved. Under this presumption, if it can be proved that the testator was sane at the time he was making a will then he will be taken as sane at the time of his death. However, where that sanity is contested then the onus is on the person making the suggestion to prove that the testator was not of sound mind at the time he made the will. If, after vigilant examination, the court feels there is no doubt that sanity prevailed, it must grant probate. Complete proof of capacity, or even proof beyond reasonable doubt, is not essential. Evidence of sanity prior to making a will may require proof of competence at the time the will was made where the will contains dispositions which are not such as an ordinary testator would make. A similar presumption of sanity applies to a person placing assets in a trust or setting up a foundation.

Presumption of survivorship: If two or more persons die in a common disaster, the younger is presumed to have survived in matters concerning title to property. This is subject to the order of the court. In respect of estate duty, they are presumed to have died at the same time. *See* COMMORIENTES.

Prima facie: A case that has been supported by sufficient evidence should be taken as proved if there is no evidence to the contrary.

Primogeniture: The state of being first born which is relevant where, for example, the rule of inheritance awards the elder of twins succession to their ancestors' land to the exclusion of the other. A right of primogeniture in England was the right whereby the eldest son succeeded to all the real estate of an intestate parent. An analogous right was frequently given by will, and in marriage settlements until the rule itself was abolished by the legislative reforms of 1925, except in connection with hereditary dignities and titles of honour.

Principal mansion house: A house, other than a farmhouse or a house whose accompanying gardens occupying less than 25 acres, which is an asset comprised in a settlement of land and which, under the *Settled Land Act* 1925, goes to the tenant for life, who cannot sell without the consent of the trustees or by an order of the court.

Principal moneys: The description frequently used to refer to the sum of money lent as capital, as distinct from interest and other moneys, covenanted to be paid in a mortgage.

Priorities: In equity and in law the basic rule is that estates and interests rank in the order of priority in which they are created, i.e. the earliest interest granted takes precedence over any interest created afterwards. This rule is expressed differently in law and in equity. Generally, at law, priority depends on the capacity of a transferor to transfer a title in property to another. Under the maxim '*NEMO DAT QUOD NON HABET*' (no-one gives what he doesn't have) no person can confer a better title than he has himself and, therefore, a recipient of any interest by law takes subject to any interest already existing in the property. By this rule, priorities are established. But, in equity, the maxim is: '*qui prior est tempore potior est jure*' (he who is early in time is stronger in law), i.e. where there is equity, the person whose equity is attached to the property first will take priority over those whose interest comes later. Where land is concerned, priority depends upon registration. There are three principle systems of registration which determine the priority of interest in real property: the *Land Registration Act* 2002, which determines title to and priority of interest in registered land; the *Land Charges Act* 1972, which does the same with unregistered land; and the *Companies Act* 1985, which determines the priority of charges over company assets by the order in which a charge appears in the company's register of charges. *See* N*EMO DAT QUAD NON HABET*.

Private foundations (sometimes called Private Interest Foundations): *See* FOUNDATION, PRIVATE.

Private international law (conflict of law): The part of the law of a jurisdiction that establishes rules for dealing with cases involving a foreign element. In respect of contracts involving parties, currency or obligations and procedures that might be subject to a different law from the jurisdiction in which the contract was created, it is necessary to decide which law governs the contract's validity and interpretation. The parties may stipulate in the contract which law governs, i.e. determine the proper law by choice. This is a recognised principle and allows the parties to a contract, and many other legal relationships, including trusts and foundations, to elect the governing law. The rules applying to a written contract are dictated by the terms of the Rome Convention of 1980, which provides rules designating which law applies if the parties to a contract have not made a specific or implied choice. The principles of private international law governing trusts have been embodied in the Hague Convention on Trusts which provides:

> 'Article 6: A trust shall be governed by the law chosen by the settlor. The choice must be express or be implied in the terms of the instrument creating or the writing evidencing the trust interpreted, if necessary, in the light of the circumstances of the case.'

The second paragraph of Article 6 states:

> 'Where the law chosen under the previous paragraph does not provide for trusts or the category of trust involved, the choice shall not be effective and the law specified in Article 7 shall apply.'

Article 7 provides:

> 'Where no applicable law has been chosen a trust shall be governed by the law with which it is most closely connected.'

With foundations, in many cases the statute in a jurisdiction which sets up the ability to establish foundations often provides that any matters concerned with the foundation are to be governed by the law of that jurisdiction. Generally, private international law provides for matters relating to jurisdiction and enforcement that have now been superseded, as far as jurisdictional enforcement in EU countries is concerned, by Council Regulation (EC) 44/2001, although the preceding Conventions still apply in some cases. Private international law also covers matrimonial affairs, legitimacy, torts, contracts, trusts and financial matters. *See* HAGUE CONVENTION ON TRUSTS, EC COUNCIL REGULATION 44/2001 *and* ROME CONVENTIONS.

Private law: The part of the law that deals with aspects of relationships between individuals that is of no direct concern to the state; this includes the law of property and of trusts and foundations, family law and the law of contract, mercantile law and the law of tort.

Private trust company (PTC): Private trust companies are companies set up to act as trustees but which are owned by the family or other close interests that set up the trust. Some jurisdictions have enacted a special regulation authorising or confirming the validity of private trust companies. Private trust companies may frequently include the settlor as one of the directors, thus ensuring that the settlor's point of view can be placed easily before the trustees as a body.

Privilege: An advantage given to a person by virtue of their status or office which enables them to do, or not to do, certain acts. This is the opposite of a duty. For example, legal professional privileges protect confidential communication between a party and his lawyer, and between lawyers themselves, made during and with reference to judicial proceedings, or in anticipation of such proceedings, or relating to a client's rights or obligations. This enables those concerned with actual contemplated litigation to be able to speak freely to their legal advisers and for their legal advisers to give candid legal advice without fear of disclosure.

Privileged communication: A written document that a witness cannot be compelled to divulge. The term often applies to communications between persons, one of whom has the benefit of privilege. Where there is an action for defamation, any communication between the parties is not regarded as a privileged communication and therefore will have to be revealed in order for the action to make sense. The term also includes matters of public law, e.g. state secrets.

Privity of contract: The relationship that exists between the immediate parties to a contract and which gives each party rights under the contract, in contrast to the position of strangers who have no rights or liabilities in the contract under the original provisions in the English law. A stranger provides no consideration to the other party and therefore no contract has been created between them. A contract made between A and B does not provide any benefit for C because C has provided no consideration; any such contract is enforceable either by A or by B, but not by C. The rule rendered English law out of step with the rights of parties under contracts in the EU, where merely supplying evidence of each party's intention to be bound is sufficient. The *Contracts (Rights of Third Parties) Act* 1999 has brought partial reform and, under certain circumstances, allows C to have an enforceable interest in the contract between A and B in most everyday situations. But privity of contract remains between lessor and lessee, between tenant for life and remaindermen or reversioner, and between joint tenants.

Probate: Recognition by the Family Division of the High Court in the UK to the effect that the will of a certain person has been proved (i.e. presented to the Registrar and certified as genuine by the deceased person's executors) and registered in the court. The executor proving the will can be granted powers of administration of the estate after his sworn declaration to faithfully administer the will and to give it a true inventory and render a just account when called upon. Probate is a prior step which must be completed where a deceased person intends to set up a foundation or a trust by will. Nothing can be done until probate of the will has been granted, i.e. no property which had belonged to the deceased can be transferred to trustees until the executor has power to deal with the property. That power is given to him by the grant of probate of the will.

Procedural rules: Rules that govern how effect should be given to substantive rules and covers such matters as the service of legal process, the calling of witnesses and the procedure before, during and after court proceedings. Almost universally the LAW OF THE FORUM dictates the law that applies to procedure. This is unlike the law governing a substantive matter of law, which may be chosen by the parties. *See* SUBSTANTIVE LAW *and* CONFLICT OF LAWS.

Professional funds: *See* HEDGE FUNDS.

Profit à prendre: The right to take soil, minerals or produce from another's land (known as the servient tenement) or to graze animals on it. This may be a legal or equitable interest and may be created by express or implied grant or by statute. Profits that are *profits à prendre* are profits which are bound to arise for the benefit of another property, the dominant tenement, for example grazing rights on a farm estate where it would be beyond doubt that the property situated on that land has been, and is, used for rearing cattle; the grazing rights arise by prescription or by a presumed grant.

Profit sharing trusts: A trust into which a company that is engaged in a cyclical industry places funds for the benefit of the employees so that salaries can be paid during the quiet period of a company's year. The trustees of these trusts often purchase shares in the company.

Profits, Compensation for lack of: In an action in connection with the lack of profits to a trust caused by the default of the trustee, a successful application, generally, may choose between a payment of compensation by the defendant (the trustee) or the profits which the defendant gained by the unlawful use of the trust's property. Therefore, when there is a breach of trust, a beneficiary may claim monetary compensation from the trustee or may elect to receive the benefit which the trust could have expected to have received if there had been no breach of trust and the defendant trustee had conducted the trust business properly.

Promissory estoppel: A doctrine of equity that applies where one party, by his words or conduct, makes a clear and unequivocal promise or assurance to another party to a transaction under circumstances that are understood by both to affect their legal relationship. This is an extension to include a promise in the existing equitable doctrine of forbearance or estoppel that applied where there was a representation of an existing fact. The doctrine of estoppel was extended to a representation of intention or promise (i.e. a promise was included with representations of existing facts in gaining an influence on the relationship of the parties). This concept became prominent in a statement by Lord Denning in ***Central London Property Trust Ltd v. High Trees House Ltd.*** [1947] K.B. 130, 134. The essential element was the knowledge of the person making the promise that the other party would rely upon it. In the ***High Trees House*** case a landlord promised a potential leasehold tenant of a property that a covenant in respect of rent increases in the lease would not be enforced. This was material in persuading the tenant to enter into the lease. Lord Denning decided that the promise by the landlord must be honoured, although a promise of this nature was not a representation of an existing fact and not within the then existing scope of estoppel. This was the origin of the doctrine of promissory estoppel. This promissory estoppel was, in the ***High Trees House*** case, a defence when the landlord attempted to act contrary to his promise; that is, it was a defence to a claim for an increased rent. Promissory estoppel cannot create a cause of action; it may only be used as a defence against a party who acts contrary to a promise. Despite a varied history and the need for further consideration of the doctrine, it is now well established in English law. *See* PROPRIETARY ESTOPPEL *and* ESTOPPEL.

Proper law: *See* GOVERNING LAW *and* CHANGING THE PROPER LAW.

Proper law of contract: The system of law that, according to private international law of a jurisdiction, is the law which governs the contract as far as the judicial system of that jurisdiction is concerned and is based upon the intention of the parties to the contract and all the surrounding circumstances. The parties may have agreed which law should govern and that choice will be recognised, by virtue of the Rome Convention 1980. If the parties to the contract have not expressly agreed, the courts will try to infer the intention of the parties; if this is not possible the courts will apply the law with which the contract has its closest and most real connection. *See* PRIVATE INTERNATIONAL LAW *and* ROME CONVENTIONS.

Property Adjustment Order: A feature of the ANCILLARY RELIEF that may be granted under the *Matrimonial Causes Act* 1973, Section 21, and which deals with property rights available to the court for the purpose of arranging a just financial outcome to the parties in a divorce. The orders available are for the transfer of property, for the settlement of property and for a variation of a settlement. These orders require the party to whom they are addressed to transfer the property specified in the order in favour of the other party or to a child of the family. Also, an order may require property subject to a trust to be made available to the other party. A similar order may be made under the *Civil Partnership Act* 2004.

Proprietary estoppel: An ESTOPPEL that arises:

> '[W]here the promisor makes a representation or promise to the promisee that he will acquire an interest in land, and the promisee has acted to his detriment in that belief, the promisee has a right to apply to the court which may grant him equitable relief in support of his expectation.' *Taylor Fashions Ltd. v. Liverpool Victoria Trustee Co. Ltd* [1982] Q.B. 133.

This early definition of proprietary estoppel has been much discussed and modified by recognising acquiescence in addition to representations as an element in proprietary estoppel. Representations, however, appear to be the more prevalent factor. Proprietary estoppel was summarised by Lord Walker in *Thorner v. Major* [2009] UKHL 18 as:

> '[B]ased on three main elements ... a representation or assurance made to the claimant; reliance on it by the claimant; and detriment to the claimant in consequence of his (reasonable) reliance.'

The three elements appear to be present in cases of proprietary estoppel but by no means define and restrict what comprises this branch of estoppel. Proprietary estoppel is not a unitary doctrine. As stated by Lord Scott in *Cobbe v. Yeoman's Row Management Ltd* [2008] UKHL 55:

> '[U]nconscionability of conduct may well lead to a remedy but ... proprietary estoppel cannot be the route to it unless the ingredients for a proprietary estoppel are present.'

There is no comprehensive and uncontroversial definition of proprietary estoppel. The statement by Lord Scott continued in describing proprietary estoppel as:

> '[A] sub-species of a "promissory" estoppel – if the right claimed is a proprietary right, usually a right to or over land, but, in principle, equally available in relation to chattels or choses in action.'

This statement, however, does not explain the acquiescence principle by which proprietary estoppel can arise where a course of conduct relies on a mistaken belief in respect of land where the other party fails to assert that the person's position is unsound, i.e. there is acquiescence underlying the situation. This acquiescence-based principle lies alongside a principle where a clear representation of a state of affairs is made. Proprietary estoppel cannot be considered a completely settled concept. *See* ESTOPPEL.

Proprietary rights: The rights connected with the proprietary title that an owner has by virtue of his ownership. These rights are contrasted with mere possessory rights. A person who owns property has the proprietary right, but a bailee of that property is only given a POSSESSORY TITLE (i.e. is entitled to retain possession against all comers except the owner) to the property but receives no proprietary rights, thus giving no right to dispose of the title. *See* BAILMENT.

Prosulting trusts: A trust where the beneficial interest goes forward to someone other than the person who provided the value where a trust fails, in contrast to a resulting trust where the property goes back to the person from whom it came. A term used infrequently.

Protection, equitable: The protection of a person using equitable principles to overcome the unfair treatment of another. Foremost amongst these principles are breach of FIDUCIARY DUTY, EQUITABLE FRAUD, UNDUE INFLUENCE and others concerned with overcoming ABUSE OF CONFIDENCE and protection against UNCONSCIONABLE TRANSACTIONS. These include, for example, the lack of CAPACITY where a gift will be set aside if the donor lacks the requisite mental capacity, and this can be applied to wills, contracts and gifts where the degree of understanding of the nature of the transaction varies according to the characteristics of each transaction. Where there is lack of capacity the burden of proof shifts to the donee to demonstrate that the donor had the necessary understanding to be able to validly make a gift. With unconscionable bargains the complainant must come within one of the separate doctrines of CONSTRUCTIVE FRAUD. Attempts to group undue influence, ABUSE OF CONFIDENCE or unconscionable bargains under one umbrella of inequality of bargaining power have been abandoned, although there is a well-established equitable jurisdiction (according to Snell, *Snells Equity*, 33rd edn) to set aside unconscionable transations; for example, a purchase made from a poor and ignorant person at a considerable undervalue unless the purchaser can satisfy the court that the transaction was fair, just and reasonable. This equitable remedy can be appreciated as different from a remedy at law for undue influence because the equitable remedy does not require a pre-existing relationship between the parties to exist that is necessary for the legal remedy. In equity, however, it is necessary to show an imbalance of relationship between the parties at the time of the transaction. Unconscionable bargains also include transactions made with expectance, i.e. where reversioners or persons hope to take a benefit under a will or intestacy of a person still alive. Transactions involving money lending are now governed by the *Consumer Credit Act* 1974 but, in other circumstances, courts of equity will also set aside transactions which are frauds on third parties or upon the public generally; these include, traditionally, marriage brokerage contracts, rewards for influence of a testator and contracts in restraint of trade.

Protection of trustees: A series of circumstances where the law provides protection for trustees against claims relating to an estate that they hold. These protections include the ability of trustees to obtain a discharge of their liabilities by paying into court any trust money or property in their hands or under their control. A receipt by the court is sufficient discharge. This can be used only where trustees have no other way of obtaining a discharge or where they cannot obtain a valid receipt. It should not be used where it is uncertain who of several persons are entitled to the trust fund; this should be resolved by instituting proceedings in which those persons are named as defendants. The *Trustee Act* 1925, Section 27, provides that a trustee or a PERSONAL REPRESENTATIVE may advertise for claimants, state that their intention is to make a conveyance or distribution and require any person to send to them particulars of the circumstances on which that person bases his purported rights. Submissions must be made within a certain time, not being less than two months after the trustees advertise for claimants in the London Gazette and local newspapers. The intention is to provide protection against belated claims not only from creditors but from next of kin or beneficiaries under the will. If there is no claim, the trustee or personal representatives may convey or distribute the property without any liability arising from other persons. The advertisement does not prejudice claimants' rights to follow the property into the hands of purchasers other than those of a purchaser for value without notice, nor does it free trustees from making searches that an intending purchaser should make. Also, where the trust assets include a lease, trustees were formerly cautious in distributing the income without setting aside money to meet future liabilities. The result was that large sums were withheld from beneficiaries. This difficulty was avoided by distributing the estate under an order of the court. This protection of trustees, however, is of limited benefit and only applies to a trust, an estate or an estate of a deceased person and the benefit only applies to personal representatives as such, and not when they become assignees of the property by taking possession of it, as is the usual position. Overall, the court has power to sanction departure from the terms of a trust and may confer additional powers on trustees to allow the variation of the terms of a trust without any liability arising on the trustee. These various matters led to the *Variation of Trusts Act* 1958.

Protective trust: A trust where the interest granted to the beneficiary is terminated or restricted in the event of the beneficiary becoming insolvent or if any of his property becomes liable to seizure by creditors. The consequences vary from a complete ending of the trust to a restriction on the ability of the beneficiary to deal in or alienate his interest. Protective trusts frequently feature in offshore jurisdictions. Protective trusts are designed to protect the beneficiary and not the settlement nor the trust assets. A protective trust is set up in the UK by the settlor simply saying so in the deed or making a reference to the *Trustee Act* 1925, Section 33, which is the governing section. The settlor sets up an INTEREST IN POSSESSION trust for no longer than the beneficiary's lifetime (i.e. the beneficiary has a present interest for his life of the trust income) but if the beneficiary commits any divesting act, the trust then automatically converts into a DISCRETIONARY TRUST for the beneficiary and his family (*Trustee Act* 1925, Section 33(ii)). Divesting acts are as defined by the settlor. The settlor may use a protective trust to restrain a beneficiary from the financial consequences of an extravagant lifestyle. On the occurrence of a divesting act then the trustee applies the income, at the trustee's ABSOLUTE DISCRETION, for a class of persons that most likely includes the beneficiary and his family but where the beneficiary then no longer has any right to receive the income itself. A protective trust can be a trust for the life of a beneficiary or for any lesser period that is determined in the event of the beneficiary's bankruptcy. A protective trust may also be used where the beneficiary, for example, commits a criminal offence or fails to achieve a measurable degree of propriety expected by the settlor. Where, under the concept of protective trusts, an interest in possession trust becomes a discretionary trust there is likely to be a tax consequence.

Protector: A person who is conferred with powers under a settlement, trust or foundation to monitor the activities of the trustees or foundation council and, where authorised by the statutory documents, to supplement the administration by offering extra knowledge and experience beneficial to the trust or foundation. A protector is sometimes called a 'GUARDIAN'; other titles are also used. In international trusts, a protector may be appointed because of his intimate knowledge of the beneficiaries and their needs. Such knowledge would be difficult for the trustees to perceive when the trust is set up in an offshore jurisdiction and geographically remote from the beneficiaries. In this case, a protector may be able to offer practical and valuable suggestions to the trustees on how they might best apply their discretion because of the protector's closer and more knowledgeable relationship with the family.

Protector (foundations): A person appointed by the founder to undertake duties specified in the foundation charter or regulations with the intention of maintaining conformity with the founder's wishes as expressed in the charter and regulations. A protector of foundations acquires greater significance for the proper management of a foundation since, unlike a trust, the beneficiaries have lesser powers, and unlike a company, there are no shareholders to exercise control. *See* PROTECTOR.

Protector (settlement): The role of the protector, as far as trusts are concerned, originated with entailed interests, the form of trusts of land which was codified by the *Settled Land Act* 1925. This form of trust gave the TENANT FOR LIFE, the principal beneficiary, considerable powers in the management of the land. Also, the tenant who came after the tenant for life, the REMAINDERMAN, in tail, could bar the entail, that is, convert the land held under settlement into freehold. In order to restrain irresponsible barrings of the entail in this way, the consent of a protector would be required. The role of protector featured under the *Fines and Recoveries Act* 1833, Section 32, which provided that a settlor may appoint a special protector but, in the absence of such a person, the owner of the first estate in possession, i.e. the tenant for life under the same settlement, becomes the statutory protector. After the Act the statutory protector might be excluded by the settlor, who may appoint not more than three persons to be special protectors. The ability to set up new entailed interests of land is now barred by the *Trusts for Land and Appointment of Trustees Act* 1996; settlements of land which existed before the Act continue. The office of protector is not assignable in connection with entailed property but if he is a tenant for life under the settlement he may make provisions before giving his consent to act as the protector of the settlement. *See* ENTAILED INTEREST.

Protector (trusts): A person who is not one of the trustees but on whom the trust deed confers certain powers in respect of the administration of the trust or the dispositive powers of the trustees. Sometimes the protector can give directions to the trustees or engage in consultation prior to the exercise by the trustees of their powers. The protector may sometimes have the power to appoint and remove trustees and to approve trustees' remuneration, to require the production of accounts and to nominate the auditor. Protectors frequently occur in offshore trusts where the trustees may be geographically remote from the beneficiaries and a protector is appointed to advise the trustees on how the trustees may exercise their discretion for the best benefit of the beneficiaries. The authority of the protector depends upon the terms laid down in the trust instrument, the construction of which determines the extent of a protector's duties, although legislation may be modified by statute or by overriding public policy considerations. *See* PROTECTOR.

Proxy: Someone appointed to vote in the place of another; usually the authority to do so is in writing and allows the proxy to use his discretion. Frequently used by shareholders unable, or unwilling, to attend a general meeting of a company. The notice of a general meeting is usually accompanied by an invitation to non-attending members to appoint the chairman of the company as the shareholder's proxy. There is a similar use at meetings of creditors of a bankrupt person or in connection with elections where a proxy is appointed to vote on behalf of another elector. Marriage by proxy may be valid in English law if it is conducted in accordance with the forms and laws of the country in which it is celebrated.

Prudent investor rule: A general term applied to the policy adopted in several jurisdictions that trustees should be allowed to invest in assets of any kind as if they were beneficial owners and to delegate investment powers to investment managers and nominees. The term also calls for trustees prudently to select their investments and to exclude the hazardous or speculative use of trust money. In English law the desirability of appointing an intermediary where the trustees had substantial investments to make was recognised by the courts in ***Anker-Petersen v. Anker-Petersen*** (1998) 12 TRU.L.I. 166; [2000] WTLR 583. This position previously required an application to the court for an appropriate extension of trustees' powers under Section 57 of the *Trustee Act* 1925; these became fairly readily granted before statutory recognition of the need became widely adopted. The first statutory recognition was in New Zealand under the *Trustee Investment Act* 1998. The Uniform Investor Regimes have been adopted by the vast majority of US states and in Canada in most English-speaking provinces under the *Uniform Trustee Investment Act* 1997. The regimes have also been adopted in Australia and the Bahamas and, under the *Trustee Act* 2000, in the UK, which was followed by the Isle of Man, Singapore, Jersey, Guernsey, Cyprus and San Marino. Other offshore jurisdictions have adopted the general principles of modern portfolio theory. The prudent investor standard is based on a responsible selection of investments by the trustees considering the specific circumstances of each trust. In English law the regime is expressed in ***Armitage v. Nurse*** [1998] Ch. 243:

> 'The duty of the trustees to perform the trust honestly and in good faith to the benefit of the beneficiaries is the minimum necessary to give substance to the trusts, but in my opinion it is sufficient [Lord Millett].'

The main difference between the prudent man of business and the prudent investor rule is that the latter requires a standard of conduct. This rule is also referred to as the 'portfolio theory'. *See* GENERAL POWER OF INVESTMENT, *UNIFORM PRUDENT INVESTOR ACT* 1994 *and UNIFORM TRUSTEE INVESTMENT ACT* 1997.

Prudent man of business: The common law STANDARD OF CARE requires trustees, when carrying out administrative or dispositive duties, to take due care of the trust property. The duties of trustees are numerous, and include the proper investment of trust funds and the giving of information to beneficiaries when required and, in some cases, submitting to their direction. Trustees also must comply with directions of the courts as well as refraining from making any profit for themselves out of the trust, unless unauthorised. This is the general standard of care required but in respect of certain circumstances the *Trustee Act* 2000 imposes a statutory duty of care that applies to trusts created both before and after the commencement of the Act. A trustee's duty is to act with such care and skill as is reasonable in the circumstances with regard to any special knowledge or experience that the trustee holds himself out as having, if skilled in a relevant business or profession. This applies under the Act to the exercise of a power of investment, the exercise of a power to acquire land and to make arrangements with an agent, nominee or custodian, or when exercising any power of legal compromise. The statutory duty of care can be excluded or modified by the trust instrument but the common duty of care cannot be excluded and some trustees have special duties, such as those who are trustees in bankruptcy who owe a duty to the bankrupt which differs from the ordinary trustee's duty. The original standard of care was established in the 19th century in England and the United States by the leading case, ***Speight v. Gaunt*** (1883) 22 Ch.D 727:

> '[A] trustee ought to conduct the business of the trust in the same manner that an ordinary man of business would conduct his own ....'

This standard did not imply that trustees would be excused if they were found to have acted 'with equal foolishness in both cases', i.e. if the trustee was as foolish in his own affairs as he was in those of the trust. The rule was amplified in ***Re Whiteley*** (1886) LR 33 Ch.D 347:

> 'The duty of a trustee is not to take such care only as a prudent man would take if he had only himself to consider; the duty rather is to take such care as an ordinary prudent man would take if he were minded to make an investment for the benefit of other people for whom he felt morally bound to provide.'

Psychopathic disorder: A persistent disorder or disability of mind, including a significant impairment of intelligence which results in abnormally aggressive or seriously irresponsible conduct on the part of the person concerned.

PTC: *See* PRIVATE TRUST COMPANY.

Public benefit requirements: The *Charities Act* 2011 detailed the purposes that can be regarded as charitable but, to constitute an effective charity, there is an overriding requirement that all these purposes are carried out for public benefit. There is no presumption, for example, that the relief of poverty, or the advancement of education or religion that are included in the list, are always delivered for the public benefit. The *Charities Act* 2011 requires trustees to report annually on how they have fulfilled the public benefit requirement. The Charity Commission offers general guidance on fulfilling the test and there are two basic principles applicable to all charities. Principle 1 states that there must be an identifiable benefit or benefits. This requires that the benefit must be clear and must be related to the aims of the charity and that the benefits must be balanced against any detriment or harm. Principle 2 requires the benefit to be to the public, or a section of the public, which means that the beneficiaries must be appropriate to the aims of the charity. Benefits must not be unreasonably restricted by geographic or other restrictions where the benefits are only to a section of the public; any private benefits must be incidental. The above principles are subject to interpretation by the Charity Commissioners. The Charity Commission has published requirements relating to, inter alia, the requirement for public benefit reporting.

Public international law: *See* INTERNATIONAL LAW.

Public policy: Rules which apply to transactions or to situations that qualify the legitimacy of particular rules of private law, such as the laws of contracts or trusts whose general application is modified in the interests of public safety or public benefit. For example, property cannot be used to assist a foreign power, or support cannot be given to any activity that is aimed at breaking up a marriage or family structure, or which encourages or assists persons to act fraudulently or to defraud a state of its taxes and other legislative obligations. Another aspect of situations that are against public policy is that no property should be permanently kept out of free circulation for the public good and, to achieve this, an otherwise legitimate settlement of property makes the settlement void as a matter of public policy (*see* PERPETUITY AND ACCUMULATIONS). Generally, therefore, trusts and foundations that contravene public policy are void.

Public Trustee: A corporation established by the *Public Trustee Act* 1906 that may act alone or jointly with any other persons and which has the same duties, powers and liabilities, rights and immunities as an ordinary trustee acting in the same capacity. Technically, a Public Trustee is a corporation sole with perpetual succession, i.e. a corporation established by special Act of Parliament whose constitution is as provided by the Act. As a corporation sole, it is a different species of incorporated body from public limited liability companies. The Public Trustee cannot act for personal reward and may sue and be sued like any other corporation sole and is subject to the control of the courts in the same way as ordinary trustees. The Public Trustee must not accept various types of trusts, such as those exclusively for religious or charitable purposes, or which act solely by way of security for money, or which exists for the benefit of creditors, or the management or carrying on of a business, with exceptions. The Public Trustee may act as a custodian trustee, a judicial trustee or an ordinary trustee and, acting either alone or jointly with another person, may hold land but cannot accept trusteeship other than a settlement governed by a foreign law. The Public Trustee also has a duty to administer small estates unless there is good reason for his refusal; the small size of any trust is not a ground for refusal to act. Any liability incurred by the Public Trustee where liability is established for which he would be personally liable if he were a private trustee, is met out of government funds.

Public trusts: These trusts, which are beneficial to the community at large, do not have specific beneficiaries and therefore, as PURPOSE TRUSTS, would be void under English law unless they qualified as charities. In many offshore jurisdictions purpose trusts are permitted and public trusts would be those purpose trusts which generally were of philanthropic intent or otherwise dedicated to creating a benefit for the public. Where a charity is in the form of a trust, the same rules apply as they do to express private trusts, but with significant differences. The differences, broadly, comprise: a modification of the rules against perpetuity; the possibility of variation if the trust becomes obsolete; and the enforcement and regulation by public authorities and enforcement outside the normal limitation period. Public trusts also are subject to favourable taxation rules. So long as the trust instrument clearly indicates a charitable purpose then the trust cannot fail for uncertainty of objects and the trust property may be applied to such charitable purposes as the trustees may select. In the absence of any workable instructions, specific objects may be supplied by the court or the CHARITY COMMISSIONERS. Since non-charitable purpose trusts cannot be set up in the UK, many philanthropic operations take the form of registered companies, some of which are called 'foundations', although taking the legal form of companies. *See* CHARITIES.

Purchaser for value without notice: A person who acquires land by purchase, i.e. for money or other consideration having monetary value and, at the time of purchase, the purchaser did not know, and had no reason to know, of an encumbrance that affected the land. Such a purchaser, under a rule of equity, is not bound by equitable encumbrances: in particular, the rights of beneficiaries under a trust. Therefore, the purchaser is safe from any claims that a beneficiary may trace his interest into the asset purchased. This robs the beneficiary of a real action against the trust property and his remedy is therefore only a personal action against the trustee. The notice which may affect a purchaser may be ACTUAL, CONSTRUCTIVE or IMPLIED NOTICE. *See* EQUITY'S DARLING.

Purpose foundations: A private foundation whose objects, as they appear in the charter, are not for the benefit of individuals but where the foundation's assets are to be applied for the support of some purpose. Such purposes generally create a valid foundation whether the purposes are approved charities (in the English sense) or for some public or philanthropic good, or whether the purpose is clearly a sporting or private endeavour. In many jurisdictions a purpose foundation can be merely an asset-holding vehicle, particularly shares in the founder's family company, and this is generally perceived as being a valid purpose but, in some jurisdictions, a directly outward- related purpose may be required. *See* DIRECTLY OUTWARD-RELATED FOUNDATION PURPOSES.

Purpose trusts: A trust that does not have an identifiable individual beneficiary but which is set up for a specific purpose. These trusts are frequently authorised under laws in offshore centres although, under English trust law, purpose trusts are unenforceable unless they are set up for charitable purposes. The argument against permitting purpose trusts in English law is that there is no beneficiary capable of enforcing the trust. This statement should not be interpreted in the sense that a purpose trust is devoid of some beneficial effect. The statement merely indicates that no person entitled to that beneficial effect can be identified as acceptable to enforce the trust. This means that there is a procedural gap which prevents enforcement but, in many cases, a purpose trust conforms to the nature of a trust where any definition of a trust is built around a trustee holding property for the benefit of another: the beneficiary. This principle showed through in the decision in ***Denley's Trust Deed, Re*** [1969] 1 Ch 373, when a purpose trust to provide a playing field for a community was permitted, as the community concerned was considered to be the equivalent of beneficiaries (*see* BENEFICIAL PURPOSE). Sometimes a non-charitable purpose trust is called a trust of imperfect obligation. Purpose trusts in English law are often ineffective because 'there are no beneficiaries that are capable of enforcing the trust against the trustees'. There are a few minor exceptions, such as a trust for the care of specific animals and trusts for the provision and upkeep of tombs and monuments. The essence of the argument relating to purpose foundations that there must be an outward-related purpose may become relevant to trusts, although there is no evidence that it has been considered judicially. In jurisdictions which permit purpose trusts, the purpose is frequently simply to hold shares in a private company although the better drafted purpose trusts wrap the pure holding function as a means of providing some general benefit. *See* CHARITABLE TRUSTS *and* PURPOSE FOUNDATIONS.

Q

Qualified person: A person resident in the jurisdiction and associated with a foundation when registration is applied for. A qualified person is usually a service provider who is registered with the foundation Registrar. The criterion for registration is frequently a person experienced in and qualified to operate trust business. The qualified person is a requirement of most foundation laws and functions as the permanent link between the foundation and the Registrar in a jurisdiction. The offices of qualified persons are frequently the registered offices of foundations set up in that jurisdiction.

Qualified privilege: A defence available to persons of authority whose statements might otherwise be considered to be defamatory and which frequently concern matters of public interest made subject to a press comment. In order to qualify for the defence of qualified privilege, a comment must be one that is made at a public meeting or press conference and published without malice as a fair and accurate view permitting a right of reply and further explanation or contradiction. Qualified privilege featured in an English judge's outline of a 10-point test of responsible journalism as being reasonable to confer upon reporters and editors a degree of protection from libel actions even if they could not prove the factual allegations.

Quantum meruit: The term 'As much as he has deserved' has been adopted into the law of contract as describing the amount of recompense that the court will allow to a party under certain circumstances. A quantum meruit can be awarded to a party who confers a benefit on another at that other person's request without remuneration having been agreed beforehand by the parties. The court must decide what constitutes a reasonable amount in each case. It also applies where extra work is performed beyond that for which a contract exists (such as by a building contractor). A quantum meruit for that extra work can be recovered from the other party even though there may be no agreement in respect of that work. Quantum meruit may be applied where a contract in which remuneration had been fixed becomes void. Quantum meruit is also due to a person who renders services under an unenforceable contract, providing the contract was not unlawful. The origin of an action for quantum meruit was based on the intention of the parties that it was reasonable to expect a payment to be made. However, recently the action appears to be included in the practice of making restitution where compensation for unjust enrichment is based upon a quantum meruit calculation. This makes the quantum meruit concept applicable to areas of the law which are not based upon contract. The boundaries of such application have yet to be worked out thoroughly by the courts.

Quantum valebant: A phrase meaning 'as much as they were worth', which applies to the supply of goods. Where A supplies goods to B of a different kind to those contracted for, and B does not reject the goods, then B is not bound to pay the contracted price but should pay the actual value of the goods supplied and which he accepted. A term that applies particularly to the purchase of goods and other moveables and similar in intention to the term QUANTUM MERUIT applied to a reasonable sum payable in return for services.

Quasi: A word implying an approximation to the noun with which this word is associated, i.e. a strict compliance with the definition of the noun is not to be expected but there is a close association with it, i.e. the object concerned shares its qualities and can be regarded as an approximation to the meaning of the noun. For example, a quasi-contract indicates a liability that is not contractual and which is not attributed to any other head of law, but is a liability that is imposed upon a particular person to pay money on the grounds that non-payment of it would confer upon the non-payer an UNJUST ENRICHMENT. In other words, an arrangement that fell short of constituting a legally enforceable contract is nevertheless of a contractual nature and because the relationship is most closely aligned with it and can most easily be described as being quasi- contractual. QUASI-CONTRACT claims can be made under a mistake of fact (the mistake removes a situation from creating a contractual liability) but not a mistake of law; it applies also for money obtained by fraud or extortion. The term is not usually used in connection with trusts or foundations although sometimes a person, who is neither a trustee nor beneficiary but who receives a benefit from the trust, is sometimes called a QUASI-TRUSTEE in order to require a justification for taking the benefit and where it is right that such a person should be answerable as a trustee.

Quasi-contract: A liability that cannot be exclusively referable to any other head of law by which a person is required to pay money to another on the grounds that non-payment would confer an unjust benefit on the party not making the payment. The term has now largely been replaced by the concept of UNJUST ENRICHMENT with a remedy of RESTITUTION. There are numerous categories which could be included within the concept of quasi-contract, such as liability for money paid by the plaintiff at the request of the defendant, including payment by sureties and contribution between joint contractors, liability for necessaries supplied to an infant, money paid under an illegal contract and money paid under a void judgment or compulsion of law and money paid under contract where there is failure of consideration. The term is also used outside the restitutionary context particularly where the courts have sought to define the circumstances in which one party will be in breach of a duty of care in tort giving rise to a liability for an economic loss and where the analysis of the circumstances in tort and contract are substantially the same. These cases are often referred to as quasi-contract cases where the parties did not enter into an enforceable agreement but their relationship gave rise to a liability in tort out of circumstances which might have led to an enforceable contract.

Quasi-easement: A right enjoyed over a plot of land for the benefit of another plot of land where both are owned by the same person and which would constitute an easement if the two plots of land were owned and occupied by different persons. The quasi-easement becomes a full easement if the two plots become separately owned. *See* QUASI.

Quasi-reality: Things that are fixed to real property in law become part of the real property even though they are moveable in themselves, such as title deeds and detachable fittings. *See* QUASI.

Quasi-trustee: A person who receives a benefit from a breach of trust and thereby becomes answerable as a trustee, sometimes called a 'CONSTRUCTIVE TRUSTEE'.

Queen's (or King's) Counsel: Senior barristers and solicitor advocates. Also called 'leading counsel' and known as 'silks' on account of their wearing of silk gowns. The appointment of Queen's Counsel (referred to as QCs or KCs if the monarch is a king) originally arose in the 16th century for rendering assistance in the Sovereign's legal business. Their numbers grew beyond the need for the Sovereign's business and now the title implies a learned and senior practising lawyer, as opposed to all other barristers, who are referred to as

'JUNIOR BARRISTERS' (whatever their age). Until 2004, QCs were appointed by the Queen on advice following an assessment by the Lord Chancellor. Selection is now made by independent representative bodies from the legal professions.

Question of law: *See* QUESTIONS OF FACT.

Questions of fact: One of the three allocations of responsibility that underpin decision-making in legal processes; the other two are questions of law and mixed questions of fact and law. Questions of law are determined by judges or magistrates, whereas questions of fact are determined by the 'trier of fact', which may be the judge or may, in criminal cases, be the jury. Whether a matter falls within the classification of a question of fact or a question of law is itself a matter of law that is determined by the judge and which demonstrates that there is no inherent theoretical method of separating the two. The precise details between a question of fact and a question of law may vary from case to case and from jurisdiction to jurisdiction. In English law the content of foreign law is a question of fact which should be proved by expert evidence unless the point is regarded as being so well known that the court is prepared to take judicial notice of it, such as the fact that roulette is lawful in Monte Carlo. Also, the interpretation of the English language is a question of fact. The meaning of an ordinary word of the English language, unlike the proper construction of a statute, is not a question of law. The construction of a trust deed or foundation document depends upon the general and proper meaning of the words. That is a matter of fact. Then, their combined effect is a question of law. Invariably the action of trustees or a foundation council and their procedure is a question of fact although their interpretation of whether it conforms to the provisions of the instrument or the law itself is a question of law.

Quia Emptores: A statute of 1290, still in force, which forbids the creation of any new tenures, i.e. forbids any SUBINFEUDATION other than by the Crown. Owners wishing to transfer property may not create such new tenures but may only do so by disposing of the tenure which they hold. This is the basis of the modern system of conveying estates. However, a leasehold, creating a tenant and landlord relationship, fell outside the feudal system of which the statute *quia emptores* was designed both to protect and to restrict and this ability to create a leasehold interest is the only way to create a legal estate in land which is subject to the legal freehold estate.

***Quia timet* actions:** An action brought by a person because he is apprehensive of suffering harm from another, or an action brought by a person who has been threatened that he might incur future injury. The relief sought is an injunction, which will only be granted if the applicant can show danger of irreparable loss being imminent. The relief will not be granted if a claim is premature or if the defendant is willing to conform to what has been agreed.

Quiet enjoyment: A term often used in leases and other covenants relating to land, ensuring that the enjoyment of the land by the tenant or other occupier is protected for all usual purposes against interruption by the landlord or others claiming through him. A clause for quiet enjoyment is usually included in a lease. In the transfer of title of land, there was an implied covenant for quiet enjoyment under the *Law of Property Act* 1925, which was modified by the *Law of Property (Miscellaneous Provisions) Act* 1994 where, in the transfer documents, the mere use of the words 'demise' or 'letting' implies a common law-qualified covenant for quiet enjoyment on the landlord's part. A breach of the covenant for quiet enjoyment may lead to a claim for damages under the law of contract.

Quistclose* Trust:** A trust named after the case of ***Barclays Bank Ltd v. Quistclose Investments Ltd [1970] AC 567 in which the bank lent money to the defendant for the sole purpose of paying the defendant's creditors. This was held to be what was called a 'primary temporary trust' for that purpose. If performed (i.e. the creditors were paid), it would result in a loan existing between the bank and the company; if the purpose was not performed then the company would be regarded as holding the money on trust in the bank's favour. This was regarded as an exception to the rule against purpose trusts but raised many questions, such as: where was the beneficial interest in the money when such a trust arose? Was it in the bank or in the company's creditors or, simply, in some form of suspense account without the intervention of a trust as a form of deposit where the company's creditors could compel the company to apply the money in accordance with the reason for the bank making the advance, i.e. in accordance with the company's undertaking to pay the money to satisfy the creditors? The matter was considered again in ***Twinsectra Ltd v. Yardley and others*** [2002] WLR 802 UKHL 12, where the question of beneficial ownership being in suspense was rejected; the money at the disposal of the borrower (the equivalent to the company that borrowed the money in the ***Quistclose*** case) should be kept separate and used only for the particular purpose for which it was loaned. Until used according to that purpose, the money was held on a RESULTING TRUST for the lender. During the existence of this trust the borrower had the power to apply the money for the stated purpose. The position was summarised by Lord Millett in the ***Twinsectra*** case, as follows:

> 'Money advanced by way of loan normally becomes the property of the borrower. He is free to apply the money as he chooses, and save to the extent to which he may have taken security for repayment the lender takes the risk of the borrower's insolvency. But it is well established that a loan to a borrower for a specific purpose where the borrower is not free to apply the money for any other purpose gives rise to fiduciary obligations on the part of the borrower which a court of equity will enforce. In the earlier cases the purpose was to enable the borrower to pay his creditors or some of them, but the principle is not limited to such cases. Such arrangements are commonly described as creating "a Quistclose trust", after the well-known decision of the House in ***Quistclose Investments Ltd v. Rolls Razor Ltd*** [1970] AC 567 [an associated case to that named above] in which Lord Wilberforce confirmed the validity of such arrangements and explained their legal consequences. When the money is advanced, the lender acquires a right, enforceable in equity, to see that it is applied for the stated purpose, or more accurately to prevent its application for any other purpose.' ***Twinsectra Ltd v. Yardley and others*** [2002] WLR 802 UKHL 12.

This decision has created a considerable amount of debate on the trust principles involved in a ***Quistclose*** arrangement.

Quitclaim deed: A legal instrument used in the transfer of land that contains no title covenant and therefore offers the transferor no warranty as to the status of the property. This means that the recipient of the land is only entitled to whatever interest the transferor actually possessed at the time of the transfer, i.e. the transferor does not actually guarantee to own any interest in a property at the time of the transfer. A quitclaim deed offers no warranty and there is no recourse by the recipient over any losses. Quitclaim deeds are most often used to transfer property as gifts, particularly between family members, and are rarely used in a traditional sale. They are used in divorce situations where, for example, a husband acquires the matrimonial home; the wife can execute a quitclaim deed thereby eliminating her interest in the property and transferring full claim to the husband quickly and inexpensively. Quitclaim deeds are also used on the sale of property to recover in a public auction a homeowner's outstanding tax debt and where the creditor claims no interest in the property but is only interested in receiving cash as recompense. Under these circumstances, a purchaser does not have the benefit of any warranty and no legal recourse in the event of any loss due to defect in the title. Hence, property sold under these circumstances often appears to be sold for less than the market value.

Quoted company: A company whose ordinary share capital (equity) is available for purchase or sale on a recognised regulated stock exchange. In the UK a quoted company is defined in terms of the nature of the accounts that the company must prepare and the reports that must be made (Section 385 of the *Companies Act* 2006). The criteria to be a quoted company are twofold. First the company must qualify as a public company, under company law, and that involves the extended accounts and regulatory regime. Second, the company must seek to conform and achieve membership of a recognised stock exchange by complying with the rules of that stock exchange. These rules are, principally, concerned with investor protection, as reflected in the behaviour of the company as far as meetings are concerned and its conduct during any merger transaction. Non-compliance with the rules of the stock exchange can lead to the stock exchange suspending the quotation of the company; a sanction which most companies take care not to incur. In the UK the Financial Services Commission maintains an official list of securities of quoted companies. In the UK companies may be quoted on the official stock exchange list or on the Alternative Investment Market (AIM) whose criteria for quotation are less stringent and which is particularly suitable for companies that have not been trading for as long a period as is required by the official stock exchange. Similar regimes for quoted companies exist within the EU and in the United States for the New York Stock Exchange and NASDAQ.

R

Rack rent: A full, or nearly full, rent equal to the rent expected for the property on the open market or the maximum rent chargeable when it is under some legal restraint.

Ratification: Confirmation. A term applied principally in three areas of the law.

(a) In agency law it applies where a person, 'A', purports to act as the agent for another, the principal, 'P', in relations with a third party at the time when A had no authority to carry out the particular act. Ratification is the adoption by P of A's act whereby P becomes subject to the same legal consequences as if A had operated with actual authority. Ratification in agency law requires that A was in existence and legally competent to perform the act both at the time of the act and at the time of ratification.

(b) In the law of contract where a person does not have the precise actual authority to enter into a contract on behalf of the principal, the defect may be cured by the principal's later ratification of the contract. This ratification may be implied or express. There is no requirement that that ratification be communicated either to the person who acted without authority or to the person with whom he contracted. Ratification may be implied and mere inactivity may be sufficient to constitute ratification provided there is a conscious decision to enter into the contract with knowledge of the material circumstances and the parties' actions must unequivocally show an intention to adopt the act in question.

(c) In international law ratification is the completion of the entry by a state into a treaty obligation through some constitutional act that approves the terms of the treaty; for example, in the UK a treaty is ratified by being adopted by Parliament.

Ratio decidendi: Literally 'the reason for deciding'. The legal basis for a judicial decision that comprises only those statements of legal principles or the rules essential for reaching the decision of the question posed to a judge. Only that essential explanation of the law is used as a precedent. Any other observation on the law given by a judge, although interesting and illustrative, is known as OBITER DICTUM and does not contribute to establishing the decision as a precedent.

Real action: An action by which a person exerts his rights to real property or to rights in connection with the ownership of a ship.

Real estate investment trust (REIT): An investment in REAL PROPERTY in the UK and elsewhere. Despite its name, a REIT in the UK does not necessarily take the form of a trust but is in compliance with the requirements of the UK *Finance Act* 2006. Qualifying investments under these provisions are exempt from UK corporation tax. The principal requirements are that the investment vehicle is resident in the UK and owns at least three UK properties. The properties must be rented to third parties and at least 90% of the profits are distributed to the shareholders, who are taxed on the income as if it was rent which they received directly. These payments are not treated as dividends but as rent.

Real property: FREEHOLD land and incorporeal hereditaments, i.e. land and things attached to land so that they have become part of the land, and rights in land which were heritable. Real property excluded periodic or fixed-term tenancies, which were, before 1925, classified as personal property, leaving real property to be only that property which was litigated about by 'real actions'. From the *Law of Property Act* 1925 freehold and leasehold property were together classified as legal estates in land. The consequence of this was that the law of real property became closer to the law of personal property with a diminution of the difference between leasehold and freehold property. The term 'realty' is sometimes used loosely to mean real property. *See* INCORPOREAL HEREDITAMENT.

Realty: *See* REAL PROPERTY.

Reasonable: A term widely used with many judicial and statutory constructions and definitions in different contexts which generally apply criteria that are within the everyday meaning of 'reasonable'. Reasonable is defined in the *Compact Oxford English Dictionary* as fair and sensible, or as much as is appropriate, or fair, or moderate or fairly. In law, the word is usually used to indicate the expected behaviour of a person in circumstances where that person knows, or ought to know, what is expected. It appears many times but, in association with trusts and wills, etc., the following examples may be quoted. A direction to execute a settlement within six months or 'such further period as my trustees shall think reasonable' was not void for uncertainty (***Re Burton's Settlements, Scott v. National Provincial Bank*** [1955] Ch. 82). A legacy of a 'reasonable income for life' was held to be certain enough to be a valid provision in a will (***Re Golay's Will Trusts, Morris v. Bridgewater*** [1965] 1. W.L.R. 969). In that case the court did not take into account legally unenforceable assurances given by other beneficiaries as reasons why a smaller award should be granted (***Rajabally v. Rajabally*** (1987) 17 Fam. Law 314). Reasonableness is a criterion also applied by statutes, for example, under the *Inheritance (Provision for Family and Dependants) Act* 1975 which requires reasonable financial provision to be made in respect of close members of a family, it was held that the financial needs of an applicant were just one of the factors to be taken into account when determining a claim under that Act (***Re Krubert (dec'd)*** [1996] 3 W.L.R. 959). Also, under the *Trustee Act* 1925, Section 61, the court may relieve a trustee either wholly or partially from personal liability for a breach of trust if the trustee acted:

> '[H]onestly and reasonably, and ought fairly to be excused for omitting to obtain the direction of the court in the manner in which he committed such a breach.'

(The *Companies Act* 1985 also gives a similar power to the court to relieve a director or other officer from liability for negligence or breach of trust). The essence of the reasonableness in these situations is that the trustee is shown to have acted honestly and reasonably. This requires at least that he had to show that he acted as prudently as he would have done in relation to his own affairs. However, each case depends upon its own circumstances. Reasonableness, as a criterion, also appears in the *Trustee Act* 1925, Section 23, which included the loss of protection granted by that Act if a trustee allowed a banker or a solicitor to retain trust money longer than was reasonably necessary. However, the criteria of reasonableness disappeared after the *Trustee Act* 2000, where detailed administrative provisions are now applied and many of the circumstances which were required to be reasonable are now made by written agreement. Reasonableness is applied where a person does not make provision in his will for his dependents or dies intestate. Then, dependents who are not provided for out of the estate in accordance with the intestacy rules can apply to the court for reasonable financial provision; a spouse or civil partner may do so even though he or she already has enough for maintenance.

Reasonable financial provision: *See* REASONABLE.

Receiver: A person appointed by a court to ensure that property can be made available to the person(s) properly entitled to it according to the law or a court judgment. A receiver is an officer of the court and the court determines his remuneration. A receiver is likely to be appointed where it is just or convenient that he should intervene because of a person's incompetence or because the proper receipt of money by a person is put in jeopardy. This power, contained in Section 37 of the *Senior Courts Act* 1981, may be used to recover rents and profits from real property or to retrieve personal property in the execution of a judgment. A receiver may be appointed until such time as the matters become clear between the parties; for example, when there is a need to settle financial matters on the dissolution of a partnership. In connection with trusts, a receiver would only be appointed over individual trustees' affairs or under the *Insolvency Act* 1986 in the event that a trustee became bankrupt. With a foundation, a receiver may be appointed in a way analogous to the appointment of a receiver over a company's affairs. Many foundation laws do not make specific provision for the appointment of receivers (in all likelihood due to the frequent prohibition on foundations engaging in trading operations) but, generally, the possibility exists if a court finds it necessary to do so. *The Foundations (Guernsey) Law* 2012 states that in connection with the MIGRATION of an overseas foundation into Guernsey, any incoming foundation will not be registered that is bankrupt or over the assets of which a liquidator, receiver or administrator has been appointed. A mortgagee may appoint a receiver of the mortgaged property if empowered to do so by the mortgage deed or by a separate instrument when money becomes due from a mortgaged property. A receiver may be authorised under mortgage documentation or a debenture or appointed by the court to realise assets which have been charged. Generally a court may appoint receivers under certain other circumstances, especially where it is necessary to protect property during the course of litigation.

Recitals: Statements in a deed or in an agreement or other formal instrument, including enactments, which introduce and explain what is contained in the instrument and may either be narrative recitals which set forth the facts on which the instrument is based, or the introductory recitals which explain the motive for the subsequent operative part. In trust deeds the recitals state that the person named as settlor intends to form a trust on the terms which follow for the benefit of the persons also named in the operative part of the deed. This is a useful preamble as it can be used in evidence, if necessary, that the intention of the person entering the deed, the settlor, was to set up a trust. Although not conclusive, it is strong evidence that it was the intention from the beginning to set up a trust.

Recognition and enforcement of foreign judgments: An aspect of the CONFLICT OF LAWS that is relevant when a judgment of a court needs to be enforced in another jurisdiction. To succeed, the foreign court must have jurisdiction over the matter and the appellant must be able to show at that foreign court that the judgment was obtained according to the law where the action was brought. The appellant then has to approach the court as if presenting a new action, i.e. a court action may be required to secure the foreign court's recognition of the judgment obtained elsewhere and to order its enforcement. This lengthy process is now abbreviated under treaty provisions. For example, with trusts, the Hague Convention provides for the enforcement of judgments concerning trusts in countries that have acceded to the

Convention. Also, apart from the Hague Convention on Trusts, the EU Directive 44/2001 cuts across the normal public international law regimes and purports to simplify recognition and enforcement. *See* HAGUE CONVENTION ON TRUSTS *and* EUROPEAN REGULATION ON JURISDICTION.

***Recognition of Trusts Act* 1987:** Gave effect in the United Kingdom to the *Hague Convention on the Law Applicable to Trusts and on Their Recognition. See* HAGUE CONVENTION.

Reconversion: A process by which a prior constructive conversion in which real property is regarded as personal property, or vice versa, is annulled and the property restored, as far as the law is concerned, to its original status. For example, real estate devised to A upon trust to sell and to pay the proceeds to B means that the real property by virtue of being held in an ABSOLUTE TRUST is constructively converted into personal estate, i.e. the real property is regarded as personal property, e.g., money. Reconversion will take place if B expresses a wish to take the property as land, i.e. the conversion in law by which the land is treated as personal property (cash) is undone. The result is that the property is reconverted and A is then required to convey the land to B accordingly. There is a limit on how far reconversion can go. Reconversion cannot be exercised to prejudice other persons such as joint owners. Reconversion may take place by operation of the law where property that was originally directed to be converted comes into the possession of the person absolutely entitled to it. If that person would prefer personal property to real property then he is in the position where he is able to bring about the conversion from real property to personal property, i.e. he can sell the land. Reconversion, under the diminished application of the doctrine of conversion, can now largely be considered as redundant but may still be relevant in considering old wills.

Rectification: Where a document does not correctly express the intention of the parties then it may be corrected with the consent of the court, which will be careful to exercise great caution and act only on the most cogent evidence. Documents subject to rectification may be conveyances, leases, contracts and certain registers of companies. If the parties agree, rectification can take place without the court's consent provided the rights of third parties are not prejudiced. Rectification is one method of correcting a trust deed which does not represent the settlor's intention. Rectification must be distinguished from rescission; the two doctrines are frequently confused. *See* RESCISSION.

Rectification of will: The court has power, under the *Administration of Justice Act* 1982, Section 20(1)(a), to rectify a will that fails to carry out the intentions of the testator. In order to permit this, the court must be satisfied that the failure was caused by a clerical error or through a misunderstanding of the testator's instructions. The expression 'clerical error' in Section 20(1)(a) of the Act has neither a technical nor a precise nor well-established meaning; it is capable of covering a mistake out of a relatively routine office function. Recently the Supreme Court held that where husband and wife made identical wills but the solicitor handed the wrong will to each spouse to sign this situation could be remedied by rectification. The wife's will was signed by the husband. The error did not come to light until the second death, that of the husband. The children of the marriage claimed that the will of the husband was invalid. Eventually the Supreme Court held that there was no doubt that the signed will could not be hers; the husband had the intention that what he had signed should be his will. The mistake of the solicitor was judged to be a clerical error and capable of rectification by the court. This case, ***Marley v. Rawlings & Anor*** [2014] UKSC 2, provides an opportunity for such mistakes to be remedied by rectification where otherwise the matter would have been dealt with in negligence. Application for rectification must generally be made within six months of the date on which the grant of representation was first taken out.

Red Cross trusts: DISCRETIONARY TRUSTS with numerous beneficiaries, one of which is a well-known charity such as the Red Cross. There is no real intention that the body chosen (the Red Cross in this example) will receive benefit from the trust, it being assumed that the discretion of the trustees will be exercised to dispose of the trust assets in favour of other named discretionary beneficiaries, but the presence of a named international organisation in the documentation gives credence to the arrangement by designating the organisation to receive the trust assets if they are not previously distributed. This is done with the intention of avoiding any resulting trust arising back to the settlor if the funds are not distributed, the intention being that the settlor wishes to emphasize his clear intention of setting up a trust by providing that in no circumstances is the settlor ever in a position of receiving any benefit from the trust if the list of real beneficiaries is exhausted before all the trust assets are distributed. Trusts of this nature are frequently called 'Red Cross Trusts' whatever the nature of the body elected as the default beneficiary.

Redeem up, foreclose down: The practice of discontinuing a MORTGAGE by a mortgagee where there are successive mortgages on the same property. A mortgagee, who is second or below in the order of priority, may then buy out or redeem an earlier mortgagee so as to take his place higher in the order of priority. Where other persons consider that they may suffer by such an action, they may state their objection in court. Otherwise, mortgages may be redeemed out of court. The purpose of redeeming up is to remove a prior mortgagee from having an interest in the property and removing the rights of a prior mortgagee to foreclose if the mortgagor does not perform as required by the mortgage. Foreclosing down refers to the process by which a mortgagee exercises his rights under the mortgage by recovering the property on default by the mortgagor (i.e. failure to pay interest or capital as agreed). This can be illustrated by considering a situation where there is more than one mortgage over a property. Thus, the first mortgagor lending, say, 70% of the purchase price of the property mortgaged stands in priority to the second mortgagee, who advances, say, 20% of the price of the property (i.e. on a second mortgage). If the mortgagor fails to fulfil the repayment terms or other clauses in favour of the first mortgagee, the first mortgagee can then foreclose and seize the property, usually for the purposes of resale. This means that the second mortgagee may not recover anything unless the resale price obtained is sufficient to repay both the outstanding loan from the first mortgagee and then leave sufficient to recompense the second mortgagee. If any money is then available after paying the mortgagee it is returned to the mortgagor.

Redemption: Literally meaning to 'buy back', which applies where a person, having the right to do so, pays off a mortgage debt on property and thereby is entitled to be released from the mortgage deed and to hold the property free of the debt. *See* EQUITY OF REDEMPTION.

Re-domiciliation: *See* MIGRATION.

Referential settlement: A settlement that incorporates by reference terms of an earlier settlement, either with or without variations. If the two settlements are inconsistent, a referential settlement may give rise to difficult questions relating to the precise meaning of the documents when taken together.

Register: A book, file or similar repository where formal records are maintained of acts or minutes to which recourse will be had to determine questions of fact. For example, a register of charges is where a company must keep records of all charges and mortgages and, similarly, a register of directors and secretaries is a record of company officers. Large and complex trusts may maintain a register of decisions of trustees where additional matters, such as the minutes of the meeting of trustees, are recorded. This is an essential means of securing consistency in the management of trusts as trustees and others change from time to time and it may be necessary to determine what decisions were made over a number of years. This is frequently neglected to the embarrassment of all, should there be a need to change trustees and the new trustees need to determine exactly what action the previous trustees have taken and what benefits have been conferred on beneficiaries. Similarly, with charitable trusts, which operate more like companies, the register of minutes is even more important as this may be challenged by the CHARITY COMMISSIONERS or other official supervisors of charities. Similar attention to record-keeping is required by foundation councils, the responsibility for which may be devolved upon a foundation secretary whose duties need to be specified in the foundation's regulations or subsidiary rules and are likely to be similar to those of a company secretary.

Registered agent: An individual or a firm resident in a jurisdiction where, under the local law, that person, individual or corporate, is registered as a FIT AND PROPER person to conduct corporate, trust or foundation business. A registered agent is frequently required by law in an offshore jurisdiction in connection with the setting up of trusts and foundations to undertake the responsibility for compliance.

Registration: A process by which the law requires that stated events are placed in official records maintained by the authorities and which may be available for inspection by the public. Trusts in many jurisdictions require no registration either in connection with the structure of the trust or the formation. In some offshore centres, the mere registration of a trust and its name is recorded but no other information as to the beneficiaries or settlor is placed on the register. With foundations registration may be necessary to obtain incorporation. In some jurisdictions registration of a foundation is merely evidence of such formation where the charter is registered and available for public inspection. With registered companies the basic constitutional documents, the Memorandum and Articles and various subsidiary matters, are registered, such as the register of directors and company secretaries, share capital and charges over the company's assets. All of these are available for public inspection. Partnerships, apart from registering the partnership name as a trading name, require no registration of their constitutional matters. Registration of some sort is usually required in order to engage in business involving financial matters.

Registration of trustees: In the UK the registration is necessary under the *Money Laundering Regulations* 2007, Regulation 25(i), of trustees and company service providers who are not already registered with their professional supervisory bodies in compliance with the *Proceeds of Crime Act* 2002 or the *Terrorism Act* 2000. Only persons registered in one form or another may act as a trustee or as a company service provider with the exclusion of members of the public who set up private trusts and others whose trustee activities are incidental (as defined) to other commercial activities.

Reinsurance: A method used by insurers to protect themselves against large, unmanageable liabilities arising from claims on insurance policies to which they are committed. Reinsurance is effected by entering into contracts with other insurers who agree to pay, or share the costs of, any claim if called upon to pay out under the contract of insurance so reinsured. This is particularly important in the case of marine insurance, where reinsurance receives statutory recognition in the *Marine Insurance Act* 1906, Section 91(1), whereby liability for the loss or damage to a vessel is spread across a large part of the marine insurance industry. Reinsurance is also a prevalent practice with fire insurance companies.

REIT: *See* REAL ESTATE INVESTMENT TRUST.

Release: A term with numerous and sometimes imprecise meanings. Generally, release refers to a gift or the renunciation of a right of action which is sometimes used with a technical meaning; for example, when applied to persons in mere possession of property who become the legal owners, i.e. possessors of land, and are then converted into the freeholders. Also a term sometimes used, perhaps inaccurately, to describe where trust property, the legal ownership of which exists in trustees, is released to beneficiaries by the trustees conveying or transferring their rights to the beneficiary. Where trustees transfer property to the beneficiaries, the trustees are released from their obligations under the trust. The term is applied to the formal discharge given by beneficiaries to trustees under the winding up of a trust. Releases are usually given under seal but, in respect of trustees and their beneficiaries, a seal may not always be required and a simple receipt may be adequate unless a deed is used.

Relevant property trust: A UK tax term which, from April 2008, means any trust that is not an interest in possession trust, an AGE 18-TO-25 TRUST or a trust established for a bereaved minor or disabled person. A relevant property trust is subject to inheritance tax and is taxed on creation or whenever there is a distribution to a beneficiary and, thereafter, on each 10th anniversary of the date of settlement.

Relief: An appellant's action to require a defendant to remedy a wrong before any harm has occurred. Relief includes an order from the court to prevent a threatened wrong, such as a potential breach of trust, or for the enforcement of a right, such as the exercise by the trustees of their discretion. Relief may be sought in addition to damages or cash compensation. Another meaning of relief is the leniency that may be exercised by a court; for example, under the *Trustee Act* 1925, Section 61, where the court may relieve a trustee wholly or partly from personal liability for a breach of trust if he:

> '[A]cted honestly and reasonably, and ought fairly to be excused for the breach of trust and for omitting to obtain the directions of the court in the matter in which he committed such breach.'

Relief is also granted to a trustee who is a beneficiary who receives or retains trust assets that subsequently appear to be excessive and beyond his true entitlement. The relief is to make the trustee, after the limitation period, liable only to repay the trust the excess over his legitimate entitlement and not the whole amount which may be claimed by a new party. This relief, under the *Limitation Amendment Act* 1980, is only available if the trustee acted honestly and reasonably in making the initial distribution.

Religious charities: *See* CHARITY.

Rem, action in: A claim made against property or the proceeds of property that is relevant to the claim made. For example, a beneficiary who has exhausted the possibilities of personal actions against trustees for breach of trust can pursue an action in respect of the trust property even after it has left the ownership of the trustees. Thus, an action IN REM allows a substantially wider range of remedies than a personal action against the trustees, or allows trust assets to be followed or traced into the hands of a third party under certain circumstances. Outside of trusts, actions in rem are particularly brought in connection with shipping and Admiralty matters. A beneficiary under a foundation who has been allotted a share in the foundation assets is likely to be able to bring an action in rem for the recovery of those assets. *See* TRACING *and* FOLLOWING.

Remainder: An interest in land that comes into possession after a prior private interest ends. For example, in a trust where A settles land on B for life and then on C in fee simple: C's interest is in remainder until B dies. Since C's interest is not a fee simple absolute in possession, it is an equitable interest. A settlement may create several successive remainders in favour of different persons who are called remaindermen. The nature of a FEE SIMPLE ABSOLUTE IN POSSESSION means there can be no remaindermen.

Remainderman: A person entitled to an estate after the expiry of a previous interest. *See* REMAINDER.

Remarriage and revocation of wills: A will is revoked, i.e. made void, by marriage or remarriage or entry into a civil partnership by the testator unless the will is made expressly in the expectation of a particular marriage or civil partnership. Where there is a mutual will, expressed to be valid until the death of the first mutual testator, the mutual will will be revoked by the subsequent marriage or entry into civil partnership of one of the testators during the life of the other. *See* REVOCATION.

Remedial constructive trust: A concept that a constructive trust can arise in favour of a successful litigant to designate the assets owned by an unsuccessful defendant as a source of damages or compensation awarded by a court. Such a remedial constructive trust would arise independently of any court order and depends on the facts of the judgment. At one time it was thought that a constructive trust might arise as a remedy and be imposed whenever justice or good conscience required, such as over assets awarded by a court; a remedial constructive trust would be regarded as arising in favour of the person to whom the assets were awarded. It is now considered that this type of trust can arise only in accordance with an order of the court. The current practice in English law is that the prevention of inequitable and unconscionable conduct is treated as UNJUST ENRICHMENT leading to an order for RESTITUTION. This now precludes the recognition of a remedial constructive trust in English law. *See* INSTITUTIONAL TRUSTS.

Remedy: The means by which a violation of a right is prevented from having an adverse effect on the person against whom it is perpetrated. This may be either by prevention, compensation or other redress of the violation. Remedies fall into four categories; by the act of the party who suffers an injury or loss, such as (i) self-defence, distress and seizure, etc., or (ii) by the operation of the law, or (iii) by agreement between the parties by restitution or arbitration, or (iv) by judicial remedy following an action or application for relief. The first three categories are called extra-judicial and the latter a judicial remedy.

Remittance basis: A method by which a person who is resident in the UK, but not domiciled there, is subject to income tax only on the income acquired outside the UK that is remitted to the UK. For the first six years a resident non-domiciled person can be taxed on this basis and thereafter those who have been resident for seven out of nine tax years can continue on this basis if a yearly tax charge of £30,000 is paid in each tax year (*Finance Act* 2000, Schedule 7). For a non-domiciled person who has been resident in the UK for 12 of the previous 14 years the figure is increased to £50,000 per year. This annual charge is in addition to any tax payable by a non-domiciled person on investments and gains from UK investments, or on the benefits of a UK employment, or from a UK-based company. During the remittance basis period any income from a foreign source that is not remitted to the UK is not subject to UK income tax. Capital gains arising from a disposal of foreign assets by a non-domiciled person are subject to UK capital gains tax only to the extent that those gains are remitted to the taxpayer in the UK. For this purpose remittance means the transfer of money or the remittance of the proceeds of the sale of goods purchased abroad.

Remoteness of damage: A test that assesses whether there is adequate connection between a wrong and damage to justify a claim by the person who suffered the damage for compensation against the wrongdoer as defendant. In other words, a defendant must be sufficiently close to the cause of the appellant's loss that he is reasonably considered to be liable to pay compensation for all or part of the loss. The criterion is that a reasonable man, knowing what he knew or ought to have known, would have come to the conclusion that, in the usual course of events, damage would have followed his actions. A breach of trust by trustees of the trustees' standard duty of care is sufficiently close to any loss that no argument on remoteness of damages is likely to be a successful defence. A term used mainly in connection with assessing liability in the law of tort, in particular with negligence, and in the law of contract.

Remuneration of members of a foundation council: There is no extensive, generally applicable law on this subject but a comparison with the position of directors of companies suggests that there is an absence of an inherent right to remuneration for members of a foundation council and therefore a need for a particular provision allowing for remuneration in the foundation charter or regulations.

Remuneration of trustees: The general principle is that a trustee is not entitled to any remittance or allowance for his trouble or for loss of time, or to any payment for professional or other services. Exceptions to this rule, based on the principle of preventing a conflict between duty and personal interest, are extensive. Particularly relevant is where there is a charging clause in the trust instrument which traditionally allows that trustees, in carrying out professional duties (such as conveyancing real property by a solicitor), may charge their usual professional charges. This exception is associated with a trustee's entitlement to be indemnified out of the trust assets against costs and expenses incurred in carrying out the trusteeship. *See* Beddoe Orders. The rule is a general rule that applies to all fiduciary positions; for example, a director of a company is not entitled to remuneration for services rendered as a director unless there is a provision in the company's Articles of Association authorising remuneration. The *Trustee Act* 2000 modified the general position of trustees and where there is a remuneration clause in the trust instrument this is now treated as remuneration for services rather than as a gift. Also, the previous provision that a trustee could charge for professional services was interpreted strictly, resulting in no remuneration being allowed for such parts of his duties as were capable of being performed by a lay trustee. This restrictive interpretation has now been removed and, generally, a trustee is now entitled to receive reasonable remuneration out of the trust assets for services provided to, or on behalf of, the trust even to the extent of remuneration to lay trustees. This does not apply to charitable trusts or to sole trustees, nor does it apply where there is a remuneration clause in the trust instrument. A trustee charging for his services may be required to obtain the other trustees' agreement in writing. A further exception is where the beneficiaries (where they are all SUI JURIS) can enter into a contract with a trustee for the trustee's compensation. This is interpreted stringently by the court. The court also has inherent jurisdiction to authorise a prospective or existing trustee to receive remuneration if there is no provision in the trust instrument. The court's jurisdiction must balance the principle that the office of a trustee is generally gratuitous on the one hand and, on the other hand, that the trust should be well administered.

Rent: The consideration paid for the occupancy or use of property contained in a lease or other contract between landlord and tenant or landlord and licensee. Usually applied in connection with the occupancy of real property, but the term frequently applies under long-term contracts for the usage of personal property, such as machinery and motor cars, where the arrangement is called a 'lease' and the payments made under that lease are colloquially referred to as rent. Rent is usually in the form of money but it may be any other form of property or services. Where property, especially real property, is supplied to the use of another in return for long service or out of family affiliations, it is frequently achieved through entering into a normal lease arrangement and, where the rent is of nominal value (but essentially of some value in order to constitute consideration) under the contractual element in the arrangement; the payment of a rose at midsummer is a well-known example of such nominal rent.

Rent charge: Periodical payment of money charged on land. Under the *Rent Charges Act* 1977, Section 2(1), the creation of rent charges is now prohibited both in law and equity subject to a few exceptions. Existing rent charges are being extinguished over a period of 60 years. Land subject to a rent charge is bound to provide a sum of money for the benefit of the current owner. This is different from a contractual right to make a payment, as a rent charge is a right IN REM, i.e. it is a right of property and not a personal contractual obligation.

Renvoi: A principle of the CONFLICT OF LAWS applied to resolve the ambiguity in a reference to the law of a country, such as to the 'law of England' or to the 'law of Italy'. Such a reference in its narrowest sense means the domestic law of the country, i.e. the law applied where there is no foreign element. In a wider sense, the law includes the country's conflict of law rules, i.e. the law of England would mean whatever law an English court would apply. For example, if a British person died intestate while domiciled in Italy leaving some moveables in England, a court may have to decide to whom these moveables should pass. An English court might simply apply the domestic law of Italy and decide in favour of the law of the deceased's domicile in accordance with Italian domestic law. However, the court may examine the situation more deeply and, in applying Italian law, include the Italian conflict of laws which may result in the application of the law of the nationality of the deceased being applied. This will then require the English court to decide whether it is English domestic law which applies or some other law, such as whether by the law of England the deceased's nationality has any part to play. Renvoi is the passing of a court's assessment from one jurisdiction to another and the reference back has been called the theory of total or double renvoi. Complications and variations can be complex. For example, an English court, having the matter referred back to it to apply the law of the deceased's domicile, might find that the law of Scotland applies. The question then arises as to whether it is purely the domestic law of Scotland or whether the conflict of laws regime of Scotland applies. The doctrine of renvoi has been subject to immense literature and in recent years has attracted rather little judicial attention in England. But the High Court of Australia in ***Neilsen v. Overseas Projects Corporation of Victoria Limited*** [2005] HCA 54 recently gave little support to the existence of the renvoi principles. Dicey, Morris and Collins in the *Conflict of Laws* (15th edn, Vol. 1) refer to the history of renvoi in the doctrine of English law as the history of a chapter of accidents. The English renvoi doctrine has been applied principally in deciding the validity of wills and in cases of intestate succession. Outside the field of succession it has been applied only to legitimation by subsequent marriage. The doctrine is not appropriate to the construction of wills or settling disputes in contract or torts. Many of the decisions of the English courts on the renvoi principle may no longer be applicable, the need having been replaced by international conventions and by the harmonisation of rules of enforcement and recognition. In connection with trusts, the Hague Convention avoids many of the conflicts involved and supports the existing substantial argument supporting the non-application of renvoi to testamentary trusts of moveables. *See* CHOICE OF LAW *and* HAGUE CONVENTIONS.

Reparation claims: A term used in some jurisdictions for claims by beneficiaries that trustees should make good the harm suffered as a consequence of their breach of duty. These claims depend upon the assertion that the trustees have committed a wrong, for example, by failing to follow the requisite duty of care by negligently making an unauthorised investment which declines in value or that fails to strike a fair balance between a life tenant (who is interested in income) and a remainderman (who is interested in capital). Beneficiaries must show that the loss has been caused by the trustees' breach of duty using a 'but for' causation test, i.e. that the harm would not have been incurred 'but for' the action of the trustee. In other words, the harm was a direct cause of the trustee's breach of trust. In Canadian courts claims are subject to the principle of *NOVUS ACTUS INTERVENIENS* and beneficiaries who behave unreasonably after becoming aware that the trustees cannot be trusted will be judged to have incurred the loss because of their unreasonable behaviour and that the loss had not been caused as a result of the breach by the trustees.

Replacement and removal of members of a foundation council: The power to remove or replace members of a foundation council can be contained in the foundation charter or regulations where the power may be given either to the founder, as one of his reserved powers, or to the protector or guardian, or to the foundation council itself.

Replacement of trustees/Removal of trustees: The removal and replacement of trustees are two associated topics. Under the *Trustee Act* 1925, Section 36, considerable powers exist to appoint new trustees subject to any contrary provision in the trust instrument. These powers generally apply when vacancies arise through natural causes, death, incapacity or removal under a power in the trust instrument. The power to appoint new trustees was considerably extended by the *Trusts of Land and Appointment of Trustees Act* 1996, where the beneficiaries are entitled to appoint new trustees or to require existing trustees to retire. In addition, the court has considerable fallback powers under the *Judicial Trustees Act* 1896 where, on application by the settlor, trustee or beneficiary, the court may appoint any fit and proper person who is an officer of the court and is nominated in the application to be a judicial trustee. The court also has power to appoint the public trustee, who may be appointed as a new or additional trustee even though there is a contrary clause in the trust instrument. The most useful means of replacing trustees remains where there is a specific power in the trust instrument and such power may be conferred upon the trust protector, if there is one. A settlor, unless he has reserved the power to do so, has no power to appoint trustees after the trust is set up unless any of the circumstances that may be specified in the trust instrument applies. The power to appoint new trustees is a fiduciary one and this suggests that the donee of the power, probably the settlor, should not appoint himself; however, the question rarely arises due to statutory powers.

Report, law: *See* LAW REPORTS.

Representative action: Actions brought by one person on behalf of others where they have identical interests in a claim. This is provided for in the UK by Part 19 of the *Civil Procedures Rules* 1998. Thus, an action against trustees for breach of trust where there is a wide range of beneficiaries, each with identical interests, could be the subject of a representative action where one or several of the beneficiaries brings an action on behalf of the others and where the judgment would apply to the whole class of beneficiaries. This is only relevant where the grounds for the action are identical.

Repugnancy: A doctrine that renders void clauses in a will or other documents if they are contrary or inconsistent with a separate statement; for example, if A grants land to B in fee simple, any subsequent expression of a condition that B shall not alienate the land is void, as such a condition is contrary to and repugnant with the concept of fee simple. This rule of construction depends upon whether the matter is contained in a deed or in a will. The difference is that in a will, the latter of two contradictory clauses prevails but in other writings the earlier statement is followed. Therefore, if assets are transferred to trustees or to a foundation (by a deed) and these transfers are made absolutely, such as the transfer of land in fee simple or a transfer of securities made by completing the necessary transfer procedures, any later restriction as to the fate or use of these assets is repugnant and therefore void. The principle may be summarised as follows:

> 'If the whole of the beneficial interest is given to one beneficiary, subject to the right of other beneficiaries to an uncertain part of it, the direction as to the uncertain part fails and leaves the principal beneficiary entitled to the whole.' (Snell's Equity, 33rd edn at 599)

See ABSOLUTE GIFT *and* LASSENCE *v.* TIERNEY, RULE IN (1849) 1 Mac & G 552.

Rescission: A term used where one of the parties is entitled to avoid a transaction and elects to do so by giving notice of his intention to the other party. A frequent use of rescission is where a contract is entered into by a fraud or misrepresentation by the other party. The term may also be used in connection with settlements in the event that there is a mistake that is not purely factual but which is connected with the legal effect of the terms of the settlement, despite the proposition that mistakes of law cannot be relieved in equity. Under these circumstances a settlement or a trust can be set aside on the basis that the concept that equity will never relieve against mistakes of law was a principle that was too widely stated. Rescission must be distinguished from RECTIFICATION; they are two distinct remedies with different threshold requirements.

Reserved judgment: A judgment that is not given immediately by the judge after a court has heard the evidence and argument. The judge gives his judgment after a period of reflection.

Reserved powers trusts: A name given to a trust in which the settlor reserves powers or interests to himself or to a third party. This is not a legal term but is applied particularly in the Cayman Islands since the introduction of the *Trusts (Amendment) (Immediate Effect and Reserved Powers) Law* 1998, which confirmed that the reservation or grant by the settlor of certain powers, if used according to the provisions of the law, do not invade upon the core principles of a trust so as to invalidate it. The law and the trusts formed thereunder confirm the common law limits of powers to administer a trust being in the hands of persons other than the trustees. These trusts are useful in the reservation of investment powers, particularly where a settlor wishes to deal directly with brokers and others in making trust investments.

Resettlement: The action by trustees who have an express power of advancement in the trust deed or who can take advantage of a statutory power (as in Section 32 of the *Trustee Act* 1925) to make a new trust for a beneficiary under an existing trust. An essential element in the validity of this power is that the trustees consider their action to be for the benefit of the beneficiary of the existing trust, although the benefit need not be connected personally to the beneficiary himself and the power of resettlement is not dependent upon achieving some special purpose associated with the beneficiary. For example, tax mitigation that will benefit other beneficiaries is sufficient. The new trust need not be in the same jurisdiction as the trust from which the funds were obtained but resettlement should be done with caution where the beneficiary is about to take an absolute interest, although a capital gains tax advantage may justify the trustees action. Although doubts have been expressed as to whether the statutory power on advancement in Section 32 of the *Trustee Act* 1925 gives sufficient power to resettle an entire trust, the current view supports resettlement if it is clear that the benefit gained is sufficiently broad to have been achievable by a less comprehensive exercise of the power. The trust property advanced is treated as leaving the original trust entirely so that the new trustees then exercise their own powers and not powers delegated to them by the old trustees. The beneficiary's interest is paramount but this does not necessarily make a new settlement invalid by the inclusion of the wife and descendants of the beneficiary in the new settlement (*Lewin on Trusts*, 19th edn at 1467-68). It may be difficult to decide whether a new settlement has been created, especially as the question usually arises in connection with taxation. The inclination is that settlors and beneficiaries exposed to a tax claim under the original settlement rely on a purported resettlement as a completely new situation free from the tentacles of the tax authority. Consequently, most attempted resettlements are subject to a challenge by the tax authorities. The Revenue in the UK, particularly, considers that in connection with capital gains tax an appointment or advancement does not create a new settlement if the appointment is revocable or if the new settlement does not exhaust the assets of the old settlement. Settlements which contain a general power for the trustees to resettle may be a useful provision to avoid consequences of the *Matrimonial Causes Act* 1973 for ANCILLARY RELIEF by making the original settlor remote from the beneficiaries in the new settlement. It is a matter of construction. Resettlement was frequently practised with entailed interest to perpetuate a family's interest in an estate of land.

Resident: A term with significant application in determining liability for taxation. The term is defined in connection with international tax by Article 4(1) of the OECD Model Tax Convention on Income and of Capital, which states that:

'The term "resident of a Contracting State" means any person who, under the laws of that State, is liable to tax therein by reason of his domicile, residence, place of management or any other criterion of a similar nature, and also includes that State and any political sub-division or local authority thereof. This term, however, does not include any person who is liable to tax in that State in respect only of income from sources in that State or capital situated therein.'

The Commentary on this Article gives the various functions of the concept and lists three cases of importance: (a) in determining a Convention's personal scope of application; (b) in solving cases where double taxation arises in consequence of double residence; and (c) in solving cases where double taxation arises as a consequence of taxation in the state of residence and the state of source or situs. As far as individuals are concerned, a person is considered a resident by the jurisdiction in which he has his domicile or residence by a presence of a specified number of days spent in that jurisdiction in a tax year. In the UK a person is resident in the UK who spends 183 or more days in the UK in a tax year (*Income Tax Act* 2007, Section 83). Any person who qualifies for residence in the UK is subject to a comprehensive liability for tax. Persons other than individuals, such as companies, foundations and, for this purpose, trusts, are deemed to be resident only in the state where the effective place of management is situated. The comprehensive liability means, for example, that a person or company which is resident in the UK is liable for tax arising anywhere in the world, and a person who is not resident in the UK is subject to UK income tax or UK corporation tax only on income arising from a source within the UK. As far as capital gains is concerned, a person resident in the UK is subject to UK capital gains tax or corporation tax on capital gains on gains arising from the disposal of assets anywhere in the world. A person not resident in the UK is not subject to UK tax unless the gain is made on the disposal of an asset of the UK's resident's permanent establishment. Also, every company incorporated within the UK is considered to be resident there under a statutory anti-tax avoidance measure (*Finance Act* 1998, Section 66(1)) and every company that has its central control and management in the UK is considered resident there.

Res judicata: Meaning the matter has already been adjudicated and it is therefore outside the normal practice of the court to bring second proceedings on the same matter. Where a matter has been finally adjudicated in a court of competent jurisdiction, it may not be reopened or challenged by the original parties or their successors. It does not preclude an appeal or challenge to the jurisdiction of the court. It may frequently arise in international trust cases where a matter has been adjudicated upon by a court in one jurisdiction but beneficiaries or other interested parties in another jurisdiction would like the matter to be considered by their own court. The plaintiff or respondent is estopped from bringing the matter again on the basis that it is desirable that litigation should end between the parties and that a person should not vexatiously be pursued in litigation in regard to matters which have already been decided. *See* ESTOPPEL.

Restitutio in integrum: A phrase taken from civil law that means the rescinding of a contract or transaction so as to place the parties to it in the same position with respect to each other as they occupied before the contract was made or the transaction took place. The term is sometimes used in English law to denote the equitable relief of rescinding contracts on the grounds of fraud where both parties can be restored to their original position.

Restitution: Return of property to the owner or person who is entitled to possession following an unjust transmission of either property or money. Restitution is ordered so that the person who unjustifiably is enriched, or retains an unjust advantage, does not retain that advantage. In certain circumstances the courts may make a restitution order in respect of the property. The concept of UNJUST ENRICHMENT resulting in a possible order of restitution now occupies a large part of the jurisdiction relating to contracts and to claims against trustees for breaches of trust (the *Powers of Criminal Courts (Sentencing) Act* 2000). This is achieved by a Restitution order. This is an order made under the powers of the *Criminal Courts (Sentencing) Act* 2002, Section 148, against a person in possession or control of stolen goods. By the terms of the order, that person is required to restore them to the person entitled to recover them or to pay to that person a sum of money not exceeding the value of the stolen goods. The word 'restitution' is also used in criminal law where a person who is convicted of a criminal offence relating to stolen property is required to make restitution to the lawful owner.

Restraint of marriage: An attempt by offering an advantage such as a favourable contract, or benefits under a trust or foundation, to restrain a person from marrying. Marriage being an institution encouraged by the state means that any such arrangement is void where the object is to restrain a person from marrying. This rule also applies if there is any clause in a trust instrument by which a beneficiary can be awarded a benefit under the trust on condition that that person does not marry. However, a provision is valid in a trust that makes marriage to a particular person a precondition of the grant of a benefit under the trust.

Restraint on alienation: *See* ALIENATION.

Restrictive Covenant: A COVENANT or clause in a deed or agreement which restricts the activities of a user of land except for restrictive terms made between lessor and lessee. A restrictive covenant can always be enforced between the original covenantee and the original covenantor under a doctrine of 'PRIVITY OF CONTRACT'. At common law the benefit of a covenant could run with the benefit in land if the covenant is concerned with the land of the covenantee. The successor in title derives his authority from the covenantee who owns the legal estate in the benefiting land; however, a burden of a covenant does not run with the servient land at common law but, under the rule of ***Tulk v. Moxhay*** (1848) 41 ER 1143, the burden may run in equity.

Resulting trust: A trust arising by operation of the law because of a legal presumption that the person who transfers the property intends it to be the subject of a trust. For example, if A transfers property to B and it is unclear on the facts whether A intends B to have the benefit of the property then B may hold the property on a resulting trust for A. This trust is not expressed and arises by operation of the law following that legal presumption. For example, resulting trusts can arise where the settlor conveys property upon trusts under terms which do not exhaust the whole of the beneficial interest in the property, such as where A creates a trust for B for life and then equally upon B's children but B dies childless, thus leaving the beneficial interest not completely disposed of. Then there is a resulting trust for A, i.e. the trustees hold the land with A as the beneficiary. Under these circumstances if A has died, then the trustees hold the property for the benefit of whoever succeeds to A's property by will or on intestacy. Importantly, a resulting trust arises where a trust fails; for example, if a trust is found to be a sham despite the property having been transferred to trustees, then the trustees hold that property on a resulting trust for the original settlor. Similarly, where property is transferred to a foundation inadequately to exhaust all the beneficial interests, or where the foundation is found to be invalid, then the property is held on a resulting trust for the founder or his estate. *See* *QUISTCLOSE* TRUST *and* SHAMS (GENERALLY).

Retirement of trustee(s): A trustee may retire provided that after his discharge there will be either a trust corporation or at least two individuals to perform the trust, and provided the co-trustees and the person entitled to appoint new trustees consent by deed to his retirement. *See* VESTING, TRUSTEES *and* REMOVAL OF TRUSTEES.

Reverse forum shopping: The practice of a person against whom an action is commenced in a foreign court launching his own proceedings and applying for a declaration in the same court that he is not liable (as alleged in the foreign court) for an injunction to restrain proceedings abroad, as the court is foreign to him, or on account that it is a *forum non-conveniens*. *See* FORUM SHOPPING; ANTI-SUIT INJUNCTION *and* *FORUM NON-CONVENIENS*.

Reversion: Reversion is the part of a person's property that remains with him after he grants an incomplete interest in the land to another person. For example, if an owner of property in fee simple, A, grants to another, B, a life interest then the fee simple that A retains is in reversion, i.e. after the expiry of the interest which A has granted to B, a life interest, expires (i.e. B dies and his life interest ends), then the entire interest in the property reverts back to A. In these circumstances what is retained by A is called the grantor's reversion or his right to reverter. In the UK, since the *Law of Property Act* 1925, reversions after the settlement of freehold or leasehold estates are reduced to equitable interests until the reverter, when the person entitled to the reversion, is restored to complete interest in the land. Since the *Trusts of Land and Appointment of Trustees Act* 1996, Schedule 1, Para. 5, a reversion upon an entail or life estate is now also an EQUITABLE INTEREST. A reversion created out of a term of years or leasehold, however, can exist as a legal estate and will only be a reversion after the expiry of the term of years; similarly with subleases which revert to the lessee after the sublease expires.

Reversionary interest: A return to the original status in law applied to land after the expiry of another estate or interest. In the wide sense, any right of property, the enjoyment of which is deferred but, particularly, interests in property that are not reversions or remainders in the strict sense but which are analogous to them. Property limited to A for life and, after his death, to B gives B a reversionary interest. Similarly, if A gives B property with a life interest, A retains a reversionary interest. These interests usually follow from placing property in trust where the legal estate in the property is conveyed to trustees. The use of a trust is simpler than setting up a reversionary interest and more easily understood. The term 'reversionary interest' is often used to describe an interest in property that is not a reversion or a remainder in the strict sense and used imprecisely to determine someone's interest in property which is legally owned by other persons. The term is also often applied in connection with leases where a reversionary lease is one that will take effect in the future, after the expiration of a former lease. A reversionary lease cannot be created to take effect more than 21 years from the date of the instrument purporting to create it.

Reversionary property: Property to which a reversionary interest attaches, i.e. property to which enjoyment can be had some time in the future, such as personal property invested to A for life and, after his death, to B. B's reversionary interest attaches to the property so included in the grant to A for life. Therefore, to have a reversionary interest attached to property a deed or some other document, such as a will, is required.

Reversioner: A person who has a reversion interest in a property which is enlarged on the expiry of an existing estate or interest in the land.

Revocable trust: A trust that is susceptible to termination or REVOCATION by the settlor as laid down in the trust instrument. On revocation, subject to the provisions in the trust instrument, the trust assets then revert to the settlor to whom the former trustees must re-convey the trust property. A power to revoke a trust is sometimes combined in a trust instrument with the power of making a new appointment of trustees. Often a power of revocation is a necessary condition precedent to the exercise of the power of appointment because unless the old trust is revoked there could obviously be no appointment of a new one. The power may be express and made by the person who declares the trust, or it may be implied, such as where a simple power to appoint new trusts is incorporated into the trust instrument or separately in an instrument exercising a power of appointment. A simple power to appoint new trustees includes a power to revoke the existing trusts. Where a power of appointment can only be exercised with stated formalities or requirements, this must be done and then a subsequent new appointment need not observe the same formalities. A settlement may declare itself to be wholly irrevocable and a power of appointment likewise may be described as an irrevocable appointment with no power of revocation reserved.

Revocation: A withdrawal of an authority or a grant previously given. Revocation may be by the act of a party, by operation of law or by the order of a court. Revocation by law, sometimes called constructive revocation, occurs without any intention of the parties; for example, the revocation of a power of attorney by the death of the principal and the revocation of a will by the subsequent marriage or civil partnership of the testator. *See* REVOCATION OF WILLS. With wills, an exception exists in respect of powers of appointment, bequests or devises where it can be shown that the testator did not intend revocation by subsequent marriage or civil partnership. Evidence of such intention on the part of the testator should appear in the will. Revocation by a court can be ordered if any irregularity in the application for PROBATE of a will is revealed. This requires an application to the court of an interested person before the grant of probate is cancelled. In some countries, e.g. in England, under Section 18, of the *Wills Act* 1837, a marriage revokes any will made before marriage by either party. This is not the law in Scotland or in France. The applicable law is the law of the domicile of the testator at the time of the marriage and not the time of the death. Revocation by a party is sometimes called intentional or voluntary revocation when applied to trusts where a settlor is able to revoke a trust according to powers reserved to him in the trust deed. Revocation is not generally available for a voluntary trust where the provisions of the trust are brought to the settlor's intention and the settlor acknowledges that he understands the nature of the arrangements; there is no element under these circumstances which involves fraud or undue influence affecting the settlor's intention which might otherwise have led to revocation. Any attempt by the settlor to revoke a settlement places the burden of proving fraud, undue influence or mistake on him unless he alleges that a beneficiary exercised undue influence; the beneficiaries may have to prove that the settlor was aware of what he, the settlor, was undertaking. Revocation of a trust is rarely permitted where a valuable consideration to enter the trust (such as marriage) has taken place. Trustees frequently have the power of revocation provided in the trust instrument alongside the grant of a power of appointment of new trustees. Where there is a power to appoint new trusts as part of a power of ADVANCEMENT, there is an implied power to revoke existing trusts. Revocation of a foundation depends upon the provisions of the foundation law, the charter or regulations.

Rights: A right in its most general sense is either the ability to act or abstain from acting in a certain manner that is protected by law, or the power of compelling a person to a certain course of action that is enforced by law. The term is used in connection with a legal right that is a capacity of one person of controlling, with the compliance of the state, the actions of others. Rights are broadly divided into primary rights and secondary rights. Primary rights are those created without reference to other rights already in existence, such as a contractual right to receive a sum of money. Primary rights may be personal rights (such as a right to life, health and liberty of action) or public rights under which every member of the community is entitled to use certain things. The latter embraces things that belong to the state or, if belonging to a private person, are available for public use, such as the rights in respect of the sea, rivers, highways and public paths, etc. Public rights also include those rights that arise from relationships with other members of the public, including ordinary rights arising from ownership, contract and marriage. Secondary rights are those which only arise for the purpose of protecting and enforcing primary rights; these are either preventative or remedial in nature and exist to prevent the infringement or loss of primary rights. These secondary rights may require the assistance of the court or may be extrajudicial when exercised by the party concerned. The right to institute proceedings to be able to administer the estate of a deceased person and to require assistance against the commission of a crime are examples of judicial preventative rights. An extrajudicial preventative right is a right of self-defence. Rights may also be referred to as 'legal rights' when, for example, one person has the capacity of controlling, with the assent and assistance of the state, the actions of others.

Ring-fenced trust fund: An expression used to indicate that a trust fund is segregated from the trustee's own personal property and separate from any liabilities of the trustee in a different capacity whether in connection with a trustee's private creditors, spouse and/or heirs. This is a fundamental aspect of trusts which provides a valuable protection for the beneficiaries in the event of the insolvency of an individual trustee or the bankruptcy of a corporate trustee.

***Rochefoucauld v. Boustead* [1897] 1 Ch 196:** The source in case law of the principle that an oral expression of trust may be valid if it would be a fraud to allow the trustees to take the property intended for the trust for themselves. This is an exception to the general rule that before any land or any interest in land can be placed in a trust, a declaration of trust must be 'manifested and proved' by some writing signed by some person who is able to declare such a trust, or by the settlor's will. Otherwise, without the principle embodied in that case, such a trust would not be enforceable and the beneficiary would not be able to invoke the help of the court against the trustees.

Rocket launcher and the rocket, The: A distinction used in connection with the HAGUE TRUST CONVENTION by which a trust is distinguish from matters concerned with the formation of the trust. The Convention distinguishes conflict of laws aspects which affect the validity of the trust (the rocket) from matters concerned with the capacities of the parties and other preliminary aspects (the rocket launcher) which are outside the Convention's scope. The image of the launcher and the rocket was used by commentators because it will always be necessary to have a 'launcher', e.g. a will, gift or other act with legal effects, which then establishes (launches) the trust (the rocket).

Role of trustee: The role of the trustee is to take possession of the legal title to trust property and to maintain it in the interests of the beneficiaries according to the trust instrument or the established trust principles and the law. In fulfilment of this rule, the trustee has many responsibilities and duties and the exacting nature of trusteeship has been recognised by a famous statement in ***Knight v. Earl of Plymouth*** (1747) Dick. 120 at 126, in which Lord Hardwicke, Lord Chancellor, stated that:

> 'A trust is an office necessary in the concerns between man and man, and ..., if faithfully discharged, attended with no small degree of trouble and anxiety ... it is an act of great kindness in anyone to accept it.'

Rome Conventions: Two Conventions of the European Union on the laws applicable to contractual and non-contractual obligations. The Convention Applicable to Contractual Obligations (known as Rome Convention I) was enacted in the UK by the *Contracts (Applicable Law) Act* 1990. The Convention's provisions determine the law governing contracts made after April 1991 but before 17 December 2009. The Convention on non-contractual obligations, (EC) No 864/2007, (known as Rome Convention II) created a harmonised set of rules from 11 January 2009 governing the choice of law in civil and commercial matters (subject to certain exclusions). These Conventions, by their nature, do not affect trusts or private foundations, although considerable debate developed at first about the legal nature of private foundations and revolved around whether private foundations came within the definition in the Rome Conventions on contractual obligations. The Rome Conventions, like the Hague Convention on Trusts, aim at establishing a uniform choice of law that will support the Brussels Convention on Jurisdiction and Enforcement of Judgments in Civil and Commercial Matters 1968 (EC REGULATION 44/2001). Both Conventions have been made the subject of EU Regulations (Regulation (EC) No. 593/2008 on the Law Applicable to Contractual Obligations (Rome I) (OJ L177, 6, 4.7.2008) and Regulation (EC) No. 864/2007 on the Law Applicable to Non-Contractual Obligations (Rome II) (OJ L199, 40, 31.7.2007). The purpose of Convention I, which has not been received with unequivocal enthusiasm (Mann, F.A., *Note on Rome Convention.* 32, ICLQ 265, 1983 and *Notes: The Proper Law of the Contract - An Obituary.* L.Q.R., 107, 1991) was to establish uniform rules in connection with the choice between the laws of different countries. In identifying what was meant by 'contractual obligations' no clear statement was made on the position of private foundations as the use of private foundations was not then significant. The definition of 'contractual obligations' could have been made according to national laws, but an 'autonomous meaning' was preferred for the purpose of Rome Convention I. Although this overlaps with the definition in English and other laws, it is not the same. It would have been more straightforward if the Convention had been confined to what English private international law regarded as contractual. But it did not. The attempt to impose uniformity resulted in great complexity and now the rules of Convention I replace the English common law rules where the Convention is applicable. The autonomous definition covers most obligations regarded as contractual in English law and follows that used in EC Regulation 44/2001 on jurisdiction.

The main characteristic of a contractual obligation under the Convention is that it should be freely entered into by the parties. This has been interpreted to suggest that it is the relationships which should be freely entered into rather than the individual terms and conditions that need to be voluntary. This opens up the possibility of the voluntary arrangement between founder and foundation council as recorded in the charter being regarded as a contractual obligation, especially as the GIULIANO-LAGARDE REPORT (Giuliano-Lagarde, OJ C282/1, 10 [1980]) states that gifts are included within the scope of Rome Convention I, without any explanation of why they are considered to be contractual. There are other anomalies such as the exclusion of implied terms in a contract for the sale of goods. The scope of Rome Convention I is not clear due to the inadequacy of the autonomous definitions although it is clear that questions governed by the law of companies and other bodies corporate or unincorporated are excluded. This suggests that private foundations should be excluded. Trusts are excluded from Rome Convention I. There is no autonomous definition of trusts; trusts are understood to have the meaning given to the term in common law countries: a sensible treatment when denied to contracts but this position is confused by the explanations given to allow some institutions similar to trusts in civil law jurisdictions to fall within Rome Convention I simply on the grounds that they are normally contractual in origin. A contractual origin seems to have been very persuasive. One explanation is that since the source of foundations has been attributed to have been the FIDUCIA of Roman law, a vehicle of contractual origin, modern private foundations should be included within Rome Convention I. On the other hand, trusts originating in the law of property are naturally excluded from any Convention on contractual obligations. Rome Convention II is concerned with Non-contractual Obligations. This Convention excludes obligations arising between parties to a trust (recognising that the Hague Convention has dealt with this) or associated with the formation and registration of corporate and incorporate bodies, constructive trusts or restitutionary liabilities. Neither the commentary nor the leading authorities make any reference to include or exclude foundations, or *Stiftungs*.

Rule against perpetuities: A rule adopted in some common law countries that enables a court to declare void any future or postponed interest in property that will vest too far in the future. The objective is to prevent property from remaining out of commercial circulation for an excessive period of time. Trusts (especially those under the *Settled Land Act* 1925) are subject to the rule where, by means of a trust, real property could be retained by a family for a period longer than that for which finance was pledged for its maintenance. Under the rule against perpetuities, property must become enjoyable as of right within a stated period prescribed by law; this period is known as the perpetuity period. The classic statement of the rule was given in 1906 in ***Re Thompson*** [1906] 2 Ch 199, 202:

> 'The rule against perpetuities requires that every estate or interest must vest, if at all, not later than twenty-one years after the determination of some life in being at the time of the creation of such estate or interest, and not only must the person to take be ascertained, but the amount of his interest must be ascertainable within the prescribed period.'

This is a statement of a classic rule that has been substantially modified by the *Perpetuities and Accumulations Act* 1964 and the *Perpetuities and Accumulations Act* 2009. The rule against perpetuities is associated with the rule against accumulations. *See* PERPETUITIES AND ACCUMULATIONS *and* WAIT AND SEE RULE.

Rule of law: The principle that the State should be governed in accordance with the law and not arbitrarily. This rule is the underlying fundamental to such principles as pronounced in 1607 that:

> 'The King in his own person cannot adjudge any case, either criminal or betwixt party and party; but it ought to be determined and adjudged in some Court of Justice, according to the law and custom of England.'

This followed the practice after the Norman Conquest that no king gave any judgment in any cause personally. The rule was more fully stated by A.V. Dicey (*Introduction to the Study of the Law of the Constitution*) as:

> '[N]o man is punishable or can be lawfully made to suffer in body or goods except for a distinct breach of law established in the ordinary legal manner before the ordinary courts of the land.'

This rule has been restated as that all persons and all authorities within the State should be bound by and entitled to the benefit of laws publically promulgated and administered in the courts. The 'rule of law' is the background to the requirement that ministers and other persons in government should abide by the law and not make arbitrary decisions. The law of the land should apply equally to all unless objective differences justify differentiation. The law should protect fundamental human rights and provide a means of resolving bona fide civil disputes.

S

Sanderson's trusts: A trust that takes its name from the case of ***Sanderson Trust, Re*** (1857) 26 LJ 804, which avoids the unenforceability of PURPOSE TRUSTS by allowing the beneficiary, under a discretionary trust, a certain amount of money where that amount is determined by the cost of the beneficiary carrying out a purpose. For example, a total of £100,000 to be paid by the trustees to a beneficiary in amounts equal to those that the beneficiary expended on a purpose, such as on church bell restoration, with the remainder of the trust fund to go to another person. However, despite appearances, this trust is perfectly valid and is not considered to be a replacement of a human beneficiary with a purpose. The purpose element is part of a formula that defines the amount of a discretionary benefit payable to an individual beneficiary. *See* DISCRETIONARY TRUSTS.

Satisfaction: Compensation for an injury done, or for the payment of money that is due and owing, or the fulfilment of an obligation by the debtor for the performance of some act. In equity, the term is usually applied to cases where the acts or language of testators or settlors imply that an obligation is to be satisfied, although the act or language may be ambiguous. For example, a parent bequeaths a legacy to a child by way of a PORTION and afterwards, during that parent's lifetime, gives, on that child's marriage, a further sum of money which constituted a portion. Equity regards that later portion as satisfaction of the former. The child does not get both portions. Similarly, a legacy to the testator's creditor operates as satisfaction of the debt to the extent of the legacy. In equity, satisfaction means the gift of a thing which, with either express or implied intention, is to extinguish wholly or partly some prior claim or demand. Satisfaction depends upon presumed intention to carry out an obligation and in this way resembles PERFORMANCE, but with important differences. In performance, an act must be carried out which can fairly be regarded as corresponding to the precise obligation of the debtor. On the other hand, satisfaction is sometimes different from the thing agreed to be done and the question then is whether it is intended as a substitute. The questions of satisfaction usually arise where a payment, such as a legacy, is paid where there is an outstanding debt which will not be satisfied unless the legacy is as beneficial to the creditor as a straightforward payment. The doctrine of satisfaction is subject to much law in equity. The general principle applied is that the law attempts to prevent double portions.

***Saunders v. Vautier* (1841) 4 Beav 115:** A rule in English trust law that where all the beneficiaries are SUI JURIS and, together, are entitled to the whole beneficial interest, they may put an end to the trust and direct the trustees to hand over the trust property. This rule applies even if the trust instrument contains express provisions by which the trust may be terminated, or where there is an absolute vested gift made payable on a future event or where the trustees are instructed to accumulate the income until such vesting takes place. The rule applies even where the accumulation of funds in a trust is directed exclusively for the benefit of a beneficiary; the moment the beneficiary is sui juris he may put an end to the trust and demand the property. Another aspect of the rule is that where trustees are directed in their discretion to pay or apply all or some of the trust income to A and the surplus to B, A and B are both sui juris and can operate the rule. This rule, which contradicts the intention of an INTER VIVOS settlor, does not apply in all trust jurisdictions; for example, it is unknown in most of the states of the US and nullified in some offshore jurisdictions. The rule is not practical where there is a purpose trust where there are no identifiable beneficiaries and where there is no gift of the trust assets but merely a continuing gift of income to be applied at the trustees' discretion to achieve a purpose. Also, in some offshore jurisdictions, beneficiaries will have little or no information about the terms of the trust. The rule may be made inapplicable to certain types of trusts, for example, under PROTECTIVE TRUSTS or SPENDTHRIFT TRUSTS. The rule has only qualified acceptance in some other jurisdictions, such as in the Bahamas, where there is broad legislation that prohibits the beneficiaries terminating or modifying a trust which affects the property if this would defeat the material purpose of the settlor.

Search order: An order issued by the UK High Court that requires a defendant to permit a claimant or his representatives to enter the defendant's premises to inspect, copy or remove material which the defendant might otherwise destroy or remove in order to frustrate a claimant's action (*Civil Procedure Act* 1997, Section 7). An order is made subject to strict conditions, such as requiring an undertaking from the applicant in respect of any damage caused by executing the order. An order is made without notice to the defendant but is granted only in limited circumstances where the court considers that it is absolutely necessary. Making the order may qualify as an exception to the defendant's right of privacy; the necessity of an order being an exception under Article 8(2) of the European Convention on Human Rights. Until 1999 a search order was known as an ANTON PILLAR ORDER after the name of the case (***Anton Piller KG v. Manufacturing Processes Ltd*** [1976] Ch 55 All ER 779) in which it became best known. Similar orders exist in most jurisdictions. In English law, the order takes the form of an interim mandatory injunction.

Secret profits: Any profit made by an agent in breach of the agent's fiduciary position and for which he has not accounted to his principal. The term applies to bribes and secret commissions and the use by trustees for their own benefit of trust property. Secret profits may be made by directors or other senior officers of a company by usurping or diverting to another person or company with whom they are associated a maturing business opportunity which the company is actively pursuing. This principle applies to members of a foundation council.

Secret trusts: A secret trust is a trust where a testator bequeaths property to a person who by an express or implied promise agrees to hold the property in trust for another person where the existence of the trust is not revealed to any other person reading the will. The legatee becomes the legal owner, but not the beneficial owner, of the legacy. The legatee will have previously agreed with the testator that the property will be held by him on trust for the beneficiaries nominated by the testator. A secret trust needs to be valid as an express trust and enforceable against the legatee and devisee. In other words, the secrecy element does not diminish the need for the secret trust to conform to the principles of trust formation; otherwise, it would be void. Where the testator indicates publicly in his will that the recipient is to hold the property on trust but withholds the identities of the beneficiaries, this is a 'HALF-SECRET TRUST'. In this case, the testator has agreed only with the trustees who the beneficiaries are to be. In ***Rawstron & Anor v. Freud*** [2014] EWHC 2577 Ch., the Supreme Court assessed a testator's intention using the normal criteria of construction. The testator gave two named legatees the residue of the estate, which the court deduced from the surrounding facts may have been subject to a secret trust. An opposing claim made by a child of the deceased was that the will showed no clear intention to set up a half-secret trust. Therefore, in respect of the residue of the estate, there was an intestacy that would have opened the possibility for previously unnamed children to claim a part of the estate for themselves. The High Court held that there was an absolute gift to the two named individuals in their personal capacity absolutely 'and was not given to them on trust under the will.' The latter phrase is important. There was evidence that the legatees, nevertheless, held the assets on a secret trust but the obligation to operate a secret trust took effect outside the will, the existence of which, in the litigation, was not the concern of the court. The judgment emphasised that with a secret trust it is immaterial whether the trust is accepted before or after execution of the will but it must be communicated in the testator's lifetime, otherwise it cannot be enforced and the legatee will take beneficially. On the other hand, with a half-secret trust, the trust must be communicated to the trustee before the execution of the will or at least be contemporaneous with it, otherwise it will fail. Generally, secret trusts and half-secret trusts are not enforceable unless, before the death of the testator, the legatee has, in a separate document, expressed or implied that he has accepted responsibility as a trustee.

Securities: Documents, such as share certificates, debentures or bonds, that can be bought and sold as investments and which are of value. The term is more widely defined in the *Financial Services and Markets Act* 2000 to include, as well as bonds and debentures, any public securities or instruments acknowledging indebtedness, warrants and any other instruments entitling the holder to subscribe for any of these, as well as certificates giving contractual or property rights in respect of them. The term is also applied to units representing rights or interests in a collective investment scheme and may include, for certain purposes, even a stakeholder or private pension scheme. The term is extended to cover options and future contracts and contracts for differences, some insurance contracts that represent securities and certificates representing derivatives. Both the creation and marketing of securities is subject to much regulatory legislation in the UK under the *Financial Services and Markets Act* 2000 (Regulated Activities) Order 2001 (SI 2001/544) and, internationally, under the International Organization of Securities Commissions (IOSCO) measures.

Securities markets: A market on which securities are traded and which, in the United Kingdom, may be either a recognised investment exchange, such as the London Stock Exchange (LSE), or an unregulated, 'multilateral trading facility' (MTF), which is not subject to pre-trade and post-trade transparency requirements that are applicable to regulated markets. The latter may be used in connection with the EU Directive 2004/39 EC on Markets and Financial Instruments (MIFID).

Securitisation: An investment practice begun in the 1970s where assets in the form of regular payments, such as repayments of mortgage and bond loans, are transferred by the originator of the loan, a bank or finance house, to a corporate entity or to a trust referred to as a SPECIAL PURPOSE VEHICLE (SPV). After the transfer, the holder of the assets, i.e. the SPV, pools the income from the various assets transferred to it and then creates a complex range of tradable securities whose marketability depends upon the credit rating of the SPV and not directly upon the value of the individual assets placed in it. For example, a mortgage company, instead of assigning the whole interest of individual mortgage arrangements to another, can group various mortgage contracts into an SPV and sell participation or shares (if the SPV is a company). Participation in an

SPV is attractive for the sake of foreseeable dates of payment of a dividend out of its income. However, the marketing of SPVs became complex and the participators had no ability to measure the reliability of the various sources of income which provided the dividend. Securitisation exacerbated the international banking crisis of 2008, due to the irresponsible nature of the mixture of assets grouped in an SPV. 'Toxic' (i.e. worthless) loans were mixed with other receivables, mortgages or loans, and this obscured the validity of many sub-prime mortgages (mortgage loans which were excessive in view of the nature of the premises mortgaged) in the US and Europe. The failure of securitised assets contributed principally to the reduction in the confidence required for interbank lending. In many cases, securitisation comprised a complex matrix of obligations. For example, an SPV was able to raise a loan to obtain its assets and then the SPV depended upon the income towards paying off the loan, and to be able to have enough funds for distribution to the beneficiaries of the SPV, who would be beneficiaries of a trust where the SPV was a trust, or to the shareholders where the SPV was a company. These beneficiaries were usually other financial institutions. The financial crisis revolved around excessive securitisation of the same assets where different aspects were used in more than one SPV, e.g. size, geographical area and the type of asset mortgaged.

Security: A term applied to something that reinforces purely a contractual obligation and thereby renders comfort and assurance to the debtor that his rights are supported. Security may be a personal security in which a person pledges his own personal assets or it may be security raised on property. Security may also be part of the judicial process and may be required by a court in respect of the ability of the parties to be able to pay the costs of a judicial action. Also, security may be required by a court to encourage a person to behave in an appropriate manner by demanding that the person should lodge, or arrange that a third party should lodge, something of value that can be forfeited in the event of breach.

Seised: A court is seised of a matter when all the legal requirements to enable proceedings to be brought have been complied with.

Seisin: An old-fashioned word, rarely used in the present century, implying possession of land or the relationship in which a person stands to land or other HEREDITAMENTS when he holds them as freehold in possession, or the equivalent term which describes ownership that is not subject to other interests. A person holding land in an estate of freehold possession is said to be seised of the land. Seisin is contrasted with possession or mere occupation. The term is sometimes used in a broader sense but with the same concept of being legitimately in possession. *See* SEISED.

Self-assessment: A system of accounting for tax liability in the UK where the taxpayer himself completes a form and submits it to the tax authorities to provide them with information relevant to the calculation of how much tax is due. This calculation may be done by the taxpayer himself or by the Revenue authorities. Self-assessment applies in the UK to income tax and capital gains tax.

Self-benefit trust: An alternative to a BLIND TRUST, introduced in Canada in 1999. The advantage of a self-benefit trust is that any capital gains tax payable on the disposal (i.e. transfer) of assets into the trust is rolled over whereas, with a blind trust, it would be payable when the trust was set up. This advantage is only available for individual self-benefit trusts and business benefit trusts that are resident in Canada. In order to constitute a valid self-benefit trust the person, individual or business must be entitled to all the income of the trust to the exclusion of any other person. This is also subject to there being no change in the beneficial ownership of the property and no absolute or contingent right of another person to become a beneficiary under the trust.

Self-dealing rule: An attempt by a trustee or other fiduciary to act as a third party with a beneficiary. This occurs when a trustee seeks to buy trust property on behalf of the trust but also acts on his own behalf in breach of his fiduciary duties (*see* FIDUCIARY DUTY). This exposes the trustee to a claim that he has been buying at an advantageous price and exploiting the beneficiaries. The transaction is voidable by the beneficiaries. The absolute nature of this principle was summarised in *Tito v. Waddell* (No 2) [1977] Ch 106 as:

> 'If a trustee purchases trust property from himself, any beneficiary may have the sale set aside *ex debito justitiae*, however fair the transaction.'

In other words, such a transaction is VOID even though the price obtained may be the same price that the beneficiaries could have obtained on the open market. A trustee cannot be both buyer and seller. The rule is severe and applies even though the circumstances are honest and the price is fair, and irrespective of the absence of any profit made by the trustee. The beneficiary is entitled to have any transaction that offends these rules set aside. Liability under this principle is avoided if it can be shown that the profit is authorised either by the terms of the office, i.e. as far as a trust is concerned, by consent in the trust instrument or by the consent of the beneficiaries of full age and capacity after proper disclosure. Also, such a purchase may be authorised by statute or made in circumstances where the trustee has not placed himself in a position of conflict or, where there is a conflict, the conflict arises by action of the seller and not of the trustee who seeks to buy. The rule applies particularly to the grant of leases by trustees to a trust and similar operations, such as the sale of a trustee's own property to a trust, loans to and by trustees and in connection with consents to assign a lease or the exercise of an appointment. Acquiescence by the court to any proposed action also avoids the application of the self-dealing rule. The rule applies to a person other than a trustee who is in a fiduciary position, such as an executor, an administrator, an *EXECUTOR DE SON TORT* and a creditor's agent. The rule applies to members of a foundation council and to company directors, as with other fiduciaries, even after the person has resigned his fiduciary role.

Semi-secret trust: *See* HALF-SECRET TRUST.

Senior Courts: In England and Wales the Senior Courts consist of the Court of Appeal, the High Court of Justice and the Crown Court. These courts, before the *Constitutional Reform Act* 2005, were collectively referred to as the Supreme Court of England and Wales. They were renamed the Senior Courts to avoid confusion with the new SUPREME COURT OF THE UNITED KINGDOM, which took over from the House of Lords as the highest court of appeal. The Court of Appeal deals only with appeals from other courts in its civil and criminal divisions. The Civil Division considers appeals from the High Court, the County Court and some certain superior tribunals, and the Criminal Division hears appeals from the Crown Court where a trial in the High Court was commenced on indictment, i.e. for serious offences. The High Court operates in three divisions: the Queen's Bench, the Chancery Division and the Family Division. Although not separate courts, they have their separate procedures and practices. Trusts and equity matters are considered by the Chancery Division. The Crown Court is a criminal court with original and appellate jurisdiction and replaced the Assizes. The Crown Court has some civil jurisdiction and, when engaged in civil matters, is regarded as an inferior court. In English law the Senior Courts have unlimited jurisdiction within their spheres of operation which are independent of any supervisory jurisdiction of any other court (as distinct from having their judgments open to an appeal by a higher court). These courts have the power to deal with any contempt of their proceedings, wherever committed. A decision of a Senior Court is usually a definitive statement of the law that can only be overridden by an appeal to a higher court, whose decision then replaces that of the lower court. In Northern Ireland there is a similar organisation of the Senior Courts. The Scottish Senior Courts are structured differently. *See* INFERIOR COURTS.

Separate estate: The *Married Woman's Property Act* 1893, Section 1, provided that every contract entered into by a married woman, otherwise than as agent for her husband, shall be deemed to be a contract entered into by her and will bind her separate property whether she was or was not in fact possessed of or entitled to any separate property at the time when she entered into the contract. The Act binds separate property which she might at that time or thereafter be possessed of and entitled to, and that property is then exposed to being used for the enforcement of the contractual obligation. Later, the *Law Reform (Married Women and Tortfeasors) Act* 1935 provided that a married woman who was capable of acquiring, holding and disposing of property may render herself liable in tort or contract and can be sued and may sue in respect of that property. Such a married woman may also be subject to bankruptcy law and other enforcement proceedings as if she were an unmarried person. This Act was amended by the *Married Women (Restraint upon Anticipation) Act* 1949, which removed any bar on actions in tort between husband and wife.

Separation: A civil law doctrine that distinguishes between the parties and their assets to a transaction and which has become particularly relevant in the definition of the different parties to a private foundation, particularly in respect of the separation between the founder's property and the foundation assets where any attempt of a founder's creditors to attack the assets of a foundation would be contrary to the principle of separation (*Trennungsprinzip*). In this context, where a founder retains the right to revoke a foundation or to amend its constitution, a separation has not been achieved and may therefore expose the foundation assets to any attack by the founder's creditors.

Separation of assets: Occurs where the parties to a marriage or civil partnership enter into an agreement on separation to control their independent financial arrangements while living separately. Such agreements, during the lifetime of the parties, can be varied or revoked by the court, which may make any arrangements that appear to be just in the court's opinion under the *Matrimonial Causes Act* 1973, Section 35(2), or *Civil Partnership Act* 2004, Schedule 1, Para. 69. A separation agreement does not bind the court in any subsequent application for ancillary relief but may be of influence in the outcome of the court's determination.

Separation of powers: A doctrine of political theory originating in the 18th century by Montesquieu in his book *The Spirit of Laws*, by which the executive (the ministers and civil service), the legislative (the law-makers) and the judiciary (the judges and the courts) should be operated by different sets of people. The intention is to avoid freedom from arbitrary rules and to avoid tyranny. The doctrine is not strictly followed in the United Kingdom, particularly since members of the political executive are drawn from the legislature, i.e. the ministers and others are required to have a seat in Parliament, thus creating an overlap between the executive and the legislature. The system is more closely followed in the United States due to a misunderstanding by Montesquieu of the position in England and of the extent of his influence on the design of the US political and government structures of the time.

Service out of the jurisdiction: The means by which a claim can be brought against a defendant who is situated outside the jurisdiction in which the appellant wishes to bring an action. Service means the delivery to a party of the necessary papers starting an action; e.g. a WRIT or summons. Such an action may be necessary when the proposed defendant is not situated within the jurisdiction. Service out of the jurisdiction may also occur to take advantage of more amenable procedural rules or more appropriate substantive law elsewhere. Before the Judgments Regulation, EC 44/2001, the consent of the court in the UK had to be obtained before a UK resident claimant could serve process on a defendant who was not in the UK in order for an action to be brought before an English court. Now, under the Regulation, permission to serve out of the jurisdiction is not required where the defendant is domiciled in a Member State of the EU (apart from Denmark). The basic rule under the Regulation (which incorporates the provisions of the Brussels and Lugano Conventions) is that the defendant is to be sued in the court of a country in which he is domiciled, subject to a contrary agreement and various special rules. Actions against trustees are normally brought in the jurisdiction where the trustees are domiciled or where the trust is managed and controlled. In jurisdictional matters, trustees follow the same jurisdiction rules as apply to companies. The Regulation is complex and there are many exceptions to the general rules. Where the Regulation does not apply and a claim needs to be served outside the jurisdiction of England and Wales then permission is required by the claimant from the court in order to serve the necessary claim to begin the action. In England, the court will need to be satisfied that one of a number of grounds exists and that England is the proper place in which to bring the claim. These grounds are normally linked to a connection with the jurisdiction. The formalities of bringing a claim in a different jurisdiction, when the defendant is not subject to the Regulation, are relevant to making a decision whether to set up a trust in a remote international financial centre; actions against trustees domiciled in such a centre will be expensive and subject to considerable delay. These factors were one of the attractions of asset protection trusts in an offshore centre where the administrative problems of bringing an action were complex and sufficient to discourage procedures against trustees who would have been easily involved in litigation if they were within the same jurisdiction as the claimant. *See* BRUSSELS CONVENTION ON JURISDICTION AND THE ENFORCEMENT OF CIVIL AND COMMERCIAL MATTERS 1968 *and* LUGANO CONVENTION ON JURISDICTION AND THE ENFORCEMENT OF JUDGMENTS IN CIVIL AND COMMERCIAL MATTERS 1988.

Servient estate: The land over which an easement is exercised in favour of the dominant property.

Set-off: A general legal principle that allows a cross claim by defendants, faced with an action for money owing, to reduce or abolish the defendant's liability by allowing credit in the defendant's favour for money owed to him by the claimant. No set-off is allowed in favour of a trustee where there has been more than one distinct breach of trust even if, overall, there has been a gain to the trust, unless both events arose in the same transaction: ***Bartlett v. Barclays Bank Trust Co Ltd*** [1980] Ch 515 at 533-534. This prevents trustees claiming that losses caused by a breach of trust may be subject to a set-off on account of previous gains made by successful investments. In other words, trustees cannot simply look back over the life of a trust and set off losses caused by breaches of trust against gains generally on the basis that, overall, the trust had benefited from the trustees' performance. Each breach of trust must be treated distinctly from any other breach. Set-off is not permitted where beneficiaries have distinct and different interests in the trust assets; it would be too difficult to apportion between them losses against gains in separate transactions. Also, in respect of trusts of land, the interests are usually varied and set-off would be impossible; for example, where priorities would have to be negotiated in respect of the beneficial owners' equitable leases and rights in PERSONAM against the legal owners' interest. The differences of beneficiaries' interest in the income and the capital growth of a trust adds further difficulty, as do different forms of co-ownership, JOINT TENANCY and TENANCY IN COMMON. One significant feature of set-off is that an assignee of the original creditor retains the same rights of set-off as the debtor had against the original creditor. Set-off against assignees is subject to some detailed judicial precedents.

Setting trusts aside: *See* REVOCATION; BANKRUPTCY OF A SETTLOR; VOLUNTARY CONVEYANCE *and* SHAM TRUSTS.

Settled land: Land where there are two or more beneficial interests that exist in succession to one another, or land which is made subject to certain other fetters of the owners' powers. No settlements of this type can be created after the *Trusts of Land and Appointment of Trustees Act* 1996, but those settled land arrangements which were in existence before that Act can continue. The *Settled Land Act* 1925 gave statutory recognition to the term 'ENTAILED INTERESTS', which are the interests that exist after those of the then tenant in possession, the life tenant. The categories within the *Settled Land Act* 1925 that can continue until naturally coming to an end include:

(1) land held in trust for any person in succession; for example, to A for life, then to B for life and then to C in fee simple;
(2) entailed interests;
(3) land owned subject to gift over on a specified event;
(4) land owned for determinable interest;
(5) land conveyed to a person under 18 years, since a minor cannot own or convey legal estate in land;
(6) land in which there is a future interest that may come into possession on a specified event; and
(7) land charged voluntarily, i.e. without consideration, or in consideration of marriage by way of family arrangement.

Where a settlement was made during the life of the settlor, this was effected by a trust instrument, i.e. setting out one or more trusts from the categories listed above, followed by a vesting deed. The trustees were either two or more individuals or a trust corporation and were known as trustees of the settlement. The vesting deed transferred the legal estate in the settled land to the immediate beneficiary (as opposed to a transfer to the trustees in a trust for sale) and identified the trustees. When this type of settlement was set up by will there was no need for a separate trust instrument; the personal representatives would vest the property in the life tenant. The purpose of the 1925 *Settled Land Act* was to codify the existing system and balance the protection of beneficiaries and future interests against the principle that the person immediately entitled in possession should not be prevented, because of the future interests, from prudently managing and dealing with the property. Consequently, unlike other trusts, the Act conferred on the immediate beneficiary (the life tenant) the ability to sell the land at the best price obtainable. These transactions overreached (*see* OVERREACHING) the interests of subsequent beneficiaries who acquired a corresponding interest in the capital money or income arising from the proceeds of the sale. In this connection, the *Settled Land Act* 1925 imposed on the immediate beneficiary, the life tenant, a fiduciary duty equal to that of a trustee to act for all the parties who had a beneficial interest in the settled land, even though he was himself a beneficiary. When the immediate beneficiary sold or otherwise disposed of settled land, the purchaser was not concerned with the beneficiaries' interests in the sale proceeds.

Settled Land Act Trustees: Two or more individuals or a trust corporation who are trustees of settled land and whose primary function is to receive and hold capital money arising on the sale or other dispositions of the land by the immediate beneficiary (the life tenant). Any money so arising is held in trust for those entitled as subsequent beneficiaries. Also, the consent of these trustees is necessary before the immediate beneficiary, the life tenant, can validly exercise his statutory powers, such as selling, if allowed by the settlement, the principal manor house or timber cut from the land. The trustees were appointed by the trust instrument and named in the vesting deed.

Settled property: Property that is the subject matter of a settlement under the *Settled Land Act* 1925 referred to above (*see* SETTLED LAND *and* SETTLED LAND ACT TRUSTEES). These settlements could also be set up by statute (such as the *Duke of Marlborough's Annuity Act* 1706) and may be set up for the purpose of a MARRIAGE SETTLEMENT, STRICT SETTLEMENT and VOLUNTARY SETTLEMENTS, as well as settlements under the *Settled Land Act* 1925.

Settlement: A term that refers to the deed or instrument by which property, or the enjoyment of property, is limited to several persons in succession. A settlement can comprise a deed, or an instrument equivalent to a deed, such as an agreement for a settlement, may be clauses in a will, and occasionally may be by an Act of Parliament. Settlement may consist of any number of documents; where there is more than one settlement, the document may be described as a compound settlement. The most significant kinds of settlements are marriage, or ANTI-NUPTIAL SETTLEMENTS, POST-NUPTIAL SETTLEMENTS, VOLUNTARY SETTLEMENTS and FAMILY SETTLEMENT or RESETTLEMENTS A court may sometimes direct that the parties to a proceeding should enter into a settlement, such as those which may be ordered by the Chancery Division on the marriage of a ward in court, and by the Family Division which has power to order a settlement of property when a marriage is dissolved. The term 'settlement' is frequently used to denote a trust of a more formal nature such as those described above. The trust principles applied to a settlement are the same as those applied to other trusts, although in certain cases the use of the term 'settlement' imposes, in addition to general trust principles, characteristics which are unique to that type of arrangement. The term 'settlement' generally may be considered to be a trust which provides for an individual for life and others after his death, rather than other types of trusts for commercial purposes. *See* SETTLED LAND *and* SETTLED PROPERTY.

Settlement of future property: A trust of property that is expected to come into the settlor's ownership after the trust is set up. Such future property can be, for example, a valuable asset on which an expectant holder may wish to capitalise, before he becomes the owner, by selling that expectancy to another. Such a transfer is an equitable arrangement and is possible so long as value is given for that transfer. This is essential, as equity will not assist a volunteer. When the future time arrives, the legal title to the property becomes automatically vested in the person to whom the property was originally due and the transfer of the beneficial interest by the original expectant holder has the effect of a contract that the entire interest will be transferred to the settlement.

Settlor: The person who, with the intention of creating a trust, transfers assets to a trustee for the benefit of the beneficiaries; sometimes called a 'GRANTOR' in the US. The settlor may be included among a class of discretionary beneficiaries or may have a life or other interest that will end under stated circumstances or within a specified period of time.

Several: Individual as opposed to joint; as, for example, where a liability rests on more than one person and can be enforced against any of them in full, their liability is said to be several. Where the liability is joint and several, then the person on whom liability falls is entitled to claim contributions from the others.

Several tenancy: A tenancy that is separate and not held jointly with another person.

Severance: The act of separating that is often applied in the examination of the constituent elements of a power and the rejection by a court of the exercise of a power to the extent that it would be a FRAUD ON A POWER (i.e. a misuse) if fulfilled but allowing the remainder of the power to be exercised. The term is often used in connection with the conversion of an equitable joint tenancy in land into a tenancy in common. The term is also applied to separate the good parts of a contract from the bad: the latter being rejected. In respect of legal proceedings severance is applied to separate individual actions where an indictment contains more than one action where it is convenient for all parties to try each individual complaint separately. *See* JOINT TENANCY *and* TENANCY IN COMMON.

Severe mental impairment: Under the *Mental Health Act* 1983 severe mental impairment means a state of arrested or incomplete development of mind, including severe impairment of intelligence and social function, and is normally associated with abnormally aggressive or seriously irresponsible conduct on the part of the person concerned.

Shadow director: Indicates a person who is not registered as a director of a company but who nevertheless gives instructions which may expose the person who is the shadow director to the same obligations as a director properly constituted.

Sham foundations: The concept of sham can apply to an arrangement labelled as a foundation as much as to any other structure. The fact that foundations are frequently registered and receive official recognition of their formation by entry into a register is sometimes considered to be unimpeachable evidence of formation and that the structure is legitimised by this registration. However, the concept of a sham is wider than that. Although registration of a foundation may take place and the document may appear to express a genuine intention of the founder to set up a foundation, this may prove to be illusory. Despite an apparent genuine intention to set up a foundation using legitimate documentation and registration, the true intention of the founder after formation is demonstrated by his manipulation to use the foundation as purely a vehicle for his personal assets, disregarding the formalities required by the law and the documentation. This would constitute a sham foundation. *See* SHAMS (GENERALLY).

Shams (generally): A sham is a declaration of intent made with the purpose of giving a false impression to third parties and, ultimately, to the court. The declaration does not represent the true intention or motive of the parties and is made in order to obtain advantages which differ from the apparent intention as declared. There is a sham when acts or documents executed are intended by the parties who execute them to give to third parties or to the court the appearance of creating legal rights and obligations different from the actual rights and obligations that the parties intend to create. All the parties must have a common objective that the acts or documents are not intended to create the legal rights and obligations which they give the appearance of creating. This is a general rule but has been extensively applied to sham trusts, in particular where one person pretends to give property to another to hold on trust but really intends to maintain that the ownership shall not change. Equally, if the intention is that the legal owner shall hold the property on trust but the transferor does not part with the beneficial ownership of the property, this is also a sham. Where the beneficiaries have no rights to enforce a trust against the trustees and where the settlor retains the power, even with the trustees' consent, to appoint the entire trust capital to anyone, including himself (the settlor), despite an apparent power in the trust instrument to appoint a wide class of beneficiaries, this is equally a sham. *See* SHAM TRUSTS *and* SHAM FOUNDATIONS.

Sham trusts: This derived from the case of ***Snook v. London and West Ridings Investments Ltd.*** [1967] 2 QB 786, which was concerned with documents that appeared to represent a hire purchase transaction but in truth was a loan. The parties intended to secure advantages that would be obtained if the transaction had been seen to be a hire purchase contract over the restrictions imposed upon loans. This doctrine has been adopted in trust law in many jurisdictions in order to overcome the activities of settlers who pretend to set up a trust but really intend to be able to exercise their own free will over the trust assets. This became prominent in offshore trusts in the case of ***Rahman v. Chase Bank*** (C.I.) Trust Co. Ltd [1991] JLR 103. The principle in this case is now often brought up in courts in offshore jurisdictions. A leading example is in ***Minwalla v. Minwalla*** [2004] EWHC 2823, in which a husband set up a Jersey trust to hold his shares in offshore companies and other properties. An application by his wife, on divorce, for ANCILLARY RELIEF was objected to on the grounds that the husband did not have the assets in which the wife claimed a share as he had placed the assets in a trust. It was held that the trust was void as a sham and that the husband was the 'true and sole owner' of the pretended trust fund. The husband, the settlor:

> '[N]ever had the slightest intention of respecting even the formalities of the trust deed ... His purpose was only to set up a screen to shield his resources ... [His] intention was that the resources were his and would continue to be his ... and the trustees went along with his intentions.'

There are many uncertainties about the doctrine as it is yet to be considered by the Supreme Court of the United Kingdom. So far, it has been held that a provision in a lease may be a sham although the lease itself remains valid, and that certain provisions in a legal document may be so condemned without invalidating the whole. In any case, to constitute a sham it is necessary that the intention is to give a false impression. This produces difficulties because the finding of a sham carries with it an element of dishonesty; because innocent third parties may often rely upon the genuineness of the provisions, conflicts can arise. The court normally places great weight upon the existence and provisions of a formal, signed document. It is necessary to distinguish motive from intention and it has been held that a transaction is not a sham merely because it is carried out with a particular purpose or object; this distinction is expressed as:

> 'If what is done is genuinely done, it does not remain undone merely because there was an ultimate purpose in doing it.'

Difficulties with the concept arise where a settlor retains powers, interests and control. Where he does so, it does not necessarily make the trust a sham unless the settlor usurps the authority of the trustees. Trustees are usually parties to a sham, if not when the trust was formed then later when the settlor is allowed to exercise control of the trust funds; then the compliance of the trustees destroys the essence of the trust. This has led to the general rule that all parties must share the responsibility for what might appear to be a trust really being a sham. Similarly, with declarations of trusts, the settlor, in declaring that he henceforth holds property which he owns as a trustee, may have no intention of foregoing his absolute rights to the property. Other parties, such as the protector, may, in addition to the trustees, be a party to the irregularities. When a trust is a sham it is void, and assets in the hands of the trustees are then held in a resulting trust for the settlor who, in most cases, can be ordered to liquidate and thus increase his assets for division in a divorce settlement. So, an aggrieved party in a divorce can, by showing that the spouse's trust is a sham, outwit the other party's attempt to reduce his assets. Similar consequences arise in connection with a settlor's creditors, the Revenue Authority, trustees in bankruptcy, next of kin or others who are interested in the settlor's estate.

Shapeless trust: A term criticising the description of trusts given in Article 2 of the HAGUE CONVENTION ON THE LAW APPLICABLE TO TRUSTS AND ON THEIR RECOGNITION 1986. The breadth of the wording in Article 2 merely outlines the features of bodies that fall within the Convention. No concise and precise definitions are attempted. This was done purposely so as not to exclude arrangements from the Convention that does not conform to the definition of a trust as understood according to English law. In particular, there is no mention in the description of any influence of equitable principles. The draftsmen of the Convention presumably thought this was unnecessary and too restrictive to the internationalisation of the trust concept. The criticism directed at the draftsmen of the Hague Convention is principally that the intention was to shift the object of the Convention from the common law trust to an undefined realm of civil law-types of structures with a consequent broadening of the coverage. This is seen to remove the trust's basic characteristics and identity. This open-ended ability to include non-conforming structures has probably had an adverse influence, resulting in only a limited number of countries entering into the Convention. *See* HAGUE CONVENTION.

Share capital: The total nominal capital of a company in respect of the shares issued; thus, a company wishing to raise £1 million capital can issue one million shares of a nominal value of £1 each. The share capital of such a company is £1 million and is irrespective of the price at which these shares are issued (*see* SHARE PREMIUM). Any amount raised above the nominal capital is accounted for separately by placing the excess in a share premium account. The total nominal amount of shares which the company has made available for subscription is the issued share capital; this may be less than the amount that the company is authorised by its Memorandum to issue (the authorised capital). A company can raise further money by seeking further subscriptions for shares providing the 'authorised capital' is not exceeded. The authorised capital maximum can be increased by following the procedures of the applicable company law. Share capital is one way of financing a company; the other is loan capital, which is money lent to the company by creditors and which is eventually repaid by the company, in contrast to share capital that is permanently part of a company's structure and can only be returned by special procedures.

Share certificate: A printed certificate issued under seal by a company identifying the holder as a member of the company who features on the register of shareholders. The share certificate is some evidence of the named persons entitled to the shares but the company's register of members is better evidence. When the ownership of shares is transferred, the share certificate is delivered to the company with a share transfer document and a new certificate is issued to the new owner. Under the *Companies Act* 2006, listed companies in the UK operate an electronic uncertificated system which now makes share certificates redundant, their place taken by a computerised record held by the company.

Share premium: Shares may be issued by a company at a price greater than their nominal value. The difference between the nominal value and the amount received for each share is called the 'share premium' and is placed in a special account, the share premium account, which has a restricted use.

Shares: A measure of a member's interests and liability in a company limited by shares. Shares are also a means of nominating the apportionment of liability in unlimited companies and guarantee companies. Liability in a company limited by shares extends only to the unpaid amount of the shares but, with unlimited companies, the shares indicate the proportion of a total liability of the company for which the holder is liable in the event of the unlimited company becoming insolvent. In a guarantee company the shares limit the amount which each shareholder is committed to contribute in the event of that company's failure. Shares in a limited company may be ordinary shares that participate in the dividends without limit but which may be postponed to other classes of shares, such as preference shares, which take priority in the payment of dividends and in the distribution of any remaining assets of the company on liquidation. Preference shares may be denominated with special rights, such as CUMULATIVE PREFERENCE SHARES that entitle the holder to arrears of dividends whenever the profits justify payment. Redeemable shares are shares which are subject to a proviso that they may be bought back by the company if they are fully paid and the company choose to apply their profits on redemption. The term 'golden share' is sometimes used to enable the holder, usually a government, to outvote all other shareholders on certain types of company resolutions by attaching to such class of shares overwhelming voting rights.

Shariah: *See* section on ISLAMIC LAW GLOSSARY.

Signature of will: *See* EXECUTION OF WILL.

Simple contract: A contract made orally or in writing but not under seal.

Simple trust: Property vested in one person upon trust for another without the nature of the trust being specified by the settlor but left to the construction of the law. The trustee is a mere repository devoid of active management duties; the beneficiary, or *CESTUI QUE TRUST*, has the right to be put into actual possession of the property and the right to call upon the trustee to execute conveyances of the legal estate as he directs. *See* BARE TRUST. From 1 January 1997, under the *Trusts of Land and Appointment of Trustees Act* 1996, any simple trust before that date, where the asset concerned was real land or real property, became a trust of land.

Situs: The place in which an asset is located.

Sleeping partner: A person who puts money into a partnership but takes no part in the active management who is nevertheless liable for the full extent of his assets, as is any other partner, to satisfy creditors. A sleeping partner must be distinguished from a limited partner, who is protected from the exposure of all his assets, i.e. until such limited partner takes an active part in the partnership management. *See* LIMITED PARTNER.

Soft law: Rules not having the force of law, such as guidelines as to compliance or recommendations of international regulatory bodies. Although not legally enforceable, soft law is often respected and indicates codes of conduct which are influential and frequently adopted as the standards to be followed throughout the business to which it relates. Soft law is often taken as a set of acceptable principles which are adopted into enforceable domestic law or into the law of the EU.

Sole trustee: An individual or company appointed to be the only trustee of a trust. Frequently set up by large enterprises for a particular purpose where the exercise is independent from the sponsors, that is, it is off the balance sheet of the sponsor, such as pension schemes or one-off loan operations whereby the sole trustee is the managing bank of an international loan. The implication of setting up a sole trustee is that a replacement can be put into place with the minimum of delay and formality and is in the hands of the promoter or sponsor to the trust itself. Such a sponsor is in the position of a settlor but where there is a sole trustee the beneficiaries have no absolute right to the appointment of an additional trustee and the court would not appoint an additional trustee against the wishes of a sole trustee when the honesty of the sole trustee is not doubted. Where the court has jurisdiction to appoint a sole trustee, it is likely that the appointment will be made of the PUBLIC TRUSTEE. A sole trustee is able to give a receipt for all capital money. A sole trustee will not be discharged from his trust unless replaced by at least two persons or by a TRUST CORPORATION; the *Trustee Act* 1925 does not authorise the appointment of a sole trustee which is not a trust corporation and which is not able to give a valid receipt for capital money arising under the trust. The limitation on the ability of a sole trustee does not occur if the sole trustee is a trust corporation. The death of a sole trustee may sometimes produce difficulty in connection with trusts for individuals. If no one has been appointed to succeed a deceased sole trustee then the personal representatives of the estate of the deceased trustee can make an appointment. In the United States the replacement of a sole trustee depends upon the particular state law which governs the trust; the laws of many states provide that if the sole trusteeship is vacant, the title in the trust property vests in a named court of general equitable jurisdiction, which will appoint a successor. *See* SYNDICATE TRUST.

Sovereign: A body or person who is supreme and which may comprise a single ruler, a monarch, a body of persons such as an elected parliament or a Supreme Court that has the powers of enforcing the law, particularly when the positivist theory applies. *See* POSITIVE LAW.

Sovereign bonds: Bonds issued for investment or as guarantees by a sovereign authority taken up by international banks and investors.

Sovereign immunity: The exemption from the jurisdiction of the English courts of the sovereign or other head of a foreign state and foreign government department which is now contained in the UK's *State Immunity Act* 1978. *See* IMMUNITY.

Sovereign investment fund (SIV): A fund comprising the international investments of a state's surplus funds. Characteristically, oil-producing countries apply their surplus funds in making substantial equity investments in leading foreign companies.

Sovereignty: The ultimate source of authority in a state that defines the nature of that state and distinguishes a state from others. Sovereignty is zealously guarded against intrusions, both physical and legal; such intrusions are condemned as breaches of sovereignty.

Special personal representatives: A term applied to trustees of SETTLED LAND whose duties were to convey the land to the tenants for life or to the statutory owner and to act as trustees of the settlement generally. Special personal representatives are no longer applicable except to settlements established before the *Trusts of Land and Appointment of Trustees Act* 1996. *See* SETTLED LAND.

Special Purpose Vehicle: *See* SECURITISATION.

Special resolution: A resolution under the UK *Companies Act* 2006 that requires a majority of no less than 75% approval by members attending a general meeting or, in the case of a written resolution, an approval by 75% of the total voting rights of the eligible members. Special resolutions are called for to approve changes to some of the fundamental characteristics of a company, such as its name and the number of authorised shares. There is no equivalent procedure with trusts or foundations where any formality that may be required to follow a course of conduct must be specified in the trust deed or in the foundation charter or regulations which stipulate the limits of trustees and foundation councils. Both these vehicles may require the consent of a protector or similar person to approve a matter for which a corporation would require a special resolution.

Special trust: A term used to distinguish trusts where the beneficiaries are known and named from discretionary trusts. Also, the term is used to describe a trust where a trustee has active duties, such as administrative and dispositive powers, in addition to duties to preserve and enhance the trust's assets. This is in contrast to a BARE TRUST, where the person holding the property, the trustee, is a mere passive repository with no duties other than to safeguard and preserve the assets. The term is also sometimes employed to group together various trusts which have tax advantages, such as EMPLOYEE TRUSTS, PROTECTIVE TRUSTS, NEWSPAPER TRUSTS, PENSION FUNDS *and* TRUSTS FOR DISABLED PERSONS.

***Special Trust (Alternative Regime) Law* 1997 (STAR Trusts):** *See* STAR TRUSTS.

Special trusts: pension funds: A UK Revenue term applied to trusts set up as an approved superannuation scheme or as an approved personal pension arrangement that are generally exempt from tax charges; however, exemption from inheritance tax charges is subject to a potential pensioner not attempting to modify his rights under the trust.

Speciality: A contract made in writing under seal; a form known as a DEED or a COVENANT that, unlike other contracts, does not require consideration in order to be legally enforceable. In the past, speciality contracts were made by the parties attaching their seals in wax to authenticate their signatures to the written contract. Also, the document, the deed, was delivered, i.e. handed over to the other parties in a formal manner. Thus such a contract was termed as being 'signed, sealed and delivered'.

Specific legacy: *See* LEGACY.

Specific performance: A discretionary order that may be issued by a court addressed to one party to a contract requiring that party to perform his obligation. This order comes under the UK courts' equity jurisdiction, one principle of which is that equity will not assist a volunteer, and this maxim therefore makes specific performance unavailable to beneficiaries of trusts and foundations. Like other EQUITABLE REMEDIES, specific performance is based on the inadequacy of the legal remedy of awarding damages. Consequently it will not be awarded where damages at law give the offended party adequate compensation for the non-performance, for example, of a contract. That is, the equitable relief will not be granted where damages are an adequate remedy or where the contract concerned requires the use of a personal skill or the rendering of a personal service.

Spendthrift trusts: A term used in North American trust practice to describe a trust that has a similar purpose to a PROTECTIVE TRUST under English law.

Stamp duty: A tax on certain written instruments required to render those instruments valid as evidence of the underlying transaction. Stamp duty consists of a fixed or AD VALOREM fee paid by the affixing and cancelling of a stamp on the document. Under modern practice, stamps are impressed on the documents and adhesive stamps can only be used when expressly provided for. Where an unstamped document is presented, or one which is insufficiently stamped, it may be received in evidence on payment to the officer of the court of the unpaid duty, interest or penalty. In connection with land transfers, stamp duty has since 2003 been replaced by Stamp Duty Land Tax, which has become chargeable on any 'land transaction' whether or not the instrument is executed in the United Kingdom and whether or not any party to the transaction is present or resident there.

Stamp Duty Land Tax (SDLT): A tax that replaced, in the UK, the previous stamp duty provisions which related to the disposal of land and which principally introduced higher rates of tax. *See* STAMP DUTY.

Standard investment criteria: The criteria relating to trust investment, brought into effect on 1 February 2001 by Part 2 of the *Trustee Act* 2000, which replaced the existing complex rules on investment of trust funds. Under the Act a trustee may make any kind of investment that he could make if he were absolutely entitled to the assets of the trust (Section 3(1) of the Act). This is the 'general power of investment' applicable to existing trusts and those created after the commencement of the Act. This GENERAL POWER OF INVESTMENT is in addition to other powers of investment conferred on the trustees and is subject to any restrictions or exclusions contained in the trust instrument. But, in any case, under (Sections 4(3)(a) and (b)) of the Act, the standard investment criteria require the investments to be suitable generally as trust investments and any particular investment should contribute to the diversification in so far as is appropriate to the circumstances of the trust. The general power of investment does not permit a trustee to invest in land other than in loans secured on land (Section 3(3)), although Section 8 of the Act confers a power on a trustee to acquire land for investment and other purposes. The Act also provides a review of investments to be made from time to time having regard to the standard investment criteria and whether any variation is appropriate. Generally, a trustee must take proper advice on investments from a person who is reasonably believed by the trustee to be qualified, by ability and experience, to give such advice. However, a trustee may not do so if he concludes it is unnecessary or inappropriate. Failure to select an appropriate investment adviser may expose trustees to an action of negligence. Also, the *Financial Services & Markets Act* 2000 (FSMA 2000) defines investment by establishing a list of broadly defined market activities. The list ranges widely from securities in the form of shares to contracts of insurance and loans that are secured on land, etc. However, these categories are not referred to in the *Trustee Act* 2000 but nevertheless the duty of care required of trustees is relevant to the context in which the trustee is acting. Financial services regulations are concerned with the context of any investment which, if applied to trusts, would require the trustees, as the service provider under the Act, to categorise the level of expertise of a client, but it is difficult to reconcile the level of expertise of a trustee and that of the beneficiaries as a whole. However, the obligation is to deal with the client in a way in which investments are suitable to the trustee's own level of experience. This, at its simplest, is often referred to as the 'PORTFOLIO THEORY'.

Standard of care: The degree of watchfulness, attention, caution and prudence that a reasonable person would in the circumstances exercise in engaging in any activity. Failing to meet the standard of care may result in a claim for NEGLIGENCE. The standard of care which must be maintained in daily events to prevent a cause of action for negligence was laid down in ***Donoghue v. Stevenson*** [1932] UKHL 100:

> 'The rule that you are to love your neighbour becomes in law, you must not injure your neighbour; and the lawyer's question, "Who is my neighbour?" receives a restricted reply. You must take reasonable care to avoid acts or omissions which you can reasonably foresee would be likely to injure your neighbour. Who, then, in law, is my neighbour? The answer seems to be – persons who are so closely and directly affected by my act that I ought reasonably to have them in contemplation as being so affected when I am directing my mind to the acts or omissions which are called in question.' (Lord Atkin)

On this broad rule, the modern law of negligence has developed in many directions into the major TORT. The standard defined by Lord Atkin, subject to subsequent refinements, is the general standard of care under English law, as in the standard of care required by trustees in investing trust assets under the PRUDENT INVESTOR RULE.

Standard of proof: The degree of persuasion or the amount of proof that is required to convince a judge that the party presenting the case has succeeded. Only two standards of proof are recognised by the common law: proof on the balance of probabilities in civil cases and proof beyond reasonable doubt in criminal procedures.

STAR trusts: A form of trust introduced into the Cayman Islands by the *Special Trust (Alternative Regime) Law* 1997, now incorporated into the *Trust Law (Revision)* 2001. A wide variety of trusts may be set up under this legislation. This includes non-charitable purpose trusts, trusts for beneficiaries, or any combination. This is said to assist settlors who may wish to include both beneficiaries and purposes within the same vehicle. STAR trusts have certain interesting characteristics. STAR trusts cannot directly or indirectly own any interest in land in the Cayman Islands but may hold an interest in a company, partnership or other entity that holds land in the islands or an interest in such land for the purpose of its business. A special provision is made for administration and enforcement. STAR trusts may only be enforced by persons appointed to be enforcers by the terms of the trust or by an order of the court, whether or not that person is a beneficiary. A beneficiary does not otherwise have any enforcement powers. A person appointed as an enforcer has a fiduciary duty and has the same rights as a trustee to protection and indemnity and may make applications to the court for an opinion or advice. A special provision is made under the Act for the administration of STAR trusts, which may be administrative or dispositive or both and may be fixed or discretionary. STAR trusts may be endowed with powers that trustees may apply but are not obliged to do so. By making some activity the subject of a power and including that within the trust assets, trustees may exercise discretion as to whether to implement the power. This avoids the uncertainty that occurs in other trusts of whether a power is a pure power or a trust power.

Stare decisis: *See* COMMON LAW *and* CIVIL LAW.

Statute: One form of legislation, usually an Act of Parliament. The term 'statute' frequently indicates legislation that affects the state or other public bodies particularly in connection with constitutional affairs.

Statute of Elizabeth I: This Statute of Queen Elizabeth I (43 Eliz. 1 c.4., 1601) set out a guide for the courts on activities that are regarded in law as charitable. The contents of the Statute continued to be referred to despite the repeal of the Statute in 1888 and subsequent legislation such as the UK *Charities Act* 2011, where the definitions which first appeared in the Statute are recognisable. The Statute listed the precise nature of what was permitted to be regarded as a charity. This had a fundamental effect on the law of trusts. Purpose trusts, even if they are philanthropic, were not effective as trusts unless they met the requirements of being a charity under the Statute and were registered. The Statute of Elizabeth has had a profound influence over charities and purpose trusts and continues to do so through the modern legislation. However, in England and Wales, the test for qualification as a charity is according to the *Charities Act* 2011. Charities may also be set up as incorporated companies and, if they do not qualify according to the same criteria, are not regarded as charities although they remain valid companies. A charity has tax consequences that are denied to other philanthropic operations. Under the Statute of Elizabeth I, the following nine activities were included as charitable purposes:

(i) The relief of aged, impotent and poor people.

(ii) The maintenance of sick and maimed soldiers and mariners, schools of learning, free schools and scholars in universities.

(iii) The repair of bridges, ports, havens, causeways, churches, sea-banks and highways.

(iv) The education and preferment of orphans.

(v) The relief, stock or maintenance for houses of correction.

(vi) The marriage of poor maids.

(vii) The supportation [sic], aid and help of young tradesmen, handicraftsmen and persons decayed.

(viii) The relief or redemption of prisoners or captives.

(ix) The aid or ease of any poor inhabitants concerning payment of fifteens ('fifteens' are levies on capital of one fifteenth of the value of moveable property that was granted from time to time to the King; originated in the 12th century, the amount which each village or township was to pay was fixed by Edward III and, since it was not subsequently increased, it diminished in value and was last heard of in the reign of James I), the setting out of soldiers, and other taxes.

These categories have been interpreted by the courts and charitable purposes summarised in *PEMSEL'S CASE* as falling within four divisions: the relief of poverty; the advancement of education; the advancement of religion; and other purposes beneficial to the community not falling under the preceding heads but within the words or spirit of the Act of 1601 (***Commissioners of Income Tax v. Pemsel*** [1891] A.C. 531 at 538). The Charities Act 2011 has extended its description of qualifying organisations into 13 categories which make it easier to identify the proposed action that could be eligible for registration by the Charity Commission. The Statute of Elizabeth I has therefore been influential for centuries but the *Charities Act* 2006 replaced the four divisions with 12 charitable purposes, all of which are subject to an overriding (public benefit) test. *See* PEMSEL'S CASE *and* CHARITIES ACT 2006.

Statute of Uses 1535: A law introduced by King Henry VIII to counter the misapplication of 'the use' as a method of conveying property to another. *See* USE. The law is important as it opened the way for the development of trusts in the form in which they are now known. The Act was intended to overcome what the King believed to be the employment of uses to avoid obligations attached to the ownership of property; an early form of tax evasion. The Statute was intended to remove the equivalent to what is now regarded as the legal estate and the beneficial interest so that when a landowner passed property to another for the use of a third party, the legal title passed directly to the third party. In other words, the total interest in the property, the equivalent to the modern legal and beneficial interests, was passed immediately to the beneficiary. The intention was to ensure that the legal owner of the land should also be the beneficial owner. The King's intentions failed under the legislation because the statute only applied where one person, the 'trustee', was given land for the use of another, the 'beneficiary'. The law did not affect personal chattels, leaseholds or assets of which there could be no SEISIN in the technical sense. Neither did the statute apply where the person to whom freehold was conveyed had an active duty to perform, such as a duty to collect rents and pay them to the beneficiary; the Statute applied only if the use was purely passive. The most important exclusion was where there was a use upon a use. For example, freehold land conveyed to A to the use of B to the use of C. Then, only the first use was recognised by the statute; i.e. B was made the legal owner, but because there was no recognition at law of a use upon a use, C took nothing until the Court of Chancery interfered and enforced the use to C in the way that uses had been enforced before the Statute. This confirmed the division of freehold property into legal and equitable parts from which the modern concept of trusts developed by the practice of conveying property unto the use of T, a trustee, in favour of a beneficiary so that T became the legal owner and, as the limitation in favour of the beneficiary was not executed and was not automatically turned into a legal estate, the dual interest in freehold was able to develop into the law of trusts.

Statutory duty of care: *See* DUTY OF CARE.

Statutory limitation periods: *See* LIMITATION OF ACTIONS.

Statutory trusts: Trusts set up according to the terms of the *Law of Property Act* 1925 where assets are transferred to trustees on TRUST FOR SALE, which meant that trustees were compelled to sell the assets and hold the net value for the beneficiaries. Under the 1925 law, trustees had the power to postpone a sale unless the trust instrument required otherwise. This distinguished statutory trusts from settlements under the *Settled Land Act* 1925. Before the abolition of settlements of land by the *Trusts of Land and Appointment of Trustees Act* 1996, it was the practice of including a clause in deeds that the trust land was to be held on trust for sale, which emphasised that the trust should not be regarded as a settlement under the *Settled Land Act* 1925. The *Law of Property (Entailed Interests) Act* 1932 stated that entailed interests in undivided shares of land should continue to be held as entailed interests in the proceeds if the land was sold. The term is also used in connection with intestacy where property is held in favour of relatives and others entitled. *See* ENTAILED INTEREST.

Stet: Meaning 'let it stand'. The term is used where a correction, which is no longer required, has been marked in text to a deed or contract.

Stiftung: A Liechtenstein foundation, which is subject to the amendments to the law of the *Persons and Companies Act* of 20th of January 1926, made on the 26th of June 2008. *See ANSTALT and TREUUNTERNEHMEN.*

Stock lending: Despite the use of the word 'lending', this term indicates an outright transfer of stock by one party to another where the recipient is only bound by a personal obligation to transfer back assets of a like kind and like value at the end of a specified date; more of a transfer and re-transfer situation than actual lending and borrowing.

Stock options: A contractual right enabling one party to purchase stock from another at a predetermined price, known as a 'call option', or to sell to the other party the shares already held at a predetermined price, known as a 'put option'. Options are one of the forms of investments known as 'DERIVATIVES'. *See* OPTION.

Stop notices: May be sought as an order of the court where securities are held in the name of trustees and there is no disclosure of the existence of the trust. The notice seeks to prevent dealings with securities so as to allow sufficient notice of the intention of trustees to be given to the beneficiaries, and serves to inform beneficiaries of the risk of dealings in trust property about which they would not otherwise be entitled to information (CIVIL PROCEDURE RULES, Part 50, Rule 51).

Strict settlement: A strict settlement was a means of conferring a beneficial interest in land on a person called the 'LIFE TENANT' who held the land normally for his life, according to the terms of the settlement, and after his death the land would pass usually to his heir. Unlike other trusts (trusts for sale) the trust assets were managed by the life tenant, the chief beneficiary. Included in these management powers was the freedom to manage and enhance the land and this included power to sell the land. On such a sale the proceeds were not at the free disposal of the tenant for life but were to be held by trustees in trust for whoever's interest came after the life tenant's. The intention was to keep the land (or the proceeds of its sale) in the settlor's family. A strict settlement was frequently set up as a marriage settlement where a life interest was given to the husband with the remainder to the first son of the marriage and then to the other sons in tail followed by a further remainder to any daughter or daughters as tenants in common with a final remainder to the husband in fee simple. Provisions were made in the marriage settlement for the wife to receive financial support should she be widowed (a JOINTURE) and for support of younger children of the marriage (portions). Under the terms of the *Trusts for Land and Appointment of Trustees Act* 1996, new strict settlements cannot now be made but existing settlements can continue. Any attempt to create a strict settlement since 1997 will result in their being construed as trusts for sale. The use of such strict settlements fell in popularity due to crippling tax regulations after World War II; their place was then taken to a large extent by discretionary trusts where no beneficiary was nominated in the trust instrument. *See* ENTAILED INTEREST, TRUST FOR SALE *and* PORTION.

Strong v. Bird*, Rule in, (1874-80) All ER Rep. 230:** The rule in ***Strong v. Bird is an unusual situation where a trust becomes completely constituted without the actual transfer of the trust assets by the donor. The rule is to render a voluntary settlement valid and effectual provided that the settlor must have done everything according to the nature of the property that was necessary to be done in order to transfer the property to the trustees. This is the rule in ***Milroy v. Lord*** (1862) 4 De G.F. & J. 264, but the principle in ***Strong v. Bird*** operates where the owner of property intends to make an immediate specific gift to 'A' but, without changing his mind and before completing the gift, he dies and the intended donee, A, becomes the deceased's personal representative and, provided it was the deceased's intention to make an immediate gift to A and not to make it a gift of the same property under his will, then A's interest prevails over any contrary provision in the will. Therefore, to operate this rule requires that the property was in existence and had been specified and the donee was appointed executor or administrator. If these conditions are fulfilled, A takes the asset as a gift from the deceased despite any interests that the beneficiaries might have had under the will. This rule comes about by analysing the situation to deem that a trust of the property had been set up despite the defect in the transfer of the property. The rule is therefore an exception to the general rule of ***Milroy v. Lord***.

Subinfeudation: A process by which medieval landowners attempted to carve out and grant to others estates in land to be held of themselves so that the obligations existing at this level of tenure to provide services, military services and various income-producing duties was created between them. The consequences of this subinfeudation were that it decreased the power and wealth of the great landholders by diluting authority and increasing the number of estates in the chain. Subinfeudation was abolished by the statute *Quia Emptores* 1289, so that if B held land of A in fee simple, B could not grant another layer of fee simple to C and could only introduce C if C held the land of A and not of B, i.e. that B transferred the land to C and the direct passage of feudal tenures was then from C to A. Alongside this feudal concept of land tenure, the concept of leasehold property developed under which C could occupy land held feudally by B without the need of replacing B and without offending the ban on the subinfeudation. This was done by C taking a contractual interest in the property, i.e. he took possession of the land in exchange for a rent. From this developed leasehold interests which did not offend the ban on subinfeudation since none of the feudal consequences of land ownership passed to the tenant. Because the system of leasehold was primarily contractual, leasehold property was regarded as personal property and not real property. Leasehold, along with freehold, was the two legal estates in land recognised by the *Law of Property Act* 1925, which categorised other interests as merely equitable. *See* LEASEHOLD.

Subject to contract: A well-used phrase that makes it clear that the parties do not intend to be contractually bound. This renders an apparent agreement between the parties to be unenforceable and not subject to enforcement by an order for specific performance. The words 'subject to contract' are used especially with written offers which indicate that the party using them does not intend any proposition contained in the writing to constitute an offer that is capable of being accepted by the other party to lead to a binding contract. This indicates that the writer needs to consider other matters before making an offer that would lead to a contract. Similarly, the words are used when acknowledging the receipt of an offer and at the same time denying that the acknowledgement is an acceptance and therefore no contract has been concluded at that time. In oral negotiations a similar situation exists, although without a written document as evidence the matter rests with proving the parties' intentions whether or not this simple formula is used.

Subjects of a trust: All property, real or personal, legal or equitable, may be transferred to trustees to hold on trust. The exception lies in respect of where the law prevents the beneficial interest of property being transferred. Therefore, a trust can be declared of an equitable interest under an existing trust, such as a trust of a wife's equitable interests. This extends to include even VESTED or CONTINGENT reversions. However, interest in FUTURE PROPERTY, such as under a discretionary trust, can only be settled into a trust for value. Interest in litigation and in respect of the benefit of a contract can be placed in trust, as can a covenant against the assignment of a lease;

placing it in trust does not break the covenant. Matters which cannot be included in a trust are certain pensions, a peerage and land that is declared to be inconsistent with the tenure under which it is held. *See* EQUITABLE INTERESTS, SETTLEMENTS OF FUTURE PROPERTY *and* REVERSION.

Subpoena: A document issued by a court to compel the attendance in court of a person to provide evidence or to provide documentary evidence at a specified time. Subpoenas were replaced by WITNESS SUMMONS in all cases, including criminal proceedings, under the *Criminal Procedure (Attendance of Witnesses) Act* 1965 and the *Magistrates Court Act* 1980. Traditionally, subpoenas were of two types: a subpoena *duces tecum* required a person to attend court with documents specified in the subpoena; and a subpoena *ad testificandum* required a person to attend court to give oral evidence.

Subrogation: The right of a person to exercise a lawful claim, demand or right by another person, such as being entitled to another's right to claim a debt, remedies or securities. An insurer that settles a loss is entitled to the benefit of any right or remedy of the assured in respect of the insured loss. Typically, when the insurer pays out in respect of damage to property then the insurer takes over the right to sue the person causing the damage for the estimated costs which the insurer has paid. In the case of a total loss then the insurer becomes entitled to the object that is damaged and may dispose of it as he will.

Subsidiarity: This is a principle of EC law by which the intention is to have decisions taken at as low a level as possible. This means that there is a preference for action to be taken at the domestic level of Member States unless action at the Community level is required.

Subsidiary companies and foundations: A company controlled by another company. Even if a subsidiary company's shares are held entirely by the holding company, both companies are distinct legal entities and one company is not the agent of the other in the absence of any agreement. A company that is wholly owned by trustees, as part of trust assets, is not a subsidiary company of the trustees. Likewise, a company wholly owned by a private foundation is not a subsidiary of the foundation. Such a company would be part of the foundation assets. Private foundations, although they are legal entities, are not capable of being owned or of owning other foundations since the concept of being a subsidiary requires ownership of one organisation by another through the holding of shares. A foundation may set up another foundation but the ownership of one foundation by another is a concept that has not been developed.

Substantial performance: Performance of a contract with only slight variations from the exact terms or with unimportant omissions or defects and which may easily be remedied by a nominal amount of damages and where the incomplete performance does not merit a rescission of the contract.

Substantive law: *See* ADJECTIVE LAW.

Substantive rules: A term used to distinguish rules that affect the relationship of parties from PROCEDURAL RULES. Substantive rules are determined in accordance with the choice of law rule in contracts, trusts and foundations, rather than the law of the forum, which universally is the source of procedural rules.

Substitution: A clause in a will that contains a gift to a class of persons with a clause stating that on the death of a member of that class his share is to go to his issue. The gift to that issue is in substitution of the original gift. For example, a bequest by A to such of his children as are living at this death or, in the case that any of his children shall then have died, then to their children. The term is also used in procedural rules allowing, in CIVIL PROCEDURE RULES (CPR), Part 19, the parties in civil litigation to be substituted.

Sub-trusts: Trusts, sometimes miscalled DERIVATIVE TRUSTS, created out of another trust. The difference is illustrated by considering a trust where A holds property on trust for B and then B declares that he will hold his beneficial interest in the property for C. This declaration of trust may mean that B retains no duties to perform as a trustee of his beneficial interest on the grounds that A continues to perform all the trustee duties and B will simply drop out of the picture, leaving the original trustee, A, holding for C. This type of arrangement is a derivative trust and theoretically is not considered to be a genuine example of a sub-trust, but if B, by declaring the trust in favour of C, has some duty to perform in his capacity as trustee, i.e. B does not drop out as in the above example, then a genuine sub-trust will have been created and B retains liability to perform the specified duty.

Succession: The taking over of property, duty, office, titles or rank from a predecessor; principally a term used where a deceased person's property passes to another under a valid will. This type of succession is governed by the law relating to wills or to intestacy. The term, despite its applicability to property passing under a trust to a beneficiary, is rarely used in that context.

Sui juris: 'Of his own right' and which is used to describe in common law a person who is not a minor, nor insane, nor the subject of any other disability. In civil law, the term describes one of the classes of persons under the law and covers those persons who are not *ALIENI JURIS*. In English law the term is particularly used in trust law to describe beneficiaries and is used as one test in determining whether all beneficiaries are eligible to put an end to the trust under the doctrine in ***Saunders v. Vautier*** (1841) 4 Beav 115.

Summing up: A judge's summary of the main points of evidence presented to the court for the benefit of the jury to help them concentrate whilst considering their decision. Where a judge has some further issue to address, these extra items may be referred to as the 'judge's instructions' and the term 'summing up' is confined to highlighting the relevant matters dealt with in the final arguments of counsel to the jury.

Supplemental deed: A deed that is expressed to be supplemental to a previous deed and is taken to have the same effect as if it contained the full recital of the previous deed. Supplemental deeds may sometimes be used to add to terms of an express trust; for example, where a person entitled under a trust deed has the power to add or remove beneficiaries, this is done by supplemental deed.

Supra: Above, and used in respect of matter that has been printed earlier in the work or on a previous page. *See* INFRA.

Supreme Court of the United Kingdom: A newly constituted court which, after the *Constitutional Reform Act* 2005, took over from the House of Lords in England and Wales the role of being the final court of appeal. This term is not to be confused with the previous Supreme Courts of England and Wales, which were the Court of Appeal, the High Court of Justice and the Crown Court and which are now known as the SENIOR COURTS. These courts were given the title 'Supreme' because under the *Judicature Act* 1873 the intention was to abolish the superior appellate role of the House of Lords; before the Act came into place it was decided to keep the House of Lord's jurisdiction but the title 'Supreme Courts' was retained and so became a misnomer.

Surety: A person who enters into a contract with an actual or possible creditor of another by which the surety undertakes to be responsible to the creditor for the repayment by the debtor of whole or part of the debt. This contract is often called a contract of GUARANTEE; the surety being the guarantor. In a contract of guarantee the person who provides the security (the surety or guarantor) assumes a secondary responsibility to answer for the debtor who remains primarily liable, i.e. the original debtor continues to be expected to repay the debt and the surety/guarantor acts when the debtor does not pay. This contrasts with a contract of INDEMNITY, where the surety, or indemnifier, assumes a primary liability either jointly with the principal debtor or alone. The principal difference between a contract of guarantee and a contract of indemnity is that a contract of guarantee must be evidenced in writing and signed by the person to be charged, i.e. the guarantor. A contract of suretyship, whether guarantee or indemnity, as a contract, requires that the debtor must provide consideration for the other party's undertaking to be bound unless the contract is entered into by deed. When the contract is entered into other than by deed (i.e. by a simple contract) then it must be entered into before the debt is incurred since the consideration for entering the guarantee contract is expressed as 'in consideration of the creditor giving credit to the debtor'. Failure to enter the contract prior to the establishment of the debt will result in the guarantee being invalid for lack of consideration. In other words, a consideration to enter into that contract of guarantee refers to a debt that had been previously incurred, so it is a case of past consideration, and PAST CONSIDERATION is no consideration. Although a contract for guarantee or suretyship may be entered into as a simple contract, the consideration must also be contemporaneous with the incurring of the debt, but even with such a simple contract it is necessary that there is some evidence of such contract in writing in order to be able to enforce that contract. This is the last remaining item first enacted under the Statute of Frauds 1677, which, because of the difficulty of providing evidence of various types of transaction, required evidence in writing to be produced. *Note*: this evidence in writing is of a simple contract although other simple contracts, by law, have to be made in writing, such as a contract of marine insurance, i.e. made in writing but not necessarily by deed. A contract of suretyship is the same in law as a contract of guarantee. The term 'surety' is usually restricted to a case where the person, the surety, binds himself by a bond. For example, persons entering into an office of responsibility may often be required to obtain sureties that bind them by bonds to answer for the principal person's acts or defaults in the performance of the office. A surety, if he is called upon to satisfy the debtor's obligation, is entitled to recover the amount from the principal debtor himself. (*Note*: the same word, surety, applies to the type of transaction and to the person who is committed under it.)

Survivorship: The entitlement to property by a person who survives another person who also had an interest in the property concerned. For example, in the case of joint tenants, the rule is that on the death of one of the two joint tenants the whole property passes to the survivor. In connection with wills, there may be difficulties in deciding whether the word has a natural meaning (PER CAPITA) or a meaning associated with the concept of *PER STIRPES*. *See* *COMMORIENTES and* JOINT TENANTS.

Swaps: A financial transaction where the holder of currencies, commodities, loan transactions or other financial contracts exchanges his rights with another person who holds similar benefits under other contracts. The object is for each party to end up with more beneficial outcomes by each party being in a better position with regard to changes in the exchange rate of currencies, the price of commodities or interest rates, since they entered into their original contracts. Swap transactions normally follow the ISDA (International Swap Dealers Association) standard conditions. These standard terms are unduly complex and the subject of much controversy, particularly as the courts have refused to allow claims against banks by parties to a swap transaction for breach of contract, negligent misstatements and negligent misrepresentations, for breach of a collateral contract and for a breach of fiduciary duty where mis-selling of swap transactions is alleged. *See* ***Bankers Trust v. P.T. Dharmala*** [1996] C.L.C. 518.

Syndicate trusts: A trust set up by a group of persons engaged in a commercial venture by which the trustee, most likely to be the lead banker, manages the commercial venture and provides financial administration for the project in order to protect the capital contributions of each member of the group by monitoring the project and collecting interest and other payments. This trust arrangement is created when the preference is for a trust, rather than for the setting up of a company, by avoiding the formalities of corporate formation when the need is for immediate administration of a short-term project. If a project turns out to be successful, permanent incorporation may follow. A trust may be preferable to a company due to the greater confidentiality maintained by the trustees (the project leader) over other members of the syndicate; a trust may be off balance sheet and if the project is short-lived or unsuccessful then the unwinding of the operation is simpler. For example, a syndicate of banks contributing funds to a large loan, a syndicated loan, may often do this by way of a trust that is managed by the lead banker (the project leader), who performs the duty of trustee and monitors the payments of interest and the general conformity of the borrower with the terms of the loan agreement. *See* SOLE TRUSTEE.

T

TABOL: An acronym indicating 'trusts arising by operation of the law'.

Tail: A term derived from the French '*tailler*', meaning 'to prune', and applied in English land law where the ownership of land is less than absolute. An ESTATE TAIL is a term applied to land that is ENTAILED, i.e. the ownership is less than the absolute ownership since the occupier, the entailed tenant, does not have the right to retain money obtained from the sale of the land. This traditional way of preserving assets over several generations was codified by the *Settled Land Act* 1925, but has been severely restricted from 1 January 1997 by the *Trusts of Land and Appointment of Trustees Act* 1996, which preserved the entailed interests then in existence but prevented the formation of any new entails. *See* ENTAILED INTEREST.

Tangible property: Physical things (such as horses, houses, books, etc.), as distinct from intangible property (such as intellectual or industrial property or CHOSE IN ACTION).

Tax: A compulsory levy by the state on taxpayers, usually by means of direct taxes levied on income, capital gains, inheritances and gifts INTER VIVOS, and indirect taxes such as VAT and other duties levied on purchases. CORPORATION TAX is levied on corporate profits. There are various other types of tax, such as tax on motor vehicles and special taxes on sales of fuel and cigarettes. Liability to tax in any country depends upon a legally defined association with that country, usually by residence or some legal concept which deems residence. Tax on foundations is in many jurisdictions uncertain, and depends on how the tax authorities view private foundations. When viewed as corporations, the tax as a general rule is levied on the foundation itself and when it is viewed as the equivalent of a trust, tax is levied on beneficiaries. The taxation of trusts is complex and is riddled with anti-evasion measures, which may result in tax being levied on the founder, the trustees or the beneficiaries. Foundations and trusts may be subject to INCOME TAX and CAPITAL GAINS TAX. In many jurisdictions both foundations and trusts may be exempt from income and capital gains tax if, by the law of the jurisdiction in which they are resident, they are regarded as charities. Some offshore jurisdictions exempt trusts and foundations from tax when they are formed under their laws on condition that no property is owned within their jurisdictions.

Tax avoidance: A lawful arrangement of a person's or a company's financial affairs so as to reduce liability for tax. Originally tax avoidance was a legal form of planning, as opposed to tax evasion which was deliberately criminal. The modern attitude of tax authorities and governments is that any planning to mitigate taxation is objectionable and deserving of anti-tax avoidance measures to recoup unpaid tax. In traditional tax avoidance one test that was applied was whether a series of transactions resulted in the taxpayer reducing his liability to tax without incurring the economic consequences that those transactions would normally incur (***IRC v. Willoughby*** [1997] 1 WLR 1071 (HL)), i.e. a taxpayer arranges his affairs to secure a tax benefit that was not intended by the law. A frequent example of tax avoidance was the use of a trust where a settlor in a high-tax jurisdiction transferred assets to trustees in a low-tax jurisdiction and instructed the trustees to hold the assets on trust for his children as beneficiaries. The assets would then be invested and the trustees would accumulate the income and pay less tax than would otherwise have been incurred if the settlor had retained the legal ownership of those assets in the country in which he was resident. Tax avoidance took advantage of manipulating the law without actually breaking it. Although many arrangements were lawful, the courts developed the practice of ignoring steps in a series of transactions which added nothing of substance to the end result; in other words, loopholes in the tax law were ignored when deciding on the liability of a taxpayer. In current practice, it is likely that such measures are incorporated into statutes and place the onus on the taxpayer rather than, as formerly, on the tax authorities, to show the true tax position. Also, the present climate of tax legislation and international tax rules militates against tax avoidance by increasing the level of transparency in international asset management, which reveals where artificial steps may occur. The ongoing campaign of the OECD against transfer pricing will add to this campaign against tax avoidance by overcoming the technique of transferring assets from a high-tax jurisdiction with minimum profits to a low-tax jurisdiction where the assets are then sold and the low-tax profits accumulated. BEPS (BASE EROSION AND PROFIT SHIFTING) is aimed at corporate tax planning that will allow action by tax authorities to be brought against a parent company rather than expecting the jurisdiction where the subsidiary is situated to counter the tax planning advantages. This, when effective, will remove the tax advantages previously shown by offshore centres. A similar shift is likely under the implementation of the *US Foreign Account Tax Compliance Act* (FATCA) 2014. Such a shift will require an increase in the accounting and reporting requirements of offshore operations.

Tax evasion: An illegal activity to avoid the lawful assessment of tax; for example, by making a false statement or concealing or failing to declare income or capital gains or other taxable events.

Temporary charitable trusts: Transfers into trusts for charity that are limited for a certain period or subject to powers of revocation that take the benefit of the trust away from the charity and give it to someone else. In the UK these trusts are not taxable as such a temporary charitable trust is not relevant for the purposes of trust taxation and so does not incur the 10-year anniversary charge levied against other trusts. If a trust ceases, or a distribution is made from the funds, a liability arises to inheritance tax, but there is no charge in respect of normal discretionary payments, which continue to be taxed at the normal rate.

Tenancy at will: A tenancy in property that usually arises by implication where the owner of the land allows a person to occupy it without the formality of a fixed term or periodic tenancy, for example, where a landlord permits a tenant to occupy premises before the formal grant of a lease or before the transfer of the freehold. Under a tenancy at will, the landlord may terminate the occupation and demand repossession at any time. If the landlord begins to accept rent on a periodic basis, an ordinary periodic tenancy is created. This may result in the landlord's right of termination of the occupation and ability to repossess the property being impeded.

Tenancy in common: A form of ownership by more than one person where each has a distinct interest in the property. Tenancy in common is also called 'UNDIVIDED SHARES IN LAND'. Each tenant's interests may be identical or different from that of other tenants. Interests may exist in any type of property. Interests may arise from the same act or different acts and may exist for unequal durations. A tenancy in common differs from a joint tenancy, where joint tenants enjoy one shared interest in the whole with no individual quantifiable shares. A further difference is that a right of survivorship applies to a joint tenancy where, on the death of a joint tenant, the other tenants continue to hold all the property. Generally, a tenancy in common will be the rule where an instrument creates properties held in shares, equally or otherwise, or where the nature of the property is such as to preclude the intention of survivorship, such as the holding by partners of property for the purpose of their business where individuals may enter the partnership at different times and where the assets of a partnership varies over the years. This means that with tenants in common there is no unity of interest between each tenant, although there is a unity of possession. A voluntary deed of partition would put an end to a tenancy in common by subdividing the land and allocating a part to each tenant individually. A tenancy in common may also be upon the union of all the titles and interests in one tenant. *See* JOINT TENANCY.

Tenant: A person in possession of land by virtue of a relationship of landlord and tenant or one who holds land under an agreement for a lease. The term is sometimes applied to personal property as well as to real property; for example, someone may be a tenant for life in shares. In its broadest use, every person with an estate in land is known as a tenant, such as a person with an estate in fee simple. Also, tenants at sufferance hold the possession of land after a previous title has ended. Such a tenant may secure his possession against anyone with no better title although, under modern law, this may not apply against a tenant with a fixed term or periodic tenancy. A tenant at will is a contractual arrangement under which possession of land is allowed but which may be ended at the whim or will of the landlord (who, in any case, constitutes a person who has a better title to the land). A tenant for life is entitled to land either for his own life or for that of another person.

Tenant in tail: A person entitled, on the death of an ancestor, to an entailed interest (*see* TAIL).

Tentative trust: A term frequently used in North America that generally describes a REVOCABLE TRUST where one person deposits money in his own name as trustee for another but where the depositor's creditors can recover what is owing from the deposit. This type of trust may be regarded as a particular example of a BARE TRUST, which revolves around the revocable nature of the deposit although, with a bare trust, it is generally a trust for the depositor, whereas a tentative trust is a trust for some other person. A tentative trust may also be called a TOTTEN TRUST.

Tenure: The nature of a legal estate held in land, being either FREEHOLD or LEASEHOLD although, in respect of freehold, the term is no longer used and the only tenure of any significance is that of a tenant of leasehold property.

Term of years absolute: A term of years or lease and one of the two legal estates in land (the other is the FEE SIMPLE ABSOLUTE IN POSSESSION). Although the description 'absolute' is applied, such a term of years may be in possession or reversion, with or without a rent, and with or without impeachment for waste and which may be terminable by notice, re-entry or by law, but does not apply to any term of years determinable on death or any other estate, which, since 1925, would be an equitable estate (*Law of Property Act* 1925, Section 205(1) (xxvii)).

Terms of art: Words or phrases which have a specific and precise meaning due to being customarily applied to particular circumstances. These are usually technical words that have been interpreted in law for precise meanings and where that interpretation has been accepted by custom and judicial use. This is somewhat unreliable, however, since the expression is used to suggest certainty when, in reality, the situation is open to conflicting interpretations in different branches of the law.

Testacy: Dying after having made a valid WILL, as opposed to INTESTACY.

Testamentary capacity: The legal capacity of a person to make a valid will depends upon the absence of a disability such as infancy or mental incapacity. A person under the age of 18 does not have such capacity, except for soldiers on active military service and for mariners and seamen at sea. Mental capacity must exist at the time a person gives instructions to create a will or codicil. At the time of execution it is sufficient that the person understands the nature of the document he is being asked to execute, but not necessarily the details. Where insanity intervenes between the execution of a will or codicil and death, the will is not invalidated. When a will or codicil is entered into during a period of mental incapacity, a subsequent recovery does not remove the invalidity. Under the *Mental Health Act* 1983 there are, in the United Kingdom, four categories which may affect the capacity of a person to manage his property, MENTAL DISORDER, PSYCHOPATHIC DISORDER, SEVERE MENTAL IMPAIRMENT and mental impairment.

Testamentary disposition: The division of a testator's estate according to the terms of the testator's valid will.

Testamentary trusts: Also known as WILL TRUSTS and consist of trusts that are declared by will. When a trust of property owned by a testator is intended to take effect only on his death, and to be recoverable until then, it must be created by will or codicil and executed by the testator according to the *Wills Act* 1837. So, an attempt to create a trust which would be operative on death would be invalid under the *Wills Act*; the act of setting up the trust would not conform to the formal requirements to create a valid will. A trust that is immediately valid and operative during the settlor's lifetime by removing property from the settlor's estate is outside the *Wills Act*. For a trust to be validly set up by will, the will itself must be valid. The will must express an irrevocable declaration that a trust is to be set up with details of the trustees and beneficiaries. If the will is revoked before death, this revokes the intention to set up a will trust. When the will is granted probate this is conclusive proof of the validity of the will and therefore the validity of the intention to set up a trust. The trust comes into existence even if the persons designated as trustees are incapable or unwilling to act. The executors act as the trustees until other persons designated by the testator can be endowed with the legal ownership of the assets. *See* WILL, CODICIL *and* PROBATE.

Testate: The term applied to a person who dies having left a legally valid will, as opposed to someone who dies intestate.

Testator: A person who makes a will or testament (the feminine version, testatrix, is rarely used).

Test case: An action in court brought with the intention of obtaining a judicial decision on a point of broad application. The courts generally will not adjudicate on hypothetical situations but where a situation arises on which many appellants base their case on an unsettled point then an action on behalf of one of them will obtain judicial interpretation on that particular matter, which can be applied by other appellants to their own situation, i.e. the initial case before the court that establishes the principle is called a 'test case'.

Testimony: The evidence delivered orally in a court by a witness in reply to examination by counsel and which is sometimes called oral testimony to distinguish it from evidence provided in documentary form. The term is applied also to evidence generally, including statements that are exceptions to the hearsay rules, and to dying statements.

Thellusson Act: The name under which the *Accumulations Act* 1800 was known and that imposed restrictions on the period allowed for accumulations and which went hand in hand with the rules against perpetuities. The Act was re-enacted in 1925 and again as the *Perpetuities and Accumulations Act* 1964 with amendments. *See* PERPETUITIES AND ACCUMULATIONS.

The National Conference on Commissioners for Uniform State Laws: A body created in the United States in 1892 consisting of practising lawyers, judges and academics appointed to draft proposals for uniform and model laws. This body recognised that in many states the law on trusts was rather 'thin'. In the year 2000, a proposed uniform trust law called the Uniform Trust Code (2000) was published and amended in 2001, 2003 and 2004. By 2010, this Uniform Trust Code had been adopted by 23 states; it has been rejected by several states and is still under consideration by others.

Third party: A term used to describe a person or group who, while not a party to the transaction concerned, is ancillary and features in the transaction but not in the dispute. For example, a third party is not a party to a contractual dispute but nevertheless has a part to play in the performance of the contract.

Time and trustees conduct: Conduct of trustees is judged according to the practices and law at the time the trustees had to act after taking into account the circumstances existing at that time and which were known, or ought to have been known, by them when they acted. New trustees should make sure that the trust fund is properly invested and should review the investments in existence and ensure that the trust portfolio is sensibly balanced as far as capital and income growth are concerned, as well as being appropriate to achieve the objectives of the trust. They do not need to hunt for breaches of trust committed by former trustees but, if the new trustees do not enquire into suspicious circumstances, they may be liable if the trust assets suffer, even though the new trustees had no part in committing the original breach of trust. Apart from being stimulated by suspicious circumstances there is no obligation on new trustees to make an investigation into existing investments either as to their title or their value so long as they are authorised investments. This must be balanced by the obligation of all trustees to make periodic reviews of their trusts' investments (***Nestle v. National Westminster Bank plc*** [1993] 1 WLR, 1260).

Time is of the essence: A phrase applied to contractual obligations, which indicates that the precise time of the performance is mandatory according to the terms of the contract. Generally, time is not of the essence in contracts and to make it so, the contract must specifically state that time is of the essence.

Tipping off: Informing a suspect of information in circumstances where the information may be used to frustrate further investigation or legal proceedings. ANTI-MONEY LAUNDERING LAW makes the tipping off of a person under suspicion a criminal offence.

Title: A right, such as a right to property, referred to as a title to the property. In the UK the *Law of Property Act* 1925 uses the term 'title' in a way analogous to its use in ordinary contracts where title, i.e. the right to the property, passes from seller to buyer. The significance of title in the transfer of real property was illustrated by the old rule that the seller of property was required to show a good title, i.e. he had the right to sell or lease the property concerned. Investigating the title of the seller was one of the principal branches of conveyancing where the seller had a duty of proving that a good title would pass to the buyer on purchase; that is, the buyer obtained a good marketable right to the property. However, under modern law, LAND REGISTRATION has affected this aspect of land transfer. When land registration was introduced under the *Land Registration Act* 1925, the seller had to prove title under the provisions relating to the registration. This was done by producing copies of subsisting entries on the register, copies of title plans and copies of abstracts of relevant documents. Since 1990, the register has been open and because of computer technology the system of searching the register is simpler and cheaper. The *Land Registration Act* 2002 does not prescribe how title to a registered estate should be deduced, but an existing entry on the register is accepted as a proof of title and obtaining a good marketable right to the property has become a matter of re-registration.

TOLATA: The *Trusts of Land and Appointment of Trustees Act* 1996.

Tontine: A financial arrangement where lenders each receive a life annuity, the amount of which to each lender increases as other lenders die; the last survivor receives an annuity amounting in aggregate to the total of the original annuities for the rest of his life. A system used mostly in the 18th century in the UK.

Tort: A word used in English law to denote a civil wrong. Scottish law and civil law use the term 'delict'. A tort is a civil wrong which gives rise to an action for damages other than one which is exclusively a breach of contract, a breach of trust or other equitable obligation. English law, unlike French law, does not have an all-embracing principle of liability for causing harm and this branch of law has no unified structure but generally covers offences against persons and property and reputation in actions that are separate and subject to their individual concepts. Falling particularly within the scope of tort are negligence, trespass, libel, slander, fraud and deceit, which depend upon the intention of the person committing the offence. In other offences that constitute a tort, redress for damage can be obtained regardless of the intention, and these are known as offences of strict liability, such as certain invasions of real property by others. There are also torts that inflict pure economic loss, such as procuring breach of contract, intimidation, interference with trade by unlawful means and conspiracy. *See* DECEIT *and* FRAUD.

Tortfeasor: A person who commits a civil wrong or tort.

Totten trust: *See* TENTATIVE TRUST.

Trace: Trace is the verb expressing the process of tracing.

Tracing: The process by which a person who has been deprived of an asset may identify a new asset as a substitute for the original asset and may elect to treat the substituted asset as representing the value contained in the original; the deprived person traces the value represented in the original asset into the substituted asset. Tracing is not a claim or a remedy but a rule of evidence to prove some claim which is then enforced by a remedy that may be personal or proprietary. Different rules have been evolved at common law and in equity. The main difference is that at common law, when an asset is replaced by money, that amount of money cannot be followed through into a fund which is a mixture of the fund and other money. Tracing into a mixed fund is permissible under the equitable rules. These equitable rules have been expanded and the difference is now not as important as it used to be. In any case, the rules cannot be applied interchangeably, i.e. a failed attempt to follow money at law cannot be remedied by a claim at equity; tracing is not a series of two alternative remedies but rather a question of evidence. Equitable tracing persists rather longer than tracing at common law but will fail if the original property, or any of its traceable proceeds, ceases to exist or is dissipated. For example, although money paid out of a bank account can be traced into the next bank account that right is lost once that bank account becomes overdrawn and there is no possibility of tracing the transferred money into that second bank account because there is no money remaining. Precise rules govern the effect in a mixed fund and generally rule out, in a tracing application, money that is not attributable to the claimant or wrongdoer. The JUDICIAL COMMITTEE OF THE PRIVY COUNCIL has, however, approved the concept of BACKWARDS TRACING in one case (*see* EQUITABLE TRACING). Limits to tracing are also imposed where the defendant received the property in good faith and then suffered some change in his personal circumstances. Then the court may consider that it would be inequitable for the defendant to return the property to the claimant on the basis that the defendant acted in reliance of having acquired rights in that property. Other defences to tracing are by ESTOPPEL by representation or by a BONA FIDE purchaser for value without notice of the claimants' rights, or by a consensual transfer.

Trading foundations: Foundations that are entitled by their governing law to act as trading organisations and which, by their constitutional documents, are authorised to do so. Public foundations are subject to their own constitutional documents, which may or may not permit trading directly; foundations of a charitable nature may wish to trade to increase their charitable funds and would most likely do so through wholly owned companies established for this purpose where the shares are wholly owned by the foundation as part of their assets. Private foundations are widely prohibited by the law which governs their formation from engaging in commercial activities that are intended to produce a profit. The intention of a private foundation is to preserve and invest funds that have already been presented to the foundation as the foundation assets. However, in the foundation assets a founder may include shares of a company which will continue to trade and the profit may be handed over to the foundation as a contribution to its assets. Where a private foundation is set up for the purpose of holding the shares of a family business, this should be examined carefully and according to the law which controls the foundation, in view of the doubts placed upon the validity of such a purpose. *See* DIRECTLY OUTWARD-RELATED FOUNDATION PURPOSES.

Trading trusts: A trust that conducts business; this business may be for the benefit of the beneficiaries or for the purposes of the trust, in the case of public or charitable trusts. Any limits on trading activities will be contained in the trust instrument. Evidence that any proposed trading is lawful may be required by a prospective counterparty to a transaction. Public or charitable trusts will conduct their trading through a CUSTODIAN authorised to conduct the business on behalf of the trust. In practice, trading is best carried on through a company; if a transaction is ULTRA VIRES then the creditors will not be paid out of the trusts' assets. The decline of the ultra vires doctrine which has taken place with companies (*Companies Act* 1985, Section 35, in the UK) still exists with trusts. Similarly, a creditor will not be paid out of trust assets on a trustee's default although this can be varied in the trust deed. In the event of a trading trust becoming unable to pay its creditors, recourse may be had against the individual trustees; insolvency, for which there is a special regime for companies, does not apply to trusts.

Transactions at an undervalue: Sales of property by an individual or a company at less than the market value made in order to reduce the amount available to the creditors of the transferor. Gifts may also be regarded in this way if the intention is to deprive the creditors. A trustee in bankruptcy can bring an action for a court order to set aside such a sale or GIFT. No such action will be made if the court is satisfied that a company entered into the transaction in GOOD FAITH for the purpose of carrying on the business of the company and there were reasonable grounds for believing that the transaction would be of benefit to the company. The modern law is contained in the *Insolvency Act* 1986 (Sections 241, 341 and, in respect of trusts, under Sections 423 to 425). The latter sections allow a trust to be set aside when transfers are made to it at an undervalue. If a private foundation is involved, the court could consider for this purpose that a foundation should be treated as an incorporated body similar to a company. The acquisition of property in this way may not result in the person who took the property having to return it provided it was obtained in good faith, for value and without notice of the relevant circumstances.

Transfer of equitable interests: The assignment of an equitable right (or, more precisely, of an equitable chose) such as a legacy, a legatee's right in an unadministered estate, the surplus proceeds when a mortgage is foreclosed or a share in a trust fund, may be made by a statutory or an equitable ASSIGNMENT. The statutory assignment is governed in the UK by the *Law of Property Act* 1925, Section 36, which requires an assignment to be made in writing and to be an absolute assignment, i.e. not part of a debt or other right where a right may be assigned as an incidental to other transactions. Notice in writing must be served upon the debtor of the new identity of the creditor. Parallel with this, assignments may be made under rules of equity where there are no requirements as to the particular form but will generally be either a direct assignment to the assignee or to his trustees for him. An equitable assignment may also be made by a simple direction to the debtor to pay the debt to the assignee, or where the right to be assigned is held in trust by instructing the trustee to hold it on trust for the assignee; alternatively, there may be simply a declaration of trust made by the assignor in favour of the assignee. The absence of formal requirements to make an equitable assignment requires that there should be a visible intention to do so. With assignments of rights already held on trust, there is a statutory requirement (under the *Law of Property Act*, Section 53(1)(c)), that a transfer of 'a disposition of an equitable interest or trust subsisting at the time of the disposition must be in writing duly signed'. Equitable assignment of rights of property that are not yet in existence requires that value be given to the assignor by the assignee in order to effect the assignment. For example, an expectation of a legatee under a will may assign his rights to receive those assets but that can only be done for value, thus making it a contractual matter. Otherwise, all that is necessary is that the assignor has done everything required to be done in order to transfer the right. Also, the assignor is not required by law to give any notice of an equitable assignment to the creditor but nevertheless it is advisable to do so (so that the assignee is known as the new owner of the right). Whether the assignment is legal or equitable, the assignee does not acquire a better title to the right than the assignor had, and the assignee takes subject to all equities which existed against the assignor in respect of the right assigned.

Transformation: *See* DOCTRINE OF INCORPORATION OF INTERNATIONAL LAW.

Transparency: A doctrine requiring that the parties to financial and other transactions should be identifiable and that they should reveal essential features of their transactions to tax authorities. The intention is to facilitate compliance with tax laws and the detection of tax evasion, tax avoidance and of breaches of anti-money laundering laws. In the UK transparency is required under the *Financial Services and Markets Act* 2000 in accordance with the European Parliament and Council Directive No. 2004/109/EC requiring disclosure of information in connection with the acquisition or disposal of major holdings of securities and major shareholdings in companies. Transparency is also required by the OECD Global Forum on International Taxation on company owners and beneficiaries of trusts and foundations, especially when these structures are set up in offshore jurisdictions. *See* GLOBAL FORUM *and* TAX EVASION.

Treasury bills: An English term which is used under the *Treasury Bills Act* 1877 that authorised the Treasury to raise money by the issuing of treasury bills, the international term for which is 'government bonds'. The term 'treasury bill' is used as an indication that the money raised is repayable not more than 12 months after the date of issue; if repayable later than 12 months, the term 'note' is used.

Treaty: An agreement between states (also called 'Convention', particularly where the terms are taken from established models or precedents; for example, a Double Tax Convention between State A and State B incorporating terms taken from one of the model treaties provided by the United Nations or the OECD). When in written form (as most treaties are) they are enforceable under international law provided the treaties are signed on behalf of each state and undergo whatever ratification procedure each signatory state requires. Treaty making is a prerogative of sovereign states. In some states treaties become immediately effective and enforceable on signature while in others, such as the UK, a signed treaty does not become effective until it has been laid before Parliament and approved by both Houses, a process called ratification. A treaty, although ratified, does not give rise to rights or obligations in the UK and many other countries until its terms have been incorporated into domestic law by an Act of Parliament, although it might be relevant for other purposes, such as the interpretation of subsequent legislation. With trusts the principal treaty concerned is the multilateral Hague Convention on the Enforcement and Recognition of Trusts. *See* DOUBLE TAXATION TREATIES *and* HAGUE CONVENTION ON TRUSTS.

Treuhandverwaltung: A trust-like arrangement set up under German law by an administrator of an estate that owns property separate from other persons involved (*Sondervermogen*). The German government has made it clear that it does not intend to adopt the HAGUE TRUST CONVENTION so the question of whether this German structure complies with the Convention does not arise.

Treuhand: A term used in German-speaking jurisdictions (Austria, Germany and Liechtenstein) as a term for a trust which would be subject to the law of the jurisdiction concerned. *See* *FIDUZIARISCHE TREUHÄND*.

Treuunternehmen: A Liechtenstein body that has legal personality, sometimes called a 'trust enterprise', which is organised under the Liechtenstein *Persons and Companies Act* 1926, Article 932(a) paragraph 1-170. *Treuunternehmen* is a business-orientated entity which is described as a 'proper business trust pursuant to the law'. The trust enterprise has an unlimited range of permissible purposes; it must be registered in the Public Register and is therefore sometimes described as a registered trust. (A form of trust without legal personality is called a real trust or specific business trust (*treuhänderschaft*), which may be organised so that neither the settlor nor the trustees are liable for its debts; any trust-like enterprise that does not have legal personality is not eligible for tax privileges.) The original 1926 Act was amended to introduce the trust enterprise in 1928 and that amendment also provided a large variety of legal entities, giving rise to a range of not less than 19 different possible structures. The most commonly used are the trust, the foundation, the company limited by shares, the limited liability company, the establishment and the trust enterprise. The law on trust enterprises contained many provisions which were applicable by reference to the then current law on private foundations. Since the 2010 revision in Liechtenstein of the Foundations Law, this cross-referencing is unnecessary.

Trust: A confidence accepted by a person, called the trustee, for the benefit of another, called the *CESTUI QUE* trust or beneficiary which, in its simplest form, is a relationship between two persons, one of which, the trustee, holds property for the benefit of the other, the beneficiary. To all outward purposes, the trustee appears to be the absolute owner who is compelled to honour his obligation, both by the arrangement between the two parties, such as by a TRUST DEED, and by the GOVERNING LAW. In countries which derive their trust law from English law this is by the law of equity, including the obligations imposed by the term 'FIDUCIARY DUTY'. Trusts arise either by an act of the parties, where a settlor (in the US, a grantor) conveys assets to a trustee who, in accepting the assets, undertakes the obligation of holding them according to the settlor's wishes or subject to the trustee's own discretion for one or more beneficiaries, if so provided in the trust instrument. Express trusts are created by clear words but a trust may also arise by implication; that is, an implied trust arises when circumstances clearly indicate that a transferee is not intended to take the beneficial interest in assets transferred. Trusts may also be set up for the benefit not of individual persons but for a purpose. In English law, such a purpose trust, to be valid, must be for a charitable purpose and recognised by the CHARITY COMMISSIONERS and the Tax Authorities as a CHARITABLE TRUST. Trusts may also arise by operation of the law, as is seen in resulting and constructive trusts. These are trusts which are not declared either directly or indirectly but which result from the effect of a rule of equity from the circumstances. Trusts may also be created by will. *See* TESTAMENTARY TRUSTS *and* IMPLIED TRUSTS, CONSTRUCTIVE TRUST, RESULTING TRUST *and* FIDUCIARY RELATIONSHIP.

Trustafarians: Beneficiaries who are assured of a comfortable life and who avoid undertaking any work, career or responsibility and who live off what can be extracted from the trust by relying on the indulgence of the trustee, who acts out of respect for the settlor. The term is used to indicate disapproval of irresponsible beneficiaries. Trustafarians are sometimes called TRUST BABES.

Trust babes: *See* TRUSTAFARIANS.

Trust corporation: A company appointed by the court, or entitled to act under the *Public Trusts (Custodian Trustee) Rules* 1926, to act as a trustee and which may exercise all the powers, jointly or solely, that two individual trustees would otherwise be required to administer. A trust corporation may take the form of a company which is incorporated by a special Act or by charter, or may be a company under the *Companies Act* 1948 with an issued capital of not less than £250,000 of which £100,000 has been paid up in cash. The Treasury Solicitor is also 'a trust corporation'. A trust corporation is a particular type of trustee authorised by statute to be used when a trusteeship is required for official bodies. A trust corporation should not be confused with limited companies that act as trustees either as private trust companies or professional trustees, which may be independent operators or a subsidiary of a bank or similar organisation. *See* PRIVATE TRUST COMPANY.

Trust deed: A written document that sets up and evidences an express private trust. The word 'SETTLEMENT' is sometimes used as an alternative term for the trust instrument (the word 'settlement' also means the actual trust-based arrangement as well as the document setting it up). This document is referred to in US practice as a 'trust agreement', in contradiction to the principle that a trust is not a contract. This important document can vary in length from US trust deeds of several hundred pages to the short form of 'off the peg' trust document of many offshore jurisdictions where the detail is left to the discretion of trustees. Insurance companies may use a short form of trust deed to enable insured persons to direct that any proceeds of a life policy should be held on trust by the insurance company as trustee for distribution and thereby avoid the proceeds being included in the insured's estate and liable to tax. A trust deed is normally written under the instructions of the settlor and contains details of the objects and subject matter and the disposition of the income and of the capital of the trust. Generally, a trust deed cannot be changed (*See* VARIATION OF TRUST *and* LETTER OF WISHES). Trust deeds may be standard form documents which give little scope for a settlor's individual wishes to be incorporated, especially in investment and commercial operations.

Trust domicile: A state whose law the settlor has chosen as the governing or proper law of the trust. A trust does not have to be administered in the same state; for example, Panama trusts that have a domicile in Panama are frequently managed in Switzerland.

Trust duty: A levy similar to STAMP DUTY levied on documents in most countries and which is applied to trust instruments. For example, in the British Virgin Islands a trust duty of US$100 is charged on every instrument declaring a trust or showing evidence of a trust or an interest in a trust. The same duty is levied on instruments changing the governing law of a trust, although wills and instruments creating or terminating bare and charitable trusts and supplementary trust instruments are not chargeable. The tax is paid by the fixing of a revenue stamp to the document, which is cancelled by signing over the stamp in accordance with the provisions of the BVI Act.

Trustee: A person who holds property on trust. The office of trustee is a personal one. If there are several trustees then the trust assets are held by the trustees as joint tenants; if a trustee dies the office devolves on the surviving trustees, as does the property. Trustees of an express trust are appointed by the settlor in the trust instrument. In other types of trust, constructive or resulting trusts in particular, the law dictates who acts as trustee. The power of appointment may be held by someone who is not a trustee himself but such a person is still a fiduciary in relation to that power and sometimes, in connection with trusts outside the United Kingdom, that power lies in the hands of protectors. In the UK, if a trustee cannot safely administer a trust he may request the High Court to administer the trust by an 'Alternative Procedure for Claims' under Part 8 of the Civil Procedure Rules (CPR), formerly known as an ORIGINATING SUMMONS. Also in the UK, the High Court and the County Courts have jurisdiction, under Section 41 of the *Trustee Act* 1925, to appoint a new trustee when it is difficult or impractical to do so without the courts' assistance. The court also has an inherent jurisdiction that is wider than provided by Section 41, as the court may also simply remove a trustee without appointing a replacement. Where a trustee neglects or refuses to administer a trust, or is guilty of a breach of trust, any beneficiary may institute an action for the execution of the trust by the court. A trustee must use the same care in acting for a beneficiary as would a PRUDENT MAN OF BUSINESS acting for himself. A trustee operates under a FIDUCIARY DUTY and must not derive or attempt to derive any benefit from the trust unless he is authorised to do so. The detailed rules relating to trustees represent a substantial proportion of the law relating to trusts.

Trustee capacity: The capacity of a person to be a trustee depends upon the capacity of the person concerned to hold property. Corporations and individuals may therefore be trustees of pure personalty and of land. However, there is nothing to prevent a minor from holding property on an implied, resulting or constructive trust.

Trustee de son tort: A person not being a trustee and without the authority from a trustee who takes upon himself to intermeddle with trust matters, or do acts characteristic of the office of a trustee, makes himself 'a trustee of his own wrong', i.e. *trustee de son tort*, also termed 'CONSTRUCTIVE TRUSTEE'. Such a person is fully subject to fiduciary obligations and assumes a primary liability when he is in breach of a trustee's duty of which he should have made himself aware. Dishonesty is not a prerequisite to liability. An honest busybody who takes it upon himself to assume an active role in the management could be construed as a *trustee de son tort*. This primary liability contrasts with the secondary liability incurred by those who assist dishonestly in a breach of trust because, in that case, the offence follows a primary breach of trust by the trustees. *See* DISHONEST ASSISTANCE.

Trustee exemption clauses: Clauses in trust deeds intended to exempt trustees from liability for a breach of trust or other default, including negligence. These clauses include 'exoneration clauses', 'indemnity clauses', 'exclusion clauses' and 'exculpatory clauses', each of which may be capable of small variations in interpretation. Following ***Armitage v. Nurse*** [1997] 2 All ER 705, these clauses were recognised as valid and preserved trustees from liability for negligence and other defaults except for their own fraud. There was a strong opinion that these clauses should have a very restricted use when applied by professional trustees. The Law Commission for England and Wales considered the matter and recommended that the trust industry should adopt a non-statutory rule of practice to be enforced by the regulatory and professional bodies which govern and influence trustees and the drafters of trusts. The Law Society and the Institute of Chartered Accountants in England and Wales have introduced a regulation for their members and the Society of Trust and Estate Practitioners (STEP) has adopted a version of the rule which they intend to be obligatory on its members in England and Wales. The recommended rule governs the disclosure and explanation of clauses in trust instruments which have the effect of limiting or reducing liability for negligence. Principally, the rule requires professional paid trustees to take reasonable steps to ensure that settlors understand the meaning and effect of such clauses before they are included in trust instruments. The Law Commission Report recommended that drafters of trusts should also be subject to the rule. The Law Commission published its Recommendations in 2006, which were accepted by the Government in a statement from the Ministry of Justice in 2010.

Trustee in bankruptcy: A person in whom the property of a bankrupt is vested which is held in trust for the creditors. In the UK this type of trustee is an individual qualified to act as an insolvency practitioner. The trustee's duty is to investigate, realise and distribute amongst the creditors the assets of the person who has been declared bankrupt and, in doing so, must investigate the claims of the creditors and reject or reduce them according to the circumstances. The trustee may investigate the bankrupt's bank accounts and can be expected to enquire into the existence of any trusts or foundations that the bankrupt might have set up which could have been used to defraud creditors. The course of these proceedings is subject to inspection by a committee of the creditors. In the UK the trustee in bankruptcy is governed by the *Insolvency Act* 1986, Sections 272-297.

Trustee indemnity: A trustee is entitled to be indemnified for liability incurred in properly carrying out the terms of the trust. The trustees exercise this indemnity by making a claim against the trust assets. Such indemnity is sufficient to protect trustees for expenses incurred in connection with the management of the trust (such as legal fees). If a trustee engages in business enterprises which have been unauthorised by the trust deed, the trustee is personally liable for any losses without any indemnification from the trust assets. To avoid this complication, a business operation should be conducted by a limited company the shares of which form part of the trust assets, but such a manoeuvre does not guarantee that a trustee always avoids liability.

Trustee powers: Usually called 'powers of appointment' and which are either administrative or dispositive powers, i.e. the power may be concerned with the administration of a trust or how the trust assets are distributed. These powers are particularly significant when trustees are given discretionary powers. Administrative powers are powers to manage or dispose of particular items of trust property and these usually consist of powers of appointment, i.e. to distribute the trust assets absolutely, or powers of MAINTENANCE and ADVANCEMENT. Powers of appointment are powers that allow the holder to create or grant beneficial interest in the trust property out of a stated range of persons or a class of persons according to the trust instrument. Powers are distinguished from trusts themselves in that while trusts are imperative, powers are discretionary. This distinction is blurred by the existence of a category called 'TRUST POWERS', which involves elements of obligation, i.e. the trustee is given the power but there exists an element that it is mandatory upon him to exercise it according to the trust instrument. Such powers contrast with mere or bare powers that impose no duty to act on the holder, although individually a power may be fiduciary in character and this includes powers given by a trust instrument to a person other than a trustee. Powers of appointment may be either general powers or special powers. A general power allows the holder to appoint anyone in the world, but special powers only allow the holder to appoint from a specified class or group of individuals. It is not clear whether it is possible to confer a fiduciary power in order to achieve a particular purpose, e.g. the provision of funds restricted to provide only the salaries of employees. Powers are subject to a variety of individual judicial and academic classifications which frequently subdivide or vary the categorisation given above. Dispositive powers tend to be less confused by repeated reclassifications. (*See* POWER OF APPOINTMENT, ***Barclays Bank Limited v. Quistclose Investments Limited*** [1970] AC 567; ***Twinsectra v. Yardley*** [2002] UKHL 12 at 100 *and* TRUST POWERS.)

Trustees' conflict of interest: Persons may be appointed as trustees even though at the time they have a conflict of interest with the affairs of the trust. They may be appointed, although the court would not have made or sanctioned such an appointment. For example, two solicitors in partnership; a bank where the beneficiary is a customer; a director of a company some of whose shares are trust assets and who is a member of the class of discretionary beneficiaries. 'The law expects that if a conflict arises the trustees will handle the situation carefully and appropriately in the circumstances but no one suggests that such persons can be appointed in the first place' (***Isaac v. Isaac*** [2005] EWHC 435 (Ch.)).

Trustees' duties: *See* DUTIES OF TRUSTEES.

Trustees of charities: The responsibilities of trustees of charitable trusts are similar to those of other trustees. The number of trustees allowed for charitable trusts is not limited by statute. They need not be unanimous in exercising their powers. Trustees of charities have as their primary obligation the distribution of the assets rather than the conservation of them, but must nevertheless show the trustee's standard of care in management. *See* CY-PRES.

Trust for sale: A trust that obliges the trustees to sell the trust property and hold the proceeds of sale on trust. This was formerly important where trustees held land in order to avoid the settlement coming within the *Settled Land Act* 1925. Since the *Trusts for Land and Appointment of Trustees Act* 1996 prevented the creation of new strict settlements of land, the distinction may seem to be less important but, with trusts for land introduced as a consequence of the 1996 Act, it is still preferable to mention that any settlement is a trust for sale. The instruction to trustees to sell the trust assets can be accompanied by a clause allowing them to postpone the disposal, although such a clause sometimes causes concern to the beneficiaries, who would like to see the trust assets kept in their present state.

Trust funds: The securities mentioned in the instrument creating the trust and any other investments in securities made by the trustees that are permitted under the law, such as the *Trustee Act* 2000, unless otherwise excluded by the terms of the trust deed.

Trust instrument: The deed or other document, such as a will or a simple declaration of trust, that sets out the terms of the trust and which needs to accommodate the requirements of CERTAINTY OF INTENTION, CERTAINTY OF OBJECTS and CERTAINTY OF SUBJECT MATTER and gives the information about the first trustees to set up a valid trust. Where the trust instrument is a deed it should bear the proper AD VALOREM stamp duty.

Trust powers: A power to which there is some trust element attached, sometimes referred to as a power in the nature of a trust. These powers differ from mere or bare powers, even where they are held by a trustee or are fiduciary in nature. A trust power is distinctive in that it ordinarily imposes a duty to select who is to benefit from amongst the class of beneficiaries. Being of a trust nature, this is a compulsory obligation, as distinct from a mere or bare power that merely creates an ability to do a certain act without any obligation to actually perform. If a person to whom a trust power is given fails to execute it then the court may execute it, provided that the intention of the donor of the power can be gathered from the terms of the instrument or the surrounding circumstances.

Trust property: The assets of a trust which the trustees are required by the trust instrument to hold on trust for the beneficiaries. These assets may be either the initial endowment to the trustees by the settlor or property acquired thereafter, either by donation to the trust or as a result of trustees' investment of trust funds as allowed by the law or by the trust instrument.

Trusts against public policy: Provisions in a trust document that are considered to be invalid as being contrary to the public policy of the law, i.e. the trust attempts to achieve something which, although not specifically unlawful, is considered likely to have adverse consequences. For example, a trust will be contrary to the policy of the law if a beneficiary is given an equitable interest that survives his death. Such an interest cannot be included in a trust; attempts to do so will result in the interest being included in the beneficiary's estate. Further examples of trusts against public policy are trusts that aim to prevent or discourage beneficiaries from going to court to contest a will, to contest a lifetime trust, attempts to separate parent and child or trusts that are adverse to religion and morality. *See* NO CONTEST CLAUSES.

Trusts and settlements: *See* SETTLEMENT *and* TRUST.

Trusts for bereaved minors: A type of trust introduced in the UK *Finance Act* 2006 for persons under the age of 18 where at least one parent has died. These trusts may also be set up following the death of a grandparent who dies intestate and one of his children dies leaving children, i.e. grandchildren who are minors but who, on attaining the age of 18, will take, under the rules of intestacy, the share of the grandparent's estate that their father would have taken. The grandchildren, while under 18 years of age, qualify as bereaved minors and trusts for them will enable the property that they will acquire under the intestacy of the grandparent to be held on statutory trust for their benefit. These trusts incur no charge for inheritance tax so long as the bereaved minor receives absolute ownership before his or her 18th birthday. Without this advantage, the property could still be held on trust for the minor but would not benefit from this special inheritance tax exemption.

Trusts for disabled persons: *See* TRUSTS FOR VULNERABLE BENEFICIARIES.

Trusts for vulnerable beneficiaries: Trusts for disabled persons and children (called vulnerable beneficiaries by the UK tax authorities) have tax advantages. A vulnerable beneficiary is a person who is mentally or physically handicapped or a person under 18 years of age (called a relevant minor) who has lost a parent through death. Trusts set up for vulnerable beneficiaries enable trustees to claim special treatment for income tax and capital gains tax providing the trust fulfils various qualifying tests. The income tax and capital gains tax advantages are that the trustees claim any difference between the tax paid as trustees and what the vulnerable beneficiary would have paid if taxed directly. Also, there is no inheritance tax on transfers made to the vulnerable beneficiary and there is no 10-year inheritance tax charge, but when a beneficiary dies any assets held are treated as part of his or her estate. A trust cannot qualify if the person setting up the trust can benefit from the income; the vulnerable person must be entitled to all the income of the trust, otherwise none of the income can be applied for the benefit of anyone else. Qualifying trusts for relevant minors must be set up by the will of a parent who has died where the assets and income are used only for the relevant minor, who then receives all the trust assets at the age of 18. Alternatively, a trust can be made under the rules of intestacy. The special tax exemption must be claimed and information sent to the tax authorities. A separate claim must be made in respect of each beneficiary. Each claim only takes place from the date the appropriate form is submitted; there is a time restriction on when it should be made. The special tax treatment is not available if the vulnerable person dies or is no longer vulnerable. If in the same trust there are other beneficiaries who are not vulnerable, the assets and income for the vulnerable beneficiary must be identified and kept separate and used only for the vulnerable beneficiary.

Trusts in Scotland: Although the property law of Scotland is entirely of a civil law nature, Scottish trusts date from the 17th century. This demonstrates that there were other models on which to base Scottish trusts rather than the English version. An important source was the *fideicommissum* of Roman law which served as a basis for Scottish trusts and remained so despite the influence of English law in the 19th century. Where assets are held by a trustee for beneficiaries, the trustee holds two patrimonies (*see* PATRIMONY): one in respect of his own private assets and the other in respect of the trust assets. These two patrimonies remain separate and distinct; there can be no cross claims between them. A trust patrimony cannot become bankrupt in the same way as a private patrimony. Where a trustee dies his private patrimony passes to his heirs and is likely to be broken up between them, while the trust patrimony remains intact and lives on in the hands of a new trustee. The separation into two patrimonies means that in the event of the trustee becoming personally insolvent, and the trust patrimony having remained untouched, the beneficiary obtains the trust assets free from the claims of the trustee's personal creditors. The beneficiary in a Scottish trust has only personal rights and no rights IN REM as exist with English trusts.

Trusts of land: Under the *Trusts of Land and Appointment of Trustees Act* 1996, where land is held on trust, the distinction between the legal and the equitable owners of the land must be clear as without that that there can be no trust. To fulfil this requirement there must be two or more joint tenants of the legal title in the property to constitute trustees who hold for the benefit of the beneficiaries. Beneficiaries may be either JOINT TENANTS or TENANTS IN COMMON; if they are the former, then the doctrine of SURVIVORSHIP will allow the property rights to pass to the survivor. Where the beneficiaries are tenants in common then their rights are severable and they are at liberty to deal with the rights as they think fit within the law of trusts. A trust of land originally was a SETTLEMENT under the *Settled Land Act* 1925 but, after the *Trusts of Land and Appointment of Trustees Act* 1996, attempts to create a settlement resulted in a 'trust of land' (as the 1996 Act calls them), which are subject to the same law as applied to trusts of personal property.

Trusts of Land and Appointment of Trustees Act 1996: A UK Act that converts all settlements of land into trusts of land that are made after the Act came into force; the *Settled Land Act* 1925 no longer applies to settlements of land formed after the Act became effective. The Act also applies to bare trusts and all trusts for sale of land are made into a composite form of trusts where land forms any part of the trust property. Any BARE TRUST then in agreement, or created later, falls outside the definition of trusts for land and will be capable of being overreached. The 1996 Act also provides that where land is held by trustees subject to a TRUST FOR SALE, the land is not regarded as PERSONAL PROPERTY. On the other hand, personal property (i.e. money) that is subject to a trust for sale for the purpose of trustees acquiring land is not regarded as land, as was the case before the Act. The Act thus abolishes the doctrine of CONVERSION in this context; the doctrine of conversion sometimes produced unexpected results. Also, where previously under the doctrine of conversion land became partnership property, it was treated as personalty both between the partners and their representatives after a partner's death unless a contrary intention appeared. Now, under the 1996 Act, partnership property is regarded as REALTY. Conversion may still apply under an order of the court for the sale of realty in which two or more persons are interested. In that case conversion takes place not from the date of the sale but from the date of the order so that if one party dies before the sale his interest is therefore considered as PERSONALTY for the purpose of the devolution of his ESTATE. Also, when there is a specifically enforceable contract to sell realty, the realty is treated as part of the vendor's personalty from the moment the contract is made. Where the contract is conditional then the conversion takes place at the moment the conditions are fulfilled and if there is an OPTION to purchase realty a conversion occurs when the option is exercised. In these last two circumstances conversion may occur after the vendor's death. Conversion does not apply where there are mere pre-emption rights over the realty. These examples are based upon the rights the vendor retains after a contract of sale all lead to his right to recover and receive the purchase money on failure by the other party, i.e. receive personalty. Conversely, after a contract has been entered into, the purchaser's interest is treated as realty and the obligation to pay the purchase money devolves after the purchaser's death before completion to the person to whom realty passes. This depends upon the contract being specifically enforceable. Under the Act, a trust of land includes express trusts, constructive and resulting trusts and implied trusts, bare trusts and trusts for sale and any other description, with the exception of settled land, which was subject to the *Settled Land Act* 1925 before the 1996 Act came into force or land to which the *Universities and Colleges Estates Act* 1925 applied. *See* SETTLEMENT, OVERREACHING *and* CONVERSION.

Trusts of imperfect obligation: Where a trust has no named beneficiaries nor any means of determining who the beneficiaries are, for example, by reference to a class or group of persons, the obligation on the trustees is said to be imperfect in the sense that there is no person upon whom the trustees are required at that time to confer a benefit. It is a principle of English law that trusts set up for a general purpose, i.e. a trust with no specific or ascertainable beneficiaries, should be void. The exception is centred on the anomaly that if the purpose of the trust is charitable (which in English law means approval as such by the CHARITY COMMISSIONERS) then that trust can be enforced. In addition, there is a very small number of trusts that are not charitable and which have no ascertainable beneficiaries which are nevertheless recognised at law and termed 'trusts of imperfect obligation'. If these trusts are capable of being indirectly enforceable, the courts recognise them. These have included trusts of legacies for the erection and maintenance of tombs, for the maintenance testator's animals and even for the promotion of fox hunting. Enforcement is achieved by the legacy being paid by the executors to a legatee who undertakes to apply the funds for the object specified in the will. The residuary beneficiaries or the next of kin may apply to the court in case the legatee fails to do his duty. Since the object of the trust cannot take proceedings the legatee cannot be directly and positively compelled to fulfil the object, hence the name given: trusts of imperfect obligation. Sometimes trusts of imperfect obligation may be construed as MERE POWERS to carry out the specified purpose as a RESULTING TRUST in favour of the settlor, residuary legatee or next of kin.

Trust, variation of: The *Variation of Trusts Act* 1958 gave the court jurisdiction to vary trusts on the application of any interested party even though the variation may have been intended to avoid tax. The court has great discretion to allow or refuse a request for a variation that may be put forward for the benefit of either minors or beneficiaries with contingent interests or unborn or unascertained beneficiaries. Under the Act a variation will only be allowed if it is for the benefit of a class of beneficiaries. If the intentions of the settlor are not conclusive they may be overridden by the court. Otherwise, apart from the authority of the court and the limited variation possible under the Act, the variation of a trust is almost impossible unless provisions are provided for in the trust instrument.

Two-party rule: The rule in equity which prevents a trustee from purchasing for his own benefit land which he holds as trustee. The rule was applied at common law where a person contracted with himself and another, but that has been reversed by statute; as long as there is no precise identity of the parties, a contract may be validly made and the validity is not affected by one or more of the persons being on both sides of the contract. But the loosening of the rule at common law does not affect the position of a trustee and so a trustee cannot enter into a contract to purchase trust property. Because there is then no valid contract for purchase by the trustee, the equitable interests of the beneficiaries are not capable of being overreached, i.e. where there is a purported purchase of land and a valid transfer of legal title, there is no valid alteration of the equitable title. The property then continues to be held in the same trust as before, allowing the beneficiaries both a proprietary and a personal remedy against whoever happens to be the trustee. The proprietary remedy enables the property to be recovered for the trust *in specie* and the personal remedy enables the beneficiaries to recover from the trustee personally. *See* GENUINE TRANSACTION RULE, SELF-DEALING RULE *and* OVERREACHING.

Tynwald: The Parliamentary Assembly of the Isle of Man; it is the oldest continuous parliamentary assembly in the world. Tynwald agrees policy matters and expenditure and sets and collects its own domestic taxes and fees and proposes changes to matters concerning the people of the island, but leaves international affairs and defence matters to the UK authorities.

Types of trust – significant distinctions: Two principal distinctions between EXPRESS TRUSTS and resulting or constructive trusts are that the formal requirement that a trust of interest in land must be evidenced in writing only applies to express trusts; resulting and constructive trusts that arise by an operation of the law may be enforced in the absence of writing. Also, since the duties of an express trustee can be specified in the written instrument, the range of those duties can be more extensive than those which follow by law in respect of resulting or constructive trusts. The express trustee is an intentional undertaking of the duties and is therefore subject to the administrative powers and duties under the general law and as defined in the trust instrument, which is all subject to fiduciary obligations. This contrasts with the minimal duties of a resulting or constructive trustee, where the obligation is no more than that of a bare trustee whose only duty is to convey the property as the beneficiary directs. *See* RESULTING TRUST *and* CONSTRUCTIVE TRUST.

U

Uberrimae fidei: *See* UTMOST GOOD FAITH.

UHNWI: *See* HNWI.

Ultra vires: Beyond the 'legal' powers. Where a person exceeds his authority the act is said to be ultra vires. The term is used generally to indicate an excess beyond what is authorised as legitimate activity, in particular of ministers of governments and other public bodies. The term is applied to describe unreasonable behaviour or failure to follow correct procedures. Also, corporate bodies created under a statute cannot do anything unless authorised by an express or implied term in a company's constitutional documents. The phrase is sometimes used where a company exceeds what has been authorised by the members of the company or where a company has entered into an obligation without using the procedures required by its members or its constitution. The term is now very limited in its application to public corporations. If a trustee or a foundation council purport to engage in activities which are not provided for in the trust or foundation constitution, or something which is not reasonably incidental to the main purpose, then the trustee can be guilty of a breach of trust for acting ultra vires. A foundation council could be similarly liable for failure to observe the necessary care for which redress may be available depending upon the foundation's constitution.

Umbrella funds: A fund that holds several sub-funds, each of which has its own investment goal. The scheme is usually in the form of an ICVC (INVESTMENT COMPANY with variable capital). As ICVCs are open-ended, it allows the capital to be adjusted for each of the funds within the umbrella.

Uncertainty: A general rule in law that when a document is uncertain and it cannot be construed to perceive the intention of the person making the document then that document is void or, if the uncertainty can be separated, the remainder of the document may still be valid providing the intention is clear. In the law of wills any provision where the intention of the testator cannot be found, the gift or the provision is made void. For example, if the testator bequeaths 'some of my property' to A this is likely to be void, although courts attempt to give meaning to a testator's wishes and try not to find something that is void for uncertainty; from 1982 onwards the courts have the power to rectify a will if the will does not reflect what has been shown to be the testator's true intention. Certainty is a prime requirement in the setting up of a trust and in contracts certainty is a requirement for an arrangement to be enforceable and valid. *See* CERTAINTY.

Uncle George: The term given to a nominee settlor of an offshore trust when the identity of the real provider of the trust assets is to remain confidential. The nominee, Uncle George, sets up the trust with a nominal amount and the substantial amount of assets are then subscribed by the true investor whose name does not appear in the trust documents.

Unconscionable transaction: A transaction which no honest or sane person would have entered into may be set aside by the courts as being unconscionable. Where a transaction is shown to be unconscionable, it is not necessary to prove fraud or misrepresentation; the standard of being unconscionable is very high and is beyond being unreasonable. When an unconscionable transaction is set aside, the court will not award damages or order specific performance or in any way recognise the validity of the transaction.

Unconstitutional: An expression describing a transgression or violation of some convention on the constitution, principle or habit generally understood to be obligatory by a member of a public body. In most countries it is applied to statutes or government conduct, or court decisions, or private contracts which violate one or more of the provisions of a written constitution. In the UK the term is sometimes applied to alleged irregular conduct which appears to be in conflict with the conventions applied and expected despite the absence of a written constitution. In the US the term 'unconstitutional' can apply to both federal and state matters.

Underlease: A grant by a tenant to another person called the 'subtenant' or 'sublessee' of a part or whole of the interest covered by the original tenancy.

Undertaking: Promises made to a court by one party in the course of civil proceedings as a condition of the court making an order. Also, in a European context, undertaking is applied to commercial and business enterprises as distinct from the person or body carrying out the business. Thus, a company operating in various separate fields may sell the undertaking of one of these activities, i.e. all the business of one particular description. The sale of an undertaking, being the sale of a business or part of a business, does not indicate the corporate or branch structure of what has been sold but merely indicates a particular activity.

Undischarged bankrupt: A person who has filed a petition for bankruptcy which remains in force until it is discharged by the court on the repayment of all debts owing or an admission by the court that an entire payment is not possible. Any disposition of property in a bankrupt's estate that is made by the bankrupt person is void after the petition for bankruptcy is presented unless the court consents by making a validation order. There is an exception for any property acquired by a third party between the presentation of the bankruptcy petition and the making of a bankruptcy order when the property is acquired by a third party for value without notice of the presentation of the petition. Where a bankrupt, after making a bankruptcy order, acquires property, this is no longer automatically regarded as property of the trustee in bankruptcy. The bankrupt has a duty to give notice to the trustee of any property so acquired and the trustee can then claim the property by notice in writing.

Undisclosed principal: Where a person uses an AGENT for transactions with a third party but the relationship of agent and principal is not disclosed. The position of the parties to such a transaction has been variously interpreted by the courts, with recourse sometimes being had to the property involved in the transaction and to the neglect of agency contractual law. The position remains unsatisfactory.

Undivided shares in land: *See* JOINT TENANCY *and* TENANTS IN COMMON.

Undue influence: Influence, pressure or domination which prevents another person from exercising his free and independent will in regard to an act, such as entering into a contract or signing a will. Undue influence is presumed in certain relationships where benefits or advantages are gained, such as between guardian and ward, parent and child, trustee and beneficiary, guide and instructor, medical advisers and attendants, and aged or infirm persons. Undue influence may be presumed where there is any relationship of influence and the nature of the transaction is suspicious. The burden is then upon the party who may exercise undue influence to show that there is no evidence of such conduct and to show the person providing the benefit was acting on independent advice. The onus is shifted in the case of wills and the person alleging undue influence is called upon for proof of the allegation. Where it is impossible to remedy undue influence by restoring the parties to their original position, a court will adjust the relationship between the parties as seems just. A distinction is drawn between situations within the categories of presumed undue influence and other situations where undue influence takes place. Actual undue influence does not depend upon a pre-existing relationship between the parties and the party who alleges it must prove that he entered into the impugned transaction not as a result of his own will but under the undue influence exerted upon him.

Unfair contract terms: Contractual terms that are restricted in the UK by the *Unfair Contract Terms Act* 1977 to the extent to which civil liability for breach of contract or for negligence or other breaches of duty may be avoided. Contractual terms that exclude or restrict negligent liability for acts which result in the death or personal injury of a person are not valid. Otherwise, exclusion by contract of liability is valid if the clause satisfies a statutory requirement of reasonableness; this depends upon the circumstances that ought reasonably to have been known by the parties or in their contemplation when the contract was made. Exclusion of liability in contract is distinct from exemption clauses in trust deeds where trustees avoid liability for losses when pursued by beneficiaries; there is no contract exists between the beneficiaries and trustees. *See* TRUSTEE EXEMPTION CLAUSES.

***Uniform Prudent Investor Act* 1994:** An important change in the law of the US which requires US trustees to take into account modern investment portfolio theory, under which investments must show a 'total return'. Under this Act, a standard of prudence is applied to any investment as part of a total portfolio rather than as an individual investment. The term 'portfolio' embraces all the trust assets. The restrictions on various types of investment categories were removed allowing the trustee to invest in whatever plays an appropriate role in achieving the risk return objectives of the particular trust and which meet other requirements of prudent investing. The concept of prudent investing incorporates a long-familiar requirement that fiduciaries should diversify their investment. The much-criticised former rule of trust law that forbade the trustee from delegating investment and management functions was reversed; one of the more unusual provisions allows a trustee to make adjustments to what is to be treated as income and capital by allowing a trustee to allocate assets between the two categories. Although many states have adopted both the Act and its practices, other states have found the Act to be too vague and have passed their own rules, such as New York where trustees may select a certain percentage to be paid out as income each year. *See* *UNIFORM TRUSTEE INVESTMENT ACT* 1997 *and* GENERAL POWER OF INVESTMENT.

Uniform Trust Code: A codification of the common law of trusts of the US intended to provide states with precise, comprehensive and easily accessible guidance on trust law questions. Most of the Uniform Trust Code consists of default rules applicable only if the terms of the trust fail to include, or insufficiently cover, a particular issue. The rules may be varied for any individual trust with the exception of the default and mandatory rules which are required to ensure the validity of a trust. Other innovative provisions include the representation of beneficiaries on trust modification and termination which are expected to enhance flexibility, as well as provisions with special rules on revocable trusts. The Uniform Trust Code was last revised or amended in 2010 by the National Conference of Commissioners on Uniform State Laws and approved and recommended for enactment in all the states. The Uniform Trust Code overrides previous Uniform Acts, which are now superseded or incorporated into the Code; these include the Uniform Probate Code 1969, *Uniform Prudent Investor Act* 1994, *Uniform Trustee Powers Act* 1964 and the original *Uniform Trusts Act* 1937. Other Uniform Acts concerned with trusts are not affected.

***Uniform Trustee Investment Act* 1997:** An Act concerned with trustee investments following the work of the Uniform Law Conference of Canada which can be adopted by Canadian provinces and territories to introduce a modern portfolio theory on trustee investment. This replaces the traditional prudent investor rule and adopts the modern portfolio theory. Under the Act, a fiduciary has to have regard for the circumstances of a trust including the role of each investment within the overall trust portfolio. The Act has been incorporated into the majority of the Canadian common law provinces. *See* GENERAL POWER OF INVESTMENT *and* *UNIFORM PRUDENT INVESTOR ACT* 1994.

Unilateral contract: *See* BILATERAL CONTRACT.

Unit trust: A form of collective investment scheme where the investments are held on trust for individual investors. The general principle is that a management company purchases a diversified range of publicly quoted securities and resells parts of the aggregate block of investments as units to retail investors at a price calculated as a proportion of the total value of the investments held. In practice, a unit trust is a network of investment contracts between investors, a scheme manager and trustees, where the trustees simply act as custodians of the scheme property leaving the scheme manager to conduct the investment business. A unit trust is set up by a deed of trust which requires the trustees to work in conjunction with the managers who are empowered by the trust deed to acquire securities or investments of the types specified. The trustees usually exist as a company distinct from the management company but both companies share the fiduciary responsibilities (*see* Section 237(1) of the *Financial Services and Markets Act* 2000). The beneficiaries of the trust are the investors whose rights are strictly a pro rata share of the dividends, interest and other income, generated by the portfolio of securities which make up the trust's total assets. *See* COLLECTIVE INVESTMENT SCHEMES.

United States trusts: To be regarded as a United States trust for Federal tax purposes, trusts must comply with two specific objective tests. First, the US court must exercise primary supervision over the administration and, second, US fiduciaries must have the authority to control all substantive decisions relating to the trust.

Unjust enrichment: The obtaining of a benefit by one person at the expense of any other without justification. A wide variety of situations are included, such as where money is obtained by MISTAKE or through FRAUD or under a contract where goods or services are supplied and where the recipient fails to perform his reciprocal obligation and who therefore has obtained a benefit that is not consistent with his contractual obligation. The term is applied to many situations which have existed for centuries and to other advantages gained by one party who is challenged by another. The doctrine of unjust enrichment is a feature of the law of Scotland and various civil law countries but has not been recognised until recently under English law which, in recent years, has been acknowledged as a means by which an order for RESTITUTION may be sought. Situations giving rise to a claim for unjust enrichment may exist alongside the more traditional common law claims such as fraud or breach of contract. Applying the term indicates that one party has been financially prejudiced by the action of the other. Where unjust enrichment is alleged, this does not imply that there is an obligation to repay the money or compensate in money for the enrichment so conferred; the outcome depends upon whether the principle of restitution can be applied.

Unlawful and fraudulent ulterior purposes: A trust may be invalid on the grounds of illegality, not on the legality of the trust itself but on an ulterior purpose for which the creation of the trust was an integral part. The subject of illegality in contracts and trusts has been examined by the LAW COMMISSION. Their preliminary recommendations appeared in 'Illegal transactions: the effect of illegality on contracts and trusts' (Consultation Paper No. 154 of 1999). The final recommendations followed the earlier provisional recommendations made in Consultation Paper No. 150 of 1997, and were also made in 'The illegality defence: a consultative report' (Consultation Paper No. 189 in 2009). However, the UK government stated in March 2012 that they 'are not minded to implement the Commission's proposals' as the Government considered that the recommendations were insufficient to remove the problems created by the illegality defence in trust law after the decision of the House of Lords in 2007 (***Stack v. Dowden*** [2007] UKHL 17), which introduced further uncertainty into the law. The position in respect of foundations in this connection must therefore be regarded as unsettled.

Unlawful trusts and foundations: A trust or foundation that is unenforceable because it is made for an unlawful purpose. The unlawful nature of such a trust may vary from being a trust to create or perpetuate a criminal or similar offence such as procuring a breach of contract, interfering with marriage or to evade taxes or other public obligations. In this case, the unlawful objective is more an integral part of the unlawful intent of the creator than in the case of unlawful and fraudulent and ulterior purposes.

Unlimited company: A company where there is no limit on the liability of its members, in contrast to the more common limited company where the liability of the members is limited by its constitution to unpaid amounts on issued shares. In an unlimited company the members are obliged to contribute to the company when the company is insolvent so as to enable the company to satisfy its creditors. The members of an unlimited company have an unlimited liability to meet this obligation. Consequently, trustees rarely invest in unlimited companies in order to avoid this hazard as trustees would have a liability to contribute without limitation even though the requirement could exceed the amount of the trust fund – leaving them personally liable. As the members are subject to a potential unlimited liability, an unlimited company is usually exempt from an obligation to file annual accounts (*Companies Act 2000*, Section 448). The position could be more favourable to foundations where, although the foundation itself would have unlimited liability to contribute, the liability does not extend beyond the assets of the foundation.

Unreasonableness: 'Something so absurd that no sensible person could ever dream that it lay within the powers of the authority' (***Associated Provincial Picture Houses Ltd v. Wednesbury Corporation*** [1948] 1KB 223); also equated with irrationality in ***Council of Civil Service Unions v. Minister for Civil Services*** [1985] AC 374:

> 'A decision which is so outrageous in its defiance of logic or of accepted moral standards that no sensible person who had applied his mind to the question to be decided could have arrived at it.'

More recently a broader definition has been applied for challenging a decision. This may be based upon illogicality, oppressiveness, unfairness, uncertainty, inconsistency, ignoring established facts or an authoritative recommendation, or an undue delay in giving a decision. *See* REASONABLE.

Unregistered companies: Companies which are not registered under the *Companies Act* 2006 but to which some provisions of that Act nevertheless apply. Such companies, incorporated and having principal places of business in the UK are distinct from statutory companies, charities or open-ended investment companies.

Unregistered land: Land that has not been registered under the Land Registration Acts. Unregistered land, otherwise known as a 'qualifying estate' which is either freehold or leasehold with a term of more than seven years to run, will trigger a need to register on the occurrence of certain events. If land is not registered within two months of the event then the transfer, grant or creation of a legal estate becomes void. Certain unregistered legal estates may be registered voluntarily. On the sale of an unregistered land the seller proves his ownership by producing deeds and documents of title to show his ownership over a period of, usually, 15 years, starting with a good root of title. Certain charges over the land are void unless a land charge is registered before the completion of a purchase. *See* LAND REGISTRATION *and* LAND REGISTRY.

Unsound mind: A general term with numerous statutory and judicial interpretations in various contexts but which generally indicates that the person to whom the description is applied is incapable of rational and consistent thought, either through age, illness, drugs or alcohol, and where generally the person will be incapable of making a decision over the disposal of property and consequently is denied the status of being SUI JURIS. *See* MENTAL CAPACITY.

Unthrift: An unusual term which neatly describes a person of outrageous prodigality of which certain types of trusts generate a disproportionate high number of cases. *See* SPENDTHRIFT TRUSTS.

Upon trust: The making of a gift with the indication that the recipient does not receive the gift beneficially, i.e. the person should hold whatever is transferred upon trust; in other words, he becomes a trustee. This is to be regarded as only evidence of the intention of not conferring the beneficial interest on the recipient. The construction that a trust has resulted may not be borne out when the document in which the phrase appears is constructed as a whole.

Use: A benefit or the act of employing a thing. This literal meaning also formerly had, in law, a technical meaning associated with the benefits of land. The term 'use' is now not used in this connection but is of interest in the development of trusts and in the transfer of property. The transfer of property, originally in the 14th century, was achieved by a formal and public ceremony, 'livery of SEISEN' (a ceremony involving the cutting of a piece of turf and delivering it to the buyer with a twig before reinsertion of the turf and a verbal declaration of the sale which was witnessed by bystanders). An alternative, a livery in law, was based upon a declaration, such as:

> 'I give you yonder land to you and your heirs, and go enter into the same, and take possession thereof accordingly.'

At that time, the possessor of property was treated as the owner and therefore the owner of land was not difficult to determine. This rule of the common law was evaded by a device of monastic lawyers based on a civil law model and this developed into a second method of transferring real property by the application of the use alongside the traditional methods. The use was originally equitable in nature: the right to the beneficial ownership of property was in equity where the legal possession had been placed in the hands of another. This was achieved by A conveying land by the common law system (such as the livery in law) to B with the intention that B would hold it for the benefit of a third person C or for A himself. In common law, B was looked upon as the owner of the land but regarded in the Court of Chancery as the nominee who became known as *CESTUI QUE USE*. C had the use, the profits and the benefit of the land, which was treated like an estate and descended to the heir of the *cestui que use* and also was divisible by will, although the legal ownership of the land was not. This made a 'use' of land different from ownership at common law. There were numerous other differences. The superior tenants (freeholders in the feudal chain of legal ownership of land entitled to receive various dues from lower tenants) lost their advantage of wardship and other attributes of owning land. Uses were not subject to the payment of debts including taxes. Purchasers of uses were less secure as transfer of uses passed by declaration to that effect without any ceremony or permanent record. An earlier form of trust existed at the same time as uses. When property was transferred to a person, the FEOFFEE to uses, for practical purposes, there was little difference between uses and the then existing trusts, which can be traced back to 1377. In the reign of King Henry VIII, the *STATUTE OF USES* 1535 purported to abolish uses (an early anti-tax avoidance measure!). This was done by enacting that when any person was the owner of land to the use or trust of another, the latter was made the legal owner of that land. For example, A conveyed land to B and his heirs for the use of C and his heirs. Then B acquired the ownership of the land in the normal way but, by the Statute of Uses, the ownership passed out of B and vested in C (who, therefore, became liable for the various payments). However, the Act did not achieve this destruction of the use completely as had been the intention of King Henry. The use persisted because the Act was not sufficiently comprehensive. It did not affect uses to be set up in copyhold land and other forms of ownership other than freehold. Furthermore, it did not apply to active and constructive uses, such as where the use involved a direction to sell the estate to a second use, i.e. a use upon a use, such as where land was conveyed from A to B to hold for the use of C who held it for the use of D. The Statute only affected the first use and not the second, since a use upon a use was not then known to law. Another loophole in the Statute was that future executory or contingent uses could not be executed into legal estates by the Statute until they came into existence. The use persisted long enough to add to the development of the trust but in the 19th century the *Conveyancing Act* 1881, Section 62, provided that a limitation of freehold land to the use of a person and attempts to do so were converted into an easement over the land. The *Statute of Uses* 1535 was repealed by the *Law of Property Act* 1925 and the provisions are now contained in the *Trusts of Land and Appointment of Trustees* 1996 (Section 25 and Schedule 4). The term is now rarely used, although the words 'for the use of another' occasionally appear, usually following a requirement to hold certain property on trust. The complex and legal origin of the concept of use was not made easier by the existence of the two words from which it originated, i.e. the Latin word '*opus*' and the Norman French word '*oes*' meaning benefit, which both gave rise to the word 'use' applied in the technical sense (as explained in this entry) and which blurred 'use' as a right of property with the everyday meaning.

Utmost good faith: *UBERRIMAE FIDEI*: Contracts that are considered by the law to be *uberrimae fidei*, or of utmost good faith, require voluntary pre-disclosure of facts by each party to the other. The onus is on the party having the information to disclose. For example, with insurance contracts the insurer is entitled to a fair presentation of the risk for which he undertakes to provide compensation to the insured if the insured risk materialises. This full disclosure is required even if the insurer does not make a specific enquiry; it is essential in order to allow the insurer to fairly assess a premium. If there is no disclosure, the insurer may avoid the contract, i.e. without the insured meeting the criteria of utmost good faith, the insurer can treat the contract as voidable. Other *uberrimae fidei* contracts are guardian and ward, and solicitor and client. Contracts of suretyship and partnership are not strictly *uberrimae fidei* but, once entered into, full disclosure is required of material circumstances. A barrister applying to the court EX PARTE is under strict obligation of *uberrimae fidei*, in that he must make full disclosure of all circumstances affecting the application he is making, whether or not in his favour. A contract for the sale of land is not considered to be *uberrimae fidei* but liability could arise if there is fraudulent non-disclosure of deeds. Strictly, the doctrine is distinct from fraudulent concealment of documents or other misrepresentations which are actionable in all contracts whether *uberrimae fidei* or not. *Uberrimae fidei* is restricted to those contracts where one party may not have the means of knowing certain circumstances, such as the long-term health history of an applicant for a life insurance policy and so a positive obligation is placed on the person seeking insurance to make full disclosure.

V

Valid purpose trusts: In addition to charitable trusts, beneficial to the public, there are a few other exceptions to the no-purpose trust rule, which are all TESTAMENTARY TRUSTS. These range from the maintenance of particular animals owned by the testator to the construction and maintenance of graves and funeral monuments. Valid purpose trusts are regarded as anomalous to the general no-purpose trust rule for English trusts. *See* CHARITABLE TRUST *and* TRUSTS OF PERFECT AND IMPERFECT OBLIGATION.

Validity of settlements: Can be affected by the MENTAL CAPACITY of the settlor; although the matter is not always clear, it is thought that a settlement, INTER VIVOS, whether for value or made voluntarily by a patient with a receiver appointed under the *Mental Health Act* 1983, is void even when the settlement was made during a lucid interval. Similarly, a settlement made when the settlor was subject to a subsisting order under the *Mental Capacity* Act 2005 will be void if the settlement is made inconsistently with the provisions of the order. Otherwise, a person who is not a patient, and for whom no receiver was appointed under the Act(s) but who is nevertheless of UNSOUND MIND, can, during a lucid interval, enter into a valid settlement. A settlement made when the patient is not enjoying a lucid interval may still be valid if it is fair and BONA FIDE and made for value and the person who provided the assets had no notice of the lack of mental capacity at the time of execution of the settlement. *See* COURT OF PROTECTION.

Valuable consideration: In contracts based upon English law, an agreement is only enforceable at law if valuable consideration is given for the benefit conferred by the contract. In a simple sale the consideration for the transfer of goods or other assets is the price, and for work performed the valuable consideration is the fee paid. Valuable consideration, however, can include things other than money and can include work, performance or other assets, or even a promise to abstain from an act so long as the act concerned would have been of value. Consideration may therefore be defined as something of value given or detriment suffered in exchange for the commitment of the other party. Consideration is a feature of a common law contract and has one significant feature in that a stranger to a contract traditionally could not sue for performance of that contract on the grounds that the stranger had not provided consideration and, on those grounds, such a person is a stranger to the obligation. In civil law contracts consideration is not required; all that is required to constitute a valid contract is some indication that it is meant to be an enforceable arrangement. In English law, the value of the consideration is irrelevant in that the value may be nominal, a traditional example of which is that a lease can be entered into for property where the consideration is merely the presentation by the tenant of a rose at midsummer to the owner. This results in a nominal consideration sometimes being incorporated into an agreement in order to make it legally enforceable. For example, in consideration of £1, A agrees to assign his rights to the copyright of a work to another. This makes the assignment legal and enforceable and with the copyright goes all the benefits and liabilities. Consideration is not necessary for contracts made under seal, i.e. by DEED.

Value added tax (VAT): A tax on the final consumption of goods or services that is collected by instalments from each party from manufacturer to retailer (in the case of goods); tax is levied on the amount added by each of these parties. VAT is an EC-inspired form of taxation and was given legal standing under Directive 77-388 EEC, also known as the Sixth VAT Directive. A similar tax is imposed in many countries outside the EU on the value added component of prices of goods or of services provided. Worldwide, VAT is gradually replacing a general sales tax or purchase tax under the influence of the IMF's rescue packages, which frequently include a requirement that VAT is introduced in order to increase the tax revenue to enable repayment of loans made as part of a rescue package.

Variation of settlements: *See* TRUST, VARIATION OF.

Variation of Trusts Act 1958: *See* TRUST, VARIATION OF.

Veil of incorporation: A principle fundamental in company law that, on incorporation, the company becomes a separate legal entity and distinct from the shareholders and the directors whose own personal affairs have no part to play in the affairs of the company; the veil of incorporation is drawn between the company and the shareholders and directors. This principle can be abused and Parliament and the courts have been prepared to 'lift the veil of incorporation' to nullify the effects of abuse. A frequent abuse is where a company is operated to effect a FRAUD ON CREDITORS and this is a crime by the directors, who can be personally liable for the debts (*Companies Act* 2006, Section 993); the veil in this situation is lifted. The range of situations justifying the lifting of the veil of incorporation is not fully defined in law, but examples are found in taxation and employment law. The lifting of the veil on those responsible for a company is intended to protect public interest and particularly where a party is seeking to use the separate personality of a company to evade current legal obligations. Since a company with limited liability is formed to limit the liability of the members, it is obvious that the concept of lifting the veil of incorporation is a delicate one. A balance must be maintained between the legitimate use of a company to limit or reduce obligations on the one hand and, on the other hand, to meet modern anti-avoidance tax measures.

Vest / vested: When a person becomes entitled to a right or an estate in property, that property is said to be vested in the person. Vesting may take one of two forms: in POSSESSION or in INTEREST (2). Vested in possession occurs when there is a present right to immediate possession of the property. Where there is a present right but the possession of the property is in the future, then the property is said to be vested in interest. For example, a vested REVERSION is a present fixed right of future enjoyment of a reversion (i.e. a right now to an interest in the future). Such an interest can be valuable: it may be mortgageable. Generally vested means vested in interest as opposed to CONTINGENT. A CONTINGENT INTEREST is where the right is not possessed by a person until the occurrence of a further event. An example of vested in possession and vested in interest is where property is given to A for life and after his death to B absolutely, then A's entitlement is vested in possession but B's is only vested in interest. If B dies before his interest vests in possession his vested interest passes to his personal representatives, which therefore suggests that a vested interest is personal property and not real property. The term is also used specifically to denote a transfer under an Act of Parliament, such as the property of a bankrupt is said to vest in the trustee, i.e. the property is transferred to the trustee in the same way as if the trustee had executed a conveyance. The term 'vested' is also applied to rights, interests and expectations with which the legislature ought not to interfere without giving compensation; for example, the rights of landowners can be said to be vested and therefore should not be interfered with by compulsory purchase without compensation.

Vesting declaration: A declaration that may be contained in a deed appointing a new trustee that in many cases is sufficient to vest the trust property in the new trustee. Such a vesting of the property in the new trustee is essential to enable the new trustee to fulfil his duties. This vesting can often be done without any express conveyance or assignment under the *Trustee Act* 1925 Section 40, except in the case of mortgages, shares in companies and leaseholds held subject to a covenant against assignment.

Vesting deed: *See* VESTING INSTRUMENT.

Vesting instrument: A deed or assent that is required under the *Settled Land Act* 1925 or a vesting order of the High Court Chancery Division to vest the legal estate in land in the person beneficially entitled, particularly under the *Trustee Act* 1925, Section 44(ii). Such a vesting instrument is used by a TENANT for life to transfer property out of the SETTLEMENT. A vesting instrument may also be used by various commissioners or ministers (such as the CHARITY COMMISSIONERS) where the vesting instrument operates as a conveyance of property. Generally, applications to the High Court for a vesting order are only made if the transfer cannot be done by other less formal means. *See* CONVEYANCE.

Vesting order: *See* VESTING INSTRUMENT.

Vesting, trustees: The transfer of trust property to trustees by whatever procedure the law requires to endow the trustee with the legal ownership of the property. On every appointment of a trustee it is necessary to provide for this vesting. If the appointment of trustees is made by deed a mere vesting declaration suffices (*see* VESTING INSTRUMENT) to vest the property in them, except where it is land held by trustees by way of mortgage for securing money, land held under a lease that contains a covenant not to assign without consent, and any shares, stock, annuity or property which is only transferable in the books kept by the company. In these cases the property must be vested in the trustees by the appropriate conveyance or transfer. When a trustee retires then everything that is required to vest trust property in the trustee must be completed in favour of a new or continuing trustee. However, where a trustee voluntarily retires and his co-trustee or trustees consent to his discharge and there is a Deed of Retirement (Section 39(1) *Trustee Act* 1925) executed by the continuing and the retiring trustee to that effect, then a vesting declaration is implied; if the contrary is stated in the deed, the Deed of Retirement will then serve to vest the trust property in the continuing trustee alone, except for cases of those properties that cannot be made to vest in this way.

Vexatious action: An action instituted by a person who is not acting bona fide but merely wishes to annoy or embarrass his opponent, or where the action is merely troublemaking and not calculated to secure any practical result. It is sometimes referred to as 'frivolous and vexatious' litigation. The action may be stopped by the courts' inherent jurisdiction or as an abuse of process rules under CPR r. 3.4. *See* ABUSE OF PROCESS.

Vexatious litigant: A person who 'habitually and persistently and without any reasonable ground' institutes civil or criminal proceedings (i.e. brings vexatious actions). The Attorney General or law officer may apply to the court for an order preventing such a person from instituting or considering legal proceedings for a specified period or indefinitely.

VHNWI: Very High Net Worth Individual. *See* HNWI.

Vicarious responsibility: The liability of a person for the acts of his agent where the agent acts within the scope of his authority. This applies to trustees who, under their power of delegation, may appoint agents to conduct various functions in connection with the trust, where the trustees remain responsible under this principle of agency law.

Virtute officii: A phrase implying that to whatever it is applied (an official, property or some rule) is of impeccable origins due to its source, which is either legislation or some imperious act.

VISTA trusts: Established under the *Virgin Islands Special Trusts Act* 2003 to overcome difficulties in connection with trustees' duty to act prudently where there was a need to provide for succession to incorporated family businesses. The trustees' duty of prudence, when the trust fund consisted of a controlling shareholding in a company, requires that the trustee monitors the conduct of the director/directors of the company and intervenes when necessary. For example, to prevent the directors entering into an unduly speculative venture, or accepting a financially attractive takeover bid, or selling the company's underlying assets and reinvesting in a more diverse portfolio. These situations requiring the trustee's intervention proved in the past to be expensive and administratively difficult. Another consequence was the frequent insertion of non-intervention clauses in trust instruments prohibiting trustees from interfering with the corporate structure. Also, requirements for consent by the shareholders often involved complex structures involving voting and non-voting shares. The VISTA trust legislation enables a special form of trust to be set up to overcome these difficulties under which a shareholder can establish a trust with the shares of his company as the trust assets and where the trustee has no responsibility for the management of the company. Also, the trustee has no duty to consider disposing of the shares to allow better investments for the trust. The VISTA Trust Law removes the monitoring duties of trustees. The settlor is entitled to require that the trustee should perform in a way more suited to the trustee's ability. This includes a duty on the trustee to intervene to resolve specific problems. An example of this is where the Board is in deadlock and now under the legislation a trustee, according to the rules in the trust instrument, may appoint or remove directors. A VISTA trust must be created by written instrument and a holder of a licence under the *British Virgin Islands Banks and Trust Companies Act* 1990 must be the sole trustee, referred to as the designated trustee; any successor trustee must also be a designated trustee. A VISTA trust cannot be created by the exercise of a power of any other trust. VISTA trusts provide opportunities for people to set up trusts of shares in their company who, because of the existing prudent trustee rules, are disinclined to do so, i.e. the existing law on trustees would limit a company's directors from enterprising activities. The access to this special trust system is therefore particularly suitable for ownership of shares in private companies. This has been compared to the English *Settled Land Act* 1925 where trusts allow the beneficiaries in possession, rather than the trustees, to manage the trust property.

Void: An agreement or other relationship that has no legal effect. Where the law declares certain types of contract to be illegal, or where they are contrary to public policy, the entire contract is void. If individual clauses in a contract are void but can be separated from the rest of the contract, the remainder of the contract remains effective. A trust deed may become void if it is altered in a material manner after it has been executed. This illustrates that a document may be void either from the beginning or after it has been partly performed.

Voidable: An agreement or other act is voidable when one or more of the parties is entitled to rescind it. A voidable situation is valid until steps are taken by an injured party to avoid the arrangement. Until rescinded, the agreement or act remains valid. For example, a contract may be voidable for misrepresentation, undue influence or duress if a party has entered into the contract under any of these influences and may be declared void, allowing the contract to be rescinded. The limit on rescission is that if a third party acquires rights under a voidable contract, without notice and for value, the contract cannot be set aside if, by doing so, the third party is put in a worse position. This contrasts with a void contract or arrangement where no third party acquires rights unless the party against whom the rights are alleged affirms it. *See* KNOWING RECEIPT AND DISHONEST ASSISTANCE.

Voluntary conveyance: A transfer by way of gift or otherwise without valuable consideration is liable to be defeated, if fraudulent, by a subsequent sale for value. However, there is no assumption of the intent to defraud when there is a voluntary disposition simply because there was a subsequent transfer for value. In equity, where A makes a voluntary transfer of property to B, there is a presumption that A did not intend to make a gift to B and the property transferred is treated as being held on a RESULTING TRUST for A: equity presuming that A did not intend that B should take the property beneficially. This presumption can be rebutted by proof that A intended otherwise, i.e. A was under an equitable obligation to support B (such as where A is the husband or father of B). Then, this presumption of ADVANCEMENT negates the possibility of a resulting trust being created. There is also a presumption of a resulting trust where B purchases real or personal property using money provided by A. PAROL evidence is admissible to prove that A was the genuine purchaser. The presumptions of a resulting trust and of advancement can be rebutted by evidence of the actual intention of the purchaser, such as a clear declaration in the transfer documents. Where there is a resulting trust, it may be set aside where there is a voluntary conveyance to defraud a subsequent purchaser where the latter is entitled to treat the voluntary disposition of land as voidable.

Voluntary settlements: A settlement made by a person without any actual bargain between the settlor and trustee. This type of settlement is within the court's equitable jurisdiction to relieve the settlor if he makes a MISTAKE by the use of the EQUITABLE REMEDIES of RECTIFICATION, RESCISSION and CANCELLATION. In particular, rectification will be ordered by a court of equity where the true intention of the settlor is not recorded in the document, whether as the result of ignorance or mistake, and where a transaction has been induced by fraud, duress, mistake, misrepresentation or undue influence, the court may order the delivery up, and cancellation, of a document. It is closely related to the circumstances where under the current principle of *HASTINGS-BASS* there is a challenge to the exercise of a power that was exercised by mistake. Marriage settlements were a form of voluntary settlement, which was one of the earliest examples of rectification. Voluntary settlements generally can be rectified when they do not record the settlor's true intention. The settlor must prove the settlement does not express his true intention or the true intention of any party, such as a spouse, that is involved. It is not, however, essential for the settlor to prove that the settlement fails to express the true intention of the trustees if they have not bargained. The equitable remedies are discretionary and may be refused if the court thinks fit and if the settlor does not establish his case by convincing proof; the onus is on the person who claims rectification or other equitable remedy and an application to the court should be supported by adequate evidence. Wills fall within this category. Where there is a clerical error or a draftsman's failure to understand the testator's instructions, rectification may follow under the authority of the *Administration of Justice Act* 1982 and, apart from these rights under the Act, a will may be rectified in cases of fraud or obvious mistake.

Voluntary winding up: *See* WINDING UP.

Von Overbeck Report: An explanatory report by Alfred E. von Overbeck, helpful in resolving any doubts about the meaning of the *HAGUE TRUST CONVENTION*.

Voting trust: A voting trust is a trust whose assets comprise the proxies of shareholders of a company which then enable the trustees to operate unimpeded by the participation or interference of individual shareholders. A voting trust is often employed in matters connected with reorganisation of a company, in negotiating or resisting takeover bids and in ensuring continuous control. A voting trust enables a more simplified manipulation of the shareholders' votes and is legitimate, provided that the shareholders who do not consign their proxies to a trust have no grounds to complain that there is fraud on the minority of shareholders.

Vulnerable people: *See* TRUSTS FOR VULNERABLE BENEFICIARIES.

W

Wait and see rule: A rule introduced by the *Perpetuities and Accumulations Act* 1964 for the purpose of saving gifts which would otherwise be instantly void because of the common law rule against gifts vesting outside the perpetuity period. Section 3(1) of the 1964 Act, in respect of instruments and oral declarations of trust and similar dispositions made after 16 July 1964, states that where a disposition would be void because it might not become vested within the perpetuity period, the disposition shall be treated as valid until such time as it may become established that the vesting must occur outside the perpetuity period. This only applies to dispositions subject to the 1964 Act and particularly to interest and powers of advancement and to sums where it is clear that such sums would become immediately void at common law without the benefit of this statutory provision. A similar 'wait and see' rule appears in the 2009 *Perpetuities and Accumulations Act*.

Waiver: A renouncement or disclaim of a right or benefit. Generally effective if given for consideration or made by deed. Also, to be legally effective, a waiver must be unequivocal in its terms and accepted by the other party.

Waqf: An endowment made by a Muslim to a religious, educational or charitable cause. *See* ISLAMIC LAW – GLOSSARY.

Warranty deed: A deed which guarantees that the seller of real property owns a good title that can be conveyed, i.e. an express statement defining the title of property to be conveyed and which may be referred to as a 'grant deed'. When used, a grant deed contrasts with a 'QUITCLAIM DEED' where no warranty as to title is given.

Waste: The spoiling or destruction by a tenant of property (house, garden, trees or uncultivated land). It also applies to uncultivated, pastoral or arable land. A tenant in tail or in fee simple may commit as much waste as he likes. Actions for waste lie against a tenant whether the tenancy is for life or for years. A tenant may also be restrained from committing waste. The same applies to a mortgagor of property. *See* EQUITABLE WASTE.

Wasting assets: Property which only has a limited existence such as leasehold property. When residuary properties are given by will to trustees for persons in succession, unless the will states otherwise, the trustees must realise such parts of the property that are wasting, perishable or unauthorised by the will or by the general law. Wasting assets have been defined for the purpose of *Taxation of Chargeable Gains Act* 1992, Section 44, as assets with a predictable life not exceeding 50 years, and these assets are exempt from capital gains tax; although a good general rule, this is not a definition which is applied in all circumstances. This doctrine embraces the rule in ***Howe v. Earl of Dartmouth*** (1802) 7 Ves. 137. In this case, a residuary bequest of personal estate, to be enjoyed by persons in succession, requires the trustees to realise wasting assets; e.g., copyrights or assets of a reversionary nature, such as interests that are subject to subsisting life interests unless the will shows a contrary intention.

'Whatever is left' trust: A trust by will of a sum of money to a beneficiary for his sole use until death with the remaining part expressed as 'what is left' to go to another was held to be invalid and the first beneficiary was entitled absolutely on the grounds that it would be impossible to execute the terms of the will. ***Mussoorie***

Bank Ltd v. Raynor (1882) 7 App. Cas. 321. *See* FLOATING TRUST.

Will: A declaration made by a person called the TESTATOR to provide for the distribution or administration of his property after his death. A will is automatically revoked on marriage or entry into a civil partnership. A will becomes effective on the death of a testator who may revoke the will at any time before death. After death, a will which has not been specifically revoked will become ineffective if a later will is produced which is likely to contain a clause revoking all other wills, which, in effect, means the terms of an earlier will are then seen to be revoked after the testator's death. In other words, a will may be revoked by the testator making a subsequent will, or by him making a formal notice of revocation or by merely noting on the will itself, where his signature is witnessed, that the will is to be no longer valid. A will is usually made in writing, which must be properly executed in conformity with the internal law of the territory where it was executed. In the UK, the Principal Registry of the Family Division has a depository for wills of living persons. A will generally appoints one or more persons as executors to administer the testator's estate; if none are nominated or none of those are willing to act, the court will appoint an administrator for that purpose. The role of the executor is a fiduciary one. The executor acts in relation to the deceased's assets as trustee until the assets have been distributed according to the will. Where the will purports to set up a trust, the executors, who do not become trustees themselves, transfer the assets to the trustees with their consent at the appropriate time. *See* MUTUAL WILLS.

Will trusts: If a testator wishes to set up a trust of his assets to come into effect after his death, this may be done in two ways: (a) he may include, in his will, a legacy and instructions that the legatee should use the gift to establish a fund for the benefit of named beneficiaries. This applies particularly to a SPECIFIC LEGACY, although it may suffer ADEMPTION, and (b) he may give a legacy to a person and at the same time nominate the legatee as trustee to hold the property in trust. Here, more precision is required. An unintended LIFE INTEREST may arise when a testator gives 'all my property in trust for my wife and children'. This appears to leave it up to the court to decide whether the wife was to have a life interest or an absolute interest as a joint tenant or a tenant in common. This was clarified by Section 22 of the *Administration of Justice Act* 1982 by providing that unless there is a clear contrary intention shown in the will, there is a presumption that if the testator devises or bequeaths property to his spouse in terms which, in themselves, would give an absolute interest to the spouse, no trust arises even where the testator also purports to give his issue an interest in the same property; the gift to the spouse is absolute notwithstanding the supplementary wish in respect of the issue on the grounds of uncertainty of subject matter concerning the identity of assets for such a trust. *See* TESTAMENTARY TRUSTS.

Winding up: The process of dissolving a company or partnership after selling the assets and paying, as far as possible, the creditors. When the body is solvent, a winding up can be a members' voluntary winding up or, if insolvent, then it is a creditors' winding up. Also called a liquidation.

Withholding tax: The method by which tax is collected when a dividend, royalty or interest is paid to a non-resident of the country in which the income is earned. The appropriate amount of tax is withheld from the payment and the balance paid to the recipient. The sum withheld is paid to the tax authority of the state in which the income arose and the recipient receives a tax credit or certificate in respect of the amount that has been withheld. This method of collecting tax ensures that the tax due is collected and paid and that the non-resident recipient of the balance of the dividend or royalty or interest then has a credit against his liability in the country in which he is resident. The adoption of a withholding tax between two jurisdictions is usually provided for in a tax convention and often follows the OECD MODEL TAX CONVENTION ON INCOME AND ON CAPITAL. The term 'withholding' is also used whenever a deduction is made from a sum payable to another.

Witness summons: A summons issued under the CIVIL PROCEDURE RULES requiring a witness to attend court to give evidence or produce documents to the court or both on a date stated. A witness summons may be issued by the High Court or the County Court in aid of a court or tribunal that does not have the power itself to issue such a summons. *See also* SUBPOENA.

Woolf Report: A report on the civil justice system of England and Wales entitled 'Access to Justice' made in 1996 by the then Master of the Rolls (the third most senior judge in England and Wales). A key recommendation was made that the courts should have the final responsibility for determining what procedures were suitable for each case and now, generally, some form of mediation between the parties, before engaging in formal tedious and expensive litigation, is required. This is known as 'ALTERNATIVE DISPUTE RESOLUTION' and may take the form of an attempt by an appointed mediator to find common ground between the parties to facilitate a non-judicial resolution. Failure to accept a mediation process may result in the court refusing to award costs of litigation to a party which had refused to participate even if that party is successful in litigation on the issue. The Woolf Report's recommendations, which also included what was supposed to be a simplification in terminology, were adopted into the CIVIL PROCEDURE RULES 1998 (CPR), which introduced a fundamental reform of the ethos and procedure of civil justice in the UK.

Writ: A former vital document by which a person initiated an action in a court worded as a command to a person to whom it was addressed to do or forbear from doing some act. A writ was a document issued under the authority of the Crown which required attendance at a court or before an officer of the Crown. As far as the law was concerned, writs may have been either original or judicial. In the UK, writs were issued under the seal of the issuing court. Writs were of various types, including a 'writ of summons', which was the beginning of an action in the High Court. Writs are now known, under the CIVIL PROCEDURE RULES (CPR), as 'claim forms' in all courts where the word 'writ' was used. *See* CLAIM FORM.

Written resolution: A resolution in writing signed by members of a private company which is of equal status to resolutions passed at a members' meeting and which can be used for any purpose other than the removal of a director or an auditor. A resolution may be proposed by either directors or members of a private company and circulated to the members for signature for approval within 28 days. There may be, under individual jurisdictions' statutory provisions, the possibility of a written resolution being proposed, approved and recorded in respect of decisions of trustees or of foundation councils in the same way as laid down for corporations, but the common form of decision-making is as the trustees or the foundation council decide, according to their constitutions.

Y

Year books: The original Law Reports produced from 1290, with a few gaps, to 1535. Year books are of little interest now to the trust practitioner, although, from time to time, these books contain references to trust uses and equity. Information about early trust litigation would doubtlessly have been extended if the year books had not ceased in the same year as the *STATUTE OF USES* 1535.

Z

Zero-rating: A term indicating that certain supplies are taxable under the VAT law at a rate of nought percent (0%). This zero-rate applies when goods of that category are supplied. The supplier, however, will be able to claim a credit or a refund of the input tax associated with such goods (i.e. the VAT already charged on the material used by the supplier to make the zero-rated supply). Zero-rated supplies include certain types of food, books and newspapers. Charities are also zero rated. Zero-rated supplies differ from exempt supplies which are entirely outside of the VAT regime in respect of which no input tax can be charged at any stage in the supply chain.

Table of Acronyms

ADR	Alternative Dispute Resolution
AIFMD	Alternative Investment Fund Managers Directive
AIM	Alternative Investment Market
AML	Anti-money Laundering Law
ARTs	Automatic Resulting Trusts
BBC	British Broadcasting Corporation
BCBS	Basel Committee on Banking Supervision
BEE	Bahamas Executive Entity
BEPS	Base Erosion and Profit Shifting
CFA	Committee on Fiscal Affairs (OECD)
CIC	Community Interest Company
CPR	Civil Procedure Rules
DIFC	Dubai International Financial Centre
EC	European Community
EE	Executive Entity
EFTA	European Free Trade Zone
EU	European Union
FATCA	Foreign Account Tax Compliance Act 2014 (US)
FATF	Financial Action Task Force
FCA	Financial Conduct Authority
FDR	Financial Dispute Resolution
FHTP	Forum on Harmful Tax Practices (OECD)
FinCEN	Financial Crimes Enforcement Network
FIU	Financial Intelligence Unit
FSA	Financial Services Authority
FSB	Financial Security Bureau
FSMA	Financial Services & Markets Act
FSRB	FATF-style regional bodies
GP	General partner
HMRC	HM Revenue & Customs (UK)
HNWI	High net worth individuals
ICLR	Incorporated Counsel of Law Reporting
ICVC	Investment Company with Variable Capital
IMF	International Monetary Fund
IOSCO	International Organization of Securities Commissions
IRS	Internal Revenue Service (US)
ISDA	International Swap Dealers Association
ITELR	International Trust and Estate Law Reports
JCPC	Judicial Committee of the Privy Council
LLP	Limited Liability Partnership
LP	Limited partner
LSE	London Stock Exchange
MIFID	Markets and Financial Instruments Directive
MTF	Multilateral trading facility
NASDAQ	National Association of Securities Dealers Automated Quotations
NGO	Non-governmental organization
NLIS	National Land Information Service
OECD	Organisation for Economic Co-operation and Development
OEEC	Organisation for European Economic Co-operation
OEIC	Open-ended investment company
OGBS	Offshore Group of Banking Supervisors

PET	Potentially exempt transfer
PIRT	Presumed Intention Resulting Trust
PLC	Public Limited Company
PTC	Private Trust Company
QC	Queen's Counsel
REIT	Real Estate Investment Trust
SDLT	Stamp Duty Land Tax
SICAV	Open-ended collective investment scheme similar to OEICs
SIV	Sovereign Investment Fund
SPV	Special Purpose Vehicle
TABOL	Trusts arising by operation of the law
TFDE	Task Force on Digital Economy (OECD)
TOLATA	Trusts of Land and Appointment of Trustees Act 1996
UK	United Kingdom
UHNWI	Ultra-high net worth individuals
UN	United Nations
US	United States
UVHNWI	Ultra and very high net worth individuals
VAT	Value Added Tax
VHNWI	Very high net worth individuals
WB	World Bank

Table of Case Law Reporting Acronyms

AC	Appeal cases
All ER Rep	All England Law Reports
BCLC	Butterworth's Company Law Cases
Ch.D	Chancery Division
CLC	Company law cases
CLR	Canadian Law Reports
EHRR	European Human Rights Reports
EWCA	England and Wales Court of Appeal
FLR	Family Law Reports
ITELR	International Trust and Estate Law Reports
JLR	Jersey Law Reports
KB	King's Bench
LR	Law Reports
OJ	Official Journal (EU)
QB	Queen's Bench
UKHL	UK House of Lords
UKSC	UK Supreme Court
WLR	Weekly Law Reports

Islamic Law – Glossary

NOTE: *Transliterations into English of Arabic words and terms may vary from work to work.*

Amanah: A deposit that is held in trust for another according to an express or implied contract, such as a current account with a bank; the party with whom the deposit is made incurs no liability except when that person commits a breach of trust. Where the bank receives permission to use the deposit in its business, the relationship then becomes that of debtor/creditor when the full amount is repayable to the depositor irrespective of a loss or profit to the bank. Generally, *Amanah* is the fulfilment of a fiduciary relationship that is established by contract and which has some characteristics of a trust.

Ameen (also Amin): A term for a trustworthy person, custodian or trustee who is safeguarding others' property as if it were the holder's own and who, in the case of any damage to the property, is not liable unless negligent.

Bai (also Bay): Basically a sale but commonly used as a prefix to refer to particular types of sale such as:

Bai al-Istijrar: A contract where the supplier agrees to supply a particular product on an ongoing basis, e.g. monthly, at an agreed price and with an agreed mode of payment.

Bai al-Wafa: A contract with a condition that if the seller pays back the price of the goods sold, the buyer returns the goods to the seller.

Dain: A loan or debt; also known as *bai-al-dain*. The sale of a debt is a controversial matter where traditional Muslim jurists (*fuqaha*) are unanimous that *bai-al-dain* with discount is not allowed in Sharia. Contemporary scholars are of the same view; they regard *bai-al-dain* as a consequence of the prohibition of *riba*, or interest. *Bai-al-dain* is sometimes allowed in Malaysia, although critics say the decision is not valid unless a debt is sold at its par value – i.e. without interest.

Dhaman: A contract where a guarantor underwrites claims arising from the ownership of an asset and is the background of export credit guarantees in Islamic law. *Dhaman* also applies to a guarantee for the repayment of a debt. Simply stated, it means a liability.

DIFC (Dubai International Financial Centre): Used in connection with Law No. 11 of 2005, which enables trusts to be recognised under the common law systems in the United Arab Emirates.

Fatwa: A legal verdict or pronouncement based on *fiqh* (Islamic jurisprudence) given by a Sharia scholar or a Sharia board usually urging physical action against persons who are considered to have offended against a fundamental religious principle.

Fiqh: Islamic jurisprudence.

Fuqaha: Muslim jurist.

Gharar: A prohibition under Islamic law against uncertainty, hazards or lack of clarity regarding the subject matter of a contract, particularly when the object of a contract is not present or the sale is uncertain or the consequences of the transaction (*Aqibah*) are not known. *Gharar* also refers to elements of absolute and excessive uncertainty in any business contract. Gambling is included in this definition, as is selling goods that the seller is unable to deliver or selling goods of unknown identity and where there is a mere speculative risk. In commercial terms, this uncertainty applies where a purchaser of goods is not allowed properly to examine the goods and where the seller selling goods is unable to deliver, or is selling at an unknown price, or without giving a proper description. *See* KATAR.

Halal: Things permitted by Sharia, including acceptable items of food and drink, permissible goods and valid earnings and other matters of everyday life which are acceptable under the law. *Halal* (allowed) is one of the five criteria that define the majority of human activities. These are: *fard* (compulsory); *mustahabb* (recommended); *halal* (allowed); *makruh* (disliked) and *haram* (forbidden). Also, *mubah* is used to indicate something that is permissible or allowed.

Haq Mally: A right associated with financial assets, e.g. *haq Dayn* (debt rights) and *haq tamalluk* (ownership rights); *haq* used alone usually indicates, in general terms, a legal right.

Haram: Something prohibited by Sharia. *See* HALAL.

Hibah: A lifetime gift which, under Sharia, is generally a transfer of property without any material consideration or any broadly based claw-back principle for forced heirship purposes. There is similar freedom to make dispositions by will within the limit of one third of the total assets which, along with lifetime gifts, are an important factor that is calculated to cultivate love and cooperation amongst citizens. *Hibah* is also applied to individual gifts to a person.

Hiwalah (or Hawala): A contract that allows a debtor to transfer his debt obligation to a third party. Frequently used as a form of international money transfer where money is paid to a person who then transfers his obligation to repay to another in a different country. It is the obligation that is transferred and this is an effective way to pass money across frontiers without the involvement of an ordinary bank. The idea of *hiwalah* is frequently associated in Western countries with money laundering.

Ibra: The process by which a person withdraws his right to collect payment from a debtor who acquired a liability to repay a loan, such as where the creditor of a loan becomes a member of the debtor's family and where the repayment of the amount owing is foregone. The term is also applied where an early settlement of a debt is made in return for a reduction in the amount owing and where it is desired to give some rebate to the debtor.

Ijarah: A contract whereby a lessor or the owner of property leases out an asset or equipment to a client at an agreed rental for a determined period that is stated in the contract (*aqd*). The ownership of the item leased remains in the hands of the lessor.

Ijarah Thumma Bai: An *ijarah* contract which allows that the lessee will purchase the asset at an agreed price at the end of a lease by executing a contract of purchase (*bai*).

Ijtihad: The effort of a qualified jurist to derive or formulate a rule of law to determine the true ruling of the divine law where the revelation is not explicit or certain in the official texts.

Istisna: A contract of sale of an item to be delivered by the seller in the future and whereby the buyer requires the seller to construct the asset and deliver it according to specifications given in the contract.

Ittifaq Dhimni: A sale and repurchase of an asset at prices agreed by the parties before the completion of the contract.

Katar: A variety of *gharar*, which is where the liability of any of the parties to a contract is uncertain or contingent, such as where the delivery of one of the items is not under the control of any of the parties, or where payment is uncertain.

Khilabah: A form of fraud by which another party is induced to enter into a contract.

Khiyanah: Failure to disclose the truth relating to a contract or otherwise breaching an agreement in a deceitful way, prohibited by the Sharia.

Maisir: Any form of gambling or betting that is prohibited under the Sharia.

Mal: An item that has value and which is capable of being gainfully used according to the Sharia.

Maqasid: The objectives of Sharia, which are, primarily, the protection and preservation of religion, life, family, property, intellect and honour, and from this are derived secondary objectives that centre on establishing peace, equity, security, the preservation of moral values and the prohibition of evil deeds.

Mard al-Mawt: An impediment to a person's capacity when in the throes of death. An illness that causes death can invalidate gifts or other transactions made by a deceased person during his last 12 months of life where they were made under the apprehension of death from a terminal illness. This is really a rule about the donor's capacity and affects sales, acknowledgement of debts, divorces and even marriage. Exceptions exist from this rule in respect of arm's length transactions.

Muajjal: A credit sale; the seller sells specific goods to the buyer at an agreed price for payment in a lump sum at a fixed future date or payment by fixed instalments within a certain period.

Mudarabah: A type of partnership where one party provides the funds while the other provides expertise and management (the *Mudarib*). Any profits of this outcome are shared between the two partners on a pre-agreed basis. Any loss is borne by the provider of the capital. Used by banks as a means of financing where the customer requests the bank to make a purchase for him at an agreed profit over the cost.

Mujtahid: A scholar of Muslim law.

Muqasah: The settlement of a debt by a contra-transaction.

Murabaha: The straightforward sale for a mutually agreed profit. Technically, it is a cost-plus sale in which the seller declares his cost and the profit he is making. Also, a bank, on the request of a client, may purchase something on the client's behalf in return for a definite profit over the cost. This cost-plus sale rewards the bank for financing the client without charging anything that can be regarded as interest.

Musharakah: A partnership or joint venture between persons who provide capital toward the financing of the project in return for a share of the profits on a prearranged basis and who share any losses in proportion to their equity participation. Management of such a joint venture is by the partners or joint venturers, who may forgo their rights of management in favour of any specified partner or person.

Mutawalli: Trustees of a *Waqf*.

Qard: A non-interest bearing loan.

Qard al-Hassan: A loan given for a good cause.

Qimar: Gambling.

Rahn: The use of an asset as collateral for a debt that is available to the creditor on a debtor's default.

Riba: Literally, excess or increases. A prohibition against charging interest or usury; i.e. any increase over and above the principal amount payable in a contractual obligation that is not covered by a corresponding increase in labour, commodity, risk and expertise.

Sarf: The buying and selling of currencies.

Sharia: Islamic Sharia (or frequently spelled Shariah), literally meaning 'the way of the fountain', is a code of law or divine injunctions that regulate the conduct of human beings in their individual and collective lives and that is derived principally from the Holy *Quir'an* and *Sunna* of the holy Prophet (peace be upon him) and secondary from *Ijmaa* (consensus) and from *Qiyas* (analogy) based on the conclusions of scholars (*Ijtihad*) who have juristic expertise to resolve emerging problems and issues. Sharia law is divided into *Sunni* and *Shia* schools and these are further subdivided. The *Sunni* schools can be *Hanbali, Hanafi, Maliki* and *Shafii*, and the *Shia* schools may be *Ithna Asharis, Zaidis, Ismaelis* and *Abadis*. These different schools are particularly relevant in matters of succession of assets. The *Sharia* is the underlying philosophy of Islamic economics and comprises a system aimed at curtailing injustice in the acquisition and disposal of material resources. The *Sharia* is now recognised in England and Wales and is being adopted in many other countries in view of its attitude towards banking and finance.

Sharia compliant trust: A trust set up according to normal trust law that has been created to be *Sharia* compliant without actually removing its status as a trust and without attempting to establish a *Waqf*. In many cases a discretionary trust will accommodate the wishes of a settlor in this regard and accommodate the complexities of inheritance under Islamic law. Frequently, a trust is set up so that on the death of the settlor the trust funds are paid to the settlor's heirs in the proportion set out in Islamic law, or for the assets to be divided into separate sub-funds for each beneficiary, which are then held separately as discretionary trusts. This may be achieved by a non-binding letter of wishes where it is usual that the investments are restricted to those which are *Sharia* compliant. This involves avoiding investments that pay interest or those that are involved in forbidden activities.

Suftajah: A financial instrument to secure payment that a creditor is able to cash at a predetermined venue or at a future date; the English equivalent would be a promissory note or bill of exchange.

Sukuk: A trust certificate of entitlement representing an undivided share in the ownership of tangible assets, particular projects, specific investment activity or usufruct and services.

Sunna: The teachings and sayings of the Prophet Mohammed (peace be upon him) as documented in *Hadith*.

Ta widh: An enforceable penalty clause that may be claimed by a creditor on default by the debtor.

Tadlis al-aib: The intentional hiding of defects in the goods by the seller, which is prohibited under *Sharia* (thus substantially opposed to the English law doctrine of *caveat emptor*).

Takaful: A form of Islamic insurance based on the principle of mutual assistance (*Ta'awon*), particularly in the case of loss to life, assets and property, and which is based on a joint risk-sharing relationship.

Theimmah: An independent legal entity which in Islamic jurisprudence includes a *Waqf*; this term also includes private foundations.

Ujrah: Financial payment that may be in the form of a salary, a wage or a commission in return for the provision of services.

Uqud al-Ishtirak: Contracts of partnership.

Uqud al-Tabarruat: Charitable contracts.

Urbun: A deposit in respect of the price of goods or services that is paid in advance and which is forfeited if the depositor cancels the transactions, at which point the forfeited money is then considered as *hibah* or gift.

Wa'd: A promise used in the context of a purchase or sale of undertakings.

Wadi'ah: A deposit or *Amanah* where the trustee is not responsible for loss except in the case of negligence.

Wadiah Yad Dhamanah: Goods or deposits placed in the safekeeping of another person (the depository) who is not the owner; the arrangement is a trust and the depository becomes responsible for the repayment of the whole amount deposited or any outstanding amount when demanded by the owner. Despite the absence of a share of any profit made by the goods or deposits being available to the owner, the depository may provide some benefit to the owner as a token of appreciation.

Wakala al mutlaqa: Absolute power of attorney.

Wakalah: A contract that gives a person the power to nominate someone, a *Wakil*, to act on his behalf during his life according to agreed terms and conditions: similar to agency.

Waqf: The placing of assets with a person who is not the owner of the assets where the income or benefit is applied for a charitable purpose. That purpose may include humanitarian objectives or a specified group of people such as the members of a family. A *Waqf* may be classified as religious, philanthropic or family. *Waqf* property cannot be sold, inherited or donated to anyone. The word '*Waqf*' translates literally as forbidding or freezing; the exact legal meaning differs according to the scholars consulted; however, the basic meaning is the same for all schools. The *Hanafi* school of law understands *Waqf* as stopping any person from owning property where the benefit of the property has been dedicated to help the poor, or designated for some other charitable purpose. Under the *Hambali* school, *Waqf* is defined as 'bequeathing the property and dedicating the fruit.' The term '*Waqf*' is also used to name the body that manages the endowment. Colloquially, the word is used to imply an Islamic trust; this is only a very poor approximation, although there are similarities. These similarities include the ability to pass ownership of the subject matter when the person making the *Waqf* loses his rights over it and deposits it in Allah's trust. Thereafter, neither the person making the *Waqf* nor his heirs or anyone else is allowed to sell it, buy it or give it as a gift, inherit it or carry out any transaction or disposition of title on it; no one can claim ownership of it and the arrangement, once made, is irreversible and cannot be broken. This means that the person making the *Waqf* is not responsible (unless that person agrees otherwise) for the expenditure or the maintenance or care of the subject matter and is not obliged to repair or maintain the property. These duties are taken over by the *Waqf* and the person responsible (in English trust terms, the trustee) is called the '*Mutawalli*'. If the *Waqf* is set up for the care of a family there must be an expressed intention to convert to a charitable *Waqf* at some stage; such as, 'the fruit of the *Waqf* shall be for my inheritance and then their inheritance and then to a charitable purpose.' This is an essential condition. A *Waqf* is established by an express and clear statement that need not be in Arabic and may be quite informal. To validate a *Waqf*, no acceptance need be given on the part of the beneficiaries. In the case of a public *Waqf*, such as for the benefit of a mosque or a school, or for charity generally (*Sadquat*), no one is required to give a formal acceptance. The *Waqf* is established immediately upon the declaration. A declaration cannot be withdrawn. A declaration of a *Waqf* must be valid from the day it is made. A private *Waqf* will be valid when the property has been given for the benefit of the beneficiaries. Anyone who has heard a declaration of the setting up of a *Waqf* will have standing to bring an action in court for the registration of the *Waqf*, even if the *Waqif* refuses to do so. A declaration that property is *Waqf* 'after my death' is not valid nor is a declaration for a *Waqf* for a period of years. The *Waqif* may also be a beneficiary so long as it is provided that the poor and needy will be made beneficiaries at some stage; the poor being a permanent group always enables beneficiaries to be found. The *Waqif* has complete discretion to decide on the beneficiaries and their shares; the beneficiaries may be either a named person or a defined group. Also, the *Waqif* sets out the conditions and terms of management, decides the nature and organs of the *Waqf* and appoints the *Mutawalli*, divides the benefits and sets any terms he chooses, provided they do not contradict the spirit and general rules. A term may be included which allows the *Waqf* to be sold and other property to be bought or exchanged. The *Mutawalli* manages and protects the *Waqf* from any abuse or mismanagement. The *Mutawalli* may be one person or many, as laid down by the *Waqif*. There may be a guardian who is able to authorise the exchange of property, dismiss the *Waqif* from being the *Mutawalli* when in the interest of the *Waqf*. Because *Waqfs* exist indefinitely, large amounts of property have come into the hands of *Mutawallis*. This has created a negative attitude in some countries where *Waqfs* have been added to the public property of the government and redistributed through land and other reforms. *See also* SHARIA COMPLIANT TRUST.

Wasiyya: Purely a will. *Wasiyya* is recognised in both *Sunni* and *Sharia* law as a source of bequests up to a maximum of a third of an estate.

Wasiyya wajba: An obligatory bequest in favour of an orphaned grandchild who otherwise would be excluded from inheritance. A legislative introduction first made under Egyptian law but not yet accepted in all Islamic legal systems.

Zakat: The Islamic concept of tithing and alms consisting of an obligation on Muslims to pay 2.5% of their wealth to specified categories in society when their annual wealth exceeds a minimum level; sometimes described as a Muslim wealth tax. The obligation to pay zakat is normally included in a trust document, requiring the trustee to make annual settlements to the settlor during the latter's lifetime.

www.ingramcontent.com/pod-product-compliance
Lightning Source LLC
La Vergne TN
LVHW052222200926
848481LV00001B/181
* 9 7 8 0 9 5 7 0 8 4 3 1 5 *